D0950157

ADAM SMITH

II

An Inquiry into the Nature and Causes of the Wealth of Nations

THE GLASGOW EDITION OF THE WORKS AND CORRESPONDENCE OF ADAM SMITH

Commissioned by the University of Glasgow to celebrate the bicentenary of the Wealth of Nations

I

THE THEORY OF MORAL SENTIMENTS
Edited by D. D. RAPHAEL *and* A. L. MACFIE

II

AN INQUIRY INTO THE NATURE AND CAUSES OF THE WEALTH OF NATIONS
Edited by R. H. CAMPBELL *and* A. S. SKINNER; *textual editor* W. B. TODD

III

ESSAYS ON PHILOSOPHICAL SUBJECTS
(and Miscellaneous Pieces)
Edited by W. P. D. WIGHTMAN

IV

LECTURES ON RHETORIC AND BELLES LETTRES
Edited by J. C. BRYCE
This volume includes the *Considerations concerning the First Formation of Languages*

V

LECTURES ON JURISPRUDENCE
Edited by R. L. MEEK, D. D. RAPHAEL, *and* P. G. STEIN
This volume includes two reports of Smith's course together with the 'Early Draft' of the *Wealth of Nations*

VI

CORRESPONDENCE OF ADAM SMITH
Edited by E. C. MOSSNER *and* I. S. ROSS

Associated volumes:

ESSAYS ON ADAM SMITH
Edited by A. S. SKINNER *and* T. WILSON

LIFE OF ADAM SMITH
By I. S. ROSS

The Glasgow Edition of the Works and Correspondence of Adam Smith and the associated volumes are published in hardcover by Oxford University Press. The six titles of the Glasgow Edition, but not the associated volumes, are being published in paperback by Liberty Fund.

ADAM SMITH

An Inquiry into the Nature and Causes of the Wealth of Nations

GENERAL EDITORS

R. H. CAMPBELL

AND

A. S. SKINNER

TEXTUAL EDITOR

W. B. TODD

VOLUME 2

Liberty Fund

Indianapolis

1981

This book is published by Liberty Fund, Inc., a foundation established to encourage study of the ideal of a society of free and responsible individuals.

The cuneiform inscription that serves as our logo and as the design motif for our endpapers is the earliest-known written appearance of the word "freedom" (*amagi*), or "liberty." It is taken from a clay document written about 2300 B.C. in the Sumerian city-state of Lagash.

This Liberty Fund edition of 1981 is an exact photographic reproduction of the edition published by Oxford University Press in 1976 and reprinted here with minor corrections in 1979.

This reprint has been authorized by Oxford University Press.

© 1976 by Oxford University Press
All rights reserved
Printed in the United States of America

97   98   99   00   P   12   11   10   9

Library of Congress Cataloging-in-Publication Data
Smith, Adam. 1723–1790.
An inquiry into the nature and causes of the wealth of nations.

Reprint. Originally published: Oxford : Clarendon Press, 1979.
(Glasgow edition of the works and correspondence of Adam Smith; 2)
Includes indexes.
I. Economics. I. Campbell, Roy Harold.   II. Skinner, Andrew S.
III. Title.   IV. Series: Smith, Adam, 1723–1790. Works. 1981.
AC7.S59 1981, vol. 2 [HB161] 330.15'3s 81-15578
ISBN 0-86597-006-8 (pbk. : v. 1)[330.15'3] AACR2
ISBN 0-86597-007-6 (pbk. : v. 2)
ISBN 0-86597-008-4 (pbk. : set)

Liberty Fund, Inc.
8335 Allison Pointe Trail, Suite 300
Indianapolis, IN 46250-1687
(317) 842-0880

Cover design by JMH Corporation, Indianapolis, Indiana
Printed & bound by Edwards Brothers, Inc., Ann Arbor, Michigan

Contents

Key to Abbreviations and References

Corr.	*Correspondence*
ED	'Early Draft' of *The Wealth of Nations*
EPS	*Essays on Philosophical Subjects* (which include:)
Ancient Logics	'History of the Ancient Logics and Metaphysics'
Ancient Physics	'History of the Ancient Physics'
Astronomy	'History of Astronomy'
English and Italian Verses	'Of the Affinity between certain English and Italian Verses'
External Senses	'Of the External Senses'
Imitative Arts	'Of the Nature of that Imitation which takes place in what are called the Imitative Arts'
Music, Dancing, and Poetry	'Of the Affinity between Music, Dancing and Poetry'
Stewart	Dugald Stewart, 'Account of the Life and Writings of Adam Smith, LL.D.'
FA, FB	Two fragments on the division of labour, Buchan Papers, Glasgow University Library.
LJ(A)	*Lectures on Jurisprudence:* Report of 1762–63.
LJ(B)	*Lectures on Jurisprudence:* Report dated 1766.
LRBL	*Lectures on Rhetoric and Belles Lettres*
TMS	*The Theory of Moral Sentiments*
WN	*The Wealth of Nations*
Anderson Notes	From John Anderson's Commonplace Book, vol. i, Andersonian Library, University of Strathclyde.

References to Smith's published works are given according to the original divisions, together with the paragraph numbers added in the margin of the Glasgow edition. For example:

TMS I.iii.2.2 = *Theory of Moral Sentiments*, Part I, section iii, chapter 2, paragraph 2.

WN I.x.b.1 = *Wealth of Nations*, Book I, chapter x, section b, paragraph 1.

Astronomy, I.4 = 'History of Astronomy', Section I, paragraph 4.

The Table of Corresponding Passages appended to this volume identifies the sections into which the WN is divided and provides for each paragraph the page references in the Cannan editions of 1930 and 1937.

In the case of the lecture notes we have adopted the following practice: references to the LRBL are given in the form 'LRBL i.8' (= volume i, page 8 of the original manuscript), with references to the Lothian edition (London, 1963) in parenthesis. In the *Lectures on Jurisprudence* we have also cited the volume and page reference from the original manuscript (all of which will be included in the Glasgow edition) while retaining page references to the Cannan edition (Oxford, 1896) where appropriate. References to the *Correspondence* give date of letter and letter number from the Glasgow edition.

CHAPTER VI

Of Treaties of Commerce

1 WHEN a nation binds itself by treaty either to permit the entry of certain goods from one foreign country which it prohibits from all others, or to exempt the goods of one country from duties to which it subjects those [324] of all others, the country, or at least the merchants and manufacturers of the country, whose commerce is so favoured, must necessarily derive great advantage from the treaty. Those merchants and manufacturers enjoy a sort of monopoly in the country which is so indulgent to them. That country becomes a market both more extensive and more advantageous for their goods: more extensive, because the goods of other nations being either excluded or subjected to heavier duties, it takes off a greater quantity of theirs: more advantageous, because the merchants of the favoured country, enjoying a sort of monopoly there, will often sell their goods for a better price than if exposed to the free competition of all other nations.

2 Such treaties, however, though they may be advantageous to the merchants and manufacturers of the favoured, are necessarily disadvantageous to those of the favouring country. A monopoly is thus granted against them to a foreign nation; and they must frequently buy the foreign goods they have occasion for, dearer than if the free competition of other nations was admitted. That part of its own produce with which such a nation purchases foreign goods, must consequently be sold cheaper, because when two things are exchanged for one another, the cheapness of the one is a necessary consequence, or rather is the same thing with the dearness of the other. The exchangeable value of its annual produce, therefore, is likely to be diminished by every such treaty. This diminution, however, [325] can scarce amount to any positive loss, but only to a lessening of the gain which it might otherwise make. Though it sells its goods cheaper than it otherwise might do, it will not probably sell them for less than they cost; nor, as in the case of bounties, for a price which will not replace the capital employed in bringing them to market, together with the ordinary profits of stock. The trade could not go on long if it did. Even the favouring country, therefore, may still gain by the trade, though less than if there was a free competition.

3 Some treaties of commerce, however, have been supposed advantageous upon principles very different from these; and a commercial country has sometimes granted a monopoly of this kind against itself to certain goods of a foreign nation, because it expected that in the whole commerce between them, it would annually sell more than it would buy, and that a balance in gold and silver would be annually returned to it. It is upon this principle

that the treaty of commerce between England and Portugal, concluded in 1703 by Mr. Methuen, has been so much commended.[1] The following is a literal translation of that treaty, which consists of three articles only.

ART. I

4 His sacred royal majesty of Portugal promises, both in his own name, and that of his successors, to admit, for ever hereafter, into Portugal, the [326] woollen cloths, and the rest of the woollen manufactures of the British, as was accustomed, till they were prohibited by the law; nevertheless upon this condition:

ART. II

5 That is to say, that her sacred royal majesty of Great Britain shall, in her own name, and that of her successors, be obliged, for ever hereafter, to admit the wines of the growth of Portugal into Britain; so that at no time, whether there shall be peace or war between the kingdoms of Britain and France, any thing more shall be demanded for these wines by the name of custom or duty, or by whatsoever other title, directly or indirectly, whether they shall be imported into Great Britain in pipes or hogsheads, or other casks, than what shall be demanded for the like quantity or measure of French wine, deducting or abating a third part of the custom or duty. But if at any time this deduction or abatement of customs, which is to be made as aforesaid, shall in any manner be attempted and prejudiced, it shall be just and lawful for his sacred royal majesty of Portugal, again to prohibit the woollen cloths, and the rest of the British woollen manufactures.

ART. III

6 The most excellent lords and plenipotentiaries promise and take upon themselves, that their above-named masters shall ratify this treaty; and [327] within the space of two months the ratifications shall be exchanged.

7 By this treaty the crown of Portugal becomes bound to admit the English woollens upon the same footing as before the prohibition, that is, not to raise the duties which had been paid before that time. But it does not

---

[1] As in a dedication to Methuen's son:

Your father . . . procured for Great Britain that glorious Treaty of Commerce, by which She gained above a Million a Year.

By this Treaty we paid our Armies in *Spain* and *Portugel*, and drew from thence, in the late war, considerable Sums for our Troops in other Parts, without remitting one Farthing from England, and at the same time coin'd in the Tower above a Million of *Portugal* Gold in three years. By this Treaty we gain a greater Ballance from Portugal only, than from any other Country whatsoever . . .

By this Treaty we have increased our Exports thither.'

Charles King, *The British Merchant* (London, 1743), iii.ii. See below, IV.viii.52.

become bound to admit them upon any better terms than those of any other nation, of France or Holland, for example. The crown of Great Britain, on the contrary, becomes bound to admit the wines of Portugal, upon paying only two-thirds of the duty, which is paid for those of France, the wines most likely to come into competition with them. So far this treaty, therefore, is evidently advantageous to Portugal, and disadvantageous to Great Britain.

8   It has been celebrated, however, as a masterpiece of the commercial policy of England. Portugal receives annually from the Brazils a greater quantity of gold than can be employed in its domestick commerce, whether in the shape of coin or of plate. The surplus is too valuable to be allowed to lie idle and locked up in coffers, and as it can find no advantageous market at home, it must, notwithstanding any prohibition, be sent abroad, and exchanged for something for which there is a more advantageous market at home. A large share of it comes annually to England, in return either for English goods, or for those of other European nations that receive their returns through England. Mr. Baretti [328] was informed that the weekly packet boat from Lisbon brings, one week with another, more than fifty thousand pounds in gold to England.[2] The sum had probably been exaggerated. It would amount to more than two millions six hundred thousand pounds a year, which is more than the Brazils are supposed to afford.[3]

9   Our merchants were some years ago out of humour with the crown of Portugal. Some privileges which had been granted them, not by treaty, but by the free grace of that crown, at the solicitation, indeed, it is probable, and in return for much greater favours, defence and protection, from the crown of Great Britain, had been either infringed or revoked. The people, therefore, usually most interested in celebrating the Portugal trade, were then rather disposed to represent it as less advantageous than it had commonly been imagined. The far greater part, almost the whole, they pretended, of this annual importation of gold, was not on account of Great Britain, but of other European nations; the fruits and wines of Portugal annually imported into Great Britain nearly compensating the value of the British goods sent thither.

10   Let us suppose, however, that the whole was on account of Great

---

[2] See above, IV.i.12. Cf. J. Baretti, *Journey from London to Genoa through England, Portugal, Spain, and France* (London, 1770), i. 67: 'Almost every week a packet sails from Falmouth to Lisbon with only the mail that is sent from London. Mails are not heavy cargoes: but when a packet sails back to England, besides the returning mail, it has . . . so many bags of Portugal-coin, as often account from thirty to fifty, and even sixty thousand pounds sterling.' The circumstances in which Baretti was given the information alone make the quantity seem unlikely, and later he says: 'I have often heard it affirmed with confidence, that from Brazil alone they [the Portugese] draw yearly above two millions sterling.' (Ibid. i.68.)

[3] See above, I.xi.g.33.

Britain, and that it amounted to a still greater sum than Mr. Baretti seems to imagine: this trade would not, upon that account, be more advantageous than any other in which, for the same value sent out, we received an equal value of consumable goods in return.

11 [329] It is but a very small part of this importation which, it can be supposed, is employed as an annual addition either to the plate or to the coin of the kingdom. The rest must all be sent abroad and exchanged for consumable goods of some kind or other. But if those consumable goods were purchased directly with the produce of English industry, it would be more for the advantage of England, than first to purchase with that produce the gold of Portugal, and afterwards to purchase with that gold those consumable goods. A direct foreign trade of consumption is always more advantageous than a round-about one;[4] and to bring the same value of foreign goods to the home market, requires a much smaller capital in the one *way* than in the other. If a smaller share of its industry, therefore, had been employed in producing goods fit for the Portugal market, and a greater in producing those fit for the other markets, where those consumable goods for which there is a demand in Great Britain are to be had, it would have been more for the advantage of England. To procure both the gold, which it wants for its own use, and the consumable goods, would, in this way, employ a much smaller capital than at present. There would be a spare capital, therefore, to be employed for other purposes, in exciting an additional quantity of industry, and in raising a greater annual produce.

12 Though Britain were entirely excluded from the Portugal trade, it could find very little difficulty in procuring all the annual supplies of gold [330] which it wants, either for the purposes of plate, or of coin, or of foreign trade. Gold, like every other commodity, is always somewhere or another to be got for its value by those who have that value to give for it.[5] The annual surplus of gold in Portugal, besides, would still be sent abroad, and though not carried away by Great Britain, would be carried away by some other nation, which would be glad to sell it again for its price, in the same manner as Great Britain does at present. In buying gold of Portugal, indeed, we buy it at the first hand; whereas, in buying it of any other nation, except Spain, we should buy it at the second, and might pay somewhat dearer. This difference, however, would surely be too insignificant to deserve the publick attention.

13 Almost all our gold, it is said, comes from Portugal. With other nations the balance of trade is either against us, or not much in our favour. But we should remember, that the more gold we import from one country, the less we must necessarily import from all others. The effectual demand for gold,

a-a 2–6

---

[4] See above, II.v.28.   [5] A similar point is made at II.iii.24 and IV.iii.c.7.

like that for every other commodity, is in every country limited to a certain quantity.[6] If nine-tenths of this quantity are imported from one country, there remains a tenth only to be imported from all others. The more gold besides that is annually imported from some particular countries, over and above what is requisite for plate and for coin, the more must necessarily be exported to some others; and the more, that most insignifi-[331]cant object of modern policy, the balance of trade, appears to be in our favour with some particular countries, the more it must necessarily appear to be against us with many others.

14   It was upon this silly notion, however, that England could not subsist without the Portugal trade, that, towards the end of the late war, France and Spain, without pretending either offence or provocation, required the king of Portugal to exclude all British ships from his ports, and for the security of this exclusion, to receive into them French or Spanish garrisons. Had the king of Portugal submitted to those ignominious terms which his brother-in-law the king of Spain proposed to him, Britain would have been freed from a much greater inconveniency than the loss of the Portugal trade, the burden of supporting a very weak ally, so unprovided of every thing for his own defence, that the whole power of England, had it been directed to that single purpose, could scarce perhaps have defended him for another campaign. The loss of the Portugal trade would, no doubt, have occasioned a considerable embarrassment to the merchants at that time engaged in it, who might not, perhaps, have found out, for a year or two, any other equally advantageous method of employing their capitals; and in this would probably have consisted all the inconveniency which England could have suffered from this notable piece of commercial policy.

15   The great annual importation of gold and silver is neither for the purpose of plate nor of [332] coin, but of foreign trade. A round-about foreign trade of consumption can be carried on more advantageously by means of these metals than of almost any other goods. As they are the universal instruments of commerce, they are more readily received in return for all commodities than any other goods; and on account of their small bulk and great value, it costs less to transport them backward and forward from one place to another than almost any other sort of merchandize, and they lose less of their value by being so transported. Of all the commodities, therefore, which are bought in one foreign country, for no other purpose but to be sold or exchanged again for some other goods in another, there are none so convenient as gold and silver.[7] In facilitating all the different round-about foreign trades of consumption which are carried on in Great Britain, consists the principal advantage of the Portugal trade; and though it is not a capital advantage, it is, no doubt, a considerable one.

---

[6] See above, IV.i.12.   [7] See above, IV.i.12.

16   That any annual addition which, it can reasonably be supposed, is made either to the plate or to the coin of the kingdom, could require but a very small annual importation of gold and silver, seems evident enough; and though we had no direct trade with Portugal, this small quantity could always, somewhere or another, be very easily got.

17   Though the goldsmiths trade be very considerable in Great Britain, the far greater part of the new plate which they annually sell, is [333] made from other old plate melted down; so that the addition annually made to the whole plate of the kingdom cannot be very great, and could require but a very small annual importation.

18   It is the same case with the coin. Nobody imagines, I believe, that even the greater part of the annual coinage, amounting, for ten years together, before the late reformation of the gold coin,[8] to upwards of eight hundred thousand pounds a year in gold,[9] was an annual addition to the money before current in the kingdom. In a country where the expence of the coinage is defrayed by the government,[10] the value of the coin, even when it contains its full standard weight of gold and silver, can never be much greater than that of an equal quantity of those metals uncoined; because it requires only the trouble of going to the mint, and the delay perhaps of a few weeks, to procure for any quantity of uncoined gold and silver an equal quantity of those metals in coin. But, in every country, the greater part of the current coin is almost always more or less worn, or otherwise degenerated from its standard.[11] In Great Britain it was, before the late reformation, a good deal so, the gold being more than two per cent. and the silver more than eight per cent. below its standard weight. But if forty-four guineas and a half, containing their full standard weight, a pound weight of gold, could purchase very little more than a pound weight of uncoined gold, forty-four guineas and a half wanting a part of their weight could not purchase a pound weight, [334] and something was to be added in order to make up the deficiency. The current price of gold bullion at market, therefore, instead of being the same with the mint price, or 46*l.* 14*s.* 6*d.* was then about 47*l.* 14*s.* and sometimes about forty-eight pounds. When the greater part of the coin, however, was in this degenerate condition, forty-four guineas and a half, fresh from the mint, would purchase no more goods in the market than any other ordinary guineas, because when they *ᵇcameᵇ* into the coffers of the merchant, being confounded

---

ᵇ⁻ᵇ come *1*

[8] In 1774. See above, I.v.29ff.

[9] The same figure is cited at II.ii.54 and § 30 of this section.

[10] A similar point is made at IV.iii.a.10. It is remarked at I.v.38 that although the coinage is free in England, a delay in converting bullion into coin is equivalent in effect to the imposition of a small duty.

[11] The subjects covered in the remainder of this chapter are also considered above, especially in I.v.29–42.

with other money, they could not afterwards be distinguished without more trouble than the difference was worth. Like other guineas they were worth no more than 46*l*. 14*s*. 6*d*. If thrown into the melting pot, however, they produced, without any sensible loss, a pound weight of standard gold, which could be sold at any time for between 47*l*. 14*s*. and 48*l*. either in gold or silver, as fit for all the purposes of coin as that which had been melted down. There was an evident profit, therefore, in melting down new coined money, and it was done so instantaneously, that no precaution of government could prevent it. The operations of the mint were, upon this account, somewhat like the web of Penelope; the work that was done in the day was undone in the night.[12] The mint was employed, not so much in making daily additions to the coin, as in replacing the very best part of it which was daily melted down.

19   Were the private people, who carry their gold and silver to the mint, to pay themselves [335] for the coinage, it would add to the value of those metals in the same manner as the fashion does to that of plate.[13] Coined gold and silver would be more valuable than uncoined. The seignorage, if it was not exorbitant, would add to the bullion the whole value of the duty; because, the government having every where the exclusive privilege of coining, no coin can come to market cheaper than they think proper to afford it. If the duty was exorbitant indeed, that is, if it was very much above the real value of the labour and expence requisite for coinage, false coiners, both at home and abroad, might be encouraged, by the great difference between the value of bullion and that of coin, to pour in so great a quantity of counterfeit money as might reduce the value of the government money. In France, however, though the seignorage is eight per cent. no sensible inconveniency of this kind is found to arise from it.[14] The dangers to which a false coiner is every where exposed, if he lives in the country of which he counterfeits the coin, and to which his agents or correspondents are exposed if he lives in a foreign country, are by far too great to be incurred for the sake of a profit of six or seven per cent.

20   The seignorage in France raises the value of the coin higher than in proportion to the quantity of pure gold which it contains. Thus by the edict of January, 1726, the* mint price [336] of fine gold of twenty-four

---

* See Dictionaire des Monnoies, ᶜtom. ii.ᶜ article Seigneurage, p. 489. par M. Abot de Bazinghen, Conseiller-Comissaire en la Cour des Monnoies à Paris. [Traité des Monnoies et de la jurisdiction de la Cour des Monnoies en forme de dictionnaire (Paris, 1764), ii.589].

ᶜ⁻ᶜ tom. i *1*

[12] In Letter 115 addressed to Lord Hailes, dated 15 January 1769, Smith wrote: 'tho' in my present situation I have ... nothing to do, my own schemes of Study leave me very little leisure, which go forward too like the web of penelope, so that I scarce see any Probability of their ending.'

[13] See I.v.39, where exactly this point is made, and also IV.iii.a.10.

[14] In Letter 150 addressed to Smith, dated 1 April 1776, Hume stated that the seignorage was likely to be less than 2 per cent, and cites Necker's *Essai sur la legislation* in support. The seignorage was 3 per cent. See above, I.v.39, IV.iii.a.10.

carats was fixed at seven hundred and forty livres nine sous and one denier one-eleventh, the mark of eight Paris ounces. The gold coin of France, making an allowance for the remedy of the mint, contains twenty-one carats and three-fourths of fine gold, and two carats one-fourth of alloy. The mark of standard gold, therefore, is worth no more than about six hundred and seventy-one livres ten deniers. But in France this mark of standard gold is coined into thirty Louis-d'ors of twenty-four livres each, or into seven hundred and twenty livres. The coinage, therefore, increases the value of a mark of standard gold bullion, by the difference between six hundred and seventy-one livres ten deniers, and seven hundred and twenty livres; or by forty-eight livres nineteen sous and two deniers.

21   A seignorage will, in many cases, take away altogether, and will, in all cases, diminish the profit of melting down the new coin. This profit always arises from the difference between the quantity of bullion which the common currency ought to contain, and that which it actually does contain. If this difference is less than the seignorage, there will be loss instead of profit. If it is equal to the seignorage, there will neither be profit nor loss. If it is greater than the seignorage, there will indeed be some profit, but less than if there was no seignorage. If, before the late reformation of the gold coin, for example, there had been a seignorage of five per cent. upon the coinage, there would have [337] been a loss of three per cent. upon the melting down of the gold coin. If the seignorage had been two per cent. there would have been neither profit nor loss. If the seignorage had been one per cent. there would have been a profit, but of one per cent. only instead of two per cent. Wherever money is received by tale, therefore, and not by weight, a seignorage is the most effectual preventative of the melting down of the coin, and, for the same reason, of its exportation. It is the best and heaviest pieces that are commonly either melted down or exported; because it is upon such that the largest profits are made.[15]

22   The law for the encouragement of the coinage, by rendering it duty-free, was first enacted, during the reign of Charles II.[16] for a limited time; and afterwards continued, by different prolongations, till 1769, when it was rendered perpetual.[17] The bank of England, in order to replenish their coffers with money, are frequently obliged to carry bullion to the mint; and it was more for their interest, they probably imagined, that the coinage should be at the expence of the government, than at their own. It was, probably, out of complaisance to this great company that the government

---

[15] The melting of coin is stated to have been a felony in LJ (A) v.75, vi.147, and LJ (B) 257, ed. Cannan 201.

[16] 18 and 19 Charles II, c.5 (1666) in *Statutes of the Realm*, v. 598–600; 18 Charles II, c.5 in Ruffhead's edition. See above, I.v.38.

[17] Various temporary provisions were made perpetual by 9 George III, c.25 (1769). The Act gave £15,000 for expenses in connection with the coinage, not £14,000 as Smith states below, IV.vi.31.

agreed to render this law perpetual. Should the custom of weighing gold, however, come to be disused, as it is very likely to be on account of its inconveniency; should the gold coin of England come to be received by tale, as it was before the late re-coinage, this great company may, perhaps, find [338] that they have upon this, as upon some other occasions, mistaken their own interest not a little.

23   Before the late re-coinage, when the gold currency of England was two per cent. below its standard weight, as there was no seignorage, it was two per cent. below the value of that quantity of standard gold bullion which it ought to have contained. When this great company, therefore, bought gold bullion in order to have it coined, they were obliged to pay for it two per cent. more than it was worth after the coinage. But if there had been a seignorage of two per cent. upon the coinage, the common gold currency, though two per cent. below its standard weight, would notwithstanding have been equal in value to the quantity of standard gold which it ought to have contained; the value of the fashion compensating in this case the diminution of the weight. They would indeed have had the seignorage to pay, which being two per cent. their loss upon the whole transaction would have been two per cent. exactly the same, but no greater than it actually was.

24   If the seignorage had been five per cent. and the gold currency only two per cent. below its standard weight, the bank would in this case have gained three per cent. upon the price of the bullion; but as they would have had a seignorage of five per cent. to pay upon the coinage, their loss upon the whole transaction would, in the same manner, have been exactly two per cent.

25   [339] If the seignorage had been only one per cent. and the gold currency two per cent. below its standard weight, the bank would in this case have lost only one per cent. upon the price of the bullion; but as they would likewise have had a seignorage of one per cent. to pay, their loss upon the whole transaction would have been exactly two per cent. in the same manner as in all other cases.

26   If there was a reasonable seignorage, while at the same time the coin contained its full standard weight, as it has done very nearly since the late re-coinage, whatever the bank might lose by the seignorage, they would gain upon the price of the bullion; and whatever they might gain upon the price of the bullion, they would lose by the seignorage. They would neither lose nor gain, therefore, upon the whole transaction, and they would in this, as in all the foregoing cases, be exactly in the same situation as if there was no seignorage.

27   When the tax upon a commodity is so moderate as not to encourage smuggling,[18] the merchant who deals in it, though he advances, does not

[18] See below, V.ii.k.27, and V.ii.b.6, where it is remarked that an injudicious tax offers a 'great temptation to smuggling'. Cf. IV.iii.a.1.

properly pay the tax, as he gets it back in the price of the commodity. The tax is finally paid by the last purchaser or consumer. But money is a commodity with regard to which every man is a merchant. Nobody buys it but in order to sell it again;[19] and with regard to it there is in ordinary cases no last purchaser or consumer. When the tax upon coinage, therefore, is so moderate as not to encourage false [340] coining, though every body advances the tax, nobody finally pays it; because every body gets it back in the advanced value of the coin.

28   A moderate seignorage, therefore, would not in any case augment the expence of the bank, or of any other private persons who carry their bullion to the mint in order to be coined, and the want of a moderate seignorage does not in any case diminish it. Whether there is or is not a seignorage, if the currency contains its full standard weight, the coinage costs nothing to any body, and if it is short of that weight, the coinage must always cost the difference between the quantity of bullion which ought to be contained in it, and that which actually is contained in it.

29   The government, therefore, when it defrays the expence of coinage, not only incurs some small expence, but loses some small revenue which it might get by a proper duty; and neither the bank nor any other private persons are in the smallest degree benefited by this useless piece of publick generosity.

30   The directors of the bank, however, would probably be unwilling to agree to the imposition of a seignorage upon the authority of a speculation which promises them no gain, but only pretends to insure them from any loss. In the present state of the gold coin, and as long as it continues to be received by weight, they certainly would gain nothing by such a change. But if the custom of weighing the gold coin should ever go into disuse, as it is very likely to do, and if the gold coin should ever fall into the same state of [341] degradation in which it was before the late re-coinage, the gain, or more properly the savings of the bank, in consequence of the imposition of a seignorage, would probably be very considerable. The bank of England is the only company which sends any considerable quantity of bullion to the mint, and the burden of the annual coinage falls entirely, or almost entirely, upon it. If this annual coinage had nothing to do but to repair the unavoidable losses and necessary ^d^wear and tear^d^ of the coin, it could seldom exceed fifty thousand or at most a hundred thousand pounds. But when the coin is degraded below its standard weight, the annual coinage must, besides this, fill up the large vacuities which exportation and the melting pot are continually making in the current coin. It was upon this account that during the ten or twelve years immediately preceding the

---

^d-d^ tear and wear *1*

[19] See above, IV.i.18.

late reformation of the gold coin, the annual coinage amounted at an average to more than eight hundred and fifty thousand pounds.[20] But if there had been a seignorage of four or five per cent. upon the gold coin, it would probably, even in the state in which things then were, have put an effectual stop to the business both of exportation and of the melting pot. The bank, instead of losing every year about two and a half per cent. upon the bullion which was to be coined into more than eight hundred and fifty thousand pounds, or incurring an annual loss of more than twenty-one thousand two hundred and fifty [342] pounds, would not probably have incurred the tenth part of that loss.

31   The revenue allotted by parliament for defraying the expence of the coinage is but fourteen thousand pounds a year,[21] and the real expence which it costs the government, or the fees of the officers of the mint, do not upon ordinary occasions, I am assured, exceed the half of that sum. The saving of so very small a sum, or even the gaining of another which could not well be much larger, are objects too inconsiderable, it may be thought, to deserve the serious attention of government. But the saving of eighteen or twenty thousand pounds a year in case of an event which is not improbable, which has frequently happened before, and which is very likely to happen again, is surely an object which well deserves the serious attention even of so great a company as the bank of England.

32   Some of the foregoing reasonings and observations might perhaps have been more properly placed in those chapters of the first book which treat of the origin and use of money, and of the difference between the real and the nominal price of commodities. But as the law for the encouragement of coinage derives its origin from those vulgar prejudices which have been introduced by the mercantile system;[22] I judged it more proper to reserve them for this chapter. Nothing could be more agreeable to the spirit of that system than a sort of bounty upon the production of money, the very thing which, it sup-[343]poses, constitutes the wealth of every nation. It is one of its many admirable expedients for enriching the country.

---

[20] The same figure is cited above, § 18.

[21] The sum given was £15,000. See above, IV.vi.22. In LJ (A) v.77 the cost of coinage is stated to have been £14,000. It is also argued that free coinage was linked to the prejudices of the mercantile system, as represented by Mun, namely, that 'the more money there was in the kingdom, the greater the benefit'. The figure of £14,000 is also given in LJ (A) vi.151 and LJ (B) 260. Metal coinage is described as a much more expensive instrument than paper at II.ii.26; cf. V.iii.81ff.

[22] Smith also uses the term 'vulgar prejudice' above, II.iii.25, in reference to the mercantile system.

CHAPTER VII

Of Colonies

PART FIRST

Of the Motives for establishing new Colonies

1   THE interest which occasioned the first settlement of the different European colonies in America and the West Indies, was not altogether so plain and distinct as that which directed the establishment of those of ancient Greece and Rome.

2   All the different states of ancient Greece possessed, each of them, but a very small territory, and when the people in any one of them multiplied beyond what that territory could easily maintain, a part of them were sent in quest of a new habitation in some remote and distant part of the world; the warlike neighbours who surrounded them on all sides, rendering it difficult for any of them to enlarge very much its territory at home. The colonies of the Dorians resorted chiefly to Italy and Sicily, which in the times preceding the foundation of Rome, were inhabited by barbarous and uncivilized nations: [344] those of the Ionians and Eolians, the two other great tribes of the Greeks, to Asia Minor and the islands of the Egean Sea, of which the inhabitants seem at that time to have been pretty much in the same state as those of Sicily and Italy. The mother city, though she considered the colony as a child, at all times entitled to great favour and assistance, and owing in return much gratitude and respect, yet considered it as an emancipated child, over whom she pretended to claim no direct authority or jurisdiction. The colony settled its own form of government, enacted its own laws, elected its own magistrates, and made peace or war with its neighbours as an independent state, which had no occasion to wait for the approbation or consent of the mother city. Nothing can be more plain and distinct than the interest which directed every such establishment.[1]

3   Rome, like most of the other ancient republicks, was originally founded upon an Agrarian law, which divided the publick territory in a certain proportion among the different citizens who composed the state.[2] The course of human affairs, by marriage, by succession, and by alienation, necessarily deranged this original division, and frequently threw the

---

[1] See below, IV.vii.c.11, where it is pointed out that the Greek colonies seldom acknowledged the authority of the mother country.

[2] Cf. Montesquieu (*Considerations*, 39): 'The founders of the ancient republics had made an equal partition of the lands. This alone produced a powerful people, that is, a well regulated society.' Cf. LJ (A) i.52 where Smith comments on Greek practice with regard to the division of land in the colonies.

lands, which had been allotted for the maintenance of many different families into the possession of a single person. To remedy this disorder, for such it was supposed to be, a law was made, restricting the quantity of land which any citizen could possess to five hundred jugera, about three hundred and [345] fifty English acres. This law, however, though we read of its having been executed upon one or two occasions, was either neglected or evaded, and the inequality of fortunes went on continually increasing. The greater part of the citizens had no land, and without it the manners and customs of those times rendered it difficult for a freeman to maintain his independency. In the present times, though a poor man has no land of his own, if he has a little stock, he may either farm the lands of another, or he may carry on some little retail trade; and if he has no stock, he may find employment either as a country labourer, or as an artificer.[3] But, among the ancient Romans, the lands of the rich were all cultivated by slaves, who wrought under an overseer, who was likewise a slave; so that a poor freeman had little chance of being employed either as a farmer or as a labourer. All trades and manufactures too, even the retail trade, were carried on by the slaves of the rich for the benefit of their masters, whose wealth, authority, and protection made it difficult for a poor freeman to maintain the competition against them.[4] The citizens, therefore, who had no land, had scarce any other means of subsistence but the bounties of the candidates at the annual elections. The tribunes, when they had a mind to animate the people against the rich and the great, put them in mind of the antient division of lands, and represented that law which restricted this sort of private property as the fundamental law of the republick.[5] The people be-[346]came clamorous to get land, and the rich and the great, we may believe, were perfectly determined not to give them any part of theirs. To satisfy them in some measure, therefore, they frequently proposed to send out a new colony. But conquering Rome was, even upon such occasions, under no necessity of turning out her citizens to seek their fortune, if one may say so, through the wide world, without knowing where they were to settle. She assigned them lands generally in the conquered provinces of Italy, where, being within the dominions of the republick, they could never form any independent state; but were at best but a sort of corporation, which, though it had the power of enacting bye-laws for its own government, was at all

---

[3] See above III.iv.12 where Smith describes the position of the artizan in the modern state.

[4] This point is elaborated below, IV.ix.47.

[5] Smith commented in LRBL ii.157, ed. Lothian 150, that the method used by 'these men, who from their attachment to the populace were called Populares, was to propose laws for the equall division of lands and the distributing of corn at the publick charge, or else by largesses and bounties bestowed out of their own private fortune. Of this sort were Clodius, Marius, and others.' See above, 166 n. 4.

times subject to the correction, jurisdiction, and legislative authority of the mother city. The sending out a colony of this kind, not only gave some satisfaction to the people, but often established a sort of garrison too in a newly conquered province, of which the obedience might otherwise have been doubtful. A Roman colony, therefore, whether we consider the nature of the establishment itself, or the motives for making it, was altogether different from a Greek one. The words accordingly, which in the original languages denote those different establishments, have very different meanings. The Latin word (*Colonia*) signifies simply a plantation. The Greek word (αποιχια), on the contrary, signifies a separation of dwelling, a departure from home, a going out of the house. But, though the [347] Roman colonies were in many respects different from the Greek ones, the interest which prompted to establish them was equally plain and distinct. Both institutions derived their origin either from irresistible necessity, or from clear and evident utility.

4   The establishment of the European colonies in America and the West Indies arose from no necessity: and though the utility which has resulted from them has been very great, it is not altogether so clear and evident. It was not understood at their first establishment, and was not the motive either of that establishment or of the discoveries which gave occasion to it, and the nature, extent, and limits of that utility are not, perhaps, well understood at this day.

5   The Venetians, during the fourteenth and fifteenth centuries, carried on a very advantageous commerce in spiceries, and other East India goods, which they distributed among the other nations of Europe.[6] They purchased them ᵃchieflyᵃ in Egypt, at that time under the dominion of the Mammeluks, the enemies of the Turks, of whom the Venetians were the enemies; and this union of interest, assisted by the money of Venice, formed such a connection as gave the Venetians almost a monopoly of the trade.

6   The great profits of the Venetians tempted the avidity of the Portuguese. They had been endeavouring, during the course of the fifteenth century, to find out by sea a way to the countries from which the Moors brought them ivory and gold dust across the Desart. They discovered [348] the Madeiras, the Canaries, the Azores, the Cape de Verd islands, the coast of Guinea, that of ᵇLoango, Congo, Angola, and Benguela,ᵇ and, finally, the Cape of Good Hope. They had long wished to share in the profitable traffick of the Venetians, and this last discovery opened to

---

ᵃ⁻ᵃ 2–6   ᵇ⁻ᵇ Congo, Angola, and Loango, *1*

[6] Smith comments on the trade enjoyed by Venice and the Italian cities at III.iii.14. LJ (A) iv.111 records that goods coming from the East Indies were brought up the Red Sea and via the Nile to Cairo where they were chiefly bought by Venetian and Genoese merchants. See above, 406 n. 30.

them a probable prospect of doing so. In 1497, Vasco de Gama sailed from the port of Lisbon with a fleet of four ships, and, after a navigation of eleven months, arrived upon the coast of Indostan, and thus compleated a course of discoveries which had been pursued with great steadiness, and with very little interruption, for near a century together.

7   Some years before this, while the expectations of Europe were in suspence about the projects of the Portuguese, of which the success appeared yet to be doubtful, a Genoese pilot formed the yet more daring project of sailing to the East Indies by the West. The situation of those countries was at that time very imperfectly known in Europe. The few European travellers who had been there had magnified the distance; perhaps through simplicity and ignorance, what was really very great, appearing almost infinite to those who could not measure it; or, perhaps, in order to increase somewhat more the marvellous of their own adventures in visiting regions so immensely remote from Europe. The longer the way was by the East, Columbus very justly concluded, the shorter it would be by the West. He proposed, therefore, to take that way, as both the shortest and the surest, and he had the good fortune to con-[349]vince Isabella of Castile of the probability of his project. He sailed from the port of Palos in August 1492, near five years before the expedition of Vasco de Gama set out from Portugal, and, after a voyage of between two and three months, discovered first some of the small Bahama or Lucayan islands, and afterwards the great island of St. Domingo.

8   But the countries which Columbus discovered, either in this or in any of his subsequent voyages, had no resemblance to those which he had gone in quest of. Instead of the wealth, cultivation, and populousness of China and Indostan, he found, in St. Domingo, and in all the other parts of the new world which he ever visited, nothing but a country quite covered with wood, uncultivated, and inhabited only by some tribes of naked and miserable savages. He was not very willing, however, to believe that they were not the same with some of the countries described by Marco Polo,[7] the first European who had visited, or at least had left behind him, any description of China or the East Indies; and a very slight resemblance, such as that which he found between the name of Cibao, a mountain in St. Domingo, and that of Cipango, mentioned by Marco Polo, was frequently sufficient to make him return to this favourite prepossession, though contrary to the clearest evidence. In his letters to Ferdinand and Isabella he called the countries which he had discovered, the Indies.[8]

---

[7] Marco Polo is also mentioned at I.viii.24.'

[8] 'Ce fut alors, plus que jamais, que Christophe Colomb se persuada que son Isle Espagnole était la veritable Cipango de Marc-Paul de Venise, et la suite sera voir combien il eut de peine à revenir de cette erreur, s'il en est même jamais bien revenu.' (F. X. de Charlevoix, *Histoire de l'isle espagnole ou de S. Domingue* (Paris, 1730), i.99.)

He entertained no doubt but that they were the extremity of those which had been described by [350] Marco Polo, and that they were not very distant from the Ganges, or from the countries which had been conquered by Alexander. Even when at last convinced that they were different, he still flattered himself that those rich countries were at no great distance, and, in a subsequent voyage, accordingly, went in quest of them along the coast of Terra Firma, and towards the isthmus of Darien.

9   In consequence of this mistake of Columbus, the name of the Indies has stuck to those unfortunate countries ever since; and when it was at last clearly discovered that the new were altogether different from the old Indies, the former were called the West, in contradistinction to the latter, which were called the East Indies.

10   It was of importance to Columbus, however, that the countries which he had discovered, whatever they were, should be represented to the court of Spain as of very great consequence; and, in what constitutes the real riches of every country, the animal and vegetable productions of the soil, there was at that time nothing which could well justify such a representation of them.

11   The Cori, something between a rat and a rabbit, and supposed by Mr. Buffon to be the same with the Aperea of Brazil, was the largest viviparous quadruped in St. Domingo.⁹ This species seems never to have been very numerous, and the dogs and cats of the Spaniards are said to have long ago almost entirely extirpated it, as well as some other tribes of a still smaller size. These, however, together with a pretty large lizard, called [351] the Ivana or Iguana, constituted the principal part of the animal food which the land afforded.¹⁰

12   The vegetable food of the inhabitants, though from their want of industry not very abundant, was not altogether so scanty. It consisted in Indian corn, yams, potatoes, bananes, &c. plants which were then altogether unknown in Europe, and which have never since been very much esteemed in it, or supposed to yield a sustenance equal to what is drawn from the common sorts of grain and pulse, which have been cultivated in this part of the world time out of mind.¹¹

13   The cotton plant indeed afforded the material of a very important manufacture, and was at that time to Europeans undoubtedly the most valuable of all the vegetable productions of those islands. But though in the end of the fifteenth century the muslins and other cotton goods of the East Indies were much esteemed in every part of Europe, the cotton manu-

---

⁹ Buffon, *Histoire naturelle*, translated as *Barr's Buffon's Natural History* (London, 1797), ix.306–7. In his Letter to the *Edinburgh Review* of 1755, Smith referred to a 'compleat system of natural history' currently being undertaken by 'two gentlemen of almost universally acknowledged merit, Mr Buffon, and Mr Daubenton'.

¹⁰ F. X. de Charlevoix, *Histoire de l'isle espagnole ou de S. Domingue*, i.27 and 35–6.

¹¹ Smith comments on the nourishing qualities of potatoes at I.xi.b.41.

facture itself was not cultivated in any part of it. Even this production therefore, could not at that time appear in the eyes of Europeans to be of very great consequence.

14   Finding nothing either in the animals or vegetables of the newly discovered countries, which could justify a very advantageous representation of them, Columbus turned his view towards their minerals; and in the richness of the productions of this third kingdom, he flattered himself, he had found a full compensation for the insignificancy of those of the other two. The [352] little bits of gold with which the inhabitants ornamented their dress, and which, he was informed, they frequently found in the rivulets and torrents that fell from the mountains, were sufficient to satisfy him that those mountains abounded with the richest gold mines. St. Domingo, therefore, was represented as a country abounding with gold, and, upon that account (according to the prejudices not only of the present times, but of those times), an inexhaustible source of real wealth to the crown and kingdom of Spain. When Columbus, upon his return from his first voyage, was introduced with a sort of triumphal honours to the sovereigns of Castile and Arragon, the principal productions of the countries which he had discovered were carried in solemn procession before him. The only valuable part of them consisted in some little fillets, bracelets, and other ornaments of gold, and in some bales of cotton. The rest were mere objects of vulgar wonder and curiosity; some reeds of an extraordinary size, some birds of a very beautiful plumage, and some stuffed skins of the huge alligator and manati; all of which were preceded by six or seven of the wretched natives, whose singular colour and appearance added greatly to the novelty of the shew.

15   In consequence of the representations of Columbus, the council of Castile determined to take possession of countries of which the inhabitants were plainly incapable of defending themselves. The pious purpose of converting them to Christianity sanctified the injustice of the project. But [353] the hope of finding treasures of gold there, was the sole motive which prompted to undertake it;[12] and to give this motive the greater weight, it was proposed by Columbus that the half of all the gold and silver that should be found there should belong to the crown. This proposal was approved of by the council.

16   As long as the whole or the far greater part of the gold, which the first adventurers imported into Europe, was got by so very easy a method as the plundering of the defenceless natives, it was not perhaps very difficult to pay even this heavy tax. But when the natives were once fairly stript of all that they had, which, in St. Domingo, and in all the other countries discovered by Columbus, was done compleatly in six or eight years, and

[12] The search for gold as a motive for Spanish colonization is mentioned at I.xi.c.36 and IV.i.2.

when in order to find more it had become necessary to dig for it in the mines, there was no longer any possibility of paying this tax. The rigorous exaction of it, accordingly, first occasioned, it is said, the total abandoning of the mines of St. Domingo, which have never been wrought since. It was soon reduced therefore to a third; then to a fifth; afterwards to a tenth; and at last to a twentieth part of the gross produce of the gold mines. The tax upon ᶜsilver continued for a long timeᶜ to be a fifth of the gross produce. ᵈIt was reduced to a tenth only in the course of the present century.ᵈ¹³ But the first adventurers do not appear to have been much interested about silver. Nothing less precious than gold seemed worthy of their attention.

17   [354] All the other enterprizes of the Spaniards in the new world, subsequent to those of Columbus, seem to have been prompted by the same motive.¹⁴ It was the sacred thirst of gold that carried Oieda, Nicuessa, and Vasco Nugnes de Balboa, to the isthmus of Darien, that carried Cortez to Mexico, and Almagro and Pizzarro to Chili and Peru. When those adventurers arrived upon any unknown coast, their first enquiry was always if there was any gold to be found there; and according to the information which they received concerning this particular, they determined either to quit the country or to settle in it.

18   Of all those expensive and uncertain projects, however, which bring bankruptcy upon the greater part of the people who engage in them, there is none perhaps more perfectly ruinous than the search after new silver and gold mines. It is perhaps the most disadvantageous lottery in the world, or the one in which the gain of those who draw the prizes bears the least proportion to the loss of those who draw the blanks:¹⁵ for though the prizes are few and the blanks many, the common price of a ticket is the whole fortune of a very rich man. Projects of mining, instead of replacing the capital employed in them, together with the ordinary profits of stock, commonly absorb both capital and profit.¹⁶ They are the projects, therefore, to which of all others a prudent law-giver, who desired to increase the capital of his nation, would least chuse to give any extraordinary encouragement, or to turn to-[355]wards them a greater share of that capital than what would go to them of its own accord. Such in reality is the absurd confidence which almost all men have in their own good fortune, that wherever there is the least probability of success, too great a share of it is apt to go to them of its own accord.¹⁷

ᶜ⁻ᶜ silver, indeed, still continues *1*   ᵈ⁻ᵈ 2–6

---

¹³ Similar points are made at I.xi.c.25, 28.   ¹⁴ See above, I.xi.c.36.
¹⁵ See above, I.xi.c.26.
¹⁶ See above, II.iii.26, where it is argued that unsuccessful projects involve a destruction of capital.
¹⁷ See above, I.x.b.27, where it is stated that the 'chance of gain is naturally overvalued'.

19   But though the judgment of sober reason and experience concerning
such projects has always been extremely unfavourable, that of human
avidity has commonly been quite otherwise. The same passion which
has suggested to so many people the absurd idea of the philosopher's
stone, has suggested to others the equally absurd one of immense rich
mines of gold and silver. They did not consider that the value of those
metals has, in all ages and nations, arisen chiefly from their scarcity, and
that their scarcity has arisen from the very small quantities of them
which nature has any where deposited in one place, from the hard and
intractable substances with which she has almost every where surrounded
those small quantities, and consequently from the labour and expence
which are every where necessary in order to penetrate to and get at
them.[18] They flattered themselves that veins of those metals might in
many places be found as large and as abundant as those which are commonly found of lead, or copper, or tin, or iron. The dream of Sir Walter
Raleigh concerning the golden city and country of Eldorado,[19] may satisfy
us, that even wise men are not always exempt from such strange delusions.
More [356] than a hundred years after the death of that great man, the
Jesuit Gumila was still convinced of the reality of that wonderful country,
and expressed with great warmth, and I dare to say, with great sincerity,
how happy he should be to carry the light of the gospel to a people who
could so well reward the pious labours of their missionary.[20]

20   In the countries first discovered by the Spaniards, no gold or silver
mines are at present known which are supposed to be worth the working.
The quantities of those metals which the first adventurers are said to
have found there, had probably been very much magnified, as well as
the fertility of the mines which were wrought immediately after the first
discovery. What those adventurers were reported to have found, however,
was sufficient to inflame the avidity of all their countrymen. Every Span-
iard who sailed to America expected to find an Eldorado. Fortune too
did upon this what she has done upon very few other occasions. She

[18] See above, I.xi.c.31. Cf. Monetsquieu, *Esprit*, XXI.xxii.7–11:
The specie of Europe soon doubled, and the profit of Spain diminished in the same
proportion; they had every year the same quantity of metal, which had become by one-
half less precious ... Thus the galoons which brought to Spain the same quantity of
gold, brought a thing which really was of less value by one-half, though the expenses
attending it had been twice as high.
   If we proceed doubling and doubling, we shall find in this progression the cause
of the impotency of the wealth of Spain.
[19] See also W. Raleigh, *The Discoverie of the large and bewtiful Empire of Guina* (1596),
ed. V. T. Harlow (London, 1928), 17: 'I have been assured by such of the Spanyards
as have seene Manoa the emperiall Citie of Guina, which the Spanyards cal el Dorado,
that for the greatnes, for the riches, and for the excellent seate, it farre exceedeth any
of the world, at least of so much of the world as is knowen to the Spanish nation.'
[20] J. Gumilla, *Histoire naturelle, civile et géographique de l'Orénoque* (Avignon, 1758),
especially ii.130–42.

realized in some measure the extravagant hopes of her votaries, and in the discovery and conquest of Mexico and Peru (of which the one happened about thirty, the other about forty years after the first expedition of Columbus), she presented them with something not very unlike that profusion of the precious metals which they sought for.

21   A project of commerce to the East Indies, therefore, gave occasion to the first discovery of the West. A project of conquest gave occasion to all the establishments of the Spaniards in those [357] newly discovered countries. The motive which excited them to this conquest was a project of gold and silver mines; and a course of accidents, which no human wisdom could foresee, rendered this project much more successful than the undertakers had any reasonable grounds for expecting.

22   The first adventurers of all the other nations of Europe, who attempted to make settlements in America, were animated by the like chimerical views; but they were not equally successful. It was more than a hundred years after the first settlement of the Brazils, before any silver, gold, or diamond mines were discovered there. In the English, French, Dutch, and Danish colonies, none have ever yet been discovered; at least none that are at present supposed to be worth the working. The first English settlers in North America, however, offered a fifth of all the gold and silver which should be found there to the king, as a motive for granting them their patents. In the patents to Sir Walter Raleigh, to the London and Plymouth companies, to the council of Plymouth, &c. this fifth was accordingly reserved to the crown. To the expectation of finding gold and silver mines, those first settlers too joined that of discovering a north-west passage to the East Indies. They have hitherto been disappointed in both.

[358]   PART SECOND

Causes of the Prosperity of new Colonies

1   The colony of a civilized nation which takes possession, either of a waste country, or of one so thinly inhabited, that the natives easily give place to the new settlers, advances more rapidly to wealth and greatness than any other human society.

2   The colonists carry out with them a knowledge of agriculture and of other useful arts, superior to what can grow up of its own accord in the course of many centuries among savage and barbarous nations.[1] They carry out

[1] The natural progress of law and government among primitive peoples is described in V.i.b. and its later progress in III. See especially ED 5.2, where it is pointed out that the most important contributory factors are the difficulties of acquiring stock and the slow progress of invention. In this place Smith also made the interesting point that 'a nation is not always in a condition to imitate and copy the inventions and improvements of its more wealthy neighbours; the application of these frequently requiring a stock with which it is not furnished.'

with them too the habit of subordination, some notion of the regular government which takes place in their own country, of the system of laws which *support* it, and of a regular administration of justice; and they naturally establish something of the same kind in the new settlement.[2] But among savage and barbarous nations, the natural progress of law and government is still slower than the natural progress of arts, after law and government have been so far established, as is necessary for their protection. Every colonist gets more land than he can possibly cultivate. He has no rent, and scarce any taxes to pay.[3] No landlord shares with him in its produce, and the share of the sovereign is commonly but a trifle. He has every motive to render as great as possible a produce, which is thus to be almost en-[359]tirely his own. But his land is commonly so extensive, that with all his own industry, and with all the industry of other people whom he can get to employ, he can seldom make it produce the tenth part of what it is capable of producing. He is eager, therefore, to collect labourers from all quarters, and to reward them with the most liberal wages. But those liberal wages, joined to the plenty and cheapness of land, soon make those labourers leave him in order to become landlords themselves, and to reward, with equal liberality, other labourers, who soon leave them for the same reason that they left their first master. The liberal reward of labour encourages marriage. The children, during the tender years of infancy, are well fed and properly taken care of, and when they are grown up, the value of their labour greatly over-pays their maintenance. When arrived at maturity, the high price of labour, and the low price of land, enable them to establish themselves in the same manner as their fathers did before them.[4]

3   In other countries, rent and profit eat up wages, and the two superior orders of people oppress the inferior one. But in new colonies, the interest of the two superior orders obliges them to treat the inferior one with more generosity and humanity; at least, where that inferior one is not in a state of slavery. Waste lands, of the greatest natural fertility, are to be had for a trifle. The increase of revenue which the proprietor, who is always the undertaker, [360] expects from their improvement, constitutes his profit; which in these circumstances is commonly very great. But this great profit

---

a–a supports 5–6

[2] Smith comments on the specific advantages accruing to the British colonies as a result of her particular institutions at IV.vii.b.51. In an apparent reference to England, Montesquieu (*Esprit*, XIX. xxvii.35) remarked that: 'As men are fond of introducing into other places what they have established among themselves, they have given the people of the colonies their own form of government; and this government carrying prosperity along with it, they have raised great nations in the forests they were sent to inhabit.'

[3] See above, III.ii.20, where Smith comments on the improvement which is possible in the absence of rent payments. See also III.i.5.

[4] Smith comments at I.viii.23 on the high value of children in America.

cannot be made without employing the labour of other people in clearing and cultivating the land; and the disproportion between the great extent of the land and the small number of the people, which commonly takes place in new colonies, makes it difficult for him to get this labour. He does not, therefore, dispute about wages, but is willing to employ labour at any price. The high wages of labour encourage population. The cheapness and plenty of good land encourage improvement, and enable the proprietor to pay those high wages.[5] In those wages consists almost the whole price of the land; and though they are high, considered as the wages of labour, they are low, considered as the price of what is so very valuable. What encourages the progress of population and improvement, encourages that of real wealth and greatness.

4   The progress of many of the antient Greek colonies towards wealth and greatness, seems accordingly to have been very rapid. In the course of a century or two, several of them appear to have rivalled, and even to have surpassed their mother cities. Syracuse and Agrigentum in Sicily, Tarentum and Locri in Italy, Ephesus and Miletus in Lesser Asia, appear by all accounts to have been at least equal to any of the cities of antient Greece.[6] Though posterior in their establishment, yet all the arts of refinement, philosophy, poetry, and eloquence, seem [361] to have been cultivated as early, and to have been improved as highly in them, as in any part of the mother country.[7] The schools of the two oldest Greek philosophers, those

[5] It is stated at I.ix.11 that high wages and profits are only found together in the 'peculiar circumstances of new colonies'.

[6] Cf. Astronomy, III.4: 'Greece, and the Greek colonies in Sicily, Italy, and the Lesser Asia, were the first countries which, in these western parts of the world, arrived at a state of civilized society. It was in them, therefore, that the first philosophers, of whose doctrine we have any distinct account, appeared.' Smith commented in LRBL ii.117–19, ed. Lothian 132–3, with regard to the history of Athens, that at one stage philosophy and the arts had come to a state 'of some perfection' in the colonies:

> before they were heard of in the mother country. Thales had taught at Miletus, Pythagoras in Italy, and Empedocles in Sicily, before the time of the Persian expedition, from which time commerce, that had been cultivated in the colonies, flourished in the continent, and brought wealth, arts, and refinement along with it. Gorgias of Mitylene was the first who introduced Eloquence into Greece. He is said to have astonished them with the elegance and force of the Oration he delivered on his embassy from his country. From that time Eloquence began to be cultivated, and was soon encouraged by the addition of wealth and opulence to the Grecian States . . .

[7] Smith made a related point in LRBL ii.115, ed. Lothian 131–2: 'Opulence and commerce commonly precede the improvement of arts and refinement of every sort . . . Wherever the inhabitants of a city are rich and opulent, where they enjoy the necessaries and conveniencies of life in ease and security, there the arts will be cultivated, and refinement of manners a never-failing attendent.' He also noted in the Astronomy, III.3 that men in the savage state have little opportunity to think in terms other than of superstition: 'But when law has established order and security, and subsistence ceases to be precarious, the curiosity of mankind is increased, and their fears are diminished. The leisure which they then enjoy renders them more attentive to the appearances of nature, more observant of her smallest irregularities, and more desirous to know what is the chain which links them all together.' The point finds an echo in Hume's essay, 'Of the Rise and Progress

of Thales and Pythagoras, were established, it is remarkable, not in antient Greece, but the one in an Asiatick, the other in an Italian colony. All those colonies had established themselves in countries inhabited by savage and barbarous nations, who easily gave place to the new settlers. They had plenty of good land, and as they were altogether independent of the mother city, they were at liberty to manage their own affairs in the way that they judged was most suitable to their own interest.

5   The history of the Roman colonies is by no means so brilliant. Some of them, indeed, such as Florence, have in the course of many ages, and after the fall of the mother city, grown up to be considerable states. But the progress of no one of them seems ever to have been very rapid. They were all established in conquered provinces, which in most cases had been fully inhabited before. The quantity of land assigned to each colonist was seldom very considerable, and as the colony was not independent, they were not always at liberty to manage their own affairs in the way that they judged was most suitable to their own interest.

6   In the plenty of good land, the European colonies established in America and the West Indies resemble, and even greatly surpass, those of antient Greece.[8] In their dependency upon [362] the mother state, they resemble those of ancient Rome; but their great distance from Europe has in all of them alleviated more or less the effects of this dependency. Their situation has placed them less in the view and less in the power of their mother country. In pursuing their interest their own way, their conduct has, upon many occasions, been over-looked, either because not known or not understood in Europe; and upon some occasions it has been fairly suffered and submitted to, because their distance rendered it difficult to restrain it. Even the violent and arbitrary government of Spain has, upon many occasions, been obliged to recall or soften the orders which had been given for the government of *b*her*b* colonies, for fear of a general insurrection. The progress of all the European colonies in wealth, population, and improvement, has accordingly been very great.

7   The crown of Spain, by its share of the gold and silver, derived some revenue from its colonies, from the moment of their first establishment. It was a revenue too, of a nature to excite in human avidity the most extravagant expectations of still greater riches. The Spanish colonies, therefore, from the moment of their first establishment, attracted very much the attention of their mother country; while those of the other European

b-b its *1*

---

of the Arts and Sciences', where it is stated that 'From law arises security: from security curiosity: and from curiosity knowledge.' (*Essays Moral, Political, and Literary*, ed. Green and Grose, i. 180.)

   [8] It is remarked at I.xi.g.26 that plenty of good cheap land is a 'circumstance common to all new colonies'.

nations were for a long time in a great measure neglected. The former did not, perhaps, thrive the better in consequence of this attention; nor the latter the worse in consequence of this neglect. In proportion to the [363] extent of the country which they in some measure possess, the Spanish colonies are considered as less populous and thriving than those of almost any other European nation. The progress even of the Spanish colonies, however, in population and improvement, has certainly been very rapid and very great. The city of Lima, founded since the conquest, is represented by Ulloa, as containing fifty thousand inhabitants near thirty years ago.[9] Quito, which had been but a miserable hamlet of Indians, is represented by the same author as in his time equally populous.[10] Gemelli Carreri, a pretended traveller,[11] it is said, indeed, but who seems every where to have written upon extreme good information, represents the city of Mexico as containing a hundred thousand inhabitants; a number which, in spite of all the exaggerations of the Spanish writers, is, probably, more than five times greater than what it contained in the time of Montezuma. These numbers exceed greatly those of Boston, New York, and Philadelphia, the three greatest cities of the English colonies. Before the conquest of the Spaniards there were no cattle fit for draught, either in Mexico or Peru. The lama was their only beast of burden, and its strength seems to have been a good deal inferior to that of a common ass. The plough was unknown among them. They were ignorant of the use of iron. They had no coined money, nor any established instrument of commerce of any kind. Their commerce was carried on by barter. A sort of wooden spade was their prin-[364]cipal instrument of agriculture. Sharp stones served them for knives and hatchets to cut with; fish bones and the hard sinews of certain animals served them for needles to sew with; and these seem to have been their principal instruments of trade. In this state of things, it seems impossible, that either of those empires could have been so much improved or so well cultivated as at present, when they are plentifully furnished with all sorts of European cattle, and when the use of iron, of the plough, and of many of the arts of Europe, has been introduced among them. But the populousness of every country must be in proportion to the degree of its improvement and cultivation. In spite of the cruel destruction of the natives which followed the conquest, these two great empires are, probably, more populous now than they ever were before: and the people are surely very different; for we must acknowledge, I apprehend,

---

[9] See above, I.xi.g.26 where the number of inhabitants is stated to be 'more than fifty thousand'.

[10] Quito is given as having 'between 50 and 60,000 persons, of all ages, sexes, and ranks'. Juan and Ulloa, *Voyage historique*, i.229, trans. John Adams, i.262.

[11] J. F. G. Carreri, *A Voyage round the World*, in A. and J. Churchill, *A Collection of Voyages and Travels* (London, 1704), iv.508.

that the Spanish creoles are in many respects superior to the antient Indians.

8   After the settlements of the Spaniards, that of the Portugueze in Brazil is the oldest of any European nation in America. But as for a long time after the first discovery, neither gold nor silver mines were found in it, and as it afforded, upon that account, little or no revenue to the crown, it was for a long time in a great measure neglected; and during this state of neglect, it grew up to be a great and powerful colony. While Portugal was under the dominion of Spain, Brazil was attacked by the Dutch, who [365] got possession of seven of the fourteen provinces into which it is divided. They expected soon to conquer the other seven, when Portugal recovered its independency by the elevation of the family of Braganza to the throne. The Dutch then, as enemies to the Spaniards, became friends to the Portugueze, who were likewise the enemies of the Spaniards. They agreed, therefore, to leave that part of Brazil, which they had not conquered, to the king of Portugal, who agreed to leave that part which they had conquered to them, as a matter not worth disputing about with such good allies. But the Dutch government soon began to oppress the Portugueze colonists, who, instead of amusing themselves with complaints, took arms against their new masters, and by their own valour and resolution, with the connivance, indeed, but without any avowed assistance from the mother country, drove them out of Brazil. The Dutch, therefore, finding it impossible to keep any part of the country to themselves, were contented that it should be entirely restored to the crown of Portugal.[12] In this colony there are said to be more than six hundred thousand people, either Portugueze or descended from Portugueze, creoles, mulattoes, and a mixed race between Portugueze and Brazilians. No one colony in America is supposed to contain so great a number of people of European extraction.

9   Towards the end of the fifteenth, and during the greater part of the sixteenth century, Spain and Portugal were the two great naval powers [366] upon the ocean; for though the commerce of Venice extended to every part of Europe, its fleets had scarce ever sailed beyond the Mediterranean. The Spaniards, in virtue of the first discovery, claimed all America as their own; and though they could not hinder so great a naval power as that of Portugal from settling in Brazil, such was, at that time, the terror of their name, that the greater part of the other nations of Europe were afraid to establish themselves in any other part of that great continent. The French, who attempted to settle in Florida, were all murdered by the Spaniards. But the declension of the naval power of this latter nation, in consequence of the defeat or miscarriage of, what they called, their Invincible Armada, which happened towards the end of the sixteenth century, put it out of their power to obstruct any longer the settlements of the

[12] In 1654.

other European nations. In the course of the seventeenth century, therefore, the English, French, Dutch, Danes, and Swedes, all the great nations who had any ports upon the ocean, attempted to make some settlements in the new world.

10 The Swedes established themselves in New Jersey; and the number of Swedish families still to be found there, sufficiently demonstrates, that this colony was very likely to prosper, had it been protected by the mother country. But being neglected by Sweden, it was soon swallowed up by the Dutch colony of New York, which again, in 1674, fell under the dominion of the English.[13]

11 [367] The small islands of St. Thomas and Santa Cruz are the only countries in the new world that have ever been possessed by the Danes. These little settlements too were under the government of an exclusive company, which had the sole right, both of purchasing the surplus produce of the colonists, and of supplying them with such goods of other countries as they wanted, and which, therefore, both in its purchases and sales, had not only the power of oppressing them, but the greatest temptation to do so. The government of an exclusive company of merchants, is, perhaps, the worst of all governments for any country whatever.[14] It was not, however, able to stop altogether the progress of these colonies, though it rendered it more slow and languid. The late king of Denmark dissolved this company, and since that time the prosperity of these colonies has been very great.

12 The Dutch settlements in the West, as well as those in the East Indies, were originally put under the government of an exclusive company. The progress of some of them, therefore, though it has been considerable, in comparison with that of almost any country that has been long peopled and established, has been languid and slow in comparison with that of the greater part of new colonies. The colony of Surinam, though very considerable, is still inferior to the greater part of the sugar colonies of the other European nations. The colony of Nova Belgia, now divided into the two provinces of New York and New [368] Jersey, would probably have soon become considerable too, even though it had remained under the government of the Dutch. The plenty and cheapness of good land are such powerful causes of prosperity,[15] that the very worst government is scarce capable of checking altogether the efficacy of their operation. The great distance too from the mother country would enable the colonists to evade more or less, by smuggling, the monopoly which the company enjoyed against them. At present the company allows all Dutch ships to trade to Surinam

[13] New Amsterdam (to become New York) was occupied by the English in 1664 and ceded to the English by the Treaty of Breda in 1667. The Dutch recaptured New York in 1673 but English rule was resumed in 1674.

[14] See below, IV.vii.c.103, where it is stated that a company of merchants seems 'incapable of considering themselves as sovereigns'.

[15] See above, II.v.21 and III.iv.19.

upon paying two and a half per cent. upon the value of their cargo for a licence; and only reserves to itself exclusively the direct trade from Africa to America, which consists almost entirely in the slave trade. This relaxation in the exclusive privileges of the company, is probably the principal cause of that degree of prosperity which that colony at present enjoys. Curaçoa and Eustatia, the two principal islands belonging to the Dutch, are free ports open to the ships of all nations; and this freedom, in the midst of better colonies whose ports are open to those of one nation only, has been the great cause of the prosperity of those two barren islands.

13   The French colony of Canada was, during the greater part of the last century, and some part of the present, under the government of an exclusive company. Under so unfavourable an administration its progress was necessarily very slow in comparison with that of other new colonies; but it became much more rapid when this [369] company was dissolved after the fall of what is called the Mississippi scheme.[16] When the English got possession of this country, they found in it near double the number of inhabitants which father Charlevoix had assigned to it between twenty and thirty years before.[17] That jesuit had travelled over the whole country, and had no inclination to represent it as less considerable than it really was.

14   The French colony of St. Domingo was established by pirates and freebooters, who, for a long time, neither required the protection, nor acknowledged the authority of France; and when ᶜthatᶜ race of banditti became so far citizens as to acknowledge this authority, it was for a long time necessary to exercise it with very great gentleness. During this period the population and improvement of this colony increased very fast. Even the oppression of the exclusive company, to which it was for some time subjected, with all the other colonies of France, though it no doubt retarded, had not been able to stop its progress altogether. The course of its prosperity returned as soon as it was relieved from that oppression. It is now the most important of the sugar colonies of the West Indies, and its produce is said to be greater than that of all the English sugar colonies put together. The other sugar colonies of France are in general all very thriving.[18]

15   But there are no colonies of which the progress has been more rapid than that of the English in North America.

ᶜ⁻ᶜ the *1*

[16] See above, II.ii.78, where Smith discusses the 'real foundation' of the scheme, and below § 24.

[17] '... il est evident, qu'il ne peut être assez considérable, pour faire vivre une Colonie de vint à vint-cinq mille Ames, et pour fournier à ce qu'elle est obligée de tirer de France.' (F. X. de Charlevoix, *Histoire et description generale de la Nouvelle France* (Paris, 1744), ii.390.)

[18] Smith comments on the extent of the demand for sugar at I.xi.b.32 and on the high profits of the English colonies engaged in this trade at III.ii.10.

16   [370] Plenty of good land, and liberty to manage their own affairs their own way, seem to be the two great causes of the prosperity of all new colonies.

17   In the plenty of good land the English colonies of North America, though, no doubt, very abundantly provided, are, however, inferior to those of the Spaniards and Portugueze, and not superior to some of those possessed by the French before the late war. But the political institutions of the English colonies have been more favourable to the improvement and cultivation of this land, than those of any of the other three nations.

18   First, the engrossing of uncultivated land, though it has by no means been prevented altogether, has been more restrained in the English colonies than in any other. The colony law which imposes upon every proprietor the obligation of improving and cultivating, within a limited time, a certain proportion of his lands, and which, in case of failure, declares those neglected lands grantable to any other person; though it has not, perhaps, been very strictly executed, has, however, had some effect.

19   Secondly, in Pensylvania there is no right of primogeniture, and lands, like moveables, are divided equally among all the children of the family.[19] In three of the provinces of New England the oldest has only a double share, as in the Mosaical law. Though in those provinces, therefore, too great a quantity of land should sometimes be engrossed by a [371] particular individual, it is likely, in the course of a generation or two, to be sufficiently divided again. In the other English colonies, indeed, the right of primogeniture takes place, as in the law of England. But in all the English colonies the tenure of ᵈtheirᵈ lands, which are all held by free socage, facilitates alienation, and the grantee of any extensive tract of land generally finds it for his interest to alienate, as fast as he can, the greater part of it, reserving only a small quit-rent. In the Spanish and Portugueze colonies, what is called the right of Majorazzo* takes place in the succession of all those great estates to which any title of honour is annexed. Such estates go all to one person, and are in effect entailed and unalienable. The French colonies, indeed, are subject to the custom of Paris, which, in the inheritance of land, is much more favourable to the younger children than the law of England. But, in the French colonies, if any part of an estate, held by the noble tenure of chivalry and homage, is alienated, it is, for a limited time, subject to the right of redemption, either by the heir of the superior or by the heir of the family; and all the largest estates of the country are held by such noble tenures, which necessarily embarrass alienation. But, in a new colony, a great uncultivated estate is likely to be

* Jus Majoratus.

ᵈ⁻ᵈ the 4–6

[19] Smith comments on the origins of the right of primogeniture at III.ii.3, and its impact on the sale of land in Europe, as compared to America, at III.iv.19.

much more speedily divided by alienation than by succession. *e*The plenty and cheapness of good land, it has already been observed, are the principal causes of the rapid prosperity of new [372] colonies.[20] The engrossing of land, in effect, destroys this plenty and cheapness. The engrossing of uncultivated land, besides, is the greatest obstruction to its improvement. But*e* the labour that is employed in the improvement and cultivation of land affords the greatest and most valuable produce to the society.[21] *f*The produce of labour*f*, in this case, pays not only its own wages, and the profit of the stock which employs it, but the rent of the land too upon which it is employed. The labour of the English colonists, therefore, being more employed in the improvement and cultivation of land, is likely to afford a greater and more valuable produce, than that of any of the other three nations, which, by the engrossing of land, is more or less diverted towards other employments.

20   Thirdly, the labour of the English colonists is not only likely to afford a greater and more valuable produce, but, in consequence of the moderation of their taxes, a greater proportion of this produce belongs to themselves, which they may store up and employ in putting into motion a still greater quantity of labour.[22] The English colonists have never yet contributed any thing towards the defence of the mother country, or towards the support of its civil government. They themselves, on the contrary, have hitherto been defended almost entirely at the expence of the mother country. But the expence of fleets and armies is out of all proportion greater than the necessary expence of civil government. The expence of their own civil [373] government has always been very moderate. It has generally been confined to what was necessary for paying competent salaries to the governor, to the judges, and to some other officers of police, and for maintaining a few of the most useful publick works. The expence of the civil establishment of Massachusett's Bay, before the commencement of the present disturbances, used to be but about 18,000*l*. a year. That of New Hampshire and Rhode Island 3,500*l*. each. That of Connecticut 4,000*l*. That of New York and Pensylvania 4,500*l*. each.[23] That of New Jersey 1,200*l*. That of Virginia and South Carolina 8,000*l*. each. The civil *g*establishment*g* of Nova Scotia and Georgia are partly supported by an annual grant of parliament. But Nova Scotia pays, besides, about 7000*l*. a

---

e-e The engrossing, however, of uncultivated land, it has already been observed, is the greatest obstruction to its improvement and cultivation; and *1*
f-f Its produce *1*   *g-g* establishments *5-6*

[20] See for example, above § 3, and I.ix.11.
[21] Smith comments on the superior productivity of agriculture at II.v.12 and accounts for the rapid progress of the American colonies in § 21 of that section.
[22] A similar point is made at IV.vii.c.12,64; V.iii.92.
[23] The cost of government in Pennsylvannia is mentioned at V.ii.a.11 and the costs of the colonies as a whole at V.iii.76.

year towards the publick expences of the colony; and Georgia about 2,500*l.* a year. All the different civil establishments in North America, in short, exclusive of those of Maryland and North Carolina, of which no exact account has been got, did not, before the commencement of the present disturbances, cost the inhabitants above 64,700*l.* a year; an ever memorable example at how small an expence three millions of people may not only be governed, but well governed. The most important part of the expence of government, indeed, that of defence and protection, has constantly fallen upon the mother country. The ceremonial too of the civil government in the colonies, upon the reception of a new governor, upon the opening of a new assembly, &c. [374] though sufficiently decent, is not accompanied with any expensive pomp or parade. Their ecclesiastical government is conducted upon a plan equally frugal. Tithes are unknown among them;[24] and their clergy, who are far from being numerous, are maintained either by moderate stipends, or by the voluntary contributions of the people. The power of Spain and Portugal, on the contrary, derives some support from the taxes levied upon their colonies.[25] France, indeed, has never drawn any considerable revenue from its colonies, the taxes which it levies upon them being generally spent among them. But the colony government of all these three nations is conducted upon a much more expensive plan, and is accompanied with a much more expensive ceremonial. The sums spent upon the reception of a new viceroy of Peru, for example, have frequently been enormous.[26] Such ceremonials are not only real taxes paid by the rich colonists upon those particular occasions, but they serve to introduce among them the habit of vanity and expence upon all other occasions.[27] They are not only very grievous occasional taxes, but they contribute to establish perpetual taxes of the same kind still more grievous; the ruinous taxes of private luxury and extravagance. In the colonies of all those three nations too the ecclesiastical government is extremely oppressive. Tithes take place in all of them, and are levied with the utmost rigour in those of Spain and Portugal. All of them besides are oppressed with a numerous race of mendicant friars, whose beggary [375] being not only licensed, but consecrated by religion, is a most grievous tax upon the poor people, who are most carefully taught that it is a duty to give, and a very great sin to refuse them their charity. Over and above all this, the clergy are, in all of them, the greatest engrossers of land.

21   Fourthly, in the disposal of their surplus produce, or of what is over and above their own consumption, the English colonies have been more

---

[24] Tithes are stated to be a 'very great hindrance' to improvement at III.ii.13 and V.ii.d.3.

[25] It is stated at IV.vii.c.13 that Spain and Portugal alone among the European powers had benefited in this way.

[26] Juan and Ulloa, *Voyage historique*, i.437–42, trans. John Adams, ii.46–52.

[27] See above, II.iii.12 where Smith discusses the influence of 'manners' on economic activity, and below, IV.vii.c.61.

favoured, and have been allowed a more extensive market, than those of any other European nation. Every European nation has endeavoured more or less to monopolize to itself the commerce of its colonies, and, upon that account, has prohibited the ships of foreign nations from trading to them, and has prohibited them from importing European goods from any foreign nation. But the manner in which this monopoly has been exercised in different nations has been very different.

22   Some nations have given up the whole commerce of their colonies to an exclusive company, of whom the *ʰ*colonists*ʰ* were obliged to buy all such European goods as they wanted, and to whom they were obliged to sell the whole of their own surplus produce. It was the interest of the company, therefore, not only to sell the former as dear, and to buy the latter as cheap as possible, but to buy no more of the latter, even at this low price, than what they could dispose of for a very high price in Europe.[28] It was their interest, not only to degrade in all cases the va-[376]lue of the surplus produce of the colony, but in many cases to discourage and keep down the natural increase of its quantity. Of all the expedients that can well be contrived to stunt the natural growth of a new colony, that of an exclusive company is undoubtedly the most effectual.[29] This, however, has been the policy of Holland, though their company, in the course of the present century, has given up in many respects the exertion of their exclusive privilege. This too was the policy of Denmark till the reign of the late king. It has occasionally been the policy of France, and of late, since 1755, after it had been abandoned by all other nations, on account of its absurdity, it has become the policy of Portugal with regard at least to two of the principal provinces of Brazil, Fernambuco and Marannon.[30]

23   Other nations, without establishing an exclusive company, have confined the whole commerce of their colonies to a particular port of the mother country, from whence no ship was allowed to sail, but either in a fleet and at a particular season, or, if single, in consequence of a particular licence, which in most cases was very well paid for. This policy opened, indeed, the trade of the colonies to all the natives of the mother country, provided they traded from the proper port, at the proper season, and in the proper

---

ʰ⁻ʰ colonies 5–6

---

[28] Above, I.vii.27, where Smith stated the famous proposition that the 'price of monopoly is upon every occasion the highest which can be got'.

[29] See for example, IV.vii.c.101.

[30] 'It was not to be expected, that a nation, which, in the barbarous ages, had pursued the inestimable advantages of competition, would at last, in an enlightened age, adopt a pernicious system, which, by collecting the principles of life and motion into a small part of the body politic, leave nothing in all the rest but langour and death . . . They [the ministry] had already, ever since the 6th of June 1755, created the Maragnan company; and, far from receding, they erected the Fernambucca company, four years after, and thereby enslaved all the northern part of Brazil.' (G. T. F. Raynal, *Histoire philosophique*, iii.384–5, trans. J. Justamond, ii.434.)

vessels. But as all the different merchants, who joined their stocks in order
to fit out those licensed vessels, would find it for their interest to act in
concert, the trade which was [377] carried on in this manner would necessarily be conducted very nearly upon the same principles as that of an
exclusive company. The profit of those merchants would be almost equally
exorbitant and oppressive. The colonies would be ill supplied, and would
be obliged both to buy very dear, and to sell very cheap. This, however,
ᶦtill within these few years, hadᶦ always been the policy of Spain, and the
price of all European goods, accordingly, is said to ʲhave beenʲ enormous
in the Spanish West Indies.³¹ At Quito, we are told by Ulloa, a pound of
iron ᵏsoldᵏ for about four and sixpence, and a pound of steel for about six
and nine-pence sterling.³² But it is chiefly in order to purchase European
goods, that the colonies part with their own produce. The more, therefore,
they pay for the one, the less they really get for the other, and the dearness
of the one is the same thing with the cheapness of the other. The policy
of Portugal is in this respect the same as ˡthe antient policyˡ of Spain, with
regard to all its colonies, except Fernambuco and Marannon, and with
regard to these it has lately adopted a still worse.

24   Other nations leave the trade of their colonies free to all their subjects
who may carry it on from all the different ports of the mother country,
and who have occasion for no other licence than the common dispatches
of the customhouse. In this case the number and dispersed situation³³
of the different traders renders it impossible for them to enter into any
general combination, and their competition is sufficient to hinder them
[378] from making very exorbitant profits. Under so liberal a policy the
colonies are enabled both to sell their own produce and to buy the goods of
Europe at a reasonable price. But since the dissolution of the Plymouth
company, when our colonies were but in their infancy, this has always been
the policy of England. It has generally too been that of France, and ᵐ has
been uniformly so since the dissolution of what, in England, is commonly
called their Mississippi company.³⁴ The profits of the trade, therefore,
which France and England carry on with their colonies, though no doubt
somewhat higher than if the competition was free to all other nations, are,

---

ᶦ⁻ᶦ has *1*   ʲ⁻ʲ be *1*·   ᵏ⁻ᵏ sells *1*   ˡ⁻ˡ that *1*   ᵐ it *1*

³¹ Juan and Ulloa, *Voyage historique*, i.489 and i.523, trans. John Adams, ii.108 and
ii.148.
³² At Quito 'they also import, by way of Guayaquil, iron and steel both from Europe
and the coast of Guatemala; and though it fetches so high a price, that a quintal of iron sells
for above a hundred dollars, and the same quantity of steel for a hundred and fifty,
there is a continual demand in order to supply the peasants with the necessary instruments
of agriculture.' (Ibid. i.252, trans. John Adams, i.292.)
³³ A similar point is made with regard to ease of combination, for example, at I.x.c.23,
IV.ii.21, and IV.v.b.4.
³⁴ See above, § 13 and II.ii.78.

however, by no means exorbitant; and the price of European goods accordingly is not extravagantly high in the greater part of the colonies of either of those nations.

25   In the exportation of their own surplus produce too, it is only with regard to certain commodities that the colonies of Great Britain are confined to the market of the mother country. These commodities having been enumerated in the act of navigation[35] and in some other subsequent acts, have upon that account been called *enumerated commodities*.[36] The rest are called *non-enumerated*; and may be exported directly to other countries, provided it is in British or Plantation ships, of which the owners and three-fourths of the mariners are British subjects.

26   Among the non-enumerated commodities are some of the most important productions of Ame-[379]rica and the West Indies; grain of all sorts, lumber, salt provisions, fish, sugar, and rum.

27   Grain is naturally the first and principal object of the culture of all new colonies. By allowing them a very extensive market for it, the law encourages them to extend this culture much beyond the consumption of a thinly inhabited country, and thus to provide beforehand an ample subsistence for a continually increasing population.

28   In a country quite covered with wood, where timber consequently is of little or no value, the expence of clearing the ground is the principal obstacle to improvement. By allowing the colonies a very extensive market for their lumber, the law endeavours to facilitate improvement by raising the price of a commodity which would otherwise be of little value, and thereby enabling them to make some profit of what would otherwise be mere expence.

29   In a country neither half-peopled nor half-cultivated, cattle naturally multiply beyond the consumption of the inhabitants, and are often upon that account of little or no value. But it is necessary, it has already been shewn,[37] that the price of cattle should bear a certain proportion to that of corn before the greater part of the lands of any country can be improved. By allowing to American cattle, in all shapes, dead and alive, a very extensive market, the law endeavours to raise the value of a commodity of which the high price is so very essential to improvement. The good effects of this liberty, [380] however, must be somewhat diminished by the 4th of George III. c. 15. which puts hides and skins among the enumerated commodities, and thereby tends to reduce the value of American cattle.

30   To increase the shipping and naval power of Great Britain, by the extension of the fisheries of our colonies, is an object which the legislature

---

[35] The provisions of the act are discussed in IV.ii.24f.

[36] Sugar, tobacco, cotton-wool, indigo, ginger, fustic, and other dyeing woods are enumerated in 12 Charles II, c.18 (1660).

[37] See above, I.xi.b.7–9 and I.xi.l.1–3.

seems to have had almost constantly in view.[38] Those fisheries, upon this account, have had all the encouragement which freedom can give them, and they have flourished accordingly. The New England fishery in particular was, before the late disturbances, one of the most important, perhaps, in the world. The whale-fishery which, notwithstanding an extravagant bounty,[39] is in Great Britain carried on to so little purpose, that in the opinion of many people (which I do not, however, pretend to warrant) the whole produce does not much exceed the value of the bounties which are annually paid for it, is in New England carried on without any bounty to a very great extent. Fish is one of the principal articles with which the North Americans trade to Spain, Portugal, and the Mediterranean.

31   Sugar was originally an enumerated commodity which could be exported only to Great Britain. But in 1731, upon a representation of the sugar-planters, its exportation was permitted to all parts of the world.[40] The restrictions, however, with which this liberty was granted, joined to the high price of sugar in Great Britain, have [381] rendered it, in a great measure, ineffectual.[41] Great Britain and her colonies, still continue to be almost the sole market for all the sugar produced in the British plantations. Their consumption increases so fast that, though in consequence of the increasing improvement of Jamaica as well of the Ceded Islands,[42] the importation of sugar has increased very greatly within these twenty years, the exportation to foreign countries is said to be not much greater than before.

32   Rum is a very important article in the trade which the Americans carry on to the coast of Africa, from which they bring back negroe slaves in return.

33   If the whole surplus produce of America in grain of all sorts, in salt provisions and in fish, had been put into the enumeration, and thereby forced into the market of Great Britain, it would have interfered too much with the produce of the industry of our own people. It was probably not so much from any regard to the interest of America, as from a jealousy of this interference, that those important commodities have not only been kept out of the enumeration, but that the importation into Great Britain of all grain, except rice, and of [n] salt provisions, has, in the ordinary state of the law, been prohibited.[43]

[n] all 6

---

[38] See for example, II.v.30, IV.ii.30, and IV.v.a.27.

[39] See above, IV.v.a.26. The bounty on the herring fishery is considered in IV.v.a.28f. Bounties were granted by 11 George III, c.38 (1771).

[40] 12 George II, c.30 (1738) permitted sugar to be carried from the colonies direct to foreign ports, from 1739 not 1731. Ships had, however, to call at a British port if not bound south of Cape Finisterre.

[41] See above, I.xi.b.32, where Smith comments on the level of demand for sugar.

[42] It is stated at V.iii.46 that the government received £95,500 from the sale of the ceded islands.

[43] See above, III.iv.20, IV.ii.1, IV.ii.16, IV.v.a.23, IV.v.b.33, IV.v.b.37, and below, V.ii.k.13.

34 The non-enumerated commodities could originally be exported to all parts of the world. Lumber and rice, having been once put into the enumeration, when they were afterwards taken out of it, were confined, as to the European market, to the countries that lie south of Cape [382] Finisterre.[44] By the 6th of George III. c. 52.[45] all non-enumerated commodities were subjected to the like restriction. The parts of Europe which lie south of Cape Finisterre, are not manufacturing countries, and we were less jealous of the colony ships carrying home from them any manufactures which could interfere with our own.

35 The enumerated commodities are of two sorts: first, such as are either the peculiar produce of America, or as cannot be produced, or at least are not produced, in the mother country. Of this kind are, melasses, coffee, cacao-nuts, tobacco, pimento, ginger, whale-fins, raw silk, cotton-wool, beaver, and other peltry of America, indigo, fustick, and other dying woods: secondly, such as are not the peculiar produce of America, but which are and may be produced in the mother country, though not in such quantities as to supply the greater part of her demand, which is principally supplied from foreign countries. Of this kind are all naval stores, masts, yards, and bowsprits, tar, pitch, and turpentine, pig and bar iron, copper ore, hides and skins, pot and pearl ashes. The largest importation of commodities of the first kind could not discourage the growth or interfere with the sale of any part of the produce of the mother country. By confining them to the home market, our merchants, it was expected, would not only be enabled to buy them cheaper in the Plantations, and consequently to sell them with a better profit at home, but to establish between the Plantations and foreign countries an advantageous carrying [383] trade,[46] of which Great Britain was necessarily to be the center or emporium, as the European country into which those commodities were first to be imported. The importation of commodities of the second kind might be so managed too, it was supposed, as to interfere, not with the sale of those of the same kind which were produced at home, but with that of those which were imported from foreign countries; because, by means of proper duties, they might be rendered always somewhat dearer than the former, and yet a good deal cheaper than the latter. By confining such commodities to the home market, therefore, it was proposed to discourage the produce, not of Great Britain, but of some foreign countries with which the balance of trade was believed to be unfavourable to Great Britain.

36 The prohibition of exporting from the colonies, to any other country but Great Britain, masts, yards, and bowsprits, tar, pitch, and turpentine,

[44] Rice by 3 George II, c.28 (1729) and lumber by 5 George III, c.45 (1765). See above, IV.iv.10 and IV.vii.c.63. The enumerated commodities are also discussed, for example, at IV.vii.c.15 and IV.viii.40.

[45] 6 George III, c.52 (1766).   [46] The term is defined at II.v.24.

naturally tended to lower the price of timber in the colonies, and consequently to increase the expence of clearing their lands, the principal obstacle to their improvement. But about the beginning of the present century, in 1703, the pitch and tar company of Sweden endeavoured to raise the price of their commodities to Great Britain, by prohibiting their exportation, except in their own ships, at their own price, and in such quantities as they thought proper.[47] In order to counteract this notable piece of mercantile policy, and to render herself [384] as much as possible independent, not only of Sweden, but of all the other northern powers, Great Britain gave a bounty upon the importation of naval stores from America,[48] and the effect of this bounty was to raise the price of timber in America, much more than the confinement to the home market could lower it; and as both regulations were enacted at the same time, their joint effect was rather to encourage than to discourage the clearing of land in America.

37   Though pig and bar iron too have been put among the enumerated commodities, yet as, when imported from America, they are exempted from considerable duties to which they are subject when imported from any other country, the one part of the regulation contributes more to encourage the erection of furnaces in America, than the other to discourage it.[49] There is no manufacture which occasions so great a consumption of wood as a furnace, or which can contribute so much to the clearing of a country overgrown with it.[50]

38   The tendency of some of these regulations to raise the value of timber in America, and thereby to facilitate the clearing of the land, was neither, perhaps, intended nor understood by the legislature. Though their beneficial effects, however, have been in this respect accidental, they have not upon that account been less real.

39   The most perfect freedom of trade is permitted between the British colonies of America and the West Indies, both in the enumerated and in the non-enumerated commodities. Those colonies are [385] now becoming so populous and thriving, that each of them finds in some of the others a great and extensive market for every part of its produce. All of them taken together, they make a great internal market for the produce of one another.

---

[47] A. Anderson, *Origin of Commerce* (1764), ii.238.

[48] 3 and 4 Anne, c.9 (1704) in *Statutes of the Realm*, viii.354–6; 3 and 4 Anne, c.10 in Ruffhead's edition. See below, IV.viii.7.

[49] 23 George II, c.29 (1749), 'An Act to encourage importation of pig and bar iron from the American colonies; and to prevent the erection of any mill or other engine for slitting or rolling of iron; or any plateing forge to work with a Tilt Hammer; or any Furnace for making steel'. See below, IV.vii.b.42 and IV.viii.3.

[50] It is stated at I.xi.c.5 that in many parts of North America, the landlord 'would be much obliged to any body who would carry away the greater part of his large trees'. It is stated below that the British iron manufacture used coal as an instrument of trade, V.ii.k.12.

40　　The liberality of England, however, towards the trade of her colonies has been confined chiefly to what concerns the market for their produce, either in its rude state, or in what may be called the very first stage of manufacture. The more advanced or more refined manufactures even of the colony produce, the merchants and manufacturers of Great Britain chuse to reserve to themselves, and have prevailed upon the legislature to prevent their establishment in the colonies, sometimes by high duties, and sometimes by absolute prohibitions.[51]

41　　While, for example, Muskovado sugars from the British plantations, pay upon importation only 6*s.* 4*d.* the hundred weight; white sugars pay 1*l.* 1*s.* 1*d.*; and refined, either double or single, in loaves 4*l.* 2*s.* 5*d.*$\frac{8}{20}$. When those high duties were imposed, Great Britain was the sole, and she still continues to be the principal market to which the sugars of the British colonies could be exported. They amounted, therefore, to a prohibition, at first of claying or refining sugar for any foreign market, and at present of claying or refining it for the market, which takes off, perhaps, more than nine-tenths of the whole produce. The manufacture of claying or refining sugar accordingly, though it has flourished in all the sugar colonies of France, has [386] been little cultivated in any of those of England, except for the market of the colonies themselves. While Grenada was in the hands of the French, there was a refinery of sugar, by claying at least, upon almost every plantation. Since it fell into those of the English, almost all works of this kind have been given up, and there are at present, October 1773, I am assured, not above two or three remaining in the island. At present, how-

---

[51] Smith mentions the encouragement given to the output of rude produce at IV.vii.c.51, IV.viii.1, and V.ii.k.24. Policy with regard to the colonies may have been the reflection of a belief which Smith himself seems to have shared at the time when his lectures were delivered. See LJ (B) 319–20, ed. Cannan 246–7:

> the common prejudice that wealth consists in money has not been in this respect so hurtfull as might have been imagined, and has even given occasions to regulations not very inconvenient. Those nations to whom we give more goods than we receive, generaly send us manufactured goods; those on the contrary from whom we receive more goods than we give, or with respect to whom the balance is in our favour, generaly send us unmanufactured goods . . . This kind of trade is very advantageous, because goods in an unmanufactured and rude state afford employment and maintenance to a great number of persons.

Cantillon also observed (*Essai*, 308–9, ed. Higgs 233) that: 'It will always be found by examining particular cases that the exportation of all Manufactured articles is advantageous to the State, because in this case the Foreigner always pays and supports Workmen useful to the State: that the best returns or payments imported are specie, and in default of specie the produce of Foreign land into which there enters the least labour.' See also Harris, *Essay*, i.24 and Steuart, *Principles*, II.xxiv. Smith may have first come in contact with the 'export of work doctrine' from Hutcheson, who said that 'Foreign materials should be imported and even premiums given, when necessary, that all our hands may be employed; and that, by exporting them again manufactured, we may obtain from abroad the price of our labours.' (*System*, ii.319.) For comment, see E. A. G. Johnson, *Predecessors of Adam Smith* (New York, 1960), Chapter xxxv.

ever, by an indulgence of the customhouse, clayed or refined sugar, if reduced from loaves into powder, is commonly imported as Muskovado.

42   While Great Britain encourages in America the manufactures of pig and bar iron, by exempting them from duties to which the like commodities are subject when imported from any other country, she imposes an absolute prohibition upon the erection of steel furnaces and slitmills in any of her American plantations.[52] She will not suffer her colonists to work in those more refined manufactures even for their own consumption; but insists upon their purchasing of her merchants and manufacturers all goods of this kind which they have occasion for.

43   She prohibits the exportation from one province to another by water, and even the carriage by land upon horseback or in a cart, of hats,[53] of wools and woollen goods,[54] of the produce of America; a regulation which effectually prevents the establishment of any manufacture of such commodities for distant sale, and confines the industry of her colonists in this way to such [387] coarse and household manufactures, as a private family commonly makes for its own use, or for that of some of its neighbours in the same province.

44   To prohibit a great people, however, from making all that they can of every part of their own produce, or from employing their stock and industry in the way that they judge most advantageous to themselves, is a manifest violation of the most sacred rights of mankind. Unjust, however, as such prohibitions may be, they have not hitherto been very hurtful to the colonies. Land is still so cheap, and, consequently, labour so dear among them, that they can import from the mother country, almost all the more refined or more advanced manufactures cheaper than they could make them for themselves.[55] Though they had not, therefore, been prohibited from establishing such manufactures, yet in their present state of improvement, a regard to their own interest would, probably, have prevented them from doing so. In their present state of improvement, those prohibitions, perhaps, without cramping their industry, or restraining it from any employment to which it would have gone of its own accord, are only impertinent badges of slavery imposed upon them, without any sufficient reason, by the groundless jealousy of the merchants and manufacturers of the mother country.[56] In a more advanced state they might be really oppressive and insupportable.

[52] 23 George II, c.29 (1749). See above, IV.vii.b.37, and below, IV.viii.3.

[53] 5 George II, c.22 (1731). See above, I.x.c.6.

[54] 10 William III, c.16 (1698) in *Statutes of the Realm*, vii.524–8; 10 and 11 William, c.10 (1698) in Ruffhead's edition. Smith also comments on the restrictions imposed on the wool trade in England at IV.viii.21.

[55] See below, IV.vii.c.51, where a similar point is made. Smith also comments on the absence of manufactures in America at III.i.5 and attributes the rapid growth of America to concentration on agriculture at II.v.21.

[56] Smith refers to monopoly as the 'principal badge' of colonial dependency at IV.vii.c.64.

45   Great Britain too, as she confines to her own market some of the most
      important productions [388] of the colonies, so in compensation she gives
      to some of them an advantage in that market; sometimes by imposing
      higher duties upon the like productions when imported from other
      countries, and sometimes by giving bounties upon their importation from
      the colonies.[57] In the first way she gives an advantage in the home-market
      to the sugar, tobacco,[58] and iron of her own colonies, and in the second to
      their raw silk, to their hemp and flax, to their indigo, to their naval stores,
      and to their building-timber.[59] This second way of encouraging the colony
      produce by bounties upon importation, is, so far as I have been able to
      learn, peculiar to Great Britain. The first is not. Portugal does not content
      herself with imposing higher duties upon the importation of tobacco from
      any other country, but prohibits it under the severest penalties.

46   With regard to the importation of goods from Europe, England has
      likewise dealt more liberally with her colonies than any other nation.

47   Great Britain allows a part, almost always the half, generally a larger
      portion, and sometimes the whole of the duty which is paid upon the
      importation of foreign goods, to be drawn back upon their exportation to
      any foreign country.[60] No independent foreign country, it was easy to
      foresee, would receive them if they came to it loaded with the heavy duties
      to which almost all foreign goods are subjected on their importation into
      Great Britain. Unless, therefore, some part of those duties was drawn
      back upon ex-[389]portation, there was an end of the carrying trade; a
      trade so much favoured by the mercantile system.

48   Our colonies, however, are by no means independent foreign countries;
      and Great Britain having assumed to herself the exclusive right of supplying
      them with all goods from Europe, might have forced them (in the same
      manner as other countries have done their colonies) to receive such goods,
      loaded with all the same duties which they paid in the mother country.
      But, on the contrary, till 1763, the same drawbacks were paid upon the
      exportation of the greater part of foreign goods to our colonies as to any
      independent foreign country.[61] In 1763, indeed, by the 4th of Geo. III. c.
      15. this indulgence was a good deal abated, and it was enacted, "That no
      part of the duty called the old subsidy should be drawn back for any goods
      of the growth, production, or manufacture of Europe or the East Indies,
      which should be exported from this kingdom to any British colony or
      plantation in America; wines, white callicoes and muslins excepted."[62]
      Before this law, many different sorts of foreign goods might have been

---

[57] The bounties given to the colonies are extensively reviewed in IV.viii.
[58] Smith also comments on the restrictions imposed on the culture of tobacco in Europe
at I.xi.b.33.
[59] For details see below, IV.viii.7–14.   [60] For details see above, IV.iv.
[61] See above, IV.iv.15.
[62] 4 George III, c.15 (1764). The quotation is not quite verbatim. See also IV.iv.10,11.

bought cheaper in the plantations than in the mother country; and some may still.

49   Of the greater part of the regulations concerning the colony trade, the merchants who carry it on, it must be observed, have been the principal advisers. We must not wonder, there-[390]fore, if, in the greater part of them, their interest has been more considered than either that of the colonies or that of the mother country. In their exclusive privilege of supplying the colonies with all the goods which they wanted from Europe, and of purchasing all such parts of their surplus produce as could not interfere with any of the trades which they themselves carried on at home, the interest of the colonies was sacrificed to the interest of those merchants. In allowing the same drawbacks upon the re-exportation of the greater part of European and East India goods to the colonies, as upon their re-exportation to any independent country, the interest of the mother country was sacrificed to it, even according to the mercantile ideas of that interest. It was for the interest of the merchants to pay as little as possible for the foreign goods which they sent to the colonies, and, consequently, to get back as much as possible of the duties which they advanced upon their importation into Great Britain. They might thereby be enabled to sell in the colonies, either the same quantity of goods with a greater profit, or a greater quantity with the same profit, and, consequently, to gain something either in the one way or the other. It was, likewise, for the interest of the colonies to get all such goods as cheap and in as great abundance as possible. But this might not always be for the interest of the mother country. She might frequently suffer both in her revenue, by giving back a [391] great part of the duties which had been paid upon the importation of such goods; and in her manufactures, by being undersold in the colony market, in consequence of the easy terms upon which foreign manufactures could be carried thither by means of those drawbacks. The progress of the linen manufacture of Great Britain, it is commonly said, has been a good deal retarded by the drawbacks upon the re-exportation of German linen to the American colonies.[63]

50   But though the policy of Great Britain with regard to the trade of her colonies has been dictated by the same mercantile spirit as that of other nations, it has, however, upon the whole, been less illiberal and oppressive than that of any of them.

51   In every thing, except their foreign trade, the liberty of the English colonists to manage their own affairs their own way is complete. It is in

---

[63] In 1742 bounties were granted on exports of British linen to Africa, America, Spain, and Portugal instead of granting the demand for the withdrawal of the drawbacks. Bounties were withdrawn for two years in 1754 and gave rise to many complaints, especially because of the sharp fall in exports in those years. See above, I.viii.50. It is remarked at IV.vii.c.82 that the consumption of the Spanish and Portuguese colonies alone was valued at £3 million, much of it supplied by France, Holland, and Germany. See also IV.viii.4.

every respect equal to that of their fellow-citizens at home, and is secured
in the same manner, by an assembly of the representatives of the people,
who claim the sole right of imposing taxes for the support of the colony
government.[64] The authority of this assembly over-awes the executive
power, and neither the meanest nor the most obnoxious colonist, as long
as he obeys the law, has any thing to fear from the resentment, either of the
governor, or of any other civil or military officer in the province. The
colony assemblies, though, like the house of commons in England, they
are not always a very equal representation of the people, yet °they ap-[392]
proach more nearly to that character; and° as the executive power either
has not the means to corrupt them, or, on account of the support which it
receives from the mother country, is not under the necessity of doing so,
they are perhaps in general more influenced by the inclinations of their
constituents. The councils, which, in the colony legislatures, correspond
to the House of Lords in Great Britain, are not composed of an hereditary
nobility. In some of the colonies, as in three of the governments of New
England, those councils are not appointed by the king, but chosen by the
representatives of the people. In none of the English colonies is there any
hereditary nobility.[65] In all of them, indeed, as in all other free countries,
the descendant of an old colony family is more respected than an upstart
of equal merit and fortune:[66] but he is only more respected, and he has no
privileges by which he can be troublesome to his neighbours. Before the
commencement of the present disturbances, the colony assemblies had not
only the legislative, but a part of the executive power. In Connecticut and
Rhode Island, they elected the governor. In the other colonies they appointed the revenue officers who collected the taxes imposed by those respective
assemblies, to whom those officers were immediately responsible. There
is more equality, therefore, among the English colonists than among the
inhabitants of the mother country.[67] Their manners are more republican,
and their governments, those of three of the provinces of [393] New
England in particular, have hitherto been more republican too.[68]

°-° 2–6

---

[64] See below, IV.vii.c.79, where Smith discusses American representation in the British
Parliament. It is pointed out at V.iii.88 that the colonies owed their constitutions to the
British model; cf. IV.vii.b.2 and below, § 64. See also LJ (A) v.134–5: 'It is in Britain alone
that any consent of the people is required, and God knows it is but a very figurative metaphoricall consent which is given here. And in Scotland still more than in England, as
but very few have a vote for a member of parliament who give this metaphoricall consent
. . .' A similar point is made in LJ (B) 94, ed. Cannan 69. Smith reviews the basis of English
liberties in LJ (A) v.1–15 and LJ (B) 61–4, ed. Cannan, 43–6.

[65] Smith also comments at V.iii.90 on the absence of an 'oppressive aristocracy' in the
colonies.

[66] See for example, V.i.b.8, and cf. V.iii.36.

[67] Some of the material of this paragraph was probably derived from the Report to the
House of Commons of 1732, quoted by A. Anderson, *Origin of Commerce* (1764), ii.342–6.

[68] See below, IV.vii.c.74, where Smith comments on the sense of importance felt by

52   The absolute governments of Spain, Portugal, and France, on the contrary, take place in their colonies; and the discretionary powers which such governments commonly delegate to all their inferior officers are, on account of the great distance, naturally exercised there with more than ordinary violence. Under all absolute governments there is more liberty in the capital than in any other part of the country. The sovereign himself can never have either interest or inclination to pervert the order of justice, or to oppress the great body of the people. In the capital his presence overawes more or less all his inferior officers, who in the remoter provinces, from whence the complaints of the people are less likely to reach him, can exercise their tyranny with much more safety. But the European colonies in America are more remote than the most distant provinces of the greatest empires which had ever been known before. The government of the English colonies is perhaps the only one which, since the world began, could give perfect security to the inhabitants of so very distant a province. The administration of the French colonies, however, has always been conducted with more gentleness and moderation than that of the Spanish and Portuguese. This superiority of conduct is suitable both to the character of the French nation, and to what forms the character of every nation, the nature of their government, which though [394] arbitrary and violent in comparison with that of Great Britain, is legal and free in comparison with those of Spain and Portugal.

53   It is in the progress of the North American colonies, however, that the superiority of the English policy chiefly appears. The progress of the sugar colonies of France has been at least equal, perhaps superior, to that of the greater part of those of England; and yet the sugar colonies of England enjoy a free government nearly of the same kind with that which takes place in her colonies of North America. But the sugar colonies of France are not discouraged, like those of England, from refining their own sugar; and, what is of still greater importance, the genius of their government naturally introduces a better management of their negro slaves.[69]

54   In all European colonies the culture of the sugar-cane is carried on by negro slaves.[70] The constitution of those who have been born in the temperate climate of Europe could not, it is supposed, support the labour of digging the ground under the burning sun of the West Indies; and the culture of the sugar-cane, as it is managed at present, is all hand labour, though, in the opinion of many, the drill plough might be introduced into it with great advantage. But, as the profit and success of the cultivation which is carried on by means of cattle, depend very much upon the good

many of the leading men of the colonies, attributing this in part to the existence of representative institutions.

[69] See also V.iii.77, where Smith comments on the appropriate treatment of slaves.

[70] Smith comments on the use of slaves in the sugar colonies at III.ii.10, where it is also stated that the profits available were such as to justify their use.

management of those cattle; so the profit and success of that which is carried on by slaves, must depend equally upon the good management of
those slaves; and in the [395] good management of their slaves the French
planters, I think it is generally allowed, are superior to the English. The
law, so far as it gives some weak protection to the slave against the violence
of his master, is likely to be better executed in a colony where the government is in a great measure arbitrary, than in one where it is altogether free.
In every country where the unfortunate law of slavery is established, the
magistrate, when he protects the slave, intermeddles in some measure in the
management of the private property of the master; and, in a free country,
where the master is perhaps either a member of the colony assembly, or an
elector of such a member, he dare not do this but with the greatest caution
and circumspection. The respect which he is obliged to pay to the master,
renders it more difficult for him to protect the slave. But in a country
where the government is in a great measure arbitrary, where it is usual for
the magistrate to intermeddle even in the management of the private
property of individuals, and to send them, perhaps, a lettre de cachet if
they do not manage it according to his liking, it is much easier for him to
give some protection to the slave; and common humanity naturally disposes him to do so. The protection of the magistrate renders the slave less
contemptible in the eyes of his master, who is thereby induced to consider
him with more regard, and to treat him with more gentleness. Gentle usage
renders the slave not only more faithful, but more intelligent, and therefore,
[396] upon a double account, more useful. He approaches more to the condition of a free servant, and may possess some degree of integrity and attachment to his master's interest, virtues which frequently belong to free
servants, but which never can belong to a slave, who is treated as slaves
commonly are in countries where the master is perfectly free and secure.

55   That the condition of a slave is better under an arbitrary than under a
free government, is, I believe, supported by the history of all ages and
nations.[71] In the Roman history, the first time we read of the magistrate
interposing to protect the slave from the violence of his master, is under the
emperors. When Vedius Pollio, in the presence of Augustus, ordered one
of his slaves, who had committed a slight fault, to be cut into pieces and
thrown into his fish pond in order to feed his fishes, the emperor commanded him, with indignation, to emancipate immediately, not only that
slave, but all the others that belonged to him.[72] Under the republick no

[71] The argument that slaves are better treated in arbitrary governments is mentioned
in LJ (B) 135, ed. Cannan 96–7, and in LJ (A) iii.104. It is also noted in LJ (A) iv.142 that
'monarchicall governments are allways more gentle than republican to this order'.
[72] The case of Vedius Pollio is cited in LJ (B) 135, ed. Cannan 97, and LJ (A) iii.92–3,
where the story is repeated in this form:

We are told that Augustus once manumitted all the slaves of Vedius Pollio with whom
he supped. A slave bringing in a dish happened to break it. The slave fell at Augustus'

magistrate could have had authority enough to protect the slave, much less to punish the master.

56   The stock, it is to be observed, which has improved the sugar colonies of France, particularly the great colony of St. Domingo, has been raised almost entirely from the gradual improvement and cultivation of those colonies. It has been almost altogether the produce of the soil and *p*of*p* the industry of the colonists, or, what comes to the same thing, the price of that produce gradually accumulated by good manage-[397]ment, and employed in raising a still greater produce. But the stock which has improved and cultivated the sugar colonies of England has, a great part of it, been sent out from England, and has by no means been altogether the produce of the soil and industry of the colonists.[73] The prosperity of the English sugar colonies has been, in a great measure, owing to the great riches of England, of which a part has overflowed, if one may say so, upon those colonies. But the prosperity of the sugar colonies of France has been entirely owing to the good conduct of the colonists, which must therefore have had some superiority over that of the English; and this superiority has been remarked in nothing so much as in the good management of their slaves.

57   Such have been the general outlines of the policy of the different European nations with regard to their colonies.

58   The policy of Europe, therefore, has very little to boast of, either in the original establishment, or, *q*so far as concerns their internal government,*q* in the subsequent prosperity of the colonies of America.

59   Folly and injustice seem to have been the principles which presided over and directed the first project of establishing those colonies; the folly of hunting after gold and silver mines, and the injustice of coveting the possession of a country whose harmless natives, far from having ever injured the people of Europe, had received the [398] first adventurers with every mark of kindness and hospitality.

---

p–p 2–6   *q–q* om. *1*

---

feet and requested him, not to get his pardon of his master, for death he thought was inevitable, but that he would request his master that after he was crucified, which was the common punishment inflicted on slaves, he should not hack his body into pieces and throw it to feed the fish in his ponds, which was, it seems, his common way of treating them.

Seneca reports that: 'Caesar, shocked by such an innovation in cruelty, ordered that the boy be pardoned, and, besides, that all the crystal cups be broken before his eyes and that the fish-pond be filled up.' (*De ira*, iii.40, translated by J. W. Basore in *Seneca's Moral Essays*, Loeb Classical Library (1928), i.349.) The episode is also recorded in *Dio's Roman History*, liv.23 translated by E. Cary in Leob Classical Library (1917), vi.333–41, who adds that Vedius Pollio still left Augustus 'a good share of his estate'. Smith adds that a man entertaining Augustus at this time would have had between 900 and 1,000 slaves so that Pollio's loss through their manumission, estimated at current slave prices in Africa or America of the order of £30 or £40, would amount to between £40,000 and £50,000. See also LJ (A) iii.102–3.

[73] See above, II.v.21 and below, IV.vii.c.38 and V.iii.83.

60   The adventurers, indeed, who formed some of the later establishments, joined, to the chimerical project of finding gold and silver mines, other motives more reasonable and more laudable; but even these motives do very little honour to the policy of Europe.

61   The English puritans, ʳrestrainedʳ at home, fled for freedom to America, and established there the four governments of New England. The English catholicks, treated with ˢmuch greaterˢ injustice, established that of Maryland; the Quakers, that of Pensylvania. The Portuguese Jews, persecuted by the inquisition, stript of their fortunes, and banished to Brazil, introduced, by their example, some sort of order and industry among the transported felons and strumpets, by whom that colony was originally peopled, and taught them the culture of the sugar-cane.⁷⁴ Upon all these different occasions it was, not the wisdom and policy, but the disorder and injustice of the European governments, which peopled and cultivated America.⁷⁵

62   In effectuating some of the most important of these establishments, the different governments of Europe had as little merit as in projecting them. The conquest of Mexico was the project, not of the council of Spain, but of a governor of Cuba; and it was effectuated by the spirit of the bold adventurer to whom it was entrusted, in spite of every thing which that governor, who [399] soon repented of having trusted such a person, could do to thwart it.⁷⁶ The conquerors of Chili and Peru, and of almost all the

---

ʳ⁻ʳ persecuted *I*   ˢ⁻ˢ equal *I*

⁷⁴ 'Before these last periods, the Jews, who had been stripped of their property by the inquisition, and banished to the Brazils, were not yet totally forsaken. Many found kind relations and faithful friends; others, who were known to be honest and industrious men, obtained credit from merchants of different nations, whom they had formerly dealt with, who advanced them money. These helps enabled them to cultivate suger-canes, which they first procured from the island of Madeira.' (G. T. F. Raynal, *Histoire philosophique*, iii.324–5, trans. J. Justamond, ii.380–1.)

⁷⁵ 'Peopled gradually from England by the necessitous and indigent, who, at home, increased neither wealth nor populousness, the colonies, which were planted along that tract, [from St. Augustine to Cape Breton] have promoted the navigation, encouraged the industry, and even multiplied the inhabitants of their mother-country. The spirit of independency, which was reviving in England, here shone forth in its full lustre, and received new accessions of force from the aspiring character of those, who, being discontented with the established church and monarchy, had fought for freedom amid those savage deserts. The seeds of many a noble state have been sown in climates, kept desolate by the wild manners of the antient inhabitants; and as asylum secured, in that solitary world, for liberty and science, if ever the spreading of unlimited empire, or the inroads of barbarous nations, should again extinguish them in this turbulent and restless hemisphere.' (Hume, *History of England* (1778), vi.186.)

⁷⁶ Smith made a related point in LJ (B) 144–5, ed. Cannan 103: 'The slavery in the West Indies took place contrary to law. When that country was conquered by Spain, Isabella and Ferdinand were at the greatest pains to prevent the Indians from falling into a state of servitude, their intention being to make settlements, to trade with them and to instruct them. But Columbus and Cortez were far from the law, and obeyed not their orders but reduced them to slavery, . . .'

other Spanish settlements upon the continent of America, carried out with them no other publick encouragement, but a general permission to make settlements and conquests in the name of the king of Spain. Those adventures were all at the private risk and expence of the adventurers. The government of Spain contributed scarce any thing to any of them. That of England contributed as little towards effectuating the establishment of some of its most important colonies in North America.

63   When those establishments were effectuated, and had become so considerable as to attract the attention of the mother country, the first regulations which she made with regard to them had always in view to secure to herself the monopoly of their commerce;[77] to confine their market, and to enlarge her own at their expence, and, consequently, rather to damp and discourage, than to quicken and forward the course of their prosperity. In the different ways in which this monopoly has been exercised, consists one of the most essential differences in the policy of the different European nations with regard to their colonies.[78] The best of them all, that of England, is only somewhat less illiberal and oppressive than that of any of the rest.

64   In what way, therefore, has the policy of Europe contributed either to the first establishment, or to the present grandeur of the colonies [400] of America? In one way, and in one way only, it has contributed a good deal. *Magna virûm Mater!*[79] It bred and formed the men who were capable of atchieving such great actions, and of laying the foundation of so great an empire; and there is no other quarter of the world of which the policy is capable of forming, or has ever actually and in fact formed such men. The colonies owe to the policy of Europe the education and great views of their active and enterprizing founders; and some of the greatest and most important of them, *ʲso far as concerns their internal government,ʲ* owe to it scarce any thing else.[80]

ʲ⁻ʲ om. 1

---

[77] See below, IV.vii.c.63, where it is pointed out that regulations were only imposed on the colonies after they had attained a level of economic growth sufficient to attract the attention of the mother-country.

[78] 'The colonies they [European nations] have formed are under a kind of dependence, of which there are but very few instances in all the colonies of the ancients; whether we consider them as holding of the state itself, or of some trading company established in the state.

The design of these colonies is, to trade on more advantageous conditions than could otherwise be done with the neighbouring people, with whom all advantages are reciprocal. It has been established that the metropolis, or mother country, alone shall trade in the colonies, and that from very good reason; because the design of the settlement was the extension of commerce, not the foundation of a city or of a new empire.' (Montesquieu, *Esprit*, XXI.xxi.10–11.)

[79] 'Salve, magna parens frugum, Saturnia tellus, Magna Virum': Hail, land of Saturn, great mother of earth's fruits, great mother of men.' (Virgil, *Georgics*, ii.173–4, translated by H. R. Fairclough in Loeb Classical Library (1930), 128–9.)

[80] See above, § 51, with regard to the debt owed to British institutions.

PART THIRD

*Of the Advantages which Europe has derived from the Discovery of America,
and from that of a Passage to the East Indies by the Cape of* Good Hope.

1   SUCH are the advantages which the colonies of America have derived
from the policy of Europe.

2   What are those which Europe has derived from the discovery and
colonization of America?

3   Those advantages may be divided, first, into the general advantages
which Europe, considered as one great country, has derived from those
great events; and, secondly, into the particular advantages which each
colonizing country has derived from the colonies which particularly be-
[401]long to it, in consequence of the authority or dominion which it
exercises over them.

4   The general advantages which Europe, considered as one great country,
has derived from the discovery and colonization of America, consist, first,
in the increase of its enjoyments; and, secondly, in the augmentation of its
industry.[1]

5   The surplus produce of America, imported into Europe, furnishes the
inhabitants of this great continent with a variety of commodities which
they could not otherwise have possessed, some for conveniency and use,
some for pleasure, and some for ornament, and thereby contributes to
increase their enjoyments.

6   The discovery and colonization of America, it will readily be allowed,
have contributed to augment the industry, first, of all the countries
which trade to it directly; such as Spain, Portugal, France, and England;
and, secondly, of all those which, without trading to it directly, send,
through the medium of other countries, goods to it of their own produce;
such as Austrian Flanders, and some provinces of Germany, which,
through the medium of the countries before mentioned, send to it a
considerable quantity of linen and other goods. All such countries
have evidently gained a more extensive market for their surplus produce, and must consequently have been encouraged to increase its
quantity.[2]

7   But, that those great events should likewise have contributed to encourage the industry of countries, such as Hungary and Poland, which
[402] may never, perhaps, have sent a single commodity of their own produce to America, is not, perhaps, altogether so evident. That those events
have done so, however, cannot be doubted. Some part of the produce of
America is consumed in Hungary and Poland, and there is some demand
there for the sugar, chocolate, and tobacco, of that new quarter of the world.

----

[1] See below, § 81.
[2] The vent for surplus as a gain from trade is cited, for example, at IV.i.31.

But those commodities must be purchased with something which is either the produce of the industry of Hungary and Poland, or with something which had been purchased with some part of that produce. Those commodities of America are new values, new equivalents, introduced into Hungary and Poland to be exchanged there for the surplus produce of those countries. By being carried thither they create a new and more extensive market for that surplus produce. They raise its value, and thereby contribute to encourage its increase. Though no part of it may ever be carried to America, it may be carried to other countries which purchase it with a part of their share of the surplus produce of America; and it may find a market by means of the circulation of that trade which was originally put into motion by the surplus produce of America.

8   Those great events may even have contributed to increase the enjoyments, and to augment the industry of countries which, not only never sent any commodities to America, but never received any from it. Even such countries may have received a greater abundance of other commodities from countries of which the surplus [403] produce had been augmented by means of the American trade. This greater abundance, as it must necessarily have increased their enjoyments, so it must likewise have augmented their industry. A greater number of new equivalents of some kind or other must have been presented to them to be exchanged for the surplus produce of that industry. A more extensive market must have been created for that surplus produce, so as to raise its value, and thereby encourage its increase. The mass of commodities annually thrown into the great circle of European commerce, and by its various revolutions annually distributed among all the different nations comprehended within it, must have been augmented by the whole surplus produce of America. A greater share of this greater mass, therefore, is likely to have fallen to each of those nations, to have increased their enjoyments, and augmented their industry.

9   The exclusive trade of the mother countries tends to diminish, or, at least, to keep down below what they would otherwise rise to, both the enjoyments and industry of all those nations in general, and of the American colonies in particular. It is a dead weight upon the action of one of the great springs which puts into motion a great part of the business of mankind. By rendering the colony produce dearer in all other countries, it lessens its consumption, and thereby cramps the industry of the colonies, and both the enjoyments and the industry of all other countries, which both enjoy less when they pay more [404] for what they enjoy, and produce less when they get less for what they produce. By rendering the produce of all other countries dearer in the colonies, it cramps, in the same manner, the industry of all other countries, and both the enjoyments and the industry of the colonies. It is a clog which, for the supposed benefit of some particular countries, embarrasses the pleasures, and encumbers the industry

of all other countries; but of the colonies more than of any other. It ᵃnotᵃ
only excludes, as much as possible, all other countries from one particular
market; but it confines, as much as possible, the colonies to one particular
market: and the difference is very great between being excluded from one
particular market, when all others are open, and being confined to one
particular market, when all others are shut up. The surplus produce of the
colonies, however, is the original source of all that increase of enjoyments
and industry which Europe derives from the discovery and colonization of
America; and the exclusive trade of the mother countries tends to render
this source much less abundant than it otherwise would be.

10   The particular advantages which each colonizing country derives from
the colonies which particularly belong to it, are of two different kinds;
first, those common advantages which every empire derives from the provinces subject to its dominion; and, secondly, those peculiar advantages
which are supposed to result from provinces of so very peculiar a nature as
the European colonies of America.

11   [405] The common advantages which every empire derives from the
provinces subject to its dominion, consist, first, in the military force which
they furnish for its defence; and, secondly, in the revenue which they furnish for the support of its civil government. The Roman colonies furnished
occasionally both the one and the other. The Greek colonies, sometimes,
furnished a military force; but seldom any revenue. They seldom acknowledged themselves subject to the dominion of the mother city. They were
generally her allies in war, but very seldom her subjects in peace.[3]

12   The European colonies of America have never yet furnished any military
force for the defence of the mother country. Their military force has never
yet been sufficient for their own defence; and in the different wars in
which the mother countries have been engaged, the defence of their
colonies has generally occasioned a very considerable distraction of the
military force of those countries. In this respect, therefore, all the European colonies have, without exception, been a cause rather of weakness
than of strength to their respective mother countries.[4]

13   The colonies of Spain and Portugal only have contributed any revenue
towards the defence of the mother country, or the support of her civil government.[5] The taxes which have been levied upon those of other European

---

ᵃ⁻ᵃ 3–6

[3] Sometimes revenue was paid: 'These Cotyorites are our colonists, and it was we who
gave over to them this land, after we had taken it away from barbarians; therefore they
pay us a stated tribute, as do the people of Cerasus and Trapezus.' (Xenophon, *Anabasis*,
V.v.10, translated by C. L. Brownson in Loeb Classical Library (1921), 134–5.) The
relationship between the Greek colonies and the mother country is described at IV.vii.a.2.
[4] The military costs of the colonies to Great Britain are examined at § 64. See also
IV.vii.b.20 and V.iii.92.
[5] See above, IV.vii.b.20.

nations, upon those of England in particular, have seldom been equal to the expence laid out upon them in time of peace, and never sufficient to defray that [406] which they occasioned in time of war. Such colonies, therefore, have been a source of expence and not of revenue to their respective mother countries.

14   The advantages of such colonies to their respective mother countries, consist altogether in those peculiar advantages which are supposed to result from provinces of so very peculiar a nature as the European colonies of America; and the exclusive trade, it is acknowledged, is the sole source of all those peculiar advantages.

15   In consequence of this exclusive trade, all that part of the surplus produce of the English colonies, for example, which consists in what are called enumerated commodities,[6] can be sent to no other country but England. Other countries must afterwards buy it of her. It must be cheaper therefore in England than it can be in any other country, and must contribute more to increase the enjoyments of England, than those of any other country. It must likewise contribute more to encourage her industry. For all those parts of her own surplus produce which England exchanges for those enumerated commodities, she must get a better price than any other *b*countries*b* can get for the like parts of theirs, when they exchange them for the same commodities. The manufactures of England, for example, will purchase a greater quantity of the sugar and tobacco of her own colonies, than the like manufactures of other countries can purchase of that sugar and tobacco. So far, therefore, as the manufactures of England and those [407] of other countries are both to be exchanged for the sugar and tobacco of the English colonies, this superiority of price gives an encouragement to the former, beyond what the latter can in these circumstances enjoy. The exclusive trade of the colonies, therefore, as it diminishes, or, at least, keeps down below what they would otherwise rise to, both the enjoyments and the industry of the countries which do not possess it; so it gives an evident advantage to the countries which do possess it over those other countries.[7]

16   This advantage, however, will, perhaps, be found to be rather what may be called a relative than an absolute advantage; and to give a superiority to the country which enjoys it, rather by depressing the industry and

---

b-b country *1*

[6] The enumerated goods are described at IV.vii.b.25,35.

[7] Pownall commented on this part of Smith's argument, *Letter*, 40: 'You in words advance upon the ground of *probable reasons for believing* only, you prove by probable suppositions only; yet most people who read your book, will think you mean to set up an absolute proof, and your conclusion is drawn as though you had.' See above, II.v, where Smith advances his thesis with regard to the different employments of capital: a thesis on which much of the argument of this section would seem to depend.

produce of other countries, than by raising those of that particular country above what they would naturally rise to in the case of a free trade.

17   The tobacco of Maryland and Virginia, for example, by means of the monopoly which England enjoys of it, certainly comes cheaper to England than it can do to France, to whom England commonly sells a considerable part of it. But had France, and all other European countries been, at all times, allowed a free trade to Maryland and Virginia, the tobacco of those colonies might, by this time, have come cheaper than it actually does, not only to all those other countries, but likewise to England. The produce of tobacco, in consequence of a market so much more extensive than any which it has hitherto enjoyed, might, and probably would, by [408] this time, have been so much increased as to reduce the profits of a tobacco plantation to their natural level with those of a corn plantation, which, it is supposed, they are still somewhat above.[8] The price of tobacco might, and probably would, by this time, have fallen somewhat lower than it is at present. An equal quantity of the commodities either of England, or of those other countries, might have purchased in Maryland and Virginia a greater quantity of tobacco than it can do at present, and, consequently, have been sold there for so much a better price.[9] So far as that weed, therefore, can, by its cheapness and abundance, increase the enjoyments or augment the industry either of England or of any other country, it would, probably, in the case of a free trade, have produced both these effects in somewhat a greater degree than it can do at present. England, indeed, would not in this case have had any advantage over other countries. She might have bought the tobacco of her colonies somewhat cheaper, and, consequently, have sold some of her own commodities somewhat dearer than she actually does. But she could neither have bought the one cheaper nor sold the other dearer than any other country might have done. She might, perhaps, have gained an absolute, but she would certainly have lost a relative advantage.

18   In order, however, to obtain this relative advantage in the colony trade, in order to execute the invidious and malignant project of excluding as much as possible other nations from any share [409] in it, England, there are very probable reasons for believing, has not only sacrificed a part of the absolute advantage which she, as well as every other nation, might have derived from that trade, but has subjected herself both to an absolute and to a relative disadvantage in almost every other branch of trade.

19   When, by the act of navigation,[10] England assumed to herself the monopoly of the colony trade, the foreign capitals which had before been employed in it were necessarily withdrawn from it. The English capital, which had before carried on but a part of it, was now to carry on the whole. The capital which had before supplied the colonies with but a part of the

8 See above, I.xi.b.33.   9 See above, I.xi.b.32.
10 12 Charles II, c.18 (1660). See above, IV.ii.24–30.

goods which they wanted from Europe, was now all that was employed to supply them with the whole. But it could not supply them with the whole, and the goods with which it did supply them were necessarily sold very dear. The capital which had before bought but a part of the surplus produce of the colonies, was now all that was employed to buy the whole. But it could not buy the whole at any thing near the old price, and, therefore, whatever it did buy it necessarily bought very cheap. But in an employment of capital in which the merchant sold very dear and bought very cheap, the profit must have been very great, and much above the ordinary level of profit in other branches of trade. This superiority of profit in the colony trade could not fail to draw from other branches of trade a part of the capital which had before been employed in them. But this revulsion of capital, as it must have gra-[410]dually increased the competition of capitals in the colony trade, so it must have gradually diminished that competition in all those other branches of trade; as it must have gradually lowered the profits of the one, so it must have gradually raised those of the other, till the profits of all came to a new level, different from and somewhat higher than that at which they had been before.[11]

20   This double effect, of drawing capital from all other trades, and of raising the rate of profit somewhat higher than it otherwise would have been in all trades, was not only produced by this monopoly upon its first establishment, but has continued to be produced by it ever since.

21   First, this monopoly has been continually drawing capital from all other trades to be employed in that of the colonies.

22   Though the wealth of Great Britain has increased very much since the establishment of the act of navigation, it certainly has not increased in the same proportion as that of the colonies. But the foreign trade of every country naturally increases in proportion to its wealth, its surplus produce in proportion to its whole produce; and Great Britain having engrossed to herself almost the whole of what may be called the foreign trade of the colonies, and her capital not having increased in the same proportion as the extent of that trade, she could not carry it on without continually withdrawing from other branches of trade some part of the capital which had before been employed in them, as well as with-holding from them a great deal more which would otherwise have gone to them. Since the establishment [411] of the act of navigation, accordingly, the colony trade has been continually increasing, while many other branches of foreign trade, particularly of that to other parts of Europe, have been continually decaying. Our manufactures for foreign sale, instead of being suited, as before the act of navigation, to the neighbouring market of Europe, or to the more distant one of the countries which lie round the Mediterranean sea, have,

[11] See above, I.ix.12, where Smith comments on the increase in the rate of profit consequent on the appearance of new outlets for stock.

the greater part of them, been accommodated to the still more distant one of the colonies, to the market in which they have the monopoly, rather than to that in which they have many competitors. The causes of decay in other branches of foreign trade, which, by Sir Matthew Decker[12] and other writers, have been sought for in the excess and improper mode of taxation, in the high price of labour, in the increase of luxury, &c. may all be found in the over-growth of the colony trade. The mercantile capital of Great Britain, though very great, yet not being infinite; and though greatly increased since the act of navigation, yet not being increased in the same proportion as the colony trade, that trade could not possibly be carried on without withdrawing some part of that capital from other branches of trade, nor consequently without some decay of those other branches.

23   England, it must be observed, was a great trading country, her mercantile capital was very great and likely to become still greater and greater every day, not only before the act of navigation had established the monopoly of the [412] colony trade, but before that trade was very considerable. In the Dutch war, during the government of Cromwel, her navy was superior to that of Holland; and in that which broke out in the beginning of the reign of Charles II. it was at least equal, perhaps superior, to the united navies of France and Holland. Its superiority, perhaps, would scarce appear greater in the present times; at least if the Dutch navy was to bear the same proportion to the Dutch commerce now which it did then. But this great naval power could not, in either of those wars, be owing to the act of navigation. During the first of them the plan of that act had been but just formed; and though before the breaking out of the second it had been fully enacted by legal authority; yet no part of it could have had time to produce any considerable effect, and least of all that part which established the exclusive trade to the colonies. Both the colonies and their trade were inconsiderable then in comparison of what they are now. The island of Jamaica was an unwholesome desert, little inhabited, and less cultivated. New York and New Jersey were in the possession of the Dutch: the half of St. Christopher's in that of the French. The island of Antigua, the two Carolinas, Pensylvania, Georgia, and Nova Scotia, were not planted. Virginia, Maryland, and New England were planted; and though they were very thriving colonies, yet there was not, perhaps, at that time either in

---

12 '. . . the foreign trade of every country must decline, that lays unequal taxes and oppressive excises on its people—cramps its trade, the foundation of riches, by high customs and prohibitions—suffers many monopolies—oppresses its people by prohibiting the importation of victuals, under the pretence of raising the value of its lands—gives bounties to feed foreigners cheaper than its own people—encourages idleness by bad laws relating to its poor—tempts foreigners to carry away its coin for less than its intrinsic value—makes the obtaining justice chargeable—suffers a very heavy national debt, contracted in time of war, to continue unpaid in time of peace.' (M. Decker, *Essay on the Causes of the Decline of Foreign Trade*, 56–7.) Decker is described as an 'excellent authority' at IV.v.a.20, and also mentioned in V.ii.k.9,18 and V.iii.74.

Europe or America a single person who foresaw or even suspected the rapid progress [413] which they have since made in wealth, population and improvement. The island of Barbadoes, in short, was the only British colony of any consequence of which the condition at that time bore any resemblance to what it is at present. The trade of the colonies, of which England, even for some time after the act of navigation enjoyed but a part (for the act of navigation was not very strictly executed till several years after it was enacted), could not at that time be the cause of the great trade of England, nor of the great naval power which was supported by that trade.[13] The trade which at that time supported that great naval power was the trade of Europe, and of the countries which lie round the Mediterranean sea. But the share which Great Britain at present enjoys of that trade could not support any such great naval power. Had the growing trade of the colonies been left free to all nations, whatever share of it might have fallen to Great Britain, and a very considerable share would probably have fallen to her, must have been all an addition to this great trade of which she was before in possession. In consequence of the monopoly, the increase of the colony trade has not so much occasioned an addition to the trade which Great Britain had before, as a total change in its direction.

24   Secondly, this monopoly has necessarily contributed to keep up the rate of profit in all the different branches of British trade higher than it naturally would have been, had all nations been allowed a free trade to the British colonies.

25   [414] The monopoly of the colony trade, as it necessarily drew towards that trade a greater proportion of the capital of Great Britain than what would have gone to it of its own accord; so by the expulsion of all foreign capitals it necessarily reduced the whole quantity of capital employed in that trade below what it naturally would have been in the case of a free trade. But, by lessening the competition of capitals in that branch of trade, it necessarily raised the rate of *c* profit in that branch. By lessening too the competition of British capitals in all other branches of trade, it necessarily raised the rate of British profit in all those other branches. Whatever may have been, at any particular period, since the establishment of the act of navigation, the state or extent of the mercantile capital of Great Britain, the monopoly of the colony trade must, during the continuance of that state, have raised the ordinary rate of British profit higher than it otherwise would have been both in that and in all the other branches of British trade. If, since the establishment of the act of navigation, the ordinary rate

---

c the *1*

[13] See above, IV.ii.30. While European markets were important, the expansion of foreign trade in the eighteenth century was almost entirely the result of the growth in the colonial trade. P. Deane and W. A. Cole, *British Economic Growth, 1688–1959* (Cambridge, 1969), 34–5 and 86–7.

of British profit has fallen considerably, as it certainly has, it must have fallen still lower, had not the monopoly established by that act contributed to keep it up.

26   But whatever raises in any country the ordinary rate of profit higher than it otherwise would be, necessarily subjects that country both to an absolute and to a relative disadvantage in every branch of trade of which she has not the monopoly.

27   [415] It subjects her to an absolute disadvantage: because in such branches of trade her merchants cannot get this greater profit, without selling dearer than they otherwise would do both the goods of foreign countries which they import into their own, and the goods of their own country which they export to foreign countries. Their own country must both buy dearer and sell dearer; must both buy less and sell less; must both enjoy less and produce less, than she otherwise would do.

28   It subjects her to a relative disadvantage; because in such branches of trade it sets other countries which are not subject to the same absolute disadvantage, either more above her or less below her than they otherwise would be. It enables them both to enjoy more and to produce more in proportion to what she enjoys and produces. It renders their superiority greater or their inferiority less than it otherwise would be. By raising the price of her produce above what it otherwise would be, it enables the merchants of other countries to undersell her in foreign markets, and thereby to justle her out of almost all those branches of trade, of which she has not the monopoly.

29   Our merchants frequently complain of the high wages of British labour as the cause of their manufactures being undersold in foreign markets; but they are silent about the high profits of stock. They complain of the extravagant gain of other people; but they say nothing of their own. The high profits of British stock, however, may contribute towards raising the price of British manufactures in many cases as much, and in some perhaps more, than the high wages of British labour.[14]

30   [416] It is in this manner that the capital of Great Britain, one may justly say, has partly been drawn and partly been driven from the greater part of the different branches of trade of which she has not the monopoly; from the trade of Europe in particular, and from that of the countries which lie round the Mediterranean sea.[15]

31   It has partly been drawn from those branches of trade; by the attraction

[14] A very similar point is made above, I.ix.24. Smith also comments below, § 61, on the additional problem caused by the habits of prodigality associated with high profit levels.

[15] Pownall held that the proposition concerning the transfer of capital relates to a matter of fact 'which must not be established by an argument *a priori*' and commented rather drily that he did not find such 'an actual deduction of facts' in Smith's book. Moreover, Pownall contended that the facts did not support Smith's case, basing this opinion on the 'very useful collection of data' which had been published by Sir C. Whitworth, *Letter*, 41.

of superior profit in the colony trade in consequence of the continual increase of that trade, and of the continual insufficiency of the capital which had carried it on one year to carry it on the next.

32   It has partly been driven from them; by the advantage which the high rate of profit, established in Great Britain, gives to other countries, in all the different branches of trade of which Great Britain has not the monopoly.

33   As the monopoly of the colony trade has drawn from those other branches a part of the British capital which would otherwise have been employed in them, so it has forced into them many foreign capitals which would never have gone to them, had they not been expelled from the colony trade. In those other branches of trade it has diminished the competition of British capitals, and thereby raised the rate of British profit higher than it otherwise would have been. On the contrary, it has increased the competition of foreign capitals, and thereby sunk the rate of foreign profit lower than it otherwise would have been. Both in the one way and in the other it must evidently have subjected Great [417] Britain to a relative disadvantage in all those other branches of trade.

34   The colony trade, however, it may perhaps be said, is more advantageous to Great Britain than any other; and the monopoly, by forcing into that trade a greater proportion of the capital of Great Britain than what would otherwise have gone to it, has turned that capital into an employment more advantageous to the country than any other which it could have found.

35   The most advantageous employment of any capital to the country to which it belongs, is that which maintains there the greatest quantity of productive labour, and increases the most the annual produce of the land and labour of that country. But the quantity of productive labour which any capital employed in the foreign trade of consumption can maintain, is exactly in proportion, it has been shewn in the second book, to the frequency of its returns.[16] A capital of a thousand pounds, for example, employed in a foreign trade of consumption, of which the returns are made regularly once in the year, can keep in constant employment, in the country to which it belongs, a quantity of productive labour equal to what a thousand pounds can maintain there for a year. If the returns are made twice or thrice in the year, it can keep in constant employment a quantity of productive labour equal to what two or three thousand pounds can maintain there for a year. A foreign trade of consumption carried on with a neighbouring ^d, is, upon this account, in general, more [418] advantageous than one carried on with a distant country; and for the same reason a

---

^d country *1*

[16] Above, II.v.27.

direct foreign trade of consumption, as it has likewise been shewn in the second book,[17] is in general more advantageous than a round-about one.

36   But the monopoly of the colony trade, so far as it has operated upon the employment of the capital of Great Britain, has in all cases forced some part of it from a foreign trade of consumption carried on with a neighbouring *e*, to one carried on with a more distant country, and in many cases from a direct foreign trade of consumption to a round-about one.

37   First, the monopoly of the colony trade has in all cases forced some part of the capital of Great Britain from a foreign trade of consumption carried on with a neighbouring, to one carried on with a more distant country.

38   It has, in all cases, forced some part of that capital from the trade with Europe, and with the countries which lie round the Mediterranean sea, to that with the more distant regions of America and the West Indies, from which the returns are necessarily less frequent, not only on account of the greater distance, but on account of the peculiar circumstances of those countries.[18] New colonies, it has already been observed, are always understocked.[19] Their capital is always much less than what they could employ with great profit and advantage in the improvement and cultivation of their land. They have a constant demand, therefore, for more capital than they have of their own; and, in order to supply the defi-[419]ciency of their own, they endeavour to borrow as much as they can of the mother country, to whom they are, therefore, always in debt.[20] The most common way in which the colonists contract this debt, is not by borrowing upon bond of the rich people of the mother country, though they sometimes do this too, but by running as much in arrear to their correspondents, who supply them with goods from Europe, as those correspondents will allow them. Their annual returns frequently do not amount to more than a third, and sometimes not to so great a proportion of what they owe. The whole capital, therefore, which their correspondents advance to

---

e country *1*

[17] Above, II.v.28.
[18] Pownall argued against this that 'if you will compare notes between the merchant trading in British manufactures to Germany, and the merchant trading with British manufactures to America and the West Indies, you will find the returns of the latter upon the whole . . . not slower than those from Germany. Credit has, even before the present war, been extended in Germany, and shortened towards America: inquire after this fact in Norwich, London, and the other great manufacturing places, and you will find it so.' (*Letter*, 46.) At the same time, however, Pownall considered that the round-about trade involved in sending tobacco to England prior to its re-export to the Continent was a 'needless and very disadvantageous operation, in which some relaxation ought to be made'. See above, II.v.28 and IV.iii.c.12, where Smith comments on the advantages of trade with France as compared to America.
[19] See above, I.ix.11.
[20] Smith comments on the use of British capital in the colonies at II.v.21, IV.vii.b.56, and V.iii.83.

them is seldom returned to Britain in less than three, and sometimes not in less than four or five years. But a British capital of a thousand pounds, for example, which is returned to Great Britain only once in five years, can keep in constant employment only one-fifth part of the British industry which it could maintain if the whole was returned once in the year; and, instead of the quantity of industry which a thousand pounds could maintain for a year, can keep in constant employment the quantity only which two hundred pounds can maintain for a year.[21] The planter, no doubt, by the high price which he pays for the goods from Europe, by the interest upon the bills which he grants at distant dates, and by the commission upon the renewal of those which he grants at near dates, makes up, and probably more than makes up, all the loss which his correspondent can sustain by this delay. But, [420] though he may make up the loss of his correspondent, he cannot make up that of Great Britain. In a trade of which the returns are very distant, the profit of the merchant may be as great or greater than in one in which they are very frequent and near; but the advantage of the country in which he resides, the quantity of productive labour constantly maintained there, the annual produce of the land and labour must always be much less. That the returns of the trade to America, and still more those of that to the West Indies, are, in general, not only more distant, but more irregular, and more uncertain too, than those of the trade to any part of Europe, or even of the countries which lie round the Mediterranean sea, will readily be allowed, I imagine, by every body who has any experience of those different branches of trade.

39   Secondly, the monopoly of the colony trade has, in many cases, forced some part of the capital of Great Britain from a direct foreign trade of consumption, into a round-about one.

40   Among the enumerated commodities which can be sent to no other market but Great Britain, there are several of which the quantity exceeds very much the consumption of Great Britain, and of which a part, therefore, must be exported to other countries. But this cannot be done without forcing some part of the capital of Great Britain into a round-about foreign trade of consumption. Maryland and Virginia, for example, send annually to Great Britain upwards of ninety-six thousand hogsheads of tobacco, and [421] the consumption of Great Britain is said not to exceed fourteen thousand.[22] Upwards of eighty-two thousand hogsheads, therefore, must be exported to other countries, to France, to Holland, and to the countries which lie round the Baltick and Mediterranean seas. But, that

----

[21] On commenting on this argument, Pownall suggested that capital withheld in America 'is not withheld unprofitably to Great Britain; like that portion of harvest which is detained for seed, it is the matrix of a succeeding and increased production; . . .' (*Letter*, 43.) See above, II.v.21.

[22] The same figure is cited at II.v.34, and IV.iv.5.

part of the capital of Great Britain which brings those eighty-two thousand hogsheads to Great Britain, which re-exports them from thence to those other countries, and which brings back from those other countries to Great Britain either goods or money in return, is employed in a round-about foreign trade of consumption; and is necessarily forced into this employment in order to dispose of this great surplus. If we would compute in how many years the whole of this capital is likely to come back to Great Britain, we must add to the distance of the American returns that of the returns from those other countries. If, in the direct foreign trade of consumption which we carry on with America, the whole capital employed frequently does not come back in less than three or four years; the whole capital employed in this round-about one is not likely to come back in less than four or five. If the one can keep in constant employment but a third or a fourth part of the domestick industry which could be maintained by a capital returned once in the year, the other can keep in constant employment but a fourth or a fifth part of that industry. *f*At some of the outports a credit is commonly given to those foreign correspondents to whom they export their [422] tobacco. At the port of London, indeed, it is commonly sold for ready money. The rule is, *Weigh and pay.* At the port of London, therefore, the final returns of the whole round-about trade are more distant than the returns from America by the time only which the goods may lie unsold in the warehouse; where, however, they may sometimes lie long enough.*f* But, had not the colonies been confined to the market of Great Britain for the sale of their tobacco, very little more of it would probably have come to us than what was necessary for the home consumption. The goods which Great Britain purchases at present for her own consumption with the great surplus of tobacco which she exports to other countries, she would, in this case, probably have purchased with the immediate produce of her own industry, or with some part of her own manufactures. That produce, those manufactures, instead of being almost entirely suited to one great market, as at present, would probably have been fitted to a great number of smaller markets. Instead of one great round-about foreign trade of consumption, Great Britain would probably have carried on a great number of small direct foreign trades of the same kind. On account of the frequency of the returns, a part, and, probably, but a small part; perhaps not above a third or a fourth, of the capital which at present carries on this great round-about trade, might have been sufficient to carry on all those small direct ones, might have kept in constant employment an equal quantity of British indus-[423]try, and have equally supported the annual produce of the land and labour of Great Britain. All the purposes of this trade being, in this manner, answered by a much smaller capital, there would have been a large spare capital to apply to other purposes; to improve the lands, to increase the manufactures, and to extend the commerce of Great Britain; to come into competition at least with the other British capitals employed in all those different ways, to reduce the rate of profit in them all, and thereby to give to Great Britain, in all of them, a superiority over other countries still greater than what she at present *g*enjoys*g*.

41   The monopoly of the colony trade too has forced some part of the capital of Great Britain from all foreign trade of consumption to a carrying trade; and, consequently, from supporting more or less the industry of Great Britain, to be employed altogether in supporting partly that of the colonies, and partly that of some other countries.

42   The goods, for example, which are annually purchased with the great surplus of eighty-two thousand hogsheads of tobacco annually re-exported from Great Britain, are not all consumed in Great Britain. Part of them, linen from Germany and Holland, for example, is returned to the colonies for their particular consumption. But, that part of the capital of Great Britain which buys the tobacco with which this linen is afterwards bought, is necessarily withdrawn from supporting the industry of Great [424] Britain, to be employed altogether in supporting, partly that of the colonies, and partly that of the particular countries who pay for this tobacco with the produce of their own industry.

43   The monopoly of the colony trade besides, by forcing towards it a much greater proportion of the capital of Great Britain than what would naturally have gone to it, seems to have broken altogether that natural balance which would otherwise have taken place among all the different branches of British industry.[23] The industry of Great Britain, instead of being accommodated to a great number of small markets, has been principally suited to one great market. Her commerce, instead of running in a great number of small channels, has been taught to run principally in one great channel. But the whole system of her industry and commerce has thereby been rendered less secure; the whole state of her body politick less healthful, than it otherwise would have been. In her present condition, Great Britain resembles one of those unwholesome bodies in which some of the vital parts are overgrown, and which, upon that account, are liable to many dangerous disorders scarce incident to those in which all the parts are more properly proportioned. A small stop in that great blood-vessel, which has been artificially swelled beyond its natural dimensions, and through which an unnatural proportion of the industry and commerce of the country has

g-g possesses *1*

[23] The concept of a natural balance of industry is developed below, § 97. See also IV.ii.3, IV.ii.12,31, IV.iv.14, and IV.v.a.39.

been forced to circulate, is very likely to bring on [425] the most dangerous disorders upon the whole body politick.[24] The expectation of a rupture with the colonies, accordingly, has struck the people of Great Britain with more terror than they ever felt for a Spanish armada, or a French invasion.[25] It was this terror, whether well or ill grounded, which rendered the repeal of the stamp act[h],[26] among the merchants at least, a popular measure[h]. In the total exclusion from the colony market, was it to last only for a few years, the greater part of our merchants used to fancy that they foresaw an entire stop to their trade; the greater part of our master manufacturers, the entire ruin of their business; and the greater part of our workmen, an end of their employment.[27] A rupture with any of our neighbours upon the continent, though likely too to occasion some stop or interruption in the employments of some of all these different orders of people, is foreseen, however, without any such general emotion. The blood, of which the circulation is stopt in some of the smaller vessels, easily disgorges itself into the greater, without occasioning any dangerous disorder; but, when it is stopt in any of the greater vessels, convulsions, apoplexy, or death, are the immediate and unavoidable consequences. If but one of those overgrown manufactures, which by means either of bounties, or of the monopoly of the home and colony markets, have been artificially raised up to an unnatural height, finds some small stop or interruption in its employment, it

---

[h-h] a popular measure, among the merchants at least *1*

[24] Pownall rejected the analogy of the blood vessel and argued that the fact that trade had felt no such 'convulsions or apoplexy' on the obstruction of our 'American artery' proved that America was 'not our principal, much less our sole channel of commerce'. He rejected Smith's explanation for this fact, developed below, which relied on the impact of five unforeseen and unthought of events. *Letter*, 45.

[25] Smith was evidently very interested in the current difficulties with America, and prepared a memorandum for Alexander Wedderburn, a former pupil and latterly Solicitor-General in Lord North's administration. The document forms a part of the Rosslyn MSS. (Ann Arbor, Michigan); it is dated February 1778 and endorsed 'Smith's Thoughts on the State of the Contest with America'. It is hereinafter referred to as 'Thoughts on America'. The text is included in the volume of Correspondence which forms a part of this edition of Smith's *Works*. It was first published by G. H. Guttridge in the *American Historical Review*, 38 (1932-3), hereinafter cited as AHR.

[26] The stamp act is mentioned at I.viii.50. Stamp duties are also discussed at V.ii.h.12 where they are stated to be of 'very modern invention'.

[27] In Letter 149 addressed to Smith, dated 8 February 1776, Hume complained about the delay in publication of the WN and reminded his friend that 'If you wait till the Fate of America be decided, you may wait long.' He went on: 'The Duke of Buccleugh tells me, that you are very zealous In American Affairs. My Notion is, that the Matter is not so important as is commonly imagind. If I be mistaken, I shall probably correct my Error, when I see or read you. Our Navigation and general Commerce may suffer more than our Manufactures.' In Letter 233 addressed to William Eden, dated 15 December 1783, Smith wrote: 'I have little anxiety about what becomes of the American commerce. By an equality of treatment to all nations, we might soon open a commerce with the neighbouring nations of Europe infinitely more advantageous than that of so distant a country as America.'

frequently occasions a mutiny and disorder alarming to go-[426]vernment, and embarrassing even to the deliberations of the legislature. How great, therefore, would be the disorder and confusion, it was thought, which must necessarily be occasioned by a sudden and entire stop in the employment of so great a proportion of our principal manufacturers?

44　　Some moderate and gradual relaxation of the laws which give to Great Britain the exclusive trade to the colonies, till it is rendered in a great measure free, seems to be the only expedient which can*ⁱ*, in all future times,*ⁱ* deliver her from this danger, which can enable her or even force her to withdraw some part of her capital from this overgrown employment, and to turn it, though with less profit, towards other employments; and which, by gradually diminishing one branch of her industry and gradually increasing all the rest, can by degrees restore all the different branches of it to that natural, healthful, and proper proportion which perfect liberty necessarily establishes, and which perfect liberty can alone preserve. To open the colony trade all at once to all nations, might not only occasion some transitory inconveniency, but a great permanent loss to the greater part of those whose industry or capital is at present engaged in it. The sudden loss of the employment even of the ships which import the eighty-two thousand hogsheads of tobacco, which are over and above the consumption of Great Britain, might alone be felt very sensibly.[28] Such are the unfortunate effects of all the regulations of the mercantile [427] system! They not only introduce very dangerous disorders into the state of the body politick, but disorders which it is often difficult to remedy, without occasioning, for a time at least, still greater disorders. In what manner, therefore, the colony trade ought gradually to be opened; what are the restraints which ought first, and what are those which ought last to be taken away; or in what manner the natural system of perfect liberty and justice ought gradually to be restored, we must leave to the wisdom of future statesmen and legislators to determine.[29]

45　　Five different events, unforeseen and unthought of, have very fortunately concurred to hinder Great Britain from feeling, so sensibly as it was generally expected she would, the total exclusion which has now taken place for more than a year (from the first of December, 1774) from a very important branch of the colony trade, that of the twelve associated provinces of North America. First, those colonies, in preparing themselves for their non-importation agreement, drained Great Britain completely of all the commodities which were fit for their market: secondly, the extra-

ⁱ⁻ⁱ *2–6*

---

[28] Cf. IV.ii.42 where Smith comments favourably on the ability of the economy to absorb dramatic changes.

[29] See below, IV.ix.51, where Smith describes the system of 'perfect liberty', and cf. I.x.a.1, I.vii.6,30, and IV.ix.17.

ordinary demand of the Spanish Flota has, this year, drained Germany and the North of many commodities, linen in particular, which used to come into competition, even in the British market, with the manufactures of Great Britain: thirdly, the peace between Russia and Turkey has occasioned an extraordinary demand from the Turkey market, which, during the distress of the country, and [428] while a Russian fleet was cruizing in the Archipelago, had been very poorly supplied: fourthly, the demand of the north of Europe for the manufactures of Great Britain, has been increasing from year to year for some time past: and, fifthly, the late partition and consequential pacification of Poland, by opening the market of that great country, have this year added an extraordinary demand from thence to the increasing demand of the North. These events are all, except the fourth, in their nature transitory and accidental,[30] and the exclusion from so important a branch of the colony trade, if unfortunately it should continue much longer, may still occasion some degree of distress. This distress, however, as it will come on gradually, will be felt much less severely than if it had come on all at once; and, in the mean time, the industry and capital of the country may find a new employment and direction, so as to prevent *this distress* from ever rising to any considerable height.

46   The monopoly of the colony trade, therefore, so far as it has turned towards that trade a greater proportion of the capital of Great Britain than what would otherwise have gone to it, has in all cases turned it, from a foreign trade of consumption with a neighbouring, into one with a more distant country; in many cases, from a direct foreign trade of consumption, into a round-about one; and in some cases, from all foreign trade of consumption, into a carrying trade. It has in all cases, therefore, turned it, from a direction in which it would have main-[429]tained a greater quantity of productive labour, into one, in which it can maintain a much smaller quantity. By suiting, besides, to one particular market only, so great a part of the industry and commerce of Great Britain, it has rendered the whole state of that industry and commerce more precarious and less secure, than if their produce had been accommodated to a greater variety of markets.[31]

47   We must carefully distinguish between the effects of the colony trade and those of the monopoly of that trade. The former are always and necessarily beneficial; the latter always and necessarily hurtful. But the former are so beneficial, that the colony trade, though subject to a monopoly, and notwithstanding the hurtful effects of that monopoly, is still upon the

---

ʲ–ʲ it *1*

[30] In 1779 the official value of English domestic exports was the lowest since 1747.

[31] See below, § 97, where Smith comments further on the disadvantages involved in artificially constraining the use of stock.

whole beneficial, and greatly beneficial; though a good deal less so than it otherwise would be.

48   The effect of the colony trade in its natural and free state, is to open a great, though distant market for such parts of the produce of British industry as may exceed the demand of the markets nearer home, of those of Europe, and of the countries which lie round the Mediterranean sea. In its natural and free state, the colony trade, without drawing from those markets any part of the produce which had ever been sent to them, encourages Great Britain to increase the surplus continually, by continually presenting new equivalents to be exchanged for it. In its natural and free state, the colony trade tends to increase the quantity of productive labour in Great [430] Britain, but without altering in any respect the direction of that which had been employed there before. In the natural and free state of the colony trade, the competition of all other nations would hinder the rate of profit from rising above the common level either in the new market, or in the new employment. The new market, without drawing any thing from the old one, would create, if one may say so, a new produce for its own supply; and that new produce would constitute a new capital for carrying on the new employment, which in the same manner would draw nothing from the old one.

49   The monopoly of the colony trade, on the contrary, by excluding the competition of other nations, and thereby raising the rate of profit both in the new market and in the new employment, draws produce from the old market and capital from the old employment.[32] To augment our share of the colony trade beyond what it otherwise would be, is the avowed purpose of the monopoly. If our share of that trade were to be no greater with, than it would have been without the monopoly, there could have been no reason for establishing the monopoly. But whatever forces into a branch of trade of which the returns are slower and more distant than those of the greater part of other trades, a greater proportion of the capital of any country, than what of its own accord would go to that branch, necessarily renders the whole quantity of productive labour annually maintained there, the whole annual produce of the land and labour of [431] that country, less than they otherwise would be. It keeps down the revenue of the inhabitants of that country, below what it would naturally rise to, and thereby diminishes their power of accumulation. It not only hinders, at all times, their capital from maintaining so great a quantity of productive labour as it would otherwise maintain, but it hinders it from increasing so fast as it would otherwise increase, and consequently from maintaining a still greater quantity of productive labour.

50   The natural good effects of the colony trade, however, more than counter-

----

[32] See above, I.ix.11.

balance to Great Britain the bad effects of the monopoly, so that, monopoly and all together, that trade, even as it is carried on at present, is not only advantageous, but greatly advantageous. The new market and ^{k}the^k new employment which are opened by the colony trade, are of much greater extent than that portion of the old market and of the old employment which is lost by the monopoly. The new produce and the new capital which has been created, if one may say so, by the colony trade, maintain in Great Britain a greater quantity of productive labour, than what can have been thrown out of employment by the revulsion of capital from other trades of which the returns are more frequent. If the colony trade, however, even as it is carried on at present is advantageous to Great Britain, it is not by means of the monopoly, but in spite of the monopoly.

51   It is rather for the manufactured than for the rude produce of Europe, that the colony trade [432] opens a new market.[33] Agriculture is the proper business of all new colonies; a business which the cheapness of land renders more advantageous than any other. They abound, therefore, in the rude produce of land, and instead of importing it from other countries, they have generally a large surplus to export. In new colonies, agriculture either draws hands from all other employments, or keeps them from going to any other employment. There are few hands to spare for the necessary, and none for the ornamental manufactures. The greater part of the manufactures of both kinds, they find it cheaper to purchase of other countries than to make for themselves.[34] It is chiefly by encouraging the manufactures of Europe, that the colony trade indirectly encourages its agriculture. The manufacturers of Europe, to whom that trade gives employment, constitute a new market for the produce of the land; and the most advantageous of all markets; the home market for the corn and cattle, for the bread and butchers-meat of Europe; is thus greatly extended by means of the trade to America.

52   But that the monopoly of the trade of populous and thriving colonies is not alone sufficient to establish, or even to maintain manufactures in any country, the examples of Spain and Portugal sufficiently demonstrate. Spain and Portugal were manufacturing countries before they had any considerable colonies. Since they had the richest and most fertile in the world, they have both ceased to be so.

53   [433] In Spain and Portugal, the bad effects of the monopoly, aggravated by other causes, have^l, perhaps, nearly overbalanced^l the natural good effects of the colony trade. These causes seem to be, other monopolies of different kinds; the degradation of the value of gold and silver below what it is in most other countries;[35] the exclusion from foreign markets by

---

$^{k-k}$ 3–6 $^{l-l}$ entirely conquered *I*

[33] See above, IV.vii.b.40.   [34] See above, II.v.21 and IV.vii.b.44.
[35] See above, IV.i.13.

improper taxes upon exportation, and the narrowing of the home market, by still more improper taxes upon the transportation of goods from one part of the country to another; but above all, that irregular and partial administration of justice, which often protects the rich and powerful debtor from the pursuit of his injured creditor, and which makes the industrious part of the nation afraid to prepare goods for the consumption of those haughty and great men, to whom they dare not refuse to sell upon credit, and from whom they are altogether uncertain of repayment.[36]

54   In England, on the contrary, the natural good effects of the colony trade, assisted by other causes, have in a great measure conquered the bad effects of the monopoly. These causes seem to be, the general liberty of trade, which, notwithstanding some restraints, is at least equal, perhaps superior, to what it is in any other country; the liberty of exporting, duty free, almost all sorts of goods which are the produce of domestick industry, to almost any foreign country; and what, perhaps, is of still greater importance, the unbounded liberty of transporting them from any one part of our own country [434] to any other, without being obliged to give any account to any publick office, without being liable to question or examination of any kind;[37] but above all, that equal and impartial administration of justice which renders the rights of the meanest British subject respectable to the greatest, and which, by securing to every man the fruits of his own industry, gives the greatest and most effectual encouragement to every sort of industry.[38]

55   If the manufactures of Great Britain, however, have been advanced, as they certainly have, by the colony trade, it has not been by means of the monopoly of that trade, but in spite of the monopoly. The effect of the monopoly has been, not to augment the quantity, but to alter the quality and shape of a part of the manufactures of Great Britain, and to accommodate to a market, from which the returns are slow and distant, what would otherwise have been accommodated to one from which the returns are frequent and near. Its effect has consequently been to turn a part of the capital of Great Britain from an employment in which it would have maintained a greater quantity of manufacturing industry, to one in which it maintains a much smaller, and thereby to diminish, instead of increasing, the whole quantity of manufacturing industry maintained in Great Britain.

56   The monopoly of the colony trade, therefore, like all the other mean and malignant expedients of the mercantile system, depresses the industry [435] of all other countries, but chiefly that of the colonies, without in the

---

[36] See above, I.xi.n.1, where it is remarked that although the feudal government had been eliminated in Spain and Portugal, it had not been succeeded by a much better.

[37] The wool trade being the exception. It is stated at IV.viii.21 that the restrictions imposed upon it were 'very burdensome and oppressive'.

[38] Cf. II.iii.36 and IV.v.c.43, where Smith comments on the experience of England.

least increasing, but on the contrary diminishing, that of the country in whose favour it is established.

57   The monopoly hinders the capital of that country, whatever may at any particular time be the extent of that capital, from maintaining so great a quantity of productive labour as it would otherwise maintain, and from affording so great a revenue to the industrious inhabitants as it would otherwise afford. But as capital can be increased only by savings from revenue,[39] the monopoly, by hindering it from affording so great a revenue as it would otherwise afford, necessarily hinders it from increasing so fast as it would otherwise increase, and consequently from maintaining a still greater quantity of productive labour, and affording a still greater revenue to the industrious inhabitants of that country. One great original source of revenue, therefore, the wages of labour, the monopoly must necessarily have rendered at all times less abundant than it otherwise would have been.

58   By raising the rate of mercantile profit, the monopoly discourages the improvement of land.[40] The profit of improvement depends upon the difference between what the land actually produces, and what, by the application of a certain capital, it can be made to produce. If this difference affords a greater profit than what can be drawn from an equal capital in any mercantile employment, the improvement of land will draw capital from all mercantile employments. If [436] the profit is less, mercantile employments will draw capital from the improvement of land. Whatever therefore raises the rate of mercantile profit, either lessens the superiority or increases the inferiority of the profit of improvement; and in the one case hinders capital from going to improvement, and in the other draws capital from it. But by discouraging improvement, the monopoly necessarily retards the natural increase of another great original source of revenue, the rent of land. By raising the rate of profit too the monopoly necessarily keeps up the market rate of interest higher than it otherwise would be. But the price of land in proportion to the rent which it affords, the number of years purchase which is commonly paid for it, necessarily falls as the rate of interest rises, and rises as the rate of interest falls.[41] The monopoly, therefore, hurts the interest of the landlord two different ways, by retarding the natural increase, first, of his rent, and secondly, of the price which he would get for his land in proportion to the rent which it affords.

59   The monopoly indeed, raises the rate of mercantile profit, and thereby augments somewhat the gain of our merchants. But as it obstructs the natural increase of capital, it tends rather to diminish than to increase the sum total of the revenue which the inhabitants of the country derive

---

[39] Above, II.iii.15.
[40] Though Smith has already recognized the beneficial effects when mercantile profits are subsequently invested in land. See above, III.iv.3.
[41] Above, II.iv.17.

from the profits of stock; a small profit upon a great capital generally affording a greater revenue than a great profit upon a small one. The monopoly raises the rate of profit, but it [437] hinders the sum of profit from rising so high as it otherwise would do.

60   All the original sources of revenue, the wages of labour, the rent of land, and the profits of stock,[42] the monopoly renders much less abundant than they otherwise would be. To promote the little interest of one little order of men in one country, it hurts the interest of all other orders of men in that country, and of all [m] men in all other countries.

61   It is solely by raising the ordinary rate of profit that the monopoly either has proved or could prove advantageous to any one particular order of men. But besides all the bad effects to the country in general, which have already been mentioned as necessarily resulting from a high rate of profit; there is one more fatal, perhaps, than all these put together, but which, if we may judge from experience, is inseparably connected with it. The high rate of profit seems every where to destroy that parsimony which in other circumstances is natural to the character of the merchant.[43] When profits are high, that sober virtue seems to be superfluous, and expensive luxury to suit better the affluence of his situation. But the owners of the great mercantile capitals are necessarily the leaders and conductors of the whole industry of every nation, and their example has a much greater influence upon the manners of the whole industrious part of it than that of any other order of men. If his employer is attentive and parsimonious, the workman is very likely to be so too; but if the master is dissolute [438] and disorderly, the servant who shapes his work according to the pattern which his master prescribes to him, will shape his life too according to the example which he sets him. Accumulation is thus prevented in the hands of all those who are naturally the most disposed to accumulate; and the funds destined for the maintenance of productive labour receive no augmentation from the revenue of those who ought naturally to augment them the most. The capital of the country, instead of increasing, gradually dwindles away, and the quantity of productive labour maintained in it grows every day less and less. Have the exorbitant profits of the merchants of Cadiz and Lisbon augmented the capital of Spain and Portugal?[44] Have they alleviated the poverty, have they promoted the industry of those two beggarly countries?

---

[m] the 6

---

[42] The original sources of revenue are discussed at I.vi.17.

[43] Smith comments on the relationship between manners and frugality at II.iii.12 and IV.vii.b.20. Sir James Steuart also noted that where high profits are sustained 'for a long time, they insensibly become *consolidated*, or, as it were, transformed into the intrinsic value of the goods', thus affecting the competitive position of the country or industry concerned. See especially, *Principles*, II.x.

[44] See below, § 82, where Smith also refers to the 'sumptuous profusion' of the merchants of Cadiz and Lisbon.

Such has been the tone of mercantile expence in those two trading cities, that those exorbitant profits, far from augmenting the general capital of the country, seem scarce to have been sufficient to keep up the capitals upon which they were made. Foreign capitals are every day intruding themselves, if I may say so, more and more into the trade of Cadiz and Lisbon. It is to expel those foreign capitals from a trade which their own [n] grows every day more and more insufficient for carrying on, that the Spaniards and Portugueze endeavour every day to straiten more and more the galling bands of their absurd monopoly. Compare the mercantile manners of Cadiz and Lisbon with those of Amsterdam, and you will be sen-[439]sible how differently the conduct and character of merchants are affected by the high and by the low profits of stock.[45] The merchants of London, indeed, have not yet generally become such magnificent lords as those of Cadiz and Lisbon; but neither are they in general such attentive and parsimonious burghers as those of Amsterdam. They are supposed, however, many of them, to be a good deal richer than the greater part of the former, and not quite so rich as many of the latter. But the rate of their profit is commonly much lower than that of the former, and a good deal higher than that of the latter. Light come light go, says the proverb; and the ordinary tone of expence seems every where to be regulated, not so much according to the real ability of spending, as to the supposed facility of getting money to spend.

62 It is thus that the single advantage which the monopoly procures to a single order of men is in many different ways hurtful to the general interest of the country.

63 To found a great empire for the sole purpose of raising up a people of customers, may at first sight appear a project fit only for a nation of shopkeepers.[46] It is, however, a project altogether unfit for a nation of shopkeepers; but extremely fit for a nation [o]whose government is influenced[o] by shopkeepers. Such [p]statesmen[p], and such [q]statesmen[q] only, are capable of fancying that they will find some advantage in employing the blood and treasure of their [r]fellow citizens[r], to found and [s]to[s] maintain such an empire. Say to a shopkeeper, Buy me a good estate, and I shall always buy my cloaths at your shop, even [440] though I should pay somewhat dearer than what I can have them for at other shops; and you will not find him

[n] capital *1* [o–o] that is governed *1* [p–p] soverigns *1* [q–q] soverigns *1*
[r–r] subjects *1* [s–s] *om. 4–6*

[45] Smith refers to the low rate of return on capital in Amsterdam at V.ii.k.80, and above, I.ix.10.

[46] See below, IV.viii.53. Pownall objected to the tone of this passage, since what he called 'creating and securing' an 'encreasing nation of appropriated customers' was the only idea which he could find 'precisely to define the relation which a commercial country bears to its colonies' (*Letter*, 44,n.). Cf. the same author's *Administration of the Colonies* (4th ed., London, 1768), vol. i, chapter viii.

very forward to embrace your proposal. But should any other person buy you such an estate, the shopkeeper would be much obliged to your bene-factor if he would enjoin you to buy all your cloaths at his shop. England purchased for some of her subjects, who found themselves uneasy at home, a great estate in a distant country. The price, indeed, was very small, and instead of thirty years purchase, the ordinary price of land in the present times, it amounted to little more than the expence of the different equip-ments which made the first discovery, reconnoitred the coast, and took a fictitious possession of the country. The land was good and of great extent, and the cultivators having plenty of good ground to work upon, and being for some time at liberty to sell their produce where they pleased, became in the course of little more than thirty or forty years (between 1620 and 1660) so numerous and thriving a people, that the shopkeepers and other traders of England wished to secure to themselves the monopoly of their custom.[47] Without pretending, therefore, that they had paid any part, either of the original purchase-money, or of the subsequent expence of improvement, they petitioned the parliament that the cultivators of America might for the future be confined to their shop; first, for buying all the goods which they wanted from Europe; and, secondly, for selling all such parts of their own produce as those traders might find it convenient to buy. For [441] they did not find it convenient to buy every part of it. Some parts of it imported into England might have interfered with some of the trades which they themselves carried on at home. Those particular parts of it, therefore, they were willing that the colonists should sell where they could; the farther off the better; and upon that account proposed that their market should be confined to the countries south of Cape Finisterre. A clause in the famous act of navigation established this truly shopkeeper proposal into a law.[48]

64   The maintenance of this monopoly has hitherto been the principal, or more properly perhaps the sole end and purpose of the dominion which Great Britain assumes over her colonies. In the exclusive trade, it is sup-posed, consists the great advantage of provinces, which have never yet afforded either revenue or military force for the support of the civil government, or the defence of the mother country.[49] The monopoly is the

---

[47] See above, IV.vii.b.15–17, where Smith comments on the prosperity of the American colonies, and § 63 of the same section where it is stated that the interest taken in them by the mother country was consequent on their success.

[48] See above, IV.ii.24–31, where the main provisions of the act are reviewed.

[49] Smith also mentions the lack of an American contribution to the costs of defence in Letter 221 addressed to John Sinclair, dated 14 October 1782. Again, Pownall objected: 'I will beg leave to suggest to you some facts that induce me, and may perhaps you also, to be of a very different opinion. That very naval force, which by their armed vessels they are now so destructively exerting against our West-India trade and transports, they did very effectively in the two late wars, especially in the last, exert to the ruin of the West India commerce of France and Spain . . .' He added, with respect to the 'point of revenue'

principal badge of their dependency,⁵⁰ and it is the sole fruit which has hitherto been gathered from that dependency. Whatever expence Great Britain has hitherto laid out in maintaining this dependency, has really been laid out in order to support this monopoly. The expence of the ordinary peace establishment of the colonies amounted, before the commencement of the present disturbances, to the pay of twenty regiments of foot; to the expence of the artillery, stores, and extraordinary provisions with which it ᵗwasᵗ necessary to supply them; and to the ex-[442]pence of a very considerable naval force which ᵘwasᵘ constantly kept up, in order to guard, from the smuggling vessels of other nations, the immense coast of North America, and that of our West Indian islands. The whole expence of this peace establishment was a charge upon the revenue of Great Britain, and was, at the same time, the smallest part of what the dominion of the colonies has cost the mother country.⁵¹ If we would know the amount of the whole, we must add to the annual expence of this peace establishment the interest of the sums which, in consequence of her considering her colonies as provinces subject to her dominion, Great Britain has upon different occasions laid out upon their defence. We must add to it, in particular, the whole expence of the late war, and a great part of that ᵛof the warᵛ which preceded it. The late war was altogether a colony quarrel, and the whole expence of it, in whatever part of the world it may have been laid out, whether in Germany or ʷ the East Indies, ought justly to be stated to the account of the colonies. It amounted to more than ninety millions sterling, including not only the new debt which was contracted, but the two shillings in the pound additional land tax, and the sums which were every year borrowed from the sinking fund.⁵² The Spanish war

ᵗ⁻ᵗ is *1*   ᵘ⁻ᵘ is *1*   ᵛ⁻ᵛ 2–6   ʷ in *1*

that 'before we went to decided war, a revenue might have been had upon compact, on terms which would have established the constitutional sovereignty of this country, regulating at the same time the trade and naval powers of the colonies, if those terms might have gone, at the same time, to securing the rights of those colonies as granted by the government of that mother country.' (*Letter*, 38.)

⁵⁰ Smith uses the term 'badge' in a similar context above, IV.vii.b.44.

⁵¹ See above, IV.vii.b.20 and IV.vii.c.12.

⁵² Smith reviews the costs of wars at II.iii.35, IV.i.26, IV.viii.53, and V.iii.92; cf. V.iii.88, where he states that the colonies should contribute to costs incurred on their behalf, and IV.vii.c.13, where he remarks that only the Spanish and Portuguese colonies had so contributed. In commenting on the saving of costs to be expected from the emancipation of America, Smith pointed out that Britain's two most expensive wars, the Spanish War of 1739 and the French War of 1755, 'were undertaken, the one chiefly, the other altogether on account of the colonies'. He went on to point out that the British had at one time complained of involvement in the affairs of Hanover 'with which we should, otherwise, have had nothing to do. But we, surely, have had much more reason to complain, upon the same account, of our connexion with America.' ('Thoughts on America', § 12, AHR 717–18.) Smith restated this theme in Letter 221 addressed to Sir John Sinclair, dated 14 October 1782: 'The real futility of all distant dominions, of which the defence is necessarily most expensive, and which contribute nothing, either by revenue or military

which began in 1739, was principally a colony quarrel. Its principal object was to prevent the search of the colony ships which carried on a contraband trade with the Spanish main. This whole expence is, in reality, a bounty which has [443] been given in order to support a monopoly. The pretended purpose of it was to encourage the manufactures, and to increase the commerce of Great Britain. But its real effect has been to raise the rate of mercantile profit, and to enable our merchants to turn into a branch of trade, of which the returns are more slow and distant than those of the greater part of other trades, a greater proportion of their capital than they otherwise would have done; two events which, if a bounty could have prevented, it might perhaps have been very well while to give such a bounty.

65   Under the present system of management, therefore, Great Britain derives nothing but loss from the dominion which she assumes over her colonies.

66   To propose that Great Britain should voluntarily give up all authority over her colonies,[53] and leave them to elect their own magistrates, to enact their own laws, and to make peace and war as they might think proper, would be to propose such a measure as never was, and never will be adopted, by any nation in the world.[54] No nation ever voluntarily gave up the dominion of any province, how troublesome soever it might be to govern it, and how small soever the revenue which it afforded might be in propor-

force, to the general defence of the empire, and very little even to their own particular defence, is, I think, the subject upon which the public prejudices of Europe require most to be set right.' Sinclair had apparently commented to Smith on the bleak prospect of the American War, and that 'if we go on at this rate, the nation must be ruined', to which Smith replied: 'Be assured, my young friend, that there is a great deal of *ruin* in a nation.' Sinclair Corr., i.390-1. In Letter 158 addressed to Strahan, dated 3 June 1776, Smith wrote: 'The American Campaign had begun awkwardly. I hope, I cannot say that I expect, it will end better. England, tho' in the present times it breeds men of great professional abilities in all different ways, great Lawyers, great watch makers & Clockmakers, &c. &c., seems to breed neither Statesmen nor Generals.'

    [53] Pownall objected to Smith's conclusion that the colonies should be given up at least in so far as that conclusion was based on the general analysis of the natural progress of opulence and Smith's views as to the different employments of capital: 'If we lose our colonies, we must submit to our fate; but the idea of parting with them on the ground of system, is much like the system which an ironical proverb recommends, *'of dying to save charges.'* (37.) Pownall's criticism of Smith's views on the colony trade appears mainly at pp. 37-48 of the *Letter.*

    [54] Cf. Smith's 'Thoughts on America', with regard to the emancipation of the colonies: 'tho' this termination of the war might be really advantageous, it would not, in the eyes of Europe appear honourable to Great Britain; and when her empire was so much curtailled, her power and dignity would be supposed to be proportionably diminished. What is of still greater importance, it could scarce fail to discredit the Government in the eyes of our own people, who would probably impute to mal-administration what might, perhaps, be no more than the unavoidable effect of the natural and necessary course of things. (it) . . . would have everything to fear from their rage and indignation at the public disgrace and calamity, for such they would suppose it to be, of thus dismembering the empire.' (§ 13, AHR 718.)

tion to the expence which it occasioned.[55] Such sacrifices, though they might frequently be agreeable to the interest, are always mortifying to the pride of every nation, and what is perhaps of still greater consequence, they are always contrary to the private interest of the governing part of it, [444] who would thereby be deprived of the disposal of many places of trust and profit, of many opportunities of acquiring wealth and distinction, which the possession of the most turbulent, and, to the great body of the people, the most unprofitable province seldom fails to afford. The most visionary enthusiast would scarce be capable of proposing such a measure, with any serious hopes at least of its ever being adopted. If it was adopted, however, Great Britain would not only be immediately freed from the whole annual expence of the peace establishment of the colonies, but might settle with them such a treaty of commerce as would effectually secure to her a free trade, more advantageous to the great body of the people, though less so to the merchants, than the monopoly which she at present enjoys. By thus parting good friends, the natural affection of the colonies to the mother country, which, perhaps, our late dissentions have well nigh extinguished, would quickly revive.[56] It might dispose them not only to respect, for whole centuries together, that treaty of commerce which they had concluded with us at parting, but to favour us in war as well as in trade, and, instead of turbulent and factious subjects, to become our most faithful, affectionate, and generous allies; and the same sort of parental affection on the one side, and filial respect on the other, might revive between Great Britain and her colonies, which used to subsist between those of ancient Greece and the mother city from which they descended.[57]

67 [445] In order to render any province advantageous to the empire to which it belongs, it ought to afford, in time of peace, a revenue to the publick sufficient not only for defraying the whole expence of its own peace establishment, but for contributing its proportion to the support of the general government of the empire. Every province necessarily contributes, more

---

[55] But cf. V.iii.92, where Smith recommends that Britain should give up her imperial pretensions.

[56] Cf. 'Thoughts on America': 'tho' Canada, Nova Scotia, and the Floridas were all given up to our rebellious colonies, or were all conquered by them, yet the similarity of language and manners would in most cases dispose the Americans to prefer our alliance to that of any other nation. Their antient affection for the people of this country might revive, if they were once assured that we meant to claim no dominion over them, . . . By a federal union with America we should certainly incur much less expense, and might, at the same time, gain as real advantages, as any we have hitherto derived from all the nominal dominion we have ever exercised over them.' (§ 12, AHR 718.) It is worth observing that Smith meant by 'federal union' a set of links established by the executive (federal) power rather than the type of constitutional arrangement which was later to be adopted in America. His own preference was for an incorporating union, of the kind which was later applied to Ireland, which would have given the colonies representation at Westminster. See below, § 77–9, and V.iii.90.

[57] See above, IV.vii.a.2.

or less, to increase the expence of that general government. If any particular province, therefore, does not contribute its share towards defraying this expence, an unequal burden must be thrown upon some other part of the empire. The extraordinary revenue too which every province affords to the publick in time of war, ought, from parity of reason, to bear the same proportion to the extraordinary revenue of the whole empire which its ordinary revenue does in time of peace.[58] That neither the ordinary nor extraordinary revenue which Great Britain derives from her colonies, bears this proportion to the whole revenue of the British empire, will readily be allowed. The monopoly, it has been supposed, indeed, by increasing the private revenue of the people of Great Britain, and thereby enabling them to pay greater taxes, compensates the deficiency of the publick revenue of the colonies. But this monopoly, I have endeavoured to show, though a very grievous tax upon the colonies, and though it may increase the revenue of a particular order of men in Great Britain, diminishes instead of increasing that of the great body of the people; and consequently diminishes instead of [446] increasing the ability of the great body of the people to pay taxes.[59] The men too whose revenue the monopoly increases, constitute a particular order, which it is both absolutely impossible to tax beyond the proportion of other orders, and extremely impolitick even to attempt to tax beyond that proportion, as I shall endeavour to shew in the following book.[60] No particular resource, therefore, can be drawn from this particular order.

[58] '. . . there never was an Idea of exempting the Colonies: on the Contrary, Restraints upon their Trade, and Taxes on their Consumption, have always gone together: And together compose the System, by which they have been constantly and happily governed . . . Our Taxes have been since encreased many-fold: Their Abilities have been enlarged still faster . . . The Proportion between the publick Burthens on the Mother-country and the Colonies, as divided when they were in their Infancy, is entirely lost: And to restore that Proportion, and again to make something like a Partition of those Burthens, is no more than maintaining the System, upon which we have always acted, and to which I own I am partial, because the Colonies have flourished under it beyond all Example in History, and I cannot prefer visionary speculations and novel Doctrines to such an Experience.' (*Considerations on the Trade and Finance of the Kingdom* (London, 1766), 81, attributed to T. Whateley and often ascribed to George Grenville.)

[59] above, § 59.

[60] Below, V.ii.f.6. Cf. Hume, *History of England* (1754), i.243–4: 'To complain of the parliament's employing the power of taxation, as the means of extorting concessions from their sovereign, were to expect, that they would intirely disarm themselves, and renounce the sole expedient, provided by the constitution, for ensuring to the kingdom a just and legal administration. In all periods of English story, there occur instances of their remonstrating with their princes in the freest manner, and of their refusing supply, when disgusted with any circumstance of public conduct. 'Tis, however, certain, that this power, tho' essential to parliaments, may easily be abused, as well by the frequency and the minuteness of their remonstrances, as by their intrusion into every part of the king's councils and determinations. Under color of advice, they may give disguised orders; and in complaining of grievances, they may draw to themselves every power of government. Whatever measure is embraced, without consulting them, may be pronounced an oppression of the people; and till corrected, they may refuse the most necessary supplies to their indigent sovereign.'

68   The colonies may be taxed by their own assemblies, or by the parliament of Great Britain.

69   That the colony assemblies can ever be so managed as to levy upon their constituents a publick revenue sufficient, not only to maintain at all times their own civil and military establishment, but to pay their proper proportion of the expence of the general government of the British empire, seems not very probable. It was a long time before even the parliament of England, though placed immediately under the eye of the sovereign, could be brought under such a system of management, or could be rendered sufficiently liberal in their grants for supporting the civil and military establishments even of their own country. It was only by distributing among the particular members of parliament, a great part either of the offices, or of the disposal of the offices arising from this civil and military establishment, that such a system of management could be established even with regard to the parliament of England. But the distance of the colony assemblies from the eye of the sovereign, [447] their number, their dispersed situation, and their various constitutions, would render it very difficult to manage them in the same manner, even though the sovereign had the same means of doing it; and those means are wanting. It would be absolutely impossible to distribute among all the leading members of all the colony assemblies such a share, either of the offices or of the disposal of the offices arising from the general government of the British empire, as to dispose them to give up their popularity at home and to tax their constituents for the support of that general government, of which almost the whole emoluments were to be divided among people who were strangers to them. The unavoidable ignorance of administration, besides, concerning the relative importance of the different members of those different assemblies, the offences which must frequently be given, the blunders which must constantly be committed in attempting to manage them in this manner, seems to render such a system of management altogether impracticable with regard to them.

70   The colony assemblies, besides, cannot be supposed the proper judges of what is necessary for the defence and support of the whole empire. The care of that defence and support is not entrusted to them. It is not their business, and they have no regular means of information concerning it. The assembly of a province, like the vestry of a parish, may judge very properly concerning the affairs of its own particular district; but can have no proper means of judging [448] concerning those of the whole empire. It cannot even judge properly concerning the proportion which its own province bears to the whole empire; or concerning the relative degree of its wealth and importance, compared with the other provinces; because those other provinces are not under the inspection and superintendency of the assembly of a particular province. What is necessary for the defence and

support of the whole empire, and in what proportion each part ought to contribute, can be judged of only by that assembly which inspects and superintends the affairs of the whole empire.

71   It has been proposed, accordingly, that the colonies should be taxed by requisition, the parliament of Great Britain determining the sum which each colony ought to pay, and the provincial assembly assessing and levying it in the way that suited best the circumstances of the province. What concerned the whole empire would in this way be determined by the assembly which inspects and superintends the affairs of the whole empire; and the provincial affairs of each colony might still be regulated by its own assembly. Though the colonies should in this case have no representatives in the British parliament, yet, if we may judge by experience, there is no probability that the parliamentary requisition would be unreasonable. The parliament of England has not upon any occasion shown the smallest disposition to overburden those parts of the empire which are not represented in parliament. The islands of Guernsey and Jersey, [449] without any means of resisting the authority of parliament, are more lightly taxed than any part of Great Britain. Parliament in attempting to exercise its supposed right, whether well or ill grounded, of taxing the colonies, has never hitherto demanded of them any thing which even approached to a just proportion to what was paid by their fellow subjects at home. If the contribution of the colonies, besides, was to rise or fall in proportion to the rise or fall of the land tax, parliament could not tax them without taxing at the same time its own constituents, and the colonies might in this case be considered as virtually represented in parliament.

72   Examples are not wanting of empires in which all the different provinces are not taxed, if I may be allowed the expression, in one mass; but in which the sovereign regulates the sum which each province ought to pay, and in some provinces assesses and levies it as he thinks proper; while in others, he leaves it to be assessed and levied as the respective states of each province shall determine. In some provinces of France, the king not only imposes what taxes he thinks proper, but assesses and levies them in the way he thinks proper.[61] From others he demands a certain sum, but leaves it to the states of each province to assess and levy that sum as they think proper. According to the scheme of taxing by requisition, the parliament of Great Britain would stand nearly in the same situation towards the colony assemblies, as the king of France does towards the states of those provinces [450] which still enjoy the privilege of having states of their own, the provinces of France which are supposed to be the best governed.

73   But though, according to this scheme, the colonies could have no just reason to fear that their share of the publick burdens should ever exceed

---

[61] See below, V.ii.k.70.

the proper proportion to that of their fellow-citizens at home; Great Britain might have just reason to fear that it never would amount to that proper proportion. The parliament of Great Britain has not for some time past had the same established authority in the colonies, which the French king has in those provinces of France which still enjoy the privilege of having states of their own. The colony assemblies, if they were not very favourably disposed (and unless more skilfully managed than they ever have been hitherto, they are not very likely to be so) might still find many pretences for evading or rejecting the most reasonable requisitions of parliament. A French war breaks out, we shall suppose; ten millions must immediately be raised, in order to defend the seat of the empire. This sum must be borrowed upon the credit of some parliamentary fund mortgaged for paying the interest. Part of this fund parliament proposes to raise by a tax to be levied in Great Britain, and part of it by a requisition to all the different colony assemblies of America and the West Indies. Would people readily advance their money upon the credit of a fund, which partly depended upon the good-humour of all those assemblies, far distant from the seat of the [451] war, and sometimes, perhaps, thinking themselves not much concerned in the event of it? Upon such a fund no more money would probably be advanced than what the tax to be levied in Great Britain might be supposed to answer for. The whole burden of the debt contracted on account of the war would in this manner fall, as it always has done hitherto, upon Great Britain; upon a part of the empire, and not upon the whole empire. Great Britain is, perhaps, since the world began, the only state which, as it has extended its empire, has only increased its expence without once augmenting its resources. Other states have generally disburdened themselves upon their subject and subordinate provinces of the most considerable part of the expence of defending the empire. Great Britain has hitherto suffered her subject and subordinate provinces to disburden themselves upon her of almost this whole expence. In order to put Great Britain upon a footing of equality with her own colonies, which the law has hitherto supposed to be subject and subordinate, it seems necessary, upon the scheme of taxing them by parliamentary requisition, that parliament should have some means of rendering its requisitions immediately effectual, in case the colony assemblies[62] should attempt to evade or reject them; and what those means are, it is not very easy to conceive, and it has not yet been explained.

74   Should the parliament of Great Britain, at the same time, be ever fully established in the right of taxing the colonies, even independent of [452] the consent of their own assemblies, the importance of those assemblies would from that moment be at an end, and with it, that of all the leading

---

[62] These assemblies are described above, IV.vii.b.51.

men of British America. Men desire to have some share in the management of publick affairs chiefly on account of the importance which it gives them.[63] Upon the power which the greater part of the leading men, the natural aristocracy of every country, have of preserving or defending their respective importance, depends the stability and duration of every system of free government.[64] In the attacks which those leading men are continually making upon the importance of one another, and in the defence of their own, consists the whole play of domestick faction and ambition. The leading men of America, like those of all other countries, desire to preserve their own importance. They feel, or imagine, that if their assemblies, which they are fond of calling parliaments, and of considering as equal in authority to the parliament of Great Britain, should be so far degraded as to become the humble ministers and executive officers of that parliament, the greater part of their own importance would be at an end. They have rejected, therefore, the proposal of being taxed by parliamentary requisition, and like other ambitious and high-spirited men, have rather chosen to draw the sword in defence of their own importance.

75   Towards the declension of the Roman republick, the allies of Rome, who had borne the principal burden of defending the state and ex-[453]tending the empire, demanded to be admitted to all the privileges of Roman citizens. Upon being refused, the social war broke out. During the course of that war Rome granted those privileges to the greater part of them, one by one, and in proportion as they detached themselves from the general confederacy. The parliament of Great Britain insists upon taxing the colonies; and they refuse to be taxed by a parliament in which they are not represented. If to each colony, which should detach itself from the general confederacy, Great Britain should allow such a number of representatives as suited the proportion of what it contributed to the publick revenue of the empire,[65] in consequence of its being subjected to the same taxes, and in compensation admitted to the same freedom of trade with its fellow-subjects at home; the number of its representatives to be augmented as the proportion of its contribution might afterwards augment; a new method of acquiring importance, a new and more dazzling object of ambition would be presented to the leading men of each colony.[66] Instead of piddling for

---

[63] Smith provides another example below, V.ii.k.80, drawn from Holland.

[64] Cf. 'Thoughts on America': 'The principal security of every government arises always from the support of those whose dignity, authority and interest, depend upon its being supported.' (§ 10, AHR 716.)

[65] See below, V.iii.68, where it is stated that taxation with representation conforms to British constitutional practice.

[66] Smith points out in the 'Thoughts on America' that a form of union with America *might* be possible: 'The leading men of America, we may believe, wish to continue to be the principal people in their own country. After a union with Great Britain, they might expect to continue to be so; in the same manner as the leading men of Scotland continued to be the principal people in their own country after the union with England.' (§ 14, AHR

the little prizes which are to found in what may be called the paltry raffle of colony faction; they might then hope, from the presumption which men naturally have in their own ability and good fortune, to draw some of the great prizes which sometimes come from the wheel of the great state lottery of British politicks. Unless this or some other method is fallen upon, and there seems to be none more obvious than this, of [454] preserving the importance and of gratifying the ambition of the leading men of America, it is not very probable that they will ever voluntarily submit to us; and we ought to consider that the blood which must be shed in forcing them to do so, is, every drop of it, the blood either of those who are, or of those whom we wish to have for our fellow-citizens. They are very weak who flatter themselves that, in the state to which things have come, our colonies will be easily conquered by force alone.[67] The persons who now govern the resolutions of that they call their continental congress, feel in themselves at this moment a degree of importance which, perhaps, the greatest subjects in Europe scarce feel. From shopkeepers, tradesmen, and attornies, they are become statesmen and legislators, and are employed in contriving a new form of government for an extensive empire, which, they flatter themselves, will become, and which, indeed, seems very likely to become, one of the greatest and most formidable that ever was in the world. Five hundred different people, perhaps, who in different ways act immediately under the continental congress; and five hundred thousand, perhaps, who act under those five hundred, all feel in the same manner a proportionable rise in their own importance. Almost every individual of the governing party in America, fills, at present in his own fancy, a station superior, not only to what he had ever filled before, but to what he had ever expected to fill; and unless some new object of ambition is presented either to him or [455] to his leaders, if he has the ordinary spirit of a man, he will die in defence of that station.

76   It is a remark of the president Henaut that we now read with pleasure the account of many little transactions of the Ligue, which when they happened were not perhaps considered as very important pieces of news.

719.) It was in this context that Smith made the ingenious suggestion that should the idea of union fail, the solution might be 'An apparent restoration of the old system, so contrived as to lead necessarily, but insensibly to the total dismemberment of America, might, perhaps, satisfy both the people of Great Britain and the leading men of America: the former mistaking, and the latter understanding, the meaning of the scheme.' (§ 16.) Another ingenious suggestion, to be applied in the case of the complete emancipation of America, was that we should restore Canada to France and the Floridas to Spain, thereby rendering our own colonies the 'natural enemies of those two monarchies and consequently the natural allies of Great Britain'. In this way, Smith hoped that 'old enmities, and probably old friendships' might be revived. § 12, AHR 718.

[67] It is pointed out in V.i.a.27 that while militias are generally inferior to standing armies, this need not be the case where the former are long in the field, and that another campaign would place the American militia on a par with the British army.

But every man then, says he, fancied himself of some importance; and the innumerable memoirs which have come down to us from those times, were, the greater part of them, written by people who took pleasure in recording and magnifying events in which, they flattered themselves, they had been considerable actors.[68] How obstinately the city of Paris upon that occasion defended itself, what a dreadful famine it supported rather than submit to the best and afterwards the most beloved of all the French kings, is well known. The greater part of the citizens, or those who governed the greater part of them, fought in defence of their own importance, which they foresaw was to be at an end whenever the ancient government should be re-established. Our colonies, unless they can be induced to consent to a union, are very likely to defend themselves against the best of all mother countries, as obstinately as the city of Paris did against one of the best of kings.

77   The idea of representation was unknown in ancient times. When the people of one state were admitted to the right of citizenship in another, they had no other means of exercising that right but by coming in a body to vote and deli-[456]berate with the people of that other state. The admission of the greater part of the inhabitants of Italy to the privileges of Roman citizens, completely ruined the Roman republick. It was no longer possible to distinguish between who was and who was not a Roman citizen. No tribe could know its own members. A rabble of any kind could be introduced into the assemblies of the people, could drive out the real citizens, and decide upon the affairs of the republick as if they themselves had been such.[69] But though America ˣwasˣ to send fifty of sixty new representatives to parliament, the door-keeper of the house of commons could not find any great difficulty in distinguishing between who was and who was not a member. Though the Roman constitution, therefore, was necessarily ruined by the union of Rome with the allied states of Italy, there is not the least probability that the British constitution would be hurt by the union of Great Britain with her colonies. That constitution, on the contrary, would be completed by it, and seems to be imperfect without it.[70] The assembly which deliberates and decides concerning the affairs of every part of the empire, in order to be properly informed, ought certainly to have representatives from every part of it. That this union, however, could be easily effectuated, or that difficulties and great difficulties might not occur in the execution, I do not pretend. I have yet heard of none, however, which

ˣ⁻ˣ were 4–6

[68] C. J. F. Hénault, *Nouvel Abrégé chronologique de l'histoire de France* (Paris, 1768), 581.

[69] Cf. Montesquieu, *Considerations*, 93: 'Once the peoples of Italy became its citizens, each city brought to Rome its genius, its particular interests, and its dependence on some great protector. The distracted city no longer formed a complete whole.'

[70] See below, V.iii.89–90, where Smith elaborates on the economic and political benefits of union with regard to the colonies and Ireland.

appear insurmountable.[71] The principal perhaps arise, not from the nature of things, but from the prejudices and opinions [457] of the people both on this and ^{y}on^y the other side of the Atlantic.

78   We, on this side the water, are afraid lest the multitude of American representatives should overturn the balance of the constitution, and increase too much either the influence of the crown on the one hand, or the force of the democracy on the other. But if the number of American representatives ^{z}was^z to be in proportion to the produce of American taxation, the number of people to be managed would increase exactly in proportion to the means of managing them; and the means of managing, to the number of people to be managed. The monarchical and democratical parts of the constitution would, after the union, stand exactly in the same degree of relative force with regard to one another as they had done before.

79   The people on the other side of the water are afraid lest their distance from the seat of government might expose them to many oppressions. But their representatives in parliament, of which the number ought from the first to be considerable, would easily be able to protect them from all oppression. The distance could not much weaken the dependency of the representative upon the constituent, and the former would still feel that he owed his seat in parliament, and all the consequence which he derived from it, to the good-will of the latter. It would be the interest of the former, therefore, to cultivate that good-will by complaining, with all the authority of a member of the legislature, of every outrage which [458] any civil or military officer might be guilty of in those remote parts of the empire. The distance of America from the seat of government, besides, the ^{a}natives^a of that country might flatter themselves, with some appearance of reason too, would not be of very long continuance. Such has hitherto been the rapid progress of that country in wealth, population and improvement, that in the course of little more than a century, perhaps, the produce of American might exceed that of British taxation. The seat of the empire

---

$^{y-y}$ 2–6 $^{z-z}$ were 4–6 $^{a-a}$ nations 1

[71] Smith considered the desirability of an incorporating union in the 'Thoughts on America', somewhat along the lines of the existing union between Scotland and England, but added that such a plan as would 'certainly tend most to the prosperity, to the splendor, and to the duration of the empire, if you except here and there a solitary philosopher like myself, seems scarce to have a single advocate' (§ 11, AHR 717). He added that the Americans especially, in their 'present elevation of spirits' were unlikely to agree, and as to British opinion, he believed the most popular solution was military victory.

Both Lord Kames and Benjamin Franklin supported the idea of consolidating union, although the latter clearly recognized that delay would make it increasingly unlikely as a solution. None the less, it is interesting to recall that the First Continental Congress of 1774 debated and narrowly defeated Joseph Galloway's plan for a 'grand legislative council' which was to be responsible for controlling the affairs of the union. The whole issue of union is extensively discussed in Richard Koebner's *Empire* (Cambridge, 1961), chapter 4.

would then naturally remove itself to that part of the empire which contributed most to the general defence and support of the whole.[72]

80   The discovery of America, and that of a passage to the East Indies by the Cape of Good Hope, are the two greatest and most important events recorded in the history of mankind.[73] Their consequences have already been very great: but, in the short period of between two and three centuries which has elapsed since these discoveries were made, it is impossible that the whole extent of their consequences can have been seen. What benefits, or what misfortunes to mankind may hereafter result from those great events no human wisdom can foresee. By uniting, in some measure, the most distant parts of the world, by enabling them to relieve one another's wants, to increase one another's enjoyments, and to encourage one another's industry, their general tendency would seem to be beneficial. To the natives, however, both of the East and West Indies, all the commercial bene-[459] fits which can have resulted from those events have been sunk and lost in the dreadful misfortunes which they have occasioned.[74] These misfortunes, however, seem to have arisen rather from accident than from any thing in the nature of those events themselves. At the particular time when these discoveries were made, the superiority of force happened to be so great on the side of the Europeans, that they were enabled to commit with impunity every sort of injustice in those remote countries. Hereafter, perhaps, the natives of those countries may grow stronger, or those of Europe may grow weaker, and the inhabitants of all the different quarters of the world may arrive at that equality of courage and force which, by inspiring mutual fear, can alone overawe the injustice of independent nations into some sort of respect for the rights of one another.[75] But

[72] It is interesting to note that in reading this section of Smith's work, Hugh Blair expressed regret that he had given the colonial affair 'a representation &c. which I wish had been omitted, because it is too much like a publication for the present moment. In Subsequent editions when public Measures come to be Settled, these pages will fall to be omitted or Altered.' (Letter 151 addressed to Smith, dated 3 April 1776.) In Letter 147 addressed to Smith, dated 1 November 1775, John Roebuck, friend and former partner of James Watt, stated the opposite opinion: 'I hoped by this time to have seen your Name in the Papers. The meeting of Parlt. is the proper time for the Publication of such a work as yours. It might also have been of general use in influencing the Opinion of many in this American contest.' In Letter 153 addressed to Smith, dated 8 April 1776, William Robertson commented that: 'Many of your observations concerning the Colonies are of capital importance to me. I shall often follow you as my Guide and Instructor. I am happy to find my own ideas concerning the absurdity of the limitations upon the Colony trade established much better than I could have done myself.'

[73] See above, IV.i.33. Cf. G. T. F. Raynal, *Histoire philosophique*, i.1, trans. J. Justamond, i.1: 'The discovery of the new world, and the passages to the East Indies by the Cape of Good Hope, is one of the most important events in the history of the human species.'

[74] Smith comments on the savage injustice inflicted by the Europeans on the native populations in IV.i.32 and below, § 100.

[75] It is pointed out in LJ (B) 339, ed. Cannan 265, in the course of considering the laws of nations, that: 'where there is no supreme legislative power nor judge to settle differences, we may always expect uncertainty and irregularity.'

nothing seems more likely to establish this equality of force than that mutual communication of knowledge and of all sorts of improvements which an extensive commerce from all countries to all countries naturally, or rather necessarily, carries along with it.

81   In the mean time one of the principal effects of those discoveries has been to raise the mercantile system to a degree of splendor and glory which it could never otherwise have attained to. It is the object of that system to enrich a great nation rather by trade and manufactures than by the improvement and cultivation of land, rather by the industry of the towns than by that of the country. But, in consequence of those dis-[460] coveries, the commercial towns of Europe, instead of being the manufacturers and carriers for but a very small part of the world (that part of Europe which is washed by the Atlantic ocean, and the countries which lie round the Baltick and Mediterranean seas), have now become the manufacturers for the numerous and thriving cultivators of America, and the carriers, and in some respects the manufacturers too, for almost all the different nations of Asia, Africa, and America. Two new worlds have been opened to their industry, each of them much greater and more extensive than the old one, and the market of one of them growing still greater and greater every day.

82   The countries which possess the colonies of America, and which trade directly to the East Indies, enjoy, indeed, the whole shew and splendor of this great commerce. Other countries, however, notwithstanding all the invidious restraints by which it is meant to exclude them, frequently enjoy a greater share of the real benefit of it.[76] The colonies of Spain and Portugal, for example, give more real encouragement to the industry of other countries than to that of Spain and Portugal. In the single article of linen alone the consumption of those colonies amounts, it is said, but I do not pretend to warrant the quantity, to more than three millions sterling a year. But this great consumption is almost entirely supplied by France, Flanders, Holland, and Germany. Spain and Portugal furnish but a small part of it. The capital [461] which supplies the colonies with this great quantity of linen is annually distributed among, and furnishes a revenue to the inhabitants of those other countries. The profits of it only are spent in Spain and Portugal, where they help to support the sumptuous profusion of the merchants of Cadiz and Lisbon.[77]

83   Even the regulations by which each nation endeavours to secure to itself the exclusive trade of its own colonies, are frequently more hurtful to the countries in favour of which they are established than to those against which they are established. The unjust oppression of the industry of other countries falls back, if I may say so, upon the heads of the oppres-

---

[76] See above, IV.vii.c.6.   [77] See above, § 61.

sors, and crushes their industry more than it does that of those other countries. By those regulations, for example, the merchant of Hamburgh must send the linen which he destines for the American market to London, and he must bring back from thence the tobacco which he destines for the German market; because he can neither send the one directly to America, nor bring back the other directly from thence. By this restraint he is probably obliged to sell the one somewhat cheaper, and to buy the other somewhat dearer than he otherwise might have done; and his profits are probably somewhat abridged by means of it. In this trade, however, between Hamburgh and London, he certainly receives the returns of his capital much more quickly than he could possibly have done in the direct trade to America, even though we should suppose, [462] what is by no means the case, that the payments of America were as punctual as those of London. In the trade, therefore, to which those regulations confine the merchant of Hamburgh, his capital can keep in constant employment a much greater quantity of German industry than it possibly could have done in the trade from which he is excluded. Though the one employment, therefore, may to him perhaps be less profitable than the other, it cannot be less advantageous to his country. It is quite otherwise with the employment into which the monopoly naturally attracts, if I may say so, the capital of the London merchant. That employment may, perhaps, be more profitable to him than the greater part of other employments, but, on account of the slowness of the returns, it cannot be more advantageous to his country.

84 After all the unjust attempts, therefore, of every country in Europe to engross to itself the whole advantage of the trade of its own colonies, no country has yet been able to engross to itself any thing but the expence of supporting in time of peace and of defending in time of war the oppressive authority which it assumes over them. The inconveniencies resulting from the possession of its colonies, every country has engrossed to itself completely. The advantages resulting from their trade it has been obliged to share with many other countries.

85 At first sight, no doubt, the monopoly of the great commerce of America, naturally seems to be an acquisition of the highest value. To the [463] undiscerning eye of giddy ambition, it naturally presents itself amidst the confused scramble of politicks and war, as a very dazzling object to fight for. The dazzling splendor of the object, however, the immense greatness of the commerce, is the very quality which renders the monopoly of it hurtful, or which makes one employment, in its own nature necessarily less advantageous to the country than the greater part of other employments, absorb a much greater proportion of the capital of the country than what would otherwise have gone to it.

86 The mercantile stock of every country, it has been shewn in the second

book,[78] naturally seeks, if one may say so, the employment most advantageous to that country. If it is employed in the carrying trade, the country to which it belongs becomes the emporium of the goods of all the countries whose trade that stock carries on. But the owner of that stock necessarily wishes to dispose of as great a part of those goods as he can at home. He thereby saves himself the trouble, risk, and expence, of exportation, and he will upon that account be glad to sell them at home, not only for a much smaller price, but with somewhat a smaller profit than he might expect to make by sending them abroad. He naturally, therefore, endeavours as much as he can to turn his carrying trade into a foreign trade of consumption. If his stock again is employed in a foreign trade of consumption, he will, for the same reason, be glad to dispose of at home as great a part as he can of the home goods, which [464] he collects in order to export to some foreign market, and he will thus endeavour, as much as he can, to turn his foreign trade of consumption into a home trade. The mercantile stock of every country naturally courts in this manner the near, and shuns the distant employment; naturally courts the employment in which the returns are frequent, and shuns that in which they are distant and slow; naturally courts the employment in which it can maintain the greatest quantity of productive labour in the country to which it belongs, or in which its owner resides, and shuns that in which it can maintain there the smallest quantity. It naturally courts the employment which in ordinary cases is most advantageous, and shuns that which in ordinary cases is least advantageous to that country.

87   But if any of those distant employments, which in ordinary cases are less advantageous to the country, the profit should happen to rise somewhat higher than what is sufficient to balance the natural preference which is given to nearer employments, this superiority of profit will draw stock from those nearer employments, till the profits of all return to their proper level. This superiority of profit, however, is a proof that in the actual circumstances of the society, those distant employments are somewhat understocked in proportion to other employments, and that the stock of the society is not distributed in the properest manner among all the different employments carried on in it. It is a proof that something is either bought cheaper or sold dearer [465] than it ought to be, and that some particular class of citizens is more or less oppressed either by paying more or by getting less than what is suitable to that equality, which ought to take place, and which naturally does take place among all the different classes of them. Though the same capital never will maintain the same quantity of productive labour in a distant as in a near employment, yet a distant employment may be as necessary for the welfare of the society as a

---

[78] See above, II.v.

near one;[79] the goods which the distant employment deals in being necessary, perhaps, for carrying on many of the nearer employments. But if the
profits of those who deal in such goods are above their proper level, those
goods will be sold dearer than they ought to be, or somewhat above their
natural price, and all those engaged in the nearer employments will be
more or less oppressed by this high price. Their interest, therefore, in this
case requires that some stock should be withdrawn from those nearer
employments, and turned towards that distant *b*one*b*, in order to reduce
its profits to their proper level, and the price of the goods which it deals in
to their natural price. In this extraordinary case, the publick interest requires that some stock should be withdrawn from those employments
which in ordinary cases are more advantageous, and turned towards one
which in ordinary cases is less advantageous to the publick: and in this
extraordinary case, the natural interests and inclinations of men coincide
as exactly with the publick interest as in all other ordinary cases, [466]
and lead them to withdraw stock from the near, and to turn it towards the
distant employment.

88   It is thus that the private interests and passions of individuals naturally
dispose them to turn their stock towards the employments which in ordinary
cases are most advantageous to the society.[80] But if from this natural preference they should turn too much of it towards those employments, the
fall of profit in them and the rise of it in all others immediately dispose
them to alter this faulty distribution. Without any intervention of law,
therefore, the private interests and passions of men naturally lead them to
divide and distribute the stock of every society, among all the different
employments carried on in it, as nearly as possible in the proportion which
is most agreeable to the interest of the whole society.

89   All the different regulations of the mercantile system, necessarily derange more or less this natural and most advantageous distribution of stock.
But those which concern the trade to America and the East Indies derange
it perhaps more than any other;[81] because the trade to those two great
continents absorbs a greater quantity of stock than any two other branches
of trade. The regulations, however, by which this derangement is effected
in those two different branches of trade are not altogether the same.
Monopoly is the great engine of both; but it is a different sort of monopoly. Monopoly of one kind or another, indeed, seems to be the sole engine
of the mercantile system.[82]

90   [467] In the trade to America every nation endeavours to engross as

---

b-b employment *I*

[79] A related point is made at II.v.34.   [80] See above, IV.ii.9.
[81] See above, § 46.
[82] Smith refers to restraints on imports and the encouragement of exports as the 'two
great engines' of the mercantile system, at IV.i.35 and IV.viii.1.

much as possible the whole market of its own colonies, by fairly excluding all other nations from any direct trade to them. During the greater part of the sixteenth century, the Portugueze endeavoured to manage the trade to the East Indies in the same manner, by claiming the sole right of sailing in the Indian seas, on account of the merit of having first found out the road to them. The Dutch still continue to exclude all other European nations from any direct trade to their spice islands. Monopolies of this kind are evidently established against all other European nations, who are thereby not only excluded from a trade to which it might be convenient for them to turn some part of their stock, but are obliged to buy the goods which that trade deals in somewhat dearer, than if they could import them themselves directly from the countries which produce them.

91   But since the fall of the power of Portugal, no European nation has claimed the exclusive right of sailing in the Indian seas, of which the principal ports are now open to the ships of all European nations. Except in Portugal,[83] however, and within these few years in France, the trade to the East Indies has in every European country been subjected to an exclusive company. Monopolies of this kind are properly established against the very nation which erects them.[84] The greater part of that nation are thereby not only excluded from a trade to which it might be con-[468] venient for them to turn some part of their stock, but are obliged to buy the goods which that trade deals in, somewhat dearer than if it was open and free to all their countrymen. Since the establishment of the English East India company, for example, the other inhabitants of England, over and above being excluded from the trade, must have paid in the price of the East India goods which they have consumed, not only for all the extraordinary profits which the company may have made upon those goods in consequence of their monopoly, but for all the extraordinary waste which the fraud and abuse, inseparable from the management of the affairs of so great a company, must necessarily have occasioned. The absurdity of this second kind of monopoly, therefore, is much more manifest than that of the first.

92   Both these kinds of monopolies derange more or less the natural distribution of the stock of the society: but they do not always derange it in the same way.

93   Monopolies of the first kind always attract to the particular trade in which they are established, a greater proportion of the stock of the society than what would go to that trade of its own accord.

94   Monopolies of the second kind, may sometimes attract stock towards the particular trade in which they are established, and sometimes repel it

<hr>

[83] See below, IV.vii.c.100.

[84] See above, I.viii.26. Smith considers the disadvantages of exclusive companies with regard to the colonies at IV.vii.b.22 and offers an extensive account of their record in V.i.e.

from that trade according to different circumstances. In poor countries they naturally [469] attract towards that trade more stock than would otherwise go to it. In rich countries they naturally repel from it a good deal of stock which would otherwise go to it.

95 Such poor countries as Sweden and Denmark, for example, would probably have never sent a single ship to the East Indies, had not the trade been subjected to an exclusive company. The establishment of such a company necessarily encourages adventurers. Their monopoly secures them against all competitors in the home market, and they have the same chance for foreign markets with the traders of other nations. Their monopoly shows them the certainty of a great profit upon a considerable quantity of goods, and the chance of a considerable profit upon a great quantity. Without such extraordinary encouragement, the poor traders of such poor countries would probably never have thought of hazarding their small capitals in so very distant and uncertain an adventure as the trade to the East Indies must naturally have appeared to them.[85]

96 Such a rich country as Holland, on the contrary, would probably, in the case of a free trade, send many more ships to the East Indies than it actually does. The limited stock of the Dutch East India company probably repels from that trade many great mercantile capitals which would otherwise go to it. The mercantile capital of Holland is so great that it is, as it were, continually overflowing, sometimes into the publick funds of foreign countries, sometimes into loans [470] to private traders and adventurers of foreign countries, sometimes into the most round-about foreign trades of consumption, and sometimes into the carrying trade. All near employments being completely filled up, all the capital which can be placed in them with any tolerable profit being already placed in them, the capital of Holland necessarily flows towards the most distant employments.[86] The trade to the East Indies, if it ᶜwasᶜ altogether free, would probably absorb the greater part of this redundant capital. The East Indies offer a market both for the manufactures of Europe and for the gold and silver as well as for several other productions of America, greater and more extensive than both Europe and America put together.

97 Every derangement of the natural distribution of stock is necessarily hurtful to the society in which it takes place; whether it be by repelling from a particular trade the stock which would otherwise go to it, or by attracting towards a particular trade that which would not otherwise come

---

ᶜ⁻ᶜ were 4–6

[85] See below, V.i.e.30, where Smith defends temporary monopolies, including those granted to merchants who first establish a hazardous trade. See also § 2 of the same section.

[86] See above, II.v.35.

to it.[87] If, without any exclusive company, the trade of Holland to the East Indies would be greater than it actually is, that country must suffer a considerable loss by part of its capital being excluded from the employment most convenient for that part. And in the same manner, if, without an exclusive company, the trade of Sweden and Denmark to the East Indies would be less than it actually is, or, what perhaps is more probable, would not exist at all, those two countries must likewise suffer a con-[471]siderable loss by part of their capital being drawn into an employment which must be more or less unsuitable to their present circumstances. Better for them, perhaps, in their present circumstances, to buy East India goods of other nations, even though they should pay somewhat dearer, than to turn so great a part of their small capital to so very distant a trade, in which the returns are so very slow, in which that capital can maintain so small a quantity of productive labour at home, where productive labour is so much wanted, where so little is done, and where so much is to do.

98   Though without an exclusive company, therefore, a particular country should not be able to carry on any direct trade to the East Indies, it will not from thence follow that such a company ought to be established there, but only that such a country ought not in these circumstances to trade directly to the East Indies. That such companies are not in general necessary for carrying on the East India trade, is sufficiently demonstrated by the experience of the Portugueze, who enjoyed almost the whole of it for more than a century together without any exclusive company.

99   No private merchant, it has been said, could well have capital sufficient to maintain factors and agents in the different ports of the East Indies, in order to provide goods for the ships which he might occasionally send thither; and yet, unless he was able to do this, the difficulty of finding a cargo might frequently make his ships lose the season for returning, and the ex-[472]pence of so long a delay would not only eat up the whole profit of the adventure, but frequently occasion a very considerable loss. This argument, however, if it proved any thing at all, would prove that no one great branch of trade could be carried on without an exclusive company, which is contrary to the experience of all nations. There is no great branch of trade in which the capital of any one private merchant is sufficient, for carrying on all the subordinate branches which must be carried on, in order to carry on the principal *d*one*d*. But when a nation is ripe for any great branch of trade, some merchants naturally turn their capitals towards the principal, and some towards the subordinate branches of it; and though all the different branches of it are in this manner carried on, yet it very seldom happens that they are all carried on by the capital of one private merchant.

---

d-d branch *1*

[87] See above, § 43, and IV.ii.3 for an elaboration of this point.

If a nation, therefore, is ripe for the East India trade, a certain portion of its capital will naturally divide itself among all the different branches of that trade. Some of its merchants will find it for their interest to reside in the East Indies, and to employ their capitals there in providing goods for the ships which are to be sent out by other merchants who reside in Europe. The settlements which different European nations have obtained in the East Indies, if they were taken from the exclusive companies to which they at present belong and put under the immediate protection of the sove-reign, would render this residence both safe and easy, at least to the mer-[473]chants of the particular nations to whom those settlements belong. If at any particular time that part of the capital of any country which of its own accord tended and inclined, if I may say so, towards the East India trade, was not sufficient for carrying on all those different branches of it, it would be a proof that, at that particular time, that country was not ripe for that trade, and that it would do better to buy for some time, even at a higher price, from other European nations, the East India goods it had occasion for, than to import them itself directly from the East Indies. What it might lose by the high price of those goods could seldom be equal to the loss which it would sustain by the distraction of a large portion of its capital from other employments more necessary, or more useful, or more suitable to its circumstances and situation, than a direct trade to the East Indies.

100   Though the Europeans possess many considerable settlements both upon the coast of Africa and in the East Indies, they have not yet established in either of those countries such numerous and thriving colonies as those in the islands and continent of America. Africa, however, as well as several of the countries comprehended under the general name of the East Indies, are inhabited by barbarous nations. But those nations were by no means so weak and defenceless as the miserable and helpless Americans; and in proportion to the natural fertility of the countries which they inhabited, they were besides much more populous. The most barba-[474]rous nations either of Africa or of the East Indies were shepherds; even the Hottentots were so.[88] But the natives of every part of America, except Mexico and Peru, were only hunters; and the difference is very great be-tween the number of shepherds and that of hunters whom the same extent of equally fertile territory can maintain.[89] In Africa and the East Indies, therefore, it was more difficult to displace the natives, and to extend the European plantations over the greater part of the lands of the original inhabitants. The genius of exclusive companies, besides, is unfavourable, it has already been observed, to the growth of new colonies, and has pro-

---

[88] Smith remarked in FA that the Hottentots 'are the most barbarous nation of shep-herds that is known in the world'.

[89] This point is elaborated below, V.i.a.5.

bably been the principal cause of the little progress which they have made in the East Indies.[90] The Portugueze carried on the trade both to Africa and the East Indies without any exclusive companies,[91] and their settlements at Congo, Angola, and Benguela on the coast of Africa, and at Goa in the East Indies, though much depressed by superstition and every sort of bad government, yet bear some faint resemblance to the colonies of America, and are partly inhabited by Portugueze who have been established there for several generations. The Dutch settlements at the Cape of Good Hope and at Batavia, are at present the most considerable colonies which the Europeans have established either in Africa or in the East Indies, and both ᵉtheseᵉ settlements are peculiarly fortunate in their situation. The Cape of Good Hope was inhabited by a race of people almost as barbarous and quite as inca-[475]pable of defending themselves as the natives of America. It is besides the half-way house, if one may say so, between Europe and the East Indies, at which almost every European ship makes some stay both in going and returning. The supplying of those ships with every sort of fresh provisions, with fruit and sometimes with wine, affords alone a very extensive market for the surplus produce of the colonists. What the Cape of Good Hope is between Europe and every part of the East Indies, Batavia is between the principal countries of the East Indies. It lies upon the most frequented road from Indostan to China and Japan, and is nearly about mid-way upon that road. Almost all the ships too that sail between Europe and China touch at Batavia; and it is, over and above all this, the center and principal mart of what is called the country trade of the East Indies; not only of that part of it which is carried on by Europeans, but of that which is carried on by the native Indians; and vessels navigated by the inhabitants of China[92] and Japan, of Tonquin, Malacca, Cochin-China, and the island of Celebes, are frequently to be seen in its port. Such advantageous situations have enabled those two colonies to surmount all the obstacles which the oppressive genius of an exclusive company may have occasionally opposed to their growth. They have enabled Batavia to surmount the additional disadvantage of perhaps the most unwholesome climate in the world.

101   [476] The English and Dutch companies, though they have established no considerable colonies, except the two above mentioned, have both made considerable conquests in the East Indies. But in the manner in which they both govern their new subjects, the natural genius of an exclusive company

ᵉ⁻ᵉ those *1*

---

[90] Above, IV.vii.b.22, and cf. IV.vii.c.103.
[91] See above, IV.vii.c.91.
[92] See above, I.ix.15, where Smith comments on the discouragement to foreign trade in China.

has shown itself most distinctly.[93] In the spice islands the Dutch *are said to* burn all the spiceries which a fertile season produces beyond what they expect to dispose of in Europe with such a profit as they think sufficient.[94] In the islands where they have no settlements, they give a premium to those who collect the young blossoms and green leaves of the clove and nutmeg trees which naturally grow there, but which this *savage* policy has now, it is said, almost compleatly extirpated. Even in the islands where they have settlements they have very much reduced, it is said, the number of those trees. If the produce even of their own islands was much greater than what suited their market, the natives, they suspect, might find means to convey some part of it to other nations; and the best way, they imagine, to secure their own monopoly, is to take care that no more shall grow than what they themselves carry to market. By different arts of oppression they have reduced the population of several of the Moluccas nearly to the number which is sufficient to supply with fresh provisions and other necessaries of life their own insignificant garrisons, and such of their ships as occasionally come [477] there for a cargo of spices. Under the government even of the Portugueze, however, those islands are said to have been tolerably well inhabited. The English company have not yet had time to establish in Bengal so perfectly destructive a system. The plan of their government, however, has had exactly the same tendency. It has not been uncommon, I am well assured, for the chief, that is, the first clerk of a factory, to order a peasant to plough up a rich field of poppies, and sow it with rice or some other grain. The pretence was, to prevent a scarcity of provisions; but the real reason, to give the chief an opportunity of selling at a better price a large quantity of opium, which he happened then to have upon hand. Upon other occasions the order has been reversed; and a rich field of rice or other grain has been ploughed up, in order to make room for a plantation of poppies; when the chief foresaw that extraordinary profit was likely to be made by opium.[95] The servants of the company have upon several occasions attempted to establish in their own favour the monopoly of some of the most important branches, not only of the foreign, but of the inland trade of the country. Had they been allowed to go on, it is impossible that they should not at some time or another have attempted to restrain the production of the particular articles of which they had thus usurped the monopoly, not only to the quantity which they themselves could purchase, but to that which they could expect to sell with such a profit as they might think sufficient. In [478] the course

ᶠ⁻ᶠ 2–6   *ᵍ⁻ᵍ* barbarous *1*

[93] The English colonies in the East Indies are cited as an example of the decaying economy in I.viii.26. The history of the East India Company is reviewed at V.i.e.26–30.

[94] A similar point is made above, IV.v.b.4 and I.xi.b.33.

[95] See above, IV.v.b.6.

of a century or two, the policy of the English company would in this manner have probably proved as compleatly destructive as that of the Dutch.

102   Nothing, however, can be more directly contrary to the real interest of those companies, considered as the sovereigns of the countries which they have conquered, than this destructive plan. In almost all countries the revenue of the sovereign is drawn from that of the people. The greater the revenue of the people, therefore, the greater the annual produce of their land and labour, the more they can afford to the sovereign. It is his interest, therefore, to increase as much as possible that annual produce. But if this is the interest of every sovereign, it is peculiarly so of one whose revenue, like that of the sovereign of Bengal, arises chiefly from a land-rent.[96] That rent must necessarily be in proportion to the quantity and value of the produce, and both the one and the other must depend upon the extent of the market. The quantity will always be suited with more or less exactness to the consumption of those who can afford to pay for it, and the price which they will pay will always be in proportion to the eagerness of their competition. It is the interest of such a sovereign, therefore, to open the most extensive market for the produce of his country, to allow the most perfect freedom of commerce, in order to increase as much as possible the number and the competition of buyers; and upon this account to abolish, not only all monopolies, but [479] all restraints upon the transportation of the home produce from one part of the country to another, upon its exportation to foreign countries, or upon the importation of goods of any kind for which it can be exchanged. He is in this manner most likely to increase both the quantity and value of that produce, and consequently of his own share of it, or of his own revenue.

103   But a company of merchants are, it seems, incapable of considering themselves as sovereigns, even after they have become such.[97] Trade, or buying in order to sell again, they still consider as *their* principal business, and by a strange absurdity, regard the character of the sovereign as but an appendix to that of the merchant, as something which ought to be made subservient to it, or by means of which they may be enabled to buy cheaper in India, and thereby to sell with a better profit in Europe. They endeavour for this purpose to keep out as much as possible all competitors from the market of the countries which are subject to their government, and consequently to reduce, at least, some part of the surplus produce

h-h the *I*

---

[96] See below, V.ii.a.13, where it is pointed out that land rents have provided the funds for many a state which has escaped from the shepherd stage. Details of the land tax in Bengal are given in William Bolts, *Considerations on India Affairs, particularly respecting the Present State of Bengal and its Dependencies* (London, 1772), i, chapter XII.

[97] See above, IV.vii.b.11, where the government of merchants is described as the 'worst of all'.

of those countries to what is barely sufficient for supplying their own demand, or to what they can expect to sell in Europe with such a profit as they may think reasonable. Their mercantile habits draw them in this manner, almost necessarily, though perhaps insensibly, to prefer upon all ordinary occasions the little and transitory profit of the monopolist to the great and permanent re-[480]venue of the sovereign, and would gradually lead them to treat the countries subject to their government nearly as the Dutch treat the Moluccas. ⁱIt is the interest of the East India company, considered as sovereigns, that the European goods which are carried to their Indian dominions, should be sold there as cheap as possible; and that the Indian goods which are brought from thence should bring there as good a price, or should be sold there as dear as possible. But the reverse of this is their interest as merchants. As sovereigns, their interest is exactly the same with that of the country which they govern. As merchants their interest is directly opposite to that interest.ⁱ

104   But if the genius of such a government, even as to what concerns its direction in Europe, is in this manner essentially and perhaps incurably faulty, that of its administration in India is still more so.⁹⁸ That administration is necessarily composed of a council of merchants, a profession no doubt extremely respectable, but which in no country in the world carries along with it that sort of authority which naturally over-awes the people, and without force commands their willing obedience. Such a council can command obedience only by the military force with which they are accompanied, and their government is therefore necessarily military and despotical. Their proper business, however, is that of merchants. It is to sell, upon their masters account, the European goods consigned to them, and to buy in return Indian goods for the [481] European market. It is to sell the one as dear and to buy the other as cheap as possible, and consequently to exclude as much as possible all rivals from the particular market where they keep their shop. The genius of the administration, therefore, so far as concerns the trade of the company, is the same as that of the direction. It tends to make government subservient to the interest of monopoly, and consequently to stunt the natural growth of some parts at least of the surplus produce of the country to what is barely sufficient for answering the demand of the company.

105   All the members of the administration, besides, trade more or less upon their own account, and it is in vain to prohibit them from doing so. Nothing can be more compleatly foolish than to expect that the clerks of a great counting-house at ten thousand miles distance, and consequently almost quite out of sight, should, upon a simple order from their masters, give up

ⁱ⁻ⁱ 2–6

---

⁹⁸ Smith considers the constitutional reforms of 1773 at V.i.e.26, and see also V.ii.a.7.

at once doing any sort of business upon their own account, abandon for ever all hopes of making a fortune, of which they have the means in their hands, and content themselves with the moderate salaries which those masters allow them, and which, moderate as they are, can seldom be augmented, being commonly as large as the real profits of the company trade can afford.[99] In such circumstances, to prohibit the servants of the company from trading upon their own account, can have scarce any other effect than to enable the superior servants, under pretence of executing their masters order, to oppress such of the inferior ones [482] as have had the misfortune to fall under their displeasure. The servants naturally endeavour to establish the same monopoly in favour of their own private trade as of the publick trade of the company. If they are suffered to act as they could wish, they will establish this monopoly openly and directly, by fairly prohibiting all other people from trading in the articles in which they chuse to deal; and this, perhaps, is the best and least oppressive way of establishing it. But if by an order from Europe they are prohibited from doing this, they will, notwithstanding, endeavour to establish a monopoly of the same kind, secretly and indirectly, in a way that is much more destructive to the country. They will employ the whole authority of government, and pervert the administration of justice, in order to harass and ruin those who interfere with them in any branch of commerce which, by means of agents, either concealed, or at least not publickly avowed, they may chuse to carry on. But the private trade of the servants will naturally extend to a much greater variety of articles than the publick trade of the company. The publick trade of the company extends no further than the trade with Europe, and comprehends a part only of the foreign trade of the country. But the private trade of the servants may extend to all the different branches both of its inland and foreign trade. The monopoly of the company can tend only to stunt the natural growth of that part of the surplus produce which, in the case of a free trade, would be exported to Europe. That of the servants tends to stunt the natural growth of [483] every part of the produce in which they chuse to deal, of what is destined for home consumption, as well as of what is destined for exportation; and consequently to degrade the cultivation of the whole country, and to reduce the number of its inhabitants. It tends to reduce the quantity of every sort of produce, even that of the necessaries of life, whenever the servants of the company chuse to deal in them, to what those servants can both afford to buy and expect to sell with such a profit as pleases them.[100]

[99] See above, I.ix.21.

[100] In his *Considerations on India Affairs*, William Bolts made the same points several times, e.g. i.206–7: 'We have seen all merchants from the interior parts of Asia effectually prevented from having any mercantile intercourse with Bengal, while, at the same time, the natives in general are in fact deprived of all trade within those provinces, it being

106   From the nature of their situation too the servants must be more disposed to support with rigorous severity their own interest against that of the country which they govern, than their masters can be to support theirs. The country belongs to their masters, who cannot avoid having some regard for the interest of what belongs to them. But it does not belong to the servants. The real interest of their masters, if they were capable of understanding it, is the same with that of the country*, and it is from ignorance *k*chiefly,*k* and the meanness of mercantile prejudice, that they ever oppress it. But the real interest of the servants is by no means the same with that of the country, and the most perfect information would not necessarily put an end to their oppressions. The regulations accordingly which have been sent out from Europe, though they have been frequently weak, have *l*upon most occasions*l* been [484] well-meaning. More intelligence and perhaps less good-meaning has sometimes appeared in those established by the servants in India. It is a very singular government in which every member of the administration wishes to get out of the country, and consequently to have done with the government, as soon as he can, and to whose interest, the day after he has left it and carried his whole fortune with him, it is perfectly indifferent *m*though*m* the whole country was swallowed up by an earthquake.[101]

*j** The interest of every proprietor of India Stock, however, is by no means the same with that of the country in the government of which his vote gives him some influence. See Book V. Chap. i. Part 3d.*j*

---

j-j 3–6 In ed. 2 the note reads: This would be exactly true if those masters never had any other interest but that which belongs to them as Proprietors of India stock. But they frequently have another of much greater importance. Frequently a man of great, sometimes even a man to moderate fortune, is willing to give thirteen or fourteen hundred pounds (the present price of a thousand pounds share in India stock) merely for the influence which he expects to acquire by a vote in the Court of Proprietors. It gives him a share, though not in the plunder, yet in the appointment of the plunderers of India; the Directors, although they make those appointments, being necessarily more or less under the influence of the Court of Proprietors, which not only elects them, but sometimes over-rules their appointments. A man of great or even a man of moderate fortune, provided he can enjoy this influence for a few years, and thereby get a certain number of his friends appointed to employments in India, frequently cares little about the dividend which he can expect from so small a capital, or even about the improvement or loss of the capital itself upon which his vote is founded. About the prosperity or ruin of the great empire, in the government of which that vote gives him a share, he seldom cares at all. No other sovereigns ever were, or from the nature of things ever could be, so perfectly indifferent about the happiness or misery of their subjects, the improvement or waste of their dominions, the glory or disgrace of their administration; as, from irresistible moral causes, the greater part of the Proprietors of such a mercantile Company are, and necessarily must be. [The matter of this note is incorporated in V.i.e.25, i.e. in a section of the WN which first appeared in 2A and ed. 3.]
      k-k only *1*   *l-l* commonly *1*   *m-m* if *1*

wholly monopolized by a few Company's servants and their dependents: In such a situation, what commercial country can flourish.'
[101] Smith makes a related point at V.ii.k.74 in discussing the activities of tax-farmers who are indifferent to the fate of the people they abuse, unlike the sovereign whose proper

107   I mean not, however, by any thing which I have here said, to throw any odious imputation upon the general character of the servants of the East India company, and much less upon that of any particular persons. It is the system of government, the situation in which they ⁿareⁿ placed, that I mean to censure; not the character of those who have acted in it. They acted as their situation naturally directed, and they who have clamoured the loudest against them would, probably, not have acted better themselves.[102] In war and negociation, the councils of Madras and Calcutta have upon several occasions conducted themselves with a resolution and decisive wisdom which would have done honour to the senate of Rome in the best days of that republick. The members of those councils, however, had been bred to professions very different from war and politicks. But their situation alone, without education, experience, or even example, seems to have formed in them all at once the great qualities which it required, and to have inspired them both with abilities and virtues which they [485] themselves could not well know that they possessed. If upon some occasions, therefore, it has animated them to actions of magnanimity which could not well have been expected from them, we should not wonder if upon others it has prompted them to exploits of somewhat a different nature.

108   Such exclusive companies, therefore, are nuisances in every respect; always more or less inconvenient to the countries in which they are established, and destructive to those which have the misfortune to fall under their government.

ⁿ⁻ⁿ were *1–2*

interest it is to protect them. The example of China 'suddenly swallowed up by an earthquake' is cited in TMS III.3.4.

[102] See below, V.i.e.26, where it is pointed out that abuses of this kind often reflect the circumstances prevailing; what Smith calls 'irresistible moral causes'.

^aCHAPTER VIII

Conclusion of the Mercantile System

1   THOUGH the encouragement of exportation, and the discouragement of importation are the two great engines by which the mercantile system proposes to enrich every country, yet with regard to some particular commodities, it seems to follow an opposite plan: to discourage exportation and to encourage importation. Its ultimate object, however, it pretends, is always the same, to enrich the country by an advantageous balance of trade. It discourages the exportation of the materials of manufacture, and of the instruments of trade, in order to give our own workmen an advantage, and to enable them to undersell those of other nations in all foreign markets: and by restrain-[486]ing, in this manner, the exportation of a few commodities, of no great price, it proposes to occasion a much greater and more valuable exportation of others.[1] It encourages the importation of the materials of manufacture, in order that our own people may be enabled to work them up more cheaply, and thereby prevent a greater and more valuable importation of the manufactured commodities. I do not observe, at least in our Statute Book, any encouragement given to the importation of the instruments of trade. When manufactures have advanced to a certain pitch of greatness, the fabrication of the instruments of trade becomes itself the object of a great number of very important manufactures. To give any particular encouragement to the importation of such instruments, would interfere too much with the interest of those manufactures. Such importation, therefore, instead of being encouraged, has frequently been prohibited. Thus the importation of wool cards, except from Ireland, or when brought in as wreck or prize goods, was prohibited by the 3d of Edward IV.;[2] which prohibition was renewed by the 39th of Elizabeth,[3] and has been continued and rendered perpetual by subsequent laws.[4]

2   The importation of the materials of manufacture has sometimes been encouraged by an exemption from the duties to which other goods are subject, and sometimes by bounties.

3   The importation of sheep's wool from several different countries,[5] of

---

^{a-a} 2A–6 [all of Chapter VIII]

[1] See above, IV.i.35, where the general outlines of the mercantile policy are given.

[2] 3 Edward IV, c. 4 (1463).   [3] 39 Elizabeth I, c. 14 (1597).

[4] 3 Charles I, c. 5 (1627) in *Statutes of the Realm*, v.27–30; 3 Charles I, c. 4 in Ruffhead's edition and 14 Charles II, c. 19 (1662) in *Statutes of the Realm*, v.412; 13 and 14 Charles II, c. 19 in Ruffhead's edition.

[5] 12 George II, c. 21 (1738) allowed the import of wool from Ireland duty free. H. Saxby *The British Customs* (1757), 143, states that Spanish wool for clothing and Spanish felt-

cotton wool from all countries,[6] of undressed flax,[7] of the greater part of [487] dying drugs,[8] of the greater part of undressed hides from Ireland or the British colonies,[9] of seal skins from the British Greenland fishery,[10] of pig and bar iron from the British colonies,[11] as well as of several other materials of manufacture, has been encouraged by an exemption from all duties, if properly entered at the customhouse. The private interest of our merchants and manufacturers may, perhaps, have extorted from the legislature these exemptions, as well as the greater part of our other commercial regulations. They are, however, perfectly just and reasonable, and if, consistently with the necessities of the state, they could be extended to all the other materials of manufacture, the publick would certainly be a gainer.

4   The avidity of our great manufacturers, however, has in some cases extended these exemptions a good deal beyond what can justly be considered as the rude materials of their work. By the 24 Geo. II. chap. 46. a small duty of only one penny the pound was imposed upon the importation of foreign brown linen yarn, instead of much higher duties to which it had been subjected before, viz. of sixpence the pound upon sail yarn, of one shilling the pound upon all French and Dutch yarn, and of two ᵇpoundᵇ thirteen shillings and four pence upon the hundred weight of all spruce or Muscovia yarn.[12] But our manufacturers were not long satisfied with this reduction. By the 29th of the same king, chap. 15. the same law which gave a bounty upon the exportation of British and Irish linen of [488] which the price did not exceed eighteen pence the yard, even this small duty upon the importation of brown linen yarn was taken away.[13] In the different operations, however, which are necessary for the preparation of linen yarn, a good deal more industry is employed than in the subsequent operation of preparing linen cloth from linen yarn. To

---

ᵇ⁻ᵇ pounds 2A; 4–6

wool was also duty free. 26 George II, c. 8 (1753) permitted the importation of wool and woollen yarn from Ireland to the port of Exeter. See below, V.ii.24.

[6] 6 George III, c. 52 (1766).   [7] 4 George II, c. 27 (1730). See below, V.ii.k.24.

[8] 8 George I, c. 15 (1721). See IV.viii.38, where the drugs which may be imported are listed and their significance evaluated.

[9] 9 George III, c. 39 (1769), continued by 14 George III, c. 86 (1774) and 21 George III, c. 29 (1781). See above, I.xi.m.11.

[10] 15 George III, c. 31 (1775).

[11] 23 George II, c. 29 (1749). See above, IV.vii.b.37 and 42.

[12] 24 George II, c. 46 (1750) imposed the duties Smith cites, but the other sums quoted are the values of the various types of yarn in the Book of Rates of 12 Charles II, c. 4 (1660), and not the duties levied on them. The duty on the specified values was increased by various measures to a total of 20 per cent. H. Saxby *The British Customs* (1757), 264–5.

[13] 29 George II, c. 15 (1756), continued by 10 George III, c. 38 (1770) and 19 George III, c. 27 (1779). See below, IV.viii.5 and V.ii.k.24. In LJ (B) 232–3, ed. Cannan 180, the bounty was payable when coarse linen was 'under 12 pence a yard'.

say nothing of the industry of the flax-growers and flax-dressers, three or four spinners, at least, are necessary, in order to keep one weaver in constant employment; and more than four-fifths of the whole quantity of labour, necessary for the preparation of linen cloth, is employed in that of linen yarn; but our spinners are poor people, women commonly, scattered about in all different parts of the country, without support or protection.[14] It is not by the sale of their work, but by that of the compleat work of the weavers, that our great master manufacturers make their profits. As it is their interest to sell the compleat manufacture as dear, so is it to buy the materials as cheap as possible. By extorting from the legislature bounties upon the exportation of their own linen, high duties upon the importation of all foreign linen, and a total prohibition of the home consumption of some sorts of French linen,[15] they endeavour to sell their own goods as dear as possible. By encouraging the importation of foreign linen yarn, and thereby bringing it into competition with that which is made by our own people, they endeavour to buy the work of the poor spinners as cheap as possible. They are as in-[489]tent to keep down the wages of their own weavers, as the earnings of the poor spinners, and it is by no means for the benefit of the workman, that they endeavour either to raise the price of the compleat work, or to lower that of the rude materials. It is the industry which is carried on for the benefit of the rich and the powerful, that is principally encouraged by our mercantile system. That which is carried on for the benefit of the poor and the indigent, is too often, either neglected, or oppressed.

5   Both the bounty upon the exportation of linen, and the exemption from duty upon the importation of foreign yarn, which were granted only for fifteen years, but continued by two different prolongations,[16] expire with the end of the session of parliament which shall immediately follow the 24th of June 1786.

6   The encouragement given to the importation of the materials of manufacture by bounties, has been principally confined to such as were imported from our American plantations.[17]

7   The first bounties of this kind were those granted, about the beginning of the present century, upon the importation of naval stores from America.[18] Under this denomination were comprehended timber fit for masts, yards, and bowsprits; hemp; tar, pitch, and turpentine. The bounty, however, of one pound the ton upon masting timber, and that of six pounds

---

[14] See above, I.x.b.51, and IV.vii.b.24 and note 33.

[15] 18 George II, c. 36 (1744); 21 George II, c. 26 (1747); 32 George II, c. 32 (1758); 7 George III, c. 43 (1766). See also IV.iii.a.1 and IV.iv.7.

[16] By 10 George III, c. 38 (1770) and 19 George III, c. 27 (1779). See above, § 4.

[17] See above, IV.vii.b.45.

[18] 3 and 4 Anne, c. 9 (1704) in *Statutes of the Realm*, viii.354–6; 3 and 4 Anne, c. 10 in Ruffhead's edition. See above, IV.vii.b.36.

the ton upon hemp, were extended to such as should be imported into England from Scotland.[19] Both these bounties continued without any variation, [490] at the same rate, till they were severally allowed to expire; that upon hemp on the 1st of January 1741, and that upon masting-timber at the end of the session of parliament immediately following the 24th June 1781.

8   The bounties upon the importation of tar, pitch, and turpentine underwent, during their continuance, several alterations. Originally[20] that upon tar was four pounds the ton; that upon pitch, the same; and that upon turpentine, three pounds the ton. The bounty of four pounds the ton upon tar was afterwards confined to such as had been prepared in a particular manner; that upon other good, clean, and merchantable tar was reduced to two pounds four shillings the ton. The bounty upon pitch was likewise reduced to one pound; and that upon turpentine to one pound ten shillings the ton.[21]

9   The second bounty upon the importation of any of the materials of manufacture, according to the order of time, was that granted by the 21 Geo. II. chap. 30. upon the importation of indigo from the British plantations.[22] When the plantation indigo was worth three-fourths of the price of the best French indigo, it was by this act entitled to a bounty of sixpence the pound. This bounty, which, like most others, was granted only for a limited time, was continued by several prolongations, but was reduced to four pence the pound.[23] It was allowed to expire with the end of the session of parliament which followed the 25th March, 1781.

10   The third bounty of this kind was that granted (much about the time that we were beginning [491] sometimes to court and sometimes to quarrel with our American colonies) by the 4 Geo. III. chap. 26. upon the importation of hemp, or undressed flax, from the British plantations.[24] This bounty was granted for twenty-one years, from the 24th June 1764, to the 24th June 1785. For the first seven years it was to be at the rate of eight pounds the ton, for the second at six pounds, and for the third at

---

[19] First by 12 Anne, c. 9 (1712) in *Statutes of the Realm*, ix.768–70; 12 Anne, st. 1, c. 9 in Ruffhead's edition. 8 George I, c. 12 (1721) gave further encouragement to the importation of naval stores and encouraged the growth of hemp in Scotland. The encouragement of imports of masting timber from Scotland was extended further by 2 George II, c. 35, s. 12 (1728).

[20] By 3 and 4 Anne, c. 9 (1704) in *Statutes of the Realm*, viii.354–6; 3 and 4 Anne, c. 10 in Ruffhead's edition.

[21] 8 George I, c. 12 (1721) and especially 2 George II, c. 35 (1728).

[22] 21 George II, c. 30 (1747).

[23] 21 George II, c. 30 (1747) was continued by 28 George II, c. 25 (1755) and by 3 George III, c. 25 (1763) to the end of the parliamentary session after 25 March 1770, but the bounty was reduced to 4d. per pound. Continued until 1781 by 17 George III, c. 44 (1777).

[24] 4 George III, c. 26 (1764).

four pounds. It was not extended to Scotland of which the climate (although hemp is sometimes raised there, in small quantities and of an inferior quality) is not very fit for that produce. Such a bounty upon the importation of Scotch flax into England would have been too great a discouragement to the native produce of the southern part of the united kingdom.

11   The fourth bounty of this kind, was that granted by the 5 Geo. III. chap. 45. upon the importation of wood from America.[25] It was granted for nine years, from the 1st January 1766, to the 1st January 1775. During the first three years, it was to be for every hundred and twenty good deals, at the rate of one pound; and for every load containing fifty cubic feet of other squared timber at the rate of twelve shillings. For the second three years, it was for deals to be at the rate of fifteen shillings, and for other squared timber, at the rate of eight shillings; and for the third three years, it was for deals, to be at the rate of ten shillings, and for other squared timber, at the rate of five shillings.

12   The fifth bounty of this kind was that granted by the 9 Geo. III. chap. 38. upon the importa-[492]tion of raw silk from the British plantations.[26] It was granted for twenty-one years, from the 1st January 1770, to the 1st January 1791. For the first seven years it was to be at the rate of twenty-five pounds for every hundred pounds value; for the second, at twenty pounds; and for the third at fifteen pounds. The management of the silk-worm, and the preparation of silk, requires so much hand labour; and labour is so very dear in America,[27] that even this great bounty, I have been informed, was not likely to produce any considerable effect.

13   The sixth bounty of this kind, was that granted by 11 Geo. III. chap. 50. for the importation of pipe, hogshead, and barrel staves and heading from the British plantations. It was granted for nine years, from 1st January 1772, to the 1st January 1781.[28] For the first three years, it was for a certain quantity of each, to be at the rate of six pounds; for the second three years, at four pounds; and for the third three years, at two pounds.

14   The seventh, and last bounty of this kind, was ᶜthatᶜ granted by the 19 Geo. III. chap. 37. upon the importation of hemp from Ireland.[29] It was granted in the same manner as that for the importation of hemp and undressed flax from America, for twenty-one years, from the 24th June 1779, to the 24th June 1800. This term is divided, likewise, into three periods of seven years each; and in each of those periods, the rate of the

---

ᶜ⁻ᶜ *om.* 2A

[25] 5 George III, c. 45 (1765).   [26] 9 George III, c. 38 (1769).
[27] See above, I.ix.11 and I.viii.23.   [28] 11 George III, c. 50 (1771).
[29] 19 George III, c. 37 (1779).

Irish bounty is the same with that of the American. It does not, however, like the American bounty, extend to the importation [493] of undressed flax. It would have been too great a discouragement to the cultivation of that plant in Great Britain. When this last bounty was granted, the British and Irish legislatures were not in much better humour with one another, than the British and American had been before. But this boon to Ireland, it is to be hoped, has been granted under more fortunate auspices, than all those to America.

15   The same commodities upon which we thus gave bounties, when imported from America, were subjected to considerable duties when imported from any other country.[30] The interest of our American colonies was regarded as the same with that of the mother country. Their wealth was considered as our wealth. Whatever money was sent out to them, it was said, came all back to us by the balance of trade, and we could never become a farthing the poorer, by any expence which we could lay out upon them. They were our own in every respect, and it was an expence laid out upon the improvement of our own property, and for the profitable employment of our own people. It is unnecessary, I apprehend, at present to say any thing further, in order to expose the folly of a system, which fatal experience has now sufficiently exposed. Had our American colonies really been a part of Great Britain, those bounties might have been considered as bounties upon production, and would still have been liable to all the objections to which such bounties are liable, but to no other.[31]

16   [494] The exportation of the materials of manufacture is sometimes discouraged by absolute prohibitions, and sometimes by high duties.

17   Our woollen manufacturers have been more successful than any other class of workmen, in persuading the legislature that the prosperity of the nation depended upon the success and extension of their particular business.[32] They have not only obtained a monopoly against the consumers by an absolute prohibition of importing woollen cloths from any foreign country;[33] but they have likewise obtained another monopoly against the sheep farmers and growers of wool, by a similar prohibition of the exportation of live sheep and wool. The severity of many of the laws which have been enacted for the security of the revenue is very justly complained of, as imposing heavy penalties upon actions which antecedent to the statutes that declared them to be crimes, had always been understood to

---

[30] See above, IV.vii.b.45.

[31] Bounties on production are considered at IV.v.a.25.

[32] Cf. LJ (A) ii.91: 'some years ago the British nation took a fancy (a very whimsicall one indeed) that the wealth and strength of the nation depended entirely on the flourishing of their woolen trade, and that this could not prosper if the exportation of wool was permitted. To prevent this, it was enacted that the exportation of wool should be punished with death.' Cf. I.xi.m.11 and cf. I.xi.p.10, where Smith comments generally on the influence of sectional interests on the legislature.

[33] See IV.ii.1.

be innocent. But the cruellest of our revenue laws, I will venture to affirm, are mild and gentle, in comparison of some of those which the clamour of our merchants and manufacturers has extorted from the legislature, for the support of their own absurd and oppressive monopolies. Like the laws of Draco, these laws may be said to be all written in blood.

18   By the 8th of Elizabeth, chap. 3.[34] the exporter of sheep, lambs or rams, was for the first offence to forfeit all his goods for ever, to suffer a year's imprisonment, and then to have his left hand cut off in a market town upon a market [495] day, to be there nailed up; and for the second offence to be adjudged a felon, and to suffer death accordingly. To prevent the breed of our sheep from being propagated in foreign countries, seems to have been the object of this law. By the 13th and 14th of Charles II. chap. 18.[35] the exportation of wool was made felony, and the exporter subjected to the same penalties and forfeitures as a felon.[36]

19   For the honour of the national humanity, it is to be hoped that neither of these statutes were ever executed. The first of them, however, so far as I know, has never been directly repealed,[37] and Serjeant Hawkins seems to consider it as still in force.[38] It may however, perhaps, be considered as virtually repealed by the 12th of Charles II. chap. 32. sect. 3.[39] which, without expressly taking away the penalties imposed by former statutes, imposes a new penalty, viz. That of twenty shillings for every sheep exported, or attempted to be exported, together with the forfeiture of the sheep and of the owner's share of the ship. The second of them was expressly repealed by the 7th and 8th of William III. chap. 28. sect. 4.[40] By which it is declared that, "Whereas the statute of the 13th and 14th of King Charles II. made against the exportation of wool, among other things in the said act mentioned, doth enact the same to be deemed

---

[34] 8 Elizabeth I, c. 3 (1566).

[35] 14 Charles II, c. 18 (1662) in *Statutes of the Realm*, v.410–12; 13 and 14 Charles II, c.18 in Ruffhead's edition. See below, IV.viii.35 and V.ii.k.24.

[36] In LJ (A) v.64 counterfeiting the coin is cited as a felony, and also in LJ (B) 81, ed. Cannan 57. LJ (A) ii.92 mentioned that at one time the exporting of wool was treated as a felony, but that: 'No one would consent to the punishment of a thing in itself so innocent, by so high a penalty. They were therefore obliged to lessen the punishment to confiscation of goods and vessel.' A similar point is made in LJ (B) 182, ed. Cannan 136, where Smith also cites the case of the sentinel condemned to death for falling asleep on duty: a punishment which clearly reflected the need to protect the public good, but which was nevertheless one which 'mankind can never enter into . . . as if he had been a thief or a robber.' See TMS II.ii.3.11.

[37] 8 Elizabeth I, c. 3 (1566) was repealed by 3 George IV, c. 41, s. 4 (1822).

[38] 'By some old Statutes, and 13 & 14 Car. 2. 18 the Exportation of Wool was made Felony; but by 7 & 8 W. 3. 28 it is reduced to a Misdemeanour only, and it is subjected to severe Penalties by many late Statutes.' Hawkins then repeats the terms of 8 Elizabeth, c. 3, which indicates he considered it still in force. W. Hawkins, *A Treatise of the Pleas of the Crown* (London, 3rd ed. 1739), i.119–20.

[39] 12 Charles II, c. 32 (1660). See below, IV.viii.20, 32, 33.

[40] 7 and 8 William III, c. 28, s. 2 (1695), in *Statutes of the Realm*, vii.118.

felony; by the severity of which penalty the prosecution of offenders hath not been so effectually put in execution: Be it, therefore, enacted by the authority foresaid, that so [496] much of the said act, which relates to the making the said offence felony, be repealed and made void."[41]

20   The penalties, however, which are either imposed by this milder statute, or which, though imposed by former statutes, are not repealed by this one, are still sufficiently severe. Besides the forfeiture of the goods, the exporter incurs the penalty of three shillings for every pound weight of wool either exported or attempted to be exported, that is about four or five times the value. Any merchant or other person convicted of this offence is disabled from requiring any debt or account belonging to him from any factor or other person.[42] Let his fortune be what it will, whether he is, or is not able to pay those heavy penalties, the law means to ruin him compleatly. But as the morals of the great body of the people are not yet so corrupt as those of the contrivers of this statute, I have not heard that any advantage has ever been taken of this clause. If the person convicted of this offence is not able to pay the penalties within three months after judgment, he is to be transported for seven years, and if he returns before the expiration of that term, he is liable to the pains of felony, without benefit of clergy. The owner of the ship knowing this offence forfeits all his interest in the ship and furniture. The master and mariners knowing this offence forfeit all their goods and chattels, and suffer three months imprisonment.[43] By a subsequent statute the master suffers six months imprisonment.[44]

21   [497] In order to prevent exportation, the whole inland commerce of wool is laid under very burdensome and oppressive restrictions.[45] It cannot be packed in any box, barrel, cask, case, chest, or any other package, but only in packs of leather or pack-cloth, on which must be marked on the outside the words *wool* or *yarn*, in large letters not less than three inches long, on pain of forfeiting the same and the package, and three shillings for every pound weight, to be paid by the owner or packer.[46] It cannot be loaden on any horse or cart, or carried by land within five miles of the coast, but between sun-rising and sun-setting, on pain of forfeiting the same, the horses and carriages. The hundred next adjoining to the sea coast, out of, or through which the wool is carried or exported, forfeits

---

[41] 14 Charles II, c. 18 (1662) in *Statutes of the Realm*, v.410–12; 13 and 14 Charles II in Ruffhead's edition was finally repealed by 19 and 20 Victoria, c. 64 (1856).

[42] 12 Charles II, c. 32 (1660). See below, IV.viii.33.   [43] 4 George I, c. 11 (1717).

[44] Probably 10 William III, c. 16 (1698), vii.524–8; 10 and 11 William, c. 10 (1698) in Ruffhead's edition. See above, IV.vii.b.43.

[45] This illustrates the qualification to the general liberality of trade in England as mentioned at IV.vii.c.54. The restrictions imposed on the wool trade in the colonies are mentioned at IV.vii.b.43.

[46] 12 George II, c. 21 (1738).

twenty pounds, if the wool is under the value of ten pounds; and if of greater value, then treble that value, together with treble costs, to be sued for within the year. The execution to be against any two of the inhabitants, whom the sessions must reimburse, by an assessment on the other inhabitants, as in the cases of robbery. And if any person compounds with the hundred for less than this penalty, he is to be imprisoned for five years; and any other person may prosecute. These regulations take place through the whole kingdom.[47]

22   But in the particular counties of Kent and Sussex the restrictions are still more troublesome. Every owner of wool within ten miles of the sea-coast must give an account in writing, three days [498] after shearing, to the next officer of the customs, of the number of his fleeces, and of the places where they are lodged. And before he removes any part of them he must give the like notice of the number and weight of the fleeces, and of the name and abode of the person to whom they are sold, and of the place to which it is intended they should be carried. No person within fifteen miles of the sea, in the said counties, can buy any wool, before he enters into bond to the king, that no part of the wool which he shall so buy shall be sold by him to any other person within fifteen miles of the sea. If any wool is found carrying towards the sea-side in the said counties, unless it has been entered and security given as aforesaid, it is forfeited, and the offender also forfeits three shillings for every pound weight. If any person lays any wool, not entered as aforesaid, within fifteen miles of the sea, it must be seized and forfeited; and if, after such seizure, any person shall claim the same, he must give security to the Exchequer, that if he is cast upon trial he shall pay treble costs, besides all other penalties.[48]

23   When such restrictions are imposed upon the inland trade, the coasting trade, we may believe, cannot be left very free. Every owner of wool who carrieth or causeth to be carried any wool to any port or place on the sea-coast, in order to be from thence transported by sea to any other place or port on the coast, must first cause an entry thereof to be made at the port from whence it is intended to be conveyed, containing the [499] weight, marks, and number of the packages before he brings the same within five miles of that port; on pain of forfeiting the same, and also the horses, carts, and other carriages; and also of suffering and forfeiting, as by the other laws in force against the exportation of wool. This law, however, (1 Will. III. chap. 32.) is so very indulgent as to declare, that "this shall not hinder any person from carrying his wool home from the place of shearing, though it be within five miles of the sea, provided

---

[47] 7 and 8 William III, c. 28 (1695). See below, IV.viii.35.

[48] 9 William III, c. 40 (1697) in *Statutes of the Realm*, vii.421–3; 9 and 10 William III, c. 40 in Ruffhead's edition.

that in ten days after shearing, and before he remove the wool, he do under his hand certify to the next officer of the customs, the true number of fleeces, and where it is housed; and do not remove the same, without certifying to such officer, under his hand, his intention so to do, three days before."[49] Bond must be given that the wool to be carried coast-ways is to be landed at the particular port for which it is entered outwards; and if any part of it is landed without the presence of an officer, not only the forfeiture of the wool is incurred as in other goods, but the usual additional penalty of three shillings for every pound weight is likewise incurred.

24   Our woollen manufacturers, in order to justify their demand of such extraordinary restrictions and regulations, confidently asserted, that English wool was of a peculiar quality, superior to that of any other country; that the wool of other countries could not, without some mixture of it, be wrought up into any tolerable manufacture; that fine cloth could not be made without it; [500] that England, therefore, if the exportation of it could be totally prevented, could monopolize to herself almost the whole woollen trade of the world; and thus, having no rivals, could sell at what price she pleased, and in a short time acquire the most incredible degree of wealth by the most advantageous balance of trade. This doctrine, like most other doctrines which are confidently asserted by any considerable number of people, was, and still continues to be, most implicitly believed by a much greater number; by almost all those who are either unacquainted with the woollen trade, or who have not made particular enquiries. It is, however, so perfectly false, that English wool is in any respect necessary for the making of fine cloth, that it is altogether unfit for it. Fine cloth is made altogether of Spanish wool. English wool cannot be even so mixed with Spanish wool as to enter into the composition without spoiling and degrading, in some degree, the fabric of the cloth.[50]

25   It has been shown in the foregoing part of this work,[51] that the effect of these regulations has been to depress the price of English wool, not only below what it naturally would be in the present times, but very much below what it actually was in the time of Edward III.[52] The price

---

[49] 1 William and Mary, c. 32 in *Statutes of the Realm*, vi.96–8; 1 William and Mary, sess. 1, c. 32 in Ruffhead's edition. The quotation is not quite verbatim.

[50] 'It is well known that the real very superfine cloth everywhere must be entirely of Spanish wool.' (A. Anderson, *Origin of Commerce* (1764), ii.137.)

[51] See above, I.xi.m.9.

[52] In Letter 203 addressed to William Eden, dated 3 January 1780, Smith wrote that 'The Price of wool is now lower than in the time of Edward III; because it is now confined to the market of Great Britain; whereas then the market of the world was open to it. The low price of wool tends to debase the quality of the commodity, and may thus hurt the woollen manufacture in one way, as much as it may benefit it in another. By this prohibition, besides, the interest of the [grower] is evidently sacrificed to the interest of the manufacturer.'

of Scots wool, when in consequence of the union it became subject to the same regulations, is said to have fallen about one half.[53] It is observed by the very accurate and intelligent author of the Memoirs of Wool, the Reverend Mr. John Smith, that the price of the best English wool in [501] England is generally below what wool of a very inferior quality commonly sells for in the market of Amsterdam.[54] To depress the price of this commodity below what may be called its natural and proper price, was the avowed purpose of those regulations; and there seems to be no doubt of their having produced the effect that was expected from them.

26   This reduction of price, it may perhaps be thought, by discouraging the growing of wool, must have reduced very much the annual produce of that commodity, though not below what it formerly was, yet below what, in the present state of things, it *probably would*[d] have been, had it, in consequence of an open and free market, been allowed to rise to the natural and proper price. I am, however, disposed to believe, that the quantity of the annual produce cannot have been much, though it may perhaps have been a little, affected by these regulations. The growing of wool is not the chief purpose for which the sheep farmer employs his industry and stock. He expects his profit, not so much from the price of the fleece, as from that of the carcase; and the average or ordinary price of the latter, must even, in many cases, make up to him whatever deficiency there may be in the average or ordinary price of the former. It has been observed in the foregoing part of this work, that "Whatever regulations tend to sink the price, either of wool or of raw hides, below what it naturally would be, must, in an improved and cultivated country, have some [502] tendency to raise the price of butchers meat. The price both of the great and small cattle which are fed on improved and cultivated land, must be sufficient to pay the rent which the landlord, and the profit which the farmer has reason to expect from improved and cultivated land. If it is not, they will soon cease to feed them. Whatever part of this price, therefore, is not paid by the wool and the hide, must be paid by the carcase. The less there is paid for the one, the more must be paid for the other. In what manner this price is to be divided upon the different parts of the beast, is indifferent to the landlords and farmers, provided it is all paid to them. In an improved and cultivated country, therefore, their interest

---

[d-d] would probably 6

[53] A similar point is made at I.xi.m.13.

[54] John Smith refers to the high quality wool of England and in a footnote discusses the term 'precious fleeces'. He continues: 'how does this Encomium [precious] agree with the Weight of their Fleeces, (which are but light, like the *Spanish*) and with the Price at which they are ordinarily sold in England; which is not only below the lowest Wool of *Spain*, at Amsterdam, but even below the coarse Wools of Germany, and the yet coarser of *Tours* in *France*'. (J. Smith, *Chronicon Rusticum-Commerciale; or Memoirs of Wool*, ii.418, n.)

as landlords and farmers cannot be much affected by such regulations, though their interest as consumers may, by the rise in the price of provisions."[55] According to this reasoning, therefore, this degradation in the price of wool is not likely, in an improved and cultivated country, to occasion any diminution in the annual produce of that commodity; except so far as, by raising the price of mutton, it may somewhat diminish the demand for, and consequently the production of, that particular species of butchers meat. Its effect, however, even in this way, it is probable, is not very considerable.

27   But though its effect upon the quantity of the annual produce may not have been very considerable, its effect upon the quality, it may [503] perhaps be thought, must necessarily have been very great. The degradation in the quality of English wool, if not below what it was in former times, yet below what it naturally would have been in the present state of improvement and cultivation, must have been, it may perhaps be supposed, very nearly in proportion to the degradation of price. As the quality depends upon the breed, upon the pasture, and upon the management and cleanliness of the sheep, during the whole progress of the growth of the fleece, the attention to these circumstances, it may naturally enough be imagined, can never be greater than in proportion to the recompence which the price of the fleece is likely to make for the labour and expence which that attention requires. It happens, however, that the goodness of the fleece depends in a great measure, upon the health, growth, and bulk of the animal; the same attention which is necessary for the improvement of the carcase, is, in some respects, sufficient for that of the fleece. Notwithstanding the degradation of price, English wool is said to have been improved considerably during the course even of the present century. The improvement might perhaps have been greater if the price had been better; but the lowness of price, though it may have obstructed, yet certainly it has not altogether prevented that improvement.

28   The violence of these regulations, therefore, seems to have affected neither the quantity nor the quality of the annual produce of wool so [504] much as it might have been expected to do; (though I think it probable that it may have affected the latter a good deal more than the former) and the interest of the growers of wool, though it must have been hurt in some degree, seems, upon the whole, to have been much less hurt than could well have been imagined.

29   These considerations, however, will not justify the absolute prohibition of the exportation of *[e]* wool. But they will fully justify the imposition of a considerable tax upon that exportation.

[e] the 2A

---

[55] See above I.xi.m.12. The passage is quoted verbatim but with some minor changes of punctuation.

30 To hurt in any degree the interest of any one order of citizens, for no other purpose but to promote that of some other, is evidently contrary to that justice and equality of treatment which the sovereign owes to all the different orders of his subjects. But the prohibition certainly hurts, in some degree, the interest of the growers of wool, for no other purpose but to promote that of the manufacturers.

31 Every different order of citizens is bound to contribute to the support of the sovereign or commonwealth. A tax of five, or even of ten shillings upon the exportation of every tod of wool, would produce a very considerable revenue to the sovereign. It would hurt the interest of the growers somewhat less than the prohibition, because it would not probably lower the price of wool quite so much. It would afford a sufficient advantage to the manufacturer, because, though he might not buy his wool altogether so cheap as under the prohibition, he would still buy it, at least, five or ten shillings cheaper than [505] any foreign manufacturer could buy it, besides saving the freight and insurance, which the other would be obliged to pay. It is scarce possible to devise a tax which could produce any considerable revenue to the sovereign, and at the same time occasion so little inconveniency to any body.

32 The prohibition, notwithstanding all the penalties which guard it, does not prevent the exportation of wool. It is exported, it is well known, in great quantities. The great difference between the price in the home and that in the foreign market, presents such a temptation to smuggling, that all the rigour of the law cannot prevent it. This illegal exportation is advantageous to no body but the smuggler. A legal exportation subject to a tax, by affording a revenue to the sovereign, and thereby saving the imposition of some other, perhaps, more burdensome and inconvenient taxes, might prove advantageous to all the different subjects of the state.

33 The exportation of fuller's earth, or fuller's clay, supposed to be necessary for preparing and cleansing the woollen manufactures, has been subjected to nearly the same penalties as the exportation of wool.[56] Even tobacco-pipe clay, though acknowledged to be different from fuller's clay, yet, on account of their resemblance, and because fuller's clay might sometimes be exported as tobacco-pipe clay, has been laid under the same prohibitions and penalties.[57]

34 [506] By the 13th and 14th of Charles II. chap. 7. the exportation, not only of raw hides, but of tanned leather, except in the shape of boots, shoes, or slippers, was prohibited;[58] and the law gave a monopoly to our boot-

---

[56] 12 Charles II, c. 32 (1660). See above, IV.viii.19 and 20. See also Hume, *History of England* (1778), vi.305, for an illustration of the penalties imposed on offenders.

[57] 14 Charles II, c. 18 (1662) in *Statutes of the Realm*, v.411; 13 and 14 Charles II, c. 18 in Ruffhead's edition.

[58] 14 Charles II, c. 7 (1662) in *Statutes of the Realm*, v.378–97; 13 and 14 Charles II, c. 7 in Ruffhead's edition. See above, I.xi.m.11.

makers and shoe-makers, not only against our graziers, but against our tanners. By subsequent statutes our tanners have got themselves exempted from this monopoly, upon paying a small tax of only one shilling on the hundred weight of tanned leather, weighing one hundred and twelve pounds.[59] They have obtained likewise the drawback of two thirds of the excise duties imposed upon their commodity, even when exported without further manufacture. All manufactures of leather may be exported duty free; and the exporter is besides entitled to the drawback of the whole duties of excise.[60] Our graziers still continue subject to the old monopoly. Graziers separated from one another, and dispersed through all the different corners of the country, cannot, without great difficulty, combine together for the purpose either of imposing monopolies upon their fellow-citizens, or of exempting themselves from such, as may have been imposed upon them by other people.[61] Manufacturers of all kinds, collected together in numerous bodies in all great cities, easily can. Even the horns of cattle are prohibited to be exported; and the two insignificant trades of the horner and comb-maker enjoy, in this respect, a monopoly against the graziers.[62]

35   [507] Restraints, either by prohibitions or by taxes, upon the exportation of goods which are partially, but not completely manufactured, are not peculiar to the manufacture of leather. As long as any thing remains to be done, in order to fit any commodity for immediate use and consumption, our manufacturers think that they themselves ought to have the doing of it. Woollen yarn and worsted are prohibited to be exported under the same penalties as wool.[63] Even white cloths are subject to a duty upon exportation,[64] and our dyers have so far obtained a monopoly against our clothiers. Our clothiers would probably have been able to defend themselves against it, but it happens that the greater part of our principal clothiers are themselves likewise dyers. Watch-cases, clock-cases, and dial-plates for clocks and watches, have been prohibited to be exported.[65] Our clock-makers

---

[59] 19 and 20 Charles II, c. 10 (1667) in *Statutes of the Realm*, v.640; 20 Charles II, c. 5 in Ruffhead's edition. Provisions confirmed by 9 Anne, c. 6 (1710).

[60] 9 Anne, c. 12 (1710) in *Statutes of the Realm*, ix.405–17; 9 Anne, c. 11 in Ruffhead's edition gave two-thirds of the duty as a drawback. 13 Anne, c. 18 (1713) in *Statutes of the Realm*, ix.936–60; 12 Anne, st. 2, c. 9 in Ruffhead's edition gave a drawback of 1½d. for every pound of tanned leather.

[61] See above, IV.viii.4 and note 14.

[62] 4 Edward IV, c. 8 (1464) allowed the export of refuse horns. The Act was repealed by 1 James I, c. 25 (1603); 2 (vulgo 1) James I, c. 25 in Ruffhead's edition, but 7 James I, c. 14 (1609) introduced a general prohibition.

[63] 14 Charles II, c. 18 (1662) in *Statutes of the Realm*, v.411; 13 and 14 Charles II, c. 18 in Ruffhead's edition. See above, IV.viii.18 and 33. 7 and 8 William III, c. 28 (1695) had similar provisions. See above, IV.viii.21.

[64] 12 Charles II, c. 4 (1660), re-enforced by 14 Charles II, c. 11 (1662) in *Statutes of the Realm*, v.393–400; 13 and 14 Charles, c. 11 in Ruffhead's edition. See below, IV.viii.38.

[65] 7 and 8 William III, c. 19 (1695) prohibited the export of unwrought plate except on a certificate. 9 William III, c. 28 (1697) in *Statutes of the Realm*, vii.399–400; 9 and 10

and watch-makers are, it seems, unwilling that the price of this sort of workmanship should be raised upon them by the competition of foreigners.

36   By some old statutes of Edward III.,[66] Henry VIII.,[67] and Edward VI.,[68] the exportation of all metals was prohibited. Lead and tin were alone excepted; probably on account of the great abundance of those metals; in the exportation of which, a considerable part of the trade of the kingdom in those days consisted. For the encouragement of the mining trade, the 5th of William and Mary, chap. 17.,[69] exempted from this prohibition iron, copper, and mundic metal made from British ore. The exportation of all [508] sorts of copper bars, foreign as well as British, was afterwards permitted by the 9th and 10th of William III., chap. 26.[70] The exportation of unmanufactured brass, of what is called gun-metal, bell-metal, and shroff-metal, still continues to be prohibited. Brass manufactures of all sorts may be exported duty free.[71]

37   The exportation of the materials of manufacture, where it is not altogether prohibited, is in many cases subjected to considerable duties.

38   By the 8th George I., chap. 15.,[72] the exportation of all goods, the produce or manufacture of Great Britain, upon which any duties had been imposed by former statutes, was rendered duty free. The following goods, however, were excepted: Allum, lead, lead ore, tin, tanned leather, copperas, coals, wool cards, white woollen cloths, lapis calaminaris, skins of all sorts, glue, coney hair or wool, hares wool, hair of all sorts, horses, and litharge of lead. If you except horses, all these are either materials of manufacture, or incomplete manufactures (which may be considered as materials for still further manufacture), or instruments of trade. This statute leaves them subject to all the old duties which had ever been imposed upon them, the old subsidy and one per cent. outwards.[73]

39   By the same statute a great number of foreign drugs for dyers use, are exempted from all duties upon importation. Each of them, however, is afterwards subjected to a certain duty, not indeed a very heavy one, upon exportation. Our dyers, it seems, while they thought it for [509]

William III, c. 28 in Ruffhead's edition allowed the export of watches, etc. but prohibited the export of cases without the movement and the maker's name. The objective was to avoid frauds.

[66] 28 Edward III, c. 5 (1354).   [67] 33 Henry VIII, c. 7 (1541).

[68] 2 and 3 Edward VI, c. 37 (1548), re-enforcing 33 Henry VIII, c. 7 (1541).

[69] 5 and 6 William and Mary, c. 17 (1694) in *Statutes of the Realm*, vi.480–1, and in Ruffhead. Exporting of iron, copper, and mundic metal allowed except 'pot-metal, gun-metal, shriff metal or . . . other metal than what is made of English ore'.

[70] 9 William III, c. 26 (1697) in *Statutes of the Realm*, vii.393–7; 9 and 10 William III, c. 26 in Ruffhead's edition.

[71] 8 George I, c. 15 (1721). See above, IV.viii.3, and below, IV.viii.38 and 41.

[72] 8 George I, c. 15 (1721). See above, §§ 3 and 36, and below, § 41.

[73] The duties were imposed by 12 Charles II, c. 4 (1660) and 14 Charles II, c. 11 (1662) in *Statutes of the Realm*, v.393–400; 13 and 14 Charles II, c. 11 in Ruffhead's edition.

their interest to encourage the importation of those drugs, by an exemption from all duties, thought it likewise for their interest to throw some small discouragement upon their exportation. The avidity, however, which suggested this notable piece of mercantile ingenuity, most probably disappointed itself of its object. It necessarily taught the importers to be more careful than they might otherwise have been, that their importation should not exceed what was necessary for the supply of the home market. The home market was at all times likely to be more scantily supplied; the commodities were at all times likely to be somewhat dearer there than they would have been, had the exportation been rendered as free as the importation.

40   By the above-mentioned statute, gum senega, or gum arabic, being among the enumerated dying drugs, might be imported duty free. They were subjected, indeed, to a small poundage duty, amounting only to three pence in the hundred weight upon their re-exportation. France enjoyed, at that time, an exclusive trade to the country most productive of those drugs, that which lies in the neighbourhood of the Senegal; and the British market could not *easily be* supplied by the immediate importation of them from the place of growth.[74] By the 25th Geo. II. therefore, gum senega was allowed to be imported, (contrary to the general dispositions of the act of navigation) from any part of Europe. As the law, however, did not mean to encourage [510] this species of trade, so contrary to the general principles of the mercantile policy of England, it imposed a duty of ten shillings the hundred weight upon such importation, and no part of this duty was to be afterwards drawn back upon its exportation.[75] The successful war which began in 1755 gave Great Britain the same exclusive trade to those countries which France had enjoyed before. Our manufacturers, as soon as the peace was made, endeavoured to avail themselves of this advantage, and to establish a monopoly in their own favour, both against the growers, and against the importers of this commodity. By the 5th Geo. III. therefore, chap. 37.[76] the exportation of gum senega from his majesty's dominions in Africa was confined to Great Britain, and was subjected to all the same restrictions, regulations, forfeitures and penalties, as that of the enumerated commodities of the British colonies in America and the West Indies.[77] Its importation, indeed, was subjected to a small duty of sixpence the hundred weight, but its re-exportation was subjected to the enormous duty of one pound ten shillings the hundred weight. It was the intention of our manufacturers that the whole produce of those countries should be imported into Great

ʃ-ʃ be easily 5–6

[74] See below, V.ii.k.24.   [75] 25 George II, c. 32 (1751).
[76] 5 George III, c. 37 (1765).
[77] The enumerated commodities are described at IV.vii.b.35.

Britain, and in order that they themselves might be enabled to buy it at their own price, that no part of it should be exported again, but at such an expence as would sufficiently discourage that exportation. Their avidity, however, upon this, as well as upon many other occasions, disappointed itself of its [511] object. This enormous duty presented such a temptation to smuggling, that great quantities of this commodity were clandestinely exported, probably to all the manufacturing countries of Europe, but particularly to Holland, not only from Great Britain but from Africa. Upon this account, by the 14 Geo. III. chap. 10. this duty upon exportation was reduced to five shillings the hundred weight.[78]

41   In the book of rates, according to which the old subsidy was levied, beaver skins were estimated at six shillings and eight pence a piece, and the different subsidies and imposts, which before the year 1722 had been laid upon their importation, amounted to one-fifth part of the rate, or to sixteen pence upon each skin; all of which, except half the old subsidy, amounting only to two pence, was drawn back upon exportation.[79] This duty upon the importation of so important a material of manufacture had been thought too high, and, in the year 1722, the rate was reduced to two shillings and sixpence, which reduced the duty upon importation to sixpence, and of this only one half was to be drawn back upon exportation.[80] The same successful war put the country most productive of beaver under the dominion of Great Britain, and beaver skins being among the enumerated commodities, their exportation from America was consequently confined to the market of Great Britain.[81] Our manufacturers soon bethought themselves of the advantage which they might make of this circumstance, and in the year 1764,[82] the duty upon the importation of beaver-[512]skin was reduced to one penny, but the duty upon exportation was raised to seven pence each skin, without any drawback of the duty upon importation. By the same law, a duty of eighteen pence the pound was imposed upon the exportation of beaver-wool or wombs, without making any alteration in the duty upon the importation of that commodity, which when imported by British and in British shipping, amounted at that time to between four pence and five pence the piece.

42   Coals may be considered both as a material of manufacture and as an instrument of trade.[83] Heavy duties, accordingly, have been imposed upon their exportation, amounting at present (1783) to more than five shillings the ton, or to more than fifteen shillings the chaldron, Newcastle measure;

---

[78] 14 George III, c. 10 (1774) reduced the duty from 30s. to 5s. No duty was imposed on gum senega exported from Great Britain to Ireland under licence. See below, V.ii.k.24.

[79] 12 Charles II, c. 4 (1660). See above, IV.iv.3, IV.v.b.37, and below, V.ii.k.23.

[80] 8 George I, c. 15 (1721). See above, IV.viii.3, 36, 38.

[81] See above, IV.vii.b.35.   [82] 4 George III, c. 9 (1763).

[83] See below, V.ii.k.12, where Smith comments favourably on granting a bounty on the transport of coal.

which is in most cases more than the original value of the commodity at the coal pit, or even at the shipping port for exportation.

43   The exportation, however, of the instruments of trade, properly so called, is commonly restrained, not by high duties, but by absolute prohibitions.[84] Thus by the 7th and 8th of William III. chap. 20. sect. 8.[85] the exportation of frames or engines for knitting gloves or stockings is prohibited under the penalty, not only of the forfeiture of such frames or engines, so exported, or attempted to be exported, but of forty pounds, one half to the king, the other to the person who shall inform or sue for the same. In the same manner by the 14th Geo. III. chap. 71.[86] the exportation to foreign [513] parts, of any utensils made use of in the cotton, linen, woollen and silk manufactures, is prohibited under the penalty, not only of the forfeiture of such utensils, but of two hundred pounds, to be paid by the person who shall offend in this manner, and likewise of two hundred pounds to be paid by the master of the ship who shall knowlingly suffer such utensils to be loaded on board his ship.

44   When such heavy penalties were imposed upon the exportation of the dead instruments of trade, it could not well be expected that the living instrument, the artificer,[87] should be allowed to go free. Accordingly, by the 5 Geo. I. chap. 27.[88] the person who shall be convicted of enticing any artificer of, or in any of the manufactures of Great Britain, to go into any foreign parts in order to practice or teach his trade, is liable for the first offence to be fined in any sum not exceeding one hundred pounds, and to three months imprisonment, and until the fine shall be paid; and for the second offence, to be fined in any sum at the discretion of the court, and to imprisonment for twelve months, and until the fine shall be paid. By the 23 Geo. II. chap. 13.[89] this penalty is increased for the first offence to five hundred pounds for every artificer so enticed, and to twelve months imprisonment, and until the fine shall be paid; and for the second offence, to one thousand pounds, and to two years imprisonment, and until the fine shall be paid.

45   [514] By the former of those two statutes, upon proof that any person has been enticing any artificer, or that any artificer has promised or contracted to go into foreign parts for the purposes aforesaid, such artificer may be obliged to give security at the discretion of the court, that he shall not go beyond the seas, and may be committed to prison until he give such security.

---

[84] See above, II.i.14, where Smith refers to 'machines and instruments of trade' and cf. §§ 1 and 38 of this section.
[85] 7 and 8 William III, c. 20 (1695). See above, IV.iii.a.1.
[86] 14 George III, c. 71 (1774).
[87] Smith includes the 'living instrument' in the nations fixed capital in II.i.17; the restrictions on the freedom of movement of labour are summarized in I.x.c.
[88] 5 George I, c. 27 (1718).   [89] 23 George II, c. 13 (1749).

46   If any artificer has gone beyond the seas, and is exercising or teaching his trade in any foreign country, upon warning being given to him by any of his majesty's ministers or consuls abroad, or by one of his majesty's secretaries of state for the time being, if he does not, within six months after such warning, return into this realm, and from thenceforth abide and inhabit continually within the same, he is from thenceforth declared incapable of taking any legacy devised to him within this kingdom, or of being executor or administrator to any person, or of taking any lands within this kingdom by descent, devise, or purchase. He likewise forfeits to the king, all his lands, goods and chattels, is declared an alien in every respect, and is put out of the king's protection.

47   It is unnecessary, I imagine, to observe, how contrary such regulations are to the boasted liberty of the subject, of which we affect to be so very jealous; but which, in this case, is so plainly sacrificed to the futile interests of our merchants and manufacturers.

48   [515] The laudable motive of all these regulations, is to extend our own manufactures, not by their own improvement, but by the depression of those of all our neighbours, and by putting an end, as much as possible, to the troublesome competition of such odious and disagreeable rivals. Our master manufacturers think it reasonable, that they themselves should have the monopoly of the ingenuity of all their countrymen. Though by restraining, in some trades, the number of apprentices which can be employed at one time, and by imposing the necessity of a long apprenticeship in all trades, they endeavour, all of them, to confine the knowledge of their respective employments to as small a number as possible; they are unwilling, however, that any part of this small number should go abroad to instruct foreigners.

49   Consumption is the sole end and purpose of all production; and the interest of the producer ought to be attended to, only so far as it may be necessary for promoting that of the consumer. *g*The maxim is so perfectly self-evident, that it would be absurd to attempt to prove it. But in the mercantile system, the interest of the consumer is almost constantly sacrificed to that of the producer; and it seems to consider production, and not consumption, as the ultimate end and object of all industry and commerce.

50   In the restraints upon the importation of all foreign commodities which can come into competition with those of our own growth, or manufacture, the interest of the home-consumer is [516] evidently sacrificed to that of the producer. It is altogether for the benefit of the latter, that the former is obliged to pay that enhancement of price which this monopoly almost always occasions.

*g*new ¶6

51   It is altogether for the benefit of the producer that bounties are granted upon the exportation of some of his productions. The home-consumer is obliged to pay, first, the tax which is necessary for paying the bounty, and secondly, the still greater tax which necessarily arises from the enhancement of the price of the commodity in the home market.[90]

52   By the famous treaty of commerce with Portugal,[91] the consumer is prevented by high duties from purchasing of a neighbouring country, a commodity which our own climate does not produce, but is obliged to purchase it of a distant country, though it is acknowledged that the commodity of the distant country is of a worse quality than that of the near one. The home-consumer is obliged to submit to this inconveniency, in order that the producer may import into the distant country some of his productions upon more advantageous terms than he would otherwise have been allowed to do. The consumer, too, is obliged to pay, whatever enhancement in the price of those very productions, this forced exportation may occasion in the home-market.

53   But in the system of laws which has been established for the management of our American and West Indian colonies, the interest of the [517] home-consumer has been sacrificed to that of the producer with a more extravagant profusion than in all our other commercial regulations. A great empire has been established for the sole purpose of raising up a nation of customers who should be obliged to buy from the shops of our different producers, all the goods with which these could supply them.[92] For the sake of that little enhancement of price which this monopoly might afford our producers, the home-consumers have been burdened with the whole expence of maintaining and defending that empire. For this purpose, and for this purpose only, in the two last wars, more than two hundred millions have been spent, and a new debt of more than a hundred and seventy millions has been contracted over and above all that had been expended for the same purpose in former wars.[93] The interest of this debt alone is not only greater than the whole extraordinary profit, which, it ever could be pretended, was made by the monopoly of the colony trade, but than the whole value of that trade or than the whole value of the goods, which at an average have been annually exported to the colonies.

54   It cannot be very difficult to determine who have been the contrivers of this whole mercantile system; not the consumers, we may believe, whose interest has been entirely neglected; but the producers whose interest has been so carefully attended to; and among this latter class our merchants and manufacturers have been by [518] far the principal architects. In

---

[90] See above, IV.v.a.24.   [91] See above, IV.vi.3.   [92] See above, IV.vii.c.63.
[93] See below, V.iii.92, and above, IV.vii.c.64, IV.i.26, II.iii.35.

the mercantile regulations, which have been taken notice of in this chapter, the interest of our manufacturers has been most peculiarly attended to; and the interest, not so much of the consumers, as that of some other sets of producers, has been sacrificed to it.[a]

(At this point in *3* Smith supplies as an 'Appendix' various computations relating to IV.v which he had previously incorporated in the text of 2A. This 'Appendix' now appears at the conclusion of the present edition, pp. 948–50.)

BOOK IV

CHAPTER *IX*

Of the agricultural Systems, or of those Systems of political Œconomy, which represent the Produce of Land as either the sole or the principal Source of the Revenue and Wealth of every Country

1 THE agriculture systems of political œconomy will not require so long an explanation as that which I have thought it necessary to bestow upon the mercantile or commercial system.

2 That system which represents the produce of land as the sole source of the revenue and wealth of every country, has, so far as I know, never been adopted by any nation, and it at present exists only in the speculations of a few men of great [2] learning and ingenuity in France.[1] It would not, surely, be worth while to examine at great length the errors of a system which never has done, and probably never will do any harm in any part of the world. I shall endeavour to explain, however, as distinctly as I can, the great outlines of this very ingenious system.

3 Mr. Colbert, the famous minister of Lewis XIV. was a man of probity, of great industry and knowledge of detail; of great experience and acuteness in the examination of publick accounts, and of abilities, in short, every way fitted for introducing method and good order into the collection and expenditure of the publick revenue.[2] That minister had unfortunately embraced all the prejudices of the mercantile system *b*, in its nature and essence a system of restraint and regulation, *c*and such as*c* could scarce fail to be agreeable to a laborious and plodding man of business, who had been accustomed to regulate the different departments of publick offices, and to

a–a VIII. *1–2*   *b*. That system *1*   *c–c* 2–6

---

[1] Apart from a visit of ten days in February 1764, Smith spent some ten months in Paris from December 1765 to October 1766. He thus came into contact with the 'economists' at a time when the school was particularly active and appears to have met the main figures such as Quesnay and Mirabeau. He also attended the literary salons and seems to have recalled that of Holbach with particular pleasure. In Letter 259 addressed to Morellet, dated 1 May 1786, Smith mentioned many of the people he had met during his stay such as Helvetius, Turgot, D'Alembert, and Diderot. He particularly mentioned Holbach and asked Morellet 'to assure him of my most affectionate and respectful remembrance, and that I shall never forget the very great kindness he did me the honour to shew me during my residence at Paris'. See John Rae, *Life*, xiv and on the physiocratic school, R. L. Meek, *The Economics of Physiocracy* (London, 1962).

[2] Colbert is described at IV.ii.38 as a man of 'great abilities'.

establish the necessary checks and controuls for confining each to its proper sphere. The industry and commerce of a great country he endeavoured to regulate upon the same model as the departments of a publick office; and instead of allowing every man to pursue his own interest his own way, upon the liberal plan of equality, liberty and justice, he bestowed upon certain branches of industry extraordinary privileges, while he laid others under as extraordinary restraints. He was not only disposed, like other European ministers, to [3] encourage more the industry of the towns than that of the country; but, in order to support the industry of the towns, he was willing even to depress and keep down that of the country. In order to render provisions cheap to the inhabitants of the towns, and thereby to encourage manufactures and foreign commerce,[3] he prohibited altogether the exportation of corn, and thus excluded the inhabitants of the country from every foreign market for by far the most important part of the produce of their industry. This prohibition, joined to the restraints imposed by the antient provincial laws of France upon the transportation of corn from one province to another, and to the arbitrary and degrading taxes which are levied upon the cultivators in almost all the provinces, discouraged and kept down the agriculture of that country very much below the state to which it would naturally have risen in so very fertile a soil and so very happy a climate.[4] This state of discouragement and depression was felt more or less in every different part of the country, and many different enquiries were set on foot concerning the causes of it. One of those causes appeared to be the preference given, by the institutions of Mr. Colbert, to the industry of the towns above that of the country.

4   If the rod be bent too much one way, says the proverb, in order to make it straight you must bend it as much the other. The French philosophers, who have proposed the system which represents agriculture as the sole source of the revenue and wealth of every country, seem to have [4] adopted this proverbial maxim; and as in the plan of Mr. Colbert the industry of the towns was certainly over-valued in comparison with that of the country; so in their system it seems to be as certainly under-valued.

5   The different orders of people who have ever been supposed to contribute in any respect towards the annual produce of the land and labour of the country, they divide into three classes. The first is the class of the proprietors of land. The second is the class of the cultivators, of farmers and country labourers, whom they honour with the peculiar appellation of the productive class. The third is the class of artificers, manufacturers and merchants, whom they endeavour to degrade by the humiliating appellation of the barren or unproductive class.

[3] Smith comments on the advantage of cheap provisions at III.iii.20.
[4] The arbitrary taxes in France are reviewed at V.ii.g.6, 7 and their impact on commerce at V.ii.k.70.

6   The class of proprietors contributes to the annual produce by the expence which they may occasionally lay out upon the improvement of the land, upon the buildings, drains, enclosures and other ameliorations, which they may either make or maintain upon it, and by means of which the cultivators are enabled, with the same capital, to raise a greater produce, and consequently to pay a greater rent. This advanced rent may be considered as the interest or profit due to the proprietor upon the expence or capital which he thus employs in the improvement of his land. Such expences are in this system called ground expences (depenses foncieres).

7   The cultivators or farmers contribute to the annual produce by what are in this system called [5] the original and annual expences (depenses primitives et depenses annuelles) which they lay out upon the cultivation of the land. The original expences consist in the instruments of husbandry, in the stock of cattle, in the seed, and in the maintenance of the farmer's family, servants and cattle, during at least a great part of the first year of his occupancy, or till he can receive some return from the land. The annual expences consist in the seed, in the *d*wear and tear*d* of the instruments of husbandry, and in the annual maintenance of the farmer's servants and cattle, and of his family too, so far as any part of them can be considered as servants employed in cultivation. That part of the produce of the land which remains to him after paying the rent, ought to be sufficient, first, to replace to him within a reasonable time, at least during the term of his occupancy, the whole of his original expences, together with the ordinary profits of stock; and, secondly, to replace to him annually the whole of his annual expences, together likewise with the ordinary profits of stock. Those two sorts of expences are two capitals which the farmer employs in cultivation; and unless they are regularly restored to him, together with a reasonable profit, he cannot carry on his employment upon a level with other employments; but, from a regard to his own interest, must desert it as soon as possible, and seek some other *e*. That part of the produce of the land which is thus necessary for enabling the farmer to continue his business, ought to be considered as a fund sacred [6] to cultivation, which if the landlord violates, he necessarily *f*reduces*f* the produce of his own land, and in a few years not only disables the farmer from paying this racked rent, but from paying the reasonable rent which he might otherwise have got for his land. The rent which properly belongs to the landlord, is no more than the neat produce which remains after paying in the compleatest manner all the necessary expences which must be previously laid out in order to raise the gross, or the whole produce. It is because the labour of the cultivators, over and above paying compleatly all those necessary expences, affords a neat produce of this kind, that this class of people are

---

d-d tear and wear *1*   *e* employment *1*   *f-f* degrades *1*

in this system peculiarly distinguished by the honourable appellation of the productive class.[5] Their original and annual expences are for the same reason called, in this system, productive expences, because, over and above replacing their own value, they occasion the annual reproduction of this neat produce.

8   The ground expences, as they are called, or what the landlord lays out upon the improvement of his land, are in this system too honoured with the appellation of productive expences. Till the whole of those expences, together with the ordinary profits of stock, have been compleatly repaid to him by the advanced rent which he gets from his land, that advanced rent ought to be regarded as sacred and inviolable, both by the church and by the king; ought to be subject neither to tithe nor to taxation. If it is otherwise, by discouraging the improvement of land, [7] the church discourages the future increase of her own tithes, and the king the future increase of his own taxes. As in a well-ordered state of things, therefore, those ground expences, over and above reproducing in the compleatest manner their own value, occasion likewise after a certain time a reproduction of a neat produce, they are in this system considered as productive expences.

9   The ground expences of the landlord, however, together with the original and the annual expences of the farmer, are the only three sorts of expences which in this system are considered as productive. All other expences and all other orders of people, even those who in the common apprehensions of men are regarded as the most productive, are in this account of things represented as altogether barren and unproductive.

10   Artificers and manufacturers, in particular, whose industry, in the common apprehensions of men, increases so much the value of the rude produce of land, are in this system represented as a class of people altogether barren and unproductive. Their labour, it is said, replaces only the stock which employs them, together with its ordinary profits. That stock consists in the materials, tools, and wages, advanced to them by their employer; and is the fund destined for their employment and maintenance. Its profits are the fund destined for the maintenance of their employer. Their employer, as he advances to them the stock of materials, tools and wages necessary for their employment, so he advances [8] to himself what is necessary for his own maintenance, and this maintenance he generally proportions to the profit which he expects to make by the price of their work. Unless its price repays to him the maintenance which he advances to himself, as well as the materials, tools and wages which he advances to

[5] See above, II.iii.1 and note. Smith discusses the physiocratic single tax at V.ii.c.7 where it is stated to be the consequence of the doctrine that land alone can produce a surplus. In this place Smith declined to go into what he described as the 'disagreeable . . . metaphysical arguments' of the physiocratic case.

his workmen, it evidently does not repay ⁹to⁹ him the whole expence which
he lays out upon it. The profits of manufacturing stock, therefore, are not,
like the rent of land, a neat produce which remains after compleatly repay-
ing the whole expence which must be laid out in order to obtain them.
The stock of the farmer yields him a profit as well as that of the master
manufacturer; and it yields a rent likewise to another person, which that
of the master manufacturer does not. The expence, therefore, laid out in
employing and maintaining artificers and manufacturers, does no more
than continue, if one may say so, the existence of its own value, and does
not produce any new value. It is therefore altogether a barren and unproductive expence. The expence, on the contrary, laid out in employing
farmers and country labourers, over and above continuing the existence of
its own value, produces a new value, the rent of the landlord. It is therefore
a productive expence.

11   Mercantile stock is equally barren and unproductive with manufacturing
stock.⁶ It only continues the existence of its own value, without producing
any new value. Its profits are only the repayment of the maintenance which
its em-[9]ployer advances to himself during the time that he employs it, or
till he receives the returns of it. They are only the repayment of a part of
the expence which must be laid out in employing it.

12   The labour of artificers and manufacturers never adds any thing to the
value of the whole annual amount of the rude produce of the land. It adds
indeed greatly to the value of some particular parts of it. But the consumption which in the mean time it occasions of other parts, is precisely equal
to the value which it adds to those parts; so that the value of the whole
amount is not, at any one moment of time, in the least augmented by it.
The person who works the lace of a pair of fine ruffles, for example, will
sometimes raise the value of perhaps a pennyworth of flax to thirty pounds
sterling. But though at first sight he appears thereby to multiply the value
of a part of the rude produce about seven thousand and two hundred times,
he in reality adds nothing to the value of the whole annual amount of the
rude produce. The working of that lace costs him perhaps two years labour.
The thirty pounds which he gets for it when it is finished, is no more than
the repayment of the subsistence which he advances to himself during the
two years that he is employed about it. The value which, by every day's,
month's, or year's labour, he adds to the flax, does no more than replace
the value of his own consumption during that day, month, or year. At no
moment of time, therefore, does he add [10] any thing to the value of the
whole annual amount of the rude produce of the land: the portion of that
produce which he is continually consuming, being always equal to the

---

⁹⁻⁹ 2–6

⁶ Smith objected to the doctrine, for example, at II.v.7.

value which he is continually producing. The extreme poverty of the greater part of the persons employed in this expensive, though trifling manufacture, may satisfy us that the price of their work does not in ordinary cases exceed the value of their subsistence. It is otherwise with the work of farmers and country labourers. The rent of the landlord is a value, which, in ordinary cases, it is continually producing, over and above replacing, in the most compleat manner, the whole consumption, the whole expence laid out upon the employment and maintenance both of the workmen and of their employer.

13   Artificers, manufacturers and merchants, can augment the revenue and wealth of their society, by parsimony only; or, as it is expressed in this system, by privation, that is, by depriving themselves of a part of the funds destined for their own subsistence. They annually reproduce nothing but those funds. Unless, therefore, they annually save some part of them, unless they annually deprive themselves of the enjoyment of some part of them, the revenue and wealth of their society can never be in the smallest degree augmented by means of their industry. Farmers and country labourers, on the contrary, may enjoy compleatly the whole funds destined for their own subsistence, and yet augment at the same time the revenue and wealth of their society. [11] Over and above ʰwhat isʰ destined for their own subsistence, their industry annually affords a neat produce, of which the augmentation necessarily augments the revenue and wealth of their society. Nations, therefore, which, like France or England, consist in a great measure of proprietors and cultivators, can be enriched by industry and enjoyment. Nations, on the contrary, which, like Holland and Hamburgh, are composed chiefly of merchants, artificers and manufacturers, can grow rich only through parsimony and privation. As the interest of nations so differently circumstanced, is very different, so is likewise the common character of the people. In those of the former kind, liberality, frankness, and good fellowship, naturally make a part of that common character. In the latter, narrowness, meanness, and a selfish disposition, averse to all social pleasure and enjoyment.

14   The unproductive class, that of merchants, artificers, and manufacturers, is maintained and employed altogether at the expence of the two other classes, of that of proprietors, and of that of cultivators. They furnish it both with the materials of its work and with the fund of its subsistence, with the corn and cattle which it consumes while it is employed about that work. The proprietors and cultivators finally pay both the wages of all the workmen of the unproductive class, and the profits of all their employers. Those workmen and their employers are properly the servants of the proprietors and cultivators. They are only servants who work without doors,

---

ʰ⁻ʰ the funds *I*

[12] as menial servants work within. Both the one and the other, however, are equally maintained at the expence of the same masters. The labour of both is equally unproductive. It adds nothing to the value of the sum total of the rude produce of the land. Instead of increasing the value of that sum total, it is a charge and expence which must be paid out of it.

15   The unproductive class, however, is not only useful, but greatly useful to the other two classes. By means of the industry of merchants, artificers and manufacturers, the proprietors and cultivators can purchase both the foreign goods and the manufactured produce of their own country which they have occasion for, with the produce of a much smaller quantity of their own labour, than what they would be obliged to employ, if they were to attempt, in an aukward and unskilful manner, either to import the one, or to make the other for their own use. By means of the unproductive class, the cultivators are delivered from many cares which would otherwise distract their attention from the cultivation of land. The superiority of produce, which, in consequence of this undivided attention, they are enabled to raise, is fully sufficient to pay the whole expence which the maintenance and employment of the unproductive class costs either the proprietors, or themselves. The industry of merchants, artificers, and manufacturers, though in its own nature altogether unproductive, yet contributes in this manner indirectly to increase the produce of the land. It increases the productive [13] powers of productive labour, by leaving it at liberty to confine itself to its proper employment, the cultivation of land; and the plough goes frequently the easier and the better by means of the labour of the man whose business is most remote from the plough.

16   It can never be the interest of the proprietors and cultivators to restrain or to discourage in any respect the industry of merchants, artificers and manufacturers. The greater the liberty which this unproductive class enjoys, the greater will be the competition in all the different trades which compose it, and the cheaper will the other two classes be supplied, both with foreign goods and with the manufactured produce of their own country.

17   It can never be the interest of the unproductive class to oppress the other two classes. It is the surplus produce of the land, or what remains after deducting the maintenance, first, of the cultivators, and afterwards, of the proprietors, that maintains and employs the unproductive class. The greater this surplus, the greater must likewise be *the* maintenance and employment *of that class*. The establishment of perfect justice, of perfect liberty,[7] and of perfect equality, is the very simple secret which most effectually secures the highest degree of prosperity to all the three classes.

i-i its *1*   *j-j* 2–6

[7] For Smith's use of this term, see for example IV.vii.c.44, I.x.a.1, I.x.c.1, I.vii.6, 30, and cf. below, § 51.

18   The merchants, artificers, and manufacturers of those mercantile states which, like Holland and Hamburgh, consist chiefly of this unproductive class, are in the same manner maintained [14] and employed altogether at the expence of the proprietors and cultivators of land. The only difference is, that those proprietors and cultivators are, the greater part of them, placed at a most inconvenient distance from the merchants, artificers, and manufacturers whom they supply with the materials of their work and the fund of their subsistence, are the inhabitants of other countries, and the subjects of other governments.

19   Such mercantile states, however, are not only useful, but greatly useful to the inhabitants of those other countries. They fill up, in some measure, a very important void, and supply the place of the merchants, artificers and manufacturers, whom the inhabitants of those countries ought to find at home, but whom, from some defect in their policy, they do not find at home.

20   It can never be the interest of those landed nations, if I may call them so, to discourage or distress the industry of such mercantile states, by imposing high duties upon their trade, or upon the commodities which they furnish. Such duties, by rendering those commodities dearer, could serve only to sink the real value of the surplus produce of their own land, with which, or, what comes to the same thing, with the price of which those commodities are purchased. Such duties could serve only to discourage the increase of that surplus produce, and consequently the improvement and cultivation of their own land. The most effectual expedient, on the contrary, for raising the value of that surplus pro-[15]duce, for encouraging its increase, and consequently the improvement and cultivation of their own land, would be to allow the most perfect freedom to the trade of all such mercantile nations.

21   This perfect freedom of trade would even be the most effectual expedient for supplying them, in due time, with all the artificers, manufacturers and merchants, whom they wanted at home, and for filling up in the properest and most advantageous manner that very important void which they felt there.

22   The continual increase of the surplus produce of their land, would, in due time, create a greater capital than what could be employed with the ordinary rate of profit in the improvement and cultivation of land; and the surplus part of it would naturally turn itself to the employment of artificers and manufacturers at home. But those artificers and manufacturers, finding at home both the materials of their work and the fund of their subsistence, might immediately, even with much less art and skill, be able to work as cheap as the like artificers and manufacturers of such mercantile states, who had both to bring from a ^{k}great^k distance. Even though from want of

$^{k-k}$ greater 5–6

art and skill, they might not for some time be able to work as cheap, yet, finding a market at home, they might be able to sell their work there as cheap as that of the artificers and manufacturers of such mercantile states, which could not be brought to that market but from so great a distance; and as their art and skill im-[16]proved, they would soon be able to sell it cheaper. The artificers and manufacturers of such mercantile states, therefore, would immediately be rivalled in the market of those landed nations, and soon after undersold and justled out of it altogether. The cheapness of the manufactures of those landed nations, in consequence of the gradual improvements of art and skill, would, in due time, extend their sale beyond the home market, and carry them to many foreign markets, from which they would in the same manner gradually justle out many of the manufactures of such mercantile nations.

23   This continual increase both of the rude and manufactured produce of those landed nations would in due time create a greater capital than could, with the ordinary rate of profit, be employed either in agriculture or in manufactures. The surplus of this capital would naturally turn itself to foreign trade, and be employed in exporting, to foreign countries, such parts of the rude and manufactured produce of its own country, as exceeded the demand of the home market. In the exportation of the produce of their own country, the merchants of a landed nation would have an advantage of the same kind over those of mercantile nations, which its artificers and manufacturers had over the artificers and manufacturers of such nations; the advantage of finding at home that cargo, and those stores and provisions, which the others were obliged to seek for at a distance. With inferior art and skill in navigation, therefore, they would [17] be able to sell that cargo as cheap in foreign markets as the merchants of such mercantile nations; and with equal art and skill they would be able to sell it cheaper. They would soon, therefore, rival those mercantile nations in this branch of ^{t} foreign trade, and in due time would justle them out of it altogether.

24   According to this liberal and generous system, therefore, the most advantageous method in which a landed nation can raise up artificers, manufacturers and merchants of its own, is to grant the most perfect freedom of trade to the artificers, manufacturers and merchants of all other nations. It thereby raises the value of the surplus produce of its own land, of which the continual increase gradually establishes a fund which in due time necessarily raises up all the artificers, manufacturers and merchants whom it has occasion for.

25   When a landed nation, on the contrary, oppresses either by high duties or by prohibitions the trade of foreign nations, it necessarily hurts its own interest in two different ways. First, by raising the price of all foreign goods and of all sorts of manufactures, it necessarily sinks the real value of the

^{t} their *I*

surplus produce of its own land, with which, or, what comes to the same thing, with the price of which, it purchases those foreign goods and manufactures. Secondly, by giving a sort of monopoly of the home market to its own merchants, artificers and manufacturers, it raises the rate of mercantile and manufacturing profit in proportion to that of agricultural profit, and [18] consequently either draws from agriculture a part of the capital which had before been employed in it, or hinders from going to it a part of what would otherwise have gone to it. This policy, therefore, discourages agriculture in two different ways; first, by sinking the real value of its produce, and thereby lowering the rate of its profit; and, secondly, by raising the rate of profit in all other employments. Agriculture is rendered less advantageous, and trade and manufactures more advantageous than they otherwise would be; and every man is tempted by his own interest to turn, as much as he can, both his capital and his industry from the former to the latter employments.

26   Though, by this oppressive policy, a landed nation should be able to raise up artificers, manufacturers and merchants of its own, somewhat sooner than it could do by the freedom of trade; a matter, however, which is not a little doubtful; yet it would raise them up, if one may say so, prematurely, and before it was perfectly ripe for them. By raising up too hastily one species of industry, it would depress another more valuable species of industry. By raising up too hastily a species of industry which only replaces the stock which employs it, together with the ordinary profit, it would depress a species of industry which, over and above replacing that stock with its profit, affords likewise a neat produce, a free rent to the landlord. It would depress productive labour, by encou-[19]raging too hastily that labour which is altogether barren and unproductive.

27   In what manner, according to this system, the sum total of the annual produce of the land is distributed among the three classes above mentioned, and in what manner the labour of the unproductive class, does no more than replace the value of its own consumption, without increasing in any respect the value of that sum total, is represented by Mr. Quesnai, the very ingenious and profound author of this system, in some arithmetical formularies. The first of these formularies, which by way of eminence he peculiarly distinguishes by the name of the Oeconomical Table,[8] represents

---

[8] Quesnay's *Tableau économique* (1757–8), ed. with translation and notes by M. Kuczynski and R. L. Meek (London, 1972). It is interesting to observe that the model which Smith expounds is rather more elaborate than that offered by Quesnay in the sense that it makes allowance for the existence of rent, wages, and profit, as separate categories, and for a distinction between wage labour and the entrepreneur. This may suggest that Smith used a modified form for the purposes of exposition and/or that he may have based his account on the work done by writers such as Baudeau or Turgot. Baudeau was the founder of the *Ephémérides du Citoyen*. This journal printed Turgot's *Reflections* in 1769–70 and it is now known that Smith's holdings of the journal included the first two parts of Turgot's work. Smith met Turgot during his stay in Paris and it seems likely that they would

the manner in which he supposes this distribution takes place, in a state of the most perfect liberty, and therefore of the highest prosperity; in a state where the annual produce is such as to afford the greatest possible neat produce, and where each class enjoys its proper share of the whole annual produce. Some subsequent formularies represent the manner in which, he supposes, this distribution is made in different states of restraint and regulation; in which, either the class of proprietors, or the barren and unproductive class, is more favoured than the class of cultivators, and in which, either the one or the other encroaches more or less upon the share which ought properly to belong to this productive class.[9] Every such encroachment, every violation of that natural distribution, which the most perfect liberty would establish, must, according to this system, [20] necessarily degrade more or less, from one year to another, the value and sum total of the annual produce, and must necessarily occasion a gradual declension in the real wealth and revenue of the society; a declension of which the progress must be quicker or slower, according to the degree of this encroachment, according as that natural distribution, which the most perfect liberty would establish, is more or less violated. Those subsequent formularies represent the different degrees of declension, which, according to this system correspond to the different degrees in which this natural distribution of things is violated.

28   Some speculative physicians seem to have imagined that the health of the human body could be preserved only by a certain precise regimen of diet and exercise, of which every, the smallest, violation necessarily occasioned some degree of disease or disorder proportioned to the degree of the violation. Experience, however, would seem to show that the human

discuss matters of common interest especially since Turgot must have been working on the *Reflections* during the course of 1766. The view that the two men discussed economics is supported by Morellet in a passage which refers to Smith and then goes on: 'M. Turgot, who like me loved things metaphysical, estimated his talents greatly. We saw him several times; he was presented at the house of M. Helvetius; we talked of commercial theory, banking, public credit and several points in the great work he was meditating'. (*Mémoires* (Paris, 1823), i.244.) Smith refers to a meeting with Turgot in Letter 93 addressed to Hume, dated 6 July 1766. In Letter 248 addressed to Rochefoucauld dated 1 November 1785, Smith indicated that although he had not corresponded with, Turgot, yet 'I had the happiness of his acquaintance, and, I flattered myself, even of his friendship and esteem'. In the same letter Smith refers to the fact that Turgot had sent him a copy of the *Procès verbal*, containing a record of events following on the registration of the six edicts, which, Smith remarked, 'did so much honour to their Author, and, had they been executed without alteration, would have proved so beneficial to his country'.

[9] See for example Quesnay's *Analyse* (1766) and his essay *Problème économique* (1766) both of which appeared in *Physiocratie* (1768) edited by Dupont de Nemours, a copy of which was in Smith's Library. These works are translated by R. L. Meek and included in his *Economics of Physiocracy*. In 1788 Dupont sent a copy of his work on the Eden Treaty to Smith as a mark of respect 'pour le Livre excellent dont vous avez enrichi le monde'. Letter 277 addressed to Smith, dated 19 June 1788.

body frequently preserves, *m*to all appearance at least*m*, the most perfect
state of health under a vast variety of different regimens; even under some
which are generally believed to be very far from being perfectly wholesome.
But the healthful state of the human body, it would seem, contains in itself
some unknown principle of preservation, capable either of preventing or of
correcting, in many respects, the bad effects even of a very faulty regimen.
Mr. Quesnai, who was himself a physician, and a very speculative physician,[10] seems to [21] have entertained a notion of the same kind concerning
the political body, and to have imagined that it would thrive and prosper
only under a certain precise regimen, the exact regimen of perfect liberty
and perfect justice. He seems not to have considered that in the political
body, the natural effort which every man is continually making to better
his own condition,[11] is a principle of preservation capable of preventing
and correcting, in many respects, the bad effects of a political œconomy,
in some degree, both partial and oppressive. Such a political œconomy,
though it no doubt retards more or less, is not always capable of stopping
altogether the natural progress of a nation towards wealth and prosperity,
and still less of making it go backwards. If a nation could not prosper
without the enjoyment of perfect liberty and perfect justice, there is not in
the world a nation which could ever have prospered. In the political body,
however, the wisdom of nature has fortunately made ample provision for
remedying many of the bad effects of the folly and injustice of man; in the
same manner as it has done in the natural body, for remedying those of his
sloth and intemperance.

29   The capital error of this system, however, seems to lie in its representing
the class of artificers, manufacturers and merchants, as altogether barren
and unproductive. The following observations may serve to show the
impropriety of this representation.

30   First, this class, it is acknowledged, reproduces annually the value of its
own annual con-[22]sumption, and continues, at least, the existence of
the stock or capital which maintains and employs it. But upon this account
alone the denomination of barren or unproductive should seem to be very
improperly applied to it. We should not call a marriage barren or unproductive, though it produced only a son and a daughter, to replace the father

---

m-m at least to all appearance *1*

[10] While in Paris, Quesnay attended Smith's charge, the Duke of Buccleuch; a fact
mentioned by Smith in Letter 94 addressed to Charles Townshend, dated 26 August 1766.
Quesnay is also mentioned in Letter 97 addressed to Lady Frances Scott, dated 15 October
1766, where Smith described him as 'one of the worthiest men in France & one of the best
Physicians that is to be met with in any country. He was not only the Physician but the
friend & confident of Madame Pompadour a woman who was no contemptible Judge of
merit.' Smith seems to have thought sufficiently highly of Quesnay as to have intended to
'inscribe' the WN to him. Stewart III.12.
[11] See above, IV.v.b.43, II.iii.28,36, and III.iii.12.

and mother, and though it did not increase the number of the human species, but only continued it as it was before. Farmers and country labourers, indeed, over and above the stock which maintains and employs them, reproduce annually a neat produce, a free rent to the landlord. As a marriage which affords three children is certainly more productive than one which affords only two; so the labour of farmers and country labourers is certainly more productive than that of merchants, artificers and manufacturers. The superior produce of the one class, however, does not render the other barren or unproductive.[12]

31   Secondly, it seems, upon this account, altogether improper to consider artificers, manufacturers and merchants, in the same light as menial servants. The labour of menial servants does not continue the existence of the fund which maintains and employs them. Their maintenance and employment is altogether at the expence of their masters, and the work which they perform is not of a nature to repay that expence. That work consists in services which perish generally in the very instant of their performance, and does not fix or realize itself in any vendible [23] commodity which can replace the value of their wages and maintenance.[13] The labour, on the contrary, of artificers, manufacturers and merchants, naturally does fix and realize itself in some such vendible commodity. It is upon this account that, in the chapter in which I treat of productive and unproductive labour, I have classed artificers, manufacturers and merchants, among the productive labourers, and menial servants among the barren or unproductive.[14]

32   Thirdly, it seems, upon every supposition, improper to say, that the labour of artificers, manufacturers and merchants, does not increase the real revenue of the society. Though we should suppose, for example, as it seems to be supposed in this system, that the value of the daily, monthly, and yearly consumption of this class was exactly equal to that of its daily, monthly, and yearly production, yet it would not from thence follow that its labour added nothing to the real revenue, to the real value of the annual produce of the land and labour of the society. An artificer, for example, who in the first six months after harvest, executes ten pounds worth of work, though he should in the same time consume ten pounds worth of corn and other necessaries, yet really adds the value of ten pounds to the annual produce of the land and labour of the society. While he has been consuming a half yearly revenue of ten pounds worth of corn and other necessaries, he has produced an equal value of work capable of purchasing, either to himself or to some other person, an equal half yearly revenue. The value, therefore, of what [24] has been consumed and produced during these

[12] See above, II.v.12, where Smith comments on the superior productivity of agriculture.
[13] Cf. II.iii.2.   [14] See II.iii.

six months is equal, not to ten, but to twenty pounds. It is possible, indeed, that no more than ten pounds worth of this value, may even have existed at any one moment of time. But if the ten pounds worth of corn and other necessaries, which were consumed by the artificer, had been consumed by a soldier or by a menial servant, the value of that part of the annual produce which existed at the end of the six months, would have been ten pounds less than it actually is in consequence of the labour of the artificer. Though the value of what the artificer produces, therefore, should not at any one moment of time be supposed greater than the value he consumes, yet at every moment of time the actually existing value of goods in the market is, in consequence of what he produces, greater than it otherwise would be.

33   When the patrons of this system assert that the consumption of artificers, manufacturers and merchants, is equal to the value of what they produce, they probably mean no more than that their revenue, or the fund destined for their consumption, is equal to it. But if they had expressed themselves more accurately, and only asserted that the revenue of this class was equal to the value of what they produced, it might readily have occurred to the reader, that what would naturally be saved out of this revenue, must necessarily increase more or less the real wealth of the society. In order, therefore, to make out something like an argument, it was necessary that they should express themselves as [25] they have done; and this argument, even supposing things actually were as it seems to presume them to be, turns out to be a very inconclusive one.

34   Fourthly, farmers and country labourers can no more augment, without parsimony, the real revenue, the annual produce of the land and labour of their society, than artificers, manufacturers and merchants.[15] The annual produce of the land and labour of any society can be augmented only in two ways; either, first, by some improvement in the productive powers of the useful labour actually maintained within it; or, secondly, by some increase in the quantity of that labour.[16]

35   The improvement in the productive powers of useful labour depend, first, upon the improvement in the ability of the workman; and, secondly, upon that of the machinery with which he works. But the labour of artificers and manufacturers, as it is capable of being more subdivided, and the labour of each workman reduced to a greater simplicity of operation, than that of farmers and country labourers,[17] so it is likewise capable of both these sorts of improvement in a much higher degree*. In this respect, therefore, the class of cultivators can have no sort of advantage over that of artificers and manufacturers.

---

* See Book I. Chap. I.

[15] See above, II.iii.16.   [16] This point is made above, II.iii.32.   [17] See above, I.i.4.

36   The increase in the quantity of useful labour actually employed within any society, must de-[26]pend altogether upon the increase of the capital which employs it; and the increase of that capital again must be exactly equal to the amount of the savings from the revenue, either of the particular persons who manage and direct the employment of that capital, or of some other persons who lend it to them.[18] If merchants, artificers and manufacturers are, as this system seems to suppose, naturally more inclined to parsimony and saving than proprietors and cultivators, they are, so far, more likely to augment the quantity of useful labour employed within their society, and consequently to increase its real revenue, the annual produce of its land and labour.

37   Fifthly and lastly, though the revenue of the inhabitants of every country was supposed to consist altogether, as this system seems to suppose, in the quantity of subsistence which their industry could procure to them; yet, even upon this supposition, the revenue of a trading and manufacturing country must, other things being equal, always be much greater than that of one without trade or manufactures. By means of trade and manufactures, a greater quantity of subsistence can be annually imported into a particular country than what its own lands, in the actual state of their cultivation, could afford. The inhabitants of a town, though they frequently possess no lands of their own, yet draw to themselves by their industry such a quantity of the rude produce of the lands of other people as supplies them, not only with the materials of their work, but with the fund of their subsistence. [27] What a town always is with regard to the country in its neighbourhood, one independent state or country may frequently be with regard to other independent states or countries.[19] It is thus that Holland draws a great part of its subsistence from other countries; live cattle from Holstein and Jutland, and corn from almost all the different countries of Europe.[20] A small quantity of manufactured produce purchases a great quantity of rude produce. A trading and manufacturing country, therefore, naturally purchases with a small part of its manufactured produce a great part of the rude produce of other countries; while, on the contrary, a country without trade and manufactures is generally obliged to purchase, at the expence of a great part of its rude produce, a very small part of the manufactured produce of other countries. The one exports what can subsist and accommodate but a very few, and imports the subsistence and accommodation of a great number. The other exports the accommodation and subsistence of a great number, and imports that of a very few only. The inhabitants of the one must always enjoy a much greater quantity of subsistence than

[18] See above, II.iii.15.
[19] See, for example, III.i.1.
[20] Smith comments on the position of Holland as an importer of grain at I.xi.e.38 and I.xi.b.12.

what their own lands, in the actual state of their cultivation, could afford. The inhabitants of the other must always enjoy a much smaller quantity.

38   This system, however, with all its imperfections is, perhaps, the nearest approximation to the truth that has yet been published upon the subject of political oeconomy, and is upon that account [28] well worth the consideration of every man who wishes to examine with attention the principles of that very important science. Though in representing the labour which is employed upon land as the only productive labour, the notions which it inculcates are perhaps too narrow and confined; yet in representing the wealth of nations as consisting, not in the unconsumable riches of money, but in the consumable goods annually reproduced by the labour of the society; and in representing perfect liberty as the only effectual expedient for rendering this annual reproduction the greatest possible, its doctrine seems to be in every respect as just as it is generous and liberal. Its followers are very numerous; and as men are fond of paradoxes, and of appearing to understand what surpasses the comprehension of ordinary people, the paradox which it maintains, concerning the unproductive nature of manufacturing labour, has not perhaps contributed a little to increase the number of its admirers.[21] They have for some years past made a pretty considerable sect, distinguished in the French republick of letters by the name of, The Oeconomists. Their works have certainly been of some service to their country;[22] not only by bringing into general discussion, many subjects which had never been well examined before, but by influencing in some measure the publick administration in favour of agriculture. It has been in consequence of their representations, accordingly, that the agriculture of France has been delivered from several of the oppressions which it [29] before laboured under. The term during which such a lease can be granted, as will be valid against every future purchaser or proprietor of the land, has been prolonged from nine to twenty-seven years.[23] The antient provincial restraints upon the transportation of corn from one province of the kingdom to another, have been entirely taken away, and the liberty of exporting it to all foreign countries, has been established as the common law of the kingdom in all ordinary cases.[24] This sect,[25] in their works, which are very numerous, and which treat not only of what is properly called Political

[21] Astronomy, IV.34, refers to 'that love of paradox, so natural to the learned, and that pleasure, which they are so apt to take in exciting, by the novelty of their supposed discoveries, the amazement of mankind'.

[22] See below, V.ii.c.7.

[23] See above, III.ii.16.

[24] See I.xi.g.15, IV.v.a.5, where it is pointed out that the prohibition on the export of grain was applied until 1764.

[25] In the manner of the time, Smith would appear to have used the term 'sect' for 'school' For example, in discussing the system of eccentric spheres in his account of astronomical theories, he comments that it 'was never adopted by any one sect of philosophers' (Astronomy, IV.17). He refers to the Pythagoreans as a sect at § 28.

Oeconomy,[26] or of the nature and causes of the wealth of nations, but of every other branch of the system of civil government, all follow implicitly, and without any sensible variation, the doctrine of Mr. Quesnai.[27] There is upon this account little variety in the greater part of their works. The most distinct and best connected account of this doctrine is to be found in a little book written by Mr. Mercier de la Riviere,[28] sometime Intendant of Martinico, intitled, The natural and essential Order of Political Societies. The admiration of this whole sect for their master, who was himself a man of the greatest modesty and simplicity, is not inferior to that of any of the antient philosophers for the founders of their respective systems. "There have been, since the world began," says a very diligent and respectable author, the Marquis de Mirabeau, "three great inventions which have principally given stability to political societies, independent of many other in-[30]ventions which have enriched and adorned them. The first, is the invention of writing, which alone gives human nature the power of transmitting, without alteration, its laws, its contracts, its annals, and its discoveries. The second, is the invention of money, which binds together all the relations between civilized societies. The third, is the Oeconomical Table, the result of the other two, which completes them both by perfecting their object; the great discovery of our age, but of which our posterity will reap the benefit."[29]

39   As the political oeconomy of the nations of modern Europe, has been more favourable to manufactures and foreign trade, the industry of the towns, than to agriculture, the industry of the country; so that of other nations has followed a different plan, and has been more favourable to agriculture than to manufactures and foreign trade.

40   The policy of China favours agriculture more than all other employments.[30] In China, the condition of a labourer is said to be as much superior to that of an artificer; as in most parts of Europe, that of an artificer is to that of a labourer.[31] In China, the great ambition of every man is to

---

[26] The term 'political economy' is used, for example, at IV.i, II.v.31, IV.i.35. The physiocrats are described at V.ii.c.7. as a sect who call themselves 'the oeconomists'.

[27] For comment on this point, see R. L. Meek, *The Economics of Physiocracy*, 27.

[28] Mercier de la Riviere, *L'ordre naturel et essential des sociétés politiques* (1767). This book was in Smith's library, which also included works by Dupont de Nemours, Forbonnais, Le Trosne, Mirabeau, Morellet, and Quesnay. In addition to the *Ephémérides* Smith owned copies of the *Journal de l'Agriculture, du Commerce et de Finances* for 1765–7, which was edited by Dupont from September 1765 to October 1766.

[29] *Philosophie rurale ou économie générale et politique de l'agriculture, pour servir de suite à l'Ami des Hommes* (Amsterdam, 1766), i.52–3.

[30] 'The whole attention, in general, of the Chinese government, is directed towards agriculture.' (P. Poivre, *Voyages d'un philosophe* (1768), translated as *Travels of a Philosopher, or, Observations on the Manners and Arts of Various Nations in Africa and Asia* (Glasgow, 1790), 169.)

[31] 'L'Agriculture y est sort estimée, et les Labourers, dont la profession est regardée comme la plus nécessaire à un Etat, y tiennent un rang considérable; on leur accorde de

get possession of some little bit of land, either in property or in lease; and leases are there said to be granted upon very moderate terms, and to be sufficiently secured to the lessees.[32] The Chinese have little respect for foreign trade.[33] Your beggarly commerce! was the language in which the Mandarins of Pekin used to talk to Mr. [31] *n*De Lange*n*, the Russian envoy, concerning it*. Except with Japan, the Chinese carry on, themselves, and in their own bottoms, little or no foreign trade; and it is only into one or two ports of their kingdom that they even admit the ships of foreign nations. Foreign trade, therefore, is, in China, every way confined within a much narrower circle than that to which it would naturally extend itself, if more freedom was allowed to it, either in their own ships, of in those of foreign nations.

41   Manufactures, as in a small bulk they frequently contain a great value, and can upon that account be transported at less expence from one country to another than most *p*parts*p* of rude produce, are, in almost all countries, the principal support of foreign trade.[34] In countries, besides, less extensive and less favourably circumstanced for interior commerce than China, they generally require the support of foreign trade. Without an extensive foreign market, they could not well flourish, either in countries so moderately extensive as to afford but a narrow home market; or in countries where the communication between one province and another was so difficult, as to render it impossible for the goods of any particular place to enjoy the whole of that home market which the country could afford. The perfection of manufacturing industry, it must be remembered, depends altogether upon the division of labour; and the degree to which the di-[32]vision of labour can be introduced into any manufacture, is necessarily regulated, it has already been shown, by the extent of the market.[35] But the great extent of

---

*o** See the Journal of Mr. De Lange in Bell's Travels, vol. ii. p. 258. 276. and 293. *o*

[The mandarins told De Lange, when he asked for a free passage for the caravan by the old road of Kerlinde: 'That they expected to have been freed from their importuning the council about their beggarly commerce, after they had been told so often, that the council would not embarrass themselves any more about affairs that were only beneficial to the Russes; and that, of course, they had only to return by the way they came.' (J. Bell, *Travels from St. Petersburg in Russia to diverse parts of Asia* (Glasgow, 1763), ii.293; See also ii.258 and 276.)]

---

n–n Langlet *1*   *o–o* 2–6   *p–p* sorts *1*

---

grands privileges, et on les préfere aux Marchands et aux Artisans.' (J. B. Du Halde, *Description geographique, historique, chronologique, politique, et physique de l'Empire de la Chine et de la Tartarie Chinoise* (Paris, 1735), ii.64.)

[32] 'The lands are as free as the people; no feudal services, and no fines of alienation; . . . none of that destructive possession, hatched in the delirium of the feudal system, under these auspices arise millions of processes . . .' (P. Poivre, *Voyages d'un philosophe*, translated as *Travels of a Philosopher*, 170–1.)

[33] Smith comments on the wealth of China, despite the lack of foreign trade, at IV.iii.c. 11, II.v.22; cf. III.i.7.

[34] See above, IV.i.29 and III.iv.20.   [35] Above, I.iii.

the empire of China, the vast multitude of its inhabitants, the variety of climate, and consequently of productions in its different provinces, and the easy communication by means of water carriage between the greater part of them, render the home market of that country of so great extent, as to be alone sufficient to support very great manufactures, and to admit of very considerable subdivisions of labour.[36] The home market of China is, perhaps, in extent, not much inferior to the market of all the different countries of Europe put together.[37] A more extensive foreign trade, however, which to this great home market added the foreign market of all the rest of the world; especially if any considerable part of this trade was carried on in Chinese ships; could scarce fail to increase very much the manufactures of China, and to improve very much the productive powers of its manufacturing industry.[38] By a more extensive navigation, the Chinese would naturally learn the art of using and constructing themselves all the different machines made use of in other countries, as well as *q* the other improvements of art and industry which are practised in all the different parts of the world. Upon their present plan they have little opportunity of improving themselves by the example of any other nation; except that of the Japanese.

42   The policy of ancient Egypt too, and that of the Gentoo government of Indostan, seem to have [33] favoured agriculture more than all other employments.[39]

43   Both in ancient Egypt and *r* Indostan, the whole body of the people was divided into different casts or tribes, each of which was confined, from father to son, to a particular employment or class of employments. The son of a priest was necessarily a priest; the son of a soldier, a soldier; the son of a labourer, a labourer; the son of a weaver, a weaver; the son of a taylor, a taylor; &c. In both countries, the cast of the priests held the highest rank, and that of the soldiers the next; and in both countries, the cast of the farmers and labourers was superior to the casts of merchants and manufacturers.[40]

44   The government of both countries was particularly attentive to the interest of agriculture. The works constructed by the ancient sovereigns of Egypt for the proper distribution of the waters of the Nile were famous in antiquity; and the ruined remains of some of them are still the admiration of travellers. Those of the same kind which were constructed by the antient sovereigns of Indostan, for the proper distribution of the waters of the

---

q all *1*   *r* in *1*

[36] See above, I.iii.7, where it is stated that China's opulence was derived from an inland navigation.
[37] 'L'historien dit que le commerce qui se fait dans l'intérieur de la Chine est si grand, que celui de l'Europe ne peut pas lui être comparé.' F. Quesnay, *Oeuvres economiques et philosophiques*, ed. A. Oncken (Paris, 1888), 603.)
[38] See above, I.ix.15.   [39] See II.v.22 and IV.iii.c.11.   [40] See above, I.vii.31.

Ganges as well as of many other rivers, though they have been less celebrated, seem to have been equally great. Both countries, accordingly, though subject occasionally to dearths, have been famous for their great fertility. Though both were extremely populous, yet, in years of moderate plenty, they were both able to export great quantities of grain to their neighbours.

45 [34] The antient Egyptians had a superstitious aversion to the sea; and as the Gentoo religion does not permit its followers to light a fire, nor consequently to dress any victuals upon the water, it in effect prohibits them from all distant sea voyages. Both the Egyptians and Indians must have depended almost altogether upon the navigation of other nations for the exportation of their surplus produce; and this dependency, as it must have confined the market, so it must have discouraged the increase of this surplus produce.[41] It must have discouraged too the increase of the manufactured produce more than that of the rude produce. Manufactures require a much more extensive market than the most important parts of the rude produce of the land. A single shoemaker will make more than three hundred pairs of shoes in the year; and his own family will not perhaps wear out six pairs. Unless therefore he has the custom of at least fifty such families as his own, he cannot dispose of the whole produce of his own labour.[42] The most numerous class of artificers will seldom, in a large country, make more than one in fifty or one in a hundred of a whole number of families contained in it. But in such large countries as France and England, the number of people employed in agriculture has by some authors been computed at a half, by others at a third, and by no author that I know of, at less than a fifth of the whole inhabitants of the country. But as the produce of the agriculture of both France and England is, the far greater part of it, con-[35]sumed at home, each person employed in it must, according to these computations, require little more than the custom of one, two, or, at most, [s]of[s] four such families as his own, in order to dispose of the whole produce of his own labour. Agriculture, therefore, can support itself under the discouragement of a confined market, much better than manufactures. In both antient Egypt and Indostan, indeed, the confinement of the foreign market was in some measure compensated by the conveniency of many inland navigations, which opened, in the most advantageous manner, the whole extent of the home market to every part of the produce of every different district of those countries. The great extent of Indostan too rendered the home market of that country very great, and sufficient to support a great variety of manufactures. But the small extent of antient Egypt, which was never equal to England, must at all times have rendered

[s–s] om. *I*

[41] See above, II.v.22.

[42] See above, I.iii.2.

the home market of that country too narrow for supporting any great variety of manufactures. Bengal, accordingly, the province of Indostan, which commonly exports the greatest quantity of rice, has always been more remarkable for the exportation of a great variety of manufactures, than for that of its grain. Antient Egypt, on the contrary, though it exported some manufactures, fine linen in particular, as well as some other goods, was always most distinguished for its great exportation of grain. It was long the granary of the Roman empire.

46   [36] The sovereigns of China, of antient Egypt, and of the different kingdoms into which Indostan has at different times been divided, have always derived the whole, or by far the most considerable part, of their revenue from some sort of land-tax or land-rent. This land-tax or land-rent, like the tithe in Europe, consisted in a certain proportion, a fifth, it is said, of the produce of the land, which was either delivered in kind, or paid in money, according to a certain valuation, and which therefore varied from year to year according to all the variations of the produce. It was natural, therefore, that the sovereigns of those countries should be particularly attentive to the interests of agriculture, upon the prosperity or declension of which immediately depended the yearly increase or diminution of their own revenue.[43]

47   The policy of the antient republicks of Greece, and that of Rome, though it honoured agriculture more than manufactures or foreign trade, yet seems rather to have discouraged the latter employments, than to have given any direct or intentional encouragement to the former. In several of the antient states of Greece, foreign trade was prohibited altogether; and in several others the employments of artificers and manufacturers were considered as hurtful to the strength and agility of the human body, as rendering it incapable of those habits which their military and gymnastic exercises endeavoured to form in it, and as thereby disqualifying it more [37] or less *for* undergoing the fatigues and encountering the dangers of war.[44] Such occupations were considered as fit only for slaves, and the free citizens of the state were prohibited from exercising them.[45] Even in those states

---

– from *I*

[43] See below, V.ii.d.5.

[44] See below, V.i.f. 39–45, where Greek education is described.

[45] LJ (B) 39, ed. Cannan 27 states that 'At Rome and Athens the arts were carried on by slaves, and the Lacedemonians went so far as not to allow any freemen to be brought up to mechanic employments, because they imagined that they hurt the body.' LJ (A) iv.82 also comments on this belief, in stating that the Greeks considered, 'and I believe, with justice, that every sort of constant labour hurt the shape and rendered him less fit for military exercises, which made the chief view of all lawgivers at that time. (We can know a taylor by his gait.)' Montesquieu also noted that the Romans regarded 'commerce and the arts as the occupations of slaves: they did not practice them.' (*Considérations*, 98–9.) A similar point is made with regard to the Greeks in *Esprit*, IV.viii. Cf. Cicero, *De Officiis*, I.xlii. While confirming that most trades were sordid and mean, Cicero argued however

where no such prohibition took place, as in Rome and Athens, the great body of the people were in effect excluded from all the trades which are now commonly exercised by the lower sort of the inhabitants of towns. Such trades were, at Athens and Rome, all occupied by the slaves of the rich, who exercised them for the benefit of their masters, whose wealth, power, and protection, made it almost impossible for a poor freeman to find a market for his work, when it came into competition with that of the slaves of the rich.[46] Slaves, however, are very seldom inventive; and all the most important improvements, either in machinery, or in ᵘtheᵘ arrangement and distribution of work which facilitate and abridge labour, have been the discoveries of freemen.[47] Should a slave propose any improvement of this kind, his master would be very apt to consider the proposal as the suggestion of laziness, and ᵛ a desire to save his own labour at the master's expence.[48] The poor slave, instead of reward, would probably meet with much abuse, perhaps with some punishment. In the manufactures carried on by slaves, therefore, more labour must generally have been employed to execute the same quantity of work, than in those carried on by freemen.[49] The work of the former must, upon that account, generally have been dearer [38] than that of the latter.[50] The Hungarian mines, it is remarked by Mr. Montesquieu,[51] though not ʷricherʷ, have always been wrought with less expence, and therefore with more profit, than the Turkish mines in their neighbourhood. The Turkish mines are wrought by slaves; and the arms of those slaves are the only machines which the Turks have ever thought of employing. The Hungarian mines are wrought by freemen, who employ a ˣgreatˣ deal of machinery, by which they facilitate and abridge their own labour.[52] From the very little that is known about the price of manufactures in the times of the Greeks and Romans, it would

---

ᵘ⁻ᵘ that *1*   ᵛ of *1, 4e–5*   ʷ⁻ʷ more rich *1*   ˣ⁻ˣ good *1*

---

that 'of all the occupations by which gain is secured, none is better than agriculture, none more profitable, none more delightful, none more becoming to a freeman.' Translated by W. Miller in Loeb Classical Library (1921), 155.

[46] A very similar expression is used above, IV.vii.a.3.   [47] See above, I.i.8 and note 17.

[48] See LJ (A) vi. 41–2, and above, I.i.8. In LJ (B) 217, ed. Cannan 167, some improvements in milling are ascribed to the slave. However, it is noted in LJ (B) 299 ed. Cannan 231, that slaves cannot work as well as free men because 'they have no motive to labour but the dread of punishment, and can never invent any machine for facilitating their business'. Smith also noted that any suggestion from the slave with regard to facilitating his work was likely to be regarded as laziness.

[49] Montesquieu held that as 'A general rule: A nation in slavery labours more to preserve than to acquire; a free nation more to acquire than to preserve.' (*Esprit*, XX.iv.9.)

[50] See above, III.ii.9 and I.viii.41.

[51] 'The Turkish mines in the Bannat of Temeswaer, though richer than those of Hungary, did not yield so much; because the working of them depended entirely on the strength of their slaves.' (Montesquieu, *Esprit*, XV.viii.3.)

[52] The same point is made in LJ (B) 299–300, ed. Cannan 231, with regard to the use of labour in Turkish and Hungarian mines.

appear that those of the finer sort were excessively dear. Silk sold for its
weight in gold. It was not, indeed, in those times a European manufacture;
and as it was all brought from the East Indies, the distance of the carriage
may in some measure account for the greatness of the price. The price,
however, which a lady, it is said, would sometimes pay for a piece of very
fine linen, seems to have been equally extravagant; and as linen was always
either *ᵃ*ᵃ European, or, at farthest, an Egyptian manufacture, this high
price can be accounted for only by the great expence of the labour which
must have been employed about it, and the expence of this labour again
could arise from nothing but the aukwardness of the machinery which it
made use of. The price of fine woollens too, though not quite so extravagant, seems however to have been much above that of the present times.
Some cloths, we are told by [39] Pliny, dyed in a particular manner, cost a
hundred denarii, or three pounds six shillings and eight pence the pound
weight*.[53] Others dyed in another manner cost a thousand denarii the
pound weight, or thirty-three *ᵃ*pound*ᵃ* six shillings and eight pence. The
Roman pound, it must be remembered, contained only twelve of our
avoirdupois ounces.[54] This high price, indeed, seems to have been principally owing to the dye. But had not the cloths themselves been much dearer
than any which are made in the present times, so very expensive a dye
would not probably have been bestowed upon them. The disproportion
would have been too great between the value of the accessory and that of
the principal. The price mentioned by the same† author of some Triclinaria,
a sort of woollen pillows or cushions made use of to lean upon as they
reclined upon their couches at table, passes all credibility; some of them
being said to have cost more than thirty thousand, others more than three
hundred thousand pounds. This high price too is not said to have arisen
from the dye. In the dress of the people of fashion of both sexes, there
seems to have been much less variety, it is observed by Doctor Arbuthnot,[55]

*ᶻ** Plin. l.ix.c.39ᶻ ['Cornelius Nepos, who died in the principate of the late lamented
Augustus, says: "In my young days the violent purple dye was the vogue, a pound of
which sold at 100 denarii; and not much later the red purple of Taranto. This was followed
by the double-dyed Tyrian purple, which it was impossible to buy for 1000 denarii per
pound."' (Pliny, *Natural History*, IX.lxiii, translated by H. Rackham in Loeb Classical
Library (1950), iii.255.)]

ᵇ† Plin. l.viii.c.48ᵇ ['Metallus Scipio counts it among the charges against Capito that
Babylonian coverlets [tricliniaria] were already then sold for 800,000 sesterces, which
lately cost the Emperor Nero 4,000,000.' (Ibid. VIII.lxxiv, trans. Rackham, iii.137–9)].

    ʸ⁻ʸ an *4–6*   ᶻ⁻ᶻ *2–6*   ᵃ⁻ᵃ pounds, *1, 4–6*   ᵇ⁻ᵇ *2–6*

---

[53] See above, I.xi.k.1.   [54] See above, I.iv.10.

[55] C. Arbuthnot, *Tables of Ancient Coins, Weights and Measures* (London, 1727), 140–8.
Arbuthnot also quoted (142) the same example of extravagance concerning triclinaria as
Smith: 'It seems they were extravagant in their Triclinaria, which one may translate
Quilts or Carpets. Capito was reproached by Metellus, that he had paid for Babylonian
Triclinaria £6,458 6s. 8d. This is nothing to the price paid by Nero mentioned afterwards
viz. £32,291 13s. 4d.'

in antient than in modern times; and the very little variety which we find in that of the antient statues confirms his observation. He infers from this, that their dress must upon the whole have been cheaper than ours: but the conclusion does not seem to follow. When the expence of fashionable dress is [40] very great, the variety must be very small. But when, by the improvements in the productive powers of manufacturing art and industry, the expence of any one dress comes to be very moderate, the variety will naturally be very great. The rich not being able to distinguish themselves by the expence of any one dress, will naturally endeavour to do so by the multitude and variety of their dresses.[56]

48　　The greatest and most important branch of the commerce of every nation, it has already been observed,[57] is that which is carried on between the inhabitants of the town and those of the country. The inhabitants of the town draw from the country the rude produce which constitutes both the materials of their work and the fund of their subsistence; and they pay for this rude produce by sending back to the country a certain portion of it manufactured and prepared for immediate use. The trade which is carried on between ᶜtheseᶜ two different sets of people, consists ultimately in a certain quantity of rude produce exchanged for a certain quantity of manufactured produce. The dearer the latter, therefore, the cheaper the former; and whatever tends in any country to raise the price of manufactured produce, tends to lower that of the rude produce of the land, and thereby to discourage agriculture. The smaller the quantity of manufactured produce which any given quantity of rude produce, or, what comes to the same thing, which the price of any given quantity of rude produce is capable of purchasing, the smaller the ᵈexchangeableᵈ value of that given quantity [41] of rude produce; the smaller the encouragement which either the landlord has to increase its quantity by improving, or the farmer by cultivating the land. Whatever, besides, tends to diminish in any country the number of artificers and manufacturers, tends to diminish the home market, the most important of all markets for the rude produce of the land, and thereby still further to discourage agriculture.

49　　Those systems, therefore, which preferring agriculture to all other employments, in order to promote it, impose restraints upon manufactures and foreign trade, act contrary to the very end which they propose, and indirectly discourage that very species of industry which they mean to promote. They are so far, perhaps, more inconsistent than even the mercantile system. That system, by encouraging manufactures and foreign trade more than agriculture, turns a certain portion of the capital of the society from supporting a more advantageous, to support a less advan-

ᶜ⁻ᶜ those *1*　　　　ᵈ⁻ᵈ real *1*

---

[56] See above, I.xi.c.31.　　　[57] See above, III.i.1.

tageous species of industry. But still it really and in the end encourages that species of industry which it means to promote. Those agricultural systems, on the contrary, really and in the end discourage their own favourite species of industry.

50   It is thus that every system which endeavours, either, by extraordinary encouragements, to draw towards a particular species of industry a greater share of the capital of the society than what would naturally go to it; or, by extraordinary restraints, to force from a particular species of industry some [42] share of the capital which would otherwise be employed in it; is in reality subversive of the great purpose which it means to promote. It retards, instead of accelerating, the progress of the society towards real wealth and greatness; and diminishes, instead of increasing, the real value of the annual produce of its land and labour.[58]

51   All systems either of preference or of restraint, therefore, being thus completely taken away, the obvious and simple system of natural liberty establishes itself of its own accord.[59] Every man, as long as he does not violate the laws of justice, is left perfectly free to pursue his own interest his own way, and to bring both his industry and capital into competition with those of any other man, or order of men. The sovereign is completely discharged from a duty, in the attempting to perform which he must always be exposed to innumerable delusions, and for the proper performance of which no human wisdom or knowledge could ever be sufficient; the duty of superintending the industry of private people, and of directing it towards the employments most suitable to the interest of the society.[60] According to the system of natural liberty, the sovereign has only three duties to attend to; three duties of great importance, indeed, but plain and intelligible to common understandings: first, the duty of protecting the society from the violence and invasion of other independent societies; secondly, the duty of protecting, as far as possible, every member of the society from the injustice or oppression of every other member of it, or the duty of establishing [43] an exact administration of justice;[61] and, thirdly, the duty of erecting and maintaining certain

[58] See IV.ii.2 and note for an elaboration of this doctrine.
[59] See above, IV.vii.c.44.
[60] See also above, IV.ii.10, and below, V.i.c.18; cf. IV.vii.b.44 where Smith comments with reference to the colonies, that regulation of their activities constitutes a 'manifest violation of the most sacred rights of mankind'. Dugald Stewart (IV.25) quoted from one of Smith's (now lost) manuscripts, to the effect that 'Little else is requisite to carry a state to the highest degree of opulence, from the lowest barbarism, but peace, easy taxes, and a tolerable administration of justice.'
[61] Smith especially emphasized the need for an exact administration of justice in the TMS II.ii.3.4, in arguing that if beneficence is an ornament to society, justice must be regarded as 'the main pillar that upholds the whole edifice' so that if it was removed, the 'immense fabric of human society' must 'in a moment crumble into atoms'. It was in this context that Smith also said that: 'Society may subsist among different men, as among different merchants, from a sense of its utility, without any mutual love or affection; and

publick works and certain publick institutions, which it can never be for the interest of any individual, or small number of individuals, to erect and maintain; because the profit could never repay the expence to any individual or small number of individuals, though it may frequently do much more than repay it to a great society.[62]

52   The proper performance of those several duties of the sovereign necessarily supposes a certain expence; and this expence again necessarily requires a certain revenue to support it. In the following book, therefore, I shall endeavour to explain; first, what are the necessary expences of the sovereign or common-wealth; and which of those expences ought to be defrayed by the general contribution of the whole society; and which of them, by that of some particular part only, or of some particular members of the society: secondly, what are the different methods in which the whole society may be made to contribute towards defraying the expences incumbent on the whole society, and what are the principal advantages and inconveniencies of each of those methods: and, thirdly, what are the reasons and causes which have induced almost all modern governments to mortgage some part of this revenue, or to contract debts, and what have been the effects of those debts upon the real wealth, the annual produce of the land and labour of the society. The following book, therefore, will naturally be divided into three chapters.

though no man in it should owe any obligation, or be bound in gratitude to any other, it may still be upheld by a mercenary exchange of good offices according to an agreed valuation.' (II.ii.3.2.)

[62] A similar expression is used below, V. i.c.1.

BOOK V

Of the Revenue of the Sovereign or Commonwealth

CHAPTER I

Of the Expences of the Sovereign or Commonwealth

PART FIRST
Of the Expence of Defence

1 THE first duty of the sovereign, that of protecting the society from the violence and invasion of other independent societies, can be performed only by means of a military force.[1] But the expence both of preparing this military force in time of peace, and of employing it in time of war, is very different in the different states of society, in the different periods of improvement.[2]

2 Among nations of hunters, the lowest and rudest state of society, such

[1] LJ (A) i.1 argues that 'The first and chief design of every system of government is to maintain justice; to prevent the members of a society from incroaching on one another's property, or seizing what is not their own.' Smith goes on to add that 'it must also be necessary to have some means of protecting the state from foreign injuries'.

[2] LJ (A) i.27 comments that 'There are four distinct states which mankind passes thro . . . 1st, the Age of Hunters; 2ndly, the Age of Shepherds; 3rdly, the age of agriculture; and 4thly, the Age of Commerce.' A similar statement occurs in LJ (B) 149, ed. Cannan 107. The Anderson Notes (1–3) mention three 'states of perfection in society' which correspond very closely to the stages of hunting, shepherds, and agriculture. The idea of a division of economic stages was widespread. See especially, Kames's *Sketches* (1774), I.ii, and the same author's *Historical Law Tracts* (1758), especially Tract II, on 'Promises and Covenants'. See also Adam Ferguson's *History of Civil Society* (1767), II.ii, iii and Steuart's *Principles*, ed. Skinner lxiii–lxxii. The 'stadial' thesis is also the organizing principle behind John Millar's *Origin of the Distinction of Ranks* (1771). A similar thesis can also be found in Mirabeau's *Philosophie rurale* (1763), in R. L. Meek, *The Economics of Physiocracy*, 60–4. In addition to Rousseau's essay on the *Origin of Inequality* (1755), the thesis also features in two discourses written by Turgot which were unpublished at the time. These were 'A Philosophical Review of the Successive Advances of the Human Mind' and his 'Plan of the Discourses on Universal History'. These passages in Turgot were translated by W. Walker Stephens in his *Life and Writings of Turgot* (London, 1895); see, for example, pp. 161–2 and 176–80. The same essays are now included in R. L. Meek, *Turgot on Progress, Sociology and Economics*. Turgot also makes use of a distinction between hunting, pastoral, and agrarian stages in the *Reflections*, LIV. Cf. Montesquieu, *Esprit*, I.iii.14, where it is stated that laws 'should be in relation to the climate of each country, to the quality of its soil, to its situation and extent, to the principal occupations of the natives, whether husbandmen, huntsmen, or shepherds'. Montesquieu also considered the relationship between population and the means of 'procuring subsistence' in XVIII.x.

as we find it among the native tribes of North America, every man is a warrior as well as a hunter.[3] When he goes to war, either to defend his society, or to revenge the injuries which have been done to it by other societies, he maintains himself by his own labour, [45] in the same manner as when he lives at home. His society, for in this state of things there is properly neither sovereign nor commonwealth, is at no sort of expence, either to prepare him for the field, or to maintain him while he is in it.[4]

3   Among nations of shepherds, a more advanced state of society, such as we find it among the Tartars and Arabs, every man is, in the same manner, a warrior.[5] Such nations have commonly no fixed habitation, but live, either in tents, or in a sort of covered waggons which are easily transported from place to place. The whole tribe or nation changes its situation according to the different seasons of the year, as well as according to other accidents. When its herds and flocks have consumed the forage of one part of the country, it removes to another, and from that to a third. In the dry season, it comes down to the banks of the rivers; in the wet season it retires to the upper country.[6] When such a nation goes to war, the warriors will not trust their herds and flocks to the feeble defence of their old men, their women and children; and their old men, their women and children, will not be left behind without defence and without subsistence. The whole nation, besides, being accustomed to a wandering life, even in time of peace, easily takes the field in time of war.[7] Whether it marches as an army, or moves about as a company of herdsmen, the way of life is nearly the same, though the object proposed by it *be* very different. They all go to war together, therefore, and every one does as well as [46] he can. Among the

a-a is *I*

---

[3] It is stated at II.iii.34 that the inhabitants of Great Britain at the time of Julius Caesar's invasion were virtually in this state. The American Indians are stated to be still in the hunting stage, 'the most rude and barbarous of any', at LJ (A) ii.97. In LJ (A) iv.5 Lafitau and Charlevoix are cited as the authors who 'give us the most distinct account of the manners of those nations'.

[4] Cf. LJ (B) 19, ed. Cannan 14; 'In a nation of hunters there is properly no government at all.' The argument is developed more fully in the second part of this chapter.

[5] Cf. LJ (A) i.47: 'The introduction of shepherds made their habitation somewhat more fixed but still very uncertain.' It is remarked in LJ (A) iv.47-8, however, that partly owing to the nature of the terrain certain shepherd nations 'generally have no fixt habitations. The Tartars live in a sort of waggons, or rather houses set upon wheels; their country is altogether plain and void of wood or stones to interrupt them; not a tree nor hill over the whole country, so that they have nothing to interrupt them in their progress. A people in this state have no attachment to their particular spot where they have taken up their habitation.' Smith also refers at p. 48-9 to families being transported in waggons covered with a 'sort of felt', and added that 'the severall nations in Germany have all been in this state, though they are now removed out of it' (50).

[6] Smith considers what he calls 'stationary' as distinct from 'wandering' shepherds at § 26.

[7] Cf. LJ (A) iv.77: 'In a nation of shepherds everyone without distinction goes to war. This was the case amongst the Children of Israel, and is so at present amongst the Arabians and Tartars.' The same point is made in LJ (B) 37, 335, ed. Cannan 26 and 261, cf. LJ (A) iv.13.

Tartars, even the women have been frequently known to engage in battle. If they conquer, whatever belongs to the hostile tribe is the recompence of the victory. But if they are vanquished, all is lost, and not only their herds and flocks, but their women and children, become the booty of the conqueror. Even the greater part of those who survive the action are obliged to submit to him for the sake of immediate subsistence. The rest are commonly dissipated and dispersed in the desart.

4   The ordinary life, the ordinary exercises of a Tartar or Arab, prepare him sufficiently for war. Running, wrestling, cudgel-playing, throwing the javelin, drawing the bow, &c. are the common pastimes of those who live in the open air, and are all of them the images of war. When a Tartar or Arab actually goes to war, he is maintained, by his own herds and flocks which he carries with him, in the same manner as in peace. His chief or sovereign, for those nations have all chiefs or sovereigns, is at no sort of expence in preparing him for the field; and when he is in it, the chance of plunder is the only pay which he either expects or requires.

5   An army of hunters can seldom exceed two or three hundred men. The precarious subsistence which the chace affords could seldom allow a greater number to keep together for any considerable time.[8] An army of shepherds, on the contrary, may sometimes amount to two or three hundred thousand. As long as nothing stops their progress, as long as they can go on from [47] one district, of which they have consumed the forage, to another which is yet entire; there seems to be scarce any limit to the number who can march on together. A nation of hunters can never be formidable to the civilized nations in their neighbourhood. A nation of shepherds may. Nothing can be more contemptible than an Indian war in North America.[9] Nothing,

---

[8] Smith compared the numbers of hunters and shepherds in FA: 'In a savage tribe of North Americans, who are generally hunters, the greatest number who can subsist easily together seldom exceeds one hundred, or one hundred & fifty persons.' By contrast: 'In a tribe of Tartars or wild Arabs, who are generally shepherds, a greater number can live conveniently in one place. They do not depend upon the precarious accidents of the chace for subsistence, but upon the milk & flesh of their herds & flocks, who graze in the fields adjoining to the village.' Smith also pointed out in this connection that the larger social groupings gave greater scope to the division of labour, citing the authority of Peter Kolben in support. See above, IV.vii.c.100. Montesquieu also comments on 'population in the relation it bears to the manner of procuring subsistence' and states that peoples who do not cultivate the earth 'can scarcely form a great nation. If they are herdsmen and shepherds, they have need of an extensive country to furnish subsistence for a small number; if they live by hunting, their number must be still less, and in order to find the means of life they must constitute a very small nation.' (*Esprit*, XVIII.x.2.) Cf. Cantillon, *Essai*, 90–1, ed. Higgs, 69, where the limitation on population growth among the tribes of North America is also attributed to the mode of earning subsistence. Sir James Steuart developed a rather similar argument, *Principles* I.iii–v, ed. Skinner lxiii–lxvi, lxxi.

[9] Cf. LJ (A) iv.38–9: 'hunters cannot form any very great schemes, nor can their expeditions be very formidable. It is impossible that 200 hunters could live together for a fortnight . . . So that there can be no great danger from such a nation. And the great astonishment our colonies in America are in on account of these expeditions, proceeds

on the contrary, can be more dreadful than a Tartar invasion has frequently been in Asia.[10] The judgment of Thucydides,[11] that both Europe and Asia could not resist the Scythians united, has been verified by the experience of all ages.[12] The inhabitants of the extensive, but defenceless plains of Scythia or Tartary, have been frequently united under the dominion of the chief of some conquering horde or clan; and the havock and devastation of Asia have always signalized their union. The inhabitants of the inhospitable desarts of Arabia, the other great nation of shepherds, have never been united but once; under Mahomet and his immediate successors. Their union, which was more the effect of religious enthusiasm than of conquest, was signalized in the same manner. If the hunting nations of America should ever become shepherds, their neighbourhood would be much more dangerous to the European colonies than it is at present.

6   In a yet more advanced state of society; among those nations of husbandmen who have little foreign commerce and no other manufactures, but those coarse and houshold ones which almost [48] every private family prepares for its own use; every man, in the same manner, either is a warrior, or easily becomes such.[13] They who live by agriculture generally pass the

intirely from their unacquaintedness with arms, for tho they may plague them and hurt some of the back settlements they could never injure the body of the people.' Cf. LJ (B) 28, ed. Cannan 20.

[10] LJ (A) iii.41 remarks that the 'Tartars, a savage nation, have overrun all Asia severall times, and Persia above twelve times.' Smith also refers to the power of the nomadic hordes in LJ (B) 29–30, 288, ed. Cannan 20–1, 224. In LJ (A) iv.40 he refers to the exploits of Mahomet and Tamerlane who invaded Asia with 'above 1,000,000 of men' and credited Ghengis Khan with even greater numbers. He added however that the ease with which the Tartars combined together was related to the nature of the terrain, which was lacking in 'mountains or rough ground . . . barriers or woods'. Cf. Montesquieu, *Esprit*, XVIII. xi.2. See also XVIII.xix, where he comments on the 'liberty of the Arabs and the Servitude of the Tartars'.

[11] 'Not only are the nations of Europe unable to compete, but even in Asia, nation against nation, there is none which can make a stand against the Scythians if they all act in concert.' (Thucydides, *History of the Peloponnesian War*, ii.97, translated by C. F. Smith in Loeb Classical Library (1919), i.446–7.) It is stated in LRBL ii.25, ed. Lothian 90, that there is 'no author who has more distinctly explained the causes of events than Thucydides'. It is also stated at ii.49, ed. Lothian 102, that Thucydides' 'was a proper design of historicall writing'. Smith also says in LJ (A) iv.65 that this author together with Homer, had provided 'the best account which is to be had of the ancient state of Greece'. Hume shared Smith's enthusiasm for Thucydides in remarking in his essay 'Of the Populousness of Ancient Nations' that 'the first page of Thucydides is, in my opinion, the commencement of real history' (*Essays Moral, Political, and Literary*, ed. Green and Grose, i.414).

[12] See also § 44 where it is pointed out that modern arms have redressed the balance between civilized and primitive peoples.

[13] Cf. LJ (A) i.29: 'We find . . . that in almost all countries the age of shepherds preceded that of agriculture. The Tartars and Arabians subsist almost entirely by their flocks and herds. The Arabs have a little agriculture, but the Tartars none at all. The whole of the savage nations which subsist by flocks have no notion of cultivating the ground. The only instance that has the appearance of an objection to this rule is the state of the North American Indians. They, tho they have no conception of flocks and herds, have nevertheless some notion of agriculture.' The same point is made in LJ (B) 150, ed. Cannan 108.

whole day in the open air, exposed to all the inclemencies of the seasons. The hardiness of their ordinary life prepares them for the fatigues of war, to some of which their necessary occupations bear a ᵇgreatᵇ analogy.[14] The necessary occupation of a ditcher prepares him to work in the trenches, and to fortify a camp as well as to enclose a field. The ordinary pastimes of such husbandmen are the same as those of shepherds, and are in the same manner the images of war. But as husbandmen have less leisure than shepherds, they are not so frequently employed in those pastimes. They are soldiers, but soldiers not quite so much masters of their exercise. Such as they are, however, it seldom costs the sovereign or commonwealth any expence to prepare them for the field.

7   Agriculture, even in its rudest and lowest state, supposes a settlement; some sort of fixed habitation which cannot be abandoned without great loss. When a nation of mere husbandmen, therefore, goes to war, the whole people cannot take the field together. The old men, the women and children, at least, must remain at home to take care of the habitation.[15] All the men of the military age, however, may take the field, and, in small nations of this kind, have frequently done so. In every nation the men of the military age are supposed to amount to about a fourth or ᶜaᶜ fifth part of the whole body of the [49] people. If the campaign too should begin after seed-time, and end before harvest, both the husbandman and his principal labourers can be spared from the farm without much loss. He trusts that the work which must be done in the mean time can be well enough executed by the old men, the women and the children. He is not unwilling, therefore, to serve without pay during ᵈa shortᵈ campaign, and it frequently costs the sovereign or commonwealth as little to maintain him in the field as to prepare him for it. The citizens of all the different states of antient Greece seem to have served in this manner till after the second Persian war; and the people of Peloponesus till after the Peloponesian war.[16] The Peloponesians, Thucydides observes,[17] generally left the field in the summer,

---

ᵇ⁻ᵇ good deal of *1*   ᶜ⁻ᶜ *2–6*   ᵈ⁻ᵈ so short a *1*

---

[14] See below, V.ii.a.15, where it is pointed out that retainers in the feudal period were also generally fit for war by virtue of their occupations.

[15] It is also remarked in FA that: 'By means of agriculture the same quantity of ground not only produces corn but is made capable of supporting a much greater number of cattle than before. A much greater number of people, therefore, may easily subsist in the same place.'

[16] Cf. LRBL ii.143, ed. Lothian 144: 'The Battle of Platea, where by the advice of Pericles the soldiers first received pay from the publick, gave the first beginning to the democraticall government; and the commerce which followed it strengthened that change.' LJ (B) 308, ed. Cannan 238, comments that 'every one of the Athenians went to war at his own expence. The same was the case with our feudal lords, the burthen of going to war was connected with the duty of the tenant or vassal.' Cf. V.ii.a.14,15.

[17] 'For before this summer the enemy's invasions, being of short duration, did not prevent the Athenians from making full use of the land during the rest of the year; but

and returned home to reap the harvest.[18] The Roman people under their kings, and during the first ages of the republick, served in the same manner.[19] It was not till the siege of Veii, that they, who staid at home, began to contribute something towards maintaining those who went to war.[20] In the European monarchies, which were founded upon the ruins of the Roman empire, both before and for some time after the establishment of what is properly called the feudal law,[21] the great lords, with all their immediate dependents, used to serve the crown at their own expence. In the field, in the same manner as at home, they maintained themselves by their own revenue, and not by any stipend or pay which they received from the king upon that particular occasion.

8   [50] In a more advanced state of society, two different causes contribute to render it altogether impossible that they, who take the field, should maintain themselves at their own expence. Those two causes are, the progress of manufactures, and the improvement in the art of war.[22]

9   Though a husbandman should be employed in an expedition, provided it begins after seed-time and ends before harvest, the interruption of his business will not always occasion any considerable diminution of his revenue. Without the intervention of his labour, nature does herself the

at this time, the occupation being continuous . . . the Athenians were suffering great damage.' (Thucydides, *History of the Peloponnesian War*, vii.27, translated by C. F. Smith in Loeb Classical Library (1923), iv.48–9.)

[18] Cf. LJ (A) iv.77–8: 'In this state the campaigns were only summer ones. They continued but three or four months in the middle of the summer, after the spring and before the harvest work. They could easily be absent in the intermediate time, as the corn grows and the crop comes on, if the season favours, as well as if they were at home. A shepherds flock feeds tho he is not with it. Nothing therefore detains them. This was the case with the Peloponesians at the time of the Peloponnesian war, and had been so some time before at Athens, as Lysias mentions . . .' See also LJ (B) 38, ed. Cannan 26.

[19] 'As the Roman generals hoped more from a siege than from an assault, they even began the erection of winter quarters—a new thing to the Roman soldier—and planned to carry the campaign on, straight through the winter . . . the young men . . . were no longer free, even in winter and the stormy season, to see to their homes and their affairs.' (Livy, v.2, translated by B. O. Foster in Loeb Classical Library (1924), iii.4–7.)

[20] '. . . the senate . . . granted the people the most seasonable boon which has ever been bestowed on them by the chiefs of state, when they decreed, without waiting for any suggestion by the plebs or their tribunes, that the soldiers should be paid from the public treasury, whereas till then every man had served at his own costs.' (Livy, iv.59, trans. Foster, ii.450–5.)

[21] Allodial is distinguished from feudal at III.iv.8.

[22] In LJ (A) iv Smith cited two causes of decline in military effectiveness: manufactures and improvements in the art of war. The thesis is illustrated by reference to Greece and Rome at pp. 75–87 and 87–104. See also LJ (B) 37–43, ed. Cannan 26–30. It is noted at 335, ed. Cannan 260–1, that in the early stages of society war was thought of as an honourable occupation, and therefore as suitable for the higher classes: 'But when arts and manufactures encreased and were thought worthy of attention, and men found that they could rise in dignity by applying to them, and it became inconvenient for the rich to go out to war, from a principle of avarice, these arts which were at first despised by the active and ambitious soon came to claim their whole attention.' As a result, Smith suggested, military duties fell to the 'meanest' classes, 'our present condition in Great Brittain.'

greater part of the work which remains to be done. But the moment that an artificer, a smith, a carpenter, or a weaver, for example, quits his work-house, the sole source of his revenue is completely dried up.[23] Nature does nothing for him, he does all for himself. When he takes the field, therefore, in defence of the publick, as he has no revenue to maintain himself, he must necessarily be maintained by the publick. But in a country of which a great part of the inhabitants are artificers and manufacturers, a great part of the people who go to war must be drawn from those classes, and must there-fore be maintained by the publick as long as they are employed in its service.[24]

10   When the art of war too has gradually grown up to be a very intricate and complicated science, when the event of war ceases to be determined, as in the first ages of society, by a single irregular skirmish or battle, but when the contest is generally spun out through several different cam-[51] paigns, each of which lasts during the greater part of the year; it becomes universally necessary that the publick should maintain those who serve the publick in war, at least while they are employed in that service. What-ever in time of peace might be the ordinary occupation of those who go to war, so very tedious and expensive a service would otherwise be by far too heavy a burden upon them. After the second Persian war, accordingly, the armies of Athens seem to have been generally composed of mercenary troops; consisting, indeed, partly of citizens, but partly too of foreigners;[25] and all of them equally hired and paid at the expence of the state. From the time of the siege of Veii, the armies of Rome received pay for their service during the time which they remained in the field. Under the feudal govern-ments the military service both of the great lords and of their immediate dependents was, after a certain period, universally exchanged for a payment in money, which was employed to maintain those who served in their stead.

11   The number of those who can go to war, in proportion to the whole number of the people, is necessarily much smaller in a civilized, than in a rude state of society. In a civilized society, as the soldiers are maintained altogether by the labour of those who are not soldiers, the number of the former *can never* exceed what the latter can maintain, over and above maintaining, in a manner suitable to their respective stations, both them-selves and the other officers of government, and [52] law, whom they are obliged to maintain. In the little agrarian states of antient Greece, a fourth

e-e never can *I*

---

[23] Cf. LJ (A) iv.79: 'Every hour a smith or a weaver is absent from his loom or the anvill his work is at a stop, which is not the case with the flocks of a shepherd or the fields of the husbandman.'

[24] See above, II.iii.2.

[25] LJ (A) iv.84–5 comments that 'This effect commerce and arts had on all the states of Greece. We see Demosthenes urging them to go out to battle themselves, instead of their mercenaries which their army then consisted of.'

or a fifth part of the whole body of the people considered themselves as soldiers, and would sometimes, it is said, take the field.[26] Among the civilized nations of modern Europe, it is commonly computed, that not more than one hundredth part of the inhabitants of any country can be employed as soldiers, without ruin to the country *f*which pays the expence of their service*f*.

12   The expence of preparing the army for the field seems not to have become considerable in any nation, till long after that of maintaining it in the field had devolved entirely upon the sovereign or commonwealth. In all the different republicks of antient Greece, to learn his military exercises, was a necessary part of education imposed by the state upon every free citizen.[27] In every city there seems to have been a publick field, in which, under the protection of the publick magistrate, the young people were taught their different exercises by different masters. In this very simple institution, consisted the whole expence which any Grecian state seems ever to have been at, in preparing its citizens for war. In antient Rome the exercises of the Campus Martius answered the same purpose with those of the Gymnasium in antient Greece. Under the feudal governments, the many publick ordinances that the citizens of every district should practise archery as well as several other military exercises, were intended for promoting the same purpose, but do not seem to have promoted it so [53] well. Either from want of interest in the officers entrusted with the execution of those ordinances, or from some other cause, they appear to have been universally neglected; and in the progress of all those governments, military exercises seem to have gone gradually into disuse among the great body of the people.

13   In the republicks of antient Greece and Rome, during the whole period of their existence, and under the feudal governments for a considerable time after their first establishment, the trade of a soldier was not a separate, distinct trade, which constituted the sole or principal occupation of a

f–f at whose expence they are employed *1*

---

[26] It is stated in LJ (A) iv.78–80 that advance in arts and improvement must diminish the military power of the state by reducing the number of people fitted for war. In the case of Greece the proportion available was stated to be one in four, falling to one in a hundred as the society progressed economically. The same figure is cited for Britain, 81. Similar points are made in LJ (B) 38, ed. Cannan 26–7. Smith discusses a related issue at 331–2, ed. Cannan 257–8, in commenting on the decline of martial spirit which is consequent on economic advance. He cites the inroads made by the savage Highlanders during the Rebellion of 1745 as evidence in support of his general contention.

LJ (B) 347, ed. Cannan 272, does cite one improvement which followed on the development of commerce, namely in the treatment of prisoners. In contrasting the situation of ancient and modern republics, Montesquieu remarked that 'Today the proportion of soldiers to the rest of the people is one to a hundred, whereas with them it could easily be one to eight.' (*Considérations*, 39.) The problems attending the decline in martial spirit as a result of economic 'advance' were particularly emphasized by Kames, *Sketches*, II.vi–vii.

[27] Public education in Greece and Rome is described at V.i.f.39–45.

particular class of citizens. Every subject of the state, whatever might be the ordinary trade or occupation by which he gained his livelihood, considered himself, upon all ordinary occasions, as fit likewise to exercise the trade of a soldier, and upon many extraordinary occasions as bound to exercise it.

14   The art of war, however, as it is certainly the noblest of all arts, so in the progress of improvement it necessarily becomes one of the most complicated among them. The state of the mechanical, as well as of some other arts, with which it is necessarily connected, determines the degree of perfection to which it is capable of being carried at any particular time. But in order to carry it to this degree of perfection, it is necessary that it should become the sole or principal occupation of a particular class of citizens, and the division of labour is as necessary for the improvement of this, as of every other art. Into [54] other arts the division of labour is naturally introduced by the prudence of individuals, who find that they promote their private interest better by confining themselves to a particular trade, than by exercising a great number. But it is the wisdom of the state only which can render the trade of a soldier a particular trade separate and distinct from all others.[28] A private citizen who, in time of profound peace, and without any particular encouragement from the publick, should spend the greater part of his time in military exercises, might, no doubt, both improve himself very much in them, and amuse himself very well; but he certainly would not promote his own interest. It is the wisdom of the state only which can render it for his interest to give up the greater part of his time to this peculiar occupation: and states have not always had this wisdom, even when their circumstances had become such, that the preservation of their existence required that they should have it.

15   A shepherd has a great deal of leisure; a husbandman, in the rude state of husbandry, has some; an artificer or manufacturer has none at all. The first may, without any loss, employ a great deal of his time in martial exercises; the second may employ some part of it; but the last cannot employ a single hour in them without some loss, and his attention to his own interest naturally leads him to neglect them altogether. *g*These*g* improvements in husbandry too, which the progress of arts and manufactures necessarily introduces, *h*leave*h* the husbandman as little leisure [55] as the artificer. Military exercises come to be as much neglected by the inhabitants of the country as by those of the town, and the great body of the people becomes altogether unwarlike. That wealth, at the same time, which always follows the improvements of agriculture and manufactures, and which in reality is no more than the accumulated produce of those improvements, provokes the invasion of all their neighbours. An industrious, and upon

---

g-g Those *1, 5–6*   *h-h* leaves *2*

[28] See above, § 18.

that account a wealthy nation, is of all nations the most likely to be attacked; and unless the state takes some new measures for the publick defence, the natural habits of the people render them altogether incapable of defending themselves.[29]

16   In these circumstances, there seem to be but two methods, by which the state can make any tolerable provision for the publick defence.

17   It may either, first, by means of a very rigorous police, and in spite of the whole bent of the interest, genius and inclinations of the people, enforce the practice of military exercises, and oblige either all the citizens of the military age, or a certain number of them, to join in some measure the trade of a soldier to whatever other trade or profession they may happen to carry on.

18   Or, secondly, by maintaining and employing a certain number of citizens in the constant practice of military exercises, it may render the trade of a soldier a particular trade, separate and distinct from all others.

19   If the state has recourse to the first of those two expedients, its military force is said to con-[56]sist in a militia; if to the second, it is said to consist in a standing army.[30] The practice of military exercises is the sole or principal occupation of the soldiers of a standing army, and the maintenance or pay which the state affords them is the principal and ordinary fund of their subsistence. The practice of military exercises is only the occasional occupation of the soldiers of a militia, and they derive the principal and ordinary fund of their subsistence from some other occupation. In a militia, the character of the labourer, artificer, or tradesman, predominates over that of the soldier: in a standing army, that of the soldier predominates over every other character; and in this distinction seems to consist the essential difference between those two different species of military force.

20   Militias have been of several different kinds. In some countries the citizens destined for defending the state, seem to have been exercised only, without being, if I may say so, regimented; that is, without being divided into separate and distinct bodies of troops, each of which performed its exercises under its own proper and permanent officers. In the republicks of antient Greece and Rome, each citizen, as long as he remained at home, seems to have practised his exercises either separately and independently, or with such of his equals as he liked best; and not to have been attached to any particular body of troops till he was actually called upon to take the

---

[29] Smith comments below, V.i.f.59, on the problem presented by a decline in martial spirit which generally follows 'improvement'.

[30] In LJ (B) 337, ed. Cannan 263, Smith discusses two kinds of standing army: 'The first is when the government gives offices to particular persons and so much for every man they levy. From such a standing army as this, which is the model of our own, there is less danger than from the second kind, when the government makes a stump bargain with a general to lead out a certain number of troops for their assistance, which is the model of the standing armies in some little states of Italy.'

field. In other countries, the militia has not only been exercised, but regimented. In Eng-[57]land, in Switzerland, and, I believe, in every other country of modern Europe, where any imperfect military force of this kind has been established, every militia-man is, even in time of peace, attached to a particular body of troops, which performs its exercises under its own proper and permanent officers.

21   Before the invention of fire-arms, that army was superior in which the soldiers had, each individually, the greatest skill and dexterity in the use of their arms. Strength and agility of body were of the highest consequence, and commonly determined the fate of battles. But this skill and dexterity in the use of their arms, could be acquired only, in the same manner as fencing is ^{i} at present, by practising, not in great bodies, but each man separately, in a particular school, under a particular master, or with his own particular equals and companions. Since the invention of fire-arms, strength and agility of body, or even extraordinary dexterity and skill in the use of arms, though they are far from being of no consequence, are, however, of less consequence. The nature of the weapon, though it by no means puts the aukward upon a level with the skilful, puts him more nearly so than he ever was before. All the dexterity and skill, it is supposed, which are necessary for using it, can be well enough acquired by practising in great bodies.

22   Regularity, order, and prompt obedience to command, are qualities which, in modern armies, are of more importance towards determining the [58] fate of battles, than the dexterity and skill of the soldiers in the use of their arms. But the noise of fire-arms, the smoke, and the invisible death to which every man feels himself every moment exposed, as soon as he comes within cannon-shot, and frequently a long time before the battle can be well said to be engaged, must render it very difficult to maintain any considerable degree of this regularity, order, and prompt obedience, even in the beginning of a modern battle. In an antient battle there was no noise but what arose from the human voice; there was no smoke, there was no invisible cause of wounds or death. Every man, till some mortal weapon actually did approach him, saw clearly that no such weapon was near him. In these circumstances, and among troops who had some confidence in their own skill and dexterity in the use of their arms, it must have been a good deal less difficult to preserve some degree of regularity and order, not only in the beginning, but through the whole progress of an antient battle, and till one of the two armies was fairly defeated. But the habits of regularity, order, and prompt obedience to command, can be acquired only by troops which are exercised in great bodies.

23   A militia, however, in whatever manner it may be either disciplined or

^{i} acquired *1*

exercised, must always be much inferior to a well disciplined and well exercised standing army.[31]

24 The soldiers, who are exercised only once a week, or once a month, can never be so expert in the use of their arms, as those who are exer-[59]cised every day, or every other day; and though this circumstance may not be of so much consequence in modern, as it was in antient times, yet the acknowledged superiority of the Prussian troops, owing, it is said, very much to their superior expertness in their exercise, may satisfy us that it is, even at this day, of very considerable consequence.

25 The soldiers, who are bound to obey their officer only once a week or once a month, and who are at all other times at liberty to manage their own affairs their own way, without being in any respect accountable to him, can never be under the same awe in his presence, can never have the same disposition to ready obedience, with those whose whole life and conduct are every day directed by him, and who every day even rise and go to bed, or at least retire to their quarters, according to his orders. In what is called discipline, or in the habit of ready obedience, a militia must always be still more inferior to a standing army, than it may sometimes be in what is called the manual exercise, or in the management and use of its arms. But in modern war the habit of ready and instant obedience is of much greater consequence than a considerable superiority in the management of arms.

26 Those militias which, like the Tartar or Arab militia, go to war under the same chieftains whom they are accustomed to obey in peace, are by far

---

[31] In Letter 154 addressed to Smith, dated 18 April 1776, Adam Ferguson expressed himself as quite happy with Smith's provocative remarks on the Church, the merchants, and the universities, 'but you have likewise provoked the militia, and there I must be against you'. See also Letter 208 addressed to Andreas Holt, dated 26 October 1780, where Smith also commented that:

> The anonymous author of a pamphlet concerning national defense, who I have been told is a Gentleman of the name of Douglas, has Written against Me. When he Wrote his book, he had not read mine to the end. He fancies that because I insist that a Militia is in all cases inferior to a well regulated & well disciplined standing Army, that I disapprove of Militias altogether. With regard to that subject, he & I happened to be precisely of the same opinion. This Gentleman, if I am rightly informed of his name, is a man of parts and one of my acquaintance, so that I was a little surprized at his attack upon Me, and still more at the mode of it.

The work (attributed to Carlyle in Halkett and Laing's *Dictionary of Anonymous Literature*) is entitled: *A Letter from a Gentleman in Edinburgh to his Grace the Duke of Buccleugh on National Defence, with Some Remarks on Dr Smith's Chapter on that Subject in his Book, entitled 'An Inquiry into the Nature and Causes of the Wealth of Nations'* (London, 1778). The militia question also figured in other correspondence. For example, Letter 23 addressed to Gilbert Elliot, dated 7 September 1757, indicates that Smith approved of a militia. Again, in Letter 50 addressed to William Strahan, dated 4 April 1760, regarding the publication of Hooke's Memoirs, Smith remarked that he was afraid 'they are published at an unlucky time, & may throw a damp upon our militia'. It is pointed out at V.i.a.27 that a militia long in the field may become in every respect the equal of a standing army.

the best. In respect for their officers, in the habit of ready obedience, they approach nearest to standing armies. The highland militia, when it [60] served under its own chieftains, had some advantage of the same kind. As the highlanders, however, were not wandering, but stationary shepherds, as they had all a fixed habitation, and were not, in peaceable times, accustomed to follow their chieftain from place to place; so in time of war they were less willing to follow him to any considerable distance, or to continue for any long time in the field. When they had acquired any booty they were eager to return home, and his authority was seldom sufficient to detain them. In point of obedience they were always much inferior to what is reported of the Tartars and Arabs. As the highlanders too, from their stationary life, spend less of their time in the open air, they were always less accustomed to military exercises, and were less expert in the use of their arms than the Tartars and Arabs are said to be.[32]

27   A militia of any kind, it must be observed, however, which has served for several successive campaigns in the field, becomes in every respect a standing army. The soldiers are every day exercised in the use of their arms, and, being constantly under the command of their officers, are habituated to the same prompt obedience which takes place in standing armies.[33] What they were before they took the field, is of little importance. They necessarily become in every respect a standing army, after they have passed a few campaigns in it. Should the war in America drag out through another campaign, the American militia may become in every respect a match for that standing army, of which *the valour ap-[61]peared, in the last war,* at least not inferior to that of the hardiest veterans of France and Spain.[34]

28   This distinction being well understood, the history of all ages, it will be found, bears testimony to the irresistible superiority which a well-regulated standing army has over *a* militia.

29   One of the first standing armies of which we have any distinct account,

---

j-j, in the last war the valour appeared *1*   *k-k* every sort of *1*

---

[32] In LJ (A) iv.38–9 Smith comments on the small size of war bands found among hunting communities, and points out that this is also true of 'stationary shepherds' such as the Scottish Highlanders. Cf. V.i.a.5.

[33] Cf. LJ (A) iv.169: 'An army composed of gentlemen has occasion for very little discipline; and their sence of honour and character will make them do their duty. But when the army comes to be compos'd of the very meanest of the people, they must be formed into a standing army and a military discipline must be established: that is, the soldiers must be put in such a condition as to fear their officers, who are still gentlemen, more than the enemy; in this case they will fight, but not otherwise: then they will follow them rather than flie from the enemy.' A similar point is made in LJ (B) 336, ed. Cannan 262.

[34] The Seven Years War, 1756 to 1763. This remark about the growing expertise of the militia may be relevant to a comment made at IV.vii.c.75 where Smith noted that the colonies were unlikely to be subdued 'by force alone'.

in any well authenticated history, is that of Philip of Macedon. His frequent wars with the Thracians, Illyrians, Thessalians, and some of the Greek cities in the neighbourhood of Macedon, gradually formed his troops, which in the beginning were probably militia, to the exact discipline of a standing army. When he was at peace, which he was very seldom, and never for any long time together, he was careful not to disband that army. It vanquished and subdued, after a long and violent struggle, indeed, the gallant and well exercised militias of the principal republicks of antient Greece; and afterwards, with very little struggle, the effeminate and ill-exercised militia of the great Persian empire. The fall of the Greek republicks and of the Persian empire, was the effect of the irresistible superiority which a standing army has over every sort of militia.[35] It is the first great revolution in the affairs of mankind of which history has preserved any distinct or circumstantial account.[36]

30   The fall of Carthage, and the consequent elevation of Rome, is the second. All the varieties in the fortune of those two famous republicks may very well be accounted for from the same cause.

31   [62] From the end of the first to the beginning of the second Carthaginian war, the armies of Carthage were continually in the field, and employed under three great generals, who succeeded one another in the command; Amilcar, his son-in-law Asdrubal, and his son Annibal; first in chastising their own rebellious slaves, afterwards in subduing the revolted nations of Africa, and, lastly, in conquering the great kingdom of Spain. The army which Annibal led from Spain into Italy must necessarily, in those different wars, have been gradually formed to the exact discipline of a standing army. The Romans, in the mean time, though they had not been altogether at peace, yet they had not, during this period, been engaged in any war of very great consequence; and their military discipline, it is generally said, was a good deal relaxed. The Roman armies which Annibal encountered at Trebia, Thrasymenus, and Cannæ, were militia opposed to a standing army. This circumstance, it is probable, contributed more than any other to determine the fate of those battles.

32   The standing army which Annibal left behind him in Spain, had the like superiority over the militia which the Romans sent to oppose it, and

---

[35] It is pointed out in LJ (A) iv.86–7 that improvements in the art of war, and especially in seige techniques, also contributed to the Macedonian success. In this place he refers to Philip as a 'very great engineer' and to the improvements made by Alexander which served to make 'every state of this kind' hold 'its liberty by a precarious tenure'. Cf. LJ (B) 41, ed. Cannan 28.

[36] It is remarked in LRBL ii.146, ed. Lothian 145, that payment for public services made the Athenians 'idle and inactive', since the people 'received the same pay for sitting at home and doing nothing but attending the publick diversions as they did for serving their country abroad, and the former was without question the easiest duty.' Smith added that the Athenians were in this state 'when Philip of Macedon arose'. Cf. V.i.a.10, V.i.f.43.

in a few years, under the command of his brother, the younger Asdrubal, expelled them almost entirely from that country.

33   Annibal was ill supplied from home. The Roman militia, being continually in the field, became in the progress of the war a well disciplined and well exercised standing army; and the superiority of Annibal grew every day less and [63] less. Asdrubal judged it necessary to lead the whole, or almost the whole of the standing army which he commanded in Spain, to the assistance of his brother in Italy. In ˡhisˡ march he is said to have been misled by his guides; and in a country which he did not know, was surprized and attacked by another standing army, in every respect equal or superior to his own, and was entirely defeated.

34   When Asdrubal had left Spain, the great Scipio found nothing to oppose him but a militia inferior to his own. He conquered and subdued that militia, and, in the course of the war, his own militia necessarily became a well-disciplined and well-exercised standing army. That standing army was afterwards carried to Africa, where it found nothing but a militia to oppose it. In order to defend Carthage it became necessary to recall the standing army of Annibal. The disheartened and frequently defeated African militia joined it, and, at the battle of Zama, composed the greater part of the troops of Annibal. The event of that day determined the fate of the two rival republicks.

35   From the end of the second Carthaginian war till the fall of the Roman republick, the armies of Rome were in every respect standing armies. The standing army of Macedon made some resistance to their arms. In the height of their grandeur, it cost them two great wars, and three great battles, to subdue that little kingdom; of which the conquest would probably have been still more difficult, had it not been for the cowardice of its last king. The militias of all the ci-[64]vilized nations of the antient world, of Greece, of Syria, and of Egypt, made but a feeble resistance to the standing armies of Rome. The militias of some barbarous nations defended themselves much better. The Scythian or Tartar militia, which Mithridates drew from the countries north of the Euxine and Caspian seas, were the most formidable enemies ᵐwhomᵐ the Romans had to encounter after the second Carthaginian war. The Parthian and German militias too were always respectable, and, upon several occasions, gained very considerable advantages over the Roman armies. In general, however, and when the Roman armies were well commanded, they appear to have been very much superior; and if the Romans did not pursue the final conquest either of Parthia or Germany, it was probably because they judged, that it was not worth while, to add those two barbarous countries to an empire which was already too large. The antient Parthians appear to have been a nation of

---

ˡ⁻ˡ this 4–6   ᵐ⁻ᵐ which 1

Scythian or Tartar extraction, and to have always retained a good deal of the manners of their ancestors. The antient Germans were, like the Scythians or Tartars, a nation of wandering shepherds, who went to war under the same chiefs whom they were accustomed to follow in peace. Their militia was exactly of the same kind with that of the Scythians or Tartars, from whom too they were probably descended.

36   Many different causes contributed to relax the discipline of the Roman armies. Its extreme severity was, perhaps, one of those causes. In [65] the days of their grandeur, when no enemy appeared capable of opposing them, their heavy armour was laid aside as unnecessarily burdensome, their laborious exercises were neglected as unnecessarily toilsome. Under the Roman emperors besides, the standing armies of Rome, those particularly which guarded the German and Pannonian frontiers, became dangerous to their masters, against whom they used frequently to set up their own generals. In order to render them less formidable, according to some authors, Dioclesian, according to others, Constantine, first withdrew them from the frontier, where they had always before been encamped in great bodies, generally of two or three legions each, and dispersed them in small bodies through the different provincial towns, from whence they were scarce ever removed, but when it became necessary to repel an invasion. Small bodies of soldiers quartered in trading and manufacturing towns, and seldom removed from those quarters, became themselves tradesmen, artificers, and manufacturers. The civil came to predominate over the military character; and the standing armies of Rome gradually degenerated into a corrupt, neglected, and undisciplined militia, incapable of resisting the attack of the German and Scythian militias, which soon afterwards invaded the western empire. It was only by hiring the militia of some of those nations, to oppose to that of others, that the emperors were for some time able to defend themselves.[37] The fall of the western empire is the third great revolution in the affairs of [66] mankind, of which antient history has preserved any distinct or circumstantial account. It was brought about by the irresistible superiority which the militia of a barbarous, has over that of a civilized nation; which the militia of a nation of shepherds, has over that of a nation of husbandmen, artificers, and manufacturers.[38] The victories which have been gained by militias have generally been, not over standing armies, but over other militias in exercise and discipline inferior to themselves. Such were the victories which the Greek militia gained over

[37] The fall of Rome as a result of using barbarian forces is considered in LJ (A) iv.99–104, and LJ (B) 46–9, ed. Cannan 32–4. Smith uses the same argument in explaining the decline of the Saxons, Caliphs, and the Italian Republics, while pointing out that both Britain and France paid heavy subsidies to their allies for military support.

[38] See above, §15. The analysis of III.ii. begins with the collapse of the western empire and proceeds to discuss the transition from the allodial to the feudal state, and thence to the commercial system.

that of the Persian empire; and such too were those which in later times the Swiss militia gained over that of the Austrians and Burgundians.

37   The military force of the German and Scythian nations who established themselves upon the ruins of the western empire, continued for some time to be of the same kind in their new settlements, as it had been in their original country. It was a militia of shepherds and husbandmen, which, in time of war, took the field under the command of the same chieftains whom it was accustomed to obey in peace. It was, therefore, tolerably well exercised, and tolerably well disciplined. As arts and industry advanced, however, the authority of the chieftains gradually decayed,[39] and the great body of the people had less time to spare for military exercises. Both the discipline and the exercise of the feudal militia, therefore, went gradually to ruin, and standing armies were gradually introduced to supply the place of it. When the expedient of a standing army, besides, [67] had once been adopted by one civilized nation, it became necessary that all its neighbours should follow the example. They soon found that their safety depended upon their doing so, and that their own militia was altogether incapable of resisting the attack of such an army.

38   The soldiers of a standing army, though they may never have seen an enemy, yet have frequently appeared to possess all the courage of veteran troops, and the very moment that they took the field to have been fit to face the hardiest and most experienced veterans. In 1756, when the Russian army marched into Poland, the valour of the Russian soldiers did not appear inferior to that of the Prussians, at that time supposed to be the hardiest and most experienced veterans in Europe. The Russian empire, however, had enjoyed a profound peace for near twenty years before, and could at that time have very few soldiers who had ever seen an enemy. When the Spanish war broke out in 1739, England had enjoyed a profound peace for about eight and twenty years. The valour of her soldiers, however, far from being corrupted by that long peace, was never more distinguished than in the attempt upon Carthagena, the first unfortunate exploit of that unfortunate war. In a long peace the generals, perhaps, may sometimes forget their skill; but, where a well-regulated standing army has been kept up, the soldiers seem never to forget their valour.

39   When a civilized nation depends for its defence upon a militia, it is at all times exposed to [68] be conquered by any barbarous nation which happens to be in its neighbourhood. The frequent conquests of all the civilized countries in Asia by the Tartars, sufficiently [n]demonstrates[n] the natural superiority, which the militia of a barbarous, has over that of a civilized nation. A well-regulated standing army is superior to every militia. Such

---

[n-n] demonstrate *I*

[39] See above, III.iv. for an analysis of this process.

an army, as it can best be maintained by an opulent and civilized nation, so it can alone defend such a nation against the invasion of a poor and barbarous neighbour. It is only by means of a standing army, therefore, that the civilization of any country can be perpetuated, or even preserved for any considerable time.

40   As it is only by means of a well-regulated standing army that a civilized country can be defended; so it is only by means of it, that a barbarous country can be suddenly and tolerably civilized. A standing army establishes, with an irresistible force, the law of the sovereign through the remotest provinces of the empire, and maintains some degree of regular government in countries which could not otherwise admit of any. Whoever examines, with attention, the improvements which Peter the Great introduced into the Russian empire, will find that they almost all resolve themselves into the establishment of a well-regulated standing army. It is the instrument which executes and maintains all his other regulations. That degree of order and internal peace, which that empire has ever since enjoyed, is altogether owing to the influence of that army.⁴⁰

41   [69] Men of republican principles have been jealous of a standing army as dangerous to liberty.⁴¹ It certainly is so, wherever the interest of the general and that of the principal officers are not necessarily connected with the support of the constitution of the state. The standing army of Caesar destroyed the Roman republick. The standing army of Cromwell turned the long parliament out of doors.⁴² But where the sovereign is himself the general, and the principal nobility and gentry of the country the chief officers of the army; where the military force is placed under the command of those who have the greatest interest in the support of the civil authority, because they have themselves the greatest share of that authority, a stand-

---

⁴⁰ It is pointed out in LJ (A) iv.178 that the army was less dangerous in Britain than elsewhere, since: a 'system of liberty' had been established before the standing army was introduced, which was not the case with other countries.
⁴¹ Smith comments at V.i.f.59 on the 'real or imaginary' dangers which arise from a standing army.
⁴² Cf. LJ (B) 338, ed. Cannan 263: 'on some occasions a standing army has proved dangerous to the liberties of the people, when that question concerning the power of the sovereign came to be disputed, as has been the case in our own country, because the standing army generaly takes the side of the king.' Smith also made the interesting point at 62, ed. Cannan 44, that: 'A peculiar advantage which Brittain enjoyed after the accession of James 1st was, that as the dominions of Brittain were in every way bounded by the sea there was no need for a standing army . . .' Cf. LJ (A) iv.168. The danger which a standing army presented to liberty in Rome is considered in LJ (A) iv.88–90. A parallel with Cromwell is drawn in LJ (B) 42–3, ed. Cannan 29, and in LJ (A) iv.94–5 where his rise to power through the use of the army is likened to that of Marius, Sulla, and Caesar. Smith cites Hannibal and Dionysius in much the same vein. The development of a situation where the soldiers were loyal to generals such as Marius, Sulla, or Caesar, rather than to the city was cited by Montesquieu as one of the factors which contributed to the decline of Rome; the second, was the change in the laws governing citizenship. *Considerations*, 91–3, 120–1; cf. IV.vii.c.75.

ing army can never be dangerous to liberty. On the contrary, it may in some cases be favourable to liberty.[43] The security which it gives to the sovereign renders unnecessary that troublesome jealousy, which, in some modern republicks, seems to watch over the minutest actions, and to be at all times ready to disturb the peace of every citizen. Where the security of the magistrate, though supported by the principal people of the country, is endangered by every popular discontent; where a small tumult is capable of bringing about in a few hours a great revolution, the whole authority of government must be employed to suppress and punish every murmur and complaint against it. To a sovereign, on the contrary, who feels himself supported, not only by the natural aristocracy of the country, but by a well-[70]regulated standing army, the rudest, the most groundless, and the most licentious remonstrances can give little disturbance. He can safely pardon or neglect them, and his consciousness of his own superiority naturally disposes him to do so. That degree of liberty which approaches to licentiousness can be tolerated only in countries where the sovereign is secured by a well-regulated standing army. It is in such countries only, that the publick safety does not require, that the sovereign should be trusted with any discretionary power, for suppressing even the impertinent wantonness of this licentious liberty.

42   The first duty of the sovereign, therefore, that of defending the society from the violence and injustice of other independent societies, grows gradually more and more expensive, as the society advances in civilization. The military force of the society, which originally cost the sovereign no expence either in time of peace or in time of war, must, in the progress of improvement, first be maintained by him in time of war, and afterwards even in time of peace.

43   The great change introduced into the art of war by the invention of fire-arms, has enhanced still further both the expence of exercising and disciplining any particular number of soldiers in time of peace, and that of employing them in time of war.[44] Both their arms and their ammunition

[43] Cf. LJ (B) 337, ed. Cannan 263: 'a standing army like ours is not so apt to turn their arms against the government, because the officers are men of honour and have great connections in the country.' A similar point is made in LJ (A) iv.179. LJ (A) iii.43 makes a related point in stating that an hereditary nobility is that which 'chiefly supports the liberty and freedom of the people' while LJ (B) 116, ed. Cannan 84, makes the same point. Smith argued in this connection that the nobility would serve as a focus for resistance in the event of defeat or invasion, and that in the absence of such a nobility, if the standing army is beaten 'the people can never after make any opposition'. It is also remarked, in 'Thoughts on America', that the 'principal security of every government arises always from the support of those whose dignity, authority and interest, depend upon its being supported' (§ 10, AHR 716).

[44] In LJ (B) 350, ed. Cannan 274, Smith ascribes a change in modern manners to the use of fire-arms: 'Modern armies too are less irritated at one another because fire-arms keep them at a greater distance. When they always fought sword in hand their rage and

are become more expensive. A musquet is a more expensive machine than a javelin or a bow and arrows; a cannon or a mortar, than a balista or a catapulta. The powder, which is [71] spent in a modern review, is lost irrecoverably, and occasions a very considerable expence. The javelins and arrows which were thrown or shot in an antient one, could easily be picked up again, and were besides of very little value. The cannon and the mortar are, not only much dearer, but much heavier machines than the balista or catapulta, and require a greater expence, not only to prepare them for the field, but to carry them to it. As the superiority of the modern artillery too, over that of the antients, is very great; it has become much more difficult, and consequently much more expensive, to fortify a town so as to resist even for a few weeks the attack of that superior artillery. In modern times many different causes contribute to render the defence of the society more expensive. The unavoidable effects of the natural progress of improvement have, in this respect, been a good deal enhanced by a great revolution in the art cf war, to which a mere accident, the invention of gun-powder, seems to have given occasion.

44 In modern war the great expence of fire-arms gives an evident advantage to the nation which can best afford that expence; and consequently, to an opulent and civilized, over a poor and barbarous nation.[45] In antient times the opulent and civilized found it difficult to defend themselves against the poor and barbarous nations. In modern times the poor and barbarous find it difficult to defend themselves against the opulent and civilized. The invention of fire-arms, an inven-[72]tion which at first sight appears to be so pernicious, is certainly favourable both to the permanency and to the extension of civilization.[46]

PART II

Of the Expence of Justice

1 The second duty of the sovereign, that of protecting, as far as possible, every member of the society from the injustice or oppression of every other member of it, or the duty of establishing an exact administration of

fury were raised to the highest pitch, and as they are mixed with one another the slaughter was vastly greater.'

[45] See above, § 14, where Smith describes the improvements in the art of war. It is pointed out at V.ii.a.14 that in modern states, war and the preparation for war 'occasion the greater part of the necessary expence'. It is also shown at V.iii.4,5 that the institutions of the modern economy also generate the means of meeting such large and sudden expenses for military purposes.

[46] 'Even to the present times, improvements have been continually making on this furious engine [artillery], which, though it seemed contrived for the destruction of mankind, and the overthrow of empires, has in the issue rendered battles less bloody, and has given greater stability to civil societies.' (Hume, *History of England* (1778), ii.432.)

justice, requires too very different degrees of expence in the different periods of society.[1]

2   Among nations of hunters, as there is scarce any property, or at least none that exceeds the value of two or three days labour; so there is seldom any established magistrate or any regular administration of justice.[2] Men who have no property can injure one another only in their persons or reputations. But when one man kills, wounds, beats, or defames another, though he to whom the injury is done suffers, he who does it receives no benefit. It is otherwise with the injuries to property. The benefit of the person who does the injury is often equal to the loss of him who suffers it. Envy, malice, or resentment, are the only passions which can prompt one man to injure another in his person or reputation. But the greater part of men are not very frequently under the influence of those passions; [73] and the very worst men are so only occasionally. As their gratification too, how agreeable soever it may be to certain characters, is not attended with any real or permanent advantage, it is in the greater part of men commonly restrained by prudential considerations. Men may live together in society with some tolerable degree of security, though there is no civil magistrate to protect them from the injustice of those passions. But avarice and ambition in the rich, in the poor the hatred of labour and the love of present ease and enjoyment, are the passions which prompt to invade property, passions much more steady in their operation, and much more universal in their influence.[3] Wherever there is

[1] Cf. LJ (A) i.9: 'The first and chief design of all civill governments is . . . to preserve justice amongst the members of the state and to prevent all incroachments on the individualls in it, from others of the same society.' See above, V.i.a.1.

[2] It is stated in LJ (A) v.109 that 'Savages of all things hate a judge set over their heads'. LJ (A) i.33 comments with regard to the age of hunters that 'As there is almost no property amongst them, the only injury that can be done is the depriving them of their game. Few laws or regulations will be requisite in such an age of society . . .' Smith did add, however, that 'even in the age of hunters there may be fixt habitations for the families, but property would not be extended to what was without the house' (i.48). It therefore followed, that in this general situation 'there can be very little government of any sort, but what there is will be of a democraticall kind'. LJ (A) iv.4; see also LJ (A) ii.152; LJ (B) 19, 183, ed. Cannan 14 and 137. Smith comments in LJ (A) iv.74 that at this stage 'there was properly no government at all' and that there was 'no occasion for any laws or regulations, property not extending at this time beyond possession' (iv.19). He also remarks at p. 22 that 'In the age of hunters a few temporary exertions of the authority of the community will be sufficient for the few occasions of dispute which can occur. Property, the grand fund of all dispute, is not then known.' Cf. LJ (B) 25, ed. Cannan 18–19.

[3] Cf. TMS VII.iv.36:

Every system of positive law may be regarded as a more or less imperfect attempt towards a system of natural jurisprudence, or towards an enumeration of the particular rules of justice. As the violation of justice is what men will never submit to from one another, the public magistrate is under a necessity of employing the power of the commonwealth to enforce the practice of this virtue. Without this precaution, civil society would become a scene of bloodshed and disorder, every man revenging himself at his own hand whenever he fancied he was injured. [*continues*]

great property, there is great inequality. For one very rich man, there must be at least five hundred poor, and the affluence of the few supposes the indigence of the many. The affluence of the rich excites the indignation of the poor, who are often both driven by want, and prompted by envy, to invade his possessions. It is only under the shelter of the civil magistrate that the owner of that valuable property, which is acquired by the labour of many years, or perhaps of many successive generations, can sleep a single night in security. He is at all times surrounded by unknown enemies, whom, though he never provoked, he can never appease, and from whose injustice he can be protected only by the powerful arm of the civil magistrate continually held up to chastise it. The acquisition of valuable *and* extensive property, therefore, necessarily re-[74]quires the establishment of civil government. Where there is no property, or at least none that exceeds the value of two or three days labour, civil government is not so necessary.[4]

3   Civil government supposes a certain subordination. But as the necessity of civil government gradually grows up with the acquisition of valuable property, so the principal causes which naturally introduce subordination gradually grow up with the growth of that valuable property.[5]

4   The causes or circumstances which naturally introduce subordination, or which naturally, and antecedent to any civil institution, give some men some superiority over the greater part of their brethren, seem to be four in number.[6]

a-a or *1*

Smith went on to observe that 'In some countries, the rudeness and barbarism of the people hinder the natural sentiments of justice from arriving at that accuracy and precision which, in more civilised nations, they naturally attain to. Their laws are, like their manners, gross and rude, and undistinguishing.' He therefore concluded that systems of positive law, 'though they deserve the greatest authority, as the records of the sentiments of mankind in different ages and nations, yet can never be regarded as accurate systems of the rules of natural justice'.

[4] LJ (A) i.33–4 comments: 'But when flocks and herds come to be reared property then becomes of a very considerable extent; there are many opportunities for injuring one another and such injuries are extremely pernicious to the sufferer.'

[5] Smith remarks at LJ (A) iv.19 that government arose, 'not as some writers imagine, from any consent or agreement of a number of persons to submit themselves to such or such regulations, but from the natural progress which men make in society'. He went on, 'I should also say that the age of shepherds is that where government first commences. Property makes it absolutely necessary' (21). See also LJ (B) 15–18, ed. Cannan 11–13, for Smith's criticism of the 'contract' theory, and LJ (A) v.114–19 where he rejects the contract theory, as represented by Locke and Sidney.

[6] The four sources of authority are examined in LJ (B) 12, ed. Cannan 9–10. The argument of this section places a good deal of emphasis on the sources of authority and subordination and on the way in which these are affected by the mode of subsistence, or type of economy, prevailing. The argument finds a close parallel in that offered by Smith's pupil, John Millar, *Origin of the Distinction of Ranks* (1771), chapter iii. For comment on Millar and his relation to the other members of the 'Scottish Historical School', see W. C. Lehmann, *John Millar of Glasgow* (Cambridge, 1960).

5   The first of those causes or circumstances is the superiority of personal qualifications, of strength, beauty, and agility of body; of wisdom, and virtue, of prudence, justice, fortitude, and moderation of mind.[7] The qualifications of the body, unless supported by those of the mind, can give little authority in any period of society. He is a very strong man who, by mere strength of body, can force two weak ones to obey him. The qualifications of the mind can alone give very great authority. They are, however, invisible qualities; always disputable, and generally disputed. No society, whether barbarous or civilized, has ever found it convenient to settle the rules of precedency, of rank and subordination, according to those invisible qualities; but according to something that is more plain and palpable.

6   [75] The second of those causes or circumstances is the superiority of age. An old man, provided his age is not so far advanced as to give suspicion of dotage, is every where more respected than a young man of equal rank, fortune, and abilities. Among nations of hunters, such as the native tribes of North America, age is the sole foundation of rank and precedency.[8] Among them, father is the appellation of a superior; brother, of an equal; and son, of an inferior. In the most opulent and civilized nations, age regulates rank among those who are in every other respect equal, and among whom, therefore, there is nothing else to regulate it. Among brothers and among sisters, the eldest always *take* place; and in the succession of the paternal estate every thing which cannot be divided, but must go entire to one person, such as a title of honour, is in most cases given to the eldest. Age is a plain and palpable quality which admits of no dispute.

7   The third of those causes or circumstances is the superiority of fortune. The authority of riches, however, though great in every age of society, is perhaps greatest in the rudest age of society which admits of any con-

---

b-b takes 5–6

[7] Cf. LRBL ii.199, ed. Lothian 168: 'The first thing which makes men submit themselves to the authority of others is the difficulty they feel in accomodating their matters either by their own judgement or by that of their opponents, and find it most adviseable to submit it to some impartiall person. By this means some persons of eminent worth came to be settled as judges and umpires.'

[8] LJ (B) 161, ed. Cannan 118, comments: 'In the beginings of society age itself is very much respected, and to this day among the Tartars the king is not succeded by his son, but by that one of the royal family who is oldest.' Montesquieu also states that in the case of primitive peoples, the old men have great authority, 'They cannot there be distinguished by wealth, but by wisdom and valour' (*Esprit*, XVIII.xiii.3). The Anderson Notes (37) observe that in the barbarous state 'the older the wiser a good maxim in the choice of magistrates, because there are no means of acquiring knowledge by books, etc. Hence the governours or chiefs in Africa are old men.' The notes go on to comment that 'Two chiefs may often be found in such a state' without causing disruption, and that governing may become hereditary in one family 'because it is natural to transplant our love or dislike to the representative of the deceast person'.

siderable inequality of fortune.[9] A Tartar chief, the increase of whose herds and flocks is sufficient to maintain a thousand men, cannot well employ that increase in any other way than in maintaining a thousand men.[10] The rude state of his society does not afford him any manufactured produce, any trinkets or baubles of any kind, for which he can exchange that part of his rude produce [76] which is over and above his own consumption. The thousand men whom he thus maintains, depending entirely upon him for their subsistence, must both obey his orders in war, and submit to his jurisdiction in peace.[11] He is necessarily both their general and their judge, and his chieftainship is the necessary effect of the superiority of his fortune.[12] In an opulent and civilized society, a man may possess a much greater fortune, and yet not be able to command a dozen of people.[13] Though the produce of his estate may be sufficient to maintain, and may perhaps actually maintain, more than a thousand people, yet as those people pay for every thing which they get from him, as he gives scarce any thing to any body but in exchange for an equivalent, there is scarce any body who considers himself as entirely dependent upon him, and his authority extends only over a few menial servants.[14] The authority of fortune, however, is very great even in an opulent and civilized society. That it is much greater than that, either of age, or of personal qualities, has been the constant complaint of every period of society which admitted of any considerable inequality of fortune. The first period of society, that of hunters, admits of no such inequality. Universal poverty establishes ᶜthereᶜ universal equality, and the superiority, either of age, or of personal qualities, are the feeble, but the sole foundations of authority and subordination. There is therefore little or no authority or

---

ᶜ⁻ᶜ their 5

[9] Cf. LJ (A) iv.41: 'Superiority of wealth gives one in this age a greater influence and authority than the same disproportion does at any other time.' A similar point is made at p. 8. See also p. 116: 'This inequality of property would, in a country where agriculture and division of land was introduced, but not practisd, introduce still greater dependance than among shepherds, tho there too it is very great.' Cf. LJ (B) 20, ed. Cannan 16.

[10] See above, III.iv.5.

[11] Cf. V.iii.1 and also III.iv.5, 8. See also LJ (B) 21, ed. Cannan 16: 'Even at present a man may spend a great estate and yet acquire no dependents. Arts and manufactures are increased by it, but it may make very few persons dependent. In a nation of shepherds it is quite otherways. They have no possible means of spending their property, having no domestic luxury, but by giving it in presents to the poor, and by this means they attain such an influence over them as to make them in a manner their slaves.'

[12] It is remarked in LRBL ii.199, ed. Lothian 168, that: 'When men, especially in a barbarous state, are accustomed to submit themselves in some points, they naturally do it in others. The same persons therefore who judged them in peace, lead them also to battle.'

[13] Smith comments on the absence of this kind of dependence in the modern state in LJ (A) iv.8.

[14] This point is elaborated above, III.iv.11.

subordination in this period of society. The second period of society, that of [77] shepherds, admits of very great inequalities of fortune, and there is no period in which the superiority of fortune gives so great authority to those who possess it. There is no period accordingly in which authority and subordination are more perfectly established. The authority of an Arabian scherif is very great; that of a Tartar khan altogether despotical.[15]

8   The fourth of those causes or circumstances is the superiority of birth. Superiority of birth supposes an antient superiority of fortune in the family of the person who claims it. All families are equally ancient; and the ancestors of the prince, though they may be better known, cannot well be more numerous than those of the beggar. Antiquity of family means every where the antiquity either of wealth, or of that greatness which is commonly either founded upon wealth, or accompanied with it. Upstart greatness is every where less respected than antient greatness.[16] The hatred of usurpers, the love ᵈofᵈ the family of an antient monarch, are, in a great measure, founded upon the contempt which men naturally have for the former, and upon their veneration for the latter. As a military officer submits without reluctance to the authority of a superior by whom he has always been commanded, but cannot bear that his inferior should be set over his head; so men easily submit to a family to whom they and their ancestors have always submitted; but are fired with indignation when another family, in whom they [78] had never acknowledged any such superiority, assumes a dominion over them.

9   The distinction of birth, being subsequent to the inequality of fortune, can have no place in nations of hunters, among whom all men, being equal in fortune, must likewise be very nearly equal in birth.[17] The son of a wise and brave man may, indeed, even among them, be somewhat more respected than a man of equal merit who has the misfortune to be the son of a fool or a coward. The difference, however, will not be very great;

ᵈ⁻ᵈ for *I*

---

[15] In LJ (A) ii.97 Smith remarks with reference to the transition from the hunting to the shepherd state that 'The step betwixt these two is of all others the greatest in the progression of society, for by it the notion of property is extended beyond possession, to which it is in the former state confined.'

[16] See above, IV.vii.b.51. In LJ (A) iv.46 the upstart family is defined as one of those who 'have been but lately raised to dignity'. Cf. iv.162. It is also remarked in LJ (B) 13, ed. Cannan 10, that 'It is evident that an old family, that is, one which has been long distinguished, by its wealth has more authority than any other. An upstart is always disagreeable, we envy his superiority over us, and think ourself as well entitled to wealth as he.' A similar point is made in LJ (A) v.129, where it is stated that 'an old family excites no such jealousy as an upstart does', and in TMS I.ii.5.1: 'An upstart, though of the greatest merit, is generally disagreeable, and a sentiment of envy commonly prevents us from heartily sympathizing with his joy.'

[17] LJ (A) iv.42 states that 'In the age of hunters there can be no hereditary nobility or respect to families.'

and there never was, I believe, a great family in the world whose illustration was entirely derived from the inheritance of wisdom and virtue.

10   The distinction of birth not only may, but always does take place among nations of shepherds.[18] Such nations are always strangers to every sort of luxury, and great wealth can scarce ever be dissipated among them by improvident profusion. There are no nations accordingly who abound more in families revered and honoured on account of their descent from a long race of great and illustrious ancestors; because there are no nations among whom wealth is likely to continue longer in the same families.[19]

11   Birth and fortune are evidently the two circumstances which principally set one man above another.[20] They are the two great sources of personal distinction, and are therefore the principal causes which naturally establish authority and subordination among men. Among nations of [79] shepherds both those causes operate with their full force. The great shepherd or herdsman, respected on account of his great wealth, and of the great number of those who depend upon him for subsistence, and revered on account of the nobleness of his birth, and of the immemorial antiquity of his illustrious family, has a natural authority over all the inferior shepherds or herdsmen of his horde or clan. He can command the united force of a greater number of people than any of them. His military power is greater than that of any of them. In time of war they are all of them naturally disposed to muster themselves under his banner, rather than under that of any other person, and his birth and fortune thus naturally procure to him some sort of executive power. By commanding too the united force of a greater number of people than any of them, he is best able to compel any one of them who may have injured another to compensate the wrong. He is the person, therefore, to whom all those who are too weak to defend themselves naturally look up for protection. It is to him that they naturally complain of the injuries which they imagine have been done to them, and his interposition in such cases is more easily submitted to, even by the person complained of, than that of any other person would be. His birth and fortune thus naturally procure him some sort of judicial authority.

----

[18] See above, III.iv.16.

[19] LJ (A) iv.43 claims that 'in the age of shepherds descent gives one more respect and authority than perhaps in any other stage of society whatever', and cites in support of this contention the genealogies in an unidentified Tartarian history. Smith added that the Jews also pay great respect and attention to family, explaining their continuing influence by their lack of luxury; i.e. forms of expenditure which would dissipate their fortunes and therefore influence (p. 44).

[20] Smith refers at V.iii.89 to the 'natural and respectable distinctions of birth and fortune'. It is remarked in TMS VI.ii.1.20 that: 'Nature has wisely judged that the distinction of ranks, the peace and order of society, would rest more securely upon the plain and palpable difference of birth and fortune, than upon the invisible and often uncertain difference of wisdom and virtue.'

12   It is in the age of shepherds, in the second period of society, that the
inequality of fortune first begins to take place, and introduces among
[80] men a degree of authority and subordination which could not possibly exist before. It thereby introduces some degree of that civil government which is indispensably necessary for its own preservation: and it
seems to do this naturally, and even independent of the consideration of
that necessity. The consideration of that necessity comes no doubt afterwards to contribute very much to maintain and secure that authority and
subordination. The rich, in particular, are necessarily interested to support that order of things, which can alone secure them in the possession
of their own advantages. Men of inferior wealth combine to defend
those of superior wealth in the possession of their property, in order that
men of superior wealth may combine to defend them in the possession
of theirs. All the inferior shepherds and herdsmen feel that the security
of their own herds and flocks depends upon the security of those of the
great shepherd or herdsman; that the maintenance of their lesser authority
depends upon that of his greater authority, and that upon their subordination to him depends his power of keeping their inferiors in subordination to them. They constitute a sort of little nobility, who feel
themselves interested to defend the property and to support the authority
of their own little sovereign, in order that he may be able to defend their
property and to support their authority. Civil government, so far as it is
instituted for the security of property, is in reality instituted for the
defence of the rich against the poor, or of those [81] who have some
property against those who have none at all.[21]

13   The judicial authority of such a sovereign, however, far from being a
cause of expence, was for a long time a source of revenue to him. The
persons who applied to him for justice were always willing to pay for it,
and a present never failed to accompany a petition. After the authority of
the sovereign too was thoroughly established, the person found guilty,
over and above the satisfaction which he was obliged to make to the party,
was likewise forced to pay an amercement to the sovereign. He had given

---

[21] Cf. LJ (B) 20, ed. Cannan 15: 'The appropriation of herds and flocks, which introduced an inequality of fortune, was that which first gave rise to regular government.
Till there be property there can be no government, the very end of which is to secure
wealth, and to defend the rich from the poor.' LJ (A) iv.21 states that 'the age of
shepherds is that where government first commences. Property makes it absolutely
necessary.' A similar point is made at iv.7 and Smith added at iv.22–3 that 'Laws and
government may be considered in this and indeed in every case as a combination of
the rich to oppress the poor, and preserve to themselves the inequality of the goods which
would otherwise be soon destroyed by the attacks of the poor, who if not hindered by
the government would soon reduce the others to an equality with themselves by open
violence.' Cf. also LJ (B) 11, ed. Cannan 8: 'Property and civil government very much
depend on one another. The preservation of property and the inequality of possession
first formed it, and the state of property must always vary with the form of government.'

trouble, he had disturbed, he had broke the peace of his lord the king, and for those offences an amercement was thought due. In the Tartar governments of Asia, in the governments of Europe which were founded by the German and Scythian nations who overturned the Roman empire, the administration of justice was a considerable source of revenue, both to the sovereign, and to all the lesser chiefs or lords who exercised under him any particular jurisdiction, either over some particular tribe or clan, or over some particular territory or district. Originally both the sovereign and the inferior chiefs used to exercise this jurisdiction in their own persons. Afterwards they universally found it convenient to delegate it to some substitute, bailiff, or judge. This substitute, however, was still obliged to account to his principal or constituent for the profits of the jurisdiction. Whoever reads the* instructions [82] which were given to the judges of the circuit in the time of Henry II. will see clearly that those judges were a sort of itinerant factors, sent round the country for the purpose of levying certain branches of the king's revenue. In those days the administration of justice, not only afforded a certain revenue to the sovereign, but to procure this revenue seems to have been one of the principal advantages which he proposed to obtain by the administration of justice.[22]

14   This scheme of making the administration of justice subservient to the purposes of revenue, could scarce fail to be productive of several very gross abuses. The person, who applied for justice with a large present in his hand, was likely to get something more than justice; while he, who applied for it with a small one, was likely to get something less.[23] Justice too might frequently be delayed, in order that this present might be repeated.[24] The amercement, besides, of the person complained of, might

---

* They are to be found in Tyrrell's History of England. [J. Tyrrell, *General History of England both Ecclesiastical and Civil* (London, 1700), ii.402 and 457–9. Fuller information on the activities of the justices is given for the reign of Richard I, ii.542 and 576–9.]

[22] See below, V.ii.a.15.

[23] LJ (B) 307, ed. Cannan 237, remarks that 'When applications are made, everyone must bring his present and the man who pays best will be best heard'. Smith also noted that the provision of a gift to those who are to deliver judgement 'is the case among the Tartars, Arabs, and Hottentots even to this day'. Similar points are made in LJ (A) iv.32 where the Americans and Mongols are also included, together with the Saxon kings and 'some of the first of the Norman race'. It is stated at iv.16 that 'A Tartar prince cannot be spoke to without you open his ears by a gift. As this will soon increase his riches, so the number of their dependants and their power must rise proportionably, and their influence on the council will also be increased.' Cf. Montesquieu, *Esprit*, V.xvii.1: 'It is a received custom in despotic countries never to address any superior whomsoever, not excepting their kings, without making them a present. The Mogul never receives the petitions of his subjects if they come with empty hands.'

[24] TMS III.i.2.24 offers an interesting aside: 'When a man has bribed all the judges, the most unanimous decision of the court, though it may gain him his law-suit, cannot give him any assurance that he was in the right; and had he carried on his law-suit merely to satisfy himself that he was in the right, he never would have bribed the judges.'

frequently suggest a very strong reason for finding him in the wrong, even when he had not really been so. That such abuses were far from being uncommon, the antient history of every country in Europe bears witness.

15   When the sovereign or chief exercised his judicial authority in his own person, how much soever he might abuse it, it must have been scarce possible to get any redress; because there could seldom be any body powerful enough to call him to account. When he exercised it by a bailiff, indeed, redress might sometimes be had. If it [83] was for his own benefit only, that the bailiff had been guilty of any act of injustice, the sovereign himself might not always be unwilling to punish him, or to oblige him to repair the wrong. But, if it was for the benefit of his sovereign, if it was in order to make court to the person who appointed him and who might prefer him, that he had committed any act of oppression, redress would upon most occasions be as impossible as if the sovereign had committed it himself. In all barbarous governments, accordingly, in all those antient governments of Europe in particular, which were founded upon the ruins of the Roman empire, the administration of justice appears for a long time to have been extremely corrupt; far from being quite equal and impartial even under the best monarchs, and altogether profligate under the worst.

16   Among nations of shepherds, where the sovereign or chief is only the greatest shepherd or herdsman of the horde or clan, he is maintained in the same manner as any of his vassals or subjects, by the increase of his own herds or flocks.[25] Among those nations of husbandmen who are but just come out of the shepherd state, and who are not much advanced beyond that state; such as the Greek tribes appear to have been about the time of the Trojan war, and our German and Scythian ancestors when they first settled upon the ruins of the western empire; the sovereign or chief is, in the same manner, only the greatest landlord of the country, and is maintained, in the same manner as any other landlord, by a [84] revenue derived from his own private estate, or from what, in modern Europe, was called the demesne of the crown. His subjects, upon ordinary occasions, contribute nothing to his support, except when*e*, in order to protect them from the oppression of some of their fellow-subjects, they stand in need of his authority.*e* The presents which they make him upon such occasions, constitute the whole ordinary revenue, the whole of the emoluments which, except perhaps upon some very extraordinary emergencies, he derives from his dominion over them. When Agamemnon,

---

e-e they stand in need of the interposition of his authority in order to protect them from the oppression of some of their fellow subjects. *I*

---

[25] See below, V.ii.a.2. It is pointed out at I.iv.3 that in this state cattle were a common instrument of commerce.

in Homer, offers to Achilles for his friendship the sovereignty of seven Greek cities, the sole advantage which he mentions as likely to be derived from it, was, that the people would honour him with presents.[26] As long as such presents, as long as the emoluments of justice, or what may be called the fees of court, constituted in this manner the whole ordinary revenue which the sovereign derived from his sovereignty, it could not well be expected, it could not even decently be proposed that he should give them up altogether. It might, and it frequently was proposed, that he should regulate and ascertain them. But after they had been so regulated and ascertained, how to hinder a person who was all-powerful from extending them beyond those regulations, was still very difficult, not to say impossible. During the continuance of this state of things, therefore, the corruption of justice, naturally resulting from the arbitrary and uncertain nature of those presents, scarce admitted of any effectual remedy.

17   [85] But when from different causes, chiefly from the continually increasing expence of defending the nation against the invasion of other nations, the private estate of the sovereign had become altogether insufficient for defraying the expence of the sovereignty; and when it had become necessary that the people should, for their own security, contribute towards this expence by taxes of different kinds, it seems to have been very commonly stipulated that no present for the administration of justice should, under any pretence, be accepted either by the sovereign, or by his bailiffs and substitutes, the judges. Those presents, it seems to have been supposed, could more easily be abolished altogether, than effectually regulated and ascertained. Fixed salaries were appointed to the judges which were supposed to compensate to them the loss of whatever might have been their share of the antient emoluments of justice; as the taxes more than compensated to the sovereign the loss of his. Justice was then said to be administered gratis.

18   Justice, however, never was in reality administered gratis in any country. Lawyers and attornies, at least, must always be paid by the parties; and, if they were not, they would perform their duty still worse than they actually perform it. The fees annually paid to lawyers and attornies amount, in every court, to a much greater sum than the salaries of the judges. The circumstance of those salaries being paid by the crown, can no where much diminish the necessary expence of a law-suit. But it was not so

---

[26] 'Seven well-peopled cities will I give him, Cardamyle, Enope, and grassy Hire, and sacred Pherae and Antheia with deep meadows, and fair Aepeia and vine-clad Pedasus. All are nigh to the sea, on the uttermost border of sandy Pylos, and in them dwell men rich in flocks and rich in kine, men that shall honour him with gifts as though he were a god, and beneath his sceptre shall bring his ordinances to prosperous fulfilment. All this will I bring to pass for him, if he but cease from his wrath.' (Homer, *Iliad*, ix.149–57, translated by A. T. Murray in Loeb Classical Library (1965), i.392–3.)

much to diminish the expence, as to prevent the cor-[86]ruption of justice, that the judges were prohibited from receiving any present or fee from the parties.

19   The office of judge is in itself so very honourable, that men are willing to accept of it, though accompanied with very small emoluments.[27] The inferior office of justice of peace, though attended with a good deal of trouble, and in most cases with no emoluments at all, is an object of ambition to the greater part of our country gentlemen.[28] The salaries of all the different judges, high and low, together with the whole expence of the administration and execution of justice, even where it is not managed with very good œconomy, makes, in any civilized country, but a very inconsiderable part of the whole expence of government.

20   The whole expence of justice too might easily be defrayed by the fees of court; and, without exposing the administration of justice to any real hazard of corruption, the publick revenue might thus be entirely discharged from a certain, though, perhaps, but a small incumbrance. It is difficult to regulate the fees of court effectually, where a person so powerful as the sovereign is to share in them, and to derive any considerable part of his revenue from them. It is very easy, where the judge is the principal person who can reap any benefit from them. The law can very easily oblige the judge to respect the regulation, though it might not always be able to make the sovereign respect it. Where the fees of court are precisely regulated and ascertained, [87] where they are paid all at once, at a certain period of every process, into the hands of a cashier or receiver, to be by him distributed in certain known proportions among the different judges after the process is decided, and not till it is decided, there seems to be no more danger of corruption than where such fees are prohibited altogether. Those fees, without occasioning any considerable increase in the expence of a law-suit, might be rendered fully sufficient for defraying the whole expence of justice. By not being paid to the judges till the process was determined, they might be some incitement to the diligence of the court in examining and deciding it. In courts which consisted of a considerable number of judges, by proportioning the share of each judge to the number of hours and days which he had employed in examining the process, either in the court or in a committee by order of the court, those fees might give some encouragement to the diligence of each particular judge. Publick services are never better performed than when their reward comes only in consequence of their being performed, and is proportioned to the diligence employed in performing them.[29] In

---

[27] See above, I.x.b.24.
[28] LJ (A) v.5 refers to sheriffs appointed by the Crown for life as an office which 'is not attended with great dignity and no profit, so that many pay a fine of £500 to be excused from it'.   [29] This point is forcibly made below, V.i.f.4.

the different parliaments of France, the fees of court (called Epicès and vacations) constitute the far greater part of the emoluments of the judges. After all deductions are made, the neat salary paid by the crown to a counsellor or judge in the parliament of Toulouse, in rank and dignity the second parliament of the kingdom, amounts only to a hundred and fifty livres, about [88] six pounds eleven shillings sterling a year. About seven years ago that sum was in the same place the ordinary yearly wages of a common footman. The distribution of those Epicès too is according to the diligence of the judges. A diligent judge gains a comfortable, though moderate, revenue by his office: An idle one gets little more than his salary. Those parliaments are perhaps, in many respects, not very convenient courts of justice; but they have never been accused; they seem never even to have been suspected of corruption.

21   The fees of court seem originally to have been the principal support of the different courts of justice in England. Each court endeavoured to draw to itself as much business as it could, and was, upon that account, willing to take cognizance of many suits which were not originally intended to fall under its jurisdiction.[30] The court of king's bench, instituted for the trial of criminal causes only, took cognizance of civil suits; the plaintiff pretending that the defendant, in not doing him justice, had been guilty of some trespass or misdemeanor. The court of exchequer, instituted for the levying of the king's revenue, and for enforcing the payment of such debts only as were due to the king, took cognizance of all other contract debts; the plaintiff alleging that he could not pay the king, because the defendant would not pay him. In consequence of such fictions it came, in many cases, to depend altogether upon the parties before what court they would chuse to have their cause tried; and [89] each court endeavoured, by superior dispatch and impartiality, to draw to itself as many causes as it could. The present admirable constitution of the courts of justice in England was, perhaps, originally in a great measure, formed by this emulation, which antiently took place between their respective judges; each judge endeavouring to give, in his own court, the speediest and most effectual remedy, which the law would admit, for every sort of injustice. Originally the courts of law gave damages only for breach of contract. The court of chancery, as a court of conscience, first took upon it to enforce the specifick performance of agreements. When the breach of contract consisted in the non-payment of money, the damage sustained could be compensated in no other way than by ordering payment, which was equivalent to a specifick performance of the agreement. In such cases, therefore, the remedy of the courts of law was sufficient. It was

[30] Smith comments on the rivalry between the courts in LJ (A) v.25–6 and LJ (B) 69, ed. Cannan 49. The structure of the courts is described in LJ (A) v. lectures 1 and 2; LJ (B) 64–75, ed. Cannan 46–53.

not so in others. When the tenant sued his lord for having unjustly outed him of his lease, the damages which he recovered were by no means equivalent to the possession of the land. Such causes, therefore, for some time, went all to the court of chancery, to the no small loss of the courts of law. It was to draw back such causes to themselves that the courts of law are said to have invented the artificial and fictitious writ of ejectment, the most effectual remedy for an unjust outer or dispossession of land.[31]

22   A stamp-duty upon the law proceedings of each particular court, to be levied by that court, [90] and applied towards the maintenance of the judges and other officers belonging to it, might, in the same manner, afford a revenue sufficient for defraying the expence of the administration of justice, without bringing any burden upon the general revenue of the society. The judges indeed might, in this case, be under the temptation of multiplying unnecessarily the proceedings upon every cause, in order to increase, as much as possible, the produce of such a stamp-duty. It has been the custom in modern Europe to regulate, upon most occasions, the payment of the attornies and clerks of court, according to the number of pages which they had occasion to write; the court, however, requiring that each page should contain so many lines, and each line so many words. In order to increase their payment, the attornies and clerks have contrived to multiply words beyond all necessity, to the corruption of the law language of, I believe, every court of justice in Europe.[32] A like temptation might perhaps occasion a like corruption in the form of law proceedings.

23   But whether the administration of justice be so contrived as to defray its own expence, or whether the judges be maintained by fixed salaries paid to them from some other fund, it does not seem necessary that the person or persons entrusted with the executive power should be charged with the management of that fund, or with the payment of those salaries. That fund might arise from the rent of landed estates, the management of each estate being entrusted to the [91] particular court which was to be maintained by it. That fund might arise even from the interest of a sum of money, the lending out of which might, in the same manner, be entrusted to the court which was to be maintained by it. A part, though indeed but a small part, of the salary of the judges of the court of session

---

[31] This writ is also mentioned above, III.ii.14.

[32] Smith refers above, II.iv.11, to the 'conveyances of a verbose attorney'. Here as elsewhere he does not object so much to the action taken as to the circumstances within which it takes place. See for example IV.vii.c.107, where Smith comments on the activities of some members of the East India Company and below, V.i.e.26, where he refers to the 'irresistible moral causes' to which they were subject. The point is of course that while nothing can be done about the principles of human nature, it should be possible to ensure an environment within which men will find it in their interest to act in such a way as to be compatible with the effective provision of some service. Cf. I.viii.44.

in Scotland, arises from the interest of a sum of money.³³ The necessary instability of such a fund seems, however, to render it an improper one for the maintenance of an institution which ought to last for ever.

24   The separation of the judicial from the executive power seems originally to have arisen from the increasing business of the society, in consequence of its increasing improvement. The administration of justice became so laborious and so complicated a duty as to require the undivided attention of the persons to whom it was entrusted.³⁴ The person entrusted with the executive power, not having leisure to attend to the decision of private causes himself, a deputy was appointed to decide them in his stead. In the progress of the Roman greatness, the consul was too much occupied with the political affairs of the state, to attend to the administration of justice. A praetor, therefore, was appointed to administer it in his stead.³⁵ In the progress of the European monarchies which were founded upon the ruins of the Roman empire, the sovereigns and the great lords came universally to consider the administration of justice as an office, both too laborious and too ignoble for them to execute in their own persons. They universally, [92] therefore, discharged themselves of it by appointing a deputy, bailiff, or judge.

25   When the judicial is united to the executive power, it is scarce possible that justice should not frequently be sacrificed to, what is vulgarly called, politics. The persons entrusted with the great interests of the state may, even without any corrupt views, sometimes imagine it necessary to sacrifice to those interests the rights of a private man. But upon the impartial administration of justice depends the liberty of every individual, the sense

³³ In Letter 235, addressee unknown, possibly dated 1783, Smith recorded that: 'By the 10th Anne Cap. 26 Sect. 108, all the duties of customs and excise at that time payable in Scotland were made liable to the expence of keeping up the three courts of Session, Justiciary and Exchequer.'

³⁴ Cf. Anderson Notes, 39. LRBL ii.203, ed. Lothian 170, states that the separation of powers is 'one of the most happy parts of the British Constitution' and that this:

is the great advantage which modern times have over antient, and the foundation of that greater security which we now enjoy, both with regard to liberty, property, and life. It was introduced only by chance and to ease the Supreme Magistrate of this the most laborious and less glorious part of his power, and has never taken place untill the increase of refinement and the growth of society have multiplied business immensely.

LJ (B) 63, ed. Cannan 45 comments on the 'happy mixture of all the different forms of government properly restrained' which exists in Britain and adds that as an additional security, judges are appointed for life, and quite independent of the king. In LJ (A) Smith makes the above point in reviewing the basis of English liberties, and includes the power of the Commons to impeach the king's ministers, Habeas Corpus, the frequency and method of elections, etc. He concluded, however, that the most important guarantee was that 'The system of government now supposes a system of liberty as a foundation. Every one would be shocked at any attempt to alter this system, and such a change would be attended with greatest difficulties.' LJ (A) v.5. The Anderson Notes observe that 'Montesquieu's division of powers in a state [is] very just' (39).

³⁵ The scope of the office of praetor is described in LRBL ii.202, ed. Lothian 169–70.

which he has of his own security. In order to make every individual feel himself perfectly secure in the possession of every right which belongs to him, it is not only necessary that the judicial should be separated from the executive power, but that it should be rendered as much as possible independent of that power. The judge should not be liable to be removed from his office according to the caprice of that power. The regular payment of his salary should not depend upon the good-will, or even upon the good œconomy of that power.[36]

PART III

Of the Expence of publick Works and publick Institutions

1   The third and last duty of the sovereign or commonwealth is that of erecting and maintaining those publick institutions and those publick works, which, though they may be in the highest degree advantageous to a great society, are, how-[93]ever, of such a nature, that the profit could never repay the expence to any individual or small number of individuals, and which it, therefore, cannot be expected that any individual or small number of individuals should erect or maintain.[1] The performance of this duty requires too very different degrees of expence in the different periods of society.

2   After the publick institutions and publick works necessary for the defence of the society, and for the administration of justice, both of which have already been mentioned, the other works and institutions of this kind are chiefly those for facilitating the commerce of the society, and those for promoting the instruction of the people. The institutions for instruction are of two kinds; those for the education of the youth, and those for the instruction of people of all ages. The consideration of the manner in which the expence of those different sorts of publick *ᵃworksᵃ* and institutions may be most properly defrayed, will divide this third part of the present chapter into three different articles.

ᵃ⁻ᵃ work *1*

---

[36] Smith had remarked in LJ (A) v.5 on the importance of independent judges with regard to liberty; the point is underlined in Letter 117 addressed to Smith, dated 6 March 1769 and written in the violent aftermath of the Douglas Cause. Lord Hailes wrote that 'Judges must not only be free, but they must feel themselves free . . . hitherto I imagined that I was answerable for my Conduct to the laws of my Country . . . *now* there is a sovereign Tribunal at every Bonfire.' See also Letter 116 addressed to Hailes, dated 5 March 1769. In the course of this letter, Smith made the interesting remark that:

> I have read law entirely with a view to form some general notion of the great outlines of the plan according to which justice has [been] administered in different ages & nations, & I have entered very little into the detail of Particulars, . . .

[1] A similar expression is used at IV.ix.51.

ARTICLE I
Of the publick Works and Institutions for facilitating the Commerce of the Society

^a*And, first, of those which are necessary for facilitating Commerce in general*^a

1   That the erection and maintenance of the publick works which facilitate the commerce of any country, such as good roads, bridges, navi-[94] gable canals, harbours,[1] &c. must require very different degrees of expence in the different periods of society, is evident without any proof. The expence of making and maintaining the publick roads of any country must evidently increase with the annual produce of the land and labour of that country, or with the quantity and weight of the goods which it becomes necessary to fetch and carry upon those roads. The strength of a bridge must be suited to the number and weight of the carriages, which are likely to pass over it. The depth and the supply of water for a navigable canal must be proportioned to the number and tunnage of the lighters, which are likely to carry goods upon it; the extent of a harbour to the number of the shipping which are likely to take shelter in it.

2   It does not seem necessary that the expence of those publick works should be defrayed from that publick revenue, as it is commonly called, of which the collection and application ^bis^b in most countries assigned to the executive power. The greater part of such publick works may easily be so managed, as to afford a particular revenue sufficient for defraying their own expence, without bringing any burden upon the general revenue of the society.

3   A highway, a bridge, a navigable canal, for example, may in most cases be both made and maintained by a small toll upon the carriages which make use of them: a harbour, by a moderate port-duty upon the tunnage of the shipping which load or unload in it. The coinage, [95] another institution for facilitating commerce, in many countries, not only defrays its own expence, but affords a small revenue or seignorage to the sovereign.[2] The post-office, another institution for the same purpose, over and above defraying its own expence, affords in almost all countries a very considerable revenue to the sovereign.[3]

4   When the carriages which pass over a highway or a bridge, and the lighters which sail upon a navigable canal, pay toll in proportion to their weight or their tunnage, they pay for the maintenance of those publick

---

^{a–a} 3–6   ^{b–b} are 5–6

[1] Smith describes the advantages of good transport facilities at I.xi.b.5.

[2] Smith comments that government is 'properly at the expence of the coinage' at II.ii.54.

[3] It is stated at V.ii.a.5 that the post office is 'properly a mercantile project'.

works exactly in proportion to the ᶜwear and tearᶜ which they occasion of them. It seems scarce possible to invent a more equitable way of maintaining such works.⁴ This tax or toll too, though it is advanced by the carrier, is finally paid by the consumer, to whom it must always be charged in the price of the goods. As the expence of carriage, however, is very much reduced by means of such publick works, the goods, notwithstanding the toll, come cheaper to the consumer than they could otherwise have done; their price not being so much raised by the toll, as it is lowered by the cheapness of the carriage. The person who finally pays this tax, therefore, gains by the application, more than he loses by the payment of it. His payment is exactly in proportion to his gain. It is in reality no more than a part of that gain which he is obliged to give up in order to get the rest. It seems impossible to imagine a more equitable method of raising a tax.

5   [96] When the toll upon carriages of luxury, upon coaches, post-chaises, &c. is made somewhat higher in proportion to their weight, than upon carriages of necessary use, such as carts, waggons, &c. the indolence and vanity of the rich is made to contribute in a very easy manner to the relief of the poor, by rendering cheaper the transportation of heavy goods to all the different parts of the country.

6   When high roads, bridges, canals, &c. are in this manner made and supported by the commerce which is carried on by means of them, they can be made only where that commerce requires them, and consequently where it is proper to make them. Their expence too, their grandeur and magnificence, must be suited to what that commerce can afford to pay. They must be made consequently as it is proper to make them. A magnificent high road cannot be made through a desart country where there is little or no commerce, or merely because it happens to lead to the country villa of the intendant of the province, or to that of some great lord to whom the intendant finds it convenient to make his court. A great bridge cannot be thrown over a river at a place where nobody passes, or merely to embellish the view from the windows of a neighbouring palace: things which sometimes happen, in countries where works of this kind are carried on by any other revenue than that which they themselves are capable of affording.⁵

7   In several different parts of Europe the toll or lock-duty upon a canal is the property of private persons, whose private interest obliges [97] them to keep up the canal. If it is not kept in tolerable order, the navigation necessarily ceases altogether, and along with it the whole profit which they can make by the tolls. If those tolls were put under the management

---

ᶜ⁻ᶜ tear and wear *1*

⁴ But see below, § 12.   ⁵ See below, § 16.

of commissioners, who had themselves no interest in them, they might be less attentive to the maintenance of the works which produced them. The canal of Languedoc cost the king of France and the province upwards of thirteen millions of livres, which (at twenty-eight livres the mark of silver, the value of French money in the end of the last century) amounted to upwards of nine hundred thousand pounds sterling. When that great work was finished, the most likely method, it was found, of keeping it in constant repair was to make a present of the tolls to Riquet the engineer, who planned and conducted the work. Those tolls constitute at present a very large estate to the different branches of the family of that gentleman, who have, therefore, a great interest to keep the work in constant repair. But had those tolls been put under the management of commissioners, who had no such interest, they might perhaps have been dissipated in ornamental and unnecessary expences, while the most essential parts of the work were allowed to go to ruin.[6]

8   The tolls for the maintenance of a high road, cannot with any safety be made the property of private persons. A high road, though entirely neglected, does not become altogether impassable, though a canal does. The proprietors of the tolls upon a high road, therefore, might neglect [98] altogether the repair of the road, and yet continue to levy very nearly the same tolls. It is proper, therefore, that the tolls for the maintenance of such a work should be put under the management of commissioners or trustees.

9   In Great Britain, the abuses which the trustees have committed in the management of those tolls, have in many cases been very justly complained of. At many turnpikes, it has been said, the money levied is more than double of what is necessary for executing, in the compleatest manner, the work which is often executed in a very slovenly manner, and sometimes not executed at all. The system of repairing the high roads by tolls of this kind, it must be observed, is not of very long standing. We should not wonder, therefore, if it has not yet been brought to that degree of perfection of which it seems *d* capable. If mean and improper persons are frequently appointed trustees; and if proper courts of inspection and account have not yet been established for controuling their conduct, and for reducing the tolls to what is barely sufficient for executing the work to be done by them; the recency of the institution both accounts and apologizes for those defects, of which, by the wisdom of parliament, the greater part may in due time be gradually remedied.

10   The money levied at the different turnpikes in Great Britain is supposed

d to be *1*

---

[6] It is stated below, V.i.e.32, that the making and maintenance of a navigable canal is one of three trades suitable for management by a joint stock company without exclusive privilege.

to exceed so much what is necessary for repairing the roads, that the savings, which, with proper œconomy, might be made from it, have been considered, even by some [99] ministers, as a very great resource which might at some time or another be applied to the exigencies of the state. Government, it has been said, by taking the management of the turnpikes into its own hands, and by employing the soldiers, who would work for a very small addition to their pay, could keep the roads in good order at a much less expence than it can be done by trustees, who have no other workmen to employ, but such as derive their whole subsistence from their wages.[7] A great revenue, half a million, perhaps*, it has been pretended, might in this manner be gained without laying any new burden upon the people; and the turnpike roads might be made to contribute to the general expence of the state, in the same manner as the post-office does at present.

11   That a considerable revenue might be gained in this manner, I have no doubt, though probably not near so much, as the projectors of this plan have supposed. The plan itself, however, seems liable to several very important objections.

12   First, if the tolls which are levied at the turnpikes should ever be considered as one of the resources for supplying the exigencies of the state, they would certainly be augmented as those exigencies were supposed to require. According to the policy of Great Britain, therefore, they [100] would probably be augmented very fast. The facility with which a great revenue could be drawn from them, would probably encourage administration to recur very frequently to this resource. Though it may, perhaps, be more than doubtful, whether half a million could by any œconomy be saved out of the present tolls, it can scarce be doubted but that a million might be saved out of them, if they were doubled; and perhaps two millions, if they were tripled†. This great revenue too might be levied without the appointment of a single new officer to collect and receive it. But the turnpike tolls being continually augmented in this manner, instead of facilitating the inland commerce of the country, as at present, would soon become a very great incumbrance upon it.[8] The expence of transporting all heavy goods from one part of the country to another would soon be so much increased, the market for all such goods,

---

* Since publishing the two first editions of this book, I have got good reasons to believe that all the turnpike tolls levied in Great Britain do not produce a neat revenue that amounts to half a million; a sum which, under the management of Government, would not be sufficient to keep in repair five of the principal roads in the kingdom.

†I have now good reasons to believe that all these conjectural sums are by much too large.

---

e–e 3–6   *f–f* 3–6

---

[7] See above, I.x.b.48 for comment on this point.   [8] See below, V.ii.k.56.

consequently, would soon be so much narrowed; that their production would be in a great measure discouraged, and the most important branches of the domestick industry of the country annihilated altogether.⁹

13   Secondly, a tax upon carriages in proportion to their weight, though a very equal tax when applied to the sole purpose of repairing the roads, is a very unequal one, when applied to any other purpose, or to supply the common exigencies of the state. When it is applied to the sole purpose above mentioned, each carriage is [101] supposed to pay exactly for the ᵍwear and tearᵍ which that carriage occasions of the roads. But when it is applied to any other purpose, each carriage is supposed to pay for more than that ʰwear and tearʰ, and contributes to the supply of some other exigency of the state. But as the turnpike toll raises the price of goods in proportion to their weight, and not to their value, it is chiefly paid by the consumers of coarse and bulky, not by those of precious and light commodities. Whatever exigency of the state therefore this tax might be intended to supply, that exigency would be chiefly supplied at the expence of the poor, not of the rich; at the expence of those who are least able to supply it, not of those who are most able.

14   Thirdly, if government should at any time neglect the reparation of the high roads, it would be still more difficult, than it is at present, to compel the proper application of any part of the turnpike tolls. A large revenue might thus be levied upon the people, without any part of it being applied to the only purpose, to which a revenue levied in this manner ought ever to be applied. If the meanness and poverty of the trustees of turnpike roads render it sometimes difficult at present to oblige them to repair their wrong; their wealth and greatness would render it ten times more so in the case which is here supposed.

15   In France, the funds destined for the reparation of the high roads are under the immediate direction of the executive power. Those funds [102] consist, partly in ⁱa certain number ofⁱ days labour which the country people are in most parts of Europe obliged to give to the reparation of the highways; and partly in such a portion of the general revenue of the state as the king chuses to spare from his other expences.

16   By the antient law of France, as well as by that of most other parts of Europe, the ʲlabour of the country peopleʲ was under the direction of a local or provincial magistracy, which had no immediate dependency upon the king's council. But by the present practice both the ᵏlabour of the country peopleᵏ, and whatever other fund the king may chuse to assign

---

ᵍ⁻ᵍ tear and wear *1*   ʰ⁻ʰ tear and wear *1*   ⁱ⁻ⁱ the six *1*
ʲ⁻ʲ six days labour *1*   ᵏ⁻ᵏ six days labour *1*

⁹ See below, V.ii.d.5, where Smith comments on the support given by the government of China to the improvement of roads and canals.

for the reparation of the high roads in any particular province or general-ity, are entirely under the management of the intendant; an officer who is appointed and removed by the king's council, who receives his orders from it, and is in constant correspondence with it. In the progress of despotism the authority of the executive power gradually absorbs that of every other power in the state, and assumes to itself the management of every branch of revenue which is destined for any public purpose. In France, however, the great post-roads, the roads which make the communication between the principal towns of the kingdom, are in general kept in good order; and in some provinces are even a good deal superior to the greater part of the turnpike roads of England. But what we call the cross-roads, that is, the far greater part of the roads in the country, are entirely neglected, and are in many places abso-[103]lutely impassable for any heavy carriage. In some places it is even dangerous to travel on horseback, and mules are the only conveyance which can safely be trusted. The proud minister of an ostentatious court may frequently take pleasure in executing a work of splendor and magnificence, such as a great high-way which is frequently seen by the principal nobility, whose applauses, not only flatter his vanity, but even contribute to support his interest at court. But to execute a great number of little works, in which nothing that can be done can make any great appearance, or excite the smallest degree of admiration in any traveller, and which, in short, have nothing to recommend them but their extreme utility, is a business which appears in every respect too mean and paultry to merit the attention of so great a magistrate. Under such an administration, therefore, such works are almost always entirely neglected.

17   In China, and in several other governments of Asia, the executive power charges itself both with the reparation of the high roads, and with the maintenance of the navigable canals. In the instructions which are given to the governor of each province, those objects, it is said, are constantly recommended to him, and the judgment which the court forms of his conduct is very much regulated by the attention which he appears to have paid to this part of his instructions. This branch of publick police accordingly is said to be very much attended to in all those countries, but particularly in China, where the [104] high roads, and still more the navigable canals, it is pretended, exceed very much every thing of the same kind which is known in Europe. The accounts of those works, however, which have been transmitted to Europe, have generally been drawn up by weak and wondering travellers; frequently by stupid and lying missionaries.[10] If they had been examined by more intelligent eyes, and if the accounts of them had been reported by more faithful witnesses,

---

[10] Smith comments on the 'wonderful accounts' of the wealth of China at II.v.22.

they would not, perhaps, appear to be so wonderful. The account which Bernier gives of some works of this kind in Indostan, falls very much short of what had been reported of them by other travellers, more disposed to the marvellous than he was.[11] It may too, perhaps, be in those countries, as it is in France, where the great roads, the great communications which are likely to be the subjects of conversation at the court and in the capital, are attended to, and all the rest neglected. In China, besides, in Indostan, and in several other governments of Asia, the revenue of the sovereign arises almost altogether from a land-tax or land-rent, which rises or falls with the rise *and* fall of the annual produce of the land. The great interest of the sovereign, therefore, his revenue, is in such countries *necessarily* and immediately connected with the cultivation of the land, with the greatness of its produce, and with the value of its produce. But in order to render that produce both as great and as valuable as possible, it is necessary to procure to it as extensive a market as possible, and consequently to [105] establish the freest, the easiest, and the least expensive communication between all the different parts of the country; which can be done only by means of the best roads and the best navigable canals. But the revenue of the sovereign does not, in any part of Europe, arise chiefly from a land-tax or land-rent. In all the great kingdoms of Europe, perhaps, the greater part of it may ultimately depend upon the produce of the land: But that dependency is neither so immediate, nor so evident. In Europe, therefore, the sovereign does not feel himself so directly called upon to promote the increase, both in quantity and value, of the produce of the land, or, by maintaining good roads and canals, to provide the most extensive market for that produce. Though it should be true, therefore, what I apprehend is not a little doubtful, that in some parts of Asia this department of the publick police is very properly managed by the executive power, there is not the least probability that, during the present state of things, it could be tolerably managed by that power in any part of Europe.

18   Even those publick works which are of such a nature that they cannot afford any revenue for maintaining themselves, but of which the conveniency is nearly confined to some particular place or district, are always better maintained by a local or provincial revenue, under the management of a local and provincial administration, than by the general revenue of the state, of which the executive power must always have the ma-[106] nagement. Were the streets of London to be lighted and paved at the expence of the treasury, is there any probability that they would be so well

---

l-l or *I*   *m-m* necessary *4* ⟨corrected *4e–6*⟩

[11] Bernier does not give an account which would justify this statement. Translated as *Travels in the Mogul Empire by F. Bernier* by I. Brock (London, 1826).

lighted and paved as they are at present, or even at so small an expence? The expence, besides, instead of being raised by a local tax upon the inhabitants of each particular street, parish, or district in London, would, in this case, be defrayed out of the general revenue of the state, and would consequently be raised by a tax upon all the inhabitants of the kingdom, of whom the greater part derive no sort of benefit from the lighting and paving of the streets of London.

19   The abuses which sometimes creep into the local and provincial administration of a local and provincial revenue, how enormous soever they may appear, are in reality, however, almost always very trifling, in comparison of those which commonly take place in the administration and expenditure of the revenue of a great empire. They are, besides, much more easily corrected. Under the local or provincial administration of the justices of the peace in Great Britain, the six days labour which the country people are obliged to give to the reparation of the highways, is not always perhaps very judiciously applied, but it is scarce ever exacted with any circumstance of cruelty or oppression. In France, under the administration of the intendants, the application is not always more judicious, and the exaction is frequently the most cruel and oppressive.[12] Such Corvées, as they are called, make one of the principal instruments of tyranny by which ⁿthose [107] officers chastiseⁿ any parish or communeauté which has had the misfortune to fall under ᵒtheirᵒ displeasure.

ᵃOf the Publick Works and Institutions which are necessary for facilitating particular Branches of Commerce

1   The object of the publick works and institutions above mentioned is to facilitate commerce in general. But in order to facilitate some particular branches of it, particular institutions are necessary, which again require a particular and extraordinary expence.

2   Some particular branches of commerce, which are carried on with barbarous and uncivilized nations, require extraordinary protection. An ordinary store or counting-house could give little security to the goods of the merchants who trade to the western coast of Africa. To defend them from the barbarous natives, it is necessary that the place where they are deposited, should be, in some measure, fortified. The disorders in the

---

ⁿ⁻ⁿ the intendant chastises *1*   ᵒ⁻ᵒ his *1*

ᵃ⁻ᵃ 2A–6 [This includes the whole of V.i.e. In Letter 222 addressed to Thomas Cadell, dated 7 December 1782, Smith indicated that among the additions to the second edition there was 'a short, but I flatter myself, a compleat History of all the trading companies in Great Britain'. Smith also refers to the additions in Letter 227 addressed to Strahan, dated 22 May 1783, and comments on his projected 'short History, and, I presume, a full exposition of the Absurdity and hurtfulness of almost all our chartered trading companies'.]

[12] See above, III.ii.18.

government of Indostan have been supposed to render a like precaution necessary even among that mild and gentle people; and it was under pretence of securing their persons and property from violence, that both the English and French East India Companies were allowed to erect the first forts which they possessed in that country. Among other nations, whose vigorous government will suffer no strangers to possess [108] any fortified place within their territory, it may be necessary to maintain some ambassador, minister, or consul, who may both decide, according to their own customs, the differences arising among his own countrymen; and, in their disputes with the natives, may, by means of his publick character, interfere with more authority, and afford them a more powerful protection, than they could expect from any private man. The interests of commerce have frequently made it necessary to maintain ministers in foreign countries, where the purposes, either of war or alliance, would not have required any.[1] The commerce of the Turkey Company first occasioned the establishment of an ordinary ambassador at Constantinople.[2] The first English embassies to Russia arose altogether from commercial interests.[3] The constant interference which those interests necessarily occasioned between the subjects of the different states of Europe, has probably introduced the custom of keeping, in all neighbouring countries, ambassadors or ministers constantly resident even in the time of peace. This custom, unknown to antient times, seems not to be older than the end of the fifteenth or beginning of the sixteenth century; that is, than the time when commerce first began to extend itself to the greater part of the nations of Europe, and when they first began to attend to its interests.

3   It seems not unreasonable, that the extraordinary expence, which the protection of any particular branch of commerce may occasion, should be defrayed by a moderate tax upon that [109] particular branch; by a moderate fine, for example, to be paid by the traders when they first enter into it, or, what is more equal, by a particular duty of so much per cent. upon the goods which they either import into, or export out of, the particular countries with which it is carried on. The protection of trade in general, from pirates and freebooters, is said to have given occasion to the first institution of the duties of customs. But, if it was thought reasonable to lay a general tax upon trade, in order to defray the expence of protecting trade in general, it should seem equally reasonable to lay a particular tax upon a particular branch of trade, in order to defray the extraordinary expence of protecting that branch.

[1] It is pointed out in LJ (B) 353, ed. Cannan 276, that permanent ambassadors only became necessary with the growth of commerce and that the first king to employ one was Ferdinand of Spain at the beginning of the seventeenth century.
[2] A. Anderson, *Origin of Commerce* (1764), i.470, quoting T. Rymer, *Foedera*.
[3] Ibid. ii.6 and 15, quoting Rymer.

4   The protection of trade in general has always been considered as essential to the defence of the commonwealth, and, upon that account, a necessary part of the duty of the executive power. The collection and application of the general duties of customs, therefore, have always been left to that power. But the protection of any particular branch of trade is a part of the general protection of trade; a part, therefore, of the duty of that power; and if nations always acted consistently, the particular duties levied for the purposes of such particular protection, should always have been left equally to its disposal. But in this respect, as well as in many others, nations have not always acted consistently; and in the greater part of the commercial states of Europe, particular companies of merchants have had the address to perswade the legislature to entrust to [110] them the performance of this part of the duty of the sovereign, together with all the powers which are necessarily connected with it.[4]

5   These companies, though they may, perhaps, have been useful for the first introduction of some branches of commerce, by making, at their own expence, an experiment which the state might not think it prudent to make, have in the long-run proved, universally, either burdensome or useless, and have either mismanaged or confined the trade.[5]

6   When those companies do not trade upon a joint stock, but are obliged to admit any person, properly qualified, upon paying a certain fine, and agreeing to submit to the regulations of the company, each member trading upon his own stock, and at his own risk, they are called regulated companies. When they trade upon a joint stock, each member sharing in the common profit or loss in proportion to his share in this stock, they are called joint stock companies. Such companies, whether regulated or joint stock, sometimes have, and sometimes have not exclusive privileges.

7   Regulated companies resemble, in every respect, the corporations of trades, so common in the cities and towns of all the different countries of Europe; and are a sort of enlarged monopolies of the same kind.[6] As no inhabitant of a town can exercise an incorporated trade, without first obtaining his freedom in the corporation, so in most cases no subject of the state can lawfully carry on any branch of foreign trade, for [111] which a regulated company is established, without first becoming a member of that company. The monopoly is more or less strict according as the terms of admission are more or less difficult; and according as the directors of the company have more or less authority, or have it more or less

---

[4] The point is frequently emphasized, see for example I.xi.p.10, and n. 12.

[5] LJ (A) vi.88 argues that 'all companies, such as the East Indian, Turky and Hudson's bay, diminish the opulence with regard to these commodities . . .' In LJ (B) 232, ed. Cannan 179, it is stated with regard to these companies that the people engaged in them make what price they please . However, see below, § 30, where Smith defends 'temporary' monopolies, and cf. Steuart, *Principles*, II.xxx, question 8.

[6] See above, I.x.c.5.

in their power to manage, in such a manner as to confine the greater part of the trade to themselves, and their particular friends. In the most antient regulated companies the privileges of apprenticeship were the same as in other corporations;[7] and entitled the person who had served his time to a member of the company, to become himself a member, either without paying any fine, or upon paying a much smaller one than what was exacted of other people. The usual corporation spirit, wherever the law does not restrain it, prevails in all regulated companies. When they have been allowed to act according to their natural genius, they have always, in order to confine the competition to as small a number of persons as possible, endeavoured to subject the trade to many burdensome regulations. When the law has restrained them from doing this, they have become altogether useless and insignificant.

8   The regulated companies for foreign commerce, which at present subsist in Great Britain are, the antient merchant adventurers company, now commonly called the Hamburgh Company, the *b*Russia*b* Company, the Eastland Company, the Turkey Company, and the African Company. [112]

9   The terms of admission into the Hamburgh Company, are now said to be quite easy; and the directors either have it not in their power to subject the trade to any burdensome *c*restraints*c* or regulations, or, at least, have not of late exercised that power. It has not always been so. About the middle of the last century, the fine for admission was fifty, and at one time one hundred pounds,[8] and the conduct of the company was said to be extremely oppressive. In 1643, in 1645, and in 1661, the clothiers and free traders of the West of England complained of them to parliament, as of monopolists who confined the trade and oppressed the manufactures of the country.[9] Though those complaints produced no act of parliament, they had probably intimidated the company so far, as to oblige them to reform their conduct. Since that time, at least, there *d*has*d* been no complaints against them. By the 10th and 11th of William III. c. 6.[10] the fine for admission into the Russian Company was reduced to five pounds;

---

b-b Russian *2A*   *c-c* restraint *4-6*   *d-d* have *5-6*

[7] See above, I.x.c.7.

[8] Raised to £100 for Londoners and £50 for others in 1643. A. Anderson, *Origin of Commerce* (1764), ii.75.

[9] 'Many and loud Complaints had been made by the Merchants and Clothiers of Exeter and other Parts of the West of England, who, not being free of the Company of Merchant Adventurers of England, were by that Company stiled Interlopers; as particularly, in the Year 1638, to the House of Commons, and also in the Years 1643 and 1645. They were again complained of in Parliament in this Year 1661, by them; who, in their Remonstrance, termed that Company Monopolizers, and Obstructors of the Sale of our Woollen Goods.' (Ibid. ii.116–18.) Details of the complaints and answers are given.

[10] 10 William III, c. 6 (1698) in *Statutes of the Realm*, vii.462–3; 10 and 11 William III, c. 6 in Ruffhead's edition.

and by the 25th of Charles II. c. 7.[11] that for admission into the Eastland
Company, to forty shillings, while, at the same time, Sweden, Denmark
and Norway, all the countries on the north-side of the Baltick, were
exempted from their exclusive charter. The conduct of those companies
had probably given occasion to those two acts of parliament. Before that
time, Sir Josiah Child[12] had represented both these and the Hamburgh
Company as extremely oppressive, and imputed to their bad management
the low state of the trade, which [113] we at that time carried on to the
countries comprehended within their respective charters. But though
such companies may not, in the present times, be very oppressive, they
are certainly altogether useless. To be merely useless, indeed, is perhaps
the highest eulogy which can ever justly be bestowed upon a regulated
company; and all the three companies above mentioned seem, in their
present state, to deserve this eulogy.

10   The fine for admission into the Turky Company, was formerly twenty-
five pounds for all persons under twenty-six years of age, and fifty pounds
for all persons above that age. Nobody but mere merchants could be
admitted; a restriction which excluded all shop-keepers and retailers. By
a bye-law, no British manufactures could be exported to Turky but in
the general ships of the company; and as those ships sailed always from
the port of London, this restriction confined the trade to that *expensive*
port, and the traders, to those who lived in London and in its neighbourhood.
By another bye-law, no person living within twenty miles of London,
and not free of the city, could be admitted a member; another restriction,
which, joined to the foregoing, necessarily excluded all but the freemen of
London. As the time for the loading and sailing of those general ships
depended altogether upon the directors, they could easily fill them with
their own goods and those of their particular friends, to the exclusion of
others, who, they might pretend, had made their proposals too late. In
this state of things, there-[114]fore, this company was in every respect
a strict and oppressive monopoly. Those abuses gave occasion to the act
of the 26th of George II. c. 18.[13] reducing the fine for admission to twenty
pounds for all persons, without any distinction of ages, or any restriction,
either to mere merchants, or to the freemen of London; and granting to
all such persons the liberty of exporting, from all the ports of Great
Britain to any port of Turky, all British goods of which the exportation
was not prohibited; and of importing from thence all Turkish goods, of
which the importation was not prohibited, upon paying both the general
duties of customs, and the particular duties assessed for defraying the

---

e-e extensive 2*A*

[11] 25 Charles II, c. 7 (1672).
[12] Sir Josiah Child, *New Discourse of Trade* (1694), chapter iii.
[13] 26 George II, c. 18 (1753).

necessary expences of the company; and submitting, at the same time, to the lawful authority of the British ambassador and consuls resident in Turky, and to the bye-laws of the company duly enacted. To prevent any oppression by those bye-laws, it was by the same act ordained, that if any seven members of the company conceived themselves aggrieved by any bye-law which should be enacted after the passing of this act, they might appeal to the Board of Trade and Plantations (to the authority of which, a committee of the privy council has now succeeded), provided such appeal was brought within twelve months after the bye-law was enacted; and that if any seven members conceived themselves aggrieved by any bye-law which had been enacted before the passing of this act, they might bring a like appeal, provided it was within twelve [115] months after the day on which this act was to take place. The experience of one year, however, may not always be sufficient to discover to all the members of a great company the pernicious tendency of a particular bye-law; and if several of them should afterwards discover it, neither the Board of Trade, nor the committee of council can afford them any redress. The object, besides, of the greater part of the bye-laws of all regulated companies, as well as of all other corporations, is not so much to oppress those who are already members, as to discourage others from becoming so; which may be done, not only by a high fine, but by many other contrivances. The constant view of such companies is always to raise the rate of their own profit as high as they can; to keep the market, both for the goods which they export, and for those which they import, as much understocked as they can: which can be done only by restraining the competition, or by discouraging new adventurers from entering into the trade. A fine even of twenty pounds, besides, though it may not perhaps, be sufficient to discourage any man from entering into the Turky trade, with an intention to continue in it, may be enough to discourage a speculative merchant from hazarding a single adventure in it. In all trades, the regular established traders, even though not incorporated, naturally combine to raise profits, which are no-way so likely to be kept, at all times, down to their proper level, as by the occasional competition of speculative adventurers.[14] The Turky [116] trade, though in some measure laid open by this act of parliament, is still considered by many people as very far from being altogether free. The Turky company contribute to maintain an ambassador and two or three consuls, who, like other public ministers, ought to be maintained altogether by the state, and the trade laid open to all his majesty's subjects. The different taxes levied by the company, for this and other corporation purposes, might afford a revenue much more than sufficient to enable the state to maintain such ministers.

---

[14] But see above, II.iv.15 and note 17.

11   Regulated companies, it was observed by Sir Josiah Child,[15] though they had frequently supported publick ministers, had never maintained any forts or garrisons in the countries to which they traded; whereas joint stock companies frequently had. And in reality the former seem to be much more unfit for this sort of service than the latter. First, the directors of a regulated company have no particular interest in the prosperity of the general trade of the company, for the sake of which, such forts and garrisons are maintained. The decay of that general trade may even frequently contribute to the advantage of their own private trade; as by diminishing the number of their competitors, it may enable them both to buy cheaper, and to sell dearer. The directors of a joint stock company, on the contrary, having only their share in the profits which are made upon the common stock committed to their management, have no private trade of their own, of which the interest can be [117] separated from that of the general trade of the company. Their private interest is connected with the prosperity of the general trade of the company; and with the maintenance of the forts and garrisons, which are necessary for its defence. They are more likely, therefore, to have that continual and careful attention which that maintenance necessarily requires.[16] Secondly, The directors of a joint stock company have always the management of a large capital, the joint stock of the company, a part of which they may frequently employ, with propriety, in building, repairing, and maintaining such necessary forts and garrisons. But the directors of a regulated company, having the management of no common capital, have no other fund to employ in this way, but the casual revenue arising from the admission fines, and from the corporation duties, imposed upon the trade of the company. Though they had the same interest, therefore, to attend to the maintenance of such forts and garrisons, they can seldom have the same ability to render that attention effectual. The maintenance of a publick minister requiring scarce any attention, and but a moderate and limited expence, is a business much more suitable both to the temper and abilities of a regulated company.

12   Long after the time of Sir Josiah Child, however, in 1750, a regulated company was established, the present company of merchants trading to Africa, which was expressly charged at first with the maintenance of all the British forts and garrisons that lie between Cape Blanc and [118] the Cape of Good Hope, and afterwards with that of those only which lie between Cape Rouge and the Cape of Good Hope. The act which establishes this company (the 23d of George II. c. 31.)[17] seems to have had two distinct objects in view; first, to restrain effectually the oppressive and

---

[15] Sir Josiah Child, *New Discourse of Trade*, 109.   [16] See below, § 18.
[17] 23 George II, c. 31 (1749). See below § 20 for a description of the legislation governing the Royal African Company.

monopolizing spirit which is natural to the directors of a regulated company; and secondly, to force them, as much as possible, to give an attention, which is not natural to them, towards the maintenance of forts and garrisons.

13   For the first of these purposes, the fine for admission is limited to forty shillings. The company is prohibited from trading in their corporate capacity, or upon a joint stock; from borrowing money upon common seal, or from laying any restraints upon the trade which may be carried on freely from all places, and by all persons being British subjects, and paying the fine. The government is in a committee of nine persons who meet at London, but who are chosen annually by the freemen of the company at London, Bristol and Liverpool; three from each place. No committee-man can be continued in office for more than three years together. Any committee-man might be removed by the Board of Trade and Plantations; now by a committee of council, after being heard in his own defence. The committee are forbid to export negroes from Africa, or to import any African goods into Great Britain. But as they are charged with the maintenance of forts and garrisons, they may, for that purpose, export from Great Britain to Africa, [119] goods and stores of different kinds. Out of the monies which they shall receive from the company, they are allowed a sum not exceeding eight hundred pounds for the salaries of their clerks and agents at London, Bristol and Liverpool, the house rent of their office at London, and all *f* other expences of management, commission and agency in England. What remains of this sum, after defraying these different expences, they may divide among themselves, as compensation for their trouble, in what manner they think proper. By this constitution, it might have been expected, that the spirit of monopoly would have been effectually restrained, and the first of these purposes sufficiently answered. It would seem, however, that it had not. Though by the 4th of George III. c. 20.[18] the fort of Senegal, with all its dependencies, had been vested in the company of merchants trading to Africa, yet in the year following, (by the 5th of George III. c. 44.)[19] not only Senegal and its dependencies, but the whole coast, from the port of Sallee, in south Barbary, to Cape Rouge, was exempted from the jurisdiction of that company, was vested in the crown, and the trade to it declared free to all his majesty's subjects. The company had been suspected of restraining the trade, and of establishing some sort of improper monopoly. It is not, however, very easy to conceive how, under the regulations of the 23d George II. they could do so. In the printed debates of the House of Com-

---

f–f the 2A

[18] 4 George III, c. 20 (1764).
[19] 5 George III, c. 44 (1765).

mons, not always the most authentic records of truth, I observe, however, that they have been ac-[120]cused of this. The members of the committee of nine, being all merchants, and the governors and factors, in their different forts and settlements, being all dependent upon them, it is not unlikely that the latter might have given peculiar attention to the consignments and commissions of the former, which would establish a real monopoly.

14   For the second of these purposes, the maintenance of the forts and garrisons, an annual sum has been allotted to them by parliament, generally about 13,000 *l.* For the proper application of this sum, the committee is obliged to account annually to the Cursitor Baron of Exchequer; which account is afterwards to be laid before parliament. But parliament, which gives so little attention to the application of millions, is not likely to give much to that of 13,000 *l.* a-year; and the Cursitor Baron of Exchequer, from his profession and education, is not likely to be profoundly skilled in the proper expence of forts and garrisons. The captains of his majesty's navy, indeed, or any other commissioned officers, appointed by the Board of Admiralty, may enquire into the condition of the forts and garrisons, and report their observations to that board. But that board seems to have no direct jurisdiction over the committee, nor any authority to correct those whose conduct it may thus enquire into; and the captains of his majesty's navy, besides, are not supposed to be always deeply learned in the science of fortification. Removal from an office, which can be enjoyed only [121] for the term of three years, and of which the lawful emoluments, even during that term, are so very small, seems to be the utmost punishment to which any committee-man is liable, for any fault, except direct malversation, or embezzlement, either of the publick money, or of that of the company; and the fear of that punishment can never be a motive of sufficient weight to force a continual and careful attention to a business, to which he has no other interest to attend. The committee are accused of having sent out bricks and stones from England for the reparation of Cape Coast Castle on the coast of Guinea, a business for which parliament had several times granted an extraordinary sum of money. These bricks and stones too, which had thus been sent upon so long a voyage, were said to have been of so bad a quality, that it was necessary to rebuild from the foundation the walls which had been repaired with them. The forts and garrisons which lie north of Cape Rouge, are not only maintained at the expence of the state, but are under the immediate government of the executive power; and why those which lie south of that Cape, and which too are, in part at least, maintained at the expence of the state, should be under a different government, it seems not very easy even to imagine a good reason. The protection of the Mediterranean trade was the original purpose or pretence of the garrisons of

Gibraltar and Minorca,[20] and the maintenance and government of those garrisons has always been, very properly, committed, not to the Turky [122] Company, but to the executive power. In the extent of its dominion consists, in a great measure, the pride and dignity of that power; and it is not very likely to fail in attention to what is necessary for the defence of that dominion. The garrisons at Gibraltar and Minorca, accordingly, have never been neglected; though Minorca has been twice taken, and is now probably lost for ever, that disaster was never even imputed to any neglect in the executive power. I would not, however, be understood to insinuate, that either of those expensive garrisons was ever, even in the smallest degree, necessary for the purpose for which they were originally dismembered from the Spanish monarchy. That dismemberment, perhaps, never served any other real purpose than to alienate from England her natural ally the King of Spain, and to unite the two principal branches of the house of Bourbon in a much stricter and more permanent alliance than the ties of blood could ever have united them.[21]

15   Joint stock companies, established either by royal charter or by act of parliament, differ in several respects, not only from regulated companies, but from private copartneries.[22]

16   First, In a private copartnery, no partner, without the consent of the company, can transfer his share to another person, or introduce a new member into the company. Each member, however, may, upon proper warning, withdraw from the copartnery, and demand payment from them of his share of the common stock. In a joint stock company, on the contrary, no member [123] can demand payment of his share from the company; but each member can, without their consent, transfer his share to another person, and thereby introduce a new member. The value of a share in a joint stock is always the price which it will bring in the market; and this may be either greater or less, in any proportion, than the sum which its owner stands credited for in the stock of the company.

17   Secondly, In a private copartnery, each partner is bound for the debts contracted by the company to the whole extent of his fortune. In a joint

[20] Smith refers to Minorca in the course of criticizing Hume's 'utility' thesis in TMS IV.i.2.11: 'There is many an honest Englishman, who, in his private station, would be more seriously disturbed by the loss of a guinea, than by the national loss of Minorca, who yet, had it been in his power to defend that fortress, would have sacrificed his life a thousand times rather than, through his fault, have let it fall into the hands of the enemy.'

[21] In Letter 221 addressed to Sir John Sinclair, dated 14 October 1782, Smith remarked that it was to our possession of 'the barren rock of Gibralter' that 'we owe the union of France and Spain, contrary to the natural interests and inveterate prejudices of both countries, the important enmity of Spain, and the futile and expensive friendship of Portugal'.

[22] Most of the information on the trading companies given in subsequent paragraphs is from A. Anderson, *Origin of Commerce* (1764). Apart from some specific references, a general note is given at the end of most paragraphs.

stock company, on the contrary, each partner is bound only to the extent of his share.[23]

18   The trade of a joint stock company is always managed by a court of directors. The court, indeed, is frequently subject, in many respects, to the controul of a general court of proprietors. But the greater part of [g]those[g] proprietors seldom pretend to understand any thing of the business of the company; and when the spirit of faction happens not to prevail among them, give themselves no trouble about it, but receive contentedly such half yearly or yearly dividend, as the directors think proper to make to them. This total exemption from trouble and from risk, beyond a limited sum, encourages many people to become adventurers in joint stock companies, who would, upon no account, hazard their fortunes in any private copartnery.[24] Such companies, therefore, commonly draw to themselves much greater stocks than any private copartnery can boast of. The trading stock of the South Sea [124] Company, at one time, amounted to upwards of thirty-three millions eight hundred thousand pounds.[25] The divided capital of the Bank of England amounts, at present, to ten millions seven hundred and eighty thousand pounds.[26] The directors of such companies, however, being the managers rather of other people's money than of their own, it cannot well be expected, that they should watch over it with the same anxious vigilance with which the partners in a private copartnery frequently watch over their own. Like the stewards of a rich man, they are apt to consider attention to small matters as not for their master's honour, and very easily give themselves a dispensation from having it. Negligence and profusion, therefore, must always prevail, more or less, in the management of the affairs of such a company. It is upon this account that joint stock companies for foreign trade have seldom been able to maintain the competition against private adventurers.[27] They have, accordingly, very seldom succeeded without an exclusive privilege; and frequently have not succeeded with one. Without an exclusive privilege they have commonly mismanaged the trade. With an exclusive privilege they have both mismanaged and confined it.

19   The royal African Company, the predecessors of the present African

[g-g] these 6

---

[23] Joint stock companies incorporated by Royal Charter or Act of Parliament were often assumed to have limited liability even when a strict legal interpretation may have led to a different conclusion. See H. A. Shannon, 'The Coming of General Limited Liability', *Economic History*, ii (1931) and R. H. Campbell, 'The Law and the Joint-Stock Company in Scotland', in P. L. Payne, *Studies in Scottish Business History* (London, 1967), chapter 6.

[24] This may provide some qualification to the doctrine that the 'chance of loss is frequently undervalued' as stated at I.x.b.28.

[25] A. Anderson, *Origin of Commerce* (1764), ii.309. It was £37,802,203 in 1720.

[26] Ibid. ii.379. See below, V.ii.a.4.   [27] See above, § 11.

Company, had an exclusive privilege by charter;[28] but as that charter had not been confirmed by act of parliament, the trade, in consequence of the declaration of rights,[29] was, soon after the revolution, laid open [125] to all his majesty's subjects. The Hudson's Bay Company are, as to their legal rights, in the same situation as the Royal African Company. Their exclusive charter has not been confirmed by act of parliament. The South Sea Company, as long as they continued to be a trading company, had an exclusive privilege confirmed by act of parliament; as have likewise the present United Company of Merchants trading to the East Indies.

20   The Royal African Company soon found that they could not maintain the competition against private adventurers, whom, notwithstanding the declaration of rights, they continued for some time to call interlopers, and to persecute as such. In 1698, however, the private adventurers were subjected to a duty of ten per cent. upon almost all the different branches of their trade, to be employed by the company in the maintenance of their forts and garrisons[30]. But, notwithstanding this heavy tax, the company were still unable to maintain the competition. Their stock and credit gradually declined. In 1712, their debts had become so great, that a particular act of parliament was thought necessary, both for their security and for that of their creditors.[31] It was enacted, that the resolution of two-thirds of these creditors in number and value, should bind the rest, both with regard to the time which should be allowed to the company

[28] Passed the Great Seal, 1672. C. T. Carr, *Select Charters of Trading Companies* (Selden Society, xxviii), 186–92.

[29] In this paragraph Smith draws on Anderson, *Origin of Commerce*, ii. 148, 154, 225. On 2 William and Mary, c. 2, An Act declaring the Rights and Liberties of the Subject and Settling the Succession of the Crown, Anderson states (ii.148) that if this Act had 'not limited the Prerogative in the Case of exclusive Charters of Privileges, this Company would doubtless be absolute in those immense Territories. But the Case, to our great Happiness, is now quite otherwise; and, since that great Establishment of our Liberties, neither the Hudson Bay, nor any other Company, not confirmed by Act of Parliament, has any exclusive right at all.' In practice the contrast between the companies may have been less clear than Smith implies. 9 Anne, c. 15 (1710) in *Statutes of the Realm*, ix.428–447; 9 Anne, c. 21 in Ruffhead's edition authorized the grant of a monopoly of trade, which was embodied in the charter of 1711, to the South Sea Company. 6 Anne, c. 71 (1707) in *Statutes of the Realm*, viii.824–9; 6 Anne, c. 17 in Ruffhead's edition incorporated the East India Company. The positions of the Royal African Company and the Hudson's Bay Company were less clear. Various statutes implied parliamentary recognition of the charters even after the Bill of Rights, e.g. 4 William and Mary, c. 15 (1692) levied duties on the stocks of the East India, African and Hudson's Bay Companies and states that their charters will be void if the duties are not paid; and 9 William III, c. 26 (1697) settled the maintenance of forts on the Royal African Company. Modern commentators do not draw Smith's distinction. See W. R. Scott, *English, Scottish and Irish Joint Stock Companies* ii.232 and K. G. Davies, *The Royal African Company* (London, 1957), 122–35.

[30] 9 William III, c. 26 (1697).

[31] 10 Anne, c. 34 (1711) in *Statutes of the Realm*, ix. 703. 10 Anne, c. 27 in Ruffhead's edition.

for the payment of their debts; and with regard to any other agreement which it might be thought proper to make with them concerning those debts. In 1730, [126] their affairs were in so great disorder, that they were altogether incapable of maintaining their forts and garrisons, the sole purpose and pretext of their institution. From that year, till their final dissolution, the parliament judged it necessary to allow the annual sum of ten thousand pounds for that purpose.[32] In 1732, after having been for many years losers by the trade of carrying negroes to the West Indies, they at last resolved to give it up altogether; to sell to the private traders to America the negroes which they purchased upon the coast; and to employ their servants in a trade to the inland parts of Africa for gold dust, elephants teeth, dying drugs, &c. But their success in this more confined trade was not greater than in their former extensive one. Their affairs continued to go gradually to decline, till at last, being in every respect a bankrupt company, they were dissolved by act of parliament, and their forts and garrisons vested in the present regulated company of merchants trading to Africa.[33] Before the erection of the Royal African Company, there had been three other joint stock companies successively established, one after another, for the African trade.[34] They were all equally unsuccessful. They all, however, had exclusive charters which, though not confirmed by act of parliament, were in those days supposed to convey a real exclusive privilege.[35]

21   The Hudson's Bay Company, before their misfortunes in the late war, had been much more fortunate than the Royal African Company. Their [127] necessary expence is much smaller. The whole number of people whom they maintain in their different settlements and habitations, which they have honoured with the name of forts, is said not to exceed a hundred and twenty persons. This number, however, is sufficient to prepare beforehand the cargo of furs and other goods necessary for loading their ships, which, on account of the ice, can seldom remain above six or eight weeks in those seas. This advantage of having a cargo ready prepared, could not for several years be acquired by private adventurers, and without it there seems to be no possibility of trading to Hudson's Bay. The moderate capital of the company, which, it is said, does not exceed one hundred and ten thousand pounds,[36] may besides be sufficient to enable

---

[32] 'In 1744 [the sum] was increased to £20,000, but in the following year reduced to the original figure; after 1746 it was withheld entirely.' K. G. Davies, The Royal Africa Company, 345.

[33] 23 George II, c. 31 (1749) and 25 George II, c. 40 (1751). See above, §§ 12 and 13.

[34] Senegal Adventurers, 1588; Company of Adventurers of London trading to Guinea and Benin, 1618; Royal Adventurers into Africa, 1660.

[35] For information on the Royal African Company in this paragraph see Anderson, Origin of Commerce, ii.225, 326, 347.

[36] The capital was increased to £103,950 in 1720 and remained at that level until 1825. Full details are in D. MacKay, The Honourable Company (Toronto, 1938), appendix D.

them to engross the whole, or almost the whole, trade and surplus produce of the miserable, though extensive country, comprehended within their charter. No private adventurers, accordingly, have ever attempted to trade to that country in competition with them. This company, there-fore, have always enjoyed an exclusive trade in fact, though they may have no right to it in law. Over and above all this, the moderate capital of this company is said to be divided among a very small number of proprie-tors.[37] But a joint stock company, consisting of a small number of pro-prietors, with a moderate capital, approaches very nearly to the nature of a private copartnery, and may be capable of nearly the same degree of vigilance and attention. It is not to be wondered at, therefore, if, [128] in consequence of these different advantages, the Hudson's Bay Company had, before the late war, been able to carry on their trade with a con-siderable degree of success. It does not seem probable, however, that their profits ever approached to what the late Mr. Dobbs imagined them.[38] A much more sober and judicious writer, Mr. Anderson, author of The Historical and Chronological Deduction of Commerce, very justly observes, that upon examining the accounts which Mr. Dobbs himself has given for several years together, of their exports and imports, and upon making proper allowances for their extraordinary risk and expence, it does not appear that their profits deserve to be envied, or that they can much, if at all, exceed the ordinary profits of trade.[39]

22   The South Sea Company never had any forts or garrisons to maintain, and therefore were entirely exempted from one great expence, to which other joint stock companies for foreign trade are subject. But they had an immense capital divided among an immense number of proprietors.

---

[37] Dobbs, not the most reliable source, held that '. . . their Charter . . . now is con-fined to eight or nine private Merchants, who have ingrossed nine Tenths of the Com-pany's Stock, and by that Means are perpetual Directors.' (*An Account of the Countries adjoining to Hudson's Bay in the North-West Part of America . . . with an Abstract of Captain Middleton's Journal* (London, 1744), 58.) D. MacKay states that there were 109 proprietors in 1770, *The Honourable Company*, 338.

[38] '. . . the exorbitant Gain they take upon their Goods from the Natives of near 2,000 per Cent. Profit, taking a Beaver Skin, worth from eight to nine shillings in England, for a Quart of English Spirits, mixed with a Third Water, which probably may cost them a Groat; they also in Exchange value three Martins or Sable Skins at one Beaver, when the French give as much for a Martin as for a Beaver; so that the Natives carry all their best Furs to the French, and leave them the Refuse.' (Dobbs, *An Account of the Coun-tries adjoining to Hudson's Bay*, 56.) But, according to William Douglass, Dobbs 'runs much into the novel; he seems to be a wild projector, and notoriously credulous' (*British Settlements in North America*, i.275).

[39] 'Their Gains are little to be envied.' Anderson, *Origin of Commerce* ii.370. W. R. Scott considered the distribution in the half century before 1720 to be 'only a fraction higher than economic interest', though undivided profits were distributed as a stock bonus in 1690 and 1720. (*English, Scottish and Irish Joint Stock Companies*, ii.236). For information on the Hudson's Bay Company in this paragraph, see A. Anderson, ii.147, 370, 371.

It was naturally to be expected, therefore, that folly, negligence, and profusion should prevail in the whole management of their affairs. The knavery and extravagance of their stock-jobbing projects are sufficiently known, and the explication of them would be foreign to the present subject. Their mercantile projects were not much better conducted. The first trade which they engaged in was that of supplying the Spanish West Indies with negroes, of which (in con-[129]sequence of what was called the Assiento contract granted them by the treaty of Utrecht) they had the exclusive privilege.[40] But as it was not expected that much profit could be made by this trade, both the Portugueze and French companies, who had enjoyed it upon the same terms before them, having been ruined by it, they were allowed, as compensation, to send annually a ship of a certain burden to trade directly to the Spanish West Indies. Of the ten voyages which this annual ship was allowed to make, they are said to have gained considerably by one, that of the Royal Caroline in 1731, and to have been losers, more or less, by almost all the rest. Their ill success was imputed, by their factors and agents, to the extortion and oppression of the Spanish government; but was, perhaps, principally owing to the profusion and depredations of those very factors and agents; some of whom are said to have acquired great fortunes even in one year.[41] In 1734, the company petitioned the king, that they might be allowed to dispose of the trade and tunnage of their annual ship, on account of the little profit which they made by it, and to accept of such equivalent as they could obtain from the king of Spain.[42]

23   In 1724, this company had undertaken the whale-fishery. Of this, indeed, they had no monopoly; but as long as they carried it on, no other British subjects appear to have engaged in it. Of the eight voyages which their ships made to Greenland, they were gainers by one, and losers by all the rest. After their eighth and last voyage, when they had sold their ships, [130] stores, and utensils, they found that their whole loss, upon this branch, capital and interest included, amounted to upwards of two hundred and thirty-seven thousand pounds.[43]

24   In 1722, this company petitioned the parliament to be allowed to divide their immense capital of more than thirty-three millions eight hundred thousand pounds, the whole of which had been lent to government, into two equal parts: The one half, or upwards of sixteen millions nine

[40] Operated under contract by the African Company in 1713 and 1714. K. G. Davies, *The Royal African Company*, 152.
[41] The situation was more complex. See *New Cambridge Modern History*, vii (1957), 515–16.
[42] For information on the South Sea Company used in this paragraph see Anderson, *Origin of Commerce*, ii.262, 311, 334, 339, 347, 352.
[43] Anderson, *Origin of Commerce*, ii.339, states that the company lost considerably in all eight years.

hundred thousand pounds, to be put upon the same footing with other government annuities, and not to be subject to the debts contracted, or losses incurred, by the directors of the company, in the prosecution of their mercantile projects; the other half to remain, as before, a trading stock, and to be subject to those debts and losses. The petition was too reasonable not to be granted.[44] In 1733, they again petitioned the parliament, that three-fourths of their trading stock might be turned into annuity stock, and only one-fourth remain as trading stock, or exposed to the hazards arising from the bad management of their directors.[45] Both their annuity and trading stocks had, by this time, been reduced more than two millions each, by several different payments from government; so that this fourth amounted only to 3,662,784*l*. 8*s*. 6*d*.[46] In 1748, all the demands of the company upon the king of Spain, in consequence of the Assiento contract, were, by the treaty of Aix-la-Chapelle, given up for what was supposed an equivalent.[47] An end was put to their trade with the Spanish West Indies, the remainder of their trading [131] stock was turned into an annuity stock, and the company ceased in every respect to be a trading company.[48]

25   It ought to be observed, that in the trade which the South Sea Company carried on by means of their annual ship, the only trade by which it ever was expected that they could make any considerable profit, they were not without competitors, either in the foreign or in the home market. At Carthagena, Porto Bello, and La Vera Cruz, they had to encounter the competition of the Spanish merchants, who brought from Cadiz, to those markets, European goods, of the same kind with the outward cargo of their ship; and in England they had to encounter that of the English merchants, who imported from Cadiz goods of the Spanish West Indies, of the same kind with the inward cargo. The goods both of the Spanish and English merchants, indeed, were, perhaps, subject to higher duties. But the loss occasioned by the negligence, profusion, and malversation of the servants of the company, had probably been a tax much heavier than all those duties. That a joint stock company should be able to carry on successfully any branch of foreign trade, when private adventurers can come into any sort of open and fair competition with them, seems contrary to all experience.

26   The old English East India Company was established in 1600, by a charter from Queen Elizabeth. In the first twelve voyages which they

---

[44] By 9 George I, c. 6 (1722).   [45] Granted by 6 George II, c. 28 (1732).

[46] The trading capital was reduced by two-thirds, not by three-quarters, leaving £3,662,784. P. G. M. Dickson, *The Financial Revolution in England* (London, 1967), 208.

[47] Of £100,000 in 1751.

[48] For information on the South Sea Company used in this paragraph see Anderson, *Origin of Commerce*, ii.309, 316, 331, 333, 338, 346, 349, 388, 394.

fitted out for India, they appear to have traded as a regulated company, with separate [132] stocks, though only in the general ships of the company. In 1612, they united into a joint stock.[49] Their charter was exclusive, and though not confirmed by act of parliament, was in those days supposed to convey a real exclusive privilege. For many years, therefore, they were not much disturbed by interlopers. Their capital, which never exceeded seven hundred and forty-four thousand pounds,[50] and of which fifty pounds was a share, was not so exorbitant, nor their dealings so extensive, as to afford either a pretext for gross negligence and profusion, or a cover to gross malversation. Notwithstanding some extraordinary losses, occasioned partly by the malice of the Dutch East India Company, and partly by other accidents, they carried on for many years a successful trade. But in process of time, when the principles of liberty were better understood, it became every day more and more doubtful how far a royal charter, not confirmed by act of parliament, could convey an exclusive privilege. Upon this question the decisions of the courts of justice were not uniform, but varied with the authority of government and the humours of the times. Interlopers multiplied upon them; and towards the end of the reign of Charles II. through the whole of that of James II. and during a part of that of William III. reduced them to great distress.[51] In 1698, a proposal was made to parliament of advancing two millions to government at eight per cent. provided the subscribers were erected into a new East India Company with exclusive privileges. The old East India Company offered seven hundred thousand [133] pounds, nearly the amount of their capital,[52] at four per cent. upon the same conditions. But such was at that time the state of publick credit, that it was more convenient for government to borrow two millions at eight per cent. than seven hundred thousand pounds at four. The proposal of the new subscribers was accepted, and a new East India Company established in consequence.[53] The old East India Company, however, had a right to continue their trade till 1701. They had, at the same time, in the name of their treasurer, subscribed, very artfully, three hundred and fifteen thousand pounds into the stock of the new. By a negligence in the expression of the act of parliament, which vested the East India trade in the subscribers to this loan of two

---

[49] Previously the capital for each voyage was raised separately, but in 1613 it was resolved to raise capital for four voyages and describe it as the 'First Joint Stock'. Scott, *English, Scottish and Irish Joint Stock Companies*, ii.101.

[50] The nominal stock in 1693, when an equivalent sum was added.

[51] 'Although the English East-India Company's Affairs were said at this Time to have been so prosperous, that its Profits in nine Years Time, *viz.* from 1676 to 1685, amounted to £963,639 yet, as Things on Earth are unstable, a Reverse of Fortune happened at this very Time.' (Anderson, *Origin of Commerce*, ii.184.)

[52] After their existing capital of £1,574,608 had been written down to £787,304. Scott, *English, Scottish and Irish Joint Stock Companies*, ii.163–4.

[53] 9 William III, c. 44 (1697).

millions, it did not appear evident that they were all obliged to unite into a joint stock. A few private traders, whose subscriptions amounted only to seven thousand two hundred pounds, insisted upon the privilege of trading separately upon their own stocks and at their own risk.[54] The old East India Company had a right to a separate trade upon their old stock till 1701; and they had likewise, both before and after that period, a right, like that of other private traders, to a separate trade upon the three hundred and fifteen thousand pounds, which they had subscribed into the stock of the new company. The competition of the two companies with the private traders, and with one another, is said to have well nigh ruined both. Upon a subsequent occasion, in 1730, when a proposal was made to parliament for putting the trade under [134] the management of a regulated company, and thereby laying it in some measure open, the East India Company, in opposition to this proposal, represented in very strong terms, what had been, at this time, the miserable effects, as they thought them, of this competition. In India, they said, it raised the price of goods so high, that they were not worth the buying; and in England, by over-stocking the market, it sunk their price so low, that no profit could be made by them. That by a more plentiful supply, to the great advantage and conveniency of the publick, it must have reduced, very much, the price of India goods in the English market, cannot well be doubted; but that it should have raised very much their price in the Indian market, seems not very probable, as all the extraordinary demand which that competition could occasion, must have been but as a drop of water in the immense ocean of Indian commerce. The increase of demand, besides, though in the beginning it may sometimes raise the price of goods, never fails to lower it in the long run. It encourages production, and thereby increases the competition of the producers, who, in order to undersell one another, have recourse to new divisions of labour and new improvements of art, which might never otherwise have been thought of.[55] The miserable effects of which the company complained, were the cheapness of consumption and the encouragement given to production, precisely the two effects which it is the great business of political œconomy to promote. The competition, however, of which they gave this [135] doleful account, had not been allowed to be of long continuance. In 1702, the two companies were, in some measure, united by an indenture tripartite, to which the queen was the third party; and in 1708, they were, by act

---

[54] Subscribers of £23,000 of the £2,000,000 did not join either old or new joint-stock companies. The Company purchased their loan stock until the account outstanding was reduced to £7,200 in 1708. Scott, *English, Scottish and Irish Joint Stock Companies*, ii.166 and 191. They were allowed to continue trading by 6 Anne, c. 71 (1707) in *Statutes of the Realm*, viii.824–9; 6 Anne, c. 17 in Ruffhead's edition.

[55] Cf. I.xi.o.4, I.viii.57.

of parliament[56] perfectly consolidated into one company by their present name of The United Company of Merchants trading to the East Indies. Into this act it was thought worth while to insert a clause, allowing the separate traders to continue their trade till Michaelmas 1711, but at the same time empowering the directors, upon three years notice, to redeem their little capital of seven thousand two hundred pounds, and thereby to convert the whole stock of the company into a joint-stock. By the same act, the capital of the company, in consequence of a new loan to government, was augmented from two millions, to three millions two hundred thousand pounds. In 1743, the company advanced another million to government.[57] But this million being raised, not by a call upon the proprietors, but by selling annuities and contracting bond-debts, it did not augment the stock upon which the proprietors could claim a dividend. It augmented, however, their trading stock, it being equally liable with the other three millions two hundred thousand pounds, to the losses sustained and debts contracted, by the company in prosecution of their mercantile projects. From 1708, or at least from 1711, this company, being delivered from all competitors, and fully established in the monopoly of the English commerce to the East Indies, carried on a successful trade, and from their profits made [136] annually a moderate dividend to their proprietors.[58] During the French war, which began in 1741, the ambition of Mr. Dupleix, the French governor of Pondicherry, involved them in the wars of the Carnatic, and in the politics of the Indian princes. After many signal successes, and equally signal losses, they at last lost Madras, at that time their principal settlement in India. It was restored to them by the treaty of Aix-la-Chapelle; and about this time the spirit of war and conquest seems to have taken possession of their servants in India, and never since to have left them. During the French war, which began in 1755, their arms partook of the general good fortune of those of Great Britain. They defended Madras, took Pondicherry, recovered Calcutta, and acquired the revenues of a rich and extensive territory, amounting, it was then said, to upwards of three millions a-year. They remained for several years in quiet possession of this revenue: But in 1767, administration laid claim to their territorial acquisitions, and the revenue arising from them, as of right belonging to the crown; and the company, in compensation for this claim, agreed to pay to government four hundred thousand pounds a-year. They had before this gradually augmented their dividend from about

[56] 6 Anne, c. 71 (1707) in *Statutes of the Realm*, viii.824–9; 6 Anne, c. 17 in Ruffhead's edition. Details of the tripartite indenture of 1702 are given in para. XI of the Act, *Statutes of the Realm*, viii.825–6.
[57] By 17 George II, c. 17 (1743), payment had to be by 29 September 1744.
[58] For information on the East India Company used in the paragraph see Anderson, *Origin of Commerce*, i.488, ii.160, 199, 174, 184, 221–4, 230, 236–8, 246, 323–6, 372–3.

six to ten per cent.; that is, upon their capital of three millions two hundred thousand pounds, they had increased it by a hundred and twenty-eight thousand pounds, or had raised it from one hundred and ninety-two thousand, to three hundred and twenty thousand pounds a-year. They were attempting about [137] this time to raise it still further, to twelve and a half per cent. which would have made their annual payments to their proprietors equal to what they had agreed to pay annually to government, or to four hundred thousand pounds a-year. But during the two years in which their agreement with government was to take place, they were restrained from any further increase of dividend by two successive acts of parliament,[59] of which the object was to enable them to make a speedier progress in the payment of their debts, which were at this time estimated at upwards of six or seven millions sterling. In 1769, they renewed their agreement with government for five years more, and stipulated, that during the course of that period they should be allowed gradually to increase their dividend to twelve and a half per cent.; never increasing it, however, more than one per cent. in one year.[60] This increase of dividend, therefore, when it had risen to its utmost height, could augment their annual payments, to their proprietors and government together, but by six hundred and eight thousand pounds, beyond what they had been before their late territorial acquisitions. What the gross revenue of those territorial acquisitions was supposed to amount to, has already been mentioned; and by an account brought by the Cruttenden East Indiaman in 1768, the nett revenue, clear of all deductions and military charges, was stated at two millions forty-eight thousand seven hundred and forty-seven pounds. They were said at the same time to possess another revenue, arising partly from lands, but chiefly from the customs [138] established at their different settlements, amounting to four hundred and thirty-nine thousand pounds. The profits of their trade too, according to the evidence of their chairman before the House of Commons, amounted at this time to at least four hundred thousand pounds a-year; according to that of their accomptant, to at least five hundred thousand; according to the lowest account, at least equal to the highest dividend that was to be paid to their proprietors. So great a revenue might certainly have afforded an augmentation of six hundred and eight thousand pounds in their annual payments; and at the same time have left a large sinking fund sufficient for the speedy reduction of their debts. In 1773, however, their debts, instead of being reduced, were augmented by an arrear to the treasury in the payment of the four hundred thousand pounds, by another to the custom-house for duties unpaid, by a large debt to the bank for money borrowed, and by a fourth for bills drawn upon them

[59] 7 George III, c. 49 (1767) and 8 George III, c. 11 (1768).
[60] 9 George III, c. 24 (1769).

from India, and wantonly accepted, to the amount of upwards of twelve hundred thousand pounds.[61] The distress which these accumulated claims brought upon them, obliged them, not only to reduce all at once their dividend to six per cent.[62] but to throw themselves upon the mercy of government, and to supplicate, first, a release from the further payment of the stipulated four hundred thousand pounds a-year; and, secondly, a loan of fourteen hundred thousand, to save them from immediate bankruptcy. The great increase of their fortune had, it seems, only served to furnish their servants with a pretext for greater pro-[139]fusion, and a cover for greater malversation, than in proportion even to that increase of fortune. The conduct of their servants in India, and the general state of their affairs both in India and in Europe, became the ʰsubjectsʰ of a parliamentary inquiry;[63] in consequence of which several very important alterations were made in the constitution of their government, both at home and abroad.[64] In India, their principal settlements of Madras, Bombay, and Calcutta, which had before been altogether independent of one another, were subjected to a governor-general, assisted by a council of four assessors, parliament assuming to itself the first nomination of this governor and council who were to reside at Calcutta; that city having now become, what Madras was before, the most important of the English settlements in India. The court of the mayor of Calcutta, originally instituted for the trial of mercantile causes, which arose in the city and neighbourhood, had gradually extended its jurisdiction with the extension of the empire. It was now reduced and confined to the original purpose of its institution. Instead of it a new supreme court of judicature was established, consisting of a chief justice and three judges to be appointed by the crown. In Europe, the qualification necessary to entitle a proprietor to vote at their general courts was raised, from five hundred pounds, the

---

ʰ⁻ʰ subject 4–6

[61] In 1771 the sum was £1,578,000. L. S. Sutherland, *The East India Company in Eighteenth Century Politics* (Oxford, 1952), 226.

[62] Which automatically relieved the Company from paying £400,000 to the government.

[63] The printed series *Reports of Committees of the House of Commons* (First Series) iii and iv are largely devoted to the inquiry of 1772–3. The activities of the East India Company are described above, IV.vii.c.101–8. In a different connection it is perhaps interesting to note that Smith was among those mentioned as a possible adviser to the East India Company. In Letter 132 addressed to William Pulteney, dated 3 September 1772, Smith wrote: 'I think myself very much honoured and obliged to you for having mentioned me to the east India Directors as a person who could be of any use to them.' It would appear, however, that the Company invited Sir James Steuart to advise them on the currency problems of Bengal. *Principles*, ed. Skinner xlix. Steuart's report was published in 1772 as the *Principles of Money Applied to the Present State of the Coin in Bengal* and is reprinted in his *Collected Works*, v (London, 1805). For comment, see S. R. Sen, *The Economics of Sir James Steuart* (London, 1957), ch. 10.

[64] By 13 George III, c. 63 (1772).

original price of a share in the stock of the company, to a thousand pounds. In order to vote upon this qualification too, it was declared necessary that he should have possessed it, if acquired by his own purchase, and not by inheritance, for at [140] least one year, instead of six months, the term requisite before. The court of twenty-four directors had before been chosen annually; but it was now enacted that each director should, for the future, be chosen for four years; six of them, however, to go out of office by rotation every year, and not to be capable of being re-chosen at the election of the six new directors for the ensuing year. In consequence of these alterations, the courts, both of the proprietors and directors, it was expected, would be likely to act with more dignity and steadiness than they had usually done before. But it seems impossible, by any alterations, to render those courts, in any respect, fit to govern, or even to share in the government of a great empire; because the greater part of their members must always have too little interest in the prosperity of that empire, to give any serious attention to what may promote it. Frequently a man of great, sometimes even a man of small fortune, is willing to purchase a thousand pounds share in India stock, merely for the influence which he expects to acquire by a vote in the court of proprietors. It gives him a share, though not in the plunder, yet in the appointment of the plunderers of India; the court of directors, though they make that appointment, being necessarily more or less under the influence of the proprietors, who not only elect those directors, but sometimes over-rule the appointments of their servants in India. Provided he can enjoy this influence for a few years, and thereby provide for a certain number of his friends, he frequently cares little about the di-[141]vidend; or even about the value of the stock upon which his vote is founded. About the prosperity of the great empire, in the government of which that vote gives him a share, he seldom cares at all. No other sovereigns ever were, or, from the nature of things, ever could be, so perfectly indifferent about the happiness or misery of their subjects, the improvemenι or waste of their dominions, the glory or disgrace of their administration; as, from irresistible moral causes, the greater part of the proprietors of such a mercantile company are, and necessarily must be.[65] This indifference too was more likely to be increased than diminished by some of the new regulations, which were made in consequence of the parliamentary inquiry. By a resolution of the House of Commons, for example, it was declared, that when the fourteen hundred thousand pounds lent to the company by government should be paid, and their bond-debts be reduced to fifteen hundred thousand pounds, they might then, and not till then, divide eight per cent. upon their capital; and that whatever remained of

[65] See above, IV.vii.c.105, 107, where Smith comments on the point that the servants of the company naturally acted as their circumstances dictated.

their revenues and 'neat' profits at home, should be divided into four parts; three of them to be paid into the exchequer for the use of the publick, and the fourth to be reserved as a fund, either for the further reduction of their bond-debts, or for the discharge of other contingent exigencies, which the company might labour under.[66] But if the company were bad stewards, and bad sovereigns, when the whole of their nett revenue and profits belonged to themselves, and were at their own disposal, they were surely not likely to be better, [142] when three-fourths of them were to belong to other people, and the other fourth, though to be laid out for the benefit of the company, yet to be so, under the inspection, and with the approbation, of other people.

27   It might be more agreeable to the company that their own servants and dependants should have either the pleasure of wasting, or the profit of embezzling whatever surplus might remain, after paying the proposed dividend of eight per cent., than that it should come into the hands of a set of people with whom those resolutions could scarce fail to set them, in some measure, at variance. The interest of those servants and dependants might so far predominate in the court of proprietors, as sometimes to dispose it to support the authors of depredations which had been committed, in direct violation of its own authority. With the majority of proprietors, the support even of the authority of their own court might sometimes be a matter of less consequence, than the support of those who had set that authority at defiance.

28   The regulations of 1773, accordingly, did not put an end to the disorders of the company's government in India. Notwithstanding that, during a momentary fit of good conduct, they had at one time collected, into the treasury of Calcutta, more than three millions sterling; notwithstanding that they had afterwards extended, either their dominion, or their depredations, over a vast accession of some of the richest and most fertile countries in India; all was wasted and destroyed. They found themselves altogether un-[143]prepared to stop or resist the incursion of Hyder Ali; and, in consequence of those disorders, the company is now (1784) in greater distress than ever; and, in order to prevent immediate bankruptcy, is once more reduced to supplicate the assistance of government.[67] Different plans have been proposed by the different parties in parliament, for the better management of its affairs. And all those plans seem to agree in supposing, what was indeed always abundantly evident, that it is altogether unfit to govern its territorial possessions. Even the

---

ᶦ⁻ᶦ nett 2A, 6

[66] Anderson, *Origin of Commerce* (1789), iv.164.
[67] By 22 George III, c. 51 (1782), 23 George III, c. 36 (1783), and 23 George III, c. 83 (1783).

company itself seems to be convinced of its own incapacity so far, and seems, upon that account, willing to give them up to government.

29   With the right of possessing forts and garrisons, in distant and barbarous countries, is necessarily connected the right of making peace and war in those countries. The joint stock companies which have had the one right, have constantly exercised the other, and have frequently had it expressly conferred upon them. How unjustly, how capriciously, how cruelly they have commonly exercised it, is too well known from recent experience.

30   When a company of merchants undertake, at their own risk and expence, to establish a new trade with some remote and barbarous nation, it may not be unreasonable to incorporate them into a joint stock company, and to grant them, in case of their success, a monopoly of the trade for a certain number of years. It is the easiest and most natural way in which the state can recompense them for hazarding a dangerous and ex-[144] pensive experiment, of which the publick is afterwards to reap the benefit.[68] A temporary monopoly of this kind may be vindicated upon the same principles upon which a like monopoly of a new machine is granted to its inventor, and that of a new book to its author.[69] But upon the expira-

---

[68] While deploring monopoly, Pufendorf also pointed out that it was defensible where the establishing of commercial relations with distant countries was expensive, and at the outset open to risk: 'But in granting such privileges, a prudent government should see to it that they are allowed only in the case of commodities which are imported from very remote places, and over paths fraught with danger, and which concern not so much the necessities of life as its adornment and ease.' (*De Jure*, V.v.7.)

[69] Smith comments on the usefulness of temporary monopolies at V.i.e.5, IV.vii.c.95. It is pointed out in LJ (A) ii.31–3 that under British law the author of a new book, like the inventor of a new machine, enjoyed the fruits of his labour for a period of 14 years and that while exclusive privileges were generally detrimental, these could be defended on the ground of equity: 'For if the legislature should appoint pecuniary rewards for the inventors of new machines, etc., they would hardly ever be so precisely proportiond to the merit of the invention as this is. For here, if the invention be good and such as is profitable to mankind, he will probably make a fortune by it; but if it be of no value he will also reap no benefit.' Similarly with new books, Smith argued that the exclusive privilege could be regarded as 'an encouragement to the labours of learned men' and as beneficial since 'if the book be a valuable one the demand for it in that time will probably be a considerable addition to his fortune. But if it is of no value the advantage he can reap from it will be very small.' See also LJ (A) i.20 and LJ (B) 175, ed. Cannan 130.

Smith's own temporary monopoly in the property of the TMS was the subject of Letter 257 addressed to Cadell, dated 14 March 1786, where Smith commented that his 28-year property was almost expired, although he hoped to secure Cadell in the property for 14 years more. Smith may have been known to be sympathetic in matters of this kind. In Letter 145 addressed to Smith, dated 1 May 1775, Burke asked his good offices 'upon a Business which I have very much at heart': 'The renewal of Mr Champion's Patent for his China Manufacture is opposed by Mr Wedgewood, who does not so much as pretend to have ever had a Manufacture of that kind . . . He pretends indeed that he is actuated, (and so he told me) by nothing but a desire of the publick good. I confess a declaration of the lowest species of any honest self-Interest, would have much greater weight with me, from the mouth of a Tradesman.' Richard Champion dealt in ceramics at Bristol. Smith too doubted the motives of those who affected a concern with the public good, above IV.ii.9.

tion of the term, the monopoly ought certainly to determine; the forts
and garrisons, if it was found necessary to establish any, to be taken into
the hands of government, their value to be paid to the company, and the
trade to be laid open to all the subjects of the state. By a perpetual monopoly, all the other subjects of the state are taxed very absurdly in two
different ways; first, by the high price of goods, which, in the case of a
free trade, they could buy much cheaper; and, secondly, by their total
exclusion from a branch of business, which it might be both convenient
and profitable for many of them to carry on. It is for the most worthless
of all purposes too that they are taxed in this manner.[70] It is merely to
enable the company to support the negligence, profusion, and malversation of their own servants, whose disorderly conduct seldom allows the
dividend of the company to exceed the ordinary rate of profit in trades
which are altogether free, and very frequently makes it fall even a good
deal short of that rate. Without a monopoly, however, a joint stock company, it would appear from experience, cannot long carry on any branch
of foreign trade. To buy in one market, in order to sell, with profit, in
another, when there are many competitors in both; to watch over, not
only the occasional [145] variations in the demand, but the much greater
and more frequent variations in the competition, or in the supply which
that demand is likely to get from other people, and to suit with dexterity
and judgment both the quantity and quality of each assortment of goods
to all these circumstances, is a species of warfare of which the operations
are continually changing, and which can scarce ever be conducted successfully, without such an unremitting exertion of vigilance and attention, as cannot long be expected from the directors of a joint stock
company. The East India Company, upon the redemption of their funds,
and the expiration of their exclusive privilege, have a right, by act of
parliament, to continue a corporation with a joint stock, and to trade in
their corporate capacity to the East Indies in common with the rest of
their fellow-subjects. But in this situation, the superior vigilance and
attention of private adventurers would, in all probability, soon make them
weary of the trade.

31   An eminent French author, of great knowledge in matters of political
oeconomy, the Abbé Morellet,[71] gives a list of fifty-five joint stock companies for foreign trade, which have been established in different parts
of Europe since the year 1600, and which, according to him, have all
failed from mismanagement, notwithstanding they had exclusive privileges. He has been misinformed with regard to the history of two or three
of them, which were not joint stock companies and have not failed. But,

---

[70] See above, IV.vii.c.91.
[71] Smith wrote to Morellet on 1 May 1786 (Letter 259). See above, IV.ix.2, n. 1.

in compensation, there have been several joint stock companies which
have failed, and which he has omitted.

32   [146] The only trades which it seems possible for a joint stock company to
carry on successfully, without an exclusive privilege, are those, of which all
the operations are capable of being reduced to what it called a Routine,
or to such a uniformity of method as admits of little or no variation. Of
this kind is, first, the banking trade; secondly, the trade of insurance from
fire, and from sea risk and capture in time of war; thirdly, the trade of
making and maintaining a navigable cut or canal; and, fourthly, the similar
trade of bringing water for the supply of a great city.[72]

33   Though the principles of the banking trade may appear somewhat
abstruse, the practice is capable of being reduced to strict rules. To depart
upon any occasion from those rules, in consequence of some flattering
speculation of extraordinary gain, is almost always extremely dangerous,
and frequently fatal to the banking company which attempts it: But the
constitution of joint stock companies renders them in general more tena-
cious of established rules than any private copartnery.[73] Such companies,
therefore, seem extremely well fitted for this trade. The principal banking
companies in Europe, accordingly, are joint stock companies, many of
which manage their trade very successfully without any exclusive privilege.
The Bank of England has no other exclusive privilege, except that no
other banking company in England shall consist of more than six persons.[74]
The two banks of Edinburgh are joint stock companies without any exclusive privilege.[75]

34   [147] The value of the risk, either from fire, or from loss by sea, or by capture, though it cannot, perhaps, be calculated very exactly, admits, however,
of such a gross estimation as renders it, in some degree, reducible to strict
rule and method. The trade of insurance, therefore, may be carried on
successfully by a joint stock company, without any exclusive privilege.
Neither the London Assurance, nor the Royal Exchange Assurance companies, have any such privilege.[76]

35   When a navigable cut or canal has been once made, the management of it

[72] The trade of insurance is discussed above, I.x.b.28.

[73] The constitution of the joint stock company is described at V.i.e.15ff.

[74] 6 Anne c. 50 (1707) in *Statutes of the Realm*, viii.772–5; 6 Anne, c. 22 in Ruffhead's
edition. See above, II.ii.79ff., where Smith considers the history of the Bank of
England.

[75] The Bank of Scotland was incorporated by Act of Parliament in 1695. *Acts of the
Parliament of Scotland*, ix.494–5 (1695). The Royal Bank of Scotland was incorporated by
Royal Charter in 1727. See above, II.ii.41.

[76] They were granted a monopoly of marine insurance for 31 years against other joint-
stock companies (except tht East India and the South Sea Companies) but not against
individuals or partnerships without a joint-stock. Charters were issued in 1720 following the
passing of 6 George I, c. 18 (1719). Scott, *English, Scottish and Irish Joint Stock Companies*,
iii.402.

becomes quite simple and easy, and ^{j} is reducible to strict rule and method. Even the making of it is so, as it may be contracted for with undertakers at so much a mile, and so much a lock. The same thing may be said of a canal, an aqueduct, or a great pipe for bringing water to supply a great city. Such undertakings, therefore, may be, and accordingly frequently are, very successfully managed by joint stock companies without any exclusive privilege.

36   To establish a joint stock company, however, for any undertaking, merely because such a company might be capable of managing it success-fully; or to exempt a particular set of dealers from some of the general laws which take place with regard to all their neighbours, merely because they might be capable of thriving if they had such an exemption, would cer-tainly not be reasonable. To render such an establishment perfectly rea-sonable, with the circumstance of being reducible to strict rule and method, two other circumstances ought to concur. First, it [148] ought to appear with the clearest evidence, that the undertaking is of greater and more general utility than the greater part of common trades; and secondly, that it requires a greater capital than can easily be collected into a private copartnery. If a moderate capital ^{k}was^k sufficient, the great utility of the undertaking would not be a sufficient reason for establishing a joint stock company; because, in this case, the demand for what it was to produce would readily and easily be supplied by private adventurers. In the four trades above mentioned, both those circumstances concur.

37   The great and general utility of the banking trade, when prudently managed, has been fully explained in the second book of this inquiry.[77] But a publick bank which is to support publick credit, and upon particular emergencies to advance to government the whole produce of a tax, to the amount, perhaps, of several millions, a year or two before it comes in, requires a greater capital than can easily be collected into any private copartnery.

38   The trade of insurance gives great security to the fortunes of private people, and by dividing among a great many that loss which would ruin an individual, makes it fall light and easy upon the whole society. In order to give this security, however, it is necessary that the insurers should have a very large capital. Before the establishment of the two joint stock companies for insurance in London, a list, it is said, was laid before the attorney-general, of one hundred and fifty private insurers who had failed in the course of a few years.

39   [149] That navigable cuts and canals, and the works are which sometimes necessary for supplying a great city with water, are of great and general

---

^{j} it 4–6 $^{k-k}$ were 4–6

[77] See generally II.ii, esp. 27–46.

utility; while at the same time they frequently require a greater expence, than suits the fortunes of private people, is sufficiently obvious.

40   Except the four trades above mentioned, I have not been able to recollect any other in which all the three circumstances, requisite for rendering reasonable the establishment of a joint stock company, concur. The English copper company of London, the lead smelting company, the glass grinding company, have not even the pretext of any great or singular utility in the object which they pursue; nor does the pursuit of that object seem to require any expence unsuitable to the fortunes of many private men. Whether the trade which those companies carry on, is reducible to such strict rule and method as to render it fit for the management of a joint stock company, or whether they have any reason to boast of their extraordinary profits, I do not pretend to know. The mine-adventurers company has been long ago bankrupt. A share in the stock of the British Linen Company of Edinburgh[78] sells, at present, very much below par, though less so that it did some years ago. The joint stock companies, which are established for the publick spirited purpose of promoting some particular manufacture, over and above managing their own affairs ill, to the diminution of the general stock of the society, can in other respects scarce ever fail to do more harm than good. Notwithstanding the most upright intentions, the [150] unavoidable partiality of their directors to particular branches of the manufacture, of which the undertakers mislead and impose upon them, is a real discouragement to the rest, and necessarily breaks, more or less, that natural proportion which would otherwise establish itself between judicious industry and profit, and which, to the general industry of the country, is of all encouragements the greatest and the most effectual.[79]

ARTICLE II
Of the Expence of the Institutions for the Education
of *ª Youth*[1]

1   The institutions for the education of the youth may, in the same manner, furnish a revenue sufficient for defraying their own expence. The fee or

ª the *1*

[78] Still not functioning as a bank in 1776.

[79] For information used in this paragraph, see Anderson, *Origin of Commerce*, i.366, ii.197, 242–3, 250, 253. See above, IV.vii.c.61, where Smith describes the problems which arise when this 'judicious' balance is broken.

[1] Many of the views first expressed in this section appeared in Letter 143 addressed to William Cullen, dated 20 September 1774, where Smith commented on the current practice of some Scottish Universities with regard to the granting (and sale!) of medical degrees. It would appear from this letter that the organization of university education had already attracted Smith's attention: 'I have thought a great deal upon this subject, and have enquired very carefully into the constitution and history of several of the principal Universities of Europe: . . .'

honorary which the scholar pays to the master naturally constitutes a revenue of this kind.

2   Even where the reward of the master does not arise altogether from this natural revenue, it still is not necessary that it should be derived from that general revenue of the society, of which the collection and application ^bis^b, in most countries, assigned to the executive power. Through the greater part of Europe, accordingly, the endowment of schools and colleges makes either no charge upon that general revenue, or but a very small one. It every where arises chiefly from some local or provincial revenue, from the rent of some landed estate, or from the interest of some sum of money allotted and put under the management of trustees for this particular purpose, sometimes by the sovereign himself, and sometimes by some private donor.

3   [151] Have those publick endowments contributed in general to promote the end of their institution? Have they contributed to encourage the diligence, and to improve the abilities of the teachers? Have they directed the course of education towards objects more useful, both to the individual and to the publick, than those to which it would naturally have gone of its own accord? It should not seem very difficult to give at least a probable answer to each of those questions.

4   In every profession, the exertion of the greater part of those who exercise it, is always in proportion to the necessity they are under of making that exertion.[2] This necessity is greatest with those to whom the emoluments of their profession are the only source from which they expect their fortune, or even their ordinary revenue and subsistence. In order to acquire this fortune, or even to get this subsistence, they must, in the course of ^ca^c year, execute a certain quantity of work of a known value; and, where the competition is free, the rivalship of competitors, who are all endeavouring to justle one another out of employment, obliges every man to endeavour to execute his work with a certain degree of exactness. The greatness of the objects which are to be acquired by success in some particular professions may, no doubt, sometimes animate the exertion of a few men of extraordinary spirit and ambition. Great objects, however, are evidently not necessary in order to occasion the greatest exertions. Rivalship and emula-

---

^{b–b} are 5–6   ^{c–c} the 1

---

[2] See below, V.i.g.42, and above, V.i.b.20, where the point is illustrated by reference to the courts. Piece-work is discussed at I.viii.44 in connection with the problems of overexertion. In the Sixth Dialogue, Cleo. remarks that: 'you never saw Men so entirely devote themselves to their Calling, and pursue Business with that Eagerness, Dispatch and Perserverance in any Office or Preferment, in which the yearly Income is certain and unalterable, as they often do in those Professions, where the Reward continually accompanies the Labour, and the Fee immediately, either precedes the Service they do to others, as it is with the Lawyers, or follows it, as it is with the Physicians.' (*The Fable of the Bees*, pt.ii.430, ed. Kaye ii.355.)

tion render excellency, even in mean professions, an object of am-[152] bition, and frequently occasion the very greatest exertions. Great objects, on the contrary, alone and unsupported by the necessity of application, have seldom been sufficient to occasion any considerable exertion. In England, success in the profession of the law leads to some very great objects of ambition; and yet how few men, born to easy fortunes, have ever in this country been eminent in that profession!

5   The endowments of schools and colleges have necessarily diminished more or less the necessity of application in the teachers. Their subsistence, so far as it arises from their salaries, is evidently derived from a fund altogether independent of their success and reputation in their particular professions.[3]

6   In some universities the salary makes but a part, and frequently but a small part of the emoluments of the teacher, of which the greater part arises from the honoraries or fees of his pupils.[4] The necessity of application, though always more or less diminished, is not in this case entirely taken away. Reputation in his profession is still of some importance to him, and he still has some dependency upon the affection, gratitude, and favourable report of those who have attended upon his instructions; and these favourable sentiments he is likely to gain in no way so well as by deserving them, that is, by the abilities and diligence with which he discharges every part of his duty.[5]

7   In other universities the teacher is prohibited from receiving any honorary or fee from his pu-[153]pils, and his salary constitutes the whole of the revenue which he derives from his office. His interest is, in this case, set as directly in opposition to his duty as it is possible to set it. It is the interest of every man to live as much at his ease as he can; and if his emoluments are to be precisely the same, whether he does, or does not perform some very laborious duty, it is certainly his interest, at least as interest is vulgarly understood, either to neglect it altogether, or, if he is subject to some authority which will not suffer him to do this, to perform it in as careless and slovenly a manner as that authority will permit. If he is naturally active and a lover of labour, it is his interest to employ that activity in any way, from which he can derive some advantage, rather than in the performance of his duty, from which he can derive none.

---

[3] A related point is made below, § 34. It is remarked at V.i.g.39 that the situation was worsened in some countries by the fact that high levels of Church benefices drew off the best men of letters.

[4] As was the case in the Scottish universities.

[5] 'Professors should, besides their Stipends allowed 'em by the Publick, have Gratifications from every Student they teach, that Self-Interest as well as Emulation and the Love of Glory might spur them on to Labour and Assiduity . . . Universities should be publick Marts for all manner of Literature . . .' (Mandeville, *The Fable of the Bees*, pt.i.335, ed. Kaye i.293–4.)

8   If the authority to which he is subject resides in the body corporate, the
college, or university, of which he himself is a member, and in which the
greater part of the other members are, like himself, persons who either are,
or ought to be teachers; they are likely to make a common cause, to be all
very indulgent to one another, and every man to consent that his neighbour
may neglect his duty, provided he himself is allowed to neglect his own. In
the university of Oxford, the greater part of the publick professors have,
for these many years, given up altogether even the pretence of teaching.[6]

9   If the authority to which he is subject resides, not so much in the body
corporate of which he [154] is a member, as in some other extraneous persons, in the bishop of the diocese for example; in the governor of the
province; or, perhaps, in some minister of state; it is not indeed in this case
very likely that he will be suffered to neglect his duty altogether. All that
such superiors, however, can force him to do, is to attend upon his pupils a
certain number of hours, that is, to give a certain number of lectures in the
week or in the year. What those lectures shall be, must still depend upon
the diligence of the teacher; and that diligence is likely to be proportioned
to the motives which he has for exerting it. An extraneous jurisdiction of
this kind, besides, is liable to be exercised both ignorantly and capriciously.
In its nature it is arbitrary and discretionary, and the persons who exercise
it, neither attending upon the lectures of the teacher themselves, nor
perhaps understanding the sciences which it is his business to teach, are
seldom capable of exercising it with judgment. From the insolence of office
too they are frequently indifferent how they exercise it, and are very apt to
censure or deprive him of his office wantonly, and without any just cause.
The person subject to such jurisdiction is necessarily degraded by it, and,
instead of being one of the most respectable, is rendered one of the meanest

[6] See the Index s.v. 'Oxford': 'the professorships there, *sinecures*'. In Letter 1 addressed
to William Smith, dated 24 August 1740, Smith commented that 'it will be his own fault if
anyone should endanger his health at Oxford by excessive study'. In Letter 27 addressed to
Smith, dated 14 November 1758, Sir Gilbert Elliot wrote with reference to the education
of Lord Fitzmaurice's brother and commented that 'I find every thinking man here begins
to discover the very absurd constitution of the English Universitys.' Elliot went on: 'I
have very little doubt, but you might even draw a good many of the youth of this part of
the world to pass a winter or two at Glasgow, notwithstanding the distance & disadvantage
of the dialect . . .' See also Letter 32 addressed to Smith, dated 26 April 1759, wherein
Lord Shelburne expressed his satisfaction with the regimen which Smith had imposed
upon his son, and stated that: 'The great fault I find with Oxford & Cambridge, is that Boys
sent thither, instead of being Governed, become the Governors of the Colleges, & that
Birth & Fortune there are more respected than Literary Merit: . . .' In contrast, Smith
believed that 'In the present state of the Scotch Universities, I do most sincerely look upon
them as, in spite of all their faults, without exception the best seminaries of learning that
are to be found any where in Europe.' (Letter 143). William Thom, a Glasgow minister,
disagreed with Smith's assessment of the Scottish Universities, and of Glasgow in particular,
in his *Defects of an University Education, and its Unsuitableness to a Commercial People*
(Glasgow, 1762). The alleged defects of university education at this time were associated
with the rise of the academy movement in Scotland.

and most contemptible persons in the society. It is by powerful protection only that he can effectually guard himself against the bad usage to which he is at all times exposed; and this protection he is most likely to gain, not by ability [155] or diligence in his profession, but by obsequiousness to the will of his superiors, and by being ready, at all times, to sacrifice to that will the rights, the interest, and the honour of the body corporate of which he is a member. Whoever has attended for any considerable time to the administration of a French university, must have had occasion to remark the effects which naturally result from an arbitrary and extraneous jurisdiction of this kind.

10   Whatever forces a certain number of students to any college or university, independent of the merit or reputation of the teachers, tends more or less to diminish the necessity of that merit or reputation.

11   The privileges of graduates in arts, in law, *d* physick and divinity, when they can be obtained only by residing a certain number of years in certain universities, necessarily force a certain number of students to such universities, independent of the merit or reputation of the teachers. The privileges of graduates are a sort of statutes of apprenticeship, which have contributed to the improvement of education, just as *e*the*e* other statutes of apprenticeship have to that of arts and manufactures.[7]

12   The charitable foundations of scholarships, exhibitions, bursaries, &c. necessarily attach a certain number of students to certain colleges,[8]

d in *1*   *e–e* 2–6

[7] The statute of apprenticeship is discussed at I.x.c.7–14. In Letter 143 addressed to Cullen, dated 20 September 1774, Smith wrote:

> A degree which can be conferred only upon students of a certain standing, is a statute of apprenticeship which is likely to contribute to the advancement of science, just as other statutes of apprenticeship have contributed to that of arts and manufactures. Those statutes of apprenticeship, assisted by other corporation laws, have banished arts and manufactures from the greater part of towns-corporate. Such degrees, assisted by some other regulations of similar tendency, have banished almost all useful and solid education from the greater part of Universities. Bad work and high price have been the effects of the monopoly introduced by the former. Quackery, imposture, and exorbitant fees, have been the consequences of that established by the latter.

In the same letter Smith commented on the proposal that no person should be admitted to an examination for a degree in medicine, without a certificate of at least two years attendance at University and inquired:

> Would not such a regulation be oppressive upon all private teachers, such as the Hunters, Hewson, Fordyce, &c.? The scholars of such teachers surely merit whatever honour or advantage a degree can confer, much more than the greater part of those who have spent many years in some Universities . . . When a man has learnt his lesson very well, it surely can be of little importance where or from whom he has learnt it.

[8] See above, I.x.c.34. In his letter to Cullen (143) Smith gave two reasons to explain the 'present state of degradation and contempt' into which most universities and university teachers had fallen: first, the large salaries paid irrespective of industry or competence, which render them 'altogether independent of their diligence and success in their professions', and secondly 'the great number of students who, in order to get degrees or to be admitted to exercise certain professions or who, for the sake of bursaries, exhibitions,

independent altogether of the merit of those particular colleges. Were the students upon such charitable foundations left free to chuse [156] what college they liked best, such liberty might perhaps contribute to excite some emulation among different colleges. A regulation, on the contrary, which prohibited even the independent members of every particular college from leaving it, and going to any other, without leave first asked and obtained of that which they meant to abandon, would tend very much to extinguish that emulation.

13   If in each college the tutor or teacher, who was to instruct each student in all arts and sciences, should not be voluntarily chosen by the student, but appointed by the head of the college; and if, in case of neglect, inability, or bad usage, the student should not be allowed to change him for another, without leave first asked and obtained; such a regulation would not only tend very much to extinguish all emulation among the different tutors of the same college, but to diminish very much in all of them the necessity of diligence and of attention to their respective pupils. Such teachers, though very well paid by their students, might be as much disposed to neglect them, as those who are not paid by them at all, or who have no other recompence but their salary.

14   If the teacher happens to be a man of sense, it must be an unpleasant thing to him to be conscious, while he is lecturing his students, that he is either speaking or reading nonsense, or what is very little better than nonsense. It must too be unpleasant to him to observe that the greater part of his students desert his lectures; or perhaps attend upon them with plain enough marks [157] of neglect, contempt, and derision. If he is obliged, therefore, to give a certain number of lectures, these motives alone, without any other interest, might dispose him to take some pains to give tolerably good ones. Several different expedients, however, may be fallen upon which will effectually blunt the edge of all those incitements to diligence. The teacher, instead of explaining to his pupils himself, the science in which he proposes to instruct them, may read some book upon it; and if this book is written in a foreign and dead language, by interpreting it to them into their own; or, what would give him still less trouble, by making them interpret it to him, and by now and then making an occasional remark upon it, he may flatter himself that he is giving a lecture. The slightest degree of knowledge and application will enable him to do this without exposing himself to contempt or derision, or saying any thing that is really foolish, absurd, or ridiculous. The discipline of the college, at the same time, may enable him to force all his pupils to the most regular attendance upon this sham-lecture, and to maintain the most decent and respectful behaviour during the whole time of the performance.

scholarships, fellowships, &c., are obliged to resort to certain societies of this kind, whether the instructions which they are likely to receive there are or are not worth the receiving.'

15   The discipline of colleges and universities is in general contrived, not for the benefit of the students, but for the interest, or more properly speaking, for the ease of the masters. Its object is, in all cases, to maintain the authority of the master, and whether he neglects or performs his duty, to oblige the students in all cases to be-[158]have to him as if he performed it with the greatest diligence and ability. It seems to presume perfect wisdom and virtue in the one order, and the greatest weakness and folly in the other. Where the masters, however, really perform their duty, there are no examples, I believe, that the greater part of the students ever neglect theirs. No discipline is ever requisite to force attendance upon lectures which are really worth the attending, as is well known wherever any such lectures are given. Force and restraint may, no doubt, be in some degree requisite in order to oblige children, or very young boys, to attend to those parts of education which it is thought necessary for them to acquire during that early period of life; but after twelve or thirteen years of age, provided the master does his duty, force or restraint can scarce ever be necessary to carry on any part of education. Such is the generosity of the greater part of young men, that, so far from being disposed to neglect or despise the instructions of their master, provided he shows some serious intention of being of use to them, they are generally inclined to pardon a great deal of incorrectness in the performance of his duty, and sometimes even to conceal from the publick a good deal of gross negligence.

16   Those parts of education, it is to be observed, for the teaching of which there are no publick institutions, are generally the best taught. When a young man goes to a fencing or a dancing school, he does not, indeed, always learn to fence or to dance very well; but he seldom fails of [159] learning to fence or to dance. The good effects of the riding school are not commonly so evident. The expence of a riding school is so great, that in most places it is a publick institution. The three most essential parts of literary education, to read, write, and account, it still continues to be more common to acquire in private than in publick schools; and it very seldom happens that any body fails of acquiring them to the degree in which it is necessary to acquire them.

17   In England the publick schools are much less corrupted than the universities. In the schools the youth are taught, or at least may be taught, Greek and Latin, that is, every thing which the masters pretend to teach, or which, it is expected, they should teach. In the universities the youth neither are taught, nor always can find any proper means of being taught, the sciences, which it is the business of those incorporated bodies to teach. The reward of the schoolmaster in most cases depends principally, in some cases almost entirely, upon the fees or honoraries of his scholars. Schools have no exclusive privileges. In order to obtain the honours of graduation, it is not necessary that a person should bring a certificate of his

having studied a certain number of years at a publick school. If upon examination he appears to understand what is taught there, no questions are asked about the place where he learnt it.

18   The parts of education which are commonly taught in universities, it may, perhaps, be said are not very well taught. But had it not been for those institutions they would not have been [160] commonly taught at all, and both the individual and the publick would have suffered a good deal from the want of those important parts of education.

19   The present universities of Europe were originally, the greater part of them, ecclesiastical corporations; instituted for the education of churchmen. They were founded by the authority of the pope, and were so entirely under his immediate protection, that their members, whether masters or students, had all of them what was then called the benefit of *f* clergy,[9] that is, were exempted from the civil jurisdiction of the countries in which their respective universities were situated, and were amenable only to the ecclesiastical tribunals. What was taught in the greater part of those universities was, suitable to the end of their institution, either theology, or something that was merely preparatory to theology.[10]

20   When christianity was first established by law, a corrupted Latin had become the common language of all the western parts of Europe. The service of the church accordingly, and the translation of the Bible which was read in churches, were both in that corrupted Latin, that is, in the common language of the country. After the irruption of the barbarous nations who overturned the Roman empire, Latin gradually ceased to be the language of any part of Europe. But the reverence of the people naturally preserves the established forms and ceremonies of religion, long after the circumstances which first introduced and rendered them reasonable are no more.[11] Though [161] Latin, therefore, was no longer understood any where by the great body of the people, the whole service of the church still continued to be performed in that language. Two different languages were thus established in Europe, in the same manner as in antient Egypt; a language of the priests, and a language of the people; a sacred and a profane; a learned and an unlearned language. But it was necessary that the priests should understand something of that sacred and learned language in which they were to officiate; and the study of the Latin

---

f the *2*

[9] See below, V.i.g.23.
[10] In Letter 143 addressed to Cullen, Smith stated that 'All universities being ecclesiastical establishments, under the immediate protection of the Pope, a degree from one of them gave, all over Christendom, very nearly the same privileges which a degree from any other could have given; and the respect which is to this day paid to foreign degrees, even in Protestant countries, must be considered as a remnant of Popery.'
[11] Smith makes a related point at III.ii.4.

language therefore made, from the beginning, an essential part of university education.

21   It was not so with that either of the Greek, or of the Hebrew language. The infallible decrees of the church had pronounced the Latin translation of the Bible, commonly called the Latin Vulgate, to have been equally dictated by divine inspiration, and therefore of equal authority with the Greek and Hebrew originals. The knowledge of those two languages, therefore, not being indispensably requisite to a churchman, the study of them did not for a long time make a necessary part of the common course of university education. There are some Spanish universities, I am assured, in which the study of the Greek language has never yet made any part of that course. The first reformers found the Greek text of the new testament, and even the Hebrew text of the old, more favourable to their opinions than the vulgate translation, which, as might naturally be supposed, had been gradually ac-[162]commodated to support the doctrines of the catholick church. They set themselves, therefore, to expose the many errors of that translation, which the Roman catholick clergy were thus put under the necessity of defending or explaining. But this could not well be done without some knowledge of the original languages, of which the study was therefore gradually introduced into the greater part of universities; both of those which embraced, and of those which rejected, the doctrines of the reformation. The Greek language was connected with every part of that classical learning, which, though at first principally cultivated by catholicks and Italians, happened to come into fashion much about the same time that the doctrines of the reformation were set on foot. In the greater part of universities, therefore, that language was taught previous to the study of philosophy, and as soon as the student had made some progress in the Latin. The Hebrew language having no connection with classical learning, and, except the holy scriptures, being the language of not a single book in any esteem, the study of it did not commonly commence till after that of philosophy, and when the student had entered upon the study of theology.

22   Originally the first rudiments both of the Greek and Latin languages were taught in universities, and ⁹in some universities they still continue to be so.⁹ In others it is expected that the student should have previously acquired at least the rudiments of one or both of those languages, of which [163] the study continues to make every where a very considerable part of university education.

23   The antient Greek philosophy was divided into three great branches; physicks, or natural philosophy; ethicks, or moral philosophy; and logick. This general division seems perfectly agreeable to the nature of things.

---

⁹⁻⁹ they still continue to be so in some universities. *1*

24   The great phenomena of nature, the *h*revolutions*h* of the heavenly
bodies, eclipses, comets, thunder, lightning, and other extraordinary
meteors; the generation, the life, growth, and dissolution of plants and
animals; are objects which, as they *i*necessarily*i* excite the wonder, so they
*j*naturally*j* call forth the curiosity of mankind to enquire into their causes.[12]
Superstition first attempted to satisfy this curiosity by referring all those
wonderful appearances to the immediate agency of the gods.[13] Philosophy
afterwards endeavoured to account for them, from more familiar causes,
or from such as mankind were better acquainted with, than the agency of
the gods. As those great phenomena are the first objects of human curiosity, so the science which pretends to explain them must naturally have been
the first branch of philosophy that was cultivated.[14] The first philosophers,

h-h revolution *1*   *i-i* naturally *1*   *j-j* necessarily *1*

[12] Cf. Astronomy, IV.1.: 'Of all phænomena of nature, the celestial appearances are, by
their greatness and beauty, the most universal objects of the curiosity of mankind.'
In LRBL the 'grand' and the 'beautiful' are cited as the 'two sorts of objects that excite
our attention' and Smith notes at ii.v.18–v.19 ed. Lothian 87, that:

> The more lively and striking the impression is which any phaenomenon makes on the
> mind, the greater curiosity does it excite to know its causes, tho perhaps the phaeno-
> menon may not be intrinsically half so grand or important as another less striking. Thus
> it is that we have a greater curiosity to pry into the cause of thunder and lightning and
> of the celestial motions, than of gravity, because these naturally make a greater impression
> on us.

Smith also pointed out that it is the marvellous which first draws the attention of unimproved man. LRBL ii.60, ed. Lothian 107. Smith considers the sentiments of wonder and
surprise in Astronomy, I and II, arguing that we feel surprise in contemplating some
unexpected appearance or relation; a feeling which is followed by wonder, that is, a state
of 'uncertainty and anxious curiosity' arising from our feeling 'a want of connection'. The
response to this situation involves the pursuit of some explanation, which is designed to
relieve the thinker of the disutility involved in the state of wonder by exposing 'a connecting
chain of intermediate events.' Astronomy, II.9. Similar points are made in LRBL ii.32–3,
ed. Lothian 93–4, in speaking of historical composition, and see also ii.85, 197, 206, ed.
Lothian 118, 167, 172.
[13] 'Hence the origin of Polytheism, and of that vulgar superstition which ascribes all the
irregular events of nature to the favour or displeasure of intelligent, though invisible
beings . . . For it may be observed, that in all Polytheistic religions . . . it is the irregular
events of nature only that are ascribed to the agency and power of their gods. Fire burns,
and water refreshes; heavenly bodies descend, and lighter substances fly upwards, by the
necessity of their own nature; nor was the invisible hand of Jupiter ever apprehended to be
employed in those matters. But thunder and lightning, storms and sunshine, those more
irregular events, were ascribed to his favour, or his anger.' (Astronomy, III.2.) In TMS
III.5.4 Smith argued that in 'the ignorance and darkness of pagan superstition, mankind
seem to have formed the ideas of their divinities with so little delicacy, that they ascribed
to them, indiscriminately, all the passions of human nature, those not excepted which do
the least honour to our species, . . .'
[14] Although Smith argued that the development of knowledge represents a response to
the needs of the imagination, without any necessarily practical purpose, he did come closer
to D'Alembert's general position as outlined in his 'Discours préliminaire' to the *Encyclo-
pédie* of Diderot in remarking that all the arts are subservient to the natural wants of man:

> Geometry, arithmetick, and writing have all been invented originally to facilitate the
> operation of the severall arts. Writing and arithmetick have been invented to record and

accordingly, of whom history has preserved any account, appear to have been natural philosophers.

25   In every age and country of the world men must have attended to the characters, designs, and actions of one another, and many reputable rules and maxims for the conduct of human life, must have been laid down and approved of by [164] common consent.[15] As soon as writing came into fashion, wise men, or those who fancied themselves such, would naturally endeavour to increase the number of those eatablished and respected maxims, and to express their own sense of what was either proper or improper conduct, sometimes in the more artificial form of apologues, like what are called the fables of Æsop; and sometimes in the more simple one of apophthegms, or wise sayings, like the Proverbs of Solomon, the verses of Theognis and Phocyllides, and some part of the works of Hesiod. They might continue in this manner for a long time merely to multiply the number of those maxims of prudence and morality, without even attempting to arrange them in any very distinct or methodical order, much less to connect them together by one or more general principles, from which they were all deducible, like effects from their natural causes. The beauty of a systematical arrangement[16] of different observations connected by a few

set in a clear light the severall transactions of the merchant and trades man, and geometry had been originally invented (either to measure out the earth and divide it amongst the inhabitants or) to assist the workman in the fashioning of those pieces of art which require more accurate mensuration. (LJ (A) vi.18.)

Similar points are made in LJ (B) 210, ed. Cannan 160, and see below, V.i.f.55.

[15] A similar point is made in LRBL i.133, ed. Lothian 51, where it is stated that "all the Rules of Criticism and morality, when traced to their foundation, turn out to be some principles of Common Sence which every one assents to.' Smith also argues with regard to the development of language that after it has made some progress, 'it was natural to imagine that men would form some rules according to which they should regulate their language.' In the First Formation of Languages, 16, it is suggested that 'The general rule would establish itself insensibly, and by slow degrees, in consequence of that love of analogy and similarity of sound, which is the foundation of by far the greater part of the rules of grammar.' Cf. § 25. One of the main features of the TMS is the interest shown in the question of the way in which we form judgements concerning what is fit and proper to be done or to be avoided. Smith went on from this basis to argue that our ability to form judgements in particular cases enables us to form some notion of general rules of morality. Smith indicated that the content of general rules was a function of experience, and that they would be found in all societies. See TMS III, especially 4 and 5.

[16] Systematic arrangement, stemming in part from a perception of its beauty, was something of a feature of Smith's own thought. Dugald Stewart often noted his 'love of system' (see, for example, Stewart, III.15), and went so far as to claim that 'it may be doubted, with respect to Mr. Smith's Inquiry, if there exists any book beyond the circle of the mathematical and physical sciences, which is at once so agreeable . . . to the rules of sound logic, and so accessible to the examination of ordinary readers' (IV.22). The systematic character of the WN was also noted by Hugh Blair, in Letter 151 addressed to Smith, dated 3 April 1776; by Joseph Black, in Letter 152 addressed to Smith, dated April 1776; by William Robertson, in Letter 153, dated 8 April 1776; and by Edward Gibbon, in Letter 187 addressed to Smith, dated 26 November 1777. In the opening paragraph of his *Letter*, Pownall refers to the 'plan and superstructure' of the WN as having given 'a

[*continues*]

common principles, was first seen in the rude essays of those antient times towards a system of natural philosophy.[17] Something of the same kind was afterwards attempted in morals. The maxims of common life were arranged in some methodical order, and connected together by a few common principles, in the same manner as they had attempted to arrange and connect the phenomena of nature. The science which pretends to investigate and explain those connecting principles, is what is properly called moral philosophy.[18]

26   [165] Different authors gave different systems both of natural and moral philosophy. But the arguments by which they supported those different systems, far from being always demonstrations, were frequently at best but very slender probabilities, and sometimes mere sophisms, which had no other foundation but the inaccuracy and ambiguity of common language. Speculative systems have in all ages of the world been adopted for reasons too frivolous to have determined the judgment of any man of common sense, in a matter of the smallest pecuniary interest.[19] Gross sophistry has scarce ever had any influence upon the opinions of mankind, except in matters of philosophy and speculation; and in these it has frequently had the greatest. The patrons of each system of natural and moral

compleat idea of that system, which I had long wished to see the publick in possession of. A system, that might fix some first principles in the most important of sciences, the knowledge of the human community, and its operations. That might become *principia* to the knowledge of politick operations; as Mathematicks are to Mechanicks, Astronomy, and the other Sciencies.' He also refers to the WN (*Letter*, 23) as an 'Institute of the Principia *of those laws of motion*, by which the operations of the community are directed and regulated, and by which they should be examined'. Indeed, Pownall expressed the hope (*Letter*, 48) that Smith's work, no doubt duly corrected, might be taken up by 'some understanding Tutor in our Universities' as a 'basis of lectures on this subject'.

[17] Two approaches to scientific discourse, the Aristotelian and the Newtonian, are mentioned in LRBL ii.133-4, ed. Lothian 140. In the former 'method' a principle, 'commonly a new one' is used in explaining each problem, whereas in the latter case:

> in the manner of Sir Isaac Newton, we may lay down certain principles, [primary?] or proved, in the beginning, from whence we account for the severall phænomena, connecting all together by the same chain. This latter, which we may call the Newtonian method, is undoubtedly the most philosophical, and in every science, whether of Moralls or Natural Philosophy, etc., is vastly more ingenious, and for that reason more engaging, than the other. It gives us a pleasure to see the phænomena which we reckoned the most unaccountable, all deduced from some principle (commonly, a wellknown one) and all united in one chain, far superior to what we feel from the unconnected method . . .

Smith also ascribed the use of this 'method' to Descartes, explaining in this way the 'enchantment' of his philosophy.

[18] In his *Short Introduction*, Hutcheson commented on the 'multiplicity of natural desires' to which man was subject, and added: 'This complex view, I say, must at first make human nature appear a strange chaos, or a confused combination of jarring principles, until we can discover by a closer attention, some natural connexion or order among them, some governing principles naturally fitted to regulate all the rest. To discover this is the main business of Moral Philosophy, and to show how all these parts are to be ranged in order . . .' (36).

[19] Cf. the remark of Cicero, quoted at V.ii.k.14.

philosophy naturally endeavoured to expose the weakness of the arguments adduced to support the systems which were opposite to their own.[20] In examining those arguments, they were necessarily led to consider the difference between a probable and a demonstrative argument, between a fallacious and a conclusive one; and Logick, or the science of the general principles of good and bad reasoning, necessarily arose out of the observations which a scrutiny of this kind gave occasion to. Though in its origin posterior both to physicks and to ethicks, it was commonly taught, not indeed in all, but in the greater part of the antient schools of philosophy, previously to either of those sciences. The student, it seems to have been thought, ought to understand well the difference [166] between good and bad reasoning, before he was led to reason upon subjects of so great importance.

27 This antient division of philosophy into three parts was in the greater part of the universities of Europe, changed for another into five.

28 In the antient philosophy, whatever was taught concerning the nature either of the human mind or of the Deity, made a part of the system of physicks.[21] Those beings, in whatever their essence might be supposed to consist, were parts of the great system of the universe, and parts too productive of the most important effects. Whatever human reason could either conclude, or conjecture, concerning them, made, as it were, two chapters, though no doubt two very important ones, of the science which pretended to give an account of the origin and revolutions of the great system of the universe. But in the universities of Europe, where philosophy was taught only as subservient to theology, it was natural to dwell longer upon ^{k}these^k two chapters than upon any other of the science. They^l were gradually more and more extended, and were divided into many inferior chapters, till at last the doctrine of spirits, of which so little can be known, came to take up as much room in the system of philosophy as the doctrine of bodies, of which so much can be known. The doctrines concerning those two subjects were considered as making two distinct sciences. What ^{m}are^m called Metaphysicks or Pneumaticks ^{n}were^n set in opposition to

$^{k-k}$ those I ^{l} Those two chapters I $^{m-m}$ was I $^{n-n}$ was I

[20] In TMS VII.ii.4.14 Smith drew attention to an interesting difference between systems of natural and moral philosophy with regard to their plausibility: 'A system of natural philosophy may appear very plausible, and be for a long time very generally received in the world, and yet have no foundation in nature, nor yet any sort of resemblance to the truth. The vortices of Descartes were regarded by a very ingenious nation, for near a century together, as a most satisfactory account of the revolutions of the heavenly bodies . . . But it is otherwise with systems of moral philosophy, and an author who pretends to account for the origin of our moral sentiments, cannot deceive us so grossly, nor depart so very far from all resemblance to the truth.'

[21] Smith ascribes the origin of theism to the development of science in classical times: 'The unity of the system . . . suggested the idea of the unity of that principle, by whose art it was formed; and thus, as ignorance begot superstition, science gave birth to the first theism that arose among those nations, who were not enlightened by divine Revelation.' (Ancient Physics, 9.)

Physicks, and ⁰were⁰ cultivated not only as the more sublime, [167] but, for the purposes of a particular profession, as the more useful science of the two. The proper subject of experiment and observation, a subject in which a careful attention is capable of making so many useful discoveries, was almost entirely neglected. The subject in which, after a few very simple and almost obvious truths, the most careful attention can discover nothing but obscurity and uncertainty, and can consequently produce nothing but subtleties and sophisms, was greatly cultivated.

29   When those two sciences had thus been set in opposition to one another, the comparison between them naturally gave birth to a third, to what was called Ontology, or the science which treated of the qualities and attributes which were common to both the subjects of the other two sciences. But if subtleties and sophisms composed the greater part of the Metaphysicks or Pneumaticks of the schools, they composed the whole of this cobweb science of Ontology, which was likewise sometimes called Metaphysicks.

30   Wherein consisted the happiness and perfection of a man, considered not only as an individual, but as the member of a family, of a state, and of the great society of mankind, was the object which the ancient moral philosophy proposed to investigate. In that philosophy the duties of human life were treated of as subservient to the happiness and perfection of human life. But when moral, as well as natural philosophy, came to be taught only as subservient to theology, the duties of human life were treated of as chiefly [168] subservient to the happiness of a life to come. In the antient philosophy the perfection of virtue was represented as necessarily productive, to the person who possessed it, of the most perfect happiness in this life. In the modern philosophy it was frequently represented as generally, or rather as almost always inconsistent with any degree of happiness in this life; and heaven was to be earned only by penance and mortification, by the austerities and abasement of a monk; not by the liberal, generous, and spirited conduct of a man.[22] Casuistry and an ascetic morality made up, in most cases, the greater part of the moral philosophy of the schools. By far the most important of all the different branches of philosophy, became in this manner by far the most corrupted.

⁰⁻⁰ was *1*

[22] This doctrine is severely criticized in TMS III.2.35: 'To compare . . . the futile mortifications of a monastery, to the ennobling hardships and hazards of war; to suppose that one day, or one hour, employed in the former should, in the eye of the great Judge of the world, have more merit than a whole life spent honourably in the latter, is surely contrary to all our moral sentiments.' He added, however, that it is this spirit which 'while it has reserved the celestial regions for monks and friars, or for those whose conduct and conversation resembled those of monks and friars, has condemned to the infernal all the heroes, all the statesmen and lawgivers, all the poets and philosophers of former ages; all those who have invented, improved, or excelled in the arts which contribute to the subsistence, to the conveniency, or to the ornament of human life'.

31   Such, therefore, was the common course of philosophical education in the greater part of the universities ᵖinᵖ Europe. Logick was taught first: Ontology came in the second place: Pneumatology, comprehending the doctrine concerning the nature of the human soul and of the Deity, in the third: In the fourth followed a debased system of moral philosophy, which was considered as immediately connected with the doctrines of Pneumatology, with the immortality of the human soul, and with the rewards and punishments which, from the justice of the Deity, were to be expected in a life to come: A short and superficial system of Physicks usually concluded the course.

32   The alterations which the universities of Europe thus introduced into the antient course of philosophy, were all meant for the education of [169] ecclesiasticks, and to render it a more proper introduction to the study of theology. But the additional quantity of subtlety and sophistry; the casuistry and the ascetic morality which those alterations introduced into it, certainly did not render it more proper for the education of gentlemen or men of the world, or more likely either to improve the understanding, or to mend the heart.

33   This course of philosophy is what still continues to be taught in the greater part of the universities of Europe; with more or less diligence, according as the constitution of each particular university happens to render diligence more or less necessary to the teachers. In some of the richest and best endowed universities, the tutors content themselves with teaching a few unconnected shreds and parcels of this corrupted course; and even these they commonly teach very negligently and superficially.

34   The improvements which, in modern times, have been made in several different branches of philosophy, have not, the greater part of them, been made in universities; though some no doubt have. The greater part of universities have not even been very forward to adopt those improvements, after they were made;[23] and several of those learned societies have chosen to remain, for a long time, the sanctuaries in which exploded systems and obsolete prejudices found shelter and protection, after they had been hunted out of every other corner of the world. In general, the richest and best endowed universities have [170] been the slowest in adopting those improvements, and the most averse to permit any considerable change in the established plan of education. Those improvements were more easily introduced into some of the poorer universities, in which the teachers,

ᵖ⁻ᵖ of *1*

---

[23] Cf. LRBL ii.215, ed. Lothian 176: 'Antiquity is necessary to give anything a very high reputation as a matter of deep knowledge. One who reads a number of modern books, altho they be very excellent, will not get thereby the Character of a learned man: the acquaintaince of the ancients will alone procure him that name.' It is also suggested at i.61, ed. Lothian 24–5, that 'we are apt to think everything that is ancient is venerable, whether it is so or not.'

depending upon their reputation for the greater part of their subsistence, were obliged to pay more attention to the current opinions of the world.[24]

35   But though the publick schools and universities of Europe were originally intended only for the education of a particular profession, that of churchmen; and though they were not always very diligent in instructing their pupils even in the sciences which were supposed necessary for that profession, yet they gradually drew to themselves the education of almost all other people, particularly of almost all gentlemen and men of fortune. No better method, it seems, could be fallen upon of spending, with any advantage, the long interval between infancy and that period of life at which men begin to apply in good earnest to the real business of the world, the business which is to employ them during the remainder of their days. The greater part of what is taught in schools and universities, however, does not seem to be the most proper preparation for that business.

36   In England, it becomes every day more and more the custom to send young people to travel in foreign countries immediately upon their leaving school, and without sending them to any university.[25] Our young people, it is said, generally [171] return home much improved by their travels. A young man who goes abroad at seventeen or eighteen, and returns home at one and twenty, returns three or four years older than he was when he went abroad; and at that age it is very difficult not to improve a good deal in three or four years. In the course of his travels, he generally acquires some knowledge of one or two foreign languages; a knowledge, however, which is seldom sufficient to enable him either to speak or write them with propriety. In other respects he commonly returns home more conceited, more unprincipled, more dissipated, and more incapable of any serious application either to study or to business, then he could well have become in so short a time, had he lived at home. By travelling so very young, by spending in the most frivolous dissipation the most precious years of his life, at a distance from the inspection and controul of his parents and relations, every useful habit, which the earlier parts of his education might have had some tendency to form in him, instead of being rivetted and confirmed, is

[24] See above, V.i.f.6. In Letter 151 addressed to Smith, dated 3 April 1776, Blair wrote that 'There is so much good Sense & Truth in your doctrine about Universities, and it is so fit that your Doctrine should be preached to the World', that the want of this section would have been a matter for regret. Blair was less confident about Smith's treatment of the American colonies and Church affairs.

[25] TMS VI.ii.1.10 also comments that: 'The education of boys at distant great schools, of young men at distant colleges, of young ladies in distant nunneries and boarding schools, seems, in the higher ranks of life, to have hurt most essentially the domestic morals, and consequently the domestic happiness, both of France and England . . . Surely no acquirement, which can possibly be derived from what is called a public education, can make any sort of compensation for what is almost certainly and necessarily lost by it. Domestic education is the institution of nature; public education the contrivance of man. It is surely unnecessary to say, which is likely to be the wisest.'

almost necessarily either weakened or effaced. Nothing but the discredit into which the universities are allowing themselves to fall, could ever have brought into repute so very absurd a practice as that of travelling at this early period of life. By sending his son abroad, a father delivers himself, at least for some time, from so disagreeable an object as that of a son unemployed, neglected, and going to ruin before his eyes.

37   [172] Such have been the effects of some of the modern institutions for education.

38   Different plans and different institutions for education seem to have taken place in other ages and nations.

39   In the republicks of antient Greece, every free citizen was instructed, under the direction of the publick magistrate, in gymnastic exercises and in musick. By gymnastic exercises it was intended to harden his body, to sharpen his courage, and to prepare him for the fatigues and dangers of war;[26] and as the Greek militia was, by all accounts, one of the best that ever was in the world, this part of their publick education must have answered completely the purpose for which it was intended. By the other part, musick, it was proposed, at least by the philosophers and historians who have given us an account of those institutions, to humanize the mind, to soften the temper, and to dispose it for performing all the social and moral duties both of publick and private life.[27]

40   In antient Rome the exercises of the Campus Martius answered the same purpose as those of the Gymnazium in antient Greece, and they seem to have answered it equally well.[28] But among the Romans there was nothing which corresponded to the musical education of the Greeks. The morals of the Romans, however, both in private and publick life, seem to have been, not only equal, but upon the whole, a good deal superior to those of the Greeks. That they were superior in private life, we have the express testimony of Polybius[29] and of Dionysius of

---

[26] It is pointed out at IV.ix.47 that the citizens were excluded from the practice of mechanic arts in case it affected their military bearing.

[27] It is stated in LRBL ii.117, ed. Lothian 132, that 'music was added to correct the bad effects' of military education and that 'These two made the whole of the education of the youth, even in Athens'. Smith added that games were instituted and prizes given to those excelling in athletics and poetry, and that at these games 'Herodotus read his History and Isocrates his orations (at least had them read by another, for his voice was so bad that he never read himself)' (ii.120, ed. Lothian 133). Smith considers Herodotus as a historian on LRBL ii.47–9, ed. Lothian 101, and Isocrates at ii.121–2, ed. Lothian 134. The earnings of the latter are calculated in I.x.c. 39 and Vi.g.40.

[28] See above, V.i.a.12 and below, § 58.

[29] 'The laws and customs relating to the acquisition of wealth are better in Rome than at Carthage. At Carthage nothing which results in profit is regarded as disgraceful; at Rome nothing is considered more so than to accept bribes and seek gain from improper channels. ... Among the Greeks, apart from other things, members of the government, if they are entrusted with no more than a talent, though they have ten copyists and as many seals and twice as many witnesses, cannot keep their faith; whereas among the Romans those who as magistrates and legates are dealing with large sums of money maintain correct conduct just

Halicarnassus,[30] two [173] authors well acquainted with both nations; and the whole tenor of the Greek and Roman history bears witness to the superiority of the publick morals of the Romans. The good temper and moderation of contending factions seems to be the most essential circumstance in the publick morals of a free people. But the factions of the Greeks were almost always violent and sanguinary; whereas, till the time of the Gracchi, no blood had ever been shed in any Roman faction, and from the time of the Gracchi the Roman republick may be considered as in reality dissolved. Notwithstanding, therefore, the very respectable authority of Plato,[31] Aristotle,[32] and Polybius,[33] and notwithstanding the very ingenious reasons by which Mr. Montesquieu[34] endeavours to support that authority, it seems

because they have pledged their faith by oath.' (Polybius, *History*, vi. 56, translated by W. R. Paton in Loeb Classical Library (1927), iii.394–5 and 396–7.) In LRBL ii.54–5, ed. Lothian 104 Polybius is described as the first writer 'who enters into the civill history of the nations he treats of' and as both 'instructing and agreable' in view of the 'distinctness and accuracy with which he has related a series of events.'

[30] Dionysius attributes to Romulus 'that good discipline . . . by the observance of which the Romans have kept their commonwealth flourishing for many generations; for he established many good and useful laws'. Later he contrasts Roman practice with the 'lax manners of the Greeks'. Dionysius of Halicarnassus, *Roman Antiquities*, II.xxiv–xxvii. translated by E. Spelman, revised by E. Cary in Loeb Classical Library (1937), i.377–89. In LRBL ii.57, ed. Lothian 105, Livy is mentioned as having provided a particular account of the Roman constitution and Dion as one who wrote for 'Greeks unacquainted with these matters'. Dionysius is described at ii.229, ed. Lothian 182, as a 'critick of great penetration' and is among the most frequently quoted authorities in these lectures, particularly with regard to Smith's lectures on the history of historians (lecture 19).

[31] 'Then good speech and good music, and grace and good rhythm, follow good nature, not that silliness which we call good nature in compliment, but the mind that is really well and nobly constituted in character.' (Plato, *Republic*, iii.400, tranlated by A. D. Lindsay in Everyman Library (1935), 83–4.)

[32] 'It is evident what an influence music has over the disposition of the mind, and how variously it can fascinate it: and if it can do this, most certainly it is what youth ought to be instructed in.' (Aristotle, *Politics*, 1340b, translated by W. Ellis in Everyman Library (1912), 247.)

[33] 'The practice of music . . . is beneficial to all men, but to Arcadians it is a necessity.' (Polybius, *History*, iv.20, translated by W. R. Paton in Loeb Classical Library (1925), ii. 348–9.)

[34] 'That judicious writer, Polybius, informs us that music was necessary to soften the manners of the Arcadians, who lived in a cold, gloomy country . . . Plato is not afraid to affirm that there is no possibility of making a change in music without altering the frame of government. Aristotle, who seems to have written his 'Politics' only in order to contradict Plato, agrees with him, notwithstanding, in regard to the power and influence of music over the manners of the people. . . . *Esprit*, IV.viii.1. He went on: 'Thus in the Greek republics the magistrates were extremely embarrassed. They would not have the citizens apply themselves to trade, to agriculture, or to the arts, and yet they would not have them idle. They found, therefore, employment for them in gymnic and military exercises; and none else were allowed by their institution. Hence the Greeks must be considered as a society of wrestlers and boxers. Now these exercises having a natural tendency to render people hardy and fierce, there was a necessity for tempering them with others that might soften their manners. For this purpose, music, which influences the mind by means of the corporeal

probable that the musical education of the Greeks had no great effect in mending their morals, since, without any such education, those of the Romans were upon the whole superior. The respect, of those antient sages for the institutions of their ancestors, had probably disposed them to find much political wisdom in what was, perhaps, merely an antient custom, continued, without interruption, from the earliest period of those societies, to the times in which they had arrived at a considerable degree of refinement. Musick and dancing are the great amusements of almost all barbarous nations, and the great accomplishments which are supposed to fit any man for entertaining his society. It is so at this day among the negroes on the coast of Africa. It was so among the [174] antient Celtes, among the antient Scandinavians, and, as we may learn from Homer, among the antient Greeks in the times preceding the Trojan war.[35] When the Greek tribes had formed themselves into little republicks, it was natural that the study of those accomplishments should, for a long time, make a part of the publick and common education of the people.

41   The masters who instructed the young people either in musick or in military exercises, do not seem to have been paid, or even appointed by the state, either in Rome or even in Athens, the Greek republick of whose laws and customs we are the best informed. The state required that every free citizen should fit himself for defending it in war, and should, upon that account, learn his military exercises. But it left him to learn them of such masters as he could find, and it seems to have advanced nothing for this

organs, was extremely proper. It is a kind of medium between manly exercises, which harden the body, and speculative sciences, which are apt to render us unsociable and sour. It cannot be said that music inspired virtue, for this would be inconceivable: but it prevented the effects of a savage institution, and enabled the soul to have such a share in the education as it could never have had without the assistance of harmony.' (Montesquieu, *Esprit*, IV.viii.5.)

[35] For example: 'Then Odysseus of many wiles answered him and said: "Then will I tell thee what seems to me to be the best way. First bathe yourselves, and put on your tunics, and bid the handmaids in the halls to take their raiment. But let the divine minstrel with his clear-toned lyre in hand be our leader in the gladsome dance, that any man who hears the sound from without, whether a passer-by or one of those who dwell around, may say that it is a wedding feast; and so the rumour of the slaying of the wooers shall not be spread abroad throughout the city before we go forth to our well-wooded farm. There shall we afterwards devise whatever advantage the Olympians may vouchsafe us" . . . So he spoke, and they all readily hearkened and obeyed. First they bathed, and put on their tunics, and the women arrayed themselves, and the divine minstrel took the hollow lyre and aroused in them the desire of sweet song and goodly dance. So the great hall resounded all about with the tread of dancing men and of fair-girdled women.' (Homer, *Odyssey*, xxiii.129–48, translated by A. T. Murray in Loeb Classical Library (1935), ii.382–5. 'Therein fashioned he also two cities of mortal men exceeding fair. In the one there were marriages and feastings, and by the light of the blazing torches they were leading the brides from their bowers through the city, and loud rose the bridal song. And young men were whirling in the dance, and in their midst flutes and lyres sounded continually; and there the women stood each before her door and marvelled.' (Homer, *Iliad*, xviii.490–6, translated by A. T. Murray, in the Loeb Classical Library (1937), ii.334–5.)

purpose, but a publick field or place of exercise, in which he should practice and perform them.

42 In the early ages both of the Greek and Roman republicks, the other parts of education seem to have consisted in learning to read, write, and account according to the arithmetick of the times. These accomplishments the richer citizens seem frequently to have acquired at home, by the assistance of some domestic pedagogue who was generally, either a slave, or a freed-man; and the poorer citizens, in the schools of such masters as made a trade of teaching for hire. Such parts of education, however, were abandoned altogether to the care of the parents or [175] guardians of each individual. It does not appear that the state ever assumed any inspection or direction of them.[36] By a law of Solon, indeed, the children were acquitted from maintaining [q]those parents in their old age[q] who had neglected to instruct them in some profitable trade or business.[37]

43 In the progress of refinement, when philosophy and rhetorick came into fashion, the better sort of people used to send their children to the schools of philosophers and rhetoricians, in order to be instructed in [r]these[r] fashionable sciences.[38] But those schools were not supported by the publick. They were for a long time barely tolerated by it. The demand for philosophy and rhetorick was for a long time so small, that the first professed teachers of either could not find constant employment in any one city, but were obliged to travel about from place to place. In this manner lived Zeno of Elea, Protagoras, Gorgias, Hippias, and many others. As the demand increased, the schools both of philosophy and rhetorick became stationary; first in Athens, and afterwards in several other cities. The state, however, seems never to have encouraged them further than by assigning to some of them a particular place to teach in, which was sometimes done

q–q in their old age those parents *1* r–r those *1*

[36] The same phrase is used above, I.vi.6.

[37] 'He enacted a law that no son who had not been taught a trade should be compelled to support his father.' (Plutarch, *Life of Solon*, xxii, translated by B. Perrin, *Plutarch's Lives*, Loeb Classical Library (1914), i.465. See also: 'An Athenian law obliged children to provide for their fathers when fallen into poverty; it excepted those who were born of a courtesan, those whose chastity had been infamously prostituted by their father, and those to whom he had not given any means of gaining a livelihood.' (Montesquieu, Esprit, XXVI.v. 1, 2.) 'At *Athens* all *Children* were forced to assist their *Parents*, if they came to *Want*: But *Solon* made a Law, that no *Son* should be oblig'd to relieve his *Father*, who had not bred him up to any *Calling*.' (Mandeville, *The Fable of the Bees*, pt.i.46, ed. Kaye i.59.)

[38] Cf. Astronomy, IV.18: 'Philosophers, long before the age of Hipparchus, seem to have abandoned the study of nature, to employ themselves chiefly in ethical, rhetorical, and dialectical questions.' LRBL ii.213–14, ed. Lothian 175, comments: 'Whatever branch of Philosophy has been most cultivated and has made the greatest progress will necessarily be most agreable in the prosecution. This, therefore, will be the fashionable science, and a knowledge in it will give a man the Character of a deep philosopher and a man of great knowledge . . . Rhetorick and Logick or Dialectick were those undoubtedly which had made the greatest progress amongst the ancients. . .' A similar point is made with regard to Rome at ii.237, ed. Lothian 187.

too by private donors. The state seems to have assigned the Academy to Plato, the Lyceum to Aristotle, and the Portico to Zeno of Citta the founder of the Stoics. But Epicurus bequeathed his gardens to his own school. Till about the time of Marcus Antoninus, however, no teacher ap-[176]pears to have had any salary from the publick, or to have had any other emoluments, but what arose from the honoraries or fees of his scholars.[39] The bounty which that philosophical emperor, as we learn from Lucian,[40] bestowed upon ˢone ofˢ the teachers of philosophy, probably lasted no longer than his own life. There was nothing equivalent to the privileges of graduation, and to have attended any of those schools was not necessary, in order to be permitted to practise any particular trade or profession. If the opinion of their own utility could not draw scholars to them, the law neither forced any body to go to them, nor rewarded any body for having gone to them. The teachers had no jurisdiction over their pupils, nor any other authority besides that natural authority, which superior virtue and abilities never fail to procure from young people, towards those who are entrusted with any part of their education.

44   At Rome, the study of the civil law made a part of the education, not of the greater part of the citizens, but of some particular families. The young people, however, who wished to acquire knowledge in the law, had no publick school to go to, and had no other method of studying it, than by frequenting the company of such of their relations and friends, as were supposed to understand it. It is perhaps worth while to remark, that though the laws of the twelve tables were, many of them, copied from those of some antient Greek republicks, yet law never seems to have grown up to be a science in any [177] republick of antient Greece. In Rome it became a science very early, and gave a considerable degree of illustration to those citizens who had the reputation of understanding it. In the republicks of antient Greece, particularly in Athens, the ordinary courts of justice consisted of numerous and, therefore, disorderly bodies of people, who frequently decided almost at random, or as ᵗ clamour, faction and party spirit happened to determine.[41] The ignominy of an unjust decision, when

ˢ⁻ˢ 3–6   ᵗ a 2

---

[39] Smith discusses the emoluments of classical teachers at I.x.c.39. See also V.i.g.40, where it is remarked that the greater part of the eminent men of letters were public or private teachers.

[40] '. . . the Emperor has established, as you know, an allowance, not inconsiderable, for the philosophers according to sect—the Stoics, I mean, the Platonics, and the Epicureans; also those of the Walk, the same amount for each of these. It was stipulated that when one of them died another should be appointed in his stead, after being approved by vote of the first citizens. And the prize was not a shield of hide or a victim as the poet has it [Homer, *Iliad*, xxii.159], but a matter of ten thousand drachmas a year, for instructing boys.' (Lucian, *Eunuchus*, iii, translated by A. M. Harmon in Loeb Classical Library (1936), v.333. Smith comments on the excellence of Lucian's work as a writer in LRBL 9.

[41] In LJ (B) 26, ed. Cannan 19, Smith commented on the powers of the chieftains in the

it was to be divided among five hundred, a thousand, or fifteen hundred people (for some of their courts were so very numerous), could not fall very heavy upon any individual. At Rome, on the contrary, the principal courts of justice consisted either of a single judge, or of a small number of judges, whose characters, especially as they deliberated always in publick, could not fail to be very much affected by any rash or unjust decision. In doubtful cases, such courts, from their anxiety to avoid blame, would naturally endeavour to shelter themselves under the example, or precedent, of the judges who had sat before them, either in the same, or in some other court. This attention, to practice and precedent, necessarily formed the Roman law into that regular and orderly system in which it has been delivered down to us; and the like attention has had the like effects upon the laws of every other country where such attention has taken place. The superiority of character in the Romans over that of the Greeks, so much remarked by Polybius and Dionysius of Halicar-[178]nassus,⁴² was probably more owing to the better constitution of their courts of justice, than to any of the circumstances to which those authors ascribe it. The Romans are said to have been particularly distinguished for their superior respect to an oath. But the people who were accustomed to make oath only before some diligent and well-informed court of justice, would naturally be much more attentive to what they swore, than they who were accustomed to do the same thing before mobbish and disorderly assemblies.

45   The abilities, both civil and military, of the Greeks and Romans, will readily be allowed to have been, at least, equal to those of any modern nation. Our prejudice is perhaps rather to over rate them. But except in what related to military exercises, the state seems to have been at no pains to form those great abilities: for I cannot be induced to believe that the musical education of the Greeks could be of much consequence in forming

---

early period of society and stated that 'They would be afraid to trust matters of importance to a few, and accordingly we find that at Athens, there were 500 judges at the same time.' The same number is mentioned in LJ (A) iv.17; in LRBL 29 Smith examines the relationship between forms of judicial oratory and the structure of the courts and concluded that in Athens, the orators 'managed the Courts of Judicature in the same manner as the managers of a play-house do the pit. They place some of their friends in different parts of the pit, and as they clap or hiss the performers the rest join in.' (ii.207–8, ed. Lothian 173.) He added at ii.200–01, ed. Lothian 169, that: 'judges, when few in number, will be much more anxious to proceed according to equity than where there is a great number; the blame there is not so easily laid upon any particular person; they are in very little fear of censure.' In this connection Smith compared the equitable decisions of the House of Lords with those reached by Parliament or the Parlement of Paris; the performance of the praetor at Rome with that of the 500 at Athens. In Rome, with the emergence of the office of judge as a separate employment, the incumbents 'would be at much greater pains to gain honour and reputation by it. Having less power they would be more timid. They would be at pains even to strengthen their conduct by the authority of their predecessors . . . Whatever, therefore, had been practised by other judges would obtain authority with them, and be received in time as Law. This is the case in England.' (ii.200, ed. Lothian 168–9.)

⁴² See above, V.i.f.40.

them. Masters, however, had been found, it seems, for instructing the better sort of people among those nations in every art and science in which the circumstances of their society rendered it necessary or convenient for them to be instructed. The demand for such instruction produced, what it always produces, the talent for giving it; and the emulation which an unrestrained competition never fails to excite, appears to have brought that talent to a very high degree of perfection.[43] In the attention which the antient philosophers excited, in the empire which they acquired over the opinions and principles of [179] their auditors, in the faculty which they possessed of giving a certain tone and character to the conduct and conversation of those auditors; they appear to have been much superior to any modern teachers. In modern times, the diligence of publick teachers is more or less corrupted by the circumstances, which render them more or less independent of their success and reputation in their particular professions.[44] Their salaries too put the private teacher, who would pretend to come into competition with them, in the same state with a merchant who attempts to trade without a bounty, in competition with those who trade with a considerable one. If he sells his goods at nearly the same price, he cannot have the same profit, and poverty and beggary at least, if not bankruptcy and ruin, will infallibly be his lot. If he attempts to sell them much dearer, he is likely to have so few customers that his circumstances will not be much mended. The privileges of graduation, besides, are in many countries necessary, or at least extremely convenient to most men of learned professions, that is, to the far greater part of those who have occasion for a learned education. But those privileges can be obtained only by attending the lectures of the publick teachers. The most careful attendance upon the ablest instructions of any private teacher, cannot always give any title to demand them. It is from these different causes that the private teacher of any of the sciences which are commonly taught in universities, is in modern times generally considered as in the very [180] lowest order of men of letters. A man of real abilities can scarce find out a more humiliating or a more unprofitable employment to turn them to. The endowments of schools and colleges have, in this manner, not only corrupted the diligence of publick teachers, but have rendered it almost impossible to have any good private ones.

46   Were there no publick institutions for education, no system, no science would be taught for which there was not some demand; or which the circumstances of the times did not render it, either necessary, or convenient, or at least fashionable to learn. A private teacher could never find his account in teaching, either an exploded and antiquated system of

---

[43] See above, V.i.f.4, where Smith discusses the link between emulation and excellence.
[44] See above, V.i.f.7–9.

a science acknowledged to be useful,[45] or a science universally believed to be a mere useless and pedantick heap of sophistry and nonsense. Such systems, such sciences, can subsist no where, but in those incorporated societies for education whose prosperity and revenue are in a great measure independent of their reputation, and altogether independent of their industry. Were there no publick institutions for education, a gentleman, after going through, with application and abilities, the most complete course of education, which the circumstances of the times were supposed to afford, could not come into the world completely ignorant of every thing which is the common subject of conversation among gentlemen and men of the world.

47   [181] There are no publick institutions for the education of women, and there is accordingly nothing useless, absurd, or fantastical in the common course of their education. They are taught what their parents or guardians judge it necessary or useful for them to learn; and they are taught nothing else. Every part of their education tends evidently to some useful purpose; either to improve the natural attractions of their person, or to form their mind to reserve, to modesty, to chastity, and to œconomy: to render them both likely to become the mistresses of a family, and to behave properly when they have become such. In every part of her life a woman feels some conveniency or advantage from every part of her education. It seldom happens that a man, in any part of his life, derives any conveniency or advantage from some of the most laborious and troublesome parts of his education.

48   Ought the publick, therefore, to give no attention, it may be asked, to the education of the people? Or if it ought to give any, what are the different parts of education which it ought to attend to in the different orders of the people? and in what manner ought it to attend to them?

49   In some cases the state of ᵘtheᵘ society necessarily places the greater part of individuals in such situations as naturally form in them, without any attention of government, almost all the abilities and virtues which that state requires, or perhaps can admit of. In other cases the state of the society does not place the greater part of individuals in such situations, and some attention of [182] government is necessary in order to prevent the almost entire corruption and degeneracy of the great body of the people.

50   In the progress of the division of labour, the employment of the far greater part of those who live by labour, that is, of the great body of the people, comes to be confined to a ᵛfew veryᵛ simple operations; frequently to one or two. But the understandings of the greater part of men are

---

ᵘ⁻ᵘ *1–5*   ᵛ⁻ᵛ very few *1*

[45] Smith also refers to 'exploded systems' at § 34, above.

necessarily formed by their ordinary employments.[46] The man whose whole life is spent in performing a few simple operations, of which the effects too are, perhaps, always the same, or very nearly the same, has no occasion to exert his understanding, or to exercise his invention in finding out expedients for removing difficulties which never occur. He naturally loses, therefore, the habit of such exertion, and generally becomes as stupid and ignorant as it is possible for a human creature to become.[47] The torpor of his mind renders him, not only incapable of relishing or bearing a part in any rational conversation, but of conceiving any generous, noble, or tender sentiment, and consequently of forming any just judgment concerning many even of the ordinary duties of private life. Of the great and extensive interests of his country, he is altogether incapable of judging; and unless very particular pains have been taken to render him otherwise, he is equally incapable of defending his country in war.[48] The uniformity of his stationary life naturally corrupts the courage of his mind, and makes him regard with abhorrence the irregular, [183] uncertain, and adventurous life of a soldier. It corrupts even the activity of his body, and renders him incapable of exerting his strength with vigour and perseverance, in any other employment than that to which he has been bred. His dexterity at his own particular trade seems, in this manner, to be acquired at the expence of his intellectual, social, and martial virtues. But in every improved and civilized society this is the state into which the labouring poor, that is, the great body of the people, must necessarily fall, unless government takes some pains to prevent it.[49]

51   It is otherwise in the barbarous societies, as they are commonly called, of hunters, of shepherds, and even of husbandmen in that rude state of

[46] Cf. LJ (B) 329, ed. Cannan 256: 'It is remarkable that in every commercial nation the low people are exceedingly stupid. The Dutch vulgar are eminently so, and the English are more so than the Scotch.' Smith also observed in the same place that the division of labour had adversely affected education by affording an opportunity for employing people very young.

[47] The limitation on the division of labour in agriculture is mentioned above, I.i.4, and the variety of knowledge and superior understanding thus required of the agricultural worker at I.x.c.23–4. Cf. I.xi.p.8, where Smith describes the indolence of landlords.

[48] Kames also noted that 'Constant application . . . to a single operation, confines the mind to a single object, and excludes all thought and invention . . . the operator becomes dull and stupid, like a beast of burden.' (*Sketches*, V.i.) Adam Ferguson, however, provided what has become perhaps the best-known example in remarking: 'It may even be doubted, whether the measure of national capacity increases with the advancement of arts. Many mechanical arts, indeed, require no capacity; they succeed best under a total supression of sentiment and reason; and ignorance is the mother of industry as well as of superstition. Reflection and fancy are subject to err; but a habit of moving the hand, or the foot, is independent of either. Manufactures, accordingly, prosper most, where the mind is least consulted, and where the workshop may, without any great effort of imagination, be considered as an engine, the parts of which are men.' (*History of Civil Society*, IV.i., ed. Forbes (Edinburgh, 1966), 182–3.)

[49] This qualifies the advantages claimed for the division of labour in I.i. See especially I.i.8, where it is claimed the invention reflected the activities of the common workman.

husbandry which precedes the improvement of manufactures, and the extension of foreign commerce. In such societies the varied occupations of every man oblige every man to exert his capacity, and to invent expedients for removing difficulties which are continually occurring.[50] Invention is kept alive, and the *w*mind is*w* not suffered to fall into that drowsy stupidity, which, in a civilized society, seems to benumb the understanding of almost all the inferior ranks of people.[51] In those barbarous societies, as they are called, every man, it has already been observed, is a warrior. Every man too is in some measure a statesman, and can form a tolerable judgment concerning the interest of the society, and the conduct of those who govern it. How far their chiefs are good judges in peace, or good leaders in war, is obvious to the observation of almost every single [184] man among them. In such a society indeed, no man can well acquire that improved and refined understanding, which a few men sometimes possess in a more civilized state. Though in a rude society there is a good deal of variety in the occupations of every individual, there is not a great deal in those of the whole society. Every man does, or is capable of doing, almost every thing which any other man does, or is capable of doing. Every man has a considerable degree of knowledge, ingenuity, and invention; but scarce any man has a great degree. The degree, however, which is commonly possessed, is generally sufficient for conducting the whole simple business of the society. In a civilized state, on the contrary, though there is little variety in the occupations of the greater part of individuals, there is an almost infinite variety in those of the whole society. These varied occupations present an almost infinite variety of objects to the contemplation of those few, who, being attached to no particular occupation themselves, have leisure and inclination to examine the occupations of other people. The contemplation of so great a variety of objects necessarily exercises their minds in endless comparisons and combinations, and renders their understandings, in an extraordinary degree, both acute and comprehensive. Unless those few, however, happen to be placed in some very particular situations, their great abilities, though honourable to themselves, may contribute very little to the good government or happiness of their society.[52] Notwithstanding the great abi-[185]lities of those few, all the nobler parts of the human

---

w-w minds of men are *1*

[50] Cf. ED 2.14. In TMS V.i.2.8–9 Smith noted a related point with regard to the manners of savage and civilized nations in remarking that the former 'by the necessity of his situation is inured to every sort of hardship' and therefore accustomed to 'give way to none of the passions which . . . distress is apt to excite'. By contrast, 'The general security and happiness which prevail in ages of civility and politeness, afford little exercise to the contempt of danger, to patience in enduring labour, hunger, and pain.'

[51] See above, I.xi.p.8, where Smith establishes a link between intellectual indolence and security in the case of the landlords as a class.

[52] See above, I.ii.4,5.

character may be, in a great measure, obliterated and extinguished in the great body of the people.[53]

52   The education of the common people requires, perhaps, in a civilized and commercial society, the attention of the publick more than that of people of some rank and fortune. People of some rank and fortune are generally eighteen or nineteen years of age before they enter upon that particular business, profession, or trade, by which they propose to distinguish themselves in the world. They have before that full time to acquire, or at least to fit themselves for afterwards acquiring, every accomplishment which can recommend them to the publick esteem, or render them worthy of it. Their parents or guardians are generally sufficiently anxious that they should be so accomplished, and are, in most cases, willing enough to lay out the expence which is necessary for that purpose. If they are not always properly educated, it is seldom from the want of expence laid out upon their education; but from the improper application of that expence. It is seldom from the want of masters; but from the negligence and incapacity of the masters who are to be had, and from the difficulty, or rather from the impossibility which there is, in the present state of things, of finding any better. The employments too in which people of some rank or fortune spend the greater part of their lives, are not, like those of the common people, simple and uniform. They are [186] almost all of them extremely complicated, and such as exercise the head more than the hands. The understandings of those who are engaged in such employments can seldom grow torpid ˣforˣ want of exercise. The employments of people of some rank and fortune, besides, are seldom such as harass them from morning to night. They generally have a good deal of leisure, during which they may perfect themselves in every branch either of useful or ornamental knowledge of which they may have laid the foundation, or for which they may have acquired some taste in the earlier part of life.

53   It is otherwise with the common people. They have little time to spare for education. Their parents can scarce afford to maintain them even in infancy. As soon as they are able to work, they must apply to some trade

---

ˣ⁻ˣ from *1*

[53] LJ (B) 328–33, ed. Cannan 255–9, reviews the disadvantages of the commercial state and concluded by remarking that 'The minds of men are contracted, and rendered incapable of elevation, education is despised, or at least neglected, and heroic spirit is almost utterly extinguished. To remedy these defects would be an object worthy of serious attention.' This form of argument may be related to views which were advanced in the Astronomy. For example, Smith there pointed out that we do not naturally speculate even about complex processes where these are performed in the course of everyday work (II.11) and that the 'indolent imagination' does not tend to find exercise in cases where the appearances observed follow an accustomed pattern (II.7). It was essential to Smith's position that only the *unusual* encourages thought—exactly the sort of conditions which would be absent in the case of the labourer described in the text.

by which they can earn their subsistence.[54] That trade too is generally so simple and uniform as to give little exercise to the understanding; while, at the same time, their labour is both so constant and so severe, that it leaves them little leisure and less inclination to apply to, or even to think of any thing else.

54   But though the common people cannot, in any civilized society, be so well instructed as people of some rank and fortune, the most essential parts of education, however, to read, write, and account, can be acquired at so early a period of life, that the greater part even of those who are to be bred to the lowest occupations, have time to acquire them before they can be [187] employed in those occupations.[55] For a very small expence the publick can facilitate, can encourage, and can even impose upon almost the whole body of the people, the necessity of acquiring those most essential parts of education.

55   The publick can facilitate this acquisition by establishing in every parish or district a little school, where children may be taught for a reward so moderate, that even a common labourer may afford it; the master being partly, but not wholly paid by the publick; because if he was wholly, or even principally paid by it, he would soon learn to neglect his business. In Scotland the establishment of such parish schools has taught almost the whole common people to read, and a very great proportion of them to write and account. In England the establishment of charity schools has had an effect of the same kind, though not so universally, because the establishment is not so universal. If in those little schools the books, by which the children are taught to read, were a little more instructive than they commonly are: and if, instead of *ᵞaᵞ* little smattering of Latin; which the children of the common people are sometimes taught there, and which can scarce ever be of any use to them: they were instructed in the elementary parts of geometry and mechanicks, the literary education of this rank of people would perhaps be as complete as it *ᶻcan beᶻ*. There is scarce a

---

ᵞ⁻ᵞ the *ı*   *ᶻ⁻ᶻ* is capable of being *ı*

---

[54] See above, I.viii.23 and n. 17. Cf LJ (B) 329–30, ed. Cannan 256: 'A boy of 6 or 7 years of age at Birmingham can gain his 3 pence or sixpence a day, and parents find it to be their interest to set them soon to work; thus their education is neglected.' In the same place, Smith ascribed the superior education of the lower orders in Scotland, not to a different attitude to education, but to the relatively *backward* condition of the economy: 'In this country indeed, where the division of labour is not so far advanced, even the meanest porter can read and write, because the price of education is cheap, and because a parent can employ his child no other way at 6 or 7 years of age.'

[55] However, Smith noted in TMS VI.iii.49 that people 'whom nature has formed a good deal below the common level, seem sometimes to rate themselves still more below than they really are. This humility appears sometimes to sink them into idiotism.' Smith went on to note that such people, even as *adults*, may find difficulty in learning 'notwithstanding that, in their advanced age, they have had spirit enough to attempt to learn what their early education had not taught them'.

common trade which does not afford some opportunities of applying to it the principles of geometry and mechanicks, and which would not therefore gradually exercise and im-[188]prove the common people in those principles, the necessary introduction to the most sublime as well as to the most useful sciences.[56]

56   The publick can encourage the acquisition of those most essential parts of education by giving small premiums, and little badges of distinction, to the children of the common people who excel in them.[57]

57   The publick can impose upon almost the whole body of the people the necessity of acquiring those most essential parts of education, by obliging every man to undergo an examination or probation in them before he can obtain the freedom in any corporation, or be allowed to set up any trade either in a village or town corporate.[58]

58   It was in this manner, by facilitating the acquisition of their military and gymnastic exercises, by encouraging it, and even by imposing upon the whole body of the people the necessity of learning those exercises, that the Greek and Roman republicks maintained the martial spirit of their respective citizens.[59] They facilitated the acquisition of those exercises by appointing a certain place for learning and practising them, and by granting to certain masters the privilege of teaching in that place. Those masters do not appear to have had either salaries or exclusive privileges of any kind. Their reward consisted altogether in what they got from their scholars; and a citizen who had learnt his exercises in the publick Gymnasia, had no sort of legal advantage over one who had learnt them privately, provided the latter had learnt them equally well. [189] Those republicks encouraged the acquisition of those exercises, by bestowing little premiums and badges of distinction upon those who excelled in them. To have gained a prize in the Olympic, Isthmian or Nemaean games, gave illustration, not only to the person who gained it, but to his whole family and kindred. The obligation which every citizen was under to serve a certain number of years, if called upon, in the armies of the republick, sufficiently imposed the necessity of learning those exercises without which he could not be fit for that service.

59   That in the progress of improvement the practice of military exercises, unless government takes proper pains to support it, goes gradually to decay, and, together with it, the martial spirit of the great body of the people, the

---

[56] LJ (B) 330, ed. Cannan 256, adverts to 'the benefit of country schools, and, however much neglected, must acknowledge them to be an excellent institution'. In both sets of lectures, Smith associated geometry with its practical uses.

[57] See above, IV.v.a.39, where Smith defends the use of premiums designed to encourage particular artists and manufacturers.

[58] See below, V.i.g.14, where Smith refers to a rather similar plan for *imposing* educational requirements on the higher classes.

[59] Military training in Greece and Rome is also discussed at V.i.a.12.

example of modern Europe sufficiently demonstrates.[60] But the security of every society must always depend, more or less, upon the martial spirit of the great body of the people. In the present times, indeed, that martial spirit alone, and unsupported by a well-disciplined standing army, would not, perhaps, be sufficient for the defence and security of any society. But where every citizen had the spirit of a soldier, a smaller standing army would surely be requisite. That spirit, besides, would necessarily diminish very much the dangers to liberty, whether real or imaginary, which are commonly apprehended from a standing army.[61] As it would very much facilitate the operations of that army against a foreign invader, so it would obstruct them as much if unfortunately [190] they should ever be directed against the constitution of the state.

60　　The antient institutions of Greece and Rome seem to have been much more effectual, for maintaining the martial spirit of the great body of the people, than the establishment of what are called the militias of modern times. They were much more simple. When they were once established, they executed themselves, and it required little or no attention from government to maintain them in the most perfect vigour. Whereas to maintain even in tolerable execution the complex regulations of any modern militia, requires the continual and painful attention of government, without which they are constantly falling into total neglect and disuse. The influence, besides, of the antient institutions was much more universal. By means of them the whole body of the people was compleatly instructed in the use of arms. Whereas it is but a very small part of them who can ever be so instructed by the regulations of any modern militia; except, perhaps, that of Switzerland. But a coward, a man incapable either of defending or of revenging himself, evidently wants one of the most essential parts of the character of a man. He is as much mutilated and deformed in his mind, as another is in his body, who is either deprived of some of its most essential members, or has lost the use of *a*them*a*. He is evidently the more wretched and miserable of the two; because happiness and misery, which reside altogether in the mind, must necessarily depend more upon the healthful or [191] unhealthful, the mutilated or entire state of the mind, than upon that of the body. Even though the martial spirit of the people were of no use towards the defence of the society, yet to prevent that sort of mental mutilation, deformity and wretchedness, which cowardice necessarily involves in it, from spreading themselves through the great body of the people, would still deserve the most serious attention of government; in the same manner as it would deserve its most serious attention to prevent a

---

a-a those members *1*

[60] See above, V.i.a.15.
[61] Standing armies as a danger to liberty are mentioned at V.i.a.41.

leprosy or any other loathsome and offensive disease, though neither mortal nor dangerous, from spreading itself among them; though, perhaps, no other publick good might result from such attention besides the prevention of so great a publick evil.

61   The same thing may be said of the gross ignorance and stupidity which, in a civilized society, seem so frequently to benumb the understandings of all the inferior ranks of people. A man, without the proper use of the intellectual faculties of a man, is, if possible, more contemptible than even a coward, and seems to be mutilated and deformed in a still more essential part of the character of human nature. Though the state was to derive no advantage from the instruction of the inferior ranks of people, it would still deserve its attention that they should not be altogether uninstructed. The state, however, derives no inconsiderable advantage from their instruction. The more they are instructed, the less liable they are to the delusions of enthusiasm and superstition, which, among ignorant nations, [192] frequently occasion the most dreadful disorders. An instructed and intelligent people besides are always more decent and orderly than an ignorant and stupid one. They feel themselves, each individually, more respectable, and more likely to obtain the respect of their lawful superiors, and they are therefore more disposed to respect those superiors. They are more disposed to examine, and more capable of seeing through, the interested complaints of faction and sedition, and they are, upon that account, less apt to be misled into any wanton or unnecessary opposition to the measures of government. In free countries, where the safety of government depends very much upon the favourable judgment which the people may form of its conduct, it must surely be of the highest importance that they should not be disposed to judge rashly or capriciously concerning it.

ARTICLE III

Of the Expence of the Institutions for the Instruction of People of all Ages

1   The institutions for the instruction of people of all ages are chiefly those for religious instruction. This is a species of instruction of which the object is not so much to render the people good citizens in this world, as to prepare them for another and a better world in a life to come. The teachers of the doctrine which contains this instruction, in the same manner as other teachers, may either depend altogether for their subsist-[193]ence upon the voluntary contributions of their hearers; or they may derive it from some other fund to which the law of their country may entitle them; such as a landed estate, a tythe or land tax, an established salary or stipend. Their exertion, their zeal and industry, are likely to be much greater in the former situation than in the latter. In this respect the teachers of new

religions have always had a considerable advantage in attacking those
antient and established systems of which the clergy, reposing themselves
upon their benefices, had neglected to keep up the fervour of faith and
devotion in the great body of the people;[1] and having given themselves up
to indolence, were become altogether incapable of making any vigorous
exertion in defence even of their own establishment. The clergy of an
established and well-endowed religion frequently become men of learning
and elegance, who possess all the virtues of gentlemen, or which can recommend them to the esteem of gentlemen; but they are apt gradually to lose
the qualities, both good and bad, which gave them authority and influence with the inferior ranks of people, and which had perhaps been the
original causes of the success and establishment of their religion. Such a
clergy, when attacked by a set of popular and bold, though perhaps stupid
and ignorant enthusiasts, feel themselves as perfectly defenceless as the
indolent, effeminate, and full fed nations of the southern parts of Asia, when
they were invaded by the active, hardy, and hungry Tartars of the North.[2]
[194] Such a clergy, upon such an emergency, have commonly no other
resource than to call upon the civil magistrate to persecute, destroy, or
drive out their adversaries, as disturbers of the public peace. It was thus
that the Roman catholic clergy called upon the civil magistrate to persecute
the protestants; and the church of England, to persecute the dissenters;
and that in general every religious sect, when it has once enjoyed for a
century or two the security of a legal establishment, has found itself
incapable of making any vigorous defence against any new sect which chose
to attack its doctrine or discipline. Upon such occasions the advantage in
point of learning and good writing may sometimes be on the side of the
established church. But the arts of popularity, all the arts of gaining
proselytes, are constantly on the side of its adversaries. In England those
arts have been long neglected by the well-endowed clergy of the established
church, and are at present chiefly cultivated by the dissenters and by the
methodists. The independent provisions, however, which in many places
have been made for dissenting teachers, by means of voluntary subscriptions,
of trust rights, and other evasions of the law, seem very much to have abated
the zeal and activity of those teachers. They have many of them become
very learned, ingenious, and respectable men; but they have in general
ceased to be very popular preachers. The methodists, without half the
learning of the dissenters, are much more in vogue.

2   [195] In the church of Rome, the industry and zeal of the inferior clergy
*a*is*a* kept more alive by the powerful motive of self-interest, than perhaps in

---

a-a are 4–6

[1] See above, V.i.f.4, and below, § 42.
[2] See above, V.i.a.5, for comment on the Tartars.

any established protestant church. The parochial clergy derive, many of
them, a very considerable part of their subsistence from the voluntary oblations of the people; a source of revenue which confession gives them
many opportunities of improving. The mendicant orders derive their whole
subsistence from such oblations. It is with them, as with the hussars and
light infantry of some armies; no plunder, no pay. The parochial clergy
are like those teachers whose reward depends partly upon their salary,
and partly upon the fees or honoraries which they get from their pupils,
and these must always depend more or less upon their industry and reputation.[3] The mendicant orders are like those teachers whose subsistence
depends altogether upon their industry. They are obliged, therefore, to
use every art which can animate the devotion of the common people. The
establishment of the two great mendicant orders of St. Dominick and St.
Francis, it is observed by Machiavel, revived, in the thirteenth and fourteenth centuries, the languishing faith and devotion of the catholick
church.[4] In Roman catholick countries the spirit of devotion is supported
altogether by the monks and by the poorer parochial clergy. The great
dignitaries of the church, with all the accomplishments of gentlemen and
men of the world, and sometimes with those of men of learning, are careful
enough to maintain the necessary disci-[196]pline over their inferiors, but
seldom give themselves any trouble about the instruction of the people.

3   "Most of the arts and professions in a state," says by far the most
illustrious philosopher and historian of the present age, "are of such a
nature, that, while they promote the interests of the society, they are also
useful or agreeable to some individuals; and in that case, the constant rule
of the magistrate, except, perhaps, on the first introduction of any art, is,
to leave the profession to itself, and trust its encouragement to the individuals who reap the benefit of it.[5] The artizans finding their profits to
rise by the favour of their customers, increase, as much as possible, their
skill and industry; and as matters are not disturbed by any injudicious
tampering, the commodity is always sure to be at all times nearly proportioned to the demand.

4   "But there are also some callings, which, though useful and even necessary
in a state, bring no advantage or pleasure to any individual, and the
supreme power is obliged to alter its conduct with regard to the retainers of

---

[3] See above, V.i.f.5 and 55, with regard to instruction in schools and universities.

[4] 'For had not this religion of ours been brought back to its original condition by Saint
Francis and Saint Dominick, it must soon have been utterly extinguished.' (N. Machiavelli, *Discourses on the First Decade of Titus Livius*, III.i, translated by N. H. Thomson
(London, 1883), 331.) It is stated in LRBL ii.70, ed. Lothian 110–11, that 'Machiavel
is of all modern Historians the only one who has contented himself with that which is the
chief purpose of History, to relate events and connect them with their causes, without
becoming a party on either side.'

[5] The original reads 'for those who reap the benefit of it'.

those professions. It must give them publick encouragement in order to their subsistence; and it must provide against that negligence to which they will naturally be subject, either by annexing particular honours to the profession, by establishing a long subordination of ranks and a strict dependance, or by some other expedient. The persons employed in the finances, [197] fleets,[6] and magistracy, are instances of this order of men.

5   "It may naturally be thought, at first sight, that the ecclesiasticks belong to the first class, and that their encouragement, as well as that of lawyers and physicians, may safely be entrusted to the liberality of individuals, who are attached to their doctrines, and who find benefit or consolation from their spiritual ministry and assistance. Their industry and vigilance will, no doubt, be whetted by such an additional motive; and their skill in the profession, as well as their address in governing the minds of the people, must receive daily increase, from their increasing practice, study, and attention.

6   "But if we consider the matter more closely, we shall find, that this interested diligence of the clergy is what every wise legislator will study to prevent; because, in every religion except the true, it is highly pernicious, and it has even a natural tendency to pervert the true, by infusing into it a strong mixture of superstition, folly, and delusion. Each ghostly practitioner, in order to render himself more precious and sacred in the eyes of his retainers, will inspire them with the most violent abhorrence of all other sects, and continually endeavour, by some novelty, to excite the languid devotion of his audience. No regard will be paid to truth, morals, or decency in the doctrines inculcated. Every tenet will be adopted that best suits the disorderly affections [198] of the human frame. Customers will be drawn to each conventicle by new industry and address in practising on the passions and credulity of the populace. And in the end, the civil magistrate will find, that he has dearly paid for his pretended frugality, in saving a fixed establishment for the priests; and that in reality the most decent and advantageous composition, which he can make with the spiritual guides, is to bribe their indolence, by assigning stated salaries to their profession, and rendering it superfluous for them to be farther active, than merely to prevent their flock from straying in quest of new pastures. And in this manner ecclesiastical establishments, though commonly they arose at first from religious views, prove in the end advantageous to the political interests of society."[7]

7   But whatever may have been the good or bad effects of the independent provision of the clergy; it has, perhaps, been very seldom bestowed upon them from any view to those effects. Times of violent religious controversy have generally been times of equally violent political faction. Upon such

---

[6] The original reads 'finances, armies, fleets'.
[7] Hume, *History of England* (1778), iii.30–1.

occasions, each political party has either found it, or imagined it, for its interest, to league itself with some one or other of the contending religious sects. But this could be done only by adopting, or at least by favouring, the tenets of that particular sect. The sect which had the good fortune to be leagued with the conquering party, necessarily shared in the victory of its ally, by whose favour and protection it was soon en-[199]abled in some degree to silence and subdue all its adversaries. Those adversaries had generally leagued themselves with the enemies of the conquering party, and were therefore the enemies of that party. The clergy of this particular sect having thus become complete masters of the field, and their influence and authority with the great body of the people being in its highest vigour, they were powerful enough to over-awe the chiefs and leaders of their own party, and to oblige the civil magistrate to respect their opinions and inclinations. Their first demand was generally, that he should silence and subdue all their adversaries; and their second, that he should bestow an independent provision on themselves. As they had generally contributed a good deal to the victory, it seemed not unreasonable that they should have some share in the spoil. They were weary, besides, of humouring the people, and of depending upon their caprice for a subsistence. In making this demand therefore they consulted their own ease and comfort, without troubling themselves about the effect which it might have in future times upon the influence and authority of their order. The civil magistrate, who could comply with *b*this*b* demand only by giving them something which he would have chosen much rather to take, or to keep to himself, was seldom very forward to grant it. Necessity, however, always forced him to submit at last, though frequently not till after many delays, evasions, and affected excuses.

8   But if politicks had never called in the aid of religion, had the conquering party never adopted [200] the tenets of one sect more than those of another, when it had gained the victory, it would probably have dealt equally and impartially with all the different sects, and have allowed every man to chuse his own priest and his own religion as he thought proper. There would in this case, no doubt, have been a great multitude of religious sects. Almost every different congregation might probably have made a little sect by itself, or have entertained some peculiar tenets of its own. Each teacher would no doubt have felt himself under the necessity of making the utmost exertion, and of using every art both to preserve and to increase the number of his disciples. But as every other teacher would have felt himself under the same necessity, the success of no one teacher, or sect of teachers, could have been very great. The interested and active zeal of religious teachers can be dangerous and troublesome only where there is, either but one sect tolerated in the society, or where the whole of a large society is divided into

b—b their 6

two or three great sects; the teachers of each ^{c} acting by concert, and under a regular discipline and subordination. But that zeal must be altogether innocent where the society is divided into two or three hundred, or perhaps into as many thousand small sects, of which no one could be considerable enough to disturb the publick tranquillity. The teachers of each sect, seeing themselves surrounded on all sides with more adversaries than friends, would be obliged to learn that candour and moderation which is so seldom to be found among the teachers of those great sects, whose [201] tenets being supported by the civil magistrate, are held in veneration by almost all the inhabitants of extensive kingdoms and empires, and who therefore see nothing round them but followers, disciples, and humble admirers. The teachers of each little sect, finding themselves almost alone, would be obliged to respect those of almost every other sect, and the concessions which they would mutually find it both convenient and agreeable to make to one another, might in time probably reduce the doctrine of the greater part of them to that pure and rational religion, free from every mixture of absurdity, imposture, or fanaticism, such as wise men have in all ages of the world wished to see established; but such as positive law has perhaps never yet established,[8] and probably never will establish in any country: because, with regard to religion, positive law always has been, and probably always will be, more or less influenced by popular superstition and enthusiasm.[9] This plan of ecclesiastical government, or more properly of no ecclesiastical government, was what the sect called Independents, a sect no doubt of very wild enthusiasts, proposed to establish in England towards the end of the civil war.[10] If it had been established, though of a very unphilosophical origin, it would probably by this time have been productive of the most philosophical good temper and moderation with regard to every sort of religious principle. It has been established in Pensylvania, where, though the Quakers happen to be the most numerous ^{d}, the law in reality fa-[202]vours no one sect more than another, and it is there said to have been productive of this philosophical good temper and moderation.

9 But though this equality of treatment should not be productive of this good temper and moderation in all, or even in the greater part of the religious sects of a particular country; yet provided those sects were

^{c} sect *1* ^{d} sect *1*

---

[8] In Letter 151 addressed to Smith, dated 3 April 1776, Blair commented: 'Independency was at no time a popular or practicable System. The little Sects you Speak of, would for many reasons, have Combined together into greater bodies, & done much Mischief to Society. You are, I think, too favourable by much to Presbytery.'

[9] See above, IV.v.b.40, where the laws governing subsistence are likened to those of religion.

[10] 'The independents rejected all ecclesiastical establishments, and would admit of no church-courts, no government among pastors, no interposal of the magistrate in spiritual concerns, no fixed encouragement annexed to any system of doctrines or opinions.' (Hume, *History of England* (1778), vii.19.)

sufficiently numerous, and each of them consequently too small to disturb
the publick tranquillity, the excessive zeal of each [e] for its particular tenets
could not well be productive of any very hurtful effects, but, on the
contrary, of several good ones: and if the government was perfectly decided
both to let them all alone, and to oblige them all to let alone one another,
there is little danger that they would not of their own accord subdivide
themselves fast enough, so as soon to become sufficiently numerous.

10   In every civilized society, in every society where the distinction of ranks
has once been completely established, there have been always two different schemes or systems of morality current at the same time; of which
the one may be called the strict or austere; the other the liberal, or, if you
will, the loose system. The former is generally admired and revered by the
common people: The latter is commonly more esteemed and adopted by
what are called people of fashion. The degree of disapprobation with which
we ought to mark the vices of levity, the vices which are apt to arise from
great prosperity, and from the excess of gaiety and good humour, seems to
[203] constitute the principal distinction between those two opposite
schemes or systems. In the liberal or loose system, luxury, wanton and even
disorderly mirth, the pursuit of pleasure to some degree of intemperance,
the breach of chastity, at least in one of the two sexes, &c. provided they
are not accompanied with gross indecency, and do not lead to falsehood or
injustice, are generally treated with a good deal of indulgence, and are
easily either excused or pardoned altogether. In the austere system, on the
contrary, those excesses are regarded with the utmost abhorrence and
detestation. The vices of levity are always ruinous to the common people,
and a single week's thoughtlessness and dissipation is often sufficient to undo
a poor workman for ever, and to drive him through despair upon committing the most enormous crimes. The wiser and better sort of the common
people, therefore, have always the utmost abhorrence and detestation of
such excesses, which their experience tells them are so immediately fatal
to people of their condition. The disorder and extravagance of several
years, on the contrary, will not always ruin a man of fashion, and people of
that rank are very apt to consider the power of indulging in some degree of
excess as one of the advantages of their fortune, and the liberty of doing so
without censure or reproach, as one of the privileges which belong to their
station. In people of their own station, therefore, they regard such excesses
with but a small degree of disapprobation, and censure them either very
slightly or not at all.

11   [204] Almost all religious sects have begun among the common people,
from whom they have generally drawn their earliest, as well as their most
numerous proselytes. The austere system of morality has, accordingly, been
adopted by those sects almost constantly, or with very few exceptions; for

e sect *1*

there have been some. It was the system by which they could best recommend themselves to that order of people to whom they first proposed their plan of reformation upon what had been before established. Many of them, perhaps the greater part of them, have even endeavoured to gain credit by refining upon this austere system, and by carrying it to some degree of folly and extravagance; and this excessive rigour has frequently recommended them more than any thing else to the respect and veneration of the common people.[11]

12   A man of rank and fortune is by his station the distinguished member of a great society, who attend to every part of his conduct, and who thereby oblige him to attend to every part of it himself. His authority and consideration depend very much upon the respect which this society bears to him. He dare not do any thing which would disgrace or discredit him in it, and he is obliged to a very strict observation of that species of morals, whether liberal or austere, which the general consent of this society prescribes to persons of his rank and fortune. A man of low condition, on the contrary, is far from being a distinguished member of any great society. While he remains in a country village his conduct may be [205] attended to, and he may be obliged to attend to it himself. In this situation, and in this situation only, he may have what is called a character to lose. But as soon as he comes into a great city, he is sunk in obscurity and darkness.[12] His conduct is observed and attended to by nobody, and he is therefore very likely to neglect it himself, and to abandon himself to every sort of low profligacy and vice.[13] He never emerges so effectually from this obscurity, his conduct never excites so much the attention of any respectable society, as by his becoming the member of a small religious sect. He from that moment acquires a degree of consideration which he never had

---

[11] See below, V.i.g.29.

[12] Smith also comments on the problems of large manufactories at I.viii.48. He says in TMS I.iii.2.1. that men are more disposed to admire riches rather than sympathize with poverty, and that 'to feel that we are taken no notice of, necessarily damps the most agreeable hope, and disappoints the most ardent desire, of human nature. The poor man goes out and comes in unheeded, and when in the midst of a crowd is in the same obscurity as if shut up in his own hovel.' Adam Ferguson also referred to the fact that great numbers confined in cities 'are exposed to corruption, become profligate, licentious, seditious, and incapable of government or public affections' (*Institutes of Moral Philosophy* (Edinburgh, 1772; 3rd ed. 1785), 262). See also Kames, *Sketches*, II.xi, and cf. Steuart, *Principles*, I.x.

[13] Hume also remarked in his essay 'Of the Populousness of Ancient Nations' that enormous cities are 'destructive to society', and that they 'beget vice and disorder of all kinds' (*Essays Moral, Political, and Literary*, ed. Green and Grose, i.398). In LJ (B) 330, ed. Cannan 257, Smith refers to the problem of the modern worker who lacks ideas to amuse himself, so that when away from his work 'he must therefore betake himself to drunkeness and riot', citing the example of the commercial part of England where the work of one half of the week is sufficient to maintain the labourer, with the remainder passed in riot and debauchery: 'So it may very justly be said that the people who cloathe the whole world are in rags themselves.'

before. All his brother sectaries are, for the credit of the sect, interested to observe his conduct, and if he gives occasion to any scandal, if he deviates very much from those austere morals which they almost always require of one another, to punish him by what is always a very severe punishment, even where no civil effects attend it, expulsion or excommunication from the sect. In little religious sects, accordingly, the morals of the common people have been almost always remarkably regular and orderly; generally much more so than in the established church. The morals of those little sects, indeed, have frequently been rather disagreeably rigorous and unsocial.[14]

13   There are two very easy and effectual remedies, however, by whose joint operation the state might, without violence, correct whatever was unsocial or disagreeably rigorous in the morals of all the little sects into which the country was divided.

14   [206] The first of those remedies is the study of science and philosophy, which the state might render almost universal among all people of middling or more than middling rank and fortune; not by giving salaries to teachers in order to make them negligent and idle, but by instituting some sort of probation, even in the higher and more difficult sciences, to be undergone by every person before he was permitted to exercise any liberal profession, or before he could be received as a candidate for any honourable office of trust or profit. If the state imposed upon this order of men the necessity of learning, it would have no occasion to give itself any trouble about providing them with proper teachers.[15] They would soon find better teachers for themselves than any whom the state could provide for them. Science is the great antidote to the poison of enthusiasm and superstition; and where all the superior ranks of people were secured from it, the inferior ranks could not be much exposed to it.

15   The second of those remedies is the frequency and gaiety of publick diversions. The state, by encouraging, that is by giving entire liberty to all those who for their own interest would attempt, without scandal or indecency, to amuse and divert the people by painting, poetry, musick, dancing;[16] by all sorts of dramatic representations and exhibitions, would easily dissipate, in the greater part of them, that melancholy and gloomy humour which is almost always the nurse of popular superstition and enthusiasm. Publick diversions have always been the objects of dread [207] and hatred, to all the fanatical promoters of those popular frenzies. The

---

[14] The problem of faction attracted a good deal of attention in the TMS. See for example III.i.3.43, where it is asserted that 'Of all the corrupters of moral sentiments . . . faction and fanaticism have always been by far the greatest'. Smith also expressed concern over the influence exerted by 'false notions of religion' at III.i.6.12. See especially chapter 6.

[15] Smith refers to the capacity to *impose* educational standards on the poor at V.i.f.57.

[16] Persons practising such arts are described as unproductive at II.iii.2. It will be observed, however, that in the present context such people emerge as being indirectly productive of benefit to society.

gaiety and good humour which those diversions inspire were altogether inconsistent with that temper of mind, which was fittest for their purpose, or which they could best work upon. Dramatick representations besides, frequently exposing their artifices to publick ridicule, and sometimes even to publick execration, were upon that account, more than all other diversions, the objects of their peculiar abhorrence.

16　　In a country where the law favoured the teachers of no one religion more than those of another, it would not be necessary that any of them should have any particular or immediate dependency upon the sovereign or executive power; or that he should have any thing to do, either in appointing, or in dismissing them from their offices. In such a situation he would have no occasion to give himself any concern about them, further than to keep the peace among them, in the same manner as among the rest of his subjects; that is, to hinder them from persecuting, abusing, or oppressing one another. But it is quite otherwise in countries where there is an established or governing religion. The sovereign can in this case never be secure, unless he has the means of influencing in a considerable degree the greater part of the teachers of that religion.

17　　The clergy of every established church constitute a great incorporation. They can act in concert, and pursue their interest upon one plan and with one spirit, as much as if they were under [208] the direction of one man; and they are frequently too under such direction. Their interest as an incorporated body is never the same with that of the sovereign, and is sometimes directly opposite to it. Their great interest is to maintain their authority with the people; and this authority depends upon the supposed certainty and importance of the whole doctrine which they inculcate, and upon the supposed necessity of adopting every part of it with the most implicit faith, in order to avoid eternal misery. Should the sovereign have the imprudence to appear either to deride or doubt himself of the most trifling part of their doctrine, or from humanity attempt to protect those who did either the one or the other, the punctilious honour of a clergy who have no sort of dependency upon him, is immediately provoked to proscribe him as a profane person, and to employ all the terrors of religion in order to oblige the people to transfer their allegiance to some more orthodox and obedient prince. Should he oppose any of their pretensions or usurpations, the danger is equally great. The princes who have dared in this manner to rebel against the church, over and above this crime of rebellion, have generally been charged too with the additional crime of heresy, notwithstanding their solemn protestations of their faith and humble submission to every tenet which she thought proper to prescribe to them. But the authority of religion is superior to every other authority. The fears which it suggests conquer all other fears. When the authorised teachers of re-[209] ligion propagate through the great body of the people doctrines subversive of the authority of the sovereign, it is by violence only, or by the force of a standing army, that he can maintain his authority. Even a standing army cannot in this case give him any lasting security; because if the soldiers are not foreigners, which can seldom be the case, but drawn from the great body of the people, which must almost always be the case, they are likely to be soon corrupted by those very doctrines. The revolutions which the turbulence of the Greek clergy was continually occasioning at Constantinople, as long as the eastern empire subsisted; the convulsions which, during the course of several centuries, the turbulence of the Roman clergy was continually occasioning in every part of Europe, sufficiently demonstrate how precarious and insecure must always be the situation of the sovereign who has no proper means of influencing the clergy of the established and governing religion of his country.

18   Articles of faith, as well as all other spiritual matters, it is evident enough, are not within the proper department of a temporal sovereign, who, though he may be very well qualified for protecting, is seldom supposed to be so for instructing the people. With regard to such matters, therefore, his authority can seldom be sufficient to counterbalance the united authority of the clergy of the established church. The publick tranquillity, however, and his own security, may frequently depend upon the doctrines which they may think proper to propagate concerning such [210] matters. As he can seldom directly oppose their decision, therefore, with proper weight and authority, it is necessary that he should be able to influence it; and he can influence it only by the fears and expectations which he may excite in the greater part of the individuals of the order. Those fears and expectations may consist in the fear of deprivation or other punishment, and in the expectation of further preferment.

19   In all christian churches the benefices of the clergy are a sort of freeholds which they enjoy, not during pleasure, but during life, or good behaviour. If they held them by a more precarious tenure, and were liable to be turned out upon every slight disobligation either of the sovereign or of his ministers, it would perhaps be impossible for them to maintain their authority with the people, who would then consider them as mercenary dependents upon the court, in the sincerity of whose instructions they could no longer have any confidence. But should the sovereign attempt irregularly, and by violence to deprive any number of clergymen of their freeholds on account, perhaps, of their having propagated, with more than ordinary zeal, some factious or seditious doctrine, he would only render, by such persecution, both them and their doctrine ten times more popular, and therefore ten times more troublesome and dangerous than they had been before. Fear is in almost all cases a wretched instrument of government, and ought in particular never to be employed against any order of men who have the smallest pretensions to [211] independency. To attempt

to terrify them, serves only to irritate their bad humour, and to confirm them in an opposition which more gentle usage perhaps might easily induce them, either to soften, or to lay aside altogether. The violence which the French government usually employed in order to oblige all their parliaments, or sovereign courts of justice, to enregister any unpopular edict, very seldom succeeded. The means commonly employed, however, the imprisonment of all the refractory members, one would think were forcible enough. The princes of the house of Stewart sometimes employed the like means in order to influence some of the members of the parliament of England; and they generally found them equally intractable. The parliament of England is now managed in another manner; and a very small experiment which the duke of Choiseul made about twelve years ago upon the parliament of Paris, demonstrated sufficiently that all the parliaments of France might have been managed still more easily in the same manner. That experiment was not pursued. For though management and persuasion are always the easiest and the safest instruments of government, as force and violence are the worst and the most dangerous, yet such, it seems, is the natural insolence of man, that he almost always disdains to use the good instrument, except when he cannot or dare not use the bad one. The French government could and durst use force, and therefore disdained to use management and persuasion. But there is no order of men, it appears, I believe, from [212] the experience of all ages, upon whom it is so dangerous, or rather so perfectly ruinous, to employ force and violence, as upon the respected clergy of ᶠanyᶠ established church. The rights, the privileges, the personal liberty of every individual ecclesiastic, who is upon good terms with his own order, are, even in the most despotic governments, more respected than those of any other person of nearly equal rank and fortune. It is so in every gradation of despotism, from that of the gentle and mild government of Paris, to that of the violent and furious government of Constantinople. But though this order of men can scarce ever be forced, they may be managed as easily as any other; and the security of the sovereign, as well as ᵍ the publick tranquillity, seems to depend very much upon the means which he has of managing them; and those means seem to consist altogether in the preferment which he has to bestow upon them.

20   In the antient constitution of the ʰChristianʰ church, the bishop of each diocese was elected by the joint votes of the clergy and of the people of the episcopal city. The people did not long retain their right of election; and while they did retain it, they almost always acted under the influence of the clergy, who in such spiritual matters appeared to be their natural guides. The clergy, however, soon grew weary of the trouble of managing them, and found it easier to elect their own bishops themselves. The abbot, in the same manner, was elected by the monks of the monastery, at least in the

---

ᶠ⁻ᶠ an *6*   ᵍ of *6*   ʰ⁻ʰ Roman Catholic *1*

greater part of abbacies. [213] All the inferior ecclesiastical benefices comprehended within the diocese were collated by the bishop, who bestowed them upon such ecclesiastics as he thought proper. All church preferments were in this manner in the disposal of the church. The sovereign, though he might have some indirect influence in those elections, and though it was sometimes usual to ask both his consent to elect, and his approbation of the election, yet had no direct or sufficient means of managing the clergy. The ambition of every clergyman naturally led him to pay court, not so much to his sovereign, as to his own order, from which only he could expect preferment.

21   Through the greater part of Europe the Pope gradually drew to himself first the collation of almost all bishopricks and abbacies, or of what were called Consistorial benefices, and afterwards, by various machinations and pretences, of the greater part of inferior benefices comprehended within each diocese; little more being left to the bishop than what was barely necessary to give him a decent authority with his own clergy. By this arrangement, the condition of the sovereign was still worse than it had been before. The clergy of all the different countries of Europe were thus formed into a sort of spiritual army, dispersed in different quarters, indeed, but of which all the movements and operations could now be directed by one head, and conducted upon one uniform plan. The clergy of each particular country might be considered as a particular detachment of that army, of which the [214] operations could easily be supported and seconded by all the other detachments quartered in the different countries round about. Each detachment was not only independent of the sovereign of the country in which it was quartered, and by which it was maintained, but dependent upon a foreign sovereign, who could at any time turn its arms against the sovereign of that particular country, and support them by the arms of all the other detachments.[17]

22   Those arms were the most formidable that can well be imagined. In the antient state of Europe, before the establishment of arts and manufactures, the wealth of the clergy gave them the same sort of influence over the common people, which that of the great barons gave them over their respective vassals, tenants, and retainers. In the great landed estates, which the mistaken piety both of princes and private persons had bestowed upon the church, jurisdictions were established of the same kind with those of

---

[17] In LJ (B) 353–4, ed. Cannan 276–7, Smith also noted that the Pope had residents or legates in all the courts of Europe: 'The very same reason that makes embassies now so frequent induced the Pope formerly to fall upon this method. He had business in all the countries of Europe and a great part of his revenue was collected from them, and as they were continualy attempting to infringe the right he claimed, he found it necessary to have a person constantly residing at their courts to see that his priviledges were preserved.' Smith added that the fact that the Pope had representatives in all the courts of Europe made them 'more nearly connected, and he obliged them to treat one another with more humanity'.

the great barons; and for the same reason.[18] In those great landed estates, the clergy, or their bailiffs, could easily keep the peace without the support or assistance either of the king or of any other person; and neither the king nor any other person could keep the peace there without the support and assistance of the clergy. The jurisdictions of the clergy, therefore, in their particular baronies or manors, were equally independent, and equally exclusive of the authority of the king's courts, as those of the great temporal lords. The tenants of the clergy were, like those of the great barons, almost [215] all tenants at will, entirely dependent upon their immediate lords, and therefore liable to be called out at pleasure, in order to fight in any quarrel in which the clergy might think proper to engage them. Over and above the rents of those estates, the clergy possessed, in the tythes, a very large portion of the rents of all the other estates in every kingdom of Europe.[19] The revenues arising from both those species of rents were, the greater part of them, paid in kind, in corn, wine, cattle, poultry, &c. The quantity exceeded greatly what the clergy could themselves consume; and there were neither arts nor manufactures for the produce of which they could exchange the surplus. The clergy could derive advantage from this immense surplus in no other way than by employing it, as the great barons employed the like surplus of their revenues, in the most profuse hospitality, and in the most extensive charity.[20] Both the hospitality and the charity of the antient clergy, accordingly, are said to have been very great. They not only maintained almost the whole poor of every kingdom, but many knights and gentlemen had frequently no other means of subsistence than by travelling about from monastery to monastery, under pretence of devotion, but in reality to enjoy the hospitality of the clergy. The retainers of some particular prelates were often as numerous as those of the greatest lay-lords; and the retainers of all the clergy taken together were, perhaps, more numerous than those of all the lay-lords. There was always much more union among the clergy than among [216] the lay-lords. The former were under a regular discipline and subordination to the papal authority. The latter were under no regular discipline or subordination, but almost always equally jealous of one another, and of the king.[21] Though the tenants and retainers of the clergy, therefore, had both together been less numerous than those of the great lay-lords, and their tenants were probably much less numerous, yet their union would have rendered them more formidable.

[18] In LJ (A) v.30 Smith refers to the advantages which the clergy derived from having the 'directions of the consciences of dying persons'. LJ (A) i.108 mentions an additional source of benefit arising from the Bishops' position of trust (as holy men) in the distribution of inheritances. Smith states that the law was changed in the time of Edward I in order to avoid such abuses.

[19] Tithes are stated to be very unequal taxes and a great discouragement to agriculture at V.ii.d.2,3.

[20] Similar points are made regarding the power of the barons at III.iv.5.

[21] See above, III.iv.9

The hospitality and charity of the clergy too, not only gave them the command of a great temporal force, but increased very much the weight of their spiritual weapons. Those virtues procured them the highest respect and veneration among all the inferior ranks of people, of whom many were constantly, and almost all occasionally, fed by them. Every thing belonging or related to so popular an order, its possessions, its privileges, its doctrines, necessarily appeared sacred in the eyes of the common people, and every violation of them, whether real or pretended, the highest act of sacriligious wickedness and profaneness. In this state of things, if the sovereign frequently found it difficult to resist the confederacy of a few of the great nobility, we cannot wonder that he should find it still more so to resist the united force of the clergy of his own dominions, supported by that of the clergy of all the neighbouring dominions. In such circumstances the wonder is, not that he was sometimes obliged to yield, but that he ever was able to resist.

23 [217] The privileges of the clergy in those antient times (which to us who live in the present times appear the most absurd) their total exemption from the secular jurisdiction, for example, or what in England was called the benefit of clergy; were the natural or rather the necessary consequences of this state of things.[22] How dangerous must it have been for the sovereign to attempt to punish a clergyman for any crime whatever, if his own order were disposed to protect him, and to represent either the proof as insufficient for convicting so holy a man, or the punishment as too severe to be inflicted upon one whose person had been rendered sacred by religion. The sovereign could, in such circumstances, do no better than leave him to be tried by the ecclesiastical courts, who, for the honour of their own order, were interested to restrain, as much as possible, every member of it from committing enormous crimes, or even from giving occasion to such gross scandal as might disgust the minds of the people.

24 In the state in which things were through the greater part of Europe during the tenth, eleventh, twelfth, and thirteenth centuries, and for some time both before and after that period, the constitution of the church of Rome may be considered as the most formidable combination that ever was formed against the authority and security of civil government, as well

---

[22] See above, V.i.f.19. LJ (A) ii.111–13 and LJ (B) 187–8, ed. Cannan 140–1, refer to the benefit of clergy and its application to capital cases, indicating that the test of ability to read was introduced in order to restrict the application of the benefit; a qualification dispensed with by a statute of Queen Anne. LJ (A) ii.51 also points out that in Scotland, anciently, the people regarded the clergy with reverence and as the chief support of the peoples' rights in administering the Canon or Ecclesiastical Law: 'Thus an ecclesiasticall court, which in a country where the regulations of the civill government are arriv'd to a considerable perfection is one of the greatest nuisances imaginable, may be of very great benefit in a state where the civil government is baddly regulated; just in the same way as corporations may be very advantageous in a low state of the arts tho of the greatest detriment where they are carried to a considerable length.'

as against the liberty, reason, and happiness of mankind, which can flourish only where civil government is able to protect them.[23] In that constitution the grossest [218] delusions of superstition were supported in such a manner by the private interests of so great a number of people as put them out of all danger from any assault of human reason: because though human reason might perhaps have been able to unveil, even to the eyes of the common people, some of the delusions of superstition; it could never have dissolved the ties of private interest. Had this constitution been attacked by no other enemies but the feeble efforts of human reason, it must have endured forever. But that immense and well-built fabric, which all the wisdom and virtue of man could never have shaken, much less have over-turned, was by the natural course of things, first weakened, ⁱandⁱ after-wards in part destroyed, and is now likely, in the course of a few centuries more, perhaps, to crumble into ruins altogether.

25   The gradual improvements of arts, manufactures, and commerce, the same causes which destroyed the power of the great barons, destroyed in the same manner, through the greater part of Europe, the whole temporal power of the clergy. In the produce of arts, manufactures, and commerce, the clergy, like the great barons, found something for which they could exchange their rude produce, and thereby discovered the means of spend-ing their whole revenues upon their own persons, without giving any considerable share of them to other people. Their charity became gradually less extensive, their hospitality less liberal or less profuse. Their retainers became consequently less numerous, and by degrees [219] dwindled away altogether. The clergy, too, like the great barons, wished to get a better rent from their landed estates, in order to spend it, in the same manner, upon the gratification of their own private vanity and folly. But this in-crease of rent could be got only by granting leases to their tenants, who thereby became in a great measure independent of them.[24] The ties of

ⁱ⁻ⁱ 2–6

[23] LJ (A) v.66 mentions Elizabeth, Henry VIII and Edward VI as being in 'continuall danger from the plots and conspiracies of the bigotted Papists, spurred on by their Priests'. The same point is made at v.79, where it is remarked that at the times of John and Henry III the country was 'little more than a fief of the Holy See', thus making it necessary to curb the Pope's power. As a result, it became a criminal offence to bring over Papal bulls, to magnify the Pope's power or convert to his religion. Smith suggests at LJ (A) v.68 that such statutes might now be repealed, although 'altogether reasonable at that time' and added at v.73–4 that: 'The zeal of that religion is greatly abated in many points, and tho it might be reasonable to discourage it by imposing double taxes or such like penalties, it can hardly be reasonable to punish as treason the weakness of anyone who was so silly as to prefer the Roman Catholick to the Protestant religion.'

[24] It is remarked in LJ (A) iii.121 that the clergy encouraged the relaxation of the authority of the great proprietors over their villeins as a means of reducing their power and that: 'They saw too perhaps that their lands were but very ill cultivated when under the management of these villains. They therefore thought it would be more for their own ad-vantage to emancipate their villains and enter into an agreement with them with regard to

interest, which bound the inferior ranks of people to the clergy, were in this manner gradually broken and dissolved. They were even broken and dissolved sooner than those which bound the same ranks of people to the great barons: because the benefices of the church being, the greater part of them, much smaller than the estates of the great barons, the possessor of each benefice was much sooner able to spend the whole of its revenue upon his own person. During the greater part of the fourteenth and fifteenth centuries the power of the great barons was, through the greater part of Europe, in full vigour. But the temporal power of the clergy, the absolute command which they had once had over the great body of the people, was very much decayed. The power of the church was by that time very nearly reduced through the greater part of Europe to what arose from her spiritual authority; and even that spiritual authority was much weakened when it ceased to be supported by the charity and hospitality of the clergy. The inferior ranks of people no longer looked upon that order, as they had done before, as the comforters of their distress, and the relievers of their indigence. On the [220] contrary, they were provoked and disgusted by the vanity, luxury, and expence of the richer clergy, who appeared to spend upon their own pleasures what had always before been regarded as the patrimony of the poor.

26   In this situation of things, the sovereigns in the different states of Europe endeavoured to recover the influence which they had once had in the disposal of the great benefices of the church, by procuring to the deans and chapters of each diocese the restoration of their antient right of electing the bishop, and to the monks of each abbacy that of electing the abbot.[25] The re-establishing of this ancient order was the object of several statutes enacted in England during the course of the fourteenth century, ʲparticularly of what is called the statute of provisors;ʲ and of the pragmatick sanction established in France in the fifteenth century. In order to render the election valid, it was necessary that the sovereign should both consent to it before-hand, and afterwards approve of the person elected; and though the election was still supposed to be free, he had, however, all the indirect means which his situation necessarily afforded him, of influencing the clergy in his own dominions. Other regulations of a similar tendency were established in other parts of Europe. But the power of the pope in the collation of the great benefices of the church seems, before the reformation, to have been no where so effectually and so universally restrained as in France and England. The Concordat afterwards, in the sixteenth century,

ʲ⁻ʲ 2–6

---

the cultivation of their lands. In this manner slavery came to be abollished.' See also III.iii, where Smith discusses the causes of decline in the power of the temporal lords.

[25] See above, § 20–1.

gave to the [221] kings of France the absolute right of presenting to all the great^k, or what are called the^k consistorial benefices of the Gallican church.

27   Since the establishment of the Pragmatic sanction and of the Concordat, the clergy of France have in general shown less respect to the decrees of the papal court than the clergy of any other catholick country. In all the disputes which their sovereign has had with the pope, they have almost constantly taken party with the former. This independency of the clergy of France upon the court of Rome, seems to be principally founded upon the Pragmatic sanction and the Concordat. In the earlier periods of the monarchy, the clergy of France appear to have been as much devoted to the pope as those of any other country. When Robert, the second prince of the Capetian race, was most unjustly excommunicated by the court of Rome, his own servants, it is said, threw the victuals which came from his table to the dogs, and refused to taste any thing themselves which had been polluted by the contact of a person in his situation. They were taught to do so, it may very safely be presumed, by the clergy of his own dominions.

28   The claim of collating to the great benefices of the church, a claim in defence of which the court of Rome had frequently shaken, and sometimes overturned the thrones of some of the greatest sovereigns in Christendom, was in this manner either restrained or modified, or given up altogether, in many different parts of Europe, even before the time of the reformation. As the [222] clergy had now less influence over the people, so the state had more influence over the clergy. The clergy therefore had both less power and less inclination to disturb the state.

29   The authority of the church of Rome was in this state of declension, when the disputes which gave birth to the reformation, began in Germany, and soon spread themselves through every part of Europe. The new doctrines were every where received with a high degree of popular favour. They were propagated with all that enthusiastic zeal which commonly animates the spirit of party, when it attacks established authority.[26] The teachers of those doctrines, though perhaps in other respects not more learned than many of the divines who defended the established church, seem in general to have been better acquainted with ecclesiastical history, and with the origin and progress of that system of opinions upon which the authority of the church was established, and they had thereby some advantage in almost every dispute. The austerity of their manners gave them authority with the common people, who contrasted the strict regularity of their conduct with the disorderly lives of the greater part of their

---

^k-k and *I*

[26] 'These two species of religion, the superstitious and fanatical, stand in diametrical opposition to each other; and a large portion of the latter must necessarily fall to his share, who is so couragious as to control authority, and so assuming as to obtrude his own innovations upon the world.' (Hume, *History of England* (1754), i.7.)

own clergy.[27] They possessed too in a much higher degree than their adversaries, all the arts of popularity and of gaining proselytes, arts which the lofty and dignified sons of the church had long neglected, as being to them in a great measure useless.[28] The reason of the new doctrines recommended them to some, their novelty to many; the hatred and contempt of the established [223] clergy to a still greater number; but the zealous, passionate and fanatical, though frequently coarse and rustick eloquence with which they were almost every where inculcated, recommended them to by far the greatest number.

30   The success of the new doctrines was almost every where so great, that the princes who at that time happened to be on bad terms with the court of Rome, were by means of them easily enabled, in their own dominions, to overturn the church, which, having lost the respect and veneration of the inferior ranks of people, could make scarce any resistance. The court of Rome had disobliged some of the smaller princes in the northern parts of Germany, whom it had probably considered as too insignificant to be worth the managing. They universally, therefore, established the reformation in their own dominions. The tyranny of Christiern II. and of Troll archbishop of Upsal, enabled Gustavus Vasa to expel them both from Sweden. The pope favoured the tyrant and the archbishop, and Gustavus Vasa found no difficulty in establishing the reformation in Sweden. Christiern II. was afterwards deposed from the throne of Denmark, where his conduct had rendered him as odious as in Sweden. The pope, however, was still disposed to favour him, and Frederick of Holstein, who had mounted the throne in his stead, revenged himself by following the example of Gustavus Vasa. The magistrates of Berne and Zurich, who had no particular quarrel with the pope, established with great ease the reformation in their respective [224] cantons, where just before some of the clergy had, by an imposture somewhat grosser than ordinary, rendered the whole order both odious and contemptible.

31   In this critical situation of its affairs, the papal court was at sufficient pains to cultivate the friendship of the powerful sovereigns of France and Spain, of whom the latter was at that time emperor of Germany. With their assistance it was enabled, though not without great difficulty and much bloodshed, either to suppress altogether, or to obstruct very much the progress of the reformation in their dominions. It was well enough inclined too to be complaisant to the king of England. But from the circumstances of the times, it could not be so without giving offence to a still greater sovereign, Charles V. king of Spain and emperor of Germany. Henry VIII.

[27] See above, V.i.g.11.

[28] Hume commented on Scotland: 'And tho' the new preachers acquired a mighty influence over the people, it was not merely by their priestly rank or office, but by the seeming austerity of their lives, and the eloquence of their zealous lectures.' (*History of England* (1754), i.60–1.)

accordingly, though he did not embrace himself the greater part of the doctrines of the reformation, was yet enabled, by ʲtheir general prevalenceʲ, to suppress all the monasteries, and to abolish the authority of the church of Rome in his dominions. That he should go so far, though he went no further, gave some satisfaction to the patrons of the reformation, who having got possession of the government in the reign of his son and successor, completed without any difficulty the work which Henry VIII. had begun.

32   In some countries, as in Scotland, where the government was weak, unpopular, and not very firmly established, the reformation was strong enough to overturn, not only the church, but [225] the state likewise for attempting to support the church.

33   Among the followers of the reformation, dispersed in all the different countries of Europe, there was no general tribunal, which, like that of the court of Rome, or an œcumenical council, could settle all disputes among them, and with irresistible authority prescribe to all of them the precise limits of orthodoxy. When the followers of the reformation in one country, therefore, happened to differ from their brethren in another, as they had no common judge to appeal to, the dispute could never be decided; and many such disputes arose among them. Those concerning the government of the church, and the right of conferring ecclesiastical benefices, were perhaps the most interesting to the peace and welfare of civil society. They gave birth accordingly to the two principal parties or sects among the followers of the reformation, the Lutheran and Calvinistic sects, the only sects among them, of which the doctrine and discipline have ever yet been established by law in any part of Europe.

34   The followers of Luther, together with what is called the church of England, preserved more or less of the episcopal government, established subordination among the clergy, gave the sovereign the disposal of all the bishopricks, and other consistorial benefices within his dominions, and thereby rendered him the real head of the church; and without depriving the bishop of the right of collating to the smaller benefices within his diocese, they, even to those benefices, not [226] only admitted, but favoured the right of presentation both in the sovereign and in all other lay-patrons. This system of church government was from the beginning favourable to peace and good order, and to submission to the civil sovereign. It has never, accordingly, been the occasion of any tumult or civil commotion in any country in which it has once been established. The church of England in particular has always valued herself, with great reason, upon the unexceptionable loyalty of her principles. Under such a government the clergy naturally endeavour to recommend themselves to the sovereign, to the court, and to the nobility and gentry of the country, by whose

ʲ⁻ʲ the general prevalence of those doctrines *1*

influence they chiefly expect to obtain preferment. They pay court to those patrons, sometimes, no doubt, by the vilest flattery and assentation, but frequently too by cultivating all those arts which best deserve, and which are therefore most likely to gain them the esteem of people of rank and fortune; by their knowledge in all the different branches of useful and ornamental learning, by the decent liberality of their manners, by the social good humour of their conversation, and by their avowed contempt of those absurd and hypocritical austerities which fanatics inculcate and pretend to practise, in order to draw upon themselves the veneration, and upon the greater part of men of rank and fortune, who avow that they do not practise them, the abhorrence of the common people. Such a clergy, however, while they pay their court in this manner to the higher ranks of life, are very [227] apt to neglect altogether the means of maintaining their influence and authority with the lower. They are listened to, esteemed and respected by their superiors; but before their inferiors they are frequently incapable of defending, effectually and to the conviction of such hearers, their own sober and moderate doctrines against the most ignorant enthusiast who chuses to attack them.

35   The followers of Zuinglius, or more properly those of Calvin, on the contrary, bestowed upon the people of each parish, whenever the church became vacant, the right of electing their own pastor; and established at the same time the most perfect equality among the clergy. The former part of this institution, as long as it remained in vigour, seems to have been productive of nothing but disorder and confusion, and to have tended equally to corrupt the morals both of the clergy and of the people. The latter part seems never to have had any effects but what were perfectly agreeable.

36   As long as the people of each parish preserved the right of electing their own pastors, they acted almost always under the influence of the clergy, and generally of the most factious and fanatical of the order. The clergy, in order to preserve their influence in those popular elections, became, or affected to become, many of them, fanatics themselves, encouraged fanaticism among the people, and gave the preference almost always to the most fanatical candidate. So small a matter as the appointment of a parish priest occasioned almost always a violent contest, not [228] only in one parish, but in all the neighbouring parishes, who seldom failed to take ᵐpartᵐ in the quarrel. When the parish happened to be situated in a great city, it divided all the inhabitants into two parties; and when that city happened either to constitute itself a little republick, or to be the head and capital of a little republick, as is the case with many of the considerable cities in Switzerland and Holland, every paltry dispute of this kind, over and above exasperating the animosity of all their other factions, threatened to leave behind it both a new schism in the church, and a new faction in the state.

ᵐ⁻ᵐ party *1–2*

In those small republicks, therefore, the magistrate very soon found it necessary, for the sake of preserving the publick peace, to assume to himself the right of presenting to all vacant benefices. In Scotland, the most extensive country in which this presbyterian form of church government has ever been established, the rights of patronage were in effect abolished by the act which established presbytery in the beginning of the reign of William III. That act at least put it in the power of certain classes of people in each parish, to purchase, for a very small price, the right of electing their own pastor. The constitution which this act established was allowed to subsist for about two and twenty years, but was abolished by the 10th of queen Ann, ch. 12.[29] on account of the confusions and disorders which this more popular mode of election had almost every where occasioned. In so extensive a country as Scotland, however, a tumult in a remote parish was [229] not so likely to give disturbance to government, as in a smaller state. The 10th of queen Ann restored the rights of patronage. But though in Scotland the law gives the benefice without any exception to the person presented by the patron; yet the church requires sometimes (for she has not in this respect been very uniform in her decisions) a certain concurrence of the people, before she will confer upon the presentee what is called the cure of souls, or the ecclesiastical jurisdiction in the parish. She sometimes at least, from an affected concern for the peace of the parish, delays the settlement till this concurrence can be procured. The private tampering of some of the neighbouring clergy, sometimes to procure, but more frequently to prevent this concurrence, and the popular arts which they cultivate in order to enable them upon such occasions to tamper more effectually, are perhaps the causes which principally keep up whatever remains of the old fanatical spirit, either in the clergy or in the people of Scotland.

37   The equality which the presbyterian form of church government establishes among the clergy, consists, first, in the equality of authority or ecclesiastical jurisdiction; and, secondly, in the equality of benefice. In all presbyterian churches the equality of authority is perfect: that of benefice is not so. The difference, however, between one benefice and another, is seldom so considerable as commonly to tempt the possessor even of the small *n*one*n* to pay court to his patron, by the vile arts of flattery and assentation, in [230] order to get a better. In all the presbyterian churches, where the rights of patronage are thoroughly established, it is by nobler and better arts that the established clergy in general endeavour to gain the favour of their superiors; by their learning, by the irreproachable regularity of their life, and by the faithful and diligent discharge of their duty. Their patrons even frequently complain of the independency of their spirit,

n-n benefice *1*

[29] 10 Anne, c.21 (1711) in *Statutes of the Realm*, ix.680–1; 10 Anne, c.12 in Ruffhead's edition.

which they are apt to construe into ingratitude for past favours, but which at worst, perhaps, is seldom any more than that indifference which naturally arises from the consciousness that no further favours of the kind are ever to be expected. There is scarce perhaps to be found any where in Europe a more learned, decent, independent, and respectable set of men, than the greater part of the presbyterian clergy of Holland, Geneva, Switzerland, and Scotland.

38   Where the church benefices are all nearly equal, none of them can be very great, and this mediocrity of benefice, though it may no doubt be carried too far, has, however, some very agreeable effects. Nothing but the most exemplary morals can give dignity to a man of small fortune. The vices of levity and vanity necessarily render him ridiculous, and are, besides, almost as ruinous to him as they are to the common people. In his own conduct, therefore, he is obliged to follow that system of morals which the common people respect the most. He gains their esteem and affection by that plan of life which his own interest and situation would lead him to follow. [231] The common people look upon him with that kindness with which we naturally regard one who approaches somewhat to our own condition, but who, we think, ought to be in a higher. Their kindness naturally provokes his kindness. He becomes careful to instruct them, and attentive to assist and relieve them. He does not even despise the prejudices of people who are disposed to be so favourable to him, and never treats them with those contemptuous and arrogant airs which we so often meet with in the proud dignitaries of opulent and well-endowed churches. The presbyterian clergy, accordingly, have more influence over the minds of the common people than perhaps the clergy of any other established church. It is accordingly in presbyterian countries only that we ever find the common people converted, without persecution, compleatly, and almost to a man, to the established church.

39   In countries where church benefices are the greater part of them very moderate, a chair in a university is generally a better establishment than a church benefice. The universities have, in this case, the picking and chusing of their members from all the churchmen of the country, who, in every country, constitute by far the most numerous class of men of letters. Where church benefices, on the contrary, are many of them very considerable, the church naturally draws from the universities the greater part of their eminent men of letters; who generally find some patron who does himself honour by procuring them church preferment. In the former situation we [232] are likely to find the universities filled with the most eminent men of letters that are to be found in the country. In the latter we are likely to find few eminent men among them, and those few among the youngest members of the society, who are likely too to be drained away from it, before they can have acquired experience and knowledge enough to be of much use to

it. It is observed by Mr. de Voltaire, that father Porrée, a jesuit of no great eminence in the republick of letters, was the only professor they had ever had in France whose works were worth the reading.[30] In a country which has produced so many eminent men of letters, it must appear some- what singular that scarce one of them should have been a professor in a university. The famous Gassendi was, in the beginning of his life, a profes- sor in the university of Aix. Upon the first dawning of his genius, it was represented to him, that by going into the church he could easily find a much more quiet and comfortable subsistence, as well as a better situation for pursuing his studies; and he immediately followed the advice. The observation of Mr. de Voltaire may be applied, I believe, not only to France, but to all other Roman catholick countries. We very rarely find, in any of them, an eminent man of letters who is a professor in a university, except, perhaps, in the professions of law and physick; professions from which the church is not so likely to draw them. After the church of Rome, that of England is by far the richest and best endowed church in Christen- dom. In England, accord-[233]ingly, the church is continually draining the universities of all their best and ablest members; and an old college tutor, who is known and distinguished in Europe as an eminent man of letters, is as rarely to be found there as in any Roman catholick country.[31] In Geneva, on the contrary, in the protestant cantons of Switzerland, in the protestant countries of Germany, in Holland, in Scotland, in Sweden, and Denmark, the most eminent men of letters whom those countries have produced, have, not all indeed, but the far greater part of them, been profes- sors in universities. In those countries the universities are continually draining the church of all its most eminent men of letters.

40   It may, perhaps, be worth while to remark, that, if we except the poets, a few orators, and a few historians, the far greater part of the other eminent men of letters, both of Greece and Rome, appear to have been either publick or private teachers; generally either of philosophy or of rhetorick.[32] This remark will be found to hold true from the days of Lysias[33] and Iso- crates, of Plato and Aristotle, down to those of Plutarch and Epictetus, of

[30] 'Porée (Charles), né en Normandie en 1675, jésuite; du petit nombre de professeurs qui ont eu de la célébrité chez les gens du monde; éloquent dans le goût de Sénèque; poëte, et très bel esprit. Son plus grand mérite fut de faire aimer les lettres et la vertu à ses disciples.' (Voltaire, *Siècle de Louis XIV*, in *Oeuvres* (Paris, 1878), i.116–17.) In the con- cluding paragraph of his Letter to the *Edinburgh Review*, Smith refers to 'Mr Voltaire, the most universal genius perhaps which France has ever produced'. Smith greatly admired Voltaire, and it is known that while in France as tutor to Buccleuch he made a journey to Geneva in order to see him. Rae, *Life*, 189.
[31] See above, V.i.f.5, ff. where Smith considers the additional problem presented by large endowments of schools and colleges.
[32] See above, V.i.f.43. The emoluments of such teachers are considered at I.x.c.39.
[33] In LRBL ii.218, ed. Lothian 177, Lysias is described as 'the most ancient of all the Orators whose works have come to our hands'. Smith considers the demonstrative elo- quence of Plato, Isocrates, and Lysias in lecture 23.

Suetonius and Quintilian. ᵒ To impose upon any man the necessity of teaching, year after year, any particular branch of science, seems, in reality, to be the most effectual method for rendering him compleatly master of it himself. By being obliged to go every year over the same ground, if he is good for any thing, he necessarily becomes, in a few years, well acquainted with every part of it: and [234] if upon any particular point he should form too hasty an opinion one year, when he comes in the course of his lectures to re-consider the same subject the year thereafter, he is very likely to correct it. As to be a teacher of science is certainly the natural employment of a mere man of letters; so is it likewise, perhaps, the education which is most likely to render him a man of solid learning and knowledge. The mediocrity of church benefices naturally tends to draw the greater part of men of letters, in the country where it takes place, to the employment in which they can be the most useful to the publick, and, at the same time, to give them the best education, perhaps, they are capable of receiving. It tends to render their learning both as solid as possible, and as useful as possible.

41   The revenue of every established church, such parts of it excepted as may arise from particular lands or manors, is a branch, it ought to be observed, of the general revenue of the state, which is thus diverted to a purpose very different from the defence of the state. The tythe, for example, is a real land-tax, which puts it out of the power of the proprietors of land to contribute so largely towards the defence of the state as they otherwise might be able to do.³⁴ The rent of land, however, is, according to some, the sole fund, and, according to others, the principal fund, from which, in all great monarchies, the exigencies of the state must be ultimately supplied.³⁵ The more of this fund that is given to the church, the less, it is evident, can be [235] spared to the state. It may be laid down as a certain maxim, that, all other things being supposed equal, the richer the church, the poorer must necessarily be, either the sovereign on the one hand, or the people on the other; and, in all cases, the less able must the state be to defend itself. In several protestant countries, particularly in all the protestant cantons of Switzerland, the revenue which antiently belonged to the Roman catholick church, the tythes and church lands, has been found a fund sufficient, not only to afford competent salaries to the established clergy, but to defray with little or no addition, all the other expences of the state. The magistrates of the powerful canton of Berne, in particular, have accumulated out of the savings from this fund a very large

ᵒ Several of those whom we do not know with certainty to have been public teachers, appear to have been private tutors. Polybius, we know, was private tutor to Scipio Æmilianus. Dionysius of Halicarnassus, there are some probable reasons for believing, was so to the children of Marcus and Quintus Cicero. 2

³⁴ Tithes are considered below, V.ii.d.
³⁵ This is probably a reference to the physiocrats; see below, V.ii.c.7.

sum, supposed to amount to several millions, part of which is deposited in a publick treasure, and part is placed at interest in what are called the publick funds of the different indebted nations of Europe, chiefly in those of France and Great Britain.[36] What may be the amount of the whole expence which the church, either of Berne, or of any other protestant canton, costs the state, I do not pretend to know. By a very exact account it appears, that, in 1755, the whole revenue of the clergy of the church of Scotland, including their glebe or church lands, and the rent of their manses or dwelling houses, estimated according to a reasonable valuation, amounted only to 68,514*l*. 1*s*. 5*d*.$\frac{1}{12}$. This very moderate re-[236]venue affords a decent subsistence to nine hundred and forty-four ministers. The whole expence of the church, including what is occasionally laid out for the building and reparation of churches, and of the manses of ministers, cannot well be supposed to exceed eighty or eighty-five thousand pounds a-year. The most opulent church in Christendom does not maintain better the uniformity of faith, the fervour of devotion, the spirit of order, regularity, and austere morals in the great body of the people, than this very poorly endowed church of Scotland. All the good effects, both civil and religious, which an established church can be supposed to produce, are produced by it as compleatly as by any other. The greater part of the protestant churches of Switzerland, which in general are not better endowed than the church of Scotland, produce those effects in a still higher degree. In the greater part of the protestant cantons, there is not a single person to be found who does not profess himself to be of the established church. If he professes himself to be of any other, indeed, the law obliges him to leave the canton. But so severe, or rather indeed so oppressive a law, could never have been executed in such free countries, had not the diligence of the clergy before-hand converted to the established church the whole body of the people, with the exception of, perhaps, a few individuals only. In some parts of Switzerland, accordingly, where, from the accidental union of a protestant and [237] Roman catholick country, the conversion has not been so compleat, both religions are not only tolerated but established by law.

42   The proper performance of every service seems to require that its pay or recompence should be, as exactly as possible, proportioned to the nature of the service. If any service is very much under-paid, it is very apt to suffer by the meanness and incapacity of the greater part of those who are employed in it. If it is very much over-paid, it is apt to suffer, perhaps, still more by their negligence and idleness.[37] A man of a large revenue,

[36] See below, V.ii.a.9, and above, I.ix.10. Hume stated that the canton of Berne had £300,000 lent at interest and 'above six times as much in their treasury', citing the authority of Stanian. 'Of the Balance of Trade', *Essays Moral, Political, and Literary*, ed. Green and Grose, i.342.

[37] Cf. V.i.f.4.

whatever may be his profession, thinks he ought to live like other men of large revenues; and to spend a great part of his time in festivity, in vanity, and in dissipation. But in a clergyman this train of life not only consumes the time which ought to be employed in the duties of his function, but in the eyes of the common people destroys almost entirely that sanctity of character which can alone enable him to perform those duties with proper weight and authority.[38]

PART IV

Of the Expence of supporting the Dignity of the Sovereign

1   Over and above the *a*expence*a* necessary for enabling the sovereign to perform his several duties, a certain expence is requisite for the support of his dignity. This expence varies [238] both with the different periods of improvement, and with the different forms of government.

2   In an opulent and improved society, where all the different orders of people are growing every day more expensive in their houses, in their furniture, in their tables, in their dress, and in their equipage; it cannot well be expected that the sovereign should alone hold out against the fashion. He naturally, therefore, or rather necessarily becomes more expensive in all those different articles too. His dignity even seems to require that he should become so.[1]

3   As in point of dignity, a monarch is more raised above his subjects than the chief magistrate of any republick is ever supposed to be above his fellow-citizens; so a greater expence is necessary for supporting that higher dignity. We naturally expect more splendor in the court of a king, than in the mansion-house of a doge or burgo-master.

Conclusion of the Chapter

1   The expence of defending the society, and that of supporting the dignity of the chief magistrate, are both laid out for the general benefit of the whole society. It is reasonable, therefore, that they should be defrayed by the general contribution of the whole society, all the different members contributing, as nearly as possible, in proportion to their respective abilities.

2   The expence of the administration of justice too, may, no doubt, be considered as laid out for the benefit of the whole society. There is no

---

a-a expences 4–6

[38] See above, V.i.g.1,29.
[1] See below, V.iii.3.

[239] impropriety, therefore, in its being defrayed by the general contribution of the whole society. The persons, however, who give occasion to this expence are those who, by their injustice in one way or another, make it necessary to seek redress or protection from the courts of justice. The persons again most immediately benefited by this expence, are those whom the courts of justice either restore to their rights, or maintain in their rights. The expence of the administration of justice, therefore, may very properly be defrayed by the particular contribution of one or other, or both of those two different sets of persons, according as different occasions may require, that is, by the fees of court. It cannot be necessary to have recourse to the general contribution of the whole society, except for the conviction of those criminals who have not themselves any estate or fund sufficient for paying those fees.

3 Those local or provincial expences of which the benefit is local or provincial (what is laid out, for example, upon the police of a particular town or district) ought to be defrayed by a local or provincial revenue, and ought to be no burden upon the general revenue of the society. It is unjust that the whole society should contribute towards an expence of which the benefit is confined to a part of the society.

4 The expence of maintaining good roads and communications is, no doubt, beneficial to the whole society, and may, therefore, without any injustice, be defrayed by the general contribu-[240]tion of the whole society. This expence, however, is most immediately and directly beneficial to those who travel or carry goods from one place to another, and to those who consume such goods. The turnpike tolls in England, and the duties called peages in other countries,[1] lay it altogether upon those two different sets of people, and thereby discharge the general revenue of the society from a very considerable burden.

5 The expence of the institutions for education and religious instruction, is likewise, no doubt, beneficial to the whole society, and may, therefore, without injustice, be defrayed by the general contribution of the whole society. This expence, however, might perhaps with equal propriety, and even with some advantage, be defrayed altogether by those who receive the immediate benefit of such education and instruction, or by the voluntary contribution of those who think they have occasion for either the one or the other.

6 When the institutions or publick works which are beneficial to the whole society, either cannot be maintained altogether, or are not maintained altogether by the contribution of such particular members of the society as are most immediately benefited by them, the deficiency must in most cases be made up by the general contribution of the whole society.

---

[1] Peages are considered below, V.ii.k.56.

The general revenue of the society, over and above defraying the expence of defending the society, and of supporting the dignity of the chief magistrate, must make up for [241] the deficiency of many particular branches of revenue. The sources of this general or publick revenue, I shall endeavour to explain in the following chapter.

CHAPTER II

Of the Sources of the general or publick Revenue of the Society

1   The revenue which must defray, not only the expence of defending the society and of supporting the dignity of the chief magistrate, but all the other necessary expences of government, for which the constitution of the state has not provided any particular revenue, may be drawn, either, first, from some fund which peculiarly belongs to the sovereign or commonwealth, and which is independent of the revenue of the people; or, secondly, from the revenue of the people.

PART I

Of the Funds or Sources of Revenue which may peculiarly belong to the Sovereign or Commonwealth

1   The funds or sources of revenue which may peculiarly belong to the sovereign or commonwealth must consist, either in stock, or in land.

2   [242] The sovereign, like any other owner of stock, may derive a revenue from it, either by employing it himself, or by lending it. His revenue is in the one case profit, in the other interest.

3   The revenue of a Tartar or Arabian chief consists in profit. It arises principally from the milk and increase of his own herds and flocks, of which he himself superintends the management, and is the principal shepherd or herdsman of his own horde or tribe. It is, however, in this earliest and rudest state of civil government only that profit has ever made the principal part of the publick revenue of a monarchical state.[1]

4   Small republicks have sometimes derived a considerable revenue from the profit of mercantile projects. The republick of Hamburgh is said to do so from the profits of a publick wine cellar and apothecary's shop*.[2]

---

* See Memoires concernant les Droits & Impositions en Europe: tome i. page 73. This work was compiled by the order of the court for the use of a commission employed for some years past in considering the proper means for reforming the finances of France. The account of the French taxes, which takes up three volumes in quarto, may be regarded as perfectly authentic. That of those of other European nations was compiled from such informations as the French ministers at the different courts could procure. It is much shorter, and probably not quite so exact as that of the French taxes.

[*Mémoires concernant les impositions et droits en Europe* (Paris, 1768–9), by J. L. Moreau de Beaumont. Smith mentions this book in Letter 196 addressed to Sir John Sinclair, dated 24 November 1778. In this letter Smith stated that he had had frequent occasion to study a book which had never been properly published, and that he had obtained it 'by the particular favour of Mr. Turgot'. At the same time Smith expressed himself as being unwilling to send the book out of Edinburgh, since 'if any accident should happen to my book, the loss is perfectly irreperable'. Smith believed that there were as few as three copies in Britain at the time.]

---

[1] The constitution of the Tartar state is described in V.i.b.7.

[2] 'La Cave de ville & l'Apothicairerie forment encore un objet de revenu tres considerable'. De Beaumont, *Mémoires*, i.73.

The state cannot be very great of which the sovereign has leisure to carry on the trade of a wine merchant or apothecary. The profit of a publick bank has been a source of revenue to more considerable states. It has been so not only to Hamburgh, but to [243] Venice and Amsterdam.[3] A revenue of this kind has even by some people been thought not below the attention of so great an empire as that of Great Britain. Reckoning the ordinary dividend of the bank of England at five and a half per cent.[4] and its capital at ten millions seven hundred and eighty thousand pounds,[5] the neat annual profit, after paying the expence of management, must amount, it is said, to five hundred and ninety-two thousand nine hundred pounds. Government, it is pretended, could borrow this capital at three per cent. interest, and by taking the management of the bank into its own hands, might make a clear profit of two hundred and sixty-nine thousand five hundred pounds a year. The orderly, vigilant, and parsimonious administration of such aristocracies as those of Venice and Amsterdam, is extremely proper, it appears from experience, for the management of a mercantile project of this kind. But whether such a government as that of England; which, whatever may be its virtues, has never been famous for good œconomy; which, in time of peace, has generally conducted itself with the slothful and negligent profusion that is perhaps natural to monarchies; and in time of war has constantly acted with all the thoughtless extravagance that democracies are apt to fall into; could be safely trusted with the management of such a project must at least be a good deal more doubtful.[6]

5   The post office is properly a mercantile project.[7] The government advances the expence of [244] establishing the different offices, and of buying or hiring the necessary horses or carriages, and is repaid with a large profit by the duties upon what is carried. It is perhaps the only mercantile project which has been successfully managed by, I believe, every sort of government. The capital to be advanced is not very considerable. There is no mystery in the business. The returns are not only certain, but immediate.

6   Princes, however, have frequently engaged in many other mercantile projects, and have been willing, like private persons, to mend their fortunes by becoming adventurers in the common branches of trade. They have scarce ever succeeded. The profusion with which the affairs of princes are always managed, renders it almost impossible that they should. The agents of a prince regard the wealth of their master as inexhaustible; are

---

[3] The Bank of Amsterdam is described above, IV.iii.b.
[4] The same figure is cited at II.ii.84.   [5] The same figure is cited at V.i.e.18.
[6] On the extravagance of government, a frequent theme, see for example II.iii.31, 36, V.iii.8, 49, 58.
[7] See above, V.i.d.3.

careless at what price they buy; are careless at what price they sell; are careless at what expence they transport his goods from one place to another. Those agents frequently live with the profusion of princes, and sometimes too, in spite of that profusion, and by a proper method of making up their accounts, acquire the fortunes of princes. It was thus, as we are told by Machiavel, that the agents of Lorenzo of Medicis, not a prince of mean abilities, carried on his trade. The republick of Florence was several times obliged to pay the debt into which their extravagance had involved him. He found it convenient, accordingly, to give up the business of merchant, the business [245] to which his family had originally owed their fortune, and in the latter part of his life to employ both what remained of that fortune, and the revenue of the state of which he had the disposal, in projects and expences more suitable to his station.[8]

7   No two characters seem more inconsistent than those of trader and sovereign. If the trading spirit of the English East India company renders them very bad sovereigns; the spirit of sovereignty seems to have rendered them equally bad traders. While they were traders only, they managed their trade successfully, and were able to pay from their profits a moderate dividend to the proprietors of their stock. Since they became sovereigns, with a revenue which, it is said, was originally more than three millions sterling, they have been obliged to beg the extraordinary assistance of government in order to avoid immediate bankruptcy. In their former situation, their servants in India considered themselves as the clerks of merchants: In their present situation, those servants consider themselves as the ministers of sovereigns.[9]

8   A state may sometimes derive some part of its publick revenue from the interest of money, as well as from the profits of stock. If it has amassed a treasure, it may lend a part of that treasure, either to foreign states, or to its own subjects.[10]

9   The canton of Berne derives a considerable revenue by lending a part of its treasure to foreign states; that is, by placing it in the publick funds of the different indebted nations of Eu-[246]rope, chiefly in those of France and England.[11] The security of this revenue must depend, first, upon the

[8] 'In his commercial affairs he [Lorenzo de Medici] was very unfortunate, from the improper conduct of his agents, who in all their proceedings assumed the deportment of princes rather than of private persons; so that in many places, much of his property was wasted, and he had to be relieved by his country with large sums of money. To avoid similar inconvenience, he withdrew from mercantile pursuits, and invested his property in land and houses, as being less liable to vicissitude.' (N. Machiavelli, *History of Florence*, book VIII, translated (London, 1851), 400–1.)

[9] On this point see IV.vii.b.11 and generally IV.vii.c.101–8, V.i.e.26–30.

[10] See above, IV.i.25, where it is pointed out that treasures are of little importance in modern times.

[11] De Beaumont, *Mémoires*, i.155. See above, V.i.g.41 and below, V.iii.3 where Smith comments on the treasure amassed by the canton. Smith also mentioned Dutch holdings in English and French funds at I.ix.10.

security of the funds in which it is placed, or upon the good faith of the government which has the management of them; and, secondly, upon the certainty or probability of the continuance of peace with the debtor nation. In the case of a war, the very first act of hostility, on the part of the debtor nation, might be the forfeiture of the funds of its creditor. This policy of lending money to foreign states is, so far as I know, peculiar to the canton of Berne.

10   The city of Hamburgh* has established a sort of publick pawn-shop, which lends money to the subjects of the state upon pledges at six per cent. interest. This pawn-shop or Lombard, as it is called, affords a revenue, it is pretended, to the state of a hundred and fifty thousand crowns, which, at four-and-sixpence the crown, amounts to 33,750*l.* sterling.

11   The government of Pensylvania, without amassing any treasure, invented a method of lending, not money indeed, but what is equivalent to money, to its subjects. By advancing to private people, at interest, and upon land security to double the value, paper bills of credit to be redeemed fifteen years after their date, and in the mean time made transferable from hand to hand like bank notes, and declared by act of assembly to be a legal tender in all payments from one inhabitant of the province to another, it [247] raised a moderate revenue, which went a considerable way towards defraying an annual expence of about 4,500*l.* the whole ordinary expence of that frugal and orderly government.[12] The success of an expedient of this kind must have depended upon three different circumstances; first, upon the demand for some other instrument of commerce, besides gold and silver money; or upon the demand for such a quantity of consumable stock, as could not be had without sending abroad the greater part of their gold and silver money, in order to purchase it; secondly, upon the good credit of the government which made use of this expedient; and, thirdly, upon the moderation with which it was used, the whole value of the paper bills of credit never exceeding that of the gold and silver money which would have been necessary for carrying on their circulation, had there been no paper bills of credit. The same expedient was upon different occasions adopted by several other American colonies: but, from want of this moderation, it produced, in the greater part of them, much more disorder than conveniency.

12   The unstable and perishable nature of stock and credit, however, render

* See ᵃMemoires concernant les Droits & Impositiones en Europe; tome i. p. 73ᵃ ['Par ce moyen elle procure à ses point onéreuses, & elle se ménage un gain considérable, qui passeroit aux usuriers qui, avant cet établissement, exigeoient des intérêts outrés, tels que Soixante ou Quatre-vingt pour cent.' (De Beaumont, *Mémoires*, i.73.)]

ᵃ⁻ᵃ id. ibid. *1–2*

[12] The issue of colonial paper money is discussed above, II.ii.102, V.iii.81. See generally II.ii. The same figure for the expence of colonial government is cited at IV.vii.b.20.

them unfit to be trusted to, as the principal funds of that sure, steady and permanent revenue, which can alone give security and dignity to government. The government of no great nation, that was advanced beyond the shepherd state, seems ever to have derived the greater part of its publick revenue from such sources.

13   [248] Land is a fund of a more stable and permanent nature; and the rent of publick lands, accordingly, has been the principal source of the publick revenue of many a great nation that was much advanced beyond the shepherd state.[13] From the produce or rent of the publick lands, the ancient republicks of Greece and Italy derived, for a long time, the greater part of that revenue which defrayed the necessary expences of the commonwealth. The rent of the crown lands constituted for a long time the greater part of the revenue of the ancient sovereigns of Europe.

14   War and the preparation for war, are the two circumstances which in modern times occasion the greater part of the necessary expence of all great states. But in the ancient republicks of Greece and Italy every citizen was a soldier, who both served and prepared himself for service at his own expence. Neither of those two circumstances, therefore, could occasion any very considerable expence to the state.[14] The rent of a very moderate landed estate might be fully sufficient for defraying all the other necessary expences of government.[15]

15   In the ancient monarchies of Europe, the manners and customs of the times sufficiently prepared the great body of the people for war;[16] and when they took the field, they were, by the condition of their feudal tenures, to be maintained, either at their own expence, or at that of their immediate lords, without bringing any new charge upon the sovereign. The other ex-[249]pences of government were, the greater part of them, very moderate. The administration of justice, it has been shown, instead of being a cause of expence, was a source of revenue.[17] The labour of the country people, for three days before and for three days after harvest, was thought a fund sufficient for making and maintaining all the bridges, highways, and other publick works which the commerce of the country was supposed to require. In those days the principal expence of the sovereign seems to have consisted in the maintenance of his own family and houshold. The officers of his houshold, accordingly, were then the great officers of state. The lord treasurer received his rents. The lord

---

[13] The point is made with reference to Bengal at IV.vii.c.102.

[14] The expence of war in the modern, as compared to the classical state, is discussed at V.i.a.12–14 and 43. See generally V.i.a.

[15] The example of Greece is given in LJ (B) 309, ed. Cannan 238, and the comment made that: 'In all barbarous countries we find lands appropriated to the purposes of sovereignty, and therefore little occasion for taxes and customs. We shall shew that this is a bad police, and one cause of the slow progress of opulence.'

[16] See above, V.i.a.6.   [17] Above, V.i.b.13.

steward and lord chamberlain looked after the expence of his family. The care of his stables was committed to the lord constable and the lord marshal. His houses were all built in the form of castles, and seem to have been the principal fortresses which he possessed. The keepers of those houses or castles might be considered as a sort of military governors. They seem to have been the only military officers whom it was necessary to maintain in time of peace. In these circumstances the rent of a great landed estate might, upon ordinary occasions, very well defray all the necessary expences of government.[18]

16   In the present state of the greater part of the civilized monarchies of Europe, the rent of all the lands in the country, managed as they probably would be if they all belonged to one proprietor, would scarce perhaps amount to the or-[250]dinary revenue which they levy upon the people even in peaceable times. The ordinary revenue of Great Britain, for example, including not only what is necessary for defraying the current expence of the year, but for paying the interest of the publick debts, and for sinking a part of the capital of those debts, amounts to upwards of ten millions a year. But the land-tax, at four shillings in the pound, falls short of two millions a year.[19] This land-tax, as it is called, however, is supposed to be one-fifth, not only of the rent of all the land, but of that of all the houses, and of the interest of all the capital stock of Great Britain, that part of it only excepted which is either lent to the publick, or employed as farming stock in the cultivation of land. A very consider-able part of the produce of this tax arises from the rent of houses, and the interest of capital stock. The land-tax of the city of London, for example, at four shillings in the pound, amounts to 123,399*l.* 6*s.* 7*d.* That of the city of Westminster, to 63,092*l.* 1*s.* 5*d.* That of the palaces of Whitehall and St. James's, to 30,754*l.* 6*s.* 3*d.* A certain proportion of the land-tax is in the same manner assessed upon all the other cities and towns corporate in the kingdom, and arises almost altogether, either from the rent of houses, or from what is supposed to be the interest of trading and capital stock. According to the estimation, therefore, by which Great Britain is rated to the land-tax, the whole mass of revenue arising from the rent of all the lands, from that of all the houses, and from the [251] interest of all the capital stock, that part of it only excepted which is, either lent to the pub-lick, or employed in the cultivation of land, does not exceed ten millions sterling a year, the ordinary revenue which government levies upon the people even in peaceable times. The estimation by which Great Britain is rated to the land-tax is, no doubt, taking the whole kingdom at an

[18] Smith also comments on the limited expence of such government at V.iii.2.

[19] In the year ended 10 October 1776, the land and assessed taxes, and duties on pen-sions, offices, and personal estates yielded net income of £1,875,057 13*s.* *Public Income and Expenditure*, Part I, 174. *British Parliamentary Papers, 1868–69*. XXV.

average, very much below the real value; though in several particular counties and districts it is said to be nearly equal to that value. The rent of the lands alone, exclusive of that of houses, and of the interest of stock, has by many people been estimated at twenty millions, an estimation made in a great measure at random, and which, I apprehend, is as likely to be above as below the truth.[20] But if the lands of Great Britain, in the present state of their cultivation, do not afford a rent of more than twenty millions a year, they could not well afford the half, most probably not the fourth part of that rent, if they all belonged to a single proprietor, and were put under the negligent, expensive, and oppressive management of his factors and agents. The crown lands of Great Britain do not at present afford the fourth part of the rent, which could probably be drawn from them, if they were the property of private persons. If the crown lands were more extensive, it is probable, they would be still worse managed.

17   The revenue which the great body of the people derives from land is in proportion, not [252] to the rent, but to the produce of the land. The whole annual produce of the land of every country, if we except what is reserved for seed, is either annually consumed by the great body of the people, or exchanged for something else that is consumed by them. Whatever keeps down the produce of the land below what it would otherwise rise to, keeps down the revenue of the great body of the people, still more than it does that of the proprietors of land. The rent of land, that portion of the produce which belongs to the proprietors, is scarce any where in Great Britain supposed to be more than a third part of the whole produce. If the land, which in one state of cultivation affords a rent of ten millions sterling a year, would in another afford a rent of twenty millions; the rent being, in both cases, supposed a third part of the produce;[21] the revenue of the proprietors would be less than it otherwise might be by ten millions a year only; but the revenue of the great body of the people would be less than it otherwise might be by thirty millions a year, deducting only what would be necessary for seed. The population of the country would be less by the number of people which thirty millions a year, deducting always the seed, could maintain, according to the particular mode of living and expence which might take place in the different ranks of men among whom the remainder was distributed.

18   Though there is not at present, in Europe, any civilized state of any kind which derives the [253] greater part of its publick revenue from the

---

[20] In LJ (B) 289, 309, ed. Cannan 224 and 238, the land rent of England is given as 24 millions. The expenses of government are stated to be 3 millions at p. 309 and the conclusion reached that 'a land rent to serve all these purposes would be the most improper thing in the world' (310, ed. Cannan 239).

[21] The same figure is cited above, II.iii.9, I.xi.c.20.

rent of lands which are the property of the state; yet, in all the great monarchies of Europe, there are still many large tracts of land which belong to the crown. They are generally forest; and sometimes forest where, after travelling several miles, you will scarce find a single tree; a mere waste and loss of country in respect both of produce and population. In every great monarchy of Europe the sale of the crown lands would produce a very large sum of money, which, if applied to the payment of the publick debts, would deliver from mortgage a much greater revenue than any which those lands have ever afforded to the crown. In countries where lands, improved and cultivated very highly, and yielding at the time of sale as great a rent as can easily be got from them, commonly sell at thirty years purchase; the unimproved, uncultivated, and low-rented crown lands might well be expected to sell at forty, fifty, or sixty years purchase. The crown might immediately enjoy the revenue which this great price would redeem from mortgage. In the course of a few years it would probably enjoy another revenue. When the crown lands had become private property, they would, in the course of a few years, become well-improved and well-cultivated.[22] The increase of their produce would increase the population of the country, by augmenting the revenue and consumption of the people. But the revenue which the crown derives from the duties of customs and excise, would necessarily [254] increase with the revenue and consumption of the people.

19   The revenue which, in any civilized monarchy, the crown derives from the crown lands, though it appears to cost nothing to individuals, in reality costs more to the society than perhaps any other equal revenue which the crown enjoys. It would, in all cases, be for the interest of the society to replace this revenue to the crown by some other equal revenue, and to divide the lands among the people, which could not well be done better, perhaps, than by exposing them to publick sale.

20   Lands, for the purposes of pleasure and magnificence, parks, gardens, publick walks, &c. possessions which are every where considered as causes of expence, not as sources of revenue, seem to be the only lands which, in a great and civilized monarchy, ought to belong to the crown.

21   Public stock and publick lands, therefore, the two sources of revenue which may peculiarly belong to the sovereign or commonwealth, being both improper and insufficient funds for defraying the necessary expence of any great and civilized state; it remains that this expence must, the greater part of it, be defrayed by taxes of one kind or another; the people contributing a part of their own private revenue in order to make up a publick revenue to the sovereign or commonwealth.

[22] See above, III.iv.3. In commenting on the inadequacy of the land tax to meet Britain's fiscal needs, Smith remarked that the crown lands were unlikely to be even 'half as well cultivated as the rest' (LJ (B) 309, ed. Cannan 239).

[255]   PART II

                              Of Taxes

1   The private revenue of individuals, it has been shewn in the first book
of this inquiry, arises ultimately from three different sources; Rent,
Profit, and Wages.[1] Every tax must finally be paid from some one or other
of those three different sorts of revenue, or from all of them indifferently.
I shall endeavour to give the best account I can, first, of those taxes which,
it is intended, should fall upon rent; secondly, of those which, it is intended, should fall upon profit; thirdly, of those which, it is intended, should
fall upon wages; and, fourthly, of those which, it is intended, should fall
indifferently upon all those three different sources of private revenue. The
particular consideration of each of these four different sorts of taxes will
divide the second part of the present chapter into four articles, three of
which will require several other subdivisions. Many of those taxes, it will
appear from the following review, are not finally paid from the fund, or
source of revenue, upon which it was intended they should fall.

2   Before I enter upon the examination of particular taxes, it is necessary
to premise the four following maxims with regard to taxes in general.

3   I. The subjects of every state ought to contribute towards the support
of the government, as nearly as possible, in proportion to their respective
abilities; that is, in proportion to the [256] revenue which they respectively enjoy under the protection of the state. The expence of government
to the individuals of a great nation, is like the expence of management to
the joint tenants of a great estate, who are all obliged to contribute in
proportion to their respective interests in the estate. In the observation
or neglect of this maxim consists, what is called the equality or inequality
of taxation. Every tax, it must be observed once for all, which falls finally
upon one only of the three sorts of revenue above-mentioned, is necessarily unequal, in so far as it does not affect the other two. In the following examination of different taxes I shall seldom take much further notice
of this sort of inequality, but shall, in most cases, confine my observations to that inequality which is occasioned by a particular tax falling unequally even upon that particular sort of private revenue which is affected
by it.

4   II. The tax which each individual is bound to pay ought to be certain,
and not arbitrary. The time of payment, the manner of payment, the
quantity to be paid, ought all to be clear and plain to the contributor, and
to every other person. Where it is otherwise, every person subject to the
tax is put more or less in the power of the tax-gatherer, who can either
aggravate the tax upon any obnoxious contributor, or extort, by the
terror of such aggravation, some present or perquisite to himself. The

[1] Above, I.vi.16, 17.

uncertainty of taxation encourages the insolence and favours the corruption of an order of men who are naturally un-[257]popular, even where they are neither insolent nor corrupt. The certainty of what each individual ought to pay is, in taxation, a matter of so great importance, that a very considerable degree of inequality, it appears, I believe, from the experience of all nations, is not near so great an evil as a very small degree of uncertainty.

5   III. Every tax ought to be levied at the time, or in the manner in which it is most likely to be convenient for the contributor to pay it. A tax upon the rent of land or of houses, payable at the same term at which such rents are usually paid, is levied at the time when it is most likely to be convenient for the contributor to pay; or, when he is most likely to have wherewithal to pay. Taxes upon such consumable goods as are articles of luxury, are all finally paid by the consumer, and generally in a manner that is very convenient for him. He pays them by little and little, as he has occasion to buy the goods. As he is at liberty too, either to buy, or not to buy as he pleases, it must be his own fault if he ever suffers any considerable inconveniency from such taxes.²

6   IV. Every tax ought to be so contrived as both to take out and to keep out of the pockets of the people as little as possible, over and above what it brings into the publick treasury of the state. A tax may either take out or keep out of the pockets of the people a great deal more than it brings into the publick treasury, in the four following ways. First, the levying of it may require a great number of officers, whose salaries may eat up the greater part of the produce of the [258] tax, and whose perquisites may impose another additional tax upon the people. Secondly, it may obstruct the industry of the people, and discourage them from applying to certain branches of business which might give maintenance and employment to great multitudes. While it obliges the people to pay, it may thus diminish, or perhaps destroy some of the funds, which might enable them more easily to do so. Thirdly, by the forfeitures and other penalties which those unfortunate individuals incur who attempt unsuccessfully to evade the tax, it may frequently ruin them, and thereby put an end to the benefit which the community might have received from the employment of their capitals. An injudicious tax offers a great temptation to smuggling.³ But the penalties of smuggling must rise in proportion to the temptation. The law, contrary to all the ordinary principles of justice, first creates the temptation, and then punishes those who yield

---

² Montesquieu also commented that taxes on merchandise were least felt by the people, since they tended to confound them with the price. XIII.vii.5. See also XIII.xiv.3, where it is pointed out that where such taxes prevail, and the liberty of the subject is secure, the merchant in effect advances money to the government by paying the duties which he has to collect subsequently through the sale of his commodities.

³ See below, V.ii.k.27, 49, 64, 75.

to it; and it commonly enhances the punishment too in proportion to the very circumstance which ought certainly to alleviate it, the temptation to commit the crime*. Fourthly, by subjecting the people to the frequent visits, and the odious examination of the tax-gatherers,[4] it may expose them to much unnecessary trouble, vexation, and oppression; and though vexation is not, strictly speaking, expence, it is certainly equivalent to the expence at which every man would be willing to redeem himself from it. It is in some one or other of these four different ways that taxes [259] are frequently so much more burdensome to the people than they are beneficial to the sovereign.

7   The evident justice and utility of the foregoing maxims have recommended them more or less to the attention of all nations. All nations have endeavoured, to the best of their judgment, to render their taxes as equal *as they could contrive;*[a] as certain, as convenient to the contributor, both in the time and in the mode of payment, and, in proportion to the revenue which they brought to the prince, as little burdensome to the people *b*. The following short review of some of the principal taxes which

* See Sketches of the History of Man, page 474. & seq. [By Henry Home, Lord Kames (Edinburgh, 1774). Kames provided in this place the following six rules regarding taxation.

(1) 'That wher-ever there is an opportunity of smuggling, taxes ought to be moderate.'
(2) 'That taxes expensive in the levying ought to be avoided.'
(3) 'To avoid arbitrary taxes.'
(4) 'To remedy the "inequality of riches" as much as possible, by relieving the poor and burdening the rich.'
(5) 'That every tax which tends to impoverish the nation ought to be rejected with indignation.'
(6) 'To avoid taxes that require oath of party.'

While citing Kames's authority, in fact Smith's discussion of taxation as contained in LJ (B) illustrates many of the canons above mentioned; for example, equality 310, ed. Cannan 240; economy 311–12, ed. Cannan 240–1; and convenience 314–15, ed. Cannan 242–3. He also emphasized the importance of levying taxes in such a way as to avoid infringing the liberty of the subject at 313(241). In LJ (A) vi.34 Smith refers to the 'insolence and oppression' of the officers who collect taxes as being 'still more insupportable' than the tax itself. Hutcheson would also appear to have anticipated at least the canons of conveniency, economy, and equity: 'As to taxes for defraying the publick expences, these are most convenient which are laid on matters of luxury and splendour, rather than the necessaries of life; on foreign products and manufactures, rather than domestick; and such as can be easily raised without many expensive offices for collecting them. But above all, a just proportion to the wealth of people should be observed in whatever is raised from them, otherways than by duties upon foreign products and manufactures, for such duties are often necessary to encourage industry at home, tho' there were no publick expences.' (*System*, ii.340–1.) Sir James Steuart also grasped the importance of convenience, economy, certainty, and equity in discussing the canons of taxation. See for example, *Principles*, V.iv–v.]

―――――――
a-a 2–6   *b* as they could contrive *1*

―――――――
[4] See below, V.ii.k.65, V.iii.55. Montesquieu also comments on the taxgatherer 'rummaging and searching' in the houses of the people in stating that 'nothing is more contrary than this to liberty'. *Esprit*, XIII.vii.7.

have taken place in different ages and countries will show that the endeavours of all nations have not in this respect been equally successful.

ARTICLE I

Taxes upon Rent; Taxes upon the Rent of land

1   A tax upon the rent of land may either be imposed according to a certain canon, every district being valued at a certain rent, which valuation is not afterwards to be altered; or it may be imposed in such a manner as to vary with every variation in the real rent of the land, and to rise or fall with the improvement or declension of its cultivation.

2   A land tax which, like that of Great Britain, is ᵃassessed upon each districtᵃ according to a certain invariable canon, though it should be equal at the time of its first establishment, necessarily becomes unequal in process of time, according [260] to the unequal degrees of improvement or neglect in the cultivation of the different parts of the country. In England, the valuation according to which the different counties and parishes were assessed to the land-tax by the 4th of William and Mary[1] was very unequal even at its first establishment. This tax, therefore, so far offends against the first of the four maxims above-mentioned. It is perfectly agreeable to the other three. It is perfectly certain. The time of payment for the tax, being the same as that for the rent, is as convenient as it can be to the contributor. Though the landlord is in all cases the real contributor, the tax is commonly advanced by the tenant, to whom the landlord is obliged to allow it in the payment of the rent.[2] This tax is levied by a much smaller number of officers than any other which affords nearly the same revenue.[3] As the tax ᵇupon each districtᵇ does not rise with the rise of the rent,[4] the sovereign does not share in the profits of the landlord's improvements. ᶜᵈThose improvements sometimesᵈ contribute, indeed, to the discharge of the other landlords of the district. But the aggravation of the tax, which this may sometimes occasion upon a particular estate, is always so very small, that it never canᶜ discourage those improvements, nor keep down the produce of the land below what it would otherwise rise to. As it has no tendency to diminish the quantity, it can have none to raise the price of that produce. It does not obstruct the

---

ᵃ⁻ᵃ imposed *1*   ᵇ⁻ᵇ *2–6*   ᶜ⁻ᶜ The tax, therefore, does not *1*   ᵈ⁻ᵈ They *2*

[1] 4 William and Mary, c. 1 (1692).

[2] LJ (B) 312, ed. Cannan 241, states that the land-tax 'does not tend to raise the price of commodities, . . . If the tenant pays the tax he pays just so much less rent.'

[3] Cf. LJ (B) 311, ed. Cannan 240: 'Taxes upon land possessions have this great advantage, that they are levied without any great expence. The whole land-tax of England does not cost the government above 8 or 10,000 pounds.' This is in contrast to the customs and excise which required 'legions of officers'. See below, V.ii.k.62.

[4] Cf. LJ (B) 317, ed. Cannan 244: 'The land-tax in England is permanent and uniform and does not rise with the rent, which is regulated by the improvement of the land.'

industry of the people. It subjects the landlord to no other inconveniency besides the unavoidable one of paying the tax.

3   [261] The advantage, however, which the landlord has derived from the invariable constancy of the valuation by which all the lands of Great Britain are rated to the land-tax, has been principally owing to some circumstances altogether extraneous to the nature of the tax.

4   It has been owing in part to the great prosperity of almost every part of the country, the rents of almost all the estates of Great Britain having, since the time when this valuation was first established, been continually rising, and scarce any of them having fallen. The landlords, therefore, have almost all gained the difference between the tax which they would have paid, according to the present rent of their estates, and that which they actually pay according to the ancient valuation. Had the state of the country been different, had rents been gradually falling in consequence of the declension of cultivation, the landlords would almost all have lost this difference. In the state of things which has happened to take place since the revolution, the constancy of the valuation has been advantageous to the landlord and hurtful to the sovereign. In a different state of things it might have been advantageous to the sovereign and hurtful to the landlord.

5   As the tax is made payable in money, so the valuation of the land is expressed in money. Since the establishment of this valuation the value of silver has been pretty uniform, and there has been no alteration in the standard of the coin either as to weight or fineness. Had silver risen considerably in its value, as it seems to have done [262] in the course of the two centuries which preceded the discovery of the mines of America,[5] the constancy of the valuation might have proved very oppressive to the landlord. Had silver fallen considerably in its value, as it certainly did for about a century at least after the discovery of those mines,[6] the same constancy of valuation would have reduced very much this branch of the revenue of the sovereign. Had any considerable alteration been made in the standard of the money, either by sinking the same quantity of silver to a lower denomination, or by raising it to a higher; had an ounce of silver, for example, instead of being coined into five shillings and two-pence, been coined, either into pieces which bore so low a denomination as two shillings and seven-pence, or into pieces which bore so high a one as ten shillings and four-pence, it would in the one case have hurt the revenue of the proprietor, in the other that of the sovereign.

6   In circumstances, therefore, somewhat different from those which have actually taken place, this constancy of valuation might have been a very

[5] See above, I.xi.e.15, where Smith discusses the more popular and contrary view with respect to the value of silver.

[6] See above, I.xi.f, and cf. IV.i.32 for a discussion of this point.

great inconveniency, either to the contributors, or to the commonwealth. In the course of ages such circumstances, however, must, at some time or other, happen. But though empires, like all the other works of men, have all hitherto proved mortal, yet every empire aims at immortality. Every constitution, therefore, which it is meant should be as permanent as the empire itself, ought to be convenient, not in certain circumstances only, but in all circum-[263]stances; or ought to be suited, not to those circumstances which are transitory, occasional, or accidental, but to those which are necessary and therefore always the same.

7   A tax upon the rent of land which varies with every variation of the rent, or which rises and falls according to the improvement or neglect of cultivation, is recommended by that sect of men of letters in France, who call themselves the œconomists,[7] as the most equitable of all taxes.[8] All taxes, they pretend, fall ultimately upon the rent of land, and ought therefore to be imposed equally upon the fund which must finally pay them. That all taxes ought to fall as equally as possible upon the fund which must finally pay them, is certainly true. But without entering into the disagreeable discussion of the metaphysical arguments by which they support their very ingenious theory, it will sufficiently appear from the following review, what are the taxes which fall finally upon the rent of the land, and what are those which fall finally upon some other fund.

8   In the Venetian territory all the arable lands which are given in lease to farmers are taxed at a tenth of the rent*. The leases are recorded in a publick register which is kept by the officers of revenue in each province or district. When the proprietor cultivates his own lands, they are valued according to an equitable estimation and he is allowed a deduction of one-fifth of the tax, so that for such lands he pays only eight instead of ten per cent. of the supposed rent.

9   [264] A land-tax of this kind is certainly more equal than the land tax of England. It might not, perhaps, be altogether so certain, and the assessment of the tax might frequently occasion a good deal more trouble to the landlord. It might too be a good deal more expensive in the levying.

10   Such a system of administration, however, might perhaps be contrived as would, in a great measure, both prevent this uncertainty and moderate this expence.

---

* Memoires concernant les Droits, p. 240, 241. ['Les Impositions territoriales consistent principalement dans une dixme générale, ou dans un droit de Dix pour cent du revenu des terres labourables, qui sont toutes décrites dans des registres ou cadastres qui sont dans les archives des Gouverneurs des revenus. Cette dixme, quant aux terres qui sont affermées, se lève sur le prix du bail; lorsque le Propriétaire fait valoir par lui-même, la dixme se perçoit par estimation; on fait remise au Propriétaire d'un cinquième, au moyen de quoi il ne paye que Huit pour cent du revenu.' (De Beaumont, *Mémoires*, i.240.)]

---

[7] See above, IV.ix.38, and generally, IV.ix.   [8] See above, IV.ix.7.

11   The landlord and tenant, for example, might jointly be obliged to record their lease in a publick register. Proper penalties might be enacted against concealing or misrepresenting any of the conditions; and if part of those penalties ᵉwasᵉ to be paid to either of the two parties who informed against and convicted the other of such concealment or misrepresentation, it would effectually deter them from combining together in order to defraud the publick revenue. All the conditions of the lease might be sufficiently known from such a record.

12   Some landlords, instead of raising the rent, take a fine for the renewal of the lease. This practice is in most cases the expedient of a spend-thrift, who for a sum of ready money sells a future revenue of much greater value.[9] It is in most cases, therefore, hurtful to the landlord. It is frequently, hurtful to the tenant, and it is always hurtful to the community. It frequently takes from the tenant so great a part of his capital, and thereby diminishes so much his ability to cultivate the land, that he finds it [265] more difficult to pay a small rent than it would otherwise have been to pay a great one. Whatever diminishes his ability to cultivate, necessarily keeps down, below what it would otherwise have been, the most important part of the revenue of the community. By rendering the tax upon such fines a good deal heavier than upon the ordinary rent, this hurtful practice might be discouraged, to the no small advantage of all the different parties concerned, of the landlord, of the tenant, of the sovereign, and of the whole community.

13   Some leases prescribe to the tenant a certain mode of cultivation, and a certain succession of crops during the whole continuance of the lease. This condition, which is generally the effect of the landlord's conceit of his own superior knowledge (a conceit in most cases very ill founded), ought always to be considered as an additional rent; as a rent in service instead of a rent in money. In order to discourage the practice, which is generally a foolish one, this species of rent might be valued rather high, and consequently taxed somewhat higher than common money rents.[10]

14   Some landlords, instead of a rent in money, require a rent in kind, in corn, cattle, poultry, wine, oil, &c. others again require a rent in service. Such rents are always more hurtful to the tenant than beneficial to the landlord. They either take more or keep more out of the pocket of the former, than they put into that of the latter. In every country where they take place, [266] the tenants are poor and beggarly, pretty much according

ᵉ⁻ᵉ were 4–6

[9] As Smith stated in TMS IV.i.2.8 (see above, II.iii): 'The pleasure which we are to enjoy ten years hence interests us so little in comparison with that which we may enjoy today; . . .' Smith comments on the ignorance of landlords at I.xi.a.1 and on the origin of long leases at III.iv.13.

[10] A reflection of Smith's view that the landlord was unlikely to be a successful improver. See above, III.ii.7 and III.iv.3, 13.

to the degree in which they take place. By valuing, in the same manner, such rents rather high, and consequently taxing them somewhat higher than common money rents, a practice which is hurtful to the whole community might perhaps be sufficiently discouraged.[11]

15 When the landlord chose to occupy himself a part of his own lands, the rent might be valued according to an equitable arbitration of the farmers and landlords in the neighbourhood, and a moderate abatement of the tax might be granted to him, in the same manner as in the Venetian territory; provided the rent of the lands which he occupied did not exceed a certain sum. It is of importance that the landlord should be encouraged to cultivate a part of his own land. His capital is generally greater than that of the tenant, and with less skill he can frequently raise a greater produce. The landlord can afford to try experiments, and is generally disposed to do so. His unsuccessful experiments occasion only a moderate loss to himself. His successful ones contribute to the improvement and better cultivation of the whole country.[12] It might be of importance, however, that the abatement of the tax should encourage him to cultivate to a certain extent only. If the landlords should, the greater part of them, be tempted to farm the whole of their own lands, the country (instead of sober and industrious tenants, who are bound by their own interest to cultivate as well as their capital and skill will [267] allow them) would be filled with idle and profligate bailiffs, whose abusive management would soon degrade the cultivation, and reduce the annual produce of the land, to the diminution, not only of the revenue of their masters, but of the most important part of that of the whole society.

16 Such a system of administration might, perhaps, free a tax of this kind from any degree of uncertainty which could occasion either oppression or inconveniency to the contributor; and might at the same time serve to introduce into the common management of land such a plan or policy, as might contribute a good deal to the general improvement and good cultivation of the country.

17 The expence of levying a land-tax, which varied with every variation of the rent, would no doubt be somewhat greater than that of levying one which was always rated according to a fixed valuation. Some additional expence would necessarily be incurred both by the different register offices which it would be proper to establish in the different districts of the country, and by the different valuations which might occasionally be made of the lands which the proprietor chose to occupy himself. The expence

---

[11] It will be observed in these two cases that Smith defends the use of taxation as a means to control the activities of individuals as distinct from merely raising revenue. This constitutes an interesting qualification perhaps to the general position stated at IV.ix.51. Cf. V.ii.k.7, 50.

[12] Cf. III.ii.7.

of all this, however, might be very moderate, and much below what is incurred in the levying of many other taxes, which afford a very inconsiderable revenue in comparison of what might easily be drawn from a tax of this kind.

18   [268] The discouragement which a variable land-tax of this kind might give to the improvement of land, seems to be the most important objection which can be made to it.[13] The landlord would certainly be less disposed to improve, when the sovereign, who contributed nothing to the expence, was to share in the profit of the improvement.[14] Even this objection might perhaps be obviated by allowing the landlord, before he began his improvement, to ascertain, in conjunction with the officers of revenue, the actual value of his lands, according to the equitable arbitration of a certain number of landlords and farmers in the neighbourhood, equally chosen by both parties; and by rating him according to this valuation for such a number of years, as might be fully sufficient for his complete indemnification. To draw the attention of the sovereign towards the improvement of the land, from a regard to the increase of his own revenue, is one of the principal advantages proposed by this species of land-tax. The term, therefore, allowed for the indemnification of the landlord, ought not to be a great deal longer than what was necessary for that purpose; lest the remoteness of the interest should discourage too much this attention. It had better, however, be somewhat too long than in any respect too short. No incitement to the attention of the sovereign can ever counterbalance the smallest discouragement to that of the landlord. The attention of the sovereign can be at best but a very general and vague consideration of what is likely to contri-[269]bute to the better cultivation of the greater part of his dominions. The attention of the landlord is a particular and minute consideration of what is likely to be the most advantageous application of every inch of ground upon his estate. The principal attention of the sovereign ought to be to encourage, by every means in his power, the attention both of the landlord and of the farmer; by allowing both to pursue their own interest in their own way, and according to their own judgment; by giving to both the most perfect security that they shall enjoy the full recompence of their own industry; and by procuring to both the most extensive market for every part of their produce, in consequence of establishing the easiest and safest communications both by land and by water, through every part of his own dominions, as well as the most unbounded freedom of exportation to the dominions of all other princes.

[13] The same principle appears at III.ii.13 in the discussion of the historical development of leases, and see below, V.ii.d.3.

[14] Cf. LJ (B) 317, ed. Cannan 244: 'When we know that the produce is to be divided with those who lay out nothing, it hinders us from laying out what we would otherwise do upon the improvement of our lands.'

19   If by such a system of administration a tax of this kind could be so
managed as to give, not only no discouragement, but, on the contrary,
some encouragement to the improvement of land, it does not appear likely
to occasion any other inconveniency to the landlord, except always the
unavoidable one of being obliged to pay the tax.

20   In all the variations of the state of the society, in the improvement and
in the declension of agriculture; in all the variations in the value of silver,
and in all those in the standard of the coin, a tax of this kind would, of its
own accord and without any attention of government, readily [270] suit
itself to the actual situation of things; and would be equally just and
equitable in all those different changes. It would, therefore, be much
more proper to be established as a perpetual and unalterable regulation,
or as what is called a fundamental law of the commonwealth, than any
tax which was always to be levied according to a certain valuation.

21   Some states, instead of the simple and obvious expedient of a register
of leases, have had recourse to the laborious and expensive one of an
actual survey and valuation of all the lands in the country. They have
suspected, probably, that the lessor and lessee, in order to defraud the
publick revenue, might combine to conceal the real terms of the lease.
Doomsday-book seems to have been the result of a very accurate survey
of this kind.[15]

22   In the antient dominions of the king of Prussia, the land-tax is assessed
according to an actual survey and valuation, which is reviewed and altered
from time to time*. According to that valuation, the lay proprietors pay
from twenty to twenty-five per cent. of their revenue. Ecclesiastics from
forty to forty-five per cent. The survey and valuation of Silesia was made
by order of the present king; it is said with great accuracy. According to
that valuation the lands belonging to the bishop of Breslaw are taxed at
twenty-five per cent. of their rent. The [271] other revenues of the ecclesiastics of both religions, at fifty per cent. The commanderies of the Teu-
tonic order, and of that of Malta, at forty per cent. Lands held by a noble
tenure, at thirty-eight and one third per cent. Lands held by a base
tenure, at thirty-five and one third per cent.[16]

23   The survey and valuation of Bohemia is said to have been the work

---

* Memoires concernant les Droits, &c. tome i. p. 114, 115, 116, &c. ['Les terres sont
distribuées en différentes classes, selon la qualité du terrain, sa situation, ses avantages
pour le commerce; & de temps en temps, ou fait la révision de cette distribution des
terres.' 'Les Propriétaires payent environ Vingt ou Vingt-cinq pour cent de leur revenu,
c'est-à-dire à peu-près le quart; & les Ecclesiastiques payent Quarante ou Quarante-
cinq pour cent, c'est-à-dire près de moitié.' (De Beaumont, *Mémoires*, i.114 and 115.)]

[15] The Domesday Book is also mentioned at III.iii.2.

[16] 'Les impositions territoriales ont été fixées & déterminées d'après un cadastre, qui
a été formé depuis quelques années avec la plus grande attention, & dans lequel les différentes natures de biens & leur produit annuel, sont distingués avec la plus grande exacti-
tude.' (De Beaumont, *Mémoires*, i.117.) Details of the rates of taxes are given in i.119.

of more than a hundred years. It was not perfected till after the peace of
1748, by the orders of the present empress queen*. The survey of the
dutchy of Milan, which was begun in the time of Charles VI., was not
perfected till after 1760. It is esteemed one of the most accurate that has
ever been made. The survey of Savoy and Piedmont was executed under
the orders of the late king of Sardinia†.

24 In the dominions of the king of Prussia the revenue of the church is
taxed much higher than that of lay proprietors. The revenue of the church
is, the greater part of it, a burden upon the rent of land. It seldom happens
that any part of it is applied towards the improvement of land; or is so
employed as to contribute in any respect towards increasing the revenue
of the great body of the people. His Prussian majesty had probably, upon
that account, thought it reasonable that it should contribute a good deal
more towards relieving the exigencies [272] of the state.[17] In some countries the lands of the church are exempted from all taxes. In others they
are taxed more lightly than other lands. In the dutchy of Milan, the
lands which the church possessed before 1575, are rated to the tax at a
third only of their value.[18]

25 In Silesia, lands held by a noble tenure are taxed three per cent. higher
than those held by a base tenure.[19] The honours and privileges of different
kinds annexed to the former, his Prussian majesty had probably imagined,
would sufficiently compensate to the proprietor a small aggravation of the
tax; while at the same time the humiliating inferiority of the latter would
be in some measure alleviated by being taxed somewhat more lightly.
In other countries, the system of taxation, instead of alleviating, aggra-
vates this inequality. In the dominions of the king of Sardinia, and in
those provinces of France which are subject to what is called the Real
or predial taille, the tax falls altogether upon the lands held by a base
tenure. Those held by a noble one are exempted.[20]

---

* Memoires concernant les Droits, &c. tome i. p. 83, 84. [Details of the cadastral
survey of Bohemia and of the methods of assessment are in De Beaumont, *Mémoires*,
i.79 and 83–85.]

† Id. p. 280, &c. also p. 287, &c. to 316. ['Les inexactitudes [etc.] . . . ces circonstances
engagèrent l'Empereur Charles VI, à reprendre les moyens qui furent jugés les plus pro-
pres à parvenir par la voie d'un cadastre général à une imposition réelle; mais ce n'a été
qu'en 1760 que cet ouvrage a été conduit à son entière perfection par les soins de l'Im-
pératrice-Reine. Le base de cette operation a été un plan figuré & topographique de tout
le territoire de Milan . . .' (De Beaumont, *Mémoires*, i.280–1.)]

---

[17] Ibid., i.115. See above, V.ii.c.22.   [18] Ibid. i.282.   [19] Ibid., i.119.

[20] De Beaumont comments on Sardinia: 'Sous prétexte des priviléges, les Nobles &
les Ecclesiastiques, ainsi que les Châtelains, les principaux Fermiers, les Praticiens &
autres gens riches, s'exemptoient de payer les portions de taille qu'ils devoient supporter;
les communantés n'osant les y contraindre, par la crainte des mauvais traitemens, on
d'être constitués dans de grandes, dépenses par la longeur des procès.' (*Mémoires*, i.291.)
For France see below V.ii.g.7 and note.

26   A land-tax assessed according to a general survey and valuation, how equal soever it may be at first, must, in the course of a very moderate period of time, become unequal. To prevent its becoming so would require the continual and painful attention of government to all the variations in the state and produce of every different farm in the country. The governments of Prussia, of Bohemia, of Sardinia, and of the dutchy of Milan, actually exert an attention of [273] this kind; an attention so unsuitable to the nature of government, that is not likely to be of long continuance, and which, if it is continued, will probably in the long-run occasion much more trouble and vexation than it can possibly bring relief to the contributors.[21]

27   In 1666, the generality of Montauban was assessed to the Real or predial *taille* according, it is said, to a very exact survey and valuation*. By 1727, this assessment had become altogether unequal. In order to remedy this inconveniency, government has found no better expedient than to impose upon the whole generality an additional tax of a hundred and twenty thousand livres. This additional tax is rated upon all the different districts subject to the taille according to the old assessment. But it is levied only upon those which in the actual state of things are by that assessment under-taxed, and it is applied to the relief of those which by the same assessment are over-taxed. Two districts, for example, one of which ought in the actual state of things to be taxed at nine hundred, the other at eleven hundred livres, are by the old assessment both taxed at a thousand livres. Both these districts are by the additional tax rated at eleven hundred livres each. But this additional tax is levied only upon the district under-charged, and it is applied altogether to the relief of that over-charged, which consequently pays only nine hundred livres. The government neither gains nor loses by the additional tax, which is applied *altogether* to re-[274]medy the inequalities arising from the old assessment. The application is pretty much regulated according to the discretion of the intendant of the generality, and must, therefore, be in a great measure arbitrary.

Taxes which are proportioned, not to the Rent, but to the produce of Land

1   Taxes upon the produce of land are in reality taxes upon the rent; and though they may be originally advanced by the farmer, are finally paid by

---

* Memoires concernant les Droits, &c. tome ii, p. 139, &c. [cf. particularly, ii.145–7.]

– [misspelt 'tallie' here and 6 lines lower down in 2–5; also in the index under the article 'Montauban'.]

– together 2

[21] See below, V.iii.70, where Smith mentions the accurate surveys recently undertaken by the governments of Milan, Austria, Prussia and Sardinia. See also below, V.ii.g.6.

the landlord. When a certain portion of the produce is to be paid away for a tax, the farmer computes, as well as he can, what the value of this portion is, one year with another, likely to amount to, and he makes a proportionable abatement in the rent which he agrees to pay to the landlord. There is no farmer who does not compute beforehand what the church tythe, which is a land-tax of this kind, is, one year with another, likely to amount to.

2   The tythe,[1] and every other land-tax of this kind, under the appearance of perfect equality, are very unequal taxes; a certain portion of the produce being, in different situations, equivalent to a very different portion of the rent. In some very rich lands the produce is so great, that the one half of it is fully sufficient to replace to the farmer his capital employed in cultivation, together with the ordinary profits of farming stock in the neighbourhood. The other half, or, what comes to the same thing, the value of the other half, he could afford to pay as rent to the land-[275] lord, if there was no tythe. But if a tenth of the produce is taken from him in the way of tythe, he must require an abatement of the fifth part of *his* rent, otherwise he cannot get back his capital with the ordinary profit.[2] In this case the rent of the landlord, instead of amounting to a half, or five-tenths of the whole produce, will amount only to four-tenths of it. In poorer lands, on the contrary, the produce is sometimes so small, and the expence of cultivation so great, that it requires four-fifths of the whole produce to replace to the farmer his capital with the ordinary profit. In this case, though there was no tythe, the rent of the landlord could amount to no more than one-fifth or two-tenths of the whole produce. But if the farmer pays one-tenth of the produce in the way of tythe, he must require an equal abatement of the rent of the landlord, which will thus be reduced to one-tenth only of the whole produce.[3] Upon the rent of rich lands, the tythe may sometimes be a tax of no more than one fifth-part, or four shillings in the pound; whereas, upon that of poorer lands, it may sometimes be a tax of one-half, or of ten shillings in the pound.

3   The tythe, as it is frequently a very unequal tax upon the rent, so it is always a great discouragement both to the improvements of the landlord and to the cultivation of the farmer. The one cannot venture to make the most important, which are generally the most expensive improvements; nor the other to raise the most valuable, which are generally too the most

---

a-a this *1–2*

[1] Smith comments on the historical significance of tithes at V.i.g.22.

[2] A similar point is made at V.ii.g.8, and see above, I.xi.a.8, where rent is stated to be a residual.

[3] It is stated below, V.iii.70, that had there been no tythes in England or Ireland, the landed classes would have been able to pay an additional 6 or 7 millions without significantly adding to their burden.

expensive crops; [276] when the church, which lays out no part of the expence, is to share so very largely in the profit.[4] The cultivation of madder was for a long time confined by the tythe to the United Provinces, which, being presbyterian countries, and upon that account exempted from this destructive tax, enjoyed a sort of monopoly of that useful dying drug against the rest of Europe. The late attempts to introduce the culture of this plant into England, have been made only in consequence of the statute which enacted that five shillings an acre should be received in lieu of all manner of tythe upon madder.[5]

4   As through the greater part of Europe, the church, so in many different countries of Asia, the state, is principally supported by a land-tax, proportioned, not to the rent, but to the produce of the land. In China, the principal revenue of the sovereign consists in a tenth part of the produce of all the lands of the empire. This tenth part, however, is estimated so very moderately, that, in many provinces, it is said not to exceed a thirtieth part of the ordinary produce. The land-tax or land rent which used to be paid to the Mahometan government of Bengal, before that country fell into the hands of the English East India Company, is said to have amounted to about a fifth part of the produce. The land-tax of antient Egypt is said likewise to have amounted to a fifth part.[6]

5   In Asia, this sort of land-tax is said to interest the sovereign in the improvement and cultivation of land. The sovereigns of China, those [277] of Bengal while under the Mahometan government, and those of antient Egypt, are said accordingly to have been extremely attentive to the making and maintaining óf good roads and navigable canals, in order to increase, as much as possible, both the quantity and value of every part of the produce of the land, by procuring to every part of it the most extensive market which their own dominions could afford.[7] The tythe of the church is divided into such small portions, that no one of its proprietors can have any interest of this kind. The parson of a parish could never find his account in making a road or canal to a distant part of the country, in order to extend the market for the produce of his own particular parish. Such taxes, when destined for the maintenance of the state, have some advantages which may serve in some measure to balance their inconveniency. When destined for the maintenance of the church, they are attended with nothing but inconveniency.

6   Taxes upon the produce of land may be levied, either in kind; or, according to a certain valuation, in money.

[4] See above, V.ii.c.18, III.ii.13.
[5] 31 George II, c. 12 (1757), continued by 5 George III, c. 18 (1765).
[6] 'And Joseph made it a law over the land of Egypt unto this day, that Pharaoh should have the fifth part; except the land of the priests only, which became not Pharaoh's.' (Genesis 47:26.)
[7] See above, V.i.d.17 and IV.ix.45.

7   The parson of a parish, or a gentleman of small fortune who lives upon
     his estate, may sometimes, perhaps, find some advantage in receiving, the
     one his tythe, and the other his rent, in kind. The quantity to be collected,
     and the district within which it is to be collected, are so small, that they
     both can oversee, with their own eyes, the collection and disposal of every
     part of what is due to them. A gentleman of great for-[278]tune, who
     lived in the capital, would be in danger of suffering much by the neglect,
     and more by the fraud, of his factors and agents, if the rents of an estate
     in a distant province were to be paid to him in this manner. The loss of
     the sovereign, from the abuse and depredations of his tax-gatherers, would
     necessarily be much greater. The servants of the most careless private
     person are, perhaps, more under the eye of their master than those of the
     most careful prince; and a publick revenue, which was paid in kind, would
     suffer so much from the mismanagement of the collectors, that a very
     small part of what was levied upon the people would ever arrive at the
     treasury of the prince. Some part of the public revenue of China, however,
     is said to be paid in this manner. The Mandarins and other tax-gatherers
     will, no doubt, find their advantage in continuing the practice of a pay-
     ment which is so much more liable to abuse than any payment in money.

8   A tax upon the produce of land which is levied in money, may be levied
     either according to a valuation which varies with all the variations of the
     market price; or according to a fixed valuation, a bushel of wheat, for
     example, being always valued at one and the same money price, whatever
     may be the state of the market. The produce of a tax levied in the former
     way, will vary only according to the variations in the real produce of the
     land, according to the improvement or neglect of cultivation. The produce
     of a tax levied in the latter way will vary, [279] not only according to the
     variations in the produce of the land, but according to both those in the
     value of the precious metals, and those in the quantity of those metals
     which is at different times contained in coin of the same denomination.
     The produce of the former will always bear the same proportion to the
     value of the real produce of the land. The produce of the latter may, at
     different times, bear very different proportions to that value.

9   When, instead either of a certain portion of the produce of land, or of
     the price of a certain portion, a certain sum of money is to be paid in
     full compensation for all tax or tythe; the tax becomes, in this case,
     exactly of the same nature with the land-tax of England. It neither rises
     nor falls with the rent of the land. It neither encourages nor discourages
     improvement. The tythe in the greater part of those parishes which pay
     what is called a Modus in lieu of all other tythe, is a tax of this kind. During
     the Mahometan government of Bengal, instead of the payment in kind of
     a fifth part of the produce, a modus, and, it is said, a very moderate one,
     was established in the greater part of the districts or zemindaries of the

country.[8] Some of the servants of the East India Company, under pretence of restoring the publick revenue to its proper value, have, in some provinces, exchanged this modus for a payment in kind. Under their management this change is likely both to discourage cultivation, and to give new opportunities for abuse in the collection of the publick re-[280] venue, which has fallen very much below what it was said to have been, when it first fell under the management of the company. The servants of the company may, perhaps, have profited by this change, but at the expence, it is probable, both of their masters and of the country.[9]

Taxes upon the Rent of Houses

1   The rent of a house may be distinguished into two parts, of which the one may very properly be called the Building rent; the other is commonly called the Ground rent.

2   The building rent is the interest or profit of the capital expended in building the house. In order to put the trade of a builder upon a level with other trades, it is necessary that this rent should be sufficient, first, to pay him the same interest which he would have got for his capital if he had lent it upon good security; and, secondly, to keep the house in constant repair, or, what comes to the same thing, to replace, within a certain term of years, the capital which had been employed in building it. The building rent, or the ordinary profit of building is, therefore, every where regulated by the ordinary interest of money.[1] Where the market rate of interest is four per cent. the rent of a house which, over and above paying the ground rent, affords six, or six and a half per cent. upon the whole expence of building, may perhaps afford a sufficient profit to the builder. Where the market rate of interest is five per cent., it may perhaps require seven or seven and a half per cent. If, [281] in proportion to the interest of money, the trade of the builder affords at any time a much greater profit than this, it will soon draw so much capital from other trades as will reduce the profit to its proper level. If it affords at any time much less than this, other trades will soon draw so much capital from it as will again raise that profit.

3   Whatever part of the whole rent of a house is over and above what is sufficient for affording this reasonable profit, naturally goes to the ground-rent; and where the owner of the ground and the owner of the building are two different persons, is, in most cases, compleatly paid to the former. This surplus rent is the price which the inhabitant of the house pays for some real or supposed advantage of the situation. In country houses, at a

---

[8] The modus is mentioned below, V.iii.70.

[9] The government of the East India Company is considered above, IV.vii.c.102–8.

[1] See above, II.iv.17, where Smith discusses the relationship between interest and the rent of land, and I.ix.22, where he considers that between interest and profit.

distance from any great town, where there is plenty of ground to chuse upon, the ground rent is scarce any thing, or no more than what the ground which the house stands upon would pay if employed in agriculture. In country villas in the neighbourhood of some great town, it is sometimes a good deal higher; and the peculiar conveniency or beauty of situation is there frequently very well paid for.[2] Ground rents are generally highest in the capital, and in those particular parts of it where there happens to be the greatest demand for houses, whatever be the reason of that demand, whether for trade and business, for pleasure and society, or for mere vanity and fashion.

4   A tax upon house-rent, payable by the tenant and proportioned to the whole rent of each house, [282] could not, for any considerable time at least, affect the building rent. If the builder did not get his reasonable profit, he would be obliged to quit the trade; which, by raising the demand for building, would in a short time bring back his profit to its proper level with that of other trades. Neither would such a tax fall altogether upon the ground-rent; but it would divide itself in such a manner as to fall, partly upon the inhabitant of the house, and partly upon the owner of the ground.

5   Let us suppose, for example, that a particular person judges that he can afford for house-rent an expence of sixty pounds a year; and let us suppose too that a tax of four shillings in the pound, or of one-fifth, payable by the inhabitant, is laid upon house-rent. A house of sixty pounds rent will in this case cost him seventy-two pounds a year, which is twelve pounds more than he thinks he can afford. He will, therefore, content himself with a worse house, or a house of fifty pounds rent, which, with the additional ten pounds that he must pay for the tax, will make up the sum of sixty pounds a year, the expence which he judges he can afford; and in order to pay the tax he will give up a part of the additional conveniency which he might have had from a house of ten pounds a year more rent. He will give up, I say, a part of this additional conveniency; for he will seldom be obliged to give up the whole, but will, in consequence of the tax, get a better house for fifty pounds a year, than he could have got if there had been [283] no tax. For as a tax of this kind, by taking away this particular competitor, must diminish the competition for houses of sixty pounds rent, so it must likewise diminish it for those of fifty pounds rent, and in the same manner for those of all other rents, except the lowest rent, for which it would for some time increase the competition. But the rents of every class of houses for which the competition was diminished, would necessarily be more or less reduced. As no part of this reduction, however, could, for any considerable time at least, affect the building

---

[2] See above, I.xi.b.4, where Smith discusses the relationship between land rent and situation.

rent; the whole of it must in the long-run necessarily fall upon the ground-rent. The final payment of this tax, therefore, would fall, partly upon the inhabitant of the house, who, in order to pay his share, would be obliged to give up a part of his conveniency; and partly upon the owner of the ground, who, in order to pay his share, would be obliged to give up a part of his revenue. In what proportion this final payment would be divided between them, it is not perhaps very easy to ascertain. The division would probably be very different in different circumstances, and a tax of this kind might, according to those different circumstances, affect very unequally both the inhabitant of the house and the owner of the ground.

6   The inequality with which a tax of this kind might fall upon the owners of different ground-rents, would arise altogether from the accidental inequality of this division. But the inequality with which it might fall upon the inhabitants of different houses would arise, not only from this, [284] but from another cause. The proportion of the expence of house-rent to the whole expence of living, is different in the different degrees of fortune. It is perhaps highest in the highest degree, and it diminishes gradually through the inferior degrees, so as in general to be lowest in the lowest degree. The necessaries of life occasion the great expence of the poor. They find it difficult to get food, and the greater part of their little revenue is spent in getting it. The luxuries and vanities of life occasion the principal expence of the rich;[3] and a magnificent house embellishes and sets off to the best advantage all the other luxuries and vanities which they possess. A tax upon house-rents, therefore, would in general fall heaviest upon the rich; and in this sort of inequality there would not, perhaps, be any thing very unreasonable. It is not very unreasonable that the rich should contribute to the publick expence, not only in proportion to their revenue, but something more than in that proportion.

7   The rent of houses, though it in some respects resembles the rent of land, is in one respect essentially different from it. The rent of land is paid for the use of a productive subject.[4] The land which pays it produces it. The rent of houses is paid for the use of an unproductive subject. Neither the house nor the ground which it stands upon produce any thing. The person who pays the rent, therefore, must draw it from some other source of revenue, distinct from and independent of this subject.[5] A tax upon the [285] rent of houses, so far as it falls upon the inhabitants, must be drawn from the same source as the rent itself, and must be paid from their revenue, whether derived from the wages of labour, the profits of stock, or the rent of land. So far as it falls upon the inhabitants, it is one of those taxes which fall, not upon one only, but indifferently upon all the three different sources of revenue; and is in every respect of the same nature as a tax upon any other sort of consumable commodities. In general

[3] See above, I.xi.c.31.   [4] See above, II.v.12.   [5] See above, II.i.12.

there is not perhaps, any one article of expence or consumption by which the liberality or narrowness of a man's whole expence can be better judged of, than by his house rent. A proportional tax upon this particular article of expence might, perhaps, produce a more considerable revenue than any which has hitherto been drawn from it in any part of Europe. If the tax indeed was very high, the greater part of people would endeavour to evade it, as much as they could, by contenting themselves with smaller houses, and by turning the greater part of their expence into some other channel.

8		The rent of houses might easily be ascertained with sufficient accuracy, by a policy of the same kind with that which would be necessary for ascertaining the ordinary rent of land. Houses not inhabited ought to pay no tax. A tax upon them would fall altogether upon the proprietor, who would thus be taxed for a subject which afforded him neither conveniency nor revenue. Houses inhabited by the proprietor [286] ought to be rated, not according to the expence which they might have cost in building, but according to the rent which an equitable arbitration might judge them likely to bring, if leased to a tenant. If rated according to the expence which they may have cost in building, a tax of three or four shillings in the pound, joined with other taxes, would ruin almost all the rich and great families of this, and, I believe, of every other civilized country. Whoever will examine, with attention, the different town and country houses of some of the richest and greatest families in this country, will find that, at the rate of only six and a half, or seven per cent. upon the original expence of building, their house-rent is nearly equal to the whole neat rent of their estates. It is the accumulated expence of several successive generations, laid out upon objects of great beauty and magnificence, indeed; but, in proportion to what they cost, of very small exchangeable value*.

9		Ground-rents are a still more proper subject of taxation than the rent of houses. A tax upon ground-rents would not raise the rents of houses. It would fall altogether upon the owner of the ground-rent, who acts always as a monopolist, and exacts the greatest rent which can be got for the use of his ground. More or less can be got for it according as the competitors happen to be richer or poorer, or can afford to gratify their [287] fancy for a particular spot of ground at a greater or smaller expence.

ᵃ* Since the first publication of this book, a tax nearly upon the above-mentioned principles has been imposed.ᵃ [First by 18 George III, c. 26 (1778) and then by 19 George III, c. 59 (1779). Under the first statute the duty was at the rate of 6*d*. in the £ on houses of an annual value of £5 and under £50, and 1*s*. in the £ on houses of higher value. The later statute altered the rates to 6*d*. in the £ on houses of £5 and under £20 annual value, 9*d*. in the £ on those of £20 and under £40, and 1*s*. in the £ on those of higher value.]
ᵃ⁻ᵃ 3–6

In every country the greatest number of rich competitors is in the capital, and it is there accordingly that the highest ground-rents are always to be found. As the wealth of those competitors would in no respect be increased by a tax upon ground-rents, they would not probably be disposed to pay more for the use of the ground. Whether the tax was to be advanced by the inhabitant, or by the owner of the ground, would be of little importance. The more the inhabitant was obliged to pay for the tax, the less he would incline to pay for the ground; so that the final payment of the tax would fall altogether upon the owner of the ground-rent. The ground-rents of uninhabited houses ought to pay no tax.

10   Both ground-rents and the ordinary rent of land are a species of revenue which the owner, in many cases, enjoys without any care or attention of his own.[6] Though a part of this revenue should be taken from him in order to defray the expences of the state, no discouragement will thereby be given to any sort of industry. The annual produce of the land and labour of the society, the real wealth and revenue of the great body of the people, might be the same after such a tax as before. Ground-rents, and the ordinary rent of land, are, therefore, perhaps, the species of revenue which can best bear to have a peculiar tax imposed upon them.

11   Ground-rents seem, in this respect, a more proper subject of peculiar taxation than even the [288] ordinary rent of land. The ordinary rent of land is, in many cases, owing partly at least to the attention and good management of the landlord.[7] A very heavy tax might discourage too much this attention and good management. Ground-rents, so far as they exceed the ordinary rent of land, are altogether owing to the good government of the sovereign, which, by protecting the industry either of the whole people, or of the inhabitants of some particular place, enables them to pay so much more than its real value for the ground which they build their houses upon; or to make to its owner so much more than compensation for the loss which he might sustain by this use of it. Nothing can be more reasonable than that a fund which owes its existence to the good government of the state, should be taxed peculiarly, or should contribute something more than the greater part of other funds, towards the support of that government.

12   Though, in many different countries of Europe, taxes have been imposed upon the rent of houses, I do not know of any in which ground-rents have been considered as a separate subject of taxation. The contrivers of taxes have, probably, found some difficulty in ascertaining what part of the rent ought to be considered as ground-rent, and what part ought to be considered as building rent. It should not, however, seem very difficult to distinguish those two parts of the rent from one another.

[6] The same point is made at I.xi.p.8.
[7] A rather more qualified view is stated above, I.xi.a.2, and see also V.iii.54.

13   In Great Britain the rent of houses is supposed to be taxed in the same
proportion as the rent [289] of land, by what is called the annual land-
tax. The valuation, according to which each different parish and district
is assessed to this tax, is always the same. It was originally extremely
unequal, and it still continues to be so. Through the greater part of the
kingdom this tax falls still more lightly upon the rent of houses than upon
that of land. In some few districts only, which were originally rated high,
and in which the rents of houses have fallen considerably, the land tax
of three or four shillings in the pound, is said to amount to an equal proportion of the real rent of *b* houses. Untenanted houses, though by law
subject to the tax, are, in most districts, exempted from it by the favour
of the assessors; and this exemption sometimes occasions some little variation in the rate of particular houses, though that of the district is always
the same. *c*Improvements of rent; by new buildings, repairs, &c.; go to
the discharge of the district, which occasions still further variations in the
rate of particular houses.*c*

14   In the province of Holland* every house is taxed at two and half per
cent. of its value, without any regard either to the rent which it actually
pays, or to the circumstance of its being tenanted or untenanted. There
seems to be a hardship in obliging the proprietor to pay a tax for an
untenanted house, from which he can derive no revenue; especially so
very heavy a tax. In Holland, where the market rate of interest [290]
does not exceed three per cent. two and a half per cent. upon the whole
value of the house, must, in most cases, amount to more than a third of
the building-rent, perhaps of the whole rent. The valuation, indeed, according to which the houses are rated, though very unequal, is said to be
always below the real value. When a house is rebuilt, improved, or enlarged, there is a new valuation, and the tax is rated accordingly.

15   The contrivers of the several taxes which in England have, at different
times, been imposed upon houses, seem to have imagined that there was
some great difficulty in ascertaining, with tolerable exactness, what was
the real rent of every house. They have regulated their taxes, therefore,
according to some more obvious circumstance, such as they had probably
imagined would, in most cases, bear some proportion to the rent.

16   The first tax of this kind was hearth-money; or a tax of two shillings
upon every hearth.⁸ In order to ascertain how many hearths were in

---

* Memoires concernant les Droits, &c. p. 223. ['Toutes les Maisons en général, soit
qu'elles soient louées, soit qu'elles ne le soient pas, sont taxées à Deux & demi pour cent
de leur valeur, suivant l'estimation qui en est faite sans égard au prix des loyers ni aux
réparations on entretien; les estimations sont en général sont inégales, mais toujours
inférieures à la valeur réalle.' (De Beaumont, *Mémoires*, i.223.)]

---

b the *1*   *c–c* 2–6

---

⁸ 14 Charles II, c. 10 (1662); 15 Charles II, c. 13 (1663); 16 Charles II, c. 3 (1664).

the house, it was necessary that the tax-gatherer should enter every room in it. This odious visit rendered the tax odious. Soon after the revolution, therefore, it was abolished as a badge of slavery.[9]

17   The next tax of this kind was, a tax of two shillings upon every dwelling house inhabited. A house with ten windows to pay four shillings more.[10] A house with twenty windows and upwards to pay eight shillings. This tax was [291] afterwards so far altered, that houses with twenty windows, and with less than thirty, were ordered to pay ten shillings, and those with thirty windows and upwards to pay twenty shillings.[11] The number of windows can, in most cases, be counted from the outside, and, in all cases, without entering every room in the house. The visit of the tax-gatherer, therefore, was less offensive in this tax than in the hearth-money.

18   This tax was afterwards repealed, and in the room of it was established the window-tax, which has undergone too several alterations and augmentations.[12] The window-tax, as it stands at present (January, 1775), over and above the duty of three shillings upon every house in England, and of one shilling upon every house in Scotland, lays a duty upon every window, which, in England, augments gradually from two-pence, the lowest rate, upon houses with not more than seven windows; to two shillings, the highest rate, upon houses with twenty-five windows and upwards.

19   The principal objection to all such taxes is their inequality, an inequality of the worst kind, as they must frequently fall much heavier upon the poor than upon the rich. A house of ten pounds rent in a country town may sometimes have more windows than a house of five hundred pounds rent in London; and though the inhabitant of the former is likely to be a much poorer man than that of the latter, yet so far as his contribution is regulated by the window-tax, he must contribute more to the support [292] of the state. Such taxes are, therefore, directly contrary to the first of the four maxims above mentioned. They do not seem to offend much against any of the other three.

20   The natural tendency of the window-tax, and of all other taxes upon houses, is to lower rents. The more a man pays for the tax, the less, it is evident, he can afford to pay for the rent. Since the imposition of the window-tax, however, the rents of houses have upon the whole risen, more or less, in almost every town and village of Great Britain, with which I am acquainted. Such has been almost every where the increase of the demand for houses, that it has raised the rents more than the window-tax

---

[9] Abolished because 'grievous to the People' by 1 William and Mary, c. 10 (1688) in *Statutes of the Realm*, vi.61–2; 1 William and Mary, sess. 1, c. 10 in Ruffhead's edition.

[10] 7 and 8 William III, c. 18 (1695).

[11] 8 Anne, c. 10 (1709) in *Statutes of the Realm*, ix.207; 8 Anne, c. 4 in Ruffhead's edition.

[12] 20 George II, c. 3 (1746); 31 George II, c. 22 (1757).

could sink them; one of the many proofs of the great prosperity of the country, and of the increasing revenue of its inhabitants. Had it not been for the tax, rents would probably have risen still higher.

ARTICLE II
Taxes upon Profit, or upon the Revenue arising from Stock

1   The revenue or profit arising from stock naturally divides itself into two parts; that which pays the interest, and which belongs to the owner of the stock; and that surplus part which is over and above what is necessary for paying the interest.

2   This latter part of profit is evidently a subject not taxable directly. It is the compen-[293]sation, and in most cases it is no more than a very moderate compensation, for the risk and trouble of employing the stock.[1] The employer must have this compensation, otherwise he cannot, consistently with his own interest, continue the employment. If he was taxed directly, therefore, in proportion to the whole profit, he would be obliged either to raise the rate of his profit, or to charge the tax upon the interest of money; that is, to pay less interest. If he raised the rate of his profit in proportion to the tax, the whole tax, though it might be advanced by him, would be finally paid by one or other of two different sets of people, according to the different ways in which he might employ the stock of which he had the management. If he employed it as a farming stock in the cultivation of land, he could raise the rate of his profit only by retaining a greater portion, or, what comes to the same thing, the price of a greater portion of the produce of the land; and as this could be done only by a reduction of rent, the final payment of the tax would fall upon the landlord.[2] If he employed it as a mercantile or manufacturing stock, he could raise the rate of his profit only by raising the price of his goods; in which case the final payment of the tax would fall altogether upon the consumers of those goods. If he did not raise the rate of his profit, he would be obliged to charge the whole tax upon that part of it which was allotted for the interest of money. He could afford less interest for whatever stock he borrowed, and the whole [294] weight of the tax would in this case fall ultimately upon the interest of money. So far as he could not relieve himself from the tax in the one way, he would be obliged to relieve himself in the other.

3   The interest of money seems at first sight a subject equally capable of being taxed directly as the rent of land. Like the rent of land, it is a neat produce which remains after compleatly compensating the whole risk and

---

[1] See above, I.ix.18 and I.vi.18.
[2] See below, V.ii.g.8, V.ii.i.2, V.ii.k.9.

trouble of employing the stock.[3] As a tax upon the rent of land cannot raise rents; because the neat produce which remains after replacing the stock of the farmer, together with his reasonable profit, cannot be greater after the tax than before it: so, for the same reason, a tax upon the interest of money could not raise the rate of interest; the quantity of stock or money in the country, like the quantity of land, being supposed to remain the same after the tax as before it. The ordinary rate of profit, it has been shewn in the first book, is every where regulated by the quantity of stock to be employed in proportion to the quantity of the employment, or of the business which must be done by it.[4] But the quantity of the employment, or of the business to be done by stock, could neither be increased nor diminished by any tax upon the interest of money. If the quantity of the stock to be employed, therefore, was neither increased nor diminished by it, the ordinary rate of profit would necessarily remain the same. But the portion of this profit necessary for compensating the [295] risk and trouble of the employer, would likewise remain the same; that risk and trouble being in no respect altered. The residue, therefore, that portion which belongs to the owner of the stock, and which pays the interest of money, would necessarily remain the same too. At first sight, therefore, the interest of money seems to be a subject as fit to be taxed directly as the rent of land.

4   There are, however, two different circumstances which render the interest of money a much less proper subject of direct taxation than the rent of land.

5   First, the quantity and value of the land which any man possesses can never be a secret, and can always be ascertained with great exactness.[5] But the whole amount of the capital stock which he possesses is almost always a secret, and can scarce ever be ascertained with tolerable exactness. It is liable, besides, to almost continual variations. A year seldom passes away, frequently not a month, sometimes scarce a single day, in which it does not rise or fall more or less. An inquisition into every man's private circumstances, and an inquisition which, in order to accommodate the tax to them, watched over all the fluctuations of his fortune, would be a source of such continual and endless vexation as no people could support.

6   Secondly, land is a subject which cannot be removed; whereas stock easily may. The proprietor of land is necessarily a citizen of the particular country in which his estate lies. The [296] proprietor of stock is properly a citizen of the world, and is not necessarily attached to any particular

---

[3] See above, I.ix.18, 19.

[4] See above, I.ix.

[5] Cf. LJ (B) 310, ed. Cannan 239: 'It is easy to levy a tax upon land because it is evident what quantity everyone possesses, but it is very difficult to lay a tax upon stock or money without very arbitrary proceedings.'

country.[6] He would be apt to abandon the country in which he was exposed to a vexatious inquisition, in order to be assessed to a burdensome tax, and would remove his stock to some other country where he could, either carry on his business, or enjoy his fortune more at his ease. By removing his stock he would put an end to all the industry which it had maintained in the country which he left. Stock cultivates land; stock employs labour. A tax which tended to drive away stock from any particular country, would so far tend to dry up every source of revenue, both to the sovereign and to the society. Not only the profits of stock, but the rent of land and the wages of labour, would necessarily be more or less diminished by its removal.

7   The nations, accordingly, who have attempted to tax the revenue arising from stock, instead of any severe inquisition of this kind, have been obliged to content themselves with some very loose, and, therefore, more or less arbitrary estimation. The extreme inequality and uncertainty of a tax assessed in this manner, can be compensated only by its extreme moderation, in consequence of which every man finds himself rated so very much below his real revenue, that he gives himself little disturbance though his neighbour should be rated somewhat lower.[7]

8   By what is called the land-tax in England, it was intended that [a] stock should be taxed in the same proportion as land. When the tax [297] upon land was at four shillings in the pound, or at one-fifth of the supposed rent, it was intended that stock should be taxed at one-fifth of the supposed interest. When the present annual land-tax was first imposed, the legal rate of interest was six per cent.[8] Every hundred pounds stock, accordingly, was supposed to be taxed at twenty-four shillings, the fifth part of six pounds. Since the legal rate of interest has been reduced to five per cent.[9] every hundred pounds stock is supposed to be taxed at twenty shillings only. The sum to be raised, by what is called the land-tax, was divided between the country and the principal towns. The greater part of it was laid upon the country; and of what was laid upon the towns, the greater part was assessed upon the houses. What remained to be assessed

---

[a] the 6

[6] See above, II.v.14, III.iv.24, and below, V.ii.k.80, V.iii.55. The point is made by Montesquieu, *Esprit*, XX.xxiii.1, where it is also remarked that 'moveable effects, as money, notes, bills of exchange, stocks in companies, vessels, and, in fine, all merchandise, belong to the whole world in general; in this respect, it is composed of but one single state, of which all the societies upon earth are members.'

[7] LJ (B) 311, ed. Cannan 240, points out with reference to land, stock, or money that of these only land is taxed in England. He also indicates that the English avoid taxes on stock 'from a kind of delicacey with regard to examining into the circumstances of particular persons, which is apparently an infringement upon liberty' (313, ed. Cannan 241).

[8] By 12 Charles II, c. 13 (1660).

[9] By 13 Anne, c. 15 (1713) in *Statutes of the Realm*, ix.928; 12 Anne, st. 2, c. 16 in Ruffhead's edition. See above, I.ix.5, and below V.iii.27.

upon the stock or trade of the towns (for the stock upon the land was not meant to be taxed) was very much below the real value of that stock or trade. Whatever inequalities, therefore, there might be in the original assessment, gave little disturbance. Every parish and district still continues to be rated for its land, its houses, and its stock, according to the original assessment; and the almost universal prosperity of the country, which in most places has raised very much the value of all these, has rendered those inequalities of still less importance now. The rate too upon each district continuing always the same, the uncertainty of this tax, so far as it might be assessed upon the stock of any individual, has been very much diminished, as well [298] as rendered of much less consequence. If the greater part of the lands of England are not rated to the land-tax at half their actual value, the greater part of the stock of England is, perhaps, scarce rated at the fiftieth part of its actual value. In some towns the whole land-tax is assessed upon houses; as in Westminster, where stock and trade are free. It is otherwise in London.

9   In all countries a severe inquisition into the circumstances of private persons has been carefully avoided.

10   At Hamburgh* every inhabitant is obliged to pay to the state, one-fourth per cent. of all that he possesses; and as the wealth of the people of Hamburgh consists principally in stock, this tax may be considered as a tax upon stock. Every man assesses himself, and, in the presence of the magistrate, puts annually into the publick coffer a certain sum of money, which he declares upon oath to be one-fourth per cent. of all that he possesses, but without declaring what it amounts to, or being liable to any examination upon that subject. This tax is generally supposed to be paid with great fidelity. In a small republick, where the people have entire confidence in their magistrates, are convinced of the necessity of the tax for the support of the state, and believe that it will be faithfully applied to that purpose, such conscientious and [299] voluntary payment *b*may*b* sometimes be expected. It is not peculiar to the people of Hamburgh.

11   The canton of Underwald in Switzerland is frequently ravaged by storms and inundations, and *c* is thereby exposed to extraordinary expences. Upon such occasions the people assemble, and every one is said to declare with the greatest frankness what he is worth, in order to be taxed accordingly. At Zurich the law orders, that, in cases of necessity, every one

* Memoires concernant les Droits, tome i. p. 74. [De Beaumont's account is: 'La Taille consiste dans le Quart pour cent que tout habitant, sans exception, est obligé de payer de tout ce qu'il possède en meubles & immeubles. Il ne se fait aucune répartition de cette taille. Chaque bourgeois se cottise lui-même & porte son imposition à la Maison de ville, & on n'exige autre chose de lui, sinon le serment qu'il est obligé de faire que ce qu'il paye, forme véritablement ce qu'il doit acquitter.' (*Mémoires*, i.74.)]

b-b om. 5   *c* it 5–6

should be taxed in proportion to his revenue; the amount of which he is obliged to declare upon oath. They have no suspicion, it is said, that any of their fellow-citizens will deceive them. At Basil the principal revenue of the state arises from a small custom upon goods exported. All the citizens make oath that they will pay every three months all the taxes imposed by the law. All merchants and even all inn-keepers are trusted with keeping themselves the account of the goods which they sell either within or without the territory. At the end of every three months they send this account to the treasurer, with the amount of the tax computed at the bottom of it. It is not suspected that the revenue suffers by this confidence*.

12   To oblige every citizen to declare publickly upon oath the amount of his fortune, must not, it seems, in those Swiss cantons, be reckoned a hardship. At Hamburgh it would be reckoned the greatest. Merchants engaged in the hazardous [300] projects of trade, all tremble at the thoughts of being obliged at all times to expose the real state of their circumstances. The ruin of their credit and the miscarriage of their projects, they foresee, would too often be the consequence. A sober and parsimonious people, who are strangers to all such projects, do not feel that they have occasion for any such concealment.[10]

13   In Holland, soon after the exaltation of the late prince of Orange to the stadtholdership, a tax of two per cent. or the fiftieth penny, as it was called, was imposed upon the whole substance of every citizen. Every citizen assessed himself and paid his tax in the same manner as at Hamburgh; and it was in general supposed to have been paid with great

---

*d Memoires concernant les Droits,d tom. i, p. 163, 166, 171. [The accounts of the procedure in the three places cited, according to De Beaumont, is as follows:

Underwald: 'Le territoire d'Underwald est si souvent dévasté par des orages & des inondations, que ce Canton a quelquefois des dépenses extraordinaires à acquitter. Dans ces cas, le peuple s'assemble, chacun convient, avec la plus grande franchise, du bien dont il jouit, & est taxé tantôt à 5 sous, quelquefois à 10 sous par 1000 livres de capital. On décide dans la même assemblée l'espace de temps pendant lequel l'impôt doit subsister.' (*Mémoires*, i.171.)

Zurich: 'Une loi expresse porte que dans des cas de besoin, chaque Particulier sera taxé à proportion de ses revenus, en quoi qu'ils puissent consister, & qu'il indiquera sous la foi de serment.' (*Mémoires*, i.163.)

Basle: 'Le revenu le plus considérable du Canton, consiste dans les droits de Douane. Chaque Bourgeois prête tous les ans serment de payer ce qu'il devra d'impôt, & tous les trois mois le Marchand & le Cabaretier, qui forment entr'eux une très-grande partie de la bourgeoisie envoient, soit aux Trésoriers de l'État, soit aux Baillis, un compte de ce qu'ils ont vendu, soit dans le pays soit à l'étranger, & règlent au bas du compte le montant de la somme qu'ils jugent devoir légitimement payer.' (*Mémoires*, i.166-7.)]

---

d-d Id. 1-2

---

[10] LJ (B) 310, ed. Cannan 239–40, comments: 'It is a hardship upon a man in trade to oblige him to shew his books, which is the only way in which we can know how much he is worth. It is a breach of liberty, and may be productive of very bad consequences by ruining his credit. The circumstances of people in trade are at sometimes far worse than others.'

fidelity. The people had at that time the greatest affection for their new government, which they had just established by a general insurrection. The tax was to be paid but once; in order to relieve the state in a particular exigency. It was, indeed, too heavy to be permanent. In a country where the market rate of interest seldom exceeds three per cent.,[11] a tax of two per cent. amounts to thirteen shillings and fourpence in the pound upon the highest neat revenue which is commonly drawn from stock. It is a tax which very few people could pay without encroaching more or less upon their capitals. In a particular exigency the people may, from great publick zeal, make a great effort, and give up even a part of their capital, in order to relieve the state. But it is impossible that they should continue to do so for any con-[301]siderable time; and if they did, the tax would soon ruin them so compleatly as to render them altogether incapable of supporting the state.

14   The tax upon stock imposed by the land-tax bill in England, though it is proportioned to the capital, is not intended to diminish or take away any part of that capital. It is meant only to be a tax upon the interest of money proportioned to that upon the rent of land; so that when the latter is at four shillings in the pound, the former may be at four shillings in the pound too. The tax at Hamburgh, and the still more moderate taxes of Underwald and Zurich, are meant, in the same manner, to be taxes, not upon the capital, but upon the interest or neat revenue of stock. That of Holland was meant to be a tax upon the capital.

Taxes upon the Profit of particular Employments

1   In some countries extraordinary taxes are imposed upon the profits of stock; sometimes when employed in particular branches of trade, and sometimes when employed in agriculture.

2   Of the former kind are in England the tax upon hawkers and pedlars,[1] that upon hackney coaches and chairs,[2] and that which the keepers of ale-houses pay for a licence to retail ale and spirituous liquors.[3] During the late war, another tax of the same kind was proposed upon shops. The war having been undertaken, it was said, in defence of the trade of the country, the merchants who were to profit by it, ought to contribute towards the support of it.

[11] See above, I.ix.10.

[1] Among others by 8 and 9 William III, c. 25 (1696); 9 William III, c. 27 (1697) in *Statutes of the Realm*, vii.397–9; 9 and 10 William III in Ruffhead's edition; 12 and 13 William III, c. 11 (1700); 3 and 4 Anne, c. 18 (1704) in *Statutes of the Realm*, viii.370–6; 3 and 4 Anne, c. 4 in Ruffhead's edition. Hawkers and pedlars are mentioned above, III.iii.2.

[2] 14 Charles II, c. 2 (1662) in *Statutes of the Realm*, v.351–7; 13 and 14 Charles II, c. 2 in Ruffhead's edition; 9 Anne, c. 16 (1710) in *Statutes of the Realm*, ix.447–72; 9 Anne, c. 23 in Ruffhead's edition.

[3] 5 and 6 Edward VI, c. 25 (1551).

3   [302] A tax, however, upon the profits of stock employed in any particular
branch of trade, can never fall finally upon the dealers (who must in all
ordinary cases have their reasonable ᵃprofit, and, where the competition
is free, can seldom have more than that profit),ᵃ but always upon the consumers, who must be obliged to pay in the price of the goods the tax which
the dealer advances; and generally with some overcharge.

4   A tax of this kind when it is proportioned to the trade of the dealer,
is finally paid by the consumer, and occasions no oppression to the dealer.
When it is not so proportioned, but is the same upon all dealers, though
in this case too it is finally paid by the consumer, yet it favours the great,
and occasions some oppression to the small dealer. The tax of five shillings
a week upon every hackney coach, and that of ten shillings a year upon
every hackney chair, so far as it is advanced by the different keepers of
such coaches and chairs, is exactly enough proportioned to the extent of
their respective dealings. It neither favours the great, nor oppresses the
smaller dealer. The tax of twenty shillings a year for a licence to sell ale;
of forty shillings for a licence to sell spirituous liquors; and of forty
shillings more for a licence to sell wine, being the same upon all retailers,
must necessarily give some advantage to the great, and occasion some
oppression to the small dealers. The former must find it more easy to get
back the tax in the price of their goods than the latter. The moderation of
the tax, however, renders this inequality of less importance, and it may
to many [303] people appear not improper to give some discouragement
to the multiplication of little ale-houses.⁴ The tax upon shops, it was intended, should be the same upon all shops. It could not well have
been otherwise. It would have been impossible to proportion with tolerable
exactness the tax upon a shop to the extent of the trade carried on in it,
without such an inquisition as would have been altogether insupportable
in a free country. If the tax had been considerable, it would have
oppressed the small, and forced almost the whole retail trade into the hands
of the great dealers. The competition of the former being taken away,
the latter would have enjoyed a monopoly of the trade; and like all other
monopolists would soon have combined to raise their profits much beyond
what was necessary for the payment of the tax. The final payment, instead of falling upon the shopkeeper, would have fallen upon the consumer,
with a considerable over-charge to the profit of the shopkeeper. For these
reasons, the project of a tax upon shops was laid aside, and in the room of
it was substituted the subsidy 1759.⁵

ᵃ⁻ᵃ profit), and where the competition is free can seldom have more than that profit
1-4 ⟨corrected *4e-6*⟩

---

⁴ The multiplication of ale houses is mentioned at II.v.7.
⁵ 32 George II, c.10 (1758). See below, V.ii.k.23.

5   What in France is called the personal taille[6] is, perhaps, the most important tax upon the profits of stock employed in agriculture that is levied in any part of Europe.

6   In the disorderly state of Europe during the prevalence of the feudal government,[7] the sovereign was obliged to content himself with taxing those who were too weak to refuse to pay taxes. The great lords, though willing to assist [304] him upon particular emergencies, refused to subject themselves to any constant tax, and he was not strong enough to force them. The occupiers of land all over Europe were, the greater part of them, originally bond-men. Through the greater part of Europe they were gradually emancipated. Some of them acquired the property of landed estates which they held by some base or ignoble tenure, sometimes under the king, and sometimes under some other great lord, like the antient copy-holders of England. Others, without acquiring the property, obtained leases for terms of years of the lands which they occupied under their lord, and thus became less dependent upon him. The great lords seem to have beheld the degree of prosperity and independency which this inferior order of men had thus come to enjoy, with [b]a[b] malignant and contemptuous indignation, and willingly consented that the sovereign should tax them.[8] In some countries this tax was confined to the lands which were held in property by an ignoble tenure; and, in this case, the taille was said to be real. The land-tax established by the late king of Sardinia, and the taille in the provinces of Languedoc, Provence, Dauphiné, and Brittany; in the generality of Montauban, and in the elections of Agen and Condom, as well as in some other districts of France, are taxes upon lands held in property by an ignoble tenure.[9] In other countries the tax was laid upon the supposed profits of all those who held in farm or lease lands belonging to other people, whatever might be the tenure [305] by which the proprietor held them; and in this case the taille was said to be personal. In the greater part of those provinces of France, which are called the Countries of Elections, the taille is of this kind. The real taille, as it is imposed only upon a part of the lands of the country, is necessarily an unequal, but it is not always an arbitrary tax, though it is so upon some occasions. The personal taille, as it is intended to be proportioned to the profits of a certain class of people, which can only be guessed at, is necessarily both arbitrary and unequal.

7   In France the personal taille at present (1775) annually imposed upon the twenty generalities, called the Countries of Elections, amounts to

[b]–[b] 2–6

---

[6] With regard to the taille, see above, III.ii.19.

[7] Smith refers to 'times of feudal anarchy' at III.ii.7 and also V.iii.1.

[8] See above, III.ii.19. The original status of bond-men is described in III.ii and the process of change in land-tenure in III.iv.

[9] See above, V.ii.c.27.

40,107,239 livres, 16 sous*. The proportion in which this sum is assessed
upon those different provinces, varies from year to year, according to the
reports which are made to the king's council concerning the goodness or
badness of the crops, as well as other circumstances, which may either
increase or diminish their respective abilities to pay. Each generality is
divided into a certain number of elections, and the proportion in which the
sum imposed upon the whole generality is divided among those different
elections, varies likewise from year to year, according to the reports made
to the council concerning their respective abilities. It seems impossible that
the council, with the best intentions, can ever pro-[306]portion with
tolerable exactness, either of those two assessments to the real abilities of
the province or district upon which they are respectively laid. Ignorance
and misinformation must always, more or less, mislead the most upright
council. The proportion which each parish ought to support of what is
assessed upon the whole election, and that which each individual ought to
support of what is assessed upon his particular parish, are both in the same
manner varied, from year to year, according as circumstances are supposed
to require. These circumstances are judged of, in the one case, by the
officers of the election; in the other by those of the parish; and both the one
and the other are, more or less, under the direction and influence of the
intendant. Not only ignorance and misinformation, but friendship, party
animosity, and private resentment, are said frequently to mislead such
assessors. No man subject to such a tax, it is evident, can ever be certain,
before he is assessed, of what he is to pay.[10] He cannot even be certain
after he is assessed. If any person has been taxed who ought to have been
exempted; or if any person has been taxed beyond his proportion, though
both must pay in the mean time, yet if they complain and make good their
complaints, the whole parish is reimposed next year in order to reimburse
them. If any of the contributors become bankrupt or insolvent, the collector
is obliged to advance his tax, and the whole parish is reimposed next year
in order to reimburse the collector. If the collector himself [307] should
become bankrupt, the parish which elects him must answer for his conduct to the receiver-general of the election. But, as it might be troublesome for the receiver to prosecute the whole parish, he takes at his choice
five or six of the richest contributors, and obliges them to make good what
had been lost by the insolvency of the collector. The parish is afterwards
reimposed in order to reimburse those five or six. Such reimpositions are
always over and above the taille of the particular year in which they are
laid on.

8   When a tax is imposed upon the profits of stock in a particular branch

---

* Memoires concernant les Droits, &c. tome ii. p. 17.

[10] Smith refers above, IV.ix.3, to the 'arbitrary and degrading taxes' which were imposed on the cultivators in France.

of trade, the traders are all careful to bring no more goods to market than what they can sell at a price sufficient to reimburse them for advancing the tax. Some of them withdraw a part of their stocks from the trade, and the market is more sparingly supplied than before. The price of the goods rises, and the final payment of the tax falls upon the consumer. But when a tax is imposed upon the profits of stock employed in agriculture, it is not the interest of the farmers to withdraw any part of their stock from that employment. Each farmer occupies a certain quantity of land, for which he pays rent. For the proper cultivation of this land a certain quantity of stock is necessary; and by withdrawing any part of this necessary quantity, the farmer is not likely to be more able to pay either the rent or the tax. In order to pay the tax, it can never be his interest to diminish the quantity of his produce, nor con-[308]sequently to supply the market more sparingly than before. The tax, therefore, will never enable him to raise the price of his produce, ᶜso asᶜ to reimburse himself by throwing the final payment upon the consumer. The farmer, however, must have his reasonable profit as well as every other dealer, otherwise he must give up the trade. After the imposition of a tax of this kind, he can get this reasonable profit only by paying less rent to the landlord.[11] The more he is obliged to pay in the way of tax, the less he can afford to pay in the way of rent.[12] A tax of this kind imposed during the currency of a lease may, no doubt, distress or ruin the farmer. Upon the renewal of the lease it must always fall upon the landlord.

9   In the countries where the personal taille takes place, the farmer is commonly assessed in proportion to the stock which he appears to employ in cultivation. He is, upon this account, frequently afraid to have a good team of horses or oxen, but endeavours to cultivate with the meanest and most wretched instruments of husbandry that he can. Such is his distrust in the justice of his assessors, that he counterfeits poverty, and wishes to appear scarce able to pay any thing for fear of being obliged to pay too much. By this miserable policy he does not, perhaps, always consult his own interest in the most effectual manner; and he probably loses more by the diminution of his produce than he saves by that of his tax. Though, in consequence of this wretched cultivation the market is, no doubt, somewhat [309] worse supplied; yet the small rise of price which this may occasion, as it is not likely even to indemnify the farmer for the diminution of his produce, it is still less likely to enable him to pay more rent to the landlord. The publick, the farmer, the landlord, all suffer more or less by this degraded cultivation. That the personal taille tends, in many dif-

---

ᶜ⁻ᶜ nor *I*

[11] See above, V.ii.f.2. A similar point is made in the discussion of taxes on wages at V.ii.i.2 and cf. V.iii.54.

[12] A similar point is made in the discussion of taxes on tithes, V.ii.d.1.

ferent ways, to discourage cultivation, and consequently to dry up the principal source of the wealth of every great country, I have already had occasion to observe in the third book of this inquiry.[13]

10   What are called poll-taxes in the sourthern provinces of North America, and in the West ^dIndian^d islands, annual taxes of so much a head upon every negro, are properly taxes upon the profits of a certain species of stock employed in agriculture. As the planters are, the greater part of them, both farmers and landlords, the final payment of the tax falls upon them in their quality of landlords without any retribution.

11   Taxes of so much a head upon the bondmen employed in cultivation, seem antiently to have been common all over Europe. There subsists at present a tax of this kind in the empire of Russia. It is probably upon this account that poll-taxes of all kinds have often been represented as badges of slavery.[14] Every tax, however, is to the person who pays it a badge, not of slavery, but of liberty. It denotes that he is subject to government, indeed, but that, as he has some property, he cannot himself be the property of a master. A poll-tax upon slaves is [310] altogether different from a poll-tax upon freemen. The latter is paid by the persons upon whom it is imposed; the former by a different set of persons. The latter is either altogether arbitrary or altogether unequal, and in most cases is both the one and the other; the former, though in some respects unequal, different slaves being of different values, is in no respect arbitrary. Every master who knows the number of his own slaves, knows exactly what he has to pay. Those different taxes, however, being called by the same name, have been considered as of the same nature.

12   ^eThe taxes which in Holland are imposed upon men and maid servants, are taxes, not upon stock, but upon expence; and so far resemble the taxes upon consumable commodities. The tax of a guinea a head for every man servant, which has lately been imposed in Great Britain,[15] is of the same kind. It falls heaviest upon the middling rank. A man of two hundred a year may keep a single man servant. A man of ten thousand a year will not keep fifty. It does not affect the poor.^e

13   Taxes upon the profits of stock in particular employments can never affect the interest of money. Nobody will lend his money for less interest to those who exercise the taxed, than to those who exercise the untaxed employments. Taxes upon the revenue arising from stock in all employments, where the government attempts to levy them with any degree of

^{d-d} India *1*   ^{e-e} 2–6

---

[13] See above, III.ii.19.

[14] See above, III.iii.2. 'A capitation [tax] is more natural to slavery; a duty on merchandise is more natural to liberty, by reason it has not so direct a relation to the person.' (Montesquieu, *Esprit*, XIII.xiv.1.)

[15] 17 George III, c.39 (1777); 18 George III, c.30 (1778) made special arrangements for its collection in Scotland.

exactness, will, in many cases, fall upon the interest of money. [311] The Vingtieme, or twentieth penny, in France, is a tax of the same kind with what is called the land-tax in England, and is assessed, in the same manner, upon the revenue arising from land, houses, and stock. So far as it affects stock it is assessed, though not with great rigour, yet with much more exactness than that part of the land-tax of England which is imposed upon the same fund. It, in many cases, falls altogether upon the interest of money. Money is frequently sunk in France upon what are called Contracts for the constitution of a rent; that is, perpetual annuities redeemable at any time by the debtor upon *ʃrepaymentʃ* of the sum originally advanced, but of which this redemption is not exigible by the creditor except in particular cases. The Vingtieme seems not to have raised the rate of those annuities, though it is exactly levied upon them all.

APPENDIX TO ARTICLES I AND II
Taxes upon the Capital Value of Lands, Houses, and Stock

1   While property remains in the possession of the same person, whatever permanent taxes may have been imposed upon it, they have never been intended to diminish or take away any part of its capital value, but only some part of the revenue arising from it. But when property changes hands, when it is transmitted either from the dead to the living, or from the living to the [312] living, such taxes have frequently been imposed upon it as necessarily take away some part of its capital value.

2   The transference of all sorts of property from the dead to the living, and that of immoveable property, of *ᵃlandsᵃ* and houses, from the living to the living, are transactions which are in their nature either publick and notorious, or such as cannot be long concealed. Such transactions, therefore, may be taxed directly. The transference of stock, or *ᵇmoveableᵇ* property, from the living to the living, by the lending of money, is frequently a secret transaction, and may always be made so. It cannot easily, therefore, be taxed directly. It has been taxed indirectly in two different ways; first, by requiring that the deed, containing the obligation to repay, should be written upon paper or parchment which had paid a certain stamp-duty, otherwise not to be valid; secondly, by requiring, under the like penalty of invalidity, that it should be recorded either in a publick or secret register, and by imposing certain duties upon such registration. Stamp-duties and duties of registration have frequently been imposed likewise upon the deeds transferring property of all kinds from the dead to the living, and upon those transferring immoveable property from the living to the living, transactions which might easily have been taxed directly.

ʃ–ʃ payment 6
ᵃ–ᵃ land *1*   ᵇ immoveable *1* ⟨corrected *4e–6*⟩

3   The Vicesima Hereditatum, the twentieth penny of inheritances, imposed by Augustus upon the antient Romans, was a tax upon the [313] transference of property from the dead to the living.[1] Dion Cassius*, the author who writes concerning it the least indistinctly, says, that it was imposed upon all successions, legacies, and donations, in case of death, except upon those to the nearest relations, and to the poor.

4   Of the same kind is the Dutch tax upon successions†. Collateral successions are taxed, according to the degree of relation, from five to thirty per cent. upon the whole value of the succession. Testamentary donations, or legacies to collaterals, are subject to the like duties. Those from husband to wife, or from wife to husband, to the fiftieth[2] penny. The Luctuosa Hereditas, the mournful succession of ascendents to descendents, to the twentieth penny only. Direct successions, or those of descendents to ascendents, pay no tax. The death of a father, to such of his children as live in the same house with him, is seldom attended with any increase, and frequently with a considerable diminution of revenue; by the loss of his industry, of his office, or of some life-rent estate, of which he may have been in possession. That tax would be cruel and oppressive which aggravated their loss by taking from them any part of his succession. It may, however, sometimes be otherwise with those children who, in the language of the Roman [314] law, are said to be emancipated; in that of the Scotch law, to be foris-familiated; that is, who have received their portion, have got families of their own, and are supported by funds separate and independent of those of their father. Whatever part of his succession might come to such children, would be a real addition to their fortune, and might, therefore, perhaps, without more inconveniency than what attends all duties of this kind, be liable to some tax.

5   The casualties of the feudal law were taxes upon the transference of land, both from the dead to the living, and from the living to the living. In antient times they constituted in every part of Europe one of the principal branches of the revenue of the crown.

6   The heir of every immediate vassal of the crown paid a certain duty,

* Lib. 55. See also Burman de Vectigalibus pop. Rom. cap. xi. and Bouchaud de l'impot du vingtieme sur les successions [published in 1714 and 1766 respectively].

†ᶜMemoires concernant les Droits, &c. tom. i. p. 225.

ᶜ See 5–6

[1] 'When different men had proposed different schemes, he [Augustus] approved none of them, but established the tax of five per cent. on the inheritances and bequests which should be left by people at their death to any except very near relatives or very poor persons, representing that he had found this tax set down in Caesar's memoranda. It was, in fact, a method which had been introduced once before, but had been abolished later, and was now revived.' (*Dio's Roman History*, iv.25, translated by E. Cary in Loeb Classical Library (1917), vi.461.)

[2] De Beaumont says 'quinzième', and in the context of the next sentence 'fiftieth' should obviously read 'fifteenth'.

generally a year's rent, upon receiving the investiture of the estate. If the heir was a minor, the whole rents of the estate, during the continuance of the minority, devolved to the superior without any other charge, besides the maintenance of the minor, and the payment of the widow's dower, when there happened to be a dowager upon the land. When the minor came to be of age, another tax, called Relief, was still due to the superior, which generally amounted likewise to a year's rent.[3] A long minority, which in the present times so frequently disburdens a great estate of all its incumbrances, and restores the family to their antient splendor, could in those times have no such effect. The waste, and not the disincum-[315]brance of the estate, was the common effect of a long minority.[4]

7   By the feudal law the vassal could not alienate without the consent of his superior, who generally extorted a fine or composition for granting it. This fine, which was at first arbitrary, came in many countries to be regulated at a certain portion of the price of the land. In some countries, where the greater part of the other feudal customs have gone into disuse, this tax upon the alienation of land still continues to make a [d]very[d] considerable branch of the revenue of the sovereign. In the canton of Berne it is so high as a sixth part of the price of all noble fiefs; and a tenth part of that of all ignoble ones*. In the canton of Lucerne the tax upon the sale of lands is not universal, and takes place only in certain districts. But if any person sells his land, in order to remove out of the territory, he pays ten per cent. upon the whole price of the sale†. Taxes of the same kind upon the sale either of all lands, or of lands held by certain tenures, take place in many other countries, and make a more or less considerable branch of the revenue of the sovereign.

8   Such transactions may be taxed indirectly, by means either of stamp-duties, or of duties upon registration; and those duties either may or may not be proportioned to the value of the subject which is transferred.

9   [316] In Great Britain the stamp-duties are higher or lower, not so much according to the value of the property transferred (an eighteen penny or half crown stamp being sufficient upon a bond for the largest sum of

---

* Memoires concernant les Droits, &c. tome i. p. 154.

† Id. p. 157. ['. . . mais lorsqu'un particulier vent abdiquer son droit d'habitant & emporter sa fortune en pays étranger, il paye Dix pour cent de la vente de son bien.' (De Beaumont, *Mémoires*, i.157.)]

[d-d] 2–6

---

[3] LJ (B) 160, ed. Cannan 117, points out that 'As the feudal lord possessed the lands during a minority, before the minor could recover his estate he was obliged to pay what is called a relief.' LJ (A) i.125–6 discusses the burdens of wardenage and marriage, and points out that that of relief or suffrage sometimes involved more than a year's rent. See also LJ (A) ii.17–18; LJ (B) 53–7, ed. Cannan 36–40. Feudal casualties are also discussed in LJ (A) iv.127–9.

[4] See above, III.iv.9 and n.26.

money) as according to the nature of the deed. The highest do not exceed six pounds upon every sheet of paper, or skin of parchment; and these high duties fall chiefly upon grants from the crown, and upon certain law proceedings, without any regard to the value of the subject. There are in Great Britain no duties on the registration of deeds or writings, except the fees of the officers who keep the register; and these are seldom more than a reasonable recompence for their labour. The crown derives no revenue from them.

10   In Holland* there are both stamp-duties and duties upon registration; which in some cases are, and in some are not proportioned to the value of the property transferred. All testaments must be written upon stampt paper, of which the price is proportioned to the property disposed of, so that there are stamps which cost from three pence, or three stivers a sheet, to three hundred florins, equal to about twenty-seven *f*pounds*f* ten shillings of our money. If the stamp is of an inferior price to what the testator ought to have made use of, his succession is confiscated. This is over and above all their other taxes on succession. Except bills of exchange, and some other mercantile bills, all [317] other deeds, bonds, and contracts, are subject to a stamp-duty. This duty, however, does not rise in proportion to the value of the subject. All sales of land and of houses, and all mortgages upon either, must be registered, and, upon registration, pay a duty to the state of two and a half per cent. upon the amount of the price or *g*of*g* the mortgage. This duty is extended to the sale of all ships and vessels of more than two tons burthen, whether decked or undecked. These, it seems, are considered as a sort of houses upon the water. The sale of moveables, when it is ordered by a court of justice, is subject to the like duty of two and a half per cent.

11   In France there are both stamp-duties and duties upon registration. The former are considered as a branch of the aides or excise, and in the provinces where those duties take place, are levied by the excise officers. The latter are considered as a branch of the domain of the crown, and are levied by a different set of officers.

12   Those modes of taxation, by stamp-duties and by duties upon registration, are of very modern invention. In the course of little more than a century, however, stamp-duties have, in Europe, become almost universal, and duties upon registration extremely common. There is no art which one government sooner learns of another than that of draining money from the pockets of the people.[5]

---

*⁂ Memoires concernant les Droits, &c. tome*e* i. p. 213, 224, 225. [Details are given in De Beaumont, *Mémoires*, i, especially 224–5.]

e–e Id. tom. *1–2*   *f–f* pound *1*   *g–g* om. *1*

[5] In Letter 228 addressed to Grey Cooper, dated 2 June 1783, Smith wrote: 'I acknowledge, I had not the most distant idea that the stamp duties could have afforded such

13   Taxes upon the transference of property from the dead to the living,
fall finally as well as im-[318]mediately upon the person to whom the
property is transferred. Taxes upon the sale of land fall altogether upon
the seller. The seller is almost always under the necessity of selling, and
must, therefore, take such a price as he can get. The buyer is scarce ever
under the necessity of buying, and will, therefore, *ʰonly giveʰ* such a price
as he likes. He considers what the land will cost him in tax and price
together. The more he is obliged to pay in the way of tax, the less he will
be disposed to give in the way of price. Such taxes, therefore, fall almost
always upon a necessitous person, and must, therefore, be frequently very
cruel and oppressive. Taxes upon the sale of new-built houses, where the
building is sold without the ground, fall generally upon the buyer, because
the builder must generally have his profit; otherwise he must give up the
trade. If he advances the tax, therefore, the buyer must generally repay it
to him. Taxes upon the sale of old houses, for the same reason as those
upon the sale of land, fall generally upon the seller; whom in most cases
either conveniency or necessity obliges to sell. The number of new-built
houses that are annually brought to market, is more or less regulated by the
demand.[6] Unless the demand is such as to afford the builder his profit,
after paying all expences, he will build no more houses. The number of old
houses which happen at any time to come to market is regulated by accidents of which the greater part have no relation to the demand. Two or three
great bankruptcies in a mercantile [319] town, will bring many houses
to sale, which must be sold for what can be got for them. Taxes upon the
sale of ground rents fall altogether upon the seller; for the same reason as
those upon the sale of land. Stamp duties, and duties upon the registration
of bonds and contracts for borrowed money, fall altogether upon the bor-
rower, and, in fact, are always paid by him. Duties of the same kind upon
law proceedings fall upon the suitors. They reduce to both the capital value
of the subject in dispute. The more it costs to acquire any property, the
less must be the *ⁱneatⁱ* value of it when acquired.

14   All taxes upon the transference of property of every kind, so far as they
diminish the capital value of that property, tend to diminish the funds
destined for the maintenance of productive labour. They are all more or
less unthrifty taxes that increase the revenue of the sovereign, which
seldom maintains any *ʲbutʲ* unproductive labourers; at the expence of the
capital of the people, which maintains none but productive.[7]

ʰ⁻ʰ give only *1*   *ⁱ⁻ⁱ* 2–6   *ʲ⁻ʲ* om. 2–3

resources as my Lord John Cavendish had shewn that they can . . . tho' I had turned over
in my mind the subject of our national resources with as much attention as I could, I
must own that none occured to me that would be so little burdensome to the People as
these that have been fallen upon.' As Chancellor, Cavendish introduced a receipts tax in
the budget of 1782–3.

    [6] Smith comments on the demand for new houses at V.ii.e.20.   [7] Above, II.iii.2.

15   Such taxes, even when they are proportioned to the value of the property transferred, are still unequal; the frequency of transference not being always equal in property of equal value. When they are not proportioned to this value, which is the case with the greater part of the stamp-duties, and duties of registration, they are still more so. They are in no respect arbitrary, but are or may be in all cases perfectly clear and certain. Though they sometimes fall upon the person who is not very able to pay; the time of [320] payment is in most cases sufficiently convenient for him. When the payment becomes due, he must in most cases have the money to pay. They are levied at very little expence, and in general subject the contributors to no other inconveniency besides always the unavoidable one of paying the tax.

16   In France the stamp-duties are not much complained of. Those of registration, which they call the Contrôle, are. They give occasion, it is pretended, to much extortion in the officers of the farmers general who collect the tax, which is in a great measure arbitrary and uncertain. In the greater part of the libels which have been written against the present system of finances in France, the abuses of the Contrôle make a principal article. Uncertainty however, does not seem to be necessarily inherent in the nature of such taxes. If the popular complaints are well founded, the abuse must arise, not so much from the nature of the tax, as from the want of precision and distinctness in the words of the edicts or laws which impose it.

17   The registration of mortgages, and in general of all rights upon immoveable property, as it gives great security both to creditors and purchasers, is extremely advantageous to the publick. That of the greater part of deeds of other kinds is frequently inconvenient and even dangerous to individuals, without any advantage to the publick. All registers which, it is acknowledged, ought to be kept secret, ought certainly never to exist. The credit of individuals ought certainly never to depend upon so very slender a secu-[321]rity as the probity and religion of the inferior officers of revenue. But where the fees of registration have been made a source of revenue to the sovereign, register offices have commonly been multiplied without end, both for the deeds which ought to be registered, and for those which ought not. In France there are several different sorts of secret registers. This abuse, though not perhaps a necessary, it must be acknowledged, is a very natural effect of such taxes.

18   Such stamp-duties as those in England upon cards and dice, upon newspapers and periodical pamphlets, &c. are properly taxes upon consumption; the final payment falls upon the persons who use or consume such commodities. Such stamp-duties as those upon licences to retail ale, wine and spirituous liquors, though intended, perhaps, to fall upon the profits of the retailers, are likewise finally paid by the consumers of those liquors.

Such taxes, though called by the same name, and levied by the same officers and in the same manner with the stamp-duties above mentioned upon the transference of property, are however of a quite different nature, and fall upon quite different funds.[8]

ARTICLE III

Taxes upon the Wages of Labour

1   The wages of the inferior classes of workmen, I have endeavoured to show in the first book, are every where necessarily regulated by [322] two different circumstances; the demand for labour, and the ordinary or average price of provisions. The demand for labour, according as it happens to be either increasing, stationary, or declining; or to require an increasing, stationary, or declining population, regulates the subsistence of the labourer, and determines in what degree it shall be, either liberal, moderate, or scanty. The ordinary or average price of provisions determines the quantity of money which must be paid to the workman in order to enable him, one year with another, to purchase this liberal, moderate, or scanty subsistence.[1] While the demand for labour and the price of provisions, therefore, remain the same, a direct tax upon the wages of labour can have no other effect than to raise them somewhat higher than the tax. Let us suppose, for example, that in a particular place the demand for labour and the price of provisions were such, as to render ten shillings a week the ordinary wages of labour; and that a tax of one-fifth, or four shillings in the pound, was imposed upon wages. If the demand for labour and the price of provisions remained the same, it would still be necessary that the labourer should in that place earn such a subsistence as could be bought only for ten shilling a week, or that after paying the tax he should have ten shillings a week free wages. But in order to leave him such free wages after paying such a tax, the price of labour must in that place soon rise, not to twelve shillings a week only, but to twelve and sixpence; that is, in order to enable him to [323] pay a tax of one-fifth, his wages must necessarily soon rise, not one-fifth part only, but one-fourth. Whatever was the proportion of the tax, the wages of labour must in all cases rise, not only in that proportion, but in a higher proportion. If the tax, for example, was one-tenth, the wages of labour must necessarily soon rise, not one-tenth part only, but one-eighth.

2   A direct tax upon the wages of labour, therefore, though the labourer might perhaps pay it out of his hand, could not properly be said to be even advanced by him; at least if the demand for labour and the average price

---

[8] See below, V.ii.k.6, where Smith discusses the incidence of taxes on luxuries, including spirituous liquors.

[1] See above, I.viii.52.

of provisions remained the same after the tax as before it. In all such cases, not only the tax, but something more than the tax, would in reality be advanced by the person who immediately employed him. The final payment would in different cases fall upon different persons. The rise which such a tax might occasion in the wages of manufacturing labour would be advanced by the master manufacturer, who would both be entitled and obliged to charge it, with a profit, upon the price of his goods. The final payment of this rise of wages, therefore, together with the additional profit of the master manufacturer, would fall upon the consumer. The rise which such a tax might occasion in the wages of country labour would be advanced by the farmer, who, in order to maintain the same number of labourers as before, would be obliged to employ a greater capital. In order to get back this greater capital, together with the ordinary profits [324] of stock, it would be necessary that he should retain a larger portion, or what comes to the same thing, the price of a larger portion, of the produce of the land, and consequently that he should pay less rent to the landlord.[2] The final payment of this rise of wages, therefore, would in this case fall upon the landlord, together with the additional profit of the farmer who had advanced it. In all cases, a direct tax upon the wages of labour must, in the long run, occasion both a greater reduction in the rent of land, and a greater rise in the price of manufactured goods, than would have followed from the proper assessment of a sum equal to the produce of the tax, partly upon the rent of land, and partly upon consumable commodities.

3   If direct taxes upon the wages of labour have not always occasioned a proportionable rise in those wages, it is because they have generally occasioned a considerable fall in the demand for labour. The declension of industry, the decrease of employment for the poor, the diminution of the annual produce of the land and labour of the country, have generally been the effects of such taxes. In consequence of them, however, the price of labour must always be higher than it otherwise would have been in the actual state of the demand: and this enhancement of price, together with the profit of those who advance it, must always be finally paid by the landlords and consumers.

4   A tax upon the wages of country labour does not raise the price of the rude produce of land *ᵃin proportion to the taxᵃ*; for the same reason that a [325] tax upon the farmers profit does not raise that price *ᵇin that proportionᵇ*.

5   Absurd and destructive as such taxes are, however, they take place in many countries. In France that part of the taille which is charged upon

---

ᵃ⁻ᵃ 2–6   ᵇ⁻ᵇ 2–6

[2] The incidence of taxation on rent is discussed, for example, at V.ii.f.2, V.ii.g.8, V.iii.54.

the industry of workmen and day-labourers in country villages, is properly a tax of this kind. Their wages are computed according to the common rate of the district in which they reside, and that they may be as little liable as possible to any over-charge, their yearly gains are estimated at no more than two hundred working days in the year*. The tax of each individual is varied from year to year according to different circumstances, of which the collector or the commissary, whom the intendant appoints to assist him, are the judges. In Bohemia, in consequence of the alteration in the system of finances which was begun in 1748, a very heavy tax is imposed upon the industry of artificers. They are divided into four classes. The highest class pay a hundred florins a year; which, at two and twenty-pence halfpenny a florin, amounts to 9*l*. 7*s*. 6*d*. The second class are taxed at seventy; the third at fifty; and the fourth, comprehending artificers in villages, and the lowest class of those in towns, at twenty-five florins†.

6   The recompence of ingenious artists and of men of liberal professions, I have endeavoured to show in the first book,[3] necessarily keeps a certain proportion to the emoluments of inferior [326] trades. A tax upon this recompence, therefore, could have no other effect than to raise it somewhat higher than in proportion to the tax. If it did not rise in this manner, the ingenious arts and the liberal professions, being no longer upon a level with other trades, would be so much deserted that they would soon return to that level.

7   The emoluments of offices are not, like those of trades and professions, regulated by the free competition of the market, and do not, therefore, always bear a just proportion to what the nature of the employment requires.[4] They are, perhaps, in most countries, higher than it requires; the persons who have the administration of government being generally disposed to reward both themselves and their immediate dependents rather more than enough. The emoluments of offices, therefore, can in most cases very well bear to be taxed. The persons, besides, who enjoy publick offices, especially the more lucrative, are in all countries the objects of general envy; and a tax upon their emoluments, even though it should be somewhat higher than upon any other sort of revenue, is always a very popular tax. In England, for example, when by the land-tax every other sort of revenue was supposed to be assessed at four shillings in the pound, it was very popular to lay a real tax of five shillings *d*and sixpence*d* in the pound upon the salaries of offices which exceeded a hundred pounds a

---

*ᶜ Memoires concernant les Droits, &c.ᶜ tom. ii. p. 108. ['. . . leur cote sera établie sur le pied que se paye la journée dans le pays, & à raison seulement de deux cents journées de travail par année.' (De Beaumont, *Mémoires*, ii.108.)]

† Id. tom. iii. p. 37. [Not as cited, but De Beaumont, *Mémoires*, i. 87.]

ᶜ⁻ᶜ Id. *1*   *d–d* 3–6

³ I.x.b.   ⁴ See above, I.x.a.1.

year; ᵉthe pensions of the younger branches of the royal family, the pay of the officers of the army and navy,ᵉ and a [327] few others less obnoxious to envy excepted.⁵ There are in England no other direct taxes upon the wages of labour.

ARTICLE IV
Taxes which, it is intended, should fall indifferently upon every different Species of Revenue

1   The taxes which, it is intended, should fall indifferently upon every different species of revenue, are capitation taxes, and taxes upon consumable commodities. These must be paid indifferently from whatever revenue the contributors may possess; from the rent of their land, from the profits of their stock, or from the wages of their labour.

Capitation Taxes

2   Capitation taxes, if it is attempted to proportion them to the fortune or revenue of each contributor, become altogether arbitrary.¹ The state of a man's fortune varies from day to day, and without an inquisition more intolerable than any tax, and renewed at least once every year, can only be guessed at. His assessment, therefore, must in most cases depend upon the good or bad humour of his assessors, and must, therefore, be altogether arbitrary and uncertain.

3   Capitation taxes, if they are proportioned not to the supposed fortune, but to the rank of each contributor, become altogether unequal; [328] the degrees of fortune being frequently unequal in the same degree of rank.

4   Such taxes, therefore, if it is attempted to render them equal, become altogether arbitrary and uncertain; and if it is attempted to render them certain and not arbitrary, become altogether unequal. Let the tax be light or heavy, uncertainty is always a great grievance. In a light tax a considerable degree of inequality may be supported; in a heavy one it is altogether intolerable.

ᵉ⁻ᵉ those of the judges *1–2*

⁵ By 31 George II, c.22 (1757) a tax of 1*s.* in the £ was levied on offices with an income exceeding £100. Smith apparently adds 1*s.* to the 4*s.* of the land tax. 5*s.* 6*d.* is a mistake, as Smith himself became aware. In Letter 208 addressed to Andreas Holt, dated 26 October 1780, Smith cites the original formulation of this passage as a blunder, the 'grossest in the whole Book, and which arose from trusting too much to memory', even although it 'does not in the least affect the reasoning, or conclusion it was brought to support'. In correcting the passage, Smith remarked to Holt that 'The tax upon salaries amounts, not to five shillings only, but to five and sixpence in the pound; and the salaries of Judges are not exempted from it. The only salaries exempted are the pensions of the younger branches of the Royal family, and the pay of the Officers of the army and Navy.'

¹ Poll taxes and hearth money are described as 'improper taxes' in LJ (A) v.141.

5   In the different poll-taxes which took place in England during the reign
of William III. the contributors were, the greater part of them, assessed
according to the degree of their rank; as dukes, marquisses, earls, viscounts,
barons, esquires, gentlemen, the eldest and youngest sons of peers, &c.[2]
All shopkeepers and tradesmen worth more than three hundred pounds,
that is, the better sort of them, were subject to the same assessment; how
great soever might be the difference in their fortunes.[3] Their rank was more
considered than their fortune. Several of those who in the first poll-tax
were rated according to their supposed fortune, were afterwards rated
according to their rank. Serjeants, attorneys, and proctors at law, who in the
first poll-tax were assessed at three shillings in the pound of their supposed
income, were afterwards assessed as gentlemen.[4] In the assessment of a
tax which was not very heavy, a considerable degree of inequality had been
found less insupportable than any degree of uncertainty.

6   [329] In the capitation which has been levied in France without any
interruption since the beginning of the present century, the highest
orders of people are rated according to their rank by an invariable tariff;
the lower orders of people, according to what is supposed to be their
fortune, by an assessment which varies from year to year. The officers of
the king's court, the judges and other officers in the superior courts of
justice, the officers of the troops, &c. are assessed in the first manner. The
inferior ranks of people in the provinces are assessed in the second. In
France the great easily submit to a considerable degree of inequality in a
tax which, so far as it affects them, is not a very heavy one; but could not
brook the arbitrary assessment of an intendant. The inferior ranks of
people must, in that country, suffer patiently the usage which their superiors
think proper to give them.

7   In England the different poll-taxes never produced the sum which
had been expected from them, or which, it was supposed, they might
have produced, had they been exactly levied. In France the capitation
always produces the sum expected from it. The mild government of
England, when it assessed the different ranks of people to the poll-tax,
contented itself with what that assessment happened to produce; and required no compensation for the loss which the state might sustain either
by those who could not pay, or by those who would not pay (for there were
many such), and who, by the indulgent [330] execution of the law, were not
forced to pay. The more severe government of France assesses upon each
generality a certain sum, which the intendant must find as he can. If any
province complains of being assessed too high, it may, in the assessment
of next year, obtain an abatement proportioned to the over-charge of the
year before: But it must pay in the mean time. The intendant, in order to

---

[2] 1 William and Mary, sess.1, c.13 (1688).
[3] 1 William and Mary, sess.2, c.7 (1688).   [4] 3 William and Mary, c.6 (1691).

be sure of finding the sum assessed upon his generality, was impowered to assess it in a larger sum, that the failure or inability of some of the contributors might be compensated by the over-charge of the rest; and till 1765, the fixation of this surplus assessment, was left altogether to his discretion. In that year indeed the council assumed this power to itself. In the capitation of the provinces, it is observed by the perfectly well-informed author of the Memoirs upon the impositions in France, the *a*proportion*a* which falls upon the nobility, and upon those whose privileges exempt them from the taille, is the least considerable. The largest falls upon those subject to the taille, who are assessed to the capitation at so much a pound of what they pay to that other tax.[5]

8　Capitation taxes, so far as they are levied upon the lower ranks of people, are direct taxes upon the wages of labour, and are attended with all the inconveniencies of such taxes.

9　Capitation taxes are levied at little expence; and, where they are rigorously exacted, afford a very sure revenue to the state. It is upon this account that in countries where the ease, com-[331]fort, and security of the inferior ranks of people are little attended to, capitation taxes are very common. It is in general, however, but a small part of the publick revenue, which, in a great empire, has ever been drawn from such taxes; and the greatest sum which they have ever afforded, might always have been found in some other way much more convenient to the people.

Taxes upon consumable Commodities

1　The impossibility of taxing the people, in proportion to their revenue, by any capitation, seems to have given occasion to the invention of taxes upon consumable commodities. The state not knowing how to tax, directly and proportionably, the revenue of its subjects, endeavours to tax it indirectly by taxing their expence, which, it is supposed, will in most cases be nearly in proportion to their revenue. Their expence is taxed by taxing the consumable commodities upon which it is laid out.[1]

2　Consumable commodities are either necessaries or luxuries.

3　By necessaries I understand, not only the commodities which are

---

a-a portion *1*

[5] 'C'est ici le lieu d'observer que dans la masse totale de cette imposition, la Capitation de la Noblesse & des Privilégies forme dans les provinces l'objet le moins considérable, la portion la plus forte est celle qui est répartie entre les taillables & non-privilégiés, au marc la livre de la Taille.' (De Beaumont, *Mémoires*, ii.421.)

[1] LJ (B) 311, ed. Cannan 240, comments: 'When taxes are laid out upon commodities, their prices must rise, the concurrence of tradesmen must be prevented, an artificial dearth occasioned, less industry excited, and a smaller quantity of goods produced.'

indispensably necessary for the support of life, but whatever the custom of the country renders it indecent for creditable people, even of the lowest order, to be without.[2] A linen shirt, for example, is, strictly speaking, not a necessary of life. The Greeks and Romans [332] lived, I suppose, very comfortably, though they had no linen. But in the present times, through the greater part of Europe, a creditable day-labourer would be ashamed to appear in publick without a linen shirt, the want of which would be supposed to denote that disgraceful degree of poverty, which, it is presumed, no body can well fall into without extreme bad conduct. Custom, in the same manner, has rendered leather shoes a necessary of life in England. The poorest creditable person of either sex would be ashamed to appear in publick without them.[3] In Scotland, custom has rendered them a necessary of life to the lowest order of men; but not to the same order of women, who may, without any discredit, walk about bare-footed. In France, they are necessaries neither to men nor to women; the lowest rank of both sexes appearing there publickly, without any discredit, sometimes in wooden shoes, and sometimes bare-footed. Under necessaries therefore, I comprehend, not only those things which nature, but those things which the established rules of decency have rendered necessary to the lowest rank of people. All other things, I call luxuries; without meaning by this appellation, to throw the smallest degree of reproach upon the temperate use of them. Beer and ale, for example, in Great Britain, and wine, even in the wine countries, I call luxuries. A man of any rank may, without any reproach, abstain totally from tasting such liquors. Nature does [333] not

---

[2] See above, I.viii.15, where Smith indicates the difficulty of defining the subsistence wage. Writing in 1767, Adam Ferguson made a related point in stating that 'The *necessary of life* is a vague and a relative term: it is one thing in the opinion of the savage; another in that of the polished citizen: it has a reference to the fancy and to the habits of living.' (*History of Civil Society*, III.iv, ed. Forbes (Edinburgh, 1966), 142.) Sir James Steuart provides an interesting commentary on the point at issue in the *Principles*, II.xxi, in arguing that mankind have two kinds of 'necessary'; the physical needs for food, shelter, etc., and an additional set of requirements 'which distinguishes what we call *rank* in society', where the latter is determined by 'birth, education, or habit. A man with difficulty submits to descend from a higher way of living to a lower'. (*Principles*, i.312–13, ed. Skinner, i.270; see above, II.iii.40.) Steuart provided an illustration of the 'physical necessary' in his *Considerations on the Interest of the County of Lanark in Scotland* (1769) in *Works* (London, 1805), v.291–2. Referring to the conditions in the county he stated that with oatmeal at 1s. per peck, the day-labourer could subsist at the level of the 'pure physical necessary' where his wages of 3s. 6d. per week were supplemented by the produce of a cow, one half rood of ground, and his wife's spinning. He added: 'However poor this life may appear to those who do not enter into such disquisitions, such, however, in fact it is with us . . .' See above, I.viii.31 and note.

[3] Mandeville made a related point, that in seeking to be well thought of, and even to change their status, people might be led to sacrifice their standard of subsistence: 'The poorest Labourer's Wife in the Parish, who scorns to wear a strong wholesom Frize, as she might, will half starve her self and her Husband to purchase a second-hand Gown and Petticoat, that cannot do her half the Service; because, forsooth, it is more genteel.' (*The Fable of the Bees*, pt.i.132, ed. Kaye i.129.)

render them necessary for the support of life; and custom no where renders it indecent to live without them.[4]

4   As the wages of labour are every where regulated, partly by the demand for it, and partly by the average price of the necessary articles of subsistence; whatever raises this average price must necessarily raise those wages, so that the labourer may still be able to purchase that quantity of those necessary articles which the state of the demand for labour, whether increasing, stationary, or declining, requires that he should have*. A tax upon those articles necessarily raises their price somewhat higher than the amount of the tax, because the dealer, who advances the tax, must generally get it back with a profit. Such a tax must, therefore, occasion a rise in the wages of labour proportionable to this rise of price.[5]

5   It is thus that a tax upon the necessaries of life, operates exactly in the same manner as a direct tax upon the wages of labour. The labourer, though he may pay it out of his hand, cannot, for any considerable time at least, be properly said even to advance it. It must always in the long-run be advanced to him by his immediate employer in the advanced rate of his wages. His employer, if he is a manufacturer, will charge upon the price of his goods this rise of wages, together with a profit; so that the final payment of the tax, together with this over-charge, will fall upon the consumer. If his employer is a [334] farmer, the final payment, together with a like over-charge, will fall upon the rent of the landlord.

6   It is otherwise with taxes upon what I call luxuries; even upon those of the poor. The rise in the price of the taxed commodities, will not necessarily occasion any rise in the wages of labour. A tax upon tobacco, for example, though a luxury of the poor as well as of the rich, will not raise wages. Though it is taxed in England at three times, and in France at fifteen times its original price, those high duties seem to have no effect upon the wages of labour. The same thing may be said of the taxes upon tea and sugar; which in England and Holland have become luxuries of the lowest ranks of people; and of those upon chocolate, which in Spain is said to have become so. The different taxes which in Great Britain have

---

* See Book I. Chap. 8. [I.viii.52].

[4] See below, V.iii.75, where it is stated that sugar, rum, and tobacco, though not necessaries, are objects of|universal consumption and therefore suitable for taxation.

[5] It is argued in LJ (B) 230–1, ed. Cannan 178–9, that taxes on 'industry', along with those on necessities, tend to raise the market price of commodities above the natural price, and thus diminish 'public opulence'. Cf. LJ (A) vi.85. In Letter 299 addressed to Sir John Sinclair, undated, Smith wrote: 'I dislike all taxes that may affect the necessary expenses of the poor. They, according to circumstances, either oppress the people immediately subject to them, or are repaid with great interest by the rich, i.e. by their employers in the advanced wages of their labour. Taxes upon the *luxuries* of the poor, upon their beer and other spirituous liquors, for example, so long as they are so moderate as not to give much temptation to smuggling, I am so far from disapproving, that I look upon them as the best of sumptuary laws.'

in the course of the present century been imposed upon spirituous liquors, are not supposed to have had any effect upon the wages of labour. The rise in the price of porter, occasioned by an additional tax of three shillings upon the barrel of strong beer,[6] has not raised the wages of common labour in London. These were about eighteen-pence and twenty-pence a day before the tax, and they are not more now.[7]

7   The high price of such commodities does not necessarily diminish the ability of the inferior ranks of people to bring up families. Upon the sober and industrious poor, taxes upon such commodities act as sumptuary laws, and dispose them either to moderate, or to refrain altogether from [335] the use of superfluities which they can no longer easily afford.[8] Their ability to bring up families, in consequence of this forced frugality, instead of being diminished, is frequently, perhaps, increased by the tax.[9] It is the sober and industrious poor who generally bring up the most numerous families, and who principally supply the demand for useful labour. All the poor indeed are not sober and industrious, and the dissolute and disorderly might continue to indulge themselves in the use of such commodities after this rise of price in the same manner as before; without regarding the distress which this indulgence might bring upon their families. Such disorderly persons, however, seldom rear up numerous families; their children generally perishing from neglect, mismanagement, and the scantiness or unwholesomeness of their food. If by the strength of their constitution they survive the hardships to which the bad conduct of their parents exposes them; yet the example of that bad conduct commonly corrupts their morals; so that, instead of being useful to society by their industry, they become publick nuisances by their vices and disorders. Though the advanced price of the luxuries of the poor, therefore, might increase somewhat the distress of such disorderly families, and thereby diminish somewhat their ability to bring up children; it would not probably diminish much the useful population of the country.

8   Any rise in the average price of necessaries, unless it is compensated by a proportionable rise in the wages of labour, must necessarily diminish

---

[6] 1 George III, c.7 (1760).

[7] It is suggested in LJ (B) 231, ed. Cannan 179, that 'Man is an anxious animal and must have his care swept off by something that can exhilerate the spirits.' It is remarked in LJ (A) vi.85 that 'Strong liquors are allmost a necessity in every nation. Man is a carefull animall, has many wants and necessities, and is in a continuall care and anxiety for his support.' In this connection see also LJ (B) 315, ed. Cannan 243: 'when an additional tax is laid upon beer the price of it must be raised, but the mob do not directly vent their malice against the government, who are the proper objects of it, but upon the brewers, as they confound the tax price with the natural one.'

[8] See above, I.viii.35, and below, V.ii.k.50, where it is noted that current policy was designed to discourage the consumption of spirits.

[9] See above, I.viii.37. This example may suggest that tax may be used as an instrument of control as distinct from a source of revenue. See V.ii.c.12, for a further example, and cf. V.ii.k.27.

[336] more or less the ability of the poor to bring up numerous families, and consequently to supply the demand for useful labour; whatever may be the state of that demand, whether increasing, stationary, or declining; or such as requires an increasing, stationary, or declining population.

9   Taxes upon luxuries have no tendency to raise the price of any other commodities except that of the commodities taxed. Taxes upon necessaries, by raising the wages of labour, necessarily tend to raise the price of all manufactures, and consequently to diminish the extent of their sale and consumption. Taxes upon luxuries are finally paid by the consumers of the commodities taxed, without any retribution. They fall indifferently upon every species of revenue, the wages of labour, the profits of stock, and the rent of land. Taxes upon necessaries, so far as they affect the labouring poor, are finally paid, partly by landlords in the diminished rent of their lands, and partly by rich consumers, whether landlords or others, in the advanced price of manufactured goods; and always with a considerable over-charge. The advanced price of such manufactures as are real necessaries of life, and are destined for the consumption of the poor, of coarse woollens, for example, must be compensated to the poor by a farther advancement of their wages. The middling and superior ranks of people, if they understood their own interest, ought always to oppose all taxes upon the necessaries of life, as well as all direct taxes upon the wages of labour. The final pay-[337]ment of both the one and the other falls altogether upon themselves, and always with a considerable over-charge. They fall heaviest upon the landlords, who always pay in a double capacity; in that of landlords, by the reduction of their rent; and in that of rich consumers, by the increase of their expence. The observation of Sir Matthew Decker, that certain taxes are, in the price of certain goods, sometimes repeated and accumulated four or five times, is perfectly just with regard to taxes upon the necessaries of life. In the price of leather, for example, you must pay, not only for the tax upon the leather of your own shoes, but for a part of that upon those of the shoe-maker and the tanner. You must pay too for the tax upon the salt, upon the soap, and upon the candles which those workmen consume while employed in your service, and for the tax upon the leather, which the salt-maker, the soap-maker, and the candle-maker consume while employed in their service.[10]

---

[10] After examining the increase because of the leather tax, as Smith outlines it, Decker continued: 'So much for the tax on leather only: but the grazier, butcher, tanner, leather-cutter and shoe maker, use sope; that sope, like leather is taxed; and like the leather-tax must be raised; but that caused twelve advances on shoes—true; place therefore twelve advances more on shoes for the sope tax. These tradesmen use candles—twelve advances more for the tax on them; and the same for every other tax on necessities.' (*Essay on the Causes of the Decline of Foreign Trade* (London, 1740) 24–5.) Decker is cited as an 'excellent authority' at IV.v.a.20.

10   In Great Britain, the principal taxes upon the necessaries of life are those upon the four commodities just now mentioned, salt, leather, soap, and candles.[11]

11   Salt is a very ancient and a very universal subject of taxation. It was taxed among the Romans, and it is so at present in, I believe, every part of Europe. The quantity annually consumed by any individual is so small, and may be purchased so gradually, that nobody, it seems to have been thought, could feel very sensibly even a pretty heavy tax upon it. It is [338] in England taxed at three shillings *and four-pence*[a] a bushel; about three times the original price of the commodity. In some other countries the tax is still higher. Leather is a real necessary of life. The use of linen renders soap such. In countries where the winter nights are long, candles are a necessary instrument of trade. Leather and soap are in Great Britain taxed at three halfpence a pound; candles at a penny;[12] taxes which, upon the original price of leather, may amount to about eight or ten per cent.; upon that of soap to about twenty or five and twenty per cent.; and upon that of candles to about fourteen or fifteen per cent.; taxes which, though lighter than that upon salt, are still very heavy. As all those four commodities are real necessaries of life, such heavy taxes upon them must increase somewhat the expence of the sober and industrious poor, and must consequently raise more or less the wages of their labour.[13]

12   In a country where the winters are so cold as in Great Britain, fuel is, during that season, in the strictest sense of the word, a necessary of life, not only for the purpose of dressing victuals, but for the comfortable subsistence of many different sorts of workmen who work within doors; and coals are the cheapest of all fuel.[14] The price of fuel has so important an influence upon that of labour, that all over Great Britain manufactures have confined themselves principally to the coal *countries*[b]; other parts of the country, on account of the high price of this necessary article, not being able to work so cheap. In some manu-[339]factures, besides, coal is a necessary instrument of trade; as in those of glass, iron, and all other metals.[15] If a bounty could in any case be reasonable, it might perhaps be so upon the transportation of coals from those parts of the country in which they abound, to those in which they are wanted. But the legislature, instead of a bounty, has imposed a tax of three shillings and three-pence a

---

a–a om. *1* ⟨corrected *1e–6*⟩   *b–b* counties 6

[11] See above, I.viii.35.

[12] Tallow candles; wax candles were taxed at 8*d*. H. Saxby, *The British Customs* (London, 1757), 51–2.

[13] Taxes on necessities are stated to be inconsiderable in Great Britain, at V.ii.k.79.

[14] See above, I.xi.c.18.

[15] Coal is also described as an 'instrument of trade' at IV.viii.42; for further examples of the use of this term, see IV.viii.1, where it is stated that the fabrication of the instruments of trade had become a specialized function, and cf. IV.viii.38.

ton upon coal carried coastways;[16] which upon most sorts of coal is more than sixty per cent. of the original price at the coal-pit. Coals carried either by land or by inland navigation pay no duty. Where they are naturally cheap, they are consumed duty free: Where they are naturally dear, they are loaded with a heavy duty.[17]

13   Such taxes, though they raise the price of subsistence, and consequently the wages of labour, yet they afford a considerable revenue to government, which it might not be easy to find in any other way. There may, therefore, be good reasons for continuing them. The bounty upon the exportation of corn,[18] so far as it tends in the actual state of tillage to raise the price of that necessary article, produces all the like bad effects; and instead of affording any revenue, frequently occasions a very great expence to government.[19] The high duties upon the importation of foreign corn, which in years of moderate plenty amount to a prohibition;[20] and the absolute prohibition of the importation either of live cattle or of salt provisions, which takes place in the ordinary state of the law,[21] and which, [340] on account of the scarcity, is at present suspended for a limited time with regard to Ireland and the British plantations,[22] have all the bad effects of taxes upon the necessaries of life, and produce no revenue to government. Nothing seems necessary for the repeal of such regulations, but to convince the publick of the futility of that system in consequence of which they have been established.

14   Taxes upon the necessaries of life are much higher in many other countries than in Great Britain. Duties upon flour and meal when ground at the mill, and upon bread when baked at the oven, take place in many countries. In Holland the money price of the bread consumed in towns is supposed to be doubled by means of such taxes. In lieu of a part of them, the people who live in the country pay every year so much a head, according to the sort of bread they are supposed to consume. Those who consume wheaten bread, pay three gilders fifteen stivers; about six shillings and ninepence halfpenny. These, and some other taxes of the same kind, by raising the price of labour, are said to have ruined the greater part of the

---

[16] 8 Anne, c.10 (1709) in *Statutes of the Realm*, ix.207; 8 Anne, c.4 in Ruffhead's edition, and 9 Anne, c.6 (1710) and subsequent acts. H. Saxby, *The British Customs* (London, 1757), 52–5 and 307.

[17] See above, IV.viii.42.

[18] 1 William and Mary, c.12 (1688). See also I.xi.g.4, III.iv.20, IV.v.a.5, IV.v.b.37.

[19] Smith comments at IV.v.a.7 on the bounty and its supposed encouragement to tillage, and see also IV.v.a.24.

[20] 22 Charles II, c.13 (1670). See also III.iv.20, IV.ii.1, IV.ii.16, IV.v.a.23, IV.v.b.33, IV.v.b.37, IV.vii.b.33.

[21] Above, IV.ii.1.

[22] Prohibition by 18 and 19 Charles II, c.2 (1666) in *Statutes of the Realm*, v.597; 18 Charles II, c.2 in Ruffhead's edition. Imports from Ireland were allowed by 32 George II, c.11 (1758), 5 George III, c.10 (1765) and 12 George III, c.2 (1772). See above, III.iv.20 and IV.ii.1.

manufactures of Holland*. Similar taxes, though not quite so heavy, take place in the Milanese, in the states of Genoa, in the dutchy of Modena, in the dutchies of Parma, Placentia, and Guastalla, and in the ecclesiastical state. A French† author [341] of some note has proposed to reform the finances of his country, by substituting in the room of the greater part of other taxes, this most ruinous of all taxes. There is nothing so absurd, says Cicero, which has not sometimes been asserted by some philosophers.[23]

15   Taxes upon butchers meat are still more common than those upon bread. It may indeed be doubted whether butchers meat is any where a necessary of life.[24] Grain and other vegetables, with the help of milk, cheese, and butter, or oil, where butter is not to be had, it is known from experience, can, without any butchers meat, afford the most plentiful, the most wholesome, the most nourishing, and the most invigorating diet.[25] Decency no where requires that any man should eat butchers meat, as it in most places requires that he should wear a linen shirt or a pair of leather shoes.

16   Consumable commodities, whether necessaries or luxuries, may be taxed in two different ways. The consumer may either pay an annual sum on account of his using or consuming goods of a certain kind; or the goods may be taxed while they remain in the hands of the dealer, and before they are delivered to the consumer. The consumable goods which last a considerable time before they are consumed altogether, are most properly taxed in the one way.[26] Those of which the consumption is either immediate or more speedy, in the other. The coach-tax and plate-tax are examples of the former method [342] of imposing: The greater part of the other duties of excise and customs, of the latter.

* Memoires concernant les.Droits, &c. p. 210, 211 [De Beaumont, *Mémoires*, i.210–11. He also commented: 'Les Impôts sont extrêmement multipliés en Hollande: le nombre & la nature de ces différens impôts paroissent même difficiles à concilier avec ce que sembleroient exiger l'industrie & le commerce.' (*Mémoires*, i.202.) 'Les droits d'Accises sont en général trop multipliés & trop considérables. Il en résulte de jour en jour la chute des manufactures, qui ne peuvent soutenir la concurrence avec l'étranger, parce que la main-d'oeuvre y est portée à un prix excessit; ainsi les habitans des villes qui sont éloignées du commerce maritime sont pauvres, les marchands ne s'y soutiennent qu' à peine; cette même circonstance de la cherté de la main-d'oeuvre pour tous les ouvrages qui tiennent au commerce & à la marine, affecte aussi les principales branches du commerce, & notamment la pêche du Hareng & de la Baleine, & la construction des vaisseaux, ce qui influe nécessairement sur le commerce en général.' (*Mémoires*, i.233.) See below, V.ii.k.79.]

† Le Reformateur. [Steuart also cites this authority, *Principles*, ii.567, ed. Skinner, ii.727.]

[23] 'Somehow or other no statement is too absurd for some philosophers to make.' (Cicero, *De Divinatione*, ii.58, translated by W. A. Falconer in Loeb Classical Library (1922), 504–5.)
[24] See above, I.xi.e.29, where it is stated that butcher's meat normally makes a small part of the subsistence of the labourer, except in the most thriving states.
[25] See above, I.viii.33. Smith comments at I.xi.b.41 on the invigorating qualities of potatoes.
[26] Smith makes the point concerning the rate at which goods are used up, above, II.i.12.

17 A coach may, with good management, last ten or twelve years. It might be taxed, once for all, before it comes out of the hands of the coach-maker. But it is certainly more convenient for the buyer to pay four pounds a year for the privilege of keeping a coach, than to pay all at once forty or forty-eight pounds additional price to the coach-maker; or a sum equivalent to what the tax is likely to cost him during the time he uses the same coach. A service of plate, in the same manner, may last more than a century. It is certainly easier for the consumer to pay five shillings a year for every hundred ounces of plate, near one per cent. of the value, than to redeem this long annuity at five and twenty or thirty years purchase, which would enhance the price at least five and twenty or thirty per cent. The different taxes which affect houses are certainly more conveniently paid by moderate annual payments, than by a heavy tax of equal value upon the first building or sale of the house.

18 It was the well-known proposal of Sir Matthew Decker, that all commodities, even those of which the consumption is either immediate or very speedy, should be taxed in this manner;[27] the dealer advancing nothing, but the consumer paying a certain annual sum for the licence to consume certain goods. The object of his scheme was to promote all the different branches [343] of foreign trade, particularly the carrying trade, by taking away all duties upon importation and exportation, and thereby enabling the merchant to employ his whole capital and credit in the purchase of goods and the freight of ships, no part of either being diverted towards the advancing of taxes. The project, however, of taxing, in this manner, goods of immediate or speedy consumption, seems liable to the four following very important objections. First, the tax would be more unequal, or not so well proportioned to the expence and consumption of the different contributors, as in the way in which it is commonly imposed. The taxes upon ale, wine, and spirituous liquors, which are advanced by the dealers, are finally paid by the different consumers exactly in proportion to their respective consumption. But if the tax ᶜwasᶜ to be paid by purchasing a licence to drink those liquors, the sober would, in proportion to his consumption, be taxed much more heavily than the drunken consumer. A family which exercised great hospitality would be taxed much more lightly than one ᵈwhoᵈ entertained fewer guests. Secondly, this mode of taxation, by paying for an annual, half-yearly, or quarterly licence to consume certain goods, would diminish very much one of the principal conveniencies

ᶜ⁻ᶜ were *4–6*   ᵈ⁻ᵈ which *1*

---

[27] 'That all persons using, wearing, or drinking the following articles of luxury, as particularly specified [list follows], be obliged to take out a license yearly, paying each one subsidy for each article of three-halfpence in the pound only, on the computed income they should have to support the station of life they voluntarily place themselves in by the article of luxury they use, wear, or drink.' (M. Decker, *Essay on the Causes of the Decline of Foreign Trade*, 67.) See below, V.iii.74.

of taxes upon goods of speedy consumption; the piece-meal payment. In the price of three-pence halfpenny, which is at present paid for a pot of porter, the different taxes upon malt, hops, and beer, together with the extraordinary profit which the [344] brewer charges for having advanced them, may perhaps amount to about three halfpence. If a workman can conveniently spare those three halfpence, he buys a pot of porter. If he cannot, he contents himself with a pint, and, as a penny saved is a penny got, he thus gains a farthing by his temperance. He pays the tax piece-meal, as he can afford to pay it, and when he can afford to pay it; and every act of payment is perfectly voluntary, and what he can avoid if he chuses to do so. Thirdly, such taxes would operate less as sumptuary laws. When the licence was once purchased, whether the purchaser drunk much or drunk little, his tax would be the same. Fourthly, if a workman *e*was*e* to pay all at once, by yearly, half-yearly, or quarterly payments, a tax equal to what he at present pays, with little or no inconveniency, upon all the different pots and pints of porter which he drinks in any such period of time, the sum might frequently distress him very much. This mode of taxation, therefore, it seems evident, could never, without the most grievous oppression, produce a revenue nearly equal to what is derived from the present mode without any oppression. In several countries, however, commodities of an immediate or very speedy consumption are taxed in this manner. In Holland, people pay so much a head for a licence to drink tea. I have already mentioned a tax upon bread, which, so far as it is consumed in farmhouses and country villages, is there levied in the same manner.[28]

19   [345] The duties of excise are imposed chiefly upon goods of home produce destined for home consumption. They are imposed only upon a few sorts of goods of the most general use. There can never be any doubt either concerning the goods which are subject to those duties, or concerning the particular duty which each species of goods is subject to. They fall almost altogether upon what I call luxuries, excepting always the four duties abovementioned, upon salt, soap, leather, candles, and, perhaps, that upon green glass.

20   The duties of customs are much more ancient than those of excise. They seem to have been called customs, as denoting customary payments which had been in use from time immemorial.[29] They appear to have been originally considered as taxes upon the profits of merchants. During the barbarous times of feudal anarchy, merchants, like all the other inhabitants

e-e were 4-6

---

[28] Above, § 14.

[29] 'The term "Customs" was anciently used in an extensive sense for customary payments or dues of many kinds, whether regal, or episcopal, or ecclesiastical, till in process of time it was restricted to the duties payable to the King, either upon the exportation or importation, or carriage coastwise, of certain articles of commerce.' (*Public Income and Expenditure*, Part II, 405, *British Parliamentary Papers, 1868–69*, XXV.)

of burghs, were considered as little better than emancipated bondmen, whose persons were despised, and whose gains were envied.[30] The great nobility, who had consented that the king should tallage the profits of their own tenants, were not unwilling that he should tallage likewise those of an order of men whom it was much less their interest to protect.[31] In those ignorant times, it was not understood, that the profits of merchants are a subject not taxable directly; or that the final payment of all such taxes must fall, with a considerable over-charge, upon the consumers.

21   [346] The gains of alien merchants were looked upon more unfavourably than those of English merchants. It was natural, therefore, that those of the former should be taxed more heavily than those of the latter. This distinction between the duties upon aliens and those upon English merchants, which was begun from ignorance, has been continued from the spirit of monopoly, or in order to give our own merchants an advantage both in the home and in the foreign market.[32]

22   With this distinction, the ancient duties of customs were imposed equally upon all sorts of goods, necessaries as well as luxuries, goods exported as well as goods imported. Why should the dealers in one sort of goods, it seems to have been thought, be more favoured than those in another? or why should the merchant exporter be more favoured than the merchant importer?

23   The ancient customs were divided into three branches. The first, and perhaps the most ancient of all those duties, was that upon wool and leather. It seems to have been chiefly or altogether an exportation duty. When the woollen manufacture came to be established in England, lest the king should lose any part of his customs upon wool by the exportation of woollen cloths, a like duty was imposed upon them.[33] The other two branches were, first, a duty upon wine, which being imposed at so much a ton, was called a tonnage; and, secondly, a duty upon all other goods, which, being imposed at so [347] much a pound of their supposed value, was called a poundage. In the forty-seventh year of Edward III. a duty of sixpence in the pound was imposed upon all goods exported and imported, except wools, wool-fells, leather, and wines, which were subject to particular duties. In the fourteenth of Richard II. this duty was raised to one shilling in the pound; but three years afterwards, it was again reduced to sixpence. It was raised to eight-pence in the second year of Henry IV.; and in the fourth year of the same prince, to one shilling. From this time to the ninth year of William III. this duty continued at one shilling in the pound. The duties of tonnage and poundage were generally granted to the king by one

---

[30] See above, III.iii.   [31] See above, III.ii.19.
[32] Though mitigated on exports by 25 Charles II, c.6 (1672). See above, IV.ii.30, IV.iii.c.10, IV.iv.3.
[33] Cf. IV.viii.17.

and the same act of parliament, and were called the Subsidy of Tonnage and Poundage. The subsidy of poundage having continued for so long a time at one shilling in the pound, or at five per cent.; a subsidy came, in the language of the customs, to denote a general duty of this kind of five per cent. This subsidy, which is now called the Old Subsidy, still continues to be levied according to the book of rates established in the twelfth of Charles II.[34] The method of ascertaining, by a book of rates, the value of goods subject to this duty, is said to be older than the time of James I. The new subsidy imposed by the ninth and tenth of William III.,[35] was an additional five per cent. upon the greater part of goods. The one-third[36] and the two-third[37] subsidy made up between them another five per [348] cent. of which they were proportionable parts. The subsidy of 1747[38] made a fourth five per cent. upon the greater part of goods; and that of 1759,[39] a fifth upon some particular sorts of goods. Besides those five subsidies, a great variety of other duties have occasionally been imposed upon particular sorts of goods, in order sometimes to relieve the exigencies of the state, and sometimes to regulate the trade of the country, according to the principles of the mercantile system.

24   That system has come gradually more and more into fashion. The old subsidy was imposed indifferently upon exportation as well as importation. The four subsequent subsidies, as well as the other duties which have since been occasionally imposed upon particular sorts of goods, have, with a few exceptions, been laid altogether upon importation. The greater part of the ancient duties which had been imposed upon the exportation of the goods of home produce and manufacture, have either been lightened or taken away altogether. In most cases they have been taken away. Bounties have even been given upon the exportation of some of them. Drawbacks too, sometimes of the whole, and, in most cases, of a part of the duties which are paid upon the importation of foreign goods, have been granted upon their exportation. Only half the duties imposed by the old subsidy upon importation are drawn back upon exportation:[40] but the whole of those imposed by the *latter* subsidies and other imposts are, upon [349] the greater part

– later *1*

---

[34] 12 Charles II, c. 4 (1660). See also IV.iv.3, IV.v.b.37, IV.viii.41.

[35] 9 William III, c. 23 (1697) in *Statutes of the Realm*, vii.382–5; 9 and 10 William III, c. 23 in Ruffhead's edition. See IV.iv.9.

[36] 2 and 3 Anne, c. 18 (1703) in *Statutes of the Realm*, viii.295–300; 2 and 3 Anne, c. 9 in Ruffhead's edition imposed a duty of one-third of 5 per cent. See above, IV.iv.9.

[37] 3 and 4 Anne, c. 3 (1704) in *Statutes of the Realm*, viii.332–6; 3 and 4 Anne, c. 5 in Ruffhead's edition imposed a duty of two-thirds of 5 per cent. See above, IV.iv.9.

[38] 21 George II, c. 2 (1747).

[39] 32 George II, c. 10 (1758). See above, V.ii.g.4.

[40] By the second of the rules annexed to 12 Charles II, c. 4 (1660). See above, IV.iv.3, IV.v.b.37, IV.viii.41.

of goods, drawn back in the same manner.[41] This growing favour of exportation, and discouragement of importation, have suffered only a few exceptions, which chiefly concern the materials of some manufactures.[42] These,
our merchants and manufacturers are willing should come as cheap as
possible to themselves, and as dear as possible to their rivals and competitors
in other countries. Foreign materials are, upon this account, sometimes
allowed to be imported duty free; Spanish wool,[43] for example, flax,[44] and
raw linen yarn.[45] The exportation of the materials of home produce, and of
those which are the *gpeculiarg* produce of our colonies, has sometimes been
prohibited, and sometimes subjected to higher duties. The exportation of
English wool has been prohibited.[46] That of beaver skins,[47] of beaver wool,
and of gum Senega,[48] has been subjected to higher duties; Great Britain,
by the conquest of Canada and Senegal, having got almost the monopoly
of those commodities.

25   That the mercantile system has not been very favourable to the revenue
of the great body of the people, to the annual produce of the land and labour
of the country, I have endeavoured to shew in the fourth book of this
inquiry. It seems not to have been more favourable to the revenue of the
sovereign; so far at least as that revenue depends upon the duties of
customs.

26   In consequence of that system, the importation of several sorts of goods
has been prohibited altogether. This prohibition has in some cases [350]
entirely prevented, and in others *hhash* very much diminished the importation of those commodities, by reducing the importers to the necessity of
smuggling. It has entirely prevented the importation of foreign woollens;
and it has very much diminished that of foreign silks and velvets. In both
cases it has entirely annihilated the revenue of customs which might have
been levied upon such importation.

27   The high duties which have been imposed upon the importation of many
different sorts of foreign goods, in order to discourage their consumption

---

g-g particular 4–6
h-h 2–6

---

[41] 7 George I, st. 1, c. 21 (1720) standardized arrangements for drawbacks. See above,
IV.iv.3.
[42] See above, IV.vii.c.40, where Smith explained this aspect of colonial policy; see also
IV.viii.1 and, generally, IV.viii.
[43] H. Saxby, *The British Customs*, 143. See also IV.viii.3.
[44] 4 George II, c. 27 (1730). See above, IV.viii.3.
[45] 29 George II, c. 15 (1756), continued by 10 George III, c. 38 (1770) and 19 George
III, c. 27 (1779). See above, IV.viii.4.
[46] 14 Charles II, c. 18 (1662) in *Statutes of the Realm*, v.410–12; 13 and 14 Charles II,
c. 18 in Ruffhead's edition, and others. See above, IV.viii.18.
[47] See above, IV.viii.41.
[48] 5 George III, c. 37 (1765) and 14 George III, c. 10 (1774). See above, IV.viii.40.

in Great Britain, have in many cases served only to encourage smuggling;[49] and in all cases have reduced the revenue of the customs below what more moderate duties would have afforded. The saying of Dr. Swift, that in the arithmetick of the customs two and two, instead of making four, make sometimes only one,[50] ⸲holds⸲ perfectly true with regard to such heavy duties, which never could have been imposed, had not the mercantile system taught us, in many cases, to employ taxation as an instrument, not of revenue, but of monopoly.[51]

28   The bounties which are sometimes given upon the exportation of home produce and manufactures, and the drawbacks which are paid upon the re-exportation of the greater part of foreign goods, have given occasion to many frauds, and to a species of smuggling more destructive of the publick revenue than any other. In order to obtain the bounty or drawback, the goods, it is well known, are sometimes [351] shipped and sent to sea; but soon afterwards clandestinely relanded in some other part of the country. The defalcation of the revenue of customs occasioned by bounties and drawbacks, of which a great part are obtained fraudulently, is very great. The gross produce of the customs in the year which ended on the 5th of January 1755, amounted to 5,068,000*l*. The bounties which were paid out of this revenue, though in that year there was no bounty upon corn, amounted to 167,800*l*. The drawbacks which were paid upon debentures and certificates, to 2,156,800*l*. Bounties and drawbacks together, amounted to 2,324,600*l*. In consequence of these deductions the revenue of the customs amounted only to 2,743,400*l*.: from which, deducting 287,900*l*. for the expence of management in salaries and other incidents, the neat revenue of the customs for that year comes out to be 2,455,500*l*. The expence of management amounts in this manner to between five and six per cent. upon the gross revenue of the customs,[52] and to something more than ten per cent. upon what remains of that revenue, after deducting what is paid away in bounties and drawbacks.

⸲⸲ hold 2

[49] The relation between smuggling and high duties is mentioned at, for example, IV.vi.27, V.ii.b.6, V.ii.k.49, 75. It is stated at IV.iii.a.1 that trade between Britain and France was largely carried on by smuggling. In Letter 234 addressed to Smith, dated 18 December 1783, George Dempster wrote that the newly appointed 'Smuggling Committee' might seek his advice on 'the most effectual means of preventing smuggling, by which all the Information we have received has come to an alarming height, threatening the destruction of the Revenue, the fair trader, the Health & Morals of the people.'

[50] J. Swift, *An Answer to a Paper called a Memorial of the Poor Inhabitants, Tradesmen and Labourers of the Kingdom of Ireland* (Dublin, 1728), in *The Prose Works of Jonathan Swift*, ed. H. Davis (Oxford, 1955), xii.21.

[51] One some occasions Smith defended the use of taxation as an instrument of policy other than revenue raising; see, for example, V.ii.k.7, 12 and 50.

[52] See below, V.ii.k.62, where Smith discusses the revenue and expenditures for the year 1775.

29   Heavy duties being imposed upon almost all goods imported, our merchant importers smuggle as much, and make entry of as little as they can. Our merchant exporters, on the contrary, make entry of more than they export; sometimes out of vanity, and to pass for great dealers in goods which pay no duty; and sometimes to gain a [352] bounty or a drawback. Our exports, in consequence of these different frauds, appear upon the customhouse books greatly to overbalance our imports; to the unspeakable comfort of those politicians who measure the national prosperity by what they call the balance of trade.[53]

30   All goods imported, unless particularly exempted, and such exemptions are not very numerous, are liable to some duties of customs. If any goods are imported not mentioned in the book of rates, they are taxed at 4s. 9$\frac{9}{20}$d. for every twenty shillings value,[54] according to the oath of the importer, that is, nearly at five subsidies, or five poundage duties. The book of rates is extremely comprehensive, and enumerates a great variety of articles, many of them little used, and therefore not well known. It is upon this account frequently uncertain under what article a particular sort of goods ought to be classed, and consequently what duty they ought to pay. Mistakes with regard to this sometimes ruin the customhouse officer, and frequently occasion much trouble, expence, and vexation to the importer. In point of perspicuity, precision, and distinctness, therefore, the duties of customs are much inferior to those of excise.

31   In order that the greater part of the members of any society should contribute to the publick revenue in proportion to their respective expence, it does not seem necessary that every single article of that expence should be taxed. The revenue, which is levied by the duties of excise, [353] is supposed to fall as equally upon the contributors as that which is levied by the duties of customs; and the duties of excise are imposed upon a few articles only of the most general use and consumption. It has been the opinion of many people, that, by proper management, the duties of customs might likewise, without any loss to the publick revenue, and with great advantage to foreign trade, be confined to a few articles only.

32   The foreign articles, of the most general use and consumption in Great Britain, seem at present to consist chiefly in foreign wines and brandies; in some of the productions of America and the West Indies, sugar, rum, tobacco, cocoa-nuts, &c. and in some of those of the East Indies, tea, coffee, china-ware, spiceries of all kinds, several sorts of piece-goods, &c. These different articles afford, perhaps, at present, the greater part of the revenue which is drawn from the duties of customs. The taxes which at present subsist upon foreign manufactures, if you except those upon the

---

[53] See below, V.iii.85, where Smith refers to 'a certain species of politician'. The doctrine of the balance of trade is discussed at IV.i.8.
[54] H. Saxby, *The British Customs*, 266.

few contained in the foregoing enumeration, have the greater part of them been imposed for the purpose, not of revenue, but of monopoly, or to give our own merchants an advantage in the home market. By removing all prohibitions, and by subjecting all foreign manufactures to such moderate taxes, as it was found from experience afforded upon each article the greatest revenue to the publick, our own workmen might still have a considerable advantage in the home market, and many ar-[354]ticles, some of which at present afford no revenue to government, and others a very inconsiderable one, might afford a very great one.

33   High taxes, sometimes by diminishing the consumption of the taxed commodities, and sometimes by encouraging smuggling, frequently afford a smaller revenue to government than what might be drawn from more moderate taxes.

34   When the diminution of revenue is the effect of the diminution of consumption, there can be but one remedy, and that is the lowering of the tax.

35   When the diminution of *ʲtheʲ* revenue is the effect of the encouragement given to smuggling, it may perhaps be remedied in two ways; either by diminishing the temptation to smuggle, or by increasing the difficulty of smuggling. The temptation to smuggle can be diminished only by the lowering of the tax; and the difficulty of smuggling can be increased only by establishing that system of administration which is most proper for preventing it.

36   The excise laws, it appears, I believe, from experience, obstruct and embarrass the operations of the smuggler much more effectually than those of the customs. By introducing into the customs a system of administration as similar to that of the excise as the nature of the different duties will admit, the difficulty of smuggling might be very much increased. This alteration, it has been supposed by many people, might very easily be brought about.

37   [355] The importer of commodities liable to any duties of customs, it has been said, might at his option be allowed either to carry them to his own private warehouse, or to lodge them in a warehouse provided either at his own expence or at that of the publick, but under the key of the customhouse officer, and never to be opened but in his presence. If the merchant carried them to his own private warehouse, the duties to be immediately paid, and never afterwards to be drawn back; and that warehouse to be at all times subject to the visit and examination of the customhouse officer, in order to ascertain how far the quantity contained in it corresponded with that for which the duty had been paid. If he carried them to the publick warehouse, no duty to be paid till they were taken out for home consumption. If taken out for exportation, to be duty-free; proper security being always given

that they should be so exported. The dealers in those particular commodities, either by wholesale or retail, to be at all times subject to the visit and examination of the customhouse officer; and to be obliged to justify by proper certificates the payment of the duty upon the whole quantity contained in their shops or warehouses. What are called the excise-duties upon rum imported are at present levied in this manner, and the same system of administration might perhaps be extended to all duties upon goods imported; provided always that those duties were, like the duties of excise, confined to a few sorts of goods of the most general use and con-[356]sumption. If they were extended to almost all sorts of goods, as at present, publick warehouses of sufficient extent could not easily be provided, and goods of a very delicate nature, or of which the preservation required much care and attention, could not safely be trusted by the merchant in any warehouse but his own.

38   If by such a system of administration smuggling, to any considerable extent, could be prevented even under pretty high duties; and if every duty was occasionally either heightened or lowered according as it was most likely, either the one way or the other, to afford the greatest revenue to the state; taxation being always employed as an instrument of revenue and never of monopoly; it seems not improbable that a revenue, at least equal to the present neat revenue of the customs, might be drawn from duties upon the importation of only a few sorts of goods of the most general use and consumption; and that the duties of customs might thus be brought to the same degree of simplicity, certainty, and precision, as those of excise. What the revenue at present loses, by drawbacks upon the re-exportation of foreign goods which are afterwards relanded and consumed at home, would under this system be saved altogether. If to this saving, which would alone be very considerable, ᵏwasᵏ added the abolition of all bounties upon the exportation of home-produce; in all cases in which those bounties were not in reality drawbacks of some duties of excise which had before been advanced; it cannot well be doubted but that the neat revenue [357] of customs might, after an alteration of this kind, be fully equal to what it had ever been before.

39   If by such a change of system the publick revenue suffered no loss, the trade and manufactures of the country would certainly gain a very considerable advantage. The trade in the commodities not taxed, by far the greatest number, would be perfectly free, and might be carried on to and from all parts of the world with every possible advantage. Among those commodities would be comprehended all the necessaries of life, and all the materials of manufacture. So far as the free importation of the necessaries of life reduced their average money price in the home market, it would reduce the money price of labour, but without reducing in any respect its

ᵏ⁻ᵏ were 4–6

real recompence.[55] The value of money is in proportion to the quantity of the necessaries of life which it will purchase. That of the necessaries of life is altogether independent of the quantity of money which can be had for them. The reduction in the money price of labour would necessarily be attended with a proportionable one in that of all home-manufactures, which would thereby gain some advantage in all foreign markets. The price of some manufactures would be reduced in a still greater proportion by the free importation of the raw materials. If raw silk could be imported from China and Indostan duty-free, the silk manufacturers in England could greatly undersell those of both France and Italy. There would be no occasion to prohibit the importation of foreign silks and velvets. The cheapness [358] of their goods would secure to our own workmen, not only the possession of the home, but a very great command of the foreign market. Even the trade in the commodities taxed would be carried on with much more advantage than at present. If those commodities were delivered out of the publick warehouse for foreign exportation, being in this case exempted from all taxes, the trade in them would be perfectly free. The carrying trade in all sorts of goods would under this system enjoy every possible advantage. If those commodities were delivered out for home-consumption, the importer not being obliged to advance the tax till he had an opportunity of selling his goods, either to some dealer, or to some consumer, he could always afford to sell them cheaper than if he had been obliged to advance it at the moment of importation. Under the same taxes, the foreign trade of consumption even in the taxed commodities, might in this manner be carried on with much more advantage than it can at present.

40   It was the object of the famous excise scheme of Sir Robert Walpole to establish, with regard to wine and tobacco, a system not very unlike that which is here proposed.[56] But though the bill which was then brought into parliament, comprehended those two commodities only; it was generally supposed to be meant as an introduction to a more extensive scheme of the same kind. Faction, combined with the interest of smuggling merchants, raised so violent, though so unjust, a clamour against that bill, that the [359] minister thought proper to drop it; and from a dread of exciting a clamour of the same kind, none of his successors have dared to resume the project.

41   The duties upon foreign luxuries imported for home-consumption, though they sometimes fall upon the poor, fall principally upon people of middling or more than middling fortune. Such are, for example, the duties upon foreign wines, upon coffee, chocolate, tea, sugar, &c.

---

[55] See above, I.viii.52, V.ii.i.1.

[56] In 1733. Similar points are made in LJ (B) 314, ed. Cannan 242, citing the examples of Walpole and Holland. Smith here refers to the 'famous excise scheme of Sir Robert Walpole, which was at last his ruin'. Walpole is also cited at 270, ed. Cannan 210–11. See below, 926 n. 52, and Corr., Letter 28, dated 21 February, 1759.

42   The duties upon the cheaper luxuries of home-produce destined for home-consumption, fall pretty equally upon people of all ranks in proportion to their respective expence. The poor pay the duties upon malt, hops, beer, and ale, upon their own consumption: The rich, *upon both* their own consumption and *m* that of their servants.

43   The whole consumption of the inferior ranks of people, or of those below the middling rank, it must be observed, is in every country much greater, not only in quantity, but in value, than that of the middling and of those above the middling rank. The whole expence of the inferior is much greater than that of the superior ranks. In the first place, almost the whole capital of every country is annually distributed among the inferior ranks of people, as the wages of productive labour.[57] Secondly, a great part of the revenue arising *from both* the rent of land and *o* the profits of stock, is annually distributed among the same rank, in the wages and maintenance of menial servants, and other unproductive labourers. Thirdly, some part of the profits [360] of stock belongs to the same rank, as a revenue arising from the employment of their small capitals. The amount of the profits annually made by small shopkeepers, tradesmen, and retailers of all kinds, is every where very considerable, and makes a very considerable portion of the annual produce. Fourthly, and lastly, some part even of the rent of land belongs to the same rank; a considerable part to those who are somewhat below the middling rank, and a small part even to the lowest rank; common labourers sometimes possessing in property an acre or two of land. Though the expence of those inferior ranks of people, therefore, taking them individually, is very small, yet the whole mass of it, taking them collectively, amounts always to by much the largest portion of the whole expence of the society; what remains, of the annual produce of the land and labour of the country for the consumption of the superior ranks, being always much less, not only in quantity but in value. The taxes upon expence, therefore, which fall chiefly upon that of the superior ranks of people, upon the smaller portion of the annual produce, are likely to be much less productive than, either those which fall indifferently upon the expence of all ranks, or even those which fall chiefly upon that of the inferior ranks; than either those which fall indifferently upon the whole annual produce, or those which fall chiefly upon the larger portion of it. The excise upon the materials and manufacture of home-made fermented and spirituous liquors is accordingly, [361] of all the different taxes upon expence, by far the most productive; and this branch of the excise falls very much, perhaps principally, upon the expence of the common people. In the year which ended

l-l both upon *1*   *m* upon *1*
n-n both from *1*   *o* from *1*

[57] See above, II.i.8, II.iii.7, II.v.11.

on the 5th of July 1775, the gross produce of this branch of the excise amounted to [p]3,341,837*l.* 9*s.* 9*d.*[p]

44 It must always be remembered, however, that it is the luxurious and not the necessary expence of the inferior ranks of people that ought ever to be taxed. The final payment of any tax upon their necessary expence would fall altogether upon the superior ranks of people; upon the smaller portion of the annual produce, and not upon the greater. Such a tax must in all cases either raise the wages of labour, or lessen the demand for it. It could not raise the wages of labour, without throwing the final payment of the tax upon the superior ranks of people. It could not lessen the demand for labour, without lessening the annual produce of the land and labour of the country, the fund [q]from[q] which all taxes must be finally paid. Whatever might be the state to which a tax of this kind reduced the demand for labour, it must always raise wages higher than they otherwise would be in that state; and the final payment of this enhancement of wages must in all cases fall upon the superior ranks of people.

45 Fermented liquors brewed, and spirituous liquors distilled, not for sale, but for private use, are not in Great Britain liable to any duties of excise.[58] This exemption, of which the object is [r]to save[r] private families [s]from[s] the odious visit and [362] examination of the tax-gatherer, occasions the burden of those duties to fall frequently much lighter upon the rich than upon the poor. It is not, indeed, very common to distil for private use, though it is done sometimes. But in the country, many middling and almost all rich and great families brew their own beer. Their strong beer, therefore, costs them eight shillings a barrel less than it costs the common brewer, who must have his profit upon the tax, as well as upon all the other expence which he advances. Such families, therefore, must drink their beer at least nine or ten shillings a barrel cheaper than any liquor of the same quality can be drunk by the common people, to whom it is every where more convenient to buy their beer, by little and little, from the brewery or the alehouse. Malt, in the same manner, that is made for the use of a private family, is not liable to the visit or examination of the tax-gatherer; but in this case the family must compound at seven shillings and sixpence a head for the tax. Seven shillings and sixpence are equal to the excise upon ten bushels of malt; a quantity fully equal to what all the different members of any sober family, men, women, and children, are at an average likely to consume. But in rich and great families, where country hospitality is much practised, the malt liquors consumed by the members of the family make but a small part of the consumption of the house. Either on account of this composition, however, or for other reasons, it is not near so common to

[p-p] 3,314,223 *l.* 18*s.* 10$\frac{3}{4}$*d.* *1* [q-q] upon *6* [r-r] not to expose *1* [s-s] to *1*

[58] This is said to be an unjust regulation at V.ii.k.55.

malt as to brew for private use. It is difficult to imagine any equitable [363] reason why those who either brew or distil for private use, should not be subject to a composition of the same kind.

46   A greater revenue than what is at present drawn from all the heavy taxes upon malt, beer, and ale, might be raised, it has frequently been said, by a much lighter tax upon malt; the opportunities of defrauding the revenue being much greater in a brewery than in a malt-house; and those who brew for private use being exempted from all duties or composition for duties, which is not the case with those who malt for private use.

47   In the porter brewery of London, a quarter of malt is commonly brewed into more than two barrels and a half, sometimes into three barrels of porter. The different taxes upon malt amount to six shillings a quarter; those upon strong beer and ale to eight shillings a barrel. In the porter brewery therefore, the different taxes upon malt, beer and ale, amount to between twenty-six and thirty shillings upon the produce of a quarter of malt. In the country brewery for common country sale, a quarter of malt is seldom brewed into less than two barrels of strong and one barrel of small beer; frequently into two barrels and a half of strong beer. The different taxes upon small beer amount to one shilling and four-pence a barrel. In the country brewery, therefore, the different taxes upon malt, beer, and ale, seldom amount to less than twenty-three shillings and four-pence, frequently to twenty-six shillings, upon the produce of a quarter of malt. Taking the whole kingdom at an average, therefore, the whole amount of the duties upon malt, beer, [364] and ale, cannot be estimated at less than twenty-four or twenty-five shillings upon the produce of a quarter of malt. But by the taking off all the different duties upon beer and ale, and by tripling the malt-tax, or by raising it from six to eighteen shillings upon the quarter of malt, a greater revenue, it is said, might be raised by this single tax than what is at present drawn from all those heavier taxes.

	l.	s.	d.
In 1772, the old malt tax produced	722,023	11	11
The additional	356,776	7	9¾
In 1773, the old tax produced	561,627	3	7½
The additional	278,650	15	3¾
In 1774, the old tax produced	621,614	17	5¾
The additional	310,745	2	8½
In 1775, the old tax produced	657,357	–	8¼
The additional	323,785	12	6¼
	4)3,835,580	12	–¾
Average of these four years	958,895	3	–1/16

In 1772, the country excise produced	1,243,128	5	3
The London brewery	408,260	7	$2\frac{3}{4}$
In 1773, the country excise	1,245,808	3	3
The London brewery	405,406	17	$10\frac{1}{2}$
In 1774, the country excise	1,246,373	14	$5\frac{1}{2}$
The London brewery	320,601	18	$-\frac{1}{4}$
In 1775, the country excise	1,214,583	6	1
The London brewery	463,670	7	$-\frac{1}{4}$

$$4)6,547,832 \quad 19 \quad 2\tfrac{1}{4}$$

Average of these four years	1,636,958	4	$9\frac{1}{2}$
To which adding the average malt tax, or	958,895	3	$-\frac{3}{16}$

The whole amount of those different⎱ taxes come out to be ⎰	2,595,853	7	$9\frac{11}{16}$

But by tripling the malt tax, or by raising it from six to eighteen shillings upon the quarter of malt, that single tax would produce	2,876,685	9	$-\frac{9}{16}$
A sum which exceeds the foregoing by	280,832	1	$2\frac{14}{16}$

48   [365] Under the old malt tax, indeed, is comprehended a tax of four shillings upon the hogshead of cyder, and another of ten shillings upon the barrel of mum. In 1774, the tax upon cyder produced only 3083*l.* 6*s.* 8*d.* It probably fell somewhat short of its usual amount; all the different taxes upon cyder having that year produced less than ordinary. The tax upon mum, though much heavier, is still less productive, on account of the smaller consumption of that liquor. But to balance whatever may be the ordinary amount of those two taxes; there is comprehended under what is called The country excise, first, the old excise of six shillings and eight-pence upon the hogs-head of cyder; secondly, a like tax of six shillings and eight-pence upon the hogshead of verjuice; thirdly, another of eight shillings and nine-pence upon the hogshead of vinegar; and, lastly, a fourth tax of eleven-pence upon the gallon of mead or metheglin: The produce of those different taxes will probably much more than counterbalance that of the duties imposed, by what is called The annual malt tax upon cyder and mum.

49   Malt is consumed not only in the brewery of beer and ale, but in the manufacture of low wines and spirits. If the malt tax ꞌwasꞌ to be raised to eighteen shillings upon the quarter, it might be necessary to make some abatement in the different excises which are imposed upon those particular

ꞌ⁻ꞌ were 4–6

sorts of low wines and spirits of which malt makes any part of the materials. In what are called Malt spirits, it makes commonly [366] but a third part of the materials; the other two-thirds being either raw barley, or one-third barley and one-third wheat. In the distillery of malt spirits, both the opportunity and the temptation to smuggle, are much greater than either in a brewery or in a malt-house; the opportunity, on account of the smaller bulk and greater value of the commodity; and the temptation, on account of the superior height of the duties, which amount to ^{u}3s. 10⅔d^u.* upon the gallon of spirits. By increasing the duties upon malt, and reducing those upon the distillery, both the opportunities and the temptation to smuggle would be diminished, which might occasion a still further augmentation of revenue.

50   It has for some time past been the policy of Great Britain to discourage the consumption of spirituous liquors, on account of their supposed tendency to ruin the health and to corrupt the morals of the common people. According to this policy, the abatement of the taxes upon the distillery ought not to be so great as to reduce in any respect the price of those liquors. Spirituous liquors might remain as dear as ever; while at the same time the wholesome and invigorating liquors of beer and ale might be considerably reduced in their price. The people might thus be in part relieved from one of the [367] burdens of which they at present complain the most; while at the same time the revenue might be considerably augmented.[59]

51   The objections of Dr. Davenant to this alteration in the present system of excise duties, seem to be without foundation. Those objections are, that the tax, instead of dividing itself as at present pretty equally upon the profit of the maltster, upon that of the brewer, and upon that of the retailer, would, so far as it affected profit, fall altogether upon that of the maltster; that the maltster could not so easily get back the amount of the tax in the advanced price of his malt, as the brewer and retailer in the advanced price of their liquor; and that so heavy a tax upon malt might reduce the rent and profit of barley land.[60]

^{v}* Though the duties directly imposed upon proof spirits amount only to 2s. 6d. per gallon, these added to the duties upon the low wines, from which they are distilled, amount to 3s. 10⅔d. Both low wines and proof spirits are, to prevent frauds, now rated according to what they gauge in the wash.^{v}

$^{u-u}$ 2s. 6d. *1–2* ⟨corrected *2e–6*⟩ $^{v-v}$ *3–6*

[59] See V.ii.k.7. It is stated at IV.iii.c.8 that a sudden reduction in taxes on beer might occasion 'a pretty general and temporary drunkenness'.

[60] D'avenant recognized the possibility of the transfer of the tax, though he still reached the same conclusion: 'The maltster . . . cannot so easily save himself upon the buyer and consumer; it will be difficult for him to raise the price of a dear commodity a full ⅓d. at once; so that he must bear the greatest part of the burthen himself, or throw it upon the farmer, by giving less for barley, which brings the tax directly upon the land of England'. (*The Political and Commercial Works*, ed. C. Whitworth, i.223.)

52   No tax can ever reduce, for any considerable time, the rate of profit in any particular trade, which must always keep its level with other trades in the neighbourhood. The present duties upon malt, beer and ale, do not affect the profits of the dealers in those commodities, who all get back the tax with an additional profit, in the enhanced price of their goods. A tax indeed may render the goods upon which it is imposed so dear as to diminish the consumption of them. But the consumption of malt is in malt liquors; and a tax of eighteen shillings upon the quarter of malt could not well render those liquors dearer than the different taxes, amounting to twenty-four or twenty-five shillings, do at present. Those liquors, on the contrary, would probably become cheaper, and the consumption [368] of them would be more likely to increase than to diminish.

53   It is not very easy to understand why it should be more difficult for the maltster to get back eighteen shillings in the advanced price of his malt, than it is at present for the brewer to get back twenty-four or twenty-five, sometimes thirty shillings, in that of his liquor. The maltster, indeed, instead of a tax of six shillings, would be obliged to advance one of eighteen shillings upon every quarter of malt. But the brewer is at present obliged to advance a tax of twenty-four or twenty-five, sometimes thirty shillings upon every quarter of malt which he brews. It could not be more inconvenient for the maltster to advance a lighter tax, than it is at present for the brewer to advance a heavier one. The maltster doth not always keep in his granaries a stock of malt which it will require a longer time to dispose of, than the stock of beer and ale which the brewer frequently keeps in his cellars. The former, therefore, may frequently get the returns of his money as soon as the latter. But whatever inconveniency might arise to the maltster from being obliged to advance a heavier tax, ^{w}it^w could easily be remedied by granting him a few months longer credit than is at present commonly given to the brewer.

54   Nothing could reduce the rent and profit of barley land which did not reduce the demand for barley. But a change of system, which reduced the duties upon a quarter of malt brewed into beer and ale from twenty-four and twenty-five shillings to eighteen shillings, would be [369] more likely to increase than diminish that demand. The rent and profit of barley land, besides, must always be nearly equal to those of other equally fertile and equally well-cultivated land. If they were less, some part of the barley land would soon be turned to some other purpose; and if they were greater, more land would soon be turned to the raising of barley.[61] When the ordinary price of any particular produce of land is at what may be called a monopoly price,[62] a tax upon it necessarily reduces the rent and profit of

$^{w-w}$ 2–6

---

[61] See above, I.xi.b.9.   [62] Monopoly price is defined at I.vii.27.

the land which grows it. A tax upon the produce of those precious vineyards, of which the wine falls so much short of the effectual demand,[63] that
its price is always above the natural proportion to that of the produce of
other equally fertile and equally well cultivated land, would necessarily
reduce the rent and profit of those vineyards.[64] The price of the wines
being already the highest that could be got for the quantity commonly
sent to market, it could not be raised higher without diminishing that
quantity; and the quantity could not be diminished without still greater
loss, because the lands could not be turned to any other equally valuable
produce. The whole weight of the tax, therefore, would fall upon the rent
and profit; properly upon the rent of the vineyard. When it has been
proposed to lay any new tax upon sugar, our sugar planters have frequently
complained that the whole weight of such taxes fell, not upon the consumer, but upon the producer; they never having been able to [370] raise
the price of their sugar after the tax, higher than it was before. The price
had, it seems, before the tax been a monopoly price; and the argument
adduced to shew that sugar was an improper subject of taxation, demonstrated, perhaps, that it was a proper one; the gains of monopolists,
whenever they can be come at, being certainly of all subjects the most
proper. But the ordinary price of barley has never been a monopoly
price; and the rent and profit of barley land have never been above their
natural proportion to those of other equally fertile and equally well-
cultivated land. The different taxes which have been imposed upon malt,
beer, and ale, have never lowered the price of barley; have never reduced
the rent and profit of barley land. The price of malt to the brewer has
constantly risen in proportion to the taxes imposed upon it; and those
taxes, together with the different duties upon beer and ale, have constantly
either raised the price, or what comes to the same thing, reduced the
quality of those commodities to the consumer. The final payment of those
taxes has fallen constantly upon the consumer, and not upon the producer.

55   The only people likely to suffer by the change of system here proposed,
are those who brew for their own private use. But the exemption, which
this superior rank of people at present enjoy, from very heavy taxes which
are paid by the poor labourer and artificer, is surely most unjust and unequal,[65] and ought to be taken away, [371] even though this change was
never to take place. It has probably been the interest of this superior order
of people, however, which has hitherto prevented a change of system that
could not well fail both to increase the revenue and to relieve the people.

56   Besides such duties as those of customs and excise above-mentioned,
there are several others which affect the price of goods more unequally and

---

[63] The term 'effectual demand' is defined at I.vii.8.
[64] Such precious vineyards are mentioned at I.vii.24 and I.xi.b.31.
[65] See above, V.ii.k.45.

more indirectly. Of this kind are the duties which in French are called Péages, which in old Saxon times were called Duties of Passage,[66] and which seem to have been originally established for the same purpose as our turnpike tolls, or the tolls upon our canals and navigable rivers, for the maintenance of the road or of the navigation. Those duties, when applied to such purposes, are most properly imposed according to the bulk or weight of the goods. As they were originally local and provincial duties, applicable to local and provincial purposes, the administration of them was in most cases entrusted to the particular town, parish, or lordship, in which they were levied; such communities being in some way or other supposed to be accountable for the application. The sovereign, who is altogether unaccountable, has in many countries assumed to himself the administration of those duties; and though he has in most cases enhanced very much the duty, he has in many entirely neglected the application. If the turnpike tolls of Great Britain should ever become one of the resources of government, we may [372] learn, by the example of many other nations, what would probably be the consequence.[67] Such tolls *are no doubt* finally paid by the consumer; but the consumer is not taxed in proportion to his expence when he pays, not according to the value, but according to the bulk or weight of what he consumes. When such duties are imposed, not according to the bulk or weight, but according to the supposed value of the goods, they become properly a sort of inland customs or excises, which obstruct very much the most important of all branches of commerce, the interior commerce of the country.[68]

57   In some small states duties similar to those passage duties are imposed upon goods carried across the territory, either by land or by water, from one foreign country to another. These are in some countries called transit-duties. Some of the little Italian states, which are situated upon the Po, and the rivers which run into it, derive some revenue from duties of this kind, which are paid altogether by foreigners, and *which, perhaps, are* the only duties that one state can impose upon the subjects of another, without obstructing in any respect the industry or commerce of its own. The most important transit-duty in the world is that levied by the king of Denmark upon all merchant ships which pass through the Sound.

58   Such taxes upon luxuries as the greater part of the duties of customs and excise, though they *all* fall indifferently upon every different species of revenue, and are paid finally, or without any [373] retribution, by whoever consumes the commodities upon which they are imposed, yet they do not

---

^x-x no doubt are 6   ^y-y which are perhaps *1*   ^z-z 2–6

[66] Peages are discussed at V.i.i.4 and duties of passage at III.iii.2.
[67] Smith considers this problem above, V.i.d.12.
[68] See above, V.i.d.4, 13.

always fall equally or *a*proportionably*a* upon the revenue of every individual.[69] As every man's humour, regulates the degree of his consumption,
every man contributes rather according to his humour than in proportion
to his revenue; the profuse contribute more, the parsimonious less, than
their proper proportion. During the minority of a man of great fortune, he
contributes commonly very little, by his consumption, towards the support
of that state from whose protection he derives a great revenue. Those who
live in another country contribute nothing, by their consumption, towards
the support of the government of that country, in which is situated the
source of their revenue. If in this latter country there should be no land-
tax, nor any considerable duty upon the transference either of moveable or
of immoveable property, as is the case in Ireland, such absentees may
derive a great revenue from the protection of a government to the support of
which they do not contribute a single shilling. This inequality is likely to
be greatest in a country of which the government is in some respects
subordinate and dependent upon that of some other. The people who possess
the most extensive property in the dependent, will in this case generally
chuse to live in the governing country. Ireland is precisely in this situation,
and we cannot therefore wonder that the proposal of a tax upon absentees
should be so very popular in that country. It might, [374] perhaps, be a
little difficult to ascertain either what sort, or what degree of absence
*b*would*b* subject a man to be taxed as an absentee, or at what precise time
the tax should either begin or end. If you except, however, this very peculiar situation, any inequality in the contribution of individuals, which can
arise from such taxes, is much more than compensated by the very circumstance which occasions that inequality; the circumstance that every man's
contribution is altogether voluntary; it being altogether in his power either
to consume or not to consume the commodity taxed. Where such taxes,
therefore, are properly assessed and upon proper commodities, they are
paid with less grumbling than any other. When they are advanced by the
merchant or manufacturer, the consumer, who finally pays them, soon
comes to confound them with the price of the commodities, and almost
forgets that he pays any tax.[70]

59   Such taxes are or may be perfectly certain, or may be assessed so as to
leave no doubt concerning either what ought to be paid, or when it ought

---

a-a proportionally 6   *b-b* should *1*

[69] Cf. LJ (B) 311, ed. Cannan 240: 'Excepting the land-tax, our taxes are generaly
upon commodities, and in these there is a much greater inequality than in the taxes upon
land possession. The consumptions of people are not always according to what they
possess, but in proportion to their liberality.'

[70] Cf. LJ (B) 315, ed. Cannan 243: 'The taxes on consumptions are not so much mur-
mured against, because they are laid upon the merchant, who lays them on the price of
goods, and thus they are insensibly paid by the people.' See above, 872 n. 7.

to be paid; concerning either the quantity or the time of payment. Whatever uncertainty there may sometimes be, either in the duties of customs in Great Britain, or in other duties of the same kind in other countries, it cannot arise from the nature of those duties, but from the inaccurate or unskilful manner in which the law that imposes them is expressed.

60   Taxes upon luxuries generally are, and always may be, paid piece-meal, or in proportion [375] as the contributors have occasion to purchase the goods upon which they are imposed. In the time and mode of payment they are, or may be, of all taxes the most convenient. Upon the whole, such taxes, therefore, are, perhaps, as agreeable to the three first of the four general maxims concerning taxation, as any other. They offend in every respect against the fourth.[71]

61   Such taxes, in proportion to what they bring into the publick treasury of the state, always take out or keep out of the pockets of the people more than almost any other taxes. They seem to do this in all the four different ways in which it is possible to do it.

62   First, the levying of such taxes, even when imposed in the most judicious manner, requires a great number of customhouse and excise officers, whose salaries and perquisites are a real tax upon the people, which brings nothing into the treasury of the state. This expence, however, it must be acknowledged, is more moderate in Great Britain than in most other countries. In the year which ended on the fifth of July 1775, the gross produce of the different duties, under the management of the commissioners of excise in England, amounted to ^{c}5,507,308*l.* 18*s.* 8¼*d.*^{c} which was levied at an expence of little more than five and a half per cent.[72] From this gross produce, however, there must be deducted what was paid away in bounties and drawbacks upon the exportation of exciseable goods, which will reduce the neat produce below five [376] millions*. The levying of the salt duty, an excise duty, but under a different management, is much more expensive. The neat revenue of the customs does not amount to two millions and a half, which is levied at an expence of more than ten per cent. in the salaries of officers, and other incidents. But the perquisites of customhouse officers are every where much greater than their salaries; at

---

^{d}* The neat produce of that year, after deducting all expences and allowances, amounted to 4,975,652 *l.* 19*s.* 6*d.*^{d}

$^{c-c}$ 5,479,695 *l.* 7*s.* 10*d.* 1 $^{d-d}$ 2–6

[71] In his essay 'Of Taxes', Hume said that 'the best taxes are such as are levied upon consumptions' and went on: 'They seem, in some measure, voluntary; since a man may chuse how far he will use the commodity which is taxed: They are paid gradually, and insensibly: They naturally produce sobriety and frugality, if judiciously imposed: And being confounded with the natural price of the commodity, they are scarcely perceived by the consumers. Their only disadvantage is, that they are expensive in the levying.' (*Essays Moral, Political, and Literary*, ed. Green and Grose, i.358.) See also 'Of Public Credit'.
[72] See above, V.ii.k.28.

some ports more than double or triple those salaries. If the salaries of officers, and other incidents, therefore, amount to more than ten per cent. upon the neat revenue of the customs; the whole expence of levying that revenue may amount, in salaries and perquisites together, to more than twenty or thirty per cent. The officers of excise receive few or no perquisites; and the administration of that branch of the revenue being of more recent establishment, is in general less corrupted than that of the customs, into which length of time has introduced and authorized many abuses. By charging upon malt the whole revenue which is at present levied by the different duties upon malt and malt liquors, a saving, it is supposed, of more than fifty thousand pounds might be made in the annual expence of the excise. By confining the duties of customs to a few sorts of goods, and by levying those duties according to the excise laws, a much greater saving might [377] probably be made in the annual expence of the customs.

63   Secondly, such taxes necessarily occasion some obstruction or discouragement to certain branches of industry. As they always raise the price of the commodity taxed, they so far discourage its consumption, and consequently its production. If it is a commodity of home growth or manufacture, less labour comes to be employed in raising and producing it. If it is a foreign commodity of which the tax increases in this manner the price, the commodities of the same kind which are made at home may thereby, indeed, gain some advantage in the home market, and a greater quantity of domestick industry may thereby be turned *etoward*e preparing them. But though this rise of price in a foreign commodity may encourage domestick industry in one particular branch, it necessarily discourages that industry in almost every other. The dearer the Birmingham manufacturer buys his foreign wine, the cheaper he necessarily sells that part of his hardware with which, or, what comes to the same thing, with the price of which he buys it. That part of his hardware, therefore, becomes of less value to him, and he has less encouragement to work at it. The dearer the consumers in one country pay for the surplus produce of another, the cheaper they necessarily sell that part of their own surplus produce with which, or, what comes to the same thing, with the price of which they buy it. That part of their own surplus produce [378] becomes of less value to them, and they have less encouragement to increase its quantity. All taxes upon consumable commodities, therefore, tend to reduce the quantity of productive labour below what it otherwise would be, either in preparing the commodities taxed, if they are home commodities; or in preparing those with which they are purchased, if they are foreign commodities. Such taxes too always alter, more or less, the natural direction of national industry, and turn it into a channel always different from, and generally

less advantageous than that in which it would have run of its own accord.[73]

64   Thirdly, the hope of evading such taxes by smuggling gives frequent occasion to forfeitures and other penalties, which entirely ruin the smuggler; a person who, though no doubt highly blameable for violating the laws of his country, is frequently incapable of violating those of natural justice, and would have been, in every respect, an excellent citizen, had not the laws of his country made that a crime which nature never meant to be so. In those corrupted governments where there is at least a general suspicion of much unnecessary expence, and great misapplication of the publick revenue, the laws which guard it are little respected. Not many people are scrupulous about smuggling, when, without perjury, they can find any easy and safe opportunity of doing so. To pretend to have any scruple about buying smuggled goods, though a manifest encouragement to the violation of the revenue laws, and to the perjury which almost [379] always attends it, would in most countries be regarded as one of those pedantick pieces of hypocrisy which, instead of gaining credit with any body, serve only to expose the person who affects to practise them, to the suspicion of being a greater knave than most of his neighbours. By this indulgence of the publick, the smuggler is often encouraged to continue a trade which he is thus taught to consider as in some measure innocent; and when the severity of the revenue laws is ready to fall upon him, he is frequently disposed to defend with violence, what he has been accustomed to regard as his just property. From being at first, perhaps, rather imprudent than criminal, he at last too often becomes one of the hardiest and most determined violators of the laws of society. By the ruin of the smuggler, his capital, which had before been employed in maintaining productive labour, is absorbed either in the revenue of the state or in that of the revenue-officer, and is employed in maintaining unproductive, to the diminution of the general capital of the society, and of the useful industry which it might otherwise have maintained.[74]

65   Fourthly, such taxes, by subjecting at least the dealers in the taxed commodities to the frequent visits and odious examination of the tax-gatherers,[75] expose them sometimes, no doubt, to some degree of oppression, and always to much trouble and vexation; and though vexation, as has already been said, is not strictly [380] speaking expence, it is certainly equivalent to the expence at which every man would be willing to redeem himself from it. The laws of excise, though more effectual for the purpose for which they were instituted, are, in this respect, more vexatious than those of the customs. When a merchant has imported goods subject to certain duties of customs, when he has paid those duties, and lodged the

[73] See above, IV.ii.3.   [74] See above, II.v.
[75] See for example, V.ii.b.6, V.iii.55 and 74.

goods in his warehouse, he is not in most cases liable to any further trouble or vexation from the custom-house officer. It is otherwise with goods subject to duties of excise. The dealers have no respite from the continual visits and examination of the excise officers. The duties of excise are, upon this account, more unpopular than those of the customs; and so are the officers who levy them. Those officers, it is pretended, though in general, perhaps, they do their duty fully as well as those of the customs; yet, as that duty obliges them to be frequently very troublesome to some of their neighbours, commonly contract a certain hardness of character which the others frequently have not. This observation, however, may very probably be the mere suggestion of fraudulent dealers, whose smuggling is either prevented or detected by their diligence.

66   The inconveniencies, however, which are, perhaps, in some degree inseparable from taxes upon consumable commodities, fall as light upon the people of Great Britain as upon those of any other country of which the government is nearly [381] as expensive. Our state is not perfect, and might be mended; but it is as good or better than that of most of our neighbours.

67   In consequence of the notion that duties upon consumable goods were taxes upon the profits of merchants, those duties have, in some countries, been repeated upon every successive sale of the goods. If the profits of the merchant importer or merchant manufacturer were taxed, equality seemed to require that those of all the middle buyers, who intervened between either of them and the consumer, should likewise be taxed. The famous Alcavala of Spain seems to have been established upon this principle. It was at first a tax of ten per cent., afterwards of fourteen per cent., and is at present of only six per cent. upon the sale of every sort of property, whether moveable or immovable; and it is repeated every time the property is sold.* The levying of this tax requires a multitude of revenue officers sufficient to guard the transportation of goods, not only from one province to another, but from one shop to another. It subjects, not only the dealers in some sorts of goods, but those in all sorts, every farmer, every manufacturer, every merchant and shop-keeper, to the continual visits and examination of the tax-gatherers. Through the greater part of a country in which a tax of this kind is established, nothing can be produced for distant sale. The produce of every part of the country must be [382] proportioned to the consumption of the neighbourhood. It is to the Alcavala, accordingly, that Ustaritz imputes the ruin of the manufactures of Spain.[76] He might

---

* Memoires concernant les Droits, &c. tom. i. p. 455. [Details of the administration are at i.456.]

---

[76] 'I have not been able to discover in France, England, or Holland . . . that they have ever laid any duty upon the sale or barter of their own woven and other manufactures, either upon the first, or any future sale. As then I find Spain alone groaning under this burden, and it is so very oppressive, as to lay ten per cent. for the primitive Alcavala, and the four one per cents annexed to it, a duty not only chargeable on the first sale, but on

have imputed to it likewise the declension of agriculture, it being imposed not only upon manufactures, but upon the rude produce of the land.

68   In the kingdom of Naples there is a similar tax of three per cent. upon the value of all contracts, and consequently upon that of all contracts of sale. It is both lighter than the Spanish tax, and the greater part of towns and parishes are allowed to pay a composition in lieu of it. They levy this composition in what manner they please, generally in a way that gives no interruption to the interior commerce of the place. The Neapolitan tax, therefore, is not near so ruinous as the Spanish one.

69   The uniform system of taxation, which, with a few exceptions of no great consequence, takes place in all the different parts of the united kingdom of Great Britain, leaves the interior commerce of the country, the inland and coasting trade, almost entirely free. The inland trade is almost perfectly free, and the greater part of goods may be carried from one end of the kingdom to the other, without requiring any permit or let-pass, without being subject to question, visit, or examination from the revenue officers. There are a few exceptions, but they are such as can give no interruption to any important branch of the inland commerce of the country. Goods carried coastwise, indeed, require certifi-[383]cates or coast-cockets. If you except coals, however, the rest are almost all duty-free. This freedom of interior commerce, the effect of the uniformity of the system of taxation, is perhaps one of the principal causes of the prosperity of Great Britain; every great country being necessarily the best and most extensive market for the greater part of the productions of its own industry.[77] If the same freedom, in consequence of the same uniformity, could be extended to Ireland and the plantations, both the grandeur of the state and the prosperity of every part of the empire, would probably be still greater than at present.

70   In France, the different revenue laws which take place in the different provinces, require a multitude of revenue officers to surround, not only the frontiers of the kingdom, but those of almost each particular province, in order either to prevent the importation of certain goods, or to subject it to the payment of certain duties, to the no small interruption of the interior commerce of the country.[78] Some provinces are allowed to compound for

every future sale of goods, I am jealous, it is one of the principal engines, that contributed to the ruin of most of our manufactures and trade.' (G. de Uztariz, *The Theory and Practice of Commerce*, trans. John Kippax, ii.236.) An additional problem with regard to Spain is mentioned in LJ (B) 319, ed. Cannan 246: 'They have imposed a high tax upon the exportation of every commodity, and think that by this means the taxes are paid by foreigners, whereas, if they were to impose a tax upon importation, it would be paid by their own subjects, not reflecting that by bringing a burthen on the exportation of commodities they so far confine the consumption of them and diminish industry.'

[77] See above, IV.v.b.43.

[78] It is remarked in LJ (B) 317, ed. Cannan 244–5, that in contrast to the British system of customs taxes on goods: 'In France a duty is paid at the end of almost every town they go into, equal, if not greater, to what is paid by us at first. Inland industry is embarassed by theirs, and only foreign trade by ours.'

the gabelle or salt-tax. Others are exempted from it altogether. Some provinces are exempted from the exclusive sale of tobacco, which the farmers-general enjoy through the greater part of the kingdom. The aids, which correspond to the excise in England, are very different in different provinces. Some provinces are exempted from them, and pay a composition or equivalent. In those in which they take place and are in farm, there are many [384] local duties which do not extend beyond a particular town or district. The Traites, which correspond to our customs, divide the kingdom into three great parts; first, the provinces subject to the tarif of 1664, which are called the provinces of the five great farms, and under which are comprehended Picardy, Normandy, and the greater part of the interior provinces of the kingdom; secondly, the provinces subject to the tarif of 1667, which are called the provinces reckoned foreign, and under which are comprehended the greater part of the frontier provinces; and, thirdly, those provinces which are said to be treated as foreign, or which, because they are allowed a free commerce with foreign countries, are in their commerce with the other provinces of France subjected to the same duties as other foreign countries. These are Alsace, the three bishopricks of Metz, Toul, and Verdun, and the three cities of Dunkirk, Bayonne, and Marseilles. Both in the provinces of the five great farms (called so on account of an antient division of the duties of customs into five great branches, each of which was originally the subject of a particular farm, though they are now all united into one), and in those which are said to be reckoned foreign, there are many local duties which do not extend beyond a particular town or district. There are some such even in the provinces which are said to be treated as foreign, particularly in the city of Marseilles. It is unnecessary to observe how much, both the restraints upon the interior commerce of the country, and the [385] number of the revenue officers must be multiplied, in order to guard the frontiers of those different provinces and districts, which are subject to such different systems of taxation.

71   Over and above the general restraints arising from this complicated system of revenue laws, the commerce of wine, after corn perhaps the most important production of France, is in the greater part of the provinces subject to particular restraints, arising from the favour which has been shewn to the vineyards of particular provinces and districts, above those of others.[79] The provinces most famous for their wines, it will be found, I believe, are those in which the trade in that article is subject to the fewest restraints of this kind. The extensive market which such provinces enjoy, encourages good management both in the cultivation of their vineyards, and in the subsequent preparation of their wines.

72   Such various and complicated revenue laws are not peculiar to France. The little dutchy of Milan is divided into six provinces, in each of which

[79] See above, I.xi.b.27.

there is a different system of taxation with regard to several different sorts of consumable goods. The still smaller territories of the duke of Parma are divided into three or four, each of which has, in the same manner, a system of its own. Under such absurd management, nothing, but the great fertility of the soil and happiness of the climate, could preserve such countries from soon relapsing into the lowest state of poverty and barbarism.

73   [386] Taxes upon consumable commodities may either be levied by an administration of which the officers are appointed by government and are immediately accountable to government, of which the revenue must in this case vary from year to year, according to the occasional variations in the produce of the tax; or they may be lett in farm for a rent certain, the farmer being allowed to appoint his own officers, who, though obliged to levy the tax in the manner directed by the law, are under his immediate inspection, and are immediately accountable to him. The best and most frugal way of levying a tax can never be by farm.[80] Over and above what is necessary for paying the stipulated rent, the salaries of the officers, and the whole expence of administration, the farmer must always draw from the produce of the tax a certain profit proportioned at least to the advance which he makes, to the risk which he runs, to the trouble which he is at, and to the knowledge and skill which it requires to manage so very complicated a concern. Government, by establishing an administration under their own immediate inspection, of the same kind with that which the farmer establishes, might at least save this profit, which is almost always exorbitant. To farm any considerable branch of the publick revenue, requires either a great capital or a great credit; circumstances which would alone restrain the competition for such an undertaking to a very small number of people. Of the few who have this capital or credit, a still smaller number have the necessary knowledge or experience; an-[387]other circumstance which restrains the competition still further. The very few, who are in condition to become competitors, find it more for their interest to combine together; to become copartners instead of competitors, and when the farm is set up to auction, to offer no rent, but what is much below the real value. In countries where the publick revenues are in farm, the farmers are generally the most opulent people.[81] Their wealth would alone excite the publick indignation, and the vanity which almost always accompanies such upstart fortunes, the foolish ostentation with which they commonly display that wealth, *excites* that indignation still more.[82]

ᶠ⁻ᶠ excite 6

[80] The problems of raising taxes by farm are considered in LJ (B) 317–18, ed. Cannan 245.
[81] It is remarked in LJ (B) 275, ed. Cannan 215, with reference to France, that 'the farmers there are the richest in the country, and must be skilled in finances and public revenues'.
[82] See above, V.i.b.8, IV.vii.b.51, and TMS I.ii.5.1.

74   The farmers of the publick revenue never find the laws too severe, which punish any attempt to evade the payment of a tax. They have no bowels for the contributors, who are not their subjects, and whose universal bankruptcy, if it should happen the day after their farm is expired, would not much affect their interest. In the greatest exigencies of the state, when the anxiety of the sovereign for the exact payment of his revenue is necessarily the greatest, they seldom fail to complain that without laws more rigorous than those which actually take place, it will be impossible for them to pay even the usual rent. In those moments of publick distress their demands cannot be disputed. The revenue laws, therefore, become gradually more and more severe. The most sanguinary are always to be found in countries where the greater part of the publick revenue is in farm. The mildest, in [388] countries where it is levied under the immediate inspection of the sovereign. Even a bad sovereign feels more compassion for his people than can ever be expected from the farmers of his revenue. He knows that the permanent grandeur of his family depends upon the prosperity of his people, and he will never knowingly ruin that prosperity for the sake of any momentary interest of his own. It is otherwise with the farmers of his revenue, whose grandeur may frequently be the effect of the ruin, and not of the prosperity of his people.[83]

75   A tax is sometimes, not only farmed for a *g*certain rent*g*, but the farmer has, besides, the monopoly of the commodity taxed. In France, the *h*duties*h* upon tobacco and salt are levied in this manner. In such cases the farmer, instead of one, levies two exorbitant profits upon the people; the profit of the farmer, and the still more exorbitant one of the monopolist. Tobacco being a luxury, every man is allowed to buy or not to buy as he chuses. But salt being a necessary, every man is obliged to buy of the farmer a certain quantity of it; because, if he did not buy this quantity of the farmer, he would, it is presumed, buy it of some smuggler. The taxes upon both commodities are exorbitant. The temptation to smuggle consequently is to many people irresistible, while at the same time the rigour of the law, and the vigilance of the farmer's officers, render the yielding to that temptation almost certainly ruinous. The smuggling of salt and tobacco sends every year several [389] hundred people to the gallies, besides a very considerable number whom it sends to the gibbet. Those taxes levied in this manner yield a very considerable revenue to government. In 1767, the farm of tobacco was let for twenty-two millions five hundred and forty-one thousand two hundred and seventy-eight livres a year. That of salt, for thirty-six millions four hundred and ninety-two thousand four hundred and four livres. The farm in both cases was to commence in 1768, and to last for six

g-g rent certain *I*   *h-h* taxes *I*

---

[83] A similar point is made with regard to the attitude of the servants of the East India Company at IV.vii.c.106.

years. Those who consider the blood of the people as nothing in comparison with the revenue of the prince, may perhaps approve of this method of levying taxes. Similar taxes and monopolies of salt and tobacco have been established in many other countries; particularly in the Austrian and Prussian dominions, and in the greater part of the states of Italy.

76 In France, the greater part of the actual revenue of the crown is derived from eight different sources; the taille, the capitation, the two vingtiemes, the gabelles, the aides, the traites, the domaine, and the farm of tobacco. The five last are, in the greater part of the provinces, under farm. The three first are every where levied by an administration under the immediate inspection and direction of government, and it is universally acknowledged that, in proportion to what they take out of the pockets of the people, they bring more into the treasury of the prince than the other five, of which the administration is much more wasteful and expensive.

77 [390] The finances of France seem, in their present state, to admit of three very obvious reformations. First, by abolishing the taille and the capitation, and by increasing the number of vingtiemes, so as to produce an additional revenue equal to the amount of those other taxes, the revenue of the crown might be preserved; the expence of collection might be much diminished; the vexation of the inferior ranks of people, which the taille and capitation occasion, might be entirely prevented; and the superior ranks might not be more burdened than the greater part of them are at present. The vingtieme, I have already observed, is a tax very nearly of the same kind with what is called the land-tax of England. The burden of the taille, it is acknowledged, falls finally upon the proprietors of land; and as the greater part of the capitation is assessed upon those who are subject to the taille at so much a pound of that other tax, the final payment of the greater part of it must likewise fall upon the same order of people. Though the number of the vingtiemes, therefore, was increased so as to produce an additional revenue equal to the amount of both those taxes, the superior ranks of people might not be more burdened than they are at present. Many individuals no doubt would; on account of the great inequalities with which the taille is commonly assessed upon the estates and tenants of different individuals. The interest and opposition of such favoured subjects are the obstacles most likely to prevent this or any other reforma-[391]tion of the same kind. Secondly, by rendering the gabelle, the aides, ⁱthe traites,ⁱ the taxes upon tobacco, all the different customs and excises, uniform in all the different parts of the kingdom, those taxes might be levied at much less expence, and the interior commerce of the kingdom might be rendered as free as that of England. Thirdly, and lastly, by subjecting all those taxes to an administration under the immediate inspection and direction of government, the exorbitant profits of the farmers general might be added

to the revenue of the state. The opposition arising from the private interest of individuals, is likely to be as effectual for preventing the two last as the first mentioned scheme of reformation.

78   The French system of taxation seems, in every respect, inferior to the British.[84] In Great Britain ten millions sterling are annually levied upon less than eight millions of people, without its being possible to say that any particular order is oppressed.[85] From the collections of the Abbè Expilly, and the observations of the author of the Essay upon the legislation and commerce of corn, it appears probable, that France, including the provinces of Lorraine and Bar, contains about twenty-three or twenty-four millions of people; three times the number perhaps contained in Great Britain.[86] The soil and climate of France are better than those of Great Britain. The country has been much longer in a state of improvement and cultivation, and is, upon that account, better stocked with all those things which it requires a long time to raise up and ac-[392]cumulate, such as great towns, and convenient and well-built houses, both in town and country. With these advantages it might be expected that in France a revenue of thirty millions might be levied for the support of the state, with as little inconveniency as a revenue of ten millions is in Great Britain. In 1765 and 1766, the whole revenue paid into the treasury of France, according to the best, though, I acknowledge, very imperfect accounts which I could get of it, usually run between 308 and 325 millions of livres; that is, it did not amount to fifteen millions sterling;[87] not the half of what might have been expected, had the people contributed in the same proportion to their numbers as the people of Great Britain. The people of France, however, it is generally acknowledged, are much more oppressed by taxes than the people of Great Britain. France, however, is certainly the great empire in Europe which, after that of Great Britain, enjoys the mildest and most indulgent government.

79   In Holland the heavy taxes upon the necessaries of life have ruined, it is said, their principal manufactures, and are likely to discourage gradually even their fisheries and their trade in ship-building.[88] The taxes upon the necessaries of life are inconsiderable in Great Britain, and no manufacture has hitherto been ruined by them. The British taxes which bear hardest on

---

[84] Cf. LJ (B) 318, ed. Cannan 245: 'Upon the whole we may observe that the English are the best financiers in Europe, and their taxes are levied with more propriety than those of any country whatever.'   [85] See below, V.iii.76, where the same figures are cited.

[86] Expilly gives 22,014,357 and Necker gives 24,181,333. (J. J. Expilly, *Dictionnaire géographique historique et politique des Gaules et de la France* (1768) v. 808; J. Necker, *Sur la législation et le commerce des grains* (1775), in *Oeuvres*, iv, (Lausanne, 1786), 29, n. 4. See above, IV.iii.c.12. Cf. TMS VI.ii.2.4: 'France may contain, perhaps, three times the number of inhabitants which Great Britain contains.'

[87] Cf. LJ (B) 318, ed. Cannan 245: 'In France 24 millions are levied every year, and not above 12 goes to the expence of the government, the rest goes for defraying the expence of levying it and for the profit of the farmer.'   [88] See above, V.ii.k.14.

manufactures are some duties upon the importation of raw materials, particularly upon that of raw silk. The revenue of the states [393] general and of the different cities, however, is said to amount to more than five millions two hundred and fifty thousand pounds sterling; and as the inhabitants of the United Provinces cannot well be supposed to amount to more than a third part of those of Great Britain, they must, in proportion to their number, be much more heavily taxed.[89]

80   After all the proper subjects of taxation have been exhausted, if the exigencies of the state still continue to require new taxes, they must be imposed upon improper ones.[90] The taxes upon the necessaries of life, therefore, may be no impeachment of the wisdom of that republick, which, in order to acquire and to maintain its independency, has, in spite of its great frugality, been involved in such expensive wars as have obliged it to contract great debts. The singular countries of Holland and Zealand, besides, require a considerable expence even to preserve their existence, or to prevent their being swallowed up by the sea, which must have contributed to increase considerably the load of taxes in those two provinces. The republican form of government seems to be the principal support of the present grandeur of Holland. The owners of great capitals, the great mercantile families, have generally either some direct share, or some indirect influence in the administration of that government. For the sake of the respect and authority which they derive from this situation,[91] they are willing to live in a country where their capital, if they employ it themselves, will bring [394] them less profit, and if they lend it to another, less interest; and where the very moderate revenue which they can draw from it will purchase less of the necessaries and conveniencies of life than in any other part of Europe.[92] The residence of such wealthy people necessarily keeps alive, in spite of all disadvantages, a certain degree of industry in the country. Any publick calamity which should destroy the republican form of government, which should throw the whole administration into the hands of nobles and of soldiers, which should annihilate altogether the importance of those wealthy merchants, would soon render it disagreeable to them to live in a country where they were no longer likely to be much respected. They would remove both their residence and their capital to some other country, and the industry and commerce of Holland would soon follow the capitals which supported them.[93]

[89] Holland, 'loaden with greater Taxes besides than any other Nation' (Mandeville, *The Fable of the Bees*, pt. i.204, ed. Kaye i.187).   [90] See below, V.iii.58.

[91] See above, IV.vii.c.74, where Smith suggests that the actions of American statesmen at the time of the rebellion could be explained at least partly in terms of their desire to defend their new-won importance.

[92] Smith comments on the low rate of profit in Holland, for example, at I.ix.10 and V.ii.f.13.

[93] Smith comments on the ability of merchants to switch capital between countries at V.ii.f.6. See also II.v.14, V.iii.55.

CHAPTER III
Of publick Debts

1 IN that rude state of society which precedes the extension of commerce and the improvement of manufactures, when those expensive luxuries which commerce and manufactures can alone introduce, are altogether unknown, the person who possesses a large revenue, I have endeavoured to show in [395] the third book of this enquiry, can spend or enjoy that revenue in no other way than by maintaining nearly as many people as it can maintain.[1] A large revenue may at all times be said to consist in the command of a large quantity of the necessaries of life. In that rude state of things it is commonly paid in a large quantity of those necessaries, in the materials of plain food and coarse cloathing, in corn and cattle, in wool and raw hides. When neither commerce nor manufactures furnish any thing for which the owner can exchange the greater part of those materials which are over and above his own consumption, he can do nothing with the surplus but feed and cloathe nearly as many people as it will feed and cloathe. A hospitality in which there is no luxury, and a liberality in which there is no ostentation, occasion, in this situation of things, the principal expences of the rich and the great. But these, I have likewise endeavoured to shew in the same book, are expences by which people are not very apt to ruin themselves.[2] There is not, perhaps, any selfish pleasure so frivolous, of which the pursuit has not sometimes ruined even sensible men. A passion for cock-fighting has ruined many. But the instances, I believe, are not very numerous of people who have been ruined by a hospitality or liberality of this kind; though the hospitality of luxury and the liberality of ostentation have ruined many. Among our feudal ancestors, the long time during which estates used to continue in the same family, sufficiently demonstrates the general disposition of people [396] to live within their income.[3] Though the rustick hospitality, constantly exercised by the great land-holders, may not, to us in the present times, seem consistent with that order, which we are apt to consider as inseparably connected with good œconomy, yet we must certainly allow them to have been at least so far frugal as not commonly to have spent their whole income. A part of their wool and raw hides they had generally an opportunity of selling for money. Some part of this money, perhaps, they spent in purchasing the few objects of vanity and luxury, with which the circumstances of the times could furnish them; but some part of it they seem commonly to have hoarded. They could not well indeed do any thing else but hoard whatever money they saved. To trade was

---

[1] See above, III.iv.   [2] Above, III.iv.16.   [3] See above, III.iv.16, and III.ii.7.

disgraceful to a gentleman, and to lend money at interest, which at that time was considered as usury and prohibited by law, would have been still more so.[4] In those times of violence and disorder, besides, it was convenient to have a hoard of money at hand, that in case they should be driven from their own home, they might have something of known value to carry with them to some place of safety. The same violence, which made it convenient to hoard, made it equally convenient to conceal the hoard.[5] The frequency of treasure-trove, or of treasure found of which no owner was known, sufficiently demonstrates the frequency in those times both of hoarding and of concealing the hoard. Treasure-trove was then considered as an important branch of the revenue of the so-[397]vereign. All the treasure-trove of the kingdom would scarce perhaps in the present times make an important branch of the revenue of a private gentleman of a good estate.

2   The same disposition to save and to hoard prevailed in the sovereign, as well as in the subjects. Among nations to whom commerce and manufactures are little known, the sovereign, it has already been observed in the fourth book,[6] is in a situation which naturally disposes him to the parsimony requisite for accumulation. In that situation the expence even of a sovereign cannot be directed by that vanity which delights in the gaudy finery of a court. The ignorance of the times affords but few of the trinkets in which that finery consists. Standing armies are not then necessary, so that the expence even of a sovereign, like that of any other great lord, can be employed in scarce any thing but bounty to his tenants, and hospitality to his retainers.[7] But bounty and hospitality very seldom lead to extravagance; though vanity almost always does.[8] All the antient sovereigns of Europe accordingly, it has already been observed, had treasures. Every Tartar chief in the present times is said to have one.

3   In a commercial country abounding with every sort of expensive luxury, the sovereign, in the same manner as almost all the great proprietors in his dominions, naturally spends a great part of his revenue in purchasing those luxuries. His own and the neighbouring countries supply him abundantly with all the costly trinkets which [398] compose the splendid, but insignificant pageantry of a court. For the sake of an inferior pageantry of the same kind, his nobles dismiss their retainers, make their tenants independent, and become gradually themselves as insignificant as the greater part of the wealthy burghers in his dominions.[9] The same frivo-

---

[4] It is remarked in LJ (B) 300, ed. Cannan 231–2, that 'In a rude society nothing is honourable but war' and that trade in particular is held in low esteem; a feeling which is not completely extinguished even in more refined societies. Smith adds at 302, ed. Cannan 233, with reference to ruder ages that the 'mean and despicable idea which they had of merchants greatly obstructed the progress of commerce'. Cf. III.iii.1–2.

[5] See above, II.i.31.   [6] Above, IV.i.30.   [7] See above, III.iv.5.
[8] Repeated from IV.i.30.   [9] See above, III.iv.15.

lous passions, which influence their conduct, influence his. How can it be supposed that he should be the only rich man in his dominions who is insensible to pleasures of this kind?[10] If he does not, what he is very likely to do, spend upon those pleasures so great a part of his revenue as to debilitate very much the defensive power of the state, it cannot well be expected that he should not spend upon them all that part of it which is over and above what is necessary for supporting that defensive power. His ordinary expence becomes equal to his ordinary revenue, and it is well if it does not frequently exceed it. The amassing of treasure can no longer be expected, and when extraordinary exigencies require extraordinary expences, he must necessarily call upon his subjects for an extraordinary aid. The present and the late king of Prussia are the only great princes of Europe who, since the death of Henry IV. of France in 1610, are supposed to have amassed any considerable treasure.[11] The parsimony which leads to accumulation has become almost as rare in republican as in monarchical governments. The Italian republicks, the United Provinces of the Netherlands, are all in debt. The canton of Berne is the single republick in Europe which [399] has amassed any considerable treasure. The other Swiss republicks have not.[12] The taste for some sort of pageantry, for splendid buildings, at least, and other publick ornaments, frequently prevails as much in the apparently sober senate-house of a little republick, as in the dissipated court of the greatest king.

4   The want of parsimony in time of peace, imposes the necessity of contracting debt in time of war. When war comes, there is no money in the treasury but what is necessary for carrying on the ordinary expence of the peace establishment. In war an establishment of three or four times that expence becomes necessary for the defence of the state, and consequently a revenue three or four times greater than the peace revenue. Supposing that the sovereign should have, what he scarce ever has, the immediate means of augmenting his revenue in proportion to the augmentation of his expence, yet still the produce of the taxes, from which this increase of revenue must be drawn, will not begin to come into the treasury till perhaps ten or twelve months after they are imposed. But the moment in which war begins, or rather the moment in which it appears likely to begin, the army must be augmented, the fleet must be fitted out, the garrisoned towns must be put into a posture of defence; that army, that fleet, those garrisoned towns must be furnished with arms, ammunition and provisions. An immediate and great expence must be incurred in that moment of immediate danger, which will not wait for the gradual and slow re-[400]turns of the new taxes. In this exigency government can have no other resource but in borrowing.

[10] See above, V.i.h.2.   [11] See above, IV.i.25.   [12] See above, V.i.g.41, V.ii.a.9.

5   The same commercial state of society which, by the operation of moral causes, brings government in this manner into the necessity of borrowing, produces in the subjects both an ability and an inclination to lend. If it commonly brings along with it the necessity of borrowing, it likewise brings *along*ᵃ with it the facility of doing so.

6   A country abounding with merchants and manufacturers, necessarily abounds with a set of people through whose hands not only their own capitals, but the capitals of all those who either lend them money, or trust them with goods, pass as frequently, or more frequently, than the revenue of a private man, who, without trade or business, lives upon his income, passes through his hands. The revenue of such a man can regularly pass through his hands only once in ᵇaᵇ year. But the whole amount of the capital and credit of a merchant, who deals in a trade of which the returns are very quick, may sometimes pass through his hands two, three, or four times in a year.[13] A country abounding with merchants and manufacturers, therefore, necessarily abounds with a set of people who have it at all times in their power to advance, if they chuse to do so, a very large sum of money to government. Hence the ability in the subjects of a commercial state to lend.

7   Commerce and manufactures can seldom flourish long in any state which does not enjoy a regular administration of justice, in which the [401] people do not feel themselves secure in the possession of their property, in which the faith of contracts is not supported by law, and in which the authority of the state is not supposed to be regularly employed in enforcing the payment of debts from all those who are able to pay. Commerce and manufactures, in short, can seldom flourish in any state in which there is not a certain degree of confidence in the justice of government.[14] The same confidence which disposes great merchants and manufacturers, upon ordinary occasions, to trust their property to the protection of a particular government; disposes them, upon extraordinary occasions, to trust that government with the use of their property. By lending money to government, they do not even for a moment diminish their ability to carry on their trade and manufactures. On the contrary, they commonly augment it. The necessities of the state render government upon most occasions willing to borrow upon terms extremely advantageous to the lender. The security which it grants to the original creditor, is made transferable to any other creditor, and, from the universal confidence in the justice of the state, generally sells in the market for more than was originally paid for it. The merchant or monied man makes money by lending money to government, and instead of diminishing, increases

---

ᵃ⁻ᵃ *om.* 5–6   ᵇ⁻ᵇ the *1*

[13] See above, II.v.27.   [14] See, for example, III.iii.12, II.i.30.

his trading capital. He generally considers it as a favour, therefore, when the administration admits him to share in the first subscription for a new [402] loan. Hence the inclination or willingness in the subjects of a commercial state to lend.

8   The government of such a state is very apt to repose itself upon this ability and willingness of its subjects to lend it their money on extraordinary occasions. It foresees the facility of borrowing, and therefore dispenses itself from the duty of saving.

9   In a rude state of society there are no great mercantile or manufacturing capitals. The individuals who hoard whatever money they can save, and who conceal their hoard, do so from a distrust of the justice of government, from a fear that if it was known that they had a hoard, and where that hoard was to be found, they would quickly be plundered. In such a state of things few people would be able, and nobody would be willing, to lend their money to government on extraordinary exigencies. The sovereign feels that he must provide for such exigencies by saving, because he foresees the absolute impossibility of borrowing. This foresight increases still further his natural disposition to save.[15]

10   The progress of the enormous debts which at present oppress, and will in the long-run probably ruin, all the great nations of Europe, has been pretty uniform. Nations, like private men, have generally begun to borrow upon what may be called personal credit, without assigning or mortgaging any particular fund for the payment of the debt; and when this resource has [403] failed them, they have gone on to borrow upon assignments or mortgages of particular funds.

11   What is called the unfunded debt of Great Britain, is contracted in the former of those two ways. It consists partly in a debt which bears, or is supposed to bear, no interest, and which resembles the debts that a private man contracts upon account; and partly in a debt which bears interest, and which resembles what a private man contracts upon his bill or promissory note. The debts which are due either for extraordinary services, or for services either not provided for, or not paid at the time when they are performed; part of the extraordinaries of the army, navy, and ordnance, the arrears of subsidies to foreign princes, those of seamens wages, &c. usually constitute a debt of the first kind. Navy and Exchequer bills, which are issued sometimes in payment of a part of such debts and sometimes for other purposes, constitute a debt of the second kind; Exchequer bills bearing interest from the day on which they are issued, and navy bills six months after they are issued. The bank of England, either by voluntarily discounting those bills at their current value, or by agreeing with government for certain considerations to circulate Exchequer bills, that is, to receive them at par, paying the interest which

[15] See above, IV.i.30. Hume develops this theme in his essay 'Of Public Credit'.

happens to be due upon them, keeps up their value and facilitates their circulation, and thereby frequently enables government to contract a very large debt of this kind. In France, where there is no bank, the state bills (billets d'état)* have [404] sometimes sold at sixty and seventy per cent. discount. During the great re-coinage in king William's time, when the bank of England thought proper to put a stop to its usual transactions, Exchequer bills and tallies are said to have sold from twenty-five to sixty per cent. discount;[16] owing partly, no doubt, to the supposed instability of the new government established by the Revolution, but partly too to the want of the support of the bank of England.[17]

12   When this resource is exhausted, and it becomes necessary, in order to raise money, to assign or mortgage some particular branch of the publick revenue for the payment of the debt, government has upon different occasions done this in two different ways. Sometimes it has made this assignment or mortgage for a short period of time only, a year, or a few years, for example; and sometimes for perpetuity. In the one case the fund was supposed sufficient to pay, within the limited time, both principal and interest of the money borrowed. In the other it was supposed sufficient to pay the interest only, or a perpetual annuity equivalent to the interest, government being at liberty to redeem at any time this annuity, upon paying back the principal sum borrowed. When money was raised in the one way, it was said to be raised by anticipation; when in the other, by perpetual funding, or, more shortly, by funding.

13   In Great Britain the annual land and malt taxes are regularly anticipated every year, by virtue of a borrowing clause constantly inserted [405] into the acts which impose them. The bank of England generally advances at an interest, which since the Revolution has varied from eight to three per cent. the sums for which those taxes are granted, and receives payment as their produce gradually comes in. If there is a deficiency, which there always is, it is provided for in the supplies of the ensuing year. The only considerable branch of the publick revenue which yet remains unmortgaged is thus regularly spent before it comes in. Like an ᶜimprovidentᶜ spendthrift, whose pressing occasions will not allow him to wait for the regular payment of his revenue, the state is in the constant practice of borrowing of its own factors and agents, and of paying interest for the use of its own money.

14   In the reign of King William, and during a great part of that of Queen

---

* See Examen des Reflexions politiques sur les finances. [J. P. Duverney, *Examen du livre intitulé Réflexions politiques sur les finances et le commerce*, i.225.]

ᶜ⁻ᶜ unprovident *I*

---

[16] J. Postlethwayt, *History of the Public Revenue*, 14–15, and 301. See above, II.ii.80, n.

[17] See above, II.ii.79.

Anne, before we had become so familiar as we are now with the practice of perpetual funding, the greater part of the new taxes were imposed but for a short period of time (for four, five, six, or seven years only), and a great part of the grants of every year consisted in loans upon anticipations of the produce of those taxes.[18] The produce being frequently insufficient for paying within the limited term the principal and interest of the money borrowed, deficiencies arose, to make good which it became necessary to prolong the term.

15   In 1697, by the 8th of William III. c. 20. the deficiencies of several taxes were charged upon what was then called the first general mortgage or fund, consisting of a prolongation to the first [406] of August, 1706, of several different taxes, which would have expired within a shorter term, and of which the produce was accumulated into one general fund.[19] The deficiencies charged upon this prolonged term amounted to 5,160,459*l.* 14*s.* 9¼*d.*[20]

16   In 1701 those duties, with some others, were still further prolonged for the like purposes till the first of August 1710, and were called the second general mortgage or fund. The deficiencies charged upon it amounted to 2,055,999*l.* 7*s.* 11½*d.*

17   In 1707, those duties were still further prolonged, as a fund for new loans, to the first of August 1712, and were called the third general mortgage or fund. The sum borrowed upon it was 983,254*l.* 11*s.* 9¼*d.*

18   In 1708, those duties were all (except the old subsidy of tonnage and poundage, of which one moiety only was made a part of this fund, and a duty upon the importation of Scotch linen, which had been taken off by the articles of union) still further continued, as a fund for new loans, to the first of August 1714, and were called the fourth general mortgage or fund. The sum borrowed upon it was 925,176*l.* 9*s.* 2¼*d.*

19   In 1709, those duties were all (except the old subsidy of tonnage and poundage, which was now left out of this fund altogether) still further continued for the same purpose to the first of August 1716, and were called the fifth general mortgage or fund. The sum borrowed upon it was 922,029*l.* 6*s.* 0*d.*

20   [407] In 1710, those duties were again prolonged to the first of August 1720, and were called the sixth general mortgage or fund. The sum borrowed upon it was 1,296,552*l.* 9*s.* 11¾*d.*

21   In 1711, the same duties (which at this time were thus subject to four

---

[18] LJ (B) 320, ed. Cannan 247, comments that 'Soon after the Revolution, on account of the necessities of government, it was necessary to borrow money from subjects, generaly at a higher rate than common interest, to be repaid in a few years.' Smith comments on the issue of funding at 320–4, ed. Cannan 247–51.

[19] 8 and 9 William III, c. 20 (1696).

[20] The information in this paragraph and in the nine following is taken from J. Postle-thwayt, *History of Public Revenue*, 38, 40, 59, 63, 64, 68, 71, 303, 305, 311, 319, 320.

different anticipations) together with several others were continued for ever, and made a fund for paying the interest of the capital of the South Sea company, which had that year advanced to government, for paying debts and making good deficiencies, the sum of 9,177,967*l*. 15*s*. 4*d*.; the greatest loan which at that time had ever been made.

22   Before this period, the principal, so far as I have been able to observe, the only taxes which in order to pay the interest of a debt had been imposed for perpetuity, were those for paying the interest of the money which had been advanced to government by the Bank and East India company, and of what it was expected would be advanced, but which was never advanced, by a projected land-bank. The bank fund at this time amounted to 3,375,027*l*. 17*s*. 10½*d*. for which was paid an annuity or interest of 206,501*l*. 13*s*. 5*d*.[21] The East India fund amounted to 3,200,000*l*. for which was paid an annuity or interest of 160,000*l*.; the bank fund being at six per cent., the East India fund at five per cent. interest.

23   In 1715, by the first of George I. c. 12.[22] the different taxes which had been mortgaged for paying the bank annuity, together with several others which by this act were likewise rendered perpetual, were accumulated into one common [408] fund called The Aggregate Fund, which was charged, not only with the ᵈpaymentsᵈ of the bank annuity, but with several other annuities and burdens of different kinds. This fund was afterwards augmented by the third of George I. c. 8. and by the fifth of George I. c. 3. and the different duties which were then added to it were likewise rendered perpetual.

24   In 1717, by the third of George I. c. 7.[23] several other taxes were rendered perpetual, and accumulated into another common fund, called The General Fund, for the payment of certain annuities, amounting in the whole to 724,849*l*. 6*s*. 10½*d*.

25   In consequence of those different acts, the greater part of the taxes which before had been anticipated only for a short term of years, were rendered perpetual as a fund for paying, not the capital, but the interest only, of the money which had been borrowed upon them by different successive anticipations.

26   Had money never been raised but by anticipation, the course of a few years would have liberated the publick revenue, without any other attention of government besides that of not overloading the fund by charging it with more debt than it could pay within the limited term, and of not anticipating a second time before the expiration of the first anticipation. But the greater part of European governments have been incapable of

ᵈ⁻ᵈ payment *I*

---

[21] Above, II.ii.81.

[22] 1 George I, c. 12 (1714), to become effective in 1715; continued by 3 George I, c. 8 (1716) and 5 George I, c. 3 (1718).

[23] 3 George I, c. 7 (1716) to become effective in 1717.

those attentions. They have frequently overloaded the fund even upon the first anticipation; and when this happened not to be [409] the case, they have generally taken care to overload it, by anticipating a second and a third time before the expiration of the first anticipation. The fund becoming in this manner altogether insufficient for paying both principal and interest of the money borrowed upon it, it became necessary to charge it with the interest only, or a perpetual annuity equal to the interest, and such unprovident anticipations necessarily gave birth to the more ruinous practice of perpetual funding. But though this practice necessarily puts off the liberation of the publick revenue from a fixed period to one so indefinite that it is not very likely ever to arrive; yet as a greater sum can in all cases be raised by this new practice than by the old one of anticipations, the former, when men have once become familiar with it, has in the great exigencies of the state been universally preferred to the latter. To relieve the present exigency is always the object which principally interests those immediately concerned in the administration of publick affairs. The future liberation of the publick revenue, they leave to the care of posterity.

27   During the reign of queen Anne, the market rate of interest had fallen from six to five per cent., and in the twelfth year of her reign five per cent. was declared to be the highest rate which could lawfully be taken for money borrowed upon private security.[24] Soon after the greater part of the temporary taxes of Great Britain had been rendered perpetual, and distributed into the Aggregate, South Sea, and [410] General Funds, the creditors of the publick, like those of private persons, were induced to accept of five per cent. for the interest of their money, which occasioned a saving of one per cent. upon the capital of the greater part of the debts which had been thus funded for perpetuity, or of one-sixth of the greater part of the annuities which were paid out of the three great funds above mentioned. This saving left a considerable surplus in the produce of the different taxes which had been accumulated into those funds, over and above what was necessary for paying the annuities which were now charged upon them, and laid the foundation of what has since been called the Sinking Fund. In 1717, it amounted to 323,434*l.* 7*s.* 7½*d.*[25] In 1727, the interest of the greater part of the publick debts was still further reduced to four per cent.;[26] and in 1753[27] and 1757,[28] to three and a half and three per cent.; which reductions still further augmented the sinking fund.[29]

[24] 13 Anne, c. 15 (1713) in *Statutes of the Realm*, ix.928; 12 Anne, st. 2, c. 16 in Ruffhead's edition. See above, I.ix.5 and V.ii.f.8.

[25] A. Anderson, *Origin of Commerce* (1764), ii.273.

[26] 'At Midsummer this Year, the Reduction of the Interest on the National Debt from 5 to 4 per cent took place; whereby the famous Sinking-Fund was increased to above one Million per Annum.' (Ibid. ii.316.)   [27] 26 George II, c. 1 (1753).

[28] 30 George II, c. 4 (1757). See also A. Anderson, *Origin of Commerce* (1764), ii.391.

[29] In 1750 Henry Pelham 'cut the rate of interest on certain annuities held by the Bank

28   A sinking fund, though instituted for the payment of old, facilitates very much the contracting of new debts. It is a subsidiary fund always at hand to be mortgaged in aid of any other doubtful fund, upon which money is proposed to be raised in any exigency of the state. Whether the sinking fund of Great Britain has been more frequently applied to the one or to the other of those two purposes, will sufficiently appear by and by.

29   Besides those two methods of borrowing, by anticipations and by perpetual funding, there [411] are two other methods, which hold a sort of middle place between them. These are, that of borrowing upon annuities for terms of years, and that of borrowing upon annuities for lives.

30   During the reigns of king William and queen Anne, large sums were frequently borrowed upon annuities for terms of years, which were sometimes longer and sometimes shorter. In 1693, an act was passed for borrowing one million upon an annuity of fourteen per cent., or of 140,000*l.* a year for sixteen years. In 1691, an act was passed for borrowing a million upon annuities for lives, upon terms which in the present times would appear very advantageous. But the subscription was not filled up. In the following year the deficiency was made good by borrowing upon annuities for lives at fourteen per cent., or at little more than seven years purchase.[30] In 1695, the persons who had purchased those annuities were allowed to exchange them for others of ninety-six years, upon paying into the Exchequer sixty-three pounds in the hundred; that is, the difference between fourteen per cent. for life, and fourteen per cent. for ninety-six years, was sold for sixty-three pounds, or for four and a half years purchase.[31] Such was the supposed instability of government, that even these terms procured few purchasers.[32] In the reign of queen Anne, money was upon different occasions borrowed both upon annuities for lives, and upon annuities for terms of thirty-two, of eighty-nine, of ninety-eight, and of ninety-nine years. In 1719, the proprietors of [412]

[of England] to 3½, with a promise of 3 to come. In 1751 he grouped together a number of funds already, or about to be put, on a 3 per cent basis into the "three per cent consolidated annuities", the original Consols. These remained above par until 1755, and during this peaceful interval touch the highest price in the whole history of Consols down to the eighties of the nineteenth century . . . the last of the annuities due to the Bank [were brought] into line with Consols at 3 per cent as from Christmas 1757.' (J. H. Clapham, *The Bank of England*, i.97–8.)

    [30] It is not clear to which acts Smith refers. 4 William and Mary, c. 3 (1692) aimed at raising £1,000,000 and offered annuitants *either* 10 per cent until 1700, then an increasing share of a fixed total sum as annuitants died *or*, if the entire £1,000,000 was not raised by May 1693, an annuity of 14 per cent. As only £881,494 was contributed, attempts were made to raise more by 5 William and Mary, c. 5 (1693) and 5 and 6 William and Mary, c. 20 (1694).

    [31] 6 and 7 William and Mary, c. 5 (1694) and 7 and 8 William III, c. 2 (1695).

    [32] Cf. LJ (B) 322, ed. Cannan 249: 'In the reigns of King William, Q. Ann, and in the begining of that of K. George the 1st, the funds rose and fell according to the credit of the government, as there was still some risk of a revolution.'

the annuities for thirty-two years were induced to accept in lieu of them South-sea stock to the amount of eleven and a half years purchase of the annuities, together with an additional quantity of stock equal to the arrears which happened then to be due upon them.[33] In 1720, the greater part of the other annuities for terms of years both long and short were subscribed into the same fund.[34] The long annuities at that time amounted to 666,821*l*. 8*s*. 3½*d*. a year.[35] On the 5th of January, 1775, the remainder of them, or what was not subscribed at that time, amounted only to 136,453*l*. 12*s*. 8*d*.

31   During the two wars which begun in 1739 and in 1755, little money was borrowed either upon annuities for terms of years, or upon those for lives. An annuity for ninety-eight or ninety-nine years, however, is worth nearly as much money as a perpetuity, and should, therefore, one might think, be a fund for borrowing nearly as much. But those who, in order to make family settlements, and to provide for remote futurity, buy into the publick stocks, would not care to purchase into one of which the value was continually diminishing; and such people make a very considerable proportion both of the proprietors and purchasers of stock. An annuity for a long term of years, therefore, though its intrinsick value may be very nearly the same with that of a perpetual annuity, will not find nearly the same number of purchasers. The subscribers to a new loan, who mean generally to sell their subscription as soon as possible, [413] prefer greatly a perpetual annuity redeemable by parliament, to an irredeemable annuity for a long term of years of only equal amount. The value of the former may be supposed always the same, or very nearly the same; and it makes, therefore, a more convenient transferable stock than the latter.

32   During the two last mentioned wars, annuities, either for terms of years or for lives, were seldom granted but as premiums to the subscribers to a new loan, over and above the redeemable annuity or interest upon the credit of which the loan was supposed to be made. They were granted, not as the proper fund upon which the money was borrowed; but as an additional encouragement to the lender.

33   Annuities for lives have occasionally been granted in two different ways; either upon separate lives, or upon lots of lives, which in French are called Tontines, from the name of their inventor. When annuities are granted upon separate lives, the death of every individual annuitant disburthens the publick revenue so far as it was affected by his annuity. When annuities are granted upon tontines, the liberation of the publick revenue does not commence till the death of all the annuitants comprehended in one lot, which may sometimes consist of twenty or thirty persons, of whom

[33] 5 George I, c. 19 (1718).   [34] 6 George I, c. 4 (1719).
[35] A. Anderson, *Origin of Commerce* (1764), ii.286.

the survivors succeed to the annuities of all those who die before them; the last survivor succeeding to the annuities of the whole lot. Upon the same revenue more money can always be raised by ton-[414]tines than by annuities for separate lives. An annuity, with a right of survivorship, is really worth more than an equal annuity for a separate life, and from the confidence which every man naturally has in his own good fortune, the principle upon which is founded the success of all lotteries, such an annuity generally sells for something more than it is worth.[36] In countries where it is usual for government to raise money by granting annuities, tontines are upon this account generally preferred to annuities for separate lives. The expedient which will raise most money, is almost always preferred to that which is likely to bring about in the speediest manner the liberation of the publick revenue.

34   In France a much greater proportion of the publick debts consists in annuities for lives than in England. According to a memoir presented by the parliament of Bourdeaux to the king in 1764, the whole publick debt of France is estimated at twenty-four hundred millions of livres; of which the capital for which annuities for lives had been granted, is supposed to amount to three hundred millions, the eighth-part of the whole publick debt. The annuities themselves are computed to amount to thirty millions a year, the fourth part of one hundred and twenty millions, the supposed interest of that whole debt. These estimations, I know very well, are not exact, but having been presented by so very respectable a body as approximations to the truth, they may, I apprehend, be considered as such. It is not the different degrees of anxiety [415] in the two governments of France and England for the liberation of the publick revenue, which occasions this difference in their respective modes of borrowing. It arises altogether from the different views and interests of the lenders.

35   In England, the seat of government being in the greatest mercantile city in the world, the merchants are generally the people who advance money to government.[37] By advancing it they do not mean to diminish, but, on the contrary, to increase their mercantile capitals; and unless they expected to sell with some profit their share in the subscription for a new loan, they never would subscribe.[38] But if by advancing their money they were to purchase, instead of perpetual annuities, annuities for lives

[36] Above, I.x.b.26, 27.

[37] See above, II.iv.5, where Smith draws a distinction between the mercantile and the monied interest.

[38] Cf. LJ (B) 323–4, ed. Cannan 250: 'there are a great many stockholders who are merchants, and who keep their stocks in the hands of the government that they may be ready to sell out on any sudden demand and take advantage of a good bargain when it casts up'. Smith examines the fluctuations in stock prices, reflecting the expectations of their holders, at 323–4, ed. Cannan 249–51. Stock jobbing as such, including the activities of bulls and bears, is considered at 324–6, ed. Cannan 251–2, where Smith also examines the effects of speculative jobbing on the price of new issues.

only, whether their own or those of other people, they would not always be so likely to sell them with a profit. Annuities upon their own lives they would always sell with loss; because no man will give for an annuity upon the life of another, whose age and state of health are nearly the same with his own, the same price which he would give for one upon his own. An annuity upon the life of a third person, indeed, is, no doubt, of equal value to the buyer and the seller; but its real value begins to diminish from the moment it is granted, and continues to do so more and more as long as it subsists. It can never, therefore, make so convenient a transferable stock as a perpetual annuity, of which the real value may be supposed always the same, or very nearly the same.

36   [416] In France, the seat of government not being in a great mercantile city, merchants do not make so great a proportion of the people who advance money to government. The people concerned in the finances, the farmers general, the receivers of the taxes which are not in farm, the court bankers, &c. make the greater part of those who advance their money in all publick exigencies. Such people are commonly men of mean birth, but of great wealth, and frequently of great pride. They are too proud to marry their equals, and women of quality disdain to marry them. They frequently resolve, therefore, to live bachelors, and having neither any families of their own, nor much regard for those of their relations, whom they are not always very fond of acknowledging, they desire only to live in splendor during their own time, and are not unwilling that their fortune should end with themselves.[39] The number of rich people, besides, who are either averse to marry, or whose condition of life renders it either improper or inconvenient for them to do so, is much greater in France than in England. To such people, who have little or no care for posterity, nothing can be more convenient than to exchange their capital for a revenue, which is to last just as long *e*, and no longer than they wish it to do.

37   The ordinary expence of the greater part of modern governments in time of peace being equal or nearly equal to their ordinary revenue, when war comes they are both unwilling and unable to increase their revenue in proportion [417] to the increase of their expence. They are unwilling, for fear of offending the people, who, by so great and so sudden an increase of taxes, would soon be disgusted with the war; and they are unable, from not well knowing what taxes would be sufficient to produce the revenue wanted. The facility of borrowing delivers them from the embarrassment which this fear and inability would otherwise occasion. By means of borrowing they are enabled, with a very moderate increase

---

e as *1–2*

[39] Smith comments at V.ii.k.73 on the attitude to upstart fortunes and on the 'foolish ostentation' of the tax-farmers.

of taxes, to raise, from year to year, money sufficient for carrying on the war, and by the practice of ʲperpetualʲ funding they are enabled, with the smallest possible increase of taxes, to raise annually the largest possible sum of money. In great empires the people who live in the capital, and in the provinces remote from the scene of action, feel, many of them scarce any inconveniency from the war; but enjoy, at their ease, the amusement of reading in the newspapers the exploits of their own fleets and armies. To them this amusement compensates the small difference between the taxes which they pay on account of the war, and those which they had been accustomed to pay in time of peace. They are commonly dissatisfied with the return of peace, which puts an end to their amusement, and to a thousand visionary hopes of conquest and national glory, from a longer continuance of the war.[40]

38   The return of peace, indeed, seldom relieves them from the greater part of the taxes imposed during the war. These are mortgaged for the [418] interest of the debt, contracted in order to carry it on. If, over and above paying the interest of this debt, and defraying the ordinary expence of government, the old revenue, together with the new taxes, produce some surplus revenue, it may perhaps be converted into a sinking fund for paying off the debt. But, in the first place, this sinking fund, even supposing it should be applied to no other purpose, is generally altogether inadequate for paying, in the course of any period during which it can reasonably be expected that peace should continue, the whole debt contracted during the war; and, in the second place, this fund is almost always applied to other purposes.

39   The new taxes were imposed for the sole purpose of paying the interest of the money borrowed upon them. If they produce more, it is generally something which was neither intended nor expected, and is therefore seldom very considerable. Sinking funds have generally arisen, not so much from any surplus of the taxes which was over and above what was necessary for paying the interest or annuity originally charged upon them, as from a subsequent reduction of that interest. That of Holland in 1655, and that of the ecclesiastical state in 1685, were both formed in this manner.[41] Hence the usual insufficiency of such funds.

40   During the most profound peace, various events occur which require an extraordinary expence, and government finds it always more convenient to defray this expence by misapplying [419] the sinking fund than by imposing a new tax. Every new tax is immediately felt more or less by the people. It occasions always some murmur, and meets with

---

ʲ⁻ʲ perpetually *3–4*, ⟨corrected *4e–6*⟩

[40] The American war would appear to have been an exception in that it touched directly on the economic interest of the mercantile classes. See above, IV.vii.c.43.

[41] A. Anderson, *Origin of Commerce* (1764), ii.273.

some opposition. The more taxes may have been multiplied, the higher they may have been raised upon every different subject of taxation; the more loudly the people complain of every new tax, the more difficult it becomes too either to find out new subjects of taxation, or to raise much higher the taxes already imposed upon the old. A momentary suspension of the payment of debt is not immediately felt by the people, and occasions neither murmur nor complaint. To borrow of the sinking fund is always an obvious and easy expedient for getting out of the present difficulty. The more the publick debts may have been accumulated, the more neces-sary it may have become to study to reduce them, the more dangerous, the more ruinous it may be to misapply any part of the sinking fund; the less likely is the publick debt to be reduced to any considerable degree, the more likely, the more certainly is the sinking fund to be misapplied towards defraying all the extraordinary expences which occur in time of peace. When a nation is already over burdened with taxes, nothing but the necessities of a new war, nothing but either the animosity of national vengeance, or the anxiety for national security, can induce the people to submit, with tolerable patience, to a new tax. Hence the usual mis-application of the sinking fund.

41   [420] In Great Britain, from the time that we had first recourse to the ruin-ous expedient of perpetual funding, the reduction of the publick debt in time of peace, has never borne any proportion to its accumulation in time of war. It was in the war which began in 1688, and was concluded by the treaty of Ryswick in 1697, that the foundation of the present enormous debt of Great Britain was first laid.

42   On the 31st of December, 1697, the publick debts of Great Britain, funded and unfunded, amounted to 21,515,742*l.* 13*s.* 8½*d.*[42] A great part of those debts had been contracted upon short anticipations, and some part upon annuities for lives; so that before the 31st of December, 1701, in less than four years, there had partly been paid off, and partly reverted to the publick, the sum of 5,121,041*l.* 12*s.* 0¾*d.*; a greater reduction of the publick debt than has ever since been brought about in so short a period of time. The remaining debt, therefore, amounted only to 16,394,701*l.* 1*s.* 7¼*d.*

43   In the war which began in 1702, and which was concluded by the treaty of Utrecht,[43] the publick debts were still more accumulated. On the 31st of December, 1714, they amounted to 53,681,076*l.* 5*s.* 6$\frac{1}{12}$*d.* The subscription into the South Sea fund of the *⁹short and long⁹* annuities increased the capital of the publick debts, so that on the 31st of December,

---

⁹⁻⁹ long and short 1

[42] The information in this and the two subsequent paragraphs is from James Postle-thwayt, *History of the Public Revenue*, 42, 145, 147, 224, 300.

[43] In LJ (A) v.141 the peace of Utrecht is mentioned as one of 'many foolish peaces'.

1722, it amounted to 55,282,978*l*. 1*s*. 3⅚*d*. The reduction of the debt began in 1723, and went on so slowly that, on the 31st of December, 1739, [421] during seventeen years of profound peace, the whole sum paid off was no more than 8,328,354*l*. 17*s*. 11$\frac{1}{12}$*d*. the capital of the publick debt at that time amounting to 46,954,623*l*. 3*s*. 4$\frac{7}{12}$*d*.

44   The Spanish war, which began in 1739, and the French war which soon followed it, occasioned a further increase of the debt, which, on the 31st of December, 1748, after the war had been concluded by the treaty of Aix la Chapelle, amounted to 78,293,313*l*. 1*s*. 10¾*d*. The most profound peace of seventeen years continuance had taken no more than 8,328,354*l*. 17*s*. 11$\frac{3}{12}$*d*. from it. A war of less than nine years continuance added 31,338,689*l*. 18*s*. 6⅙*d*. to it*.

45   During the administration of Mr. Pelham,[44] the interest of the publick debt was reduced, or at least measures were taken for reducing it, from four to three per cent.;[45] the sinking fund was increased, and some part of the publick debt was paid off. In 1755, before the breaking out of the late war, the funded debt of Great Britain amounted to 72,289,673*l*. On the 5th of January, 1763, at the conclusion of the peace, the funded debt amounted to 122,603,336*l*. 8*s*. 2¼*d*. The unfunded debt has been stated at 13,927,589*l*. 2*s*. 2*d*. But the expence occasioned by the war did not end with the conclusion of the peace; so that though, on the 5th of January, 1764, the funded debt was increased (partly by a new loan, and partly by funding a part of the unfunded debt) to 129,586,789*l*. [422] 10*s*. 1¾*d*. there still remained (according to the very well informed author of the *Considerations on the trade and finances of Great Britain*) an un-funded debt which was brought to account in that and the following year, of 9,975,017*l*. 12*s*. 2$\frac{15}{44}$*d*.[46] In 1764, therefore, the publick debt of Great Britain, funded and unfunded together, amounted, according to this author, to ᴴ139,516,807*l*.ᴴ 2*s*. 4*d*.[47] The annuities for lives too, which had been granted as premiums to the subscribers to the new loans in 1757, estimated at fourteen years purchase, were valued at 472,500*l*.;

---

* See James Postlethwaite's history of the publick revenue.

ʰ⁻ʰ 139,561,807 *l*. *1*

[44] In LJ (A) vi.168 Pelham is mentioned as having raised 10 millions in one year, and Pitt is said to have raised 23 millions with 'greater ease than it had ever been done before'. The same point is made in LJ (B) 265, ed. Cannan 207, where it is stated that 'A late Minister of State levied in one year 23 millions with greater ease than Lord Godolphin could levy 6 in Q. Ann's time.'

[45] Above, V.iii.27.

[46] *Considerations on the Trade and Finances of the Kingdom* (London, 1766), 22, attri-buted to Thomas Whately and often ascribed to George Grenville. Most of the informa-tion in this paragraph is from the book.

[47] Not stated in *Considerations on the Trade and Finances of the Kingdom* but derived from it by adding together £129,586,789 10*s*. 1¾*d*. and £9,975,017 12*s*. 2$\frac{14}{44}$*d*., giving £139,561,807 2*s*. 4*d*. as in Ed. 1.

and the annuities for long terms of years, granted as premiums likewise, in 1761 and 1762, estimated at 27½ years purchase, were valued at 6,826,875*l*. During a peace of about seven years continuance, the prudent and truly patriot administration of Mr. Pelham, was not able to pay off an old debt of six millions. During a war of nearly the same continuance, a new debt of more than seventy-five millions was contracted.

46   On the 5th of January, 1775, the funded debt of Great Britain amounted to 124,996,086*l*. 1*s*. 6¼*d*. The unfunded, exclusive of a large civil list debt, to 4,150,236*l*. 3*s*. 11⅞*d*. Both together, to 129,146,322*l*. 5*s*. 6*d*. According to this account the whole debt paid off during eleven years profound peace amounted only to 10,415,474*l*. 16*s*. 9⅞*d*. Even this small reduction of debt, however, has not been all made from the savings out of the ordinary revenue of the state. Several extraneous sums, [423] altogether independent of that ordinary revenue, have contributed towards it. ʻAmongstʻ these we may reckon an additional shilling in the pound land tax for three years; the two millions received from the East India company, as indemnification for their territorial acquisitions; and the one hundred and ten thousand pounds received from the bank for the renewal of their charter. To these must be added several other sums which, as they arose out of the late war, ought perhaps to be considered as deductions from the expences of it. The principal are

	l.	*s.*	*d.*
The produce of French prizes	690,449	18	9
Composition for French prisoners[48]	670,000	0	0
What has been received from the sale of the ceded islands[49]	95,500	0	0
Total,	1,455,949	18	9

If we add to this sum the balance of the earl of Chatham's and Mr. Calcraft's accounts, and other army savings of the same kind, together with what has been received from the bank, the East India company, and the additional shilling in the pound land tax; the whole must be a good deal more than five millions. The debt, therefore, which since the peace has been paid out of the savings from the ordinary revenue of the state, has not, one year with another, amounted to half a million a year. The sink-

---

ʻ⁻ʻ Among *I*

---

⁴⁸ In LJ (B) 346–7, ed. Cannan 271, cartel agreements are cited as evidence of a growing humanity in the treatment of prisoners-of-war. In such treaties, Smith pointed out, 'soldiers and sailors are valued at so much and exchanged at the end of every campaign'. He added that 'In the late war indeed, we refused to enter into any such treaty with France for sailors, and by this wise regulation soon unman'd their navy, as we took a great many more than they.'

⁴⁹ The ceded islands are mentioned above, IV.vii.b.31.

ing fund, has, no doubt, been considerably augmented since the peace, by the debt which has been paid [424] off, by the reduction of the redeemable four per cents. to three per cents, and by the annuities for lives which have fallen in, and, if peace *was* to continue, a million, perhaps, might now be annually spared out of it towards the discharge of the debt. Another million, accordingly, was paid in the course of last year; but, at the same time, a large civil list debt was left unpaid, and we are now involved in a new war which, in its progress, may prove as expensive as any of our former wars*. The new debt which will probably be contracted before the end of the next campaign, may perhaps be nearly equal to all the old debt which has been paid off from the savings out of the ordinary revenue of the state. It would be altogether chimerical, therefore, to expect that the publick debt should ever be completely discharged by any savings which are likely to be made from that ordinary revenue as it stands at present.

47   The publick funds of the different indebted nations of Europe, particularly those of England, have by one author been represented as the accumulation of a great capital superadded to the other capital of the country, by means of which its trade is extended, its manufactures multiplied, and its lands cultivated and im-[425]proved much beyond what they could have been by means of that other capital only[50]. He does not consider that the capital which the first creditors of the publick advanced to government, was, from the moment in which they advanced it, a certain portion of the annual produce turned away from serving in the function of a capital, to serve in that of a revenue; from maintaining productive labourers to maintain unproductive ones, and to be spent and wasted, generally in the course of the year, without even the hope of any future reproduction. In return for the capital which they advanced they obtained, indeed, an annuity in the publick funds in most cases of more than equal value. This annuity, no doubt, replaced to them their capital, and enabled them to carry on their trade and business to the same or perhaps to a greater extent than before; that is, they were enabled either to borrow of other people a new capital upon the credit of this annuity, or by selling it to get from other people a new capital of their own, equal or superior to that which they had advanced to government. This new capital, however, which they in this manner either bought or borrowed of other people, must have existed in the country before, and must have been

---

*k** It has proved more expensive than any of our former wars; and has involved us in an additional debt of more than one hundred millions. During a profound peace of eleven years, little more than ten millions of debt was paid; during a war of seven years, more than one hundred millions was contracted.*k*

j–j were 4–6   *k–k* 3–6

[50] Cf. J. F. Melon, *Essai politique sur le Commerce* (1734), trans. D. Bindon (Dublin 1738), 330.

employed, as all capitals are, in maintaining productive labour. When it came into the hands of those who had advanced their money to government, though it was in some respects a new capital to them, it was not so to the country; but was only a capital withdrawn from certain [426] employments in order to be turned towards others. Though it replaced to them what they had advanced to government, it did not replace it to the country. Had they not advanced this capital to government, there would have been in the country two capitals, two portions of the annual produce, instead of one, employed in maintaining productive labour.

48   When for defraying the expence of government a revenue is raised within the year from the produce of free or unmortgaged taxes, a certain portion of the revenue of private people is only turned away from maintaining one species of unproductive labour, towards maintaining another. Some part of what they pay in those taxes might no doubt have been accumulated into capital, and consequently employed in maintaining productive labour; but the greater part would probably have been spent and consequently employed in maintaining unproductive labour. The publick expence, however, when defrayed in this manner, no doubt hinders more or less the further accumulation of new capital; but it does not necessarily occasion the destruction of any actually existing capital.

49   When the publick expence is defrayed by funding, it is defrayed by the annual destruction of some capital which had before existed in the country; by the perversion of some portion of the annual produce which had before been destined for the maintenance of productive labour, towards that of unproductive labour. As in this case, however, the taxes are lighter than [427] they would have been, had a revenue sufficient for defraying the same expence been raised within the year; the private revenue of individuals is necessarily less burdened, and consequently their ability to save and accumulate some part of that revenue into capital is a good deal less impaired. If the method of funding ¹destroys¹ more old capital, it at the same time hinders less the accumulation or acquisition of new capital, than that of defraying the publick expence by a revenue raised within the year. Under the system of funding, the frugality and industry of private people can more easily repair the breaches which the waste and extravagance of government may occasionally make in the general capital of the society.⁵¹

50   It is only during the continuance of war, however, that the system of funding has this advantage over the other system. Were the expence of war to be defrayed always by a revenue raised within the year, the taxes

¹⁻¹ destroy 4–6

---

⁵¹ It is also remarked at II.iii.31 that the frugality of private people is generally capable of overcoming the extravagance of government. See also below, § 57.

from which that extraordinary revenue was drawn would last no longer than the war. The ability of private people to accumulate, though less during the war, would have been greater during the peace than under the system of funding. War would not necessarily have occasioned the destruction of any old capitals, and peace would have occasioned the accumulation of many more new. Wars would in general be more speedily concluded, and less wantonly undertaken. The people feeling, during the continuance of ᵐtheᵐ war, the complete burden of it, would soon grow weary of it, [428] and government, in order to humour them, would not be under the necessity of carrying it on longer than it was necessary to do so. The foresight of the heavy and unavoidable burdens of war would hinder the people from wantonly calling for it when there was no real or solid interest to fight for. The seasons during which the ability of private people to accumulate was somewhat impaired, would occur more rarely, and be of shorter continuance. Those on the contrary, during which that ability was in the highest vigour, would be of much longer duration than they can well be under the system of funding.

51   When funding, besides, has made a certain progress, the multiplication of taxes which it brings along with it sometimes impairs as much the ability of private people to accumulate even in time of peace, as the other system would in time of war. The peace revenue of Great Britain amounts at present to more than ten millions a year. If free and unmortgaged, it might be sufficient, with proper management and without contracting a shilling of new debt, to carry on the most vigorous war. The private revenue of the inhabitants of Great Britain is at present as much encumbered in time of peace, their ability to accumulate is as much impaired as it would have been in the time of the most expensive war, had the pernicious system of funding never been adopted.

52   In the payment of the interest of the publick debt, it has been said, it is the right hand which pays the left.⁵² The money does not go out of

ᵐ⁻ᵐ *om.* 6

⁵² In LJ (B) 269, ed. Cannan 210, Smith also refers to the apology for the public debt offered by some (unspecified) authors: 'Say they, tho' we owe at present above 100 millions, we owe it to ourselves, or at least very little of it to forreigners. It is just the right hand owing the left, and on the whole can be little or no disadvantage.' Smith rejected this doctrine on the ground that the taxes paid by the industrious classes, such as the merchants, in effect reduced their stocks: 'it is to be considered that the interest of this 100 millions is paid by industrious people, and given to support idle people who are employed in gathering it. Thus industry is taxed to support idleness. If the debt had not been contracted, by prudence and œconomy the nation would have been much richer than at present.' Smith went on to point out that the contemporary clamour against the debt caused Sir Robert Walpole to try and show that 'the public debt was no inconvenience, tho' it is to be supposed that a man of his abilities saw the contrary himself' (LJ (B) 270, ed. Cannan 210–11). In his essay 'Of Public Credit' Hume described the doctrine as being based on 'loose reasonings and specious comparisons' (*Essays Moral, Political and Literary*, ed. Green and Grose, i.366). Melon stated: 'The Debts of a State are Debts due from the right hand to the left'. *Essai*, trans. Bindon, 329.

[429] the country. It is only a part of the revenue of one set of the inhabitants which is transferred to another; and the nation is not a farthing the poorer. This apology is founded altogether in the sophistry of the mercantile system, and after the long examination which I have already bestowed upon that system, it may perhaps be unnecessary to say any thing further about it. It supposes, besides, that the whole publick debt is owing to the inhabitants of the country, which happens not to be true; the Dutch, as well as several other foreign nations, having a very considerable share in our publick funds.[53] But though the whole debt were owing to the inhabitants of the country, it would not upon that account be less pernicious.

53   Land and capital stock are the two original sources of all revenue both private and publick. Capital stock pays the wages of productive labour, whether employed in agriculture, manufactures, or commerce. The management of those two original sources of revenue belongs to two different setts of people; the proprietors of land, and the owners or employers of capital stock.

54   The proprietor of land is interested for the sake of his own revenue to keep his estate in as good condition as he can, by building and repairing his tenants houses, by making and maintaining the necessary drains and enclosures, and all those other expensive improvements which it properly belongs to the landlord to make and maintain.[54] But by different landtaxes the re-[430]venue of the landlord may be so much diminished; and by different duties upon the necessaries and conveniencies of life, that diminished revenue may be rendered of so little real value, that he may find himself altogether unable to make or maintain those expensive improvements. When the landlord, however, ceases to do his part, it is altogether impossible that the tenant should continue to do his. As the distress of the landlord increases, the agriculture of the country must necessarily decline.

55   When, by different taxes upon the necessaries and conveniencies of life, the owners and employers of capital stock find, that whatever revenue they derive from it, will not, in a particular country, purchase the same quantity of those necessaries and conveniencies, which an equal revenue would in almost any other; they will be disposed to remove to some other.[55] And when, in order to raise those taxes, all or the greater part of merchants and manufacturers; that is, all or the greater part of the employers of great capitals, come to be continually exposed to the mortifying and vexatious visits of the tax-gatherers;[56] this disposition to remove will soon be changed into an actual removal. The industry of the country will

---

[53] Though Smith indicated earlier that there was a tendency to exaggerate the amount held by the Dutch. See above, I.ix.10.
[54] Cf. I.xi.a.2.   [55] See above, V.ii.f.6.   [56] Above, V.ii.b.6, V.ii.k.65 and V.iii.74.

necessarily fall with the removal of the capital which supported it, and the ruin of trade and manufactures will follow the declension of agriculture.

56   To transfer from the owners of those two great sources of revenue, land and capital stock, from the persons immediately interested in the good [431] condition of every particular portion of land, and in the good management of every particular portion of capital stock, to another set of persons (the creditors of the publick, who have no such particular interest) the greater part of the revenue arising from either, must, in the long-run, occasion both the neglect of land, and the waste or removal of capital stock. A creditor of the publick has no doubt a general interest in the prosperity of the agriculture, manufactures, and commerce of the country; and consequently in the good condition of its lands, and in the good management of its capital stock. Should there be any general failure or declension in any of these things, the produce of the different taxes might no longer be sufficient to pay him the annuity or interest which is due to him. But a creditor of the publick, considered merely as such, has no interest in the good condition of any particular portion of land, or in the good management of any particular portion of capital stock. As a creditor of the publick he has no knowledge of any such particular portion. He has no inspection of it. He can have no care about it. Its ruin may in ⁿsomeⁿ cases be unknown to him, and cannot directly affect him.

57   The practice of funding has gradually enfeebled every state which has adopted it. The Italian republicks seem to have begun it. Genoa and Venice, the only two remaining which can pretend to an independent existence, have both been enfeebled by it. Spain seems to have learned the practice from the Italian republicks, [432] and (its taxes being probably less judicious than theirs) it has, in proportion to its natural strength, been still more enfeebled. The debts of Spain are of very old standing. It was deeply in debt before the end of the sixteenth century, about a hundred years before England owed a shilling. France, notwithstanding all its natural resources, languishes under an oppressive load of the same kind. The republick of the United Provinces is as much enfeebled by its debts as either Genoa or Venice. Is it likely that in Great Britain alone a practice, which has brought either weakness or desolation into every other country, should prove altogether innocent?

58   The system of taxation established in those different countries, it may be said, is inferior to that of England. I believe it is so. But it ought to be remembered, that when the wisest government has exhausted all the proper subjects of taxation, it must, in cases of urgent necessity, have recourse to improper ones.[57] The wise republick of Holland has upon

---

ⁿ⁻ⁿ most *1*

[57] Above, V.ii.k.80.

some occasions been obliged to have recourse to taxes as inconvenient as the greater part of those of Spain. Another war begun before any considerable liberation of the publick revenue had been brought about, and growing in its progress as expensive as the last war, may, from irresistible necessity, render the British system of taxation as oppressive as that of Holland, or even as that of Spain. To the honour of our present system of taxation, indeed, it has hitherto given so little embarrassment to industry, that, during the [433] course even of the most expensive wars, the frugality and good conduct of individuals °seem° to have been able, by saving and accumulation, to repair all the breaches which the waste and extravagance of government had made in the general capital of the society.[58] At the conclusion of the late war, the most expensive that Great Britain ever waged, her agriculture was as flourishing, her manufacturers as numerous and as fully employed, and her commerce as extensive, as they had ever been before. The capital, therefore, which supported all those different branches of industry, must have been equal to what it had ever been before. Since the peace, agriculture has been still further improved, the rents of houses have risen in every town and village of the country, a proof of the increasing wealth and revenue of the people; and the annual amount of the greater part of the old taxes, of the principal branches of the excise and customs in particular, has been continually increasing, an equally clear proof of an increasing consumption, and consequently of an increasing produce, which could alone support that consumption. Great Britain seems to support with ease, a burden which, half a century ago, nobody believed her capable of supporting. Let us not, however, upon this account rashly conclude that she is capable of supporting any burden; nor even be too confident that she could support, without great distress, a burden a little greater than what has already been laid upon her.

59   [434] When national debts have once been accumulated to a certain degree, there is scarce, I believe, a single instance of their having been fairly and compleatly paid. The liberation of the publick revenue, if it has ever been brought about at all, has always been brought about by a bankruptcy; sometimes by an avowed one, but always by a real one, though frequently by a pretended payment.

60   The raising of the denomination of the coin has been the most usual expedient by which a real publick bankruptcy has been disguised under the appearance of a pretended payment.[59] If a sixpence, for example, should either by act of parliament or royal proclamation be raised to the denomination of a shilling, and twenty sixpences to that of a pound sterling; the

person who under the old denomination had borrowed twenty shillings, or near four ounces of silver, would, under the new, pay with twenty six-pences, or with something less than two ounces. A national debt of about a hundred and twenty-eight millions, nearly the capital of the funded and unfunded debt of Great Britain, might in this manner be paid with about sixty-four millions of our present money. It would indeed be a pretended payment only, and the creditors of the publick would really be defrauded of ten shillings in the pound of what was due to them. The calamity too would extend much further than to the creditors of the publick, and those of every private person would suffer a proportionable loss; and this without any advantage, but [435] in most cases with a great additional loss, to the creditors of the publick. If the creditors of the publick indeed were gener-ally much in debt to other people, they might in some measure compensate their loss by paying their creditors in the same coin in which the publick had paid them. But in most countries the creditors of the publick are, the greater part of them, wealthy people, who stand more in the relation of creditors than in that of debtors towards the rest of their fellow-citizens. A pretended payment of this kind, therefore, instead of alleviating, aggra-vates in most cases the loss of the creditors of the publick; and without any advantage to the publick, extends the calamity to a great number of other innocent people. It occasions a general and most pernicious subver-sion of the fortunes of private people; enriching in most cases the idle and profuse debtor at the expence of the industrious and frugal creditor, and transporting a great part of the national capital from the hands which were likely to increase and improve it, to those which are likely to dissipate and destroy it. When it becomes necessary for a state to declare itself bankrupt, in the same manner as when it becomes necessary for an individual to do so, a fair, open, and avowed bankruptcy is always the measure which is both least dishonourable to the debtor, and least hurtful to the creditor. The honour of a state is surely very poorly provided for, when, in order to cover the disgrace of a real bankruptcy, it has recourse to a juggling trick of this kind, so easily seen [436] through, and at the same time so extremely pernicious.

61   Almost all states, however, antient as well as modern, when reduced to this necessity, have, upon some occasions, played this very juggling trick. The Romans, at the end of the first Punic war, reduced the As, the coin or denomination by which they computed the value of all their other coins, from containing twelve ounces of copper to contain only two ounces; that is, they raised two ounces of copper to a denomination which had always before expressed the value of twelve ounces. The republick was, in this manner, enabled to pay the great debts which it had contracted with the sixth part of what it really owed. So sudden and so great a bankruptcy, we should in the present times be apt to imagine, must have occasioned a

very violent popular clamour. It does not appear to have occasioned any. The law which enacted it was, like all other laws relating to the coin, introduced and carried through the assembly of the people by a tribune, and was probably a very popular law. In Rome, as in all the other antient republicks, the poor people were constantly in debt to the rich and the great, who, in order to secure their votes at the annual elections, used to lend them money at exorbitant interest, which, being never paid, soon accumulated into a sum too great either for the debtor to pay, or for any body else to pay for him. The debtor, for fear of a very severe execution, was obliged, without any further gratuity, to vote [437] for the candidate whom the creditor recommended. In spite of all the laws against bribery and corruption, the bounty of the candidates, together with the occasional distributions of corn, which were ordered by the senate, were the principal funds from which, during the ᵖlatterᵖ times of the Roman republick, the poorer citizens derived their subsistence.⁶⁰ To deliver themselves from this subjection to their creditors, the poorer citizens were continually calling out either for an entire abolition of debts, or for what they called New Tables; that is, for a law which should entitle them to a complete acquittance, upon paying only a certain proportion of their accumulated debts. The law which reduced the coin of all denominations to a sixth part of its former value, as it enabled them to pay their debts with a sixth part of what they really owed, was equivalent to the most advantageous new tables. In order to satisfy the people, the rich and the great were, upon several different occasions, obliged to consent to laws both for abolishing debts, and for introducing new tables; and they probably were induced to consent to this law, partly for the same reason, and partly that, by liberating the publick revenue, they might restore vigour to that government of which they themselves had the principal direction. An operation of this kind would at once reduce a debt of a hundred and twenty-eight millions to twenty-one millions three hundred and thirty-three thousand three hundred and thirty-three pounds six shillings and eight-[438]pence. In the course of the second Punic war the As was still further reduced, first, from two ounces of copper to one ounce; and afterwards from one ounce to half an ounce; that is, to the twenty-fourth part of its original value.⁶¹ By combining the three Roman operations into one, a debt of a hundred and twenty-eight millions of our present money, might in this manner be reduced all at once to a debt of five millions three hundred and thirty-three thousand

---

ᵖ⁻ᵖ later *1–2*

---

⁶⁰ Smith comments at I.xi.b.12 on the adverse effect on Roman agriculture of the free distribution of corn. See also III.ii.21.

⁶¹ Pliny, *Natural History*, XXXIII.xiii, translated by H. Rackham in Loeb Classical Library (1952), ix.35–9. See above I.iv.10. These points are also made by Montesquieu, *Esprit*, XXII.xi, and see also xii.

three hundred and thirty-three pounds six shillings and eight-pence. Even the enormous debt of Great Britain might in this manner soon be paid.

62   By means of such expedients the coin of, I believe, all nations has been gradually reduced more and more below its original value, and the same nominal sum has been gradually brought to contain a smaller and a smaller quantity of silver.

63   Nations have sometimes, for the same purpose, adulterated the standard of their coin; that is, have mixed a greater quantity of alloy in it. If in the pound weight of our silver coin, for example, instead of eighteen penny weight, according to the present standard, there was mixed eight ounces of alloy; a pound sterling, or twenty shillings of such coin, would be worth little more than six shillings and eight-pence of our present money. The quantity of silver contained in six shillings and eight-pence of our present money, would thus be raised very nearly to the denomination of a pound sterling. The adulteration of the standard has exactly the same effect with what the French call an augmentation, [439] or a direct raising of the denomination of the coin.

64   An augmentation, or a direct raising of the denomination of the coin, always is, and from its nature must be, an open and avowed operation. By means of it pieces of a smaller weight and bulk are called by the same name which had before been given to pieces of a greater weight and bulk. The adulteration of the standard, on the contrary, has generally been a concealed operation. By means of it pieces were issued from the mint of the same denominations, and, as nearly as could be contrived, of the same weight, bulk, and appearance, with pieces which had been current before of much greater value. When king John of France*, in order to pay his debts, adulterated his coin, all the officers of his mint were sworn to secrecy. Both operations are unjust. But a simple augmentation is an injustice of open violence; whereas an adulteration is an injustice of treacherous fraud. This latter operation, therefore, as soon as it has been discovered, and it could never be concealed very long, has always excited much greater indignation than the former. The coin after any considerable augmentation has very seldom been brought back to its former weight; but after the greatest adulterations it has almost always been brought back to its former fineness. It has scarce ever happened that the fury and indignation of the people could otherwise be appeased.

65   [440] In the end of the reign of Henry VIII. and in the beginning of that of Edward VI. the English coin was not only raised in its denomination, but adulterated in its standard. The like frauds were practised in Scotland during the minority of James VI. They have occasionally been practised in most other countries.

* See Du Cange Glossary, voce Moneta; the Benedictine edition. [C. Du Fresne, Sieur du Cange, *Glossarium* (Paris, 1842), iv.493. See also Melon, *Essai*, trans. Bindon, 221-2.]

66   That the publick revenue of Great Britain can ^qnever^q be compleatly liberated, or even that any considerable progress can ever be made towards that liberation, while the surplus of that revenue, or what is over and above defraying the annual expence of the peace establishment, is so very small, it seems altogether in vain to expect. That liberation, it is evident, can never be brought about without either some very considerable augmentation of the publick revenue, or some equally considerable reduction of the publick expence.[62]

67   A more equal land-tax, a more equal tax upon the rent of houses, and such alterations in the present system of customs and excise as those which have been mentioned in the foregoing chapter, might, perhaps, without increasing the burden of the greater part of the people, but only distributing the weight of it more equally upon the whole, produce a considerable augmentation of revenue. The most sanguine projector, however, could scarce flatter himself that any augmentation of this kind would be such as could give any reasonable hopes, either of liberating the publick revenue altogether, or even of making such progress towards that liberation in time of peace, as [441] either to prevent or to compensate the further accumulation of the publick debt in the next war.

68   By extending the British system of taxation to all the different provinces of the empire inhabited by people ^rof either^r British or European extraction, a much greater augmentation of revenue might be expected. This, however, could scarce, perhaps, be done, consistently with the principles of the British constitution, without admitting into the British parliament, or if you will into the states-general of the British Empire, a fair and equal representation of all those different provinces, that of each province bearing the same proportion to the produce of its taxes, as the representation of Great Britain might bear to the produce of the taxes levied upon Great Britain.[63] The private interest of many powerful individuals, the

---

^{q-q} ever *1*   ^{r-r} either of *1*

[62] In Letter 203 addressed to William Eden, dated 3 January 1780, Smith wrote 'It does not occur to me that much can be added to what you have already said. The difficulty of either inventing new taxes or increasing the old, is, I apprehend, the principal cause of our embarassment.' Smith suggested three possibilities, apart from a 'strict attention to Oeconomy' first, a repeal of the bounties on exportation which in some years had reached £600,000; second, a repeal of the prohibitions on importation and the substitution of 'moderate and reasonable duties in the room of them'; third, repeal of the prohibition of exporting wool and the substitution of 'a pretty high duty in the room of it'. The reference is to William Eden's *Four Letters to the Earl of Carlisle* (London, 1779).

[63] See above, IV.vii.c.75. Smith considered that this principle would eventually lead to a transfer of the seat of empire, IV.vii.c.79. LJ (A) v.134–5 refers to the connection between taxation and representation as a doctrine derived from Locke, and added that 'It is in Britain alone that any consent of the people is required and God knows it is but a very figurative metaphoricall consent which is given here'. Cf. LJ (B) 94, ed. Cannan 69 and WN IV.vii.b.51.

confirmed prejudices of great bodies of people seem, indeed, at present, to oppose to so great a change such obstacles as it may be very difficult, perhaps altogether impossible, to surmount.[64] Without, however, pretending to determine whether such a union be practicable or impracticable, it may not, perhaps, be improper, in a speculative work of this kind, to consider how far the British system of taxation might be applicable to all the different provinces of the empire; what revenue might be expected from it if so applied, and in what manner a general union of this kind might be likely to affect the happiness and prosperity of the different provinces comprehended within it. Such a specula-[442]tion can at worst be regarded but as a new Utopia, less amusing certainly, but not more useless and chimerical than the old one.

69   The land-tax, the stamp duties, and the different duties of customs and excise, constitute the four principal branches of the British taxes.

70   Ireland is certainly as able, and our American and West Indian plantations more able to pay a land-tax than Great Britain.[65] Where the landlord is subject neither to tithe nor poors rate, he must certainly be more able to pay such a tax, than where he is subject to both those other burdens. The tithe, where there is no modus, and where it is levied in kind, diminishes more what would otherwise be the rent of the landlord, than a land-tax which really amounted to five shillings in the pound. Such a tithe will be found in most cases to amount to more than a fourth part of the real rent of the land, or of what remains after replacing compleatly the capital of the farmer, together with his reasonable profit. If all moduses and all impropriations were taken away, the compleat church tithe of Great Britain and Ireland could not well be estimated at less than six or seven millions. If there was no tithe either in Great Britain or Ireland, the landlords could afford to pay six or seven millions additional land-tax, without being more burdened than a very great part of them are at present. America pays no tithe, and could therefore very well afford to pay a land-tax. The lands in America and the West Indies, indeed, are in general not tenanted ˢnorˢ leased out [443] to farmers. They could not therefore be assessed according to any rent-roll. But neither were the lands of Great Britain, in the 4th of William and Mary, assessed according to any rent-roll, but according to a very loose and inaccurate estimation.[66] The lands in America might be assessed either in the same manner, or according to an equitable valuation in consequence of an accurate survey, like that which was lately made in the Milanese, and in the dominions of Austria, Prussia, and Sardinia.[67]

ˢ⁻ˢ or *I*

---

[64] Above, IV.vii.c.77–9.
[66] See above, V.ii.c.2.

[65] This tax is described above, V.ii.c.2.
[67] Cf. V.ii.c.26.

71   Stamp-duties, it is evident, might be levied without any variation in all countries where the forms of law process, and the deeds by which property both real and personal is transferred, are the same or nearly the same.

72   The extension of the custom-house laws of Great Britain to Ireland and the plantations, provided it was accompanied, as in justice it ought to be, with an extension of the freedom of trade, would be in the highest degree advantageous to both.[68] All the invidious restraints which at present oppress the trade of Ireland, the distinction between the enumerated and non-enumerated commodities of America, would be entirely at an end.[69] The countries north of Cape Finisterre would be as open to every part of the produce of America, as those south of that Cape are to some parts of that produce at present. The trade between all the different parts of the British empire would, in consequence of this uniformity in the *custom-house laws*, be as free as the coasting trade of Great Britain is at present. The British [444] empire would thus afford within itself an immense internal market for every part of the produce of all its different provinces. So great an extension of market would soon compensate both to Ireland and the plantations, all that they could suffer from the increase of the duties of customs.

73   The excise is the only part of the British system of taxation, which would require to be varied in any respect according as it was applied to the different provinces of the empire. It might be applied to Ireland without any variation; the produce and consumption of that kingdom being exactly of the same nature with those of Great Britain. In its application to America and the West Indies, of which the produce and consumption are so very

t-t customhouse *1*

---

[68] See below, § 89. Smith expressed agreement with regard to the beneficial consequences of free trade with Ireland in Letter 201 addressed to Henry Dundas, dated 1 November 1779: 'I cannot believe that the manufactures of G.B. can, for a century to come, suffer much from the rivalship of those of Ireland . . . Ireland has neither the Skill, nor the Stock which could enable her to rival England . . . Ireland has neither coal nor Wood.' Smith went on to point out that it would be perfectly reasonable to grant Ireland freedom to export to the most favourable markets, and to relieve her from the 'unjust and unreasonable' restraints under which her glass and woollen industries laboured. Smith supported free trade between Ireland and Britain and concluded that 'Nothing, in my opinion, would be more highly advantageous to both countries than this mutual freedom of trade. It would help to break down that absurd monopoly which we have most absurdly established against ourselves in favour of almost all the different classes of our manufacturers.' Smith expressed similar arguments in Letter 202 addressed to Carlisle, dated 8 November 1779, wherein he also commented that in addition to the lack of raw materials, Ireland also 'wants order, police, and a regular administration of justice both to protect and restrain the inferior ranks of the people, articles more essential to the progress of Industry than both coal and wood put together, and which Ireland must continue to want as long as it continues to be divided between two hostile nations, the oppressors and the oppressed, the protestants and the Papists.'

[69] Above, IV.vii.b.25.

different from those of Great Britain, some modification might be necessary, in the same manner as in its application to the cyder and beer counties
of England.

74   A fermented liquor, for example, which is called beer, but which, as it
is made of melasses, bears very little resemblance to our beer, makes a
considerable part of the common drink of the people in America. This
liquor, as it can be kept only for a few days, cannot, like our beer, be prepared and stored up for sale in great breweries; but every private family
must brew it for their own use, in the same manner as they cook their
victuals. But to subject every private family to the odious visits and examination of the tax-gatherers,[70] in the same manner as we subject the keepers of
alehouses and the brewers for publick sale, would be altogether inconsistent [445] with liberty. If for the sake of equality it was thought necessary to lay a tax upon this liquor,[71] it might be taxed by taxing the material
of which it is made, either at the place of manufacture, or, if the circumstances of the trade rendered such an excise improper, by laying a duty
upon its importation into the colony in which it was to be consumed. Besides the duty of one penny a gallon imposed by the British parliament
upon the importation of melasses into America; there is a provincial tax
of this kind upon their importation into Massachusets Bay, in ships belonging to any other colony, of eight-pence the hogshead; and another
upon their importation, from the northern colonies, into South Carolina,
of five-pence the gallon. Or if neither of these methods was found convenient, each family might compound for its consumption of this liquor,
either according to the number of persons of which it consisted, in the
same manner as private families compound for the malt-tax in England;
or according to the different ages and sexes of those persons, in the same
manner as several different taxes are levied in Holland; or nearly as Sir
Matthew Decker proposes that all taxes upon consumable commodities
should be levied in England. This mode of taxation, it has already been
observed, when applied to objects of a speedy consumption, is not a very
convenient one. It might be adopted, however, in cases where no better
could be done.[72]

75   Sugar, rum, and tobacco, are commodities which are no where necessaries of life,[73] which are [446] become objects of almost universal consumption, and which are therefore extremely proper subjects of taxation. If a
union with the colonies ᵘwasᵘ to take place, those commodities might be
taxed either before they go out of the hands of the manufacturer or grower;
or if this mode of taxation did not suit the circumstances of those persons,

ᵘ⁻ᵘ were 4–6

---

[70] See above, V.ii.b.6, V.ii.k.65 and V.iii.55.   [71] Above, V.ii.k.45,55.
[72] See above, V.ii.k.18, where Decker's proposals are considered.
[73] Smith attempts to define the 'necessaries of life' at V.ii.k.3.

they might be deposited in publick warehouses both at the place of manufacture, and at all the different ports of the empire to which they might afterwards be transported, to remain there, under the joint custody of the owner and the revenue officer, till such time as they should be delivered out either to the consumer, to the merchant retailer for home-consumption, or to the merchant exporter, the tax not to be advanced till such delivery. When delivered out for exportation, to go duty free; upon proper security being given that they should really be exported out of the empire. These are perhaps the principal commodities with regard to which a union with the colonies might require some considerable change in the present system of British taxation.

76   What might be the amount of the revenue which this system of taxation extended to all the different provinces of the empire might produce, it must, no doubt, be altogether impossible to ascertain with tolerable exactness. By means of this system there is annually levied in Great Britain, upon less than eight millions of people, more than ten millions of revenue.[74] Ireland contains more than two millions of people, and [447] according to the accounts laid before the congress, the twelve associated provinces of America contain more than three.[75] Those accounts, however, may have been exaggerated, in order, perhaps, either to encourage their own people, or to intimidate those of this country, and we shall suppose therefore that our North American and West Indian colonies taken together contain no more than three millions; or that the whole British empire, in Europe and America, contains no more than thirteen millions of inhabitants. If upon less than eight millions of inhabitants this system of taxation raises a revenue of more than ten millions sterling; it ought upon thirteen millions of inhabitants to raise a revenue of more than sixteen millions two hundred and fifty thousand pounds sterling. From this revenue, supposing that this system could produce it, must be deducted, the revenue usually raised in Ireland and the plantations for defraying the expence of their respective civil governments. The expence of the civil and military establishment of Ireland, together with the interest of the publick debt, amounts, at a medium of the two years which ended March 1775, to something less than seven hundred and fifty thousand pounds a year.[76] By a very exact account of the revenue of the principal colonies of America and the West Indies, it amounted, before the commencement of the *v*present*v* disturbances, to a hundred and forty-one thousand eight hundred pounds. In this account, however, the revenue of Maryland, of North Carolina, [448] and of all our

---

v–v late *1*

---

[74] The same figures are cited at V.ii.k.78.

[75] See above, IV.iii.c.12. Smith comments on the rapid rate of growth of population in America at I.viii.23.

[76] See above, IV.vii.b.20.

late acquisitions both upon the continent and in the islands, is omitted, which may perhaps make a difference of thirty or forty thousand pounds. For the sake of even numbers therefore, let us suppose that the revenue necessary for supporting the civil government of Ireland, and the plantations, may amount to a million. There would remain consequently a revenue of fifteen millions two hundred and fifty thousand pounds, to be applied towards defraying the general expence of the empire, and towards paying the publick debt. But if from the present revenue of Great Britain a million could in peaceable times be spared towards the payment of that debt, six millions two hundred and fifty thousand pounds could very well be spared from this improved revenue. This great sinking fund too might be augmented every year by the interest of the debt which had been discharged the year before, and might in this manner increase so very rapidly, as to be sufficient in a few years to discharge the whole debt, and thus to restore compleatly the at present debilitated and languishing vigour of the empire. In the mean time the people might be relieved from some of the most burdensome taxes; from those which are imposed either upon the necessaries of life, or upon the materials of manufacture. The labouring poor would thus be enabled to live better, to work cheaper, and to send their goods cheaper to market. The cheapness of their goods would increase the demand for them, and consequently for the labour of [449] those who produced them. This increase in the demand for labour, would both increase the numbers and improve the circumstances of the labouring poor. Their consumption would increase, and together with it the revenue arising from all those articles of their consumption upon which the taxes might be allowed to remain.

77   The revenue arising from this system of taxation, however, might not immediately increase in proportion to the number of people who were subjected to it. Great indulgence would for some time be due to those provinces of the empire which were thus subjected to burthens to which they had not before been accustomed, and even when the same taxes came to be levied every where as exactly as possible, they would not every where produce a revenue proportioned to the numbers of the people. In a poor country the consumption of the principal commodities subject to the duties of customs and excise is very small; and in a thinly inhabited country the opportunities of smuggling are very great. The consumption of malt liquors among the inferior ranks of people in Scotland is very small, and the excise upon malt, beer, and ale, produces less there than in England in proportion to the numbers of the people and the rate of the duties, which upon malt is different on account of a supposed difference of quality. In these particular branches of the excise, there is not, I apprehend, much more smuggling in the one country than in the other. The duties upon the distillery, and the greater part of the duties of customs, in [450] proportion

to the numbers of people in the respective countries, produce less in Scotland than in England, not only on account of the smaller consumption of the taxed commodities, but of the much greater facility of smuggling. In Ireland, the inferior ranks of people are still poorer than in Scotland, and many parts of the country are almost as thinly inhabited. In Ireland, therefore, the consumption of the taxed commodities might, in proportion to the number of the people, be still less than in Scotland, and the facility of smuggling nearly the same. In America and the West Indies the white people even of the lowest rank are in much better circumstances than those of the same rank in England, and their consumption of all the luxuries in which they usually indulge themselves is probably much greater. The blacks, indeed, who make the greater part of the inhabitants both of the southern colonies upon the continent and of the West *w*India*w* islands, as they are in a state of slavery, are, no doubt, in a worse condition than the poorest people either in Scotland or Ireland. We must not, however, upon that account, imagine that they are worse fed, or that their consumption of articles which might be subjected to moderate duties, is less than that even of the lower ranks of people in England. In order that they may work well, it is the interest of their master that they should be fed well and kept in good heart, in the same manner as it is his interest that his working cattle should be so.[77] The blacks accordingly have almost every where their [451] allowance of rum and of melasses or spruce beer, in the same manner as the white servants; and this allowance would not probably be withdrawn, though those articles should be subjected to moderate duties. The consumption of the taxed commodities, therefore, in proportion to the number of inhabitants, would probably be as great in America and the West Indies as in any part of the British empire. The opportunities of smuggling, indeed, would be much greater; America, in proportion to the extent of the country, being much more thinly inhabited than either Scotland or Ireland. If the revenue, however, which is at present raised by the different duties upon malt and malt liquors, *x*was*x* to be levied by a single duty upon malt, the opportunity of smuggling in the most important branch of the excise would be almost entirely taken away: And if the duties of customs, instead of being imposed upon almost all the different articles of importation, were confined to a few of the most general use and consumption, and if the levying of those duties *y*was*y* subjected to the excise laws, the opportunity of smuggling, though not so entirely taken away, would be very much diminished. In consequence of those two, apparently, very simple and easy alterations, the duties of customs and excise might probably produce a revenue as great in proportion to the consumption of

---

w-w Indian *1*   *x-x* were 4-6   *y-y* were 4-6

[77] See above, IV.vii.b.54.

the most thinly inhabited province as they do at present in proportion to
that of the most populous.

78   [452] The Americans, it has been said, indeed, have no gold or silver
money; the interior commerce of the country being carried on by a paper
currency, and the gold and silver which occasionally come among them being
all sent to Great Britain in return for the commodities which they receive
from us.[78] But without gold and silver, it is added, there is no possibility
of paying taxes. We already get all the gold and silver which they have.
How is it possible to draw from them what they have not?

79   The present scarcity of gold and silver money in America is not the effect
of the poverty of that country, or of the inability of the people there to
purchase those metals. In a country where the wages of labour are so much
higher, and the price of provisions so much lower than in England, the
greater part of the people must surely have wherewithal to purchase a
greater quantity, if it ᶻwasᶻ either necessary or convenient for them to do
so. The scarcity of those metals therefore, must be the effect of choice,
and not of necessity.

80   It is for transacting either domestick or foreign business, that gold and
silver money is either necessary or convenient.

81   The domestick business of every country, it has been shewn in the second
book of this inquiry, may, at least in peaceable times, be transacted by
means of a paper currency, with nearly the same degree of conveniency as
by gold and silver money.[79] It is convenient for the Americans, who could
always employ with [453] profit in the improvement of their lands a
greater stock than they can easily get, to save as much as possible the expence of so costly an instrument of commerce as gold and silver, and rather
to employ that part of their surplus produce which would be necessary for
purchasing those metals, in purchasing the instruments of trade, the
materials of clothing, several parts of household furniture, and the iron-
work necessary for building and extending their settlements and plantations; in purchasing, not dead stock, but active and productive stock. The
colony governments find it for their interest to supply ᵃtheᵃ people with
such a quantity of paper-money as is fully sufficient and generally more
than sufficient for transacting their domestick business. Some of those
governments, that of Pennsylvania particularly, derive a revenue from
lending this paper-money to their subjects at an interest of so much per
cent.[80] Others, like that of Massachusett's Bay, advance upon extraordinary emergencies a paper-money of this kind for defraying the publick

---

ᶻ⁻ᶻ were 4–6   ᵃ⁻ᵃ 2–6

---

[78] See above, II.ii.100.   [79] See above, II.ii.
[80] Above, V.ii.a.11. Smith comments on the moderation of the Pennsylvania government at II.ii.102 with regard to the issue of paper money.

expence, and afterwards, when it suits the conveniency of the colony, redeem it at the depreciated value to which it gradually falls.⁸¹ In 1747* that
colony paid, in this manner, the greater part of its publick debts, with the
tenth part of the money for which its bills had been granted. It suits the
conveniency of the planters to save the expence of employing gold and
silver money in their domestick trans-[454]actions; and it suits the conveniency of the colony governments to supply them with a medium, which,
though attended with some very considerable disadvantages, enables them
to save that expence. The redundancy of paper money necessarily banishes
gold and silver from the domestick transactions of the colonies, for the same
reason that it has banished those metals from the greater part of the domestick transactions ᵇinᵇ Scotland;⁸² and in both countries it is not the poverty,
but the enterprizing and projecting spirit of the people, their desire of
employing all the stock which they can get as active and productive stock,
which has occasioned this redundancy of paper money.

82   In the exterior commerce which the different colonies carry on with
Great Britain, gold and silver are more or less employed, exactly in proportion as they are more or less necessary. Where those metals are not
necessary, they seldom appear. Where they are necessary, they are generally
found.

83   In the commerce between Great Britain and the tobacco colonies, the
British goods are generally advanced to the colonists at a pretty long credit,
and are afterwards paid for in tobacco, rated at a certain price.⁸³ It is more
convenient for the colonists to pay in tobacco than in gold and silver. It
would be more convenient for any merchant to pay for the goods which his
correspondents had sold to him in some other sort of goods which he might
happen to deal in, than in money. Such a merchant would have no oc-[455]
casion to keep any part of his stock by him unemployed, and in ready
money, for answering occasional demands. He could have, at all times, a
larger quantity of goods in his shop or warehouse, and he could deal to a
greater extent. But it seldom happens to be convenient for all the correspondents of a merchant to receive payment for the goods which they sell to
him, in goods of some other kind which he happens to deal in. The

---

* See Hutchinson's Hist. of Massachusett's Bay, Vol. II. page 436 & seq. [*History of
the Colony of Massachussett's Bay*, 2nd ed., 1765–8.]

ᵇ⁻ᵇ of *1*

---

⁸¹ Douglass, always an opponent of paper money, commented on the practice in Massa-
chusetts' Bay: 'There seems to be a standing faction consisting of *wrong heads* and *fraudulent debtors*; this faction endeavours to persuade us, that one of our *invaluable* charter
privileges, is *A liberty to make paper-money, or public bills of credit*, receivable in all dealings
(specialities excepted) as a legal tender.' (W. Douglass, *British Settlements in North
America*, i.510–13.)
⁸² See above, II.ii.89, where Scottish experience is likened to that of America.
⁸³ See also IV.vii.c.38.

British merchants who trade to Virginia and Maryland happen to be a particular set of correspondents, to whom it is more convenient to receive payment for the goods which they sell to those colonies in tobacco than in gold and silver. They expect to make a profit by the sale of the tobacco. They could make none by that of the gold and silver. Gold and silver, therefore, very seldom appear in the commerce between Great Britain and the tobacco colonies. Maryland and Virginia have as little occasion for those metals in their foreign as in their domestick commerce. They are said, accordingly, to have less gold and silver money than any other colonies in America. They are reckoned, however, as thriving, and consequently as rich as any of their neighbours.

84   In the northern colonies, Pennsylvania, New York, New Jersey, the four governments of New England, &c. the value of their own produce which they export to Great Britain is not equal to that of the manufactures which they import for their own use, and for that of some of the other colonies to which they are the car-[456]riers. A balance, therefore, must be paid to the mother country in gold and silver, and this balance they generally find.

85   In the sugar colonies the value of the produce annually exported to Great Britain is much greater than that of all the goods imported from thence. If the sugar and rum annually sent to the mother country were paid for in those colonies, Great Britain would be obliged to send out every year a very large balance in money, and the trade to the West Indies would, by a certain species of politicians, be considered as extremely disadvantageous.[84] But it so happens, that many of the principal proprietors of the sugar plantations reside in Great Britain. Their rents are remitted to them in sugar and rum, the produce of their estates. The sugar and rum which the West India merchants purchase in those colonies upon their own account, are not equal in value to the goods which they annually sell there. A balance, therefore, must ᶜnecessarilyᶜ be paid to them in gold and silver, and this balance too is generally found.

86   The difficulty and irregularity of payment from the different colonies to Great Britain, have not been at all in proportion to the greatness or smallness of the balances which were respectively due from them. Payments have in general been more regular from the northern than from the tobacco colonies, though the former have generally paid a pretty large balance in money, while the latter have ᵈeither paidᵈ no balance, or a much [457] smaller one. The difficulty of getting payment from our different sugar colonies has been greater or less in proportion, not so much to

---

ᶜ⁻ᶜ generally *1*   ᵈ⁻ᵈ paid either *1*

[84] That is, the species of politician who measure national well-being in terms of the balance of trade. See V.ii.k.29.

the extent of the balances respectively due from them, as to the quantity of uncultivated land which they contained; that is, to the greater or smaller temptation which the planters have been under of over-trading, or of undertaking the settlement and plantation of greater quantities of waste land than suited the extent of their capitals. The returns from the great island of Jamaica, where there is still much uncultivated land, have, upon this account, been in general more irregular and uncertain than those from the smaller islands of Barbadoes, Antigua, and St. Christophers, which have for these many years been compleatly cultivated, and have, upon that account, afforded less field for the speculations of the planter. The new acquisitions of Grenada, Tobago, St. Vincents, and Dominica, have opened a new field for speculations of this kind; and the returns from those islands have of late been as irregular and uncertain as those from the great island of Jamaica.

87   It is not, therefore, the poverty of the colonies which occasions, in the greater part of them, the present scarcity of gold and silver money. Their great demand for active and productive stock makes it convenient for them to have as little dead stock as possible; and disposes them upon that account to content themselves with a cheaper, though less commodious instrument of commerce than gold and silver. They are [458] thereby enabled to convert the value of that gold and silver into the instruments of trade, into the materials of cloathing, into houshold furniture, and into the iron work necessary for building and extending their settlements and plantations. In those branches of business which cannot be transacted without gold and silver money, it appears that they can always find the necessary quantity of those metals; and if they frequently do not find it, their failure is generally the effect, not of their necessary poverty, but of their unnecessary and excessive enterprize. It is not because they are poor that their payments are irregular and uncertain; but because they are too eager to become excessively rich. Though all that part of the produce of the colony taxes, which was over and above what was necessary for defraying the expence of their own civil and military establishments, were to be remitted to Great Britain in gold and silver, the colonies have abundantly wherewithal to purchase the requisite quantity of those metals. They would in this case be obliged, indeed, to exchange a part of their surplus produce, with which they now purchase active and productive stock, for dead stock. In transacting their domestic business they would be obliged to employ a costly instead of a cheap instrument of commerce;[85] and the expence of purchasing this costly instrument might damp somewhat the vivacity and ardour of their excessive enterprize in the improvement of land. It might not, however, be necessary to remit any part of the American revenue in gold [459] and silver. It might be remitted in bills drawn upon and accepted by

[85] Paper is described as a cheaper instrument of commerce at II.ii.26.

particular merchants or companies in Great Britain, to whom a part of the surplus produce of America had been consigned, who would pay into the treasury the American revenue in money, after having themselves received the value of it in goods; and the whole business might frequently be transacted without exporting a single ounce of gold ^{e}or^e silver from America.

88   It is not contrary to justice that both Ireland and America should contribute towards the discharge of the publick debt of Great Britain. That debt has been contracted in support of the government established by the Revolution, a government to which the protestants of Ireland owe, not only the whole authority which they at present enjoy in their own country, but every security which they possess for their liberty, their property, and their religion; a government to which several of the colonies of America owe their present charters, and consequently their present constitution, and to which all the colonies of America owe the liberty, security, and property which they have ever since enjoyed.[86] That publick debt has been contracted in the defence, not of Great Britain alone, but of all the different provinces of the empire; the immense debt contracted in the late war in particular, and a great part of that contracted in the war before, were both properly contracted in defence of America.[87]

89   [460] By a union with Great Britain, Ireland would gain, besides the freedom of trade, other advantages much more important, and which would much more than compensate any increase of taxes that might accompany that union. By the union with England, the middling and inferior ranks of people in Scotland gained a compleat deliverance from the power of an aristocracy which had always before oppressed them. By ^{f}an^f union with Great Britain the greater part of the people of all ranks in Ireland would gain an equally compleat deliverance from a much more oppressive aristocracy; an aristocracy not founded, like that of Scotland, in the natural and respectable distinctions of birth and fortune;[88] but in the most odious of all distinctions, those of religious and political prejudices; distinctions which, more than any other, animate both the insolence of the oppressors and the hatred and indignation of the oppressed, and which commonly render the inhabitants of the same country more hostile to one another than those of different countries ever are. Without a union with Great Britain, the inhabitants of Ireland are not likely for many ages to consider themselves as one people.

90   No oppressive aristocracy has ever prevailed in the colonies.[89] Even they, however, would, in point of happiness and tranquillity, gain consider-

---

$^{e-e}$ and $\mathit{1}$ $^{f-f}$ a $\mathit{1}$

[86] The constitution of the colonies is described at IV.vii.b.51.   [87] See IV.vii.c.64.
[88] Birth and fortune as sources of authority are considered at V.i.b.11. See also TMS I.iii.2.
[89] Smith comments on the absence of an aristocracy in the colonies at IV.vii b.51.

ably by a union with Great Britain. It would, at least, deliver them from
those rancorous and virulent factions which are inseparable from [461]
small democracies, and which have so frequently divided the affections of
their people, and disturbed the tranquillity of their governments, in their
form so nearly democratical. In the case of a total separation from Great
Britain, which, unless prevented by a union of this kind, seems very likely
to take place, those factions would be ten times more virulent than ever.[90]
Before the commencement of the present disturbances, the coercive power
of the mother-country had always been able to restrain those factions from
breaking out into any thing worse than gross brutality and insult. If that
coercive power ⁹was⁹ entirely taken away, they would probably soon break
out into open violence and bloodshed. In all great countries which are
united under one uniform government, the spirit of party commonly prevails less in the remote provinces than in the centre of the empire. The distance of those provinces from the capital, from the principal seat of the
great scramble of faction and ambition, makes them enter less into the
views of any of the contending parties, and renders them more indifferent
and impartial spectators of the conduct of all.[91] The spirit of party prevails
less in Scotland than in England. In the case of a union it would probably
prevail less in Ireland than in Scotland, and the colonies would probably
soon enjoy a degree of concord and unanimity at present unknown in any
part of the British empire. Both Ireland and the colonies, indeed, would be
subjected to heavier taxes than any which they at present [462] pay. In
consequence, however, of a diligent and faithful application of the publick
revenue towards the discharge of the national debt, the greater part of those
taxes might not be of long continuance, and the publick revenue of Great
Britain might soon be reduced to what was necessary for maintaining a
moderate peace establishment.

91   The territorial acquisitions of the East India company, the undoubted
right of the crown, that is, of the state and people of Great Britain, might
be rendered another source of revenue more abundant, perhaps, than all
those already mentioned. Those countries are represented as more fertile,
more extensive; and in proportion to their extent, much richer and more
populous than Great Britain. In order to draw a great revenue from them,
it would not probably be necessary, to introduce any new system of taxation into countries which are already sufficiently and more than sufficiently
taxed. It might, perhaps, be more proper to lighten, than to aggravate,
the burden of those unfortunate countries, and to endeavour to draw a

---

⁹⁻⁹ were 4–6

---

[90] While recognizing that it was now unlikely, Smith argued that union with the American colonies would 'complete' the British constitution, IV.vii.c.77.
[91] It is interesting to recall that in the TMS the impartial spectator faces a problem of
perspective when 'at a distance' from the object of judgement. Cf. III.i.3.

revenue from them, not by imposing new taxes, but by preventing the embezzlement and misapplication of the greater part of those which they already pay.

92   If it should be found impracticable for Great Britain to draw any considerable augmentation of revenue from any of the resources above mentioned; the only resource which can remain to her is a diminution of her expence. In the mode of collecting, and in that of expending the pub-[463] lick revenue; though in both there may be still room for improvement; Great Britain seems to be at least as œconomical as any of her neighbours. The military establishment which she maintains for her own defence in time of peace, is more moderate than that of any European state which can pretend to rival her either in wealth or in power. None of those articles, therefore, seem to admit of any considerable reduction of expence. The expence of the peace establishment of the colonies was, before the commencement of the present disturbances, very considerable, and is an expence which may, and if no revenue can be drawn from them, ought certainly to be saved altogether. This constant expence in time of peace, though very great, is insignificant in comparison with what the defence of the colonies has cost us in time of war. The last war, which was undertaken altogether on account of the colonies, cost Great Britain, it has already been observed, upwards of ninety millions.[92] The Spanish war of 1739 was principally undertaken on their account; in which, and in the French war that was the consequence of it, Great Britain spent upwards of forty millions, a great part of which ought justly to be charged to the colonies. In those two wars the colonies cost Great Britain much more than double the sum which the national debt amounted to before the commencement of the first of them. Had it not been for those wars that debt might, and probably would by this time, have been compleatly paid; and had it not been for the [464] colonies, the former of those wars might not, and the latter certainly would not have been undertaken. It was because the colonies were supposed to be provinces of the British empire, that this expence was laid out upon them. But countries which contribute neither revenue nor military force towards the support of the empire, cannot be considered as provinces. They may perhaps be considered as appendages, as a sort of splendid and showy equipage of the empire. But if the empire can no longer support the expence of keeping up this equipage, it ought certainly to lay it down; and if it cannot raise its revenue in proportion to its expence, it ought, at least, to accommodate its expence to its revenue. If the colonies, notwithstanding their refusal to submit to British taxes, are still to be considered as provinces of the British empire, their defence in some future war may cost Great Britain as great an expence as it ever has done in any former war. The rulers of Great Britain have, for more than a

[92] Above, IV.i.26, IV.vii.c.64; see also II.iii.35 and IV.viii.53.

century past, amused the people with the imagination that they possessed a great empire on the west side of the Atlantic. This empire, however, has hitherto existed in imagination only. It has hitherto been, not an empire, but the project of an empire; not a gold mine, but the project of a gold mine; a project which has cost, which continues to cost, and which, if pursued in the same way as it has been hitherto, is likely to cost immense expence, without being likely to bring any profit; for the effects of the monopoly of the colony trade, it [465] has been shewn,[93] are, to the great body of the people, mere loss instead of profit. It is surely now time that our rulers should either realize this golden dream, in which they have been indulging themselves, perhaps, as well as the people; or, that they should awake from it themselves, and endeavour to awaken the people. If the project cannot be compleated, it ought to be given up. If any of the provinces of the British empire cannot be made to contribute towards the support of the whole empire, it is surely time that Great Britain should free herself from the expence of defending those provinces in time of war, and of supporting any part of their civil or military establishments in time of peace, and endeavour to accommodate her future views and designs to the real mediocrity of her circumstances.[94]

[93] See above, IV.vii.c.
[94] However, it is argued at IV.vii.c.66 that a voluntary withdrawal is a ridiculous if not a pious hope.

Appendix

THE two following Accounts are subjoined in order to illustrate and confirm what is said[a] in the Fifth Chapter of the Fourth Book[a], concerning the Tonnage bounty to the White Herring Fishery. The Reader, I believe, may depend upon the accuracy of both Accounts.

An Account of Busses fitted out in Scotland for Eleven Years, with the Number of Empty Barrels carried out, and the Number of Barrels of Herrings caught; also the Bounty at a Medium on each Barrel of Seasteeks, and on each Barrel when fully packed.

Years	Number of Busses.	Empty Barrels carried out.	Barrels of Herrings caught.	Bounty paid on the Busses.		
				£.	s.	d.
1771	29	5948	2832	2085	0	0
1772	168	41316	22237	11055	7	6
1773	190	42333	42055	12510	8	6
1774	248	59303	56365	16952	2	6
1775	275	69144	52879	19315	15	0
1776	294	76329	51863	21290	7	6
1777	240	62679	43313	17592	2	6
1778	220	56390	40958	16316	2	6
1779	206	55194	29367	15287	0	0
1780	181	48315	19885	13445	12	6
1781	135	33992	16593	9613	12	6
Total,	2186	550943	378347	155463	11	0

Seasteeks	378347	Bounty at a medium for each barrel of seasteeks, ... £. 0 8 2¼

Seasteeks   378347   Bounty at a medium for each barrel of
seasteeks, ... £. 0 8 2¼
But a barrel of seasteeks being only
reckoned two-thirds of a barrel fully
packed, one-third is deducted, which
⅓ deducted 126115⅔   brings the bounty to . . . . . £. 0 12 3¾

Barrels full⎫
    packed, ⎬   252231⅓

[a-a] above 2A [In the *Additions and Corrections*, this appendix formed part of the text: see above IV.v.a.31 and note. The appendix was printed in vol. ii of eds. 3–6.]

And if the herrings are exported, there is besides a premium of .   0   2   8

So that the bounty paid by Government in money for each
barrel, is . . . .   *£.* 0 14 11¾
But if to this, the duty of the salt usually taken credit for as expended in curing each barrel, which at a medium is of foreign,
one bushel and one-fourth of a bushel, at 10*s.* a bushel, be added,
viz.   0   12   6

The bounty on each barrel would amount to . . . . . .   *£.* 1   7   5¾

If the herrings are cured with British salt, it *b*will*b* stand thus, viz.

Bounty as before . . . .   *£.* 0 14 11¾
—but if to this bounty the duty on two bushels of Scots salt at
1*s.* 6*d.* per bushel, supposed to be the quantity at a medium used
in curing each barrel is added, to wit, ...   0   3   0

The bounty on each barrel will amount to . . . . . .   *£.* 0 17 11¾
And,
When buss herrings are entered for home consumption in Scot-
land, and pay the shilling a barrel of duty, the bounty stands thus,
to wit, as before. . . . .   *£.* 0 12   3¾
From which the 1*s.* a barrel is to be deducted   0   1   0

                                                                  0   11   3¾
But to that there is to be added again, the duty of the foreign
salt used in curing a barrel of herrings, viz.   0   12   6

So that the premium allowed for each barrel of herrings entered
for home consumption is . . . .   *£.* 1   3   9¾

If the Herrings are cured with British salt, it will stand as follows,
viz.

Bounty on each barrel brought in by the busses as above . . .   *£.* 0 12   3¾
From which deduct the 1*s.* a barrel paid at the time they are
entered for home consumption   0   1   0

                                                            £. 0 11   3¾
But if to the bounty the duty on two bushels of Scots salt at 1*s.*
6*d.* per bushel, supposed to be the quantity at a medium used in
curing each barrel, is added, to wit   0   3   0

The premium for each barrel entered for home consumption will
be . . . .   *£.* 0 14   3¾

^{b-b} would 2A

Though the loss of duties upon herrings exported cannot, perhaps, properly be considered as bounty; that upon herrings entered for home consumption certainly may.

An Account of the Quantity of Foreign Salt imported into Scotland, and of Scots Salt delivered duty free from the Works there for the Fishery, from the 5th of April 1771 to the 5th of April 1782, with a Medium of both for one year.

PERIOD	Foreign Salt imported.	Scots Salt delivered from the Works.
	Bushels.	Bushels.
From the 5th of April 1771, to the 5th of April 1782.	936974	168226
Medium for one Year	85179$\frac{5}{11}$	15293$\frac{3}{11}$

It is to be observed that the Bushel of Foreign Salt weighs 84lb. that of British Salt 56lb. only.[1]

[1] Smith's information is almost certainly derived from the Scottish Customs records. No exactly parallel documentation has been traced in the surviving records in the Scottish Record Office, though it might be possible to calculate most of the information in the account of the herring bounty from the Customs Cash Accounts (SRO/E/502), which give payments of bounties to vessels engaged in the herring fishery, 1752–96, and from the supporting detailed vouchers (SRO/E/508), which give particulars of vessels, crews and catches.

The Third Report from the Committee appointed to enquire into the State of the British Fisheries, 1785, reproduced in Journal of the House of Commons (First Series), x, 18, gives the account of the herring bounty paid as follows:

$$
\begin{array}{lrrr}
1771— & £\ 2,085 & \text{os.} & \text{rod.} \\
1772— & 11,103 & 7 & 6 \\
1773— & 12,510 & 8 & 6 \\
1774— & 17,025 & 5 & 0 \\
1775— & 19,609 & 15 & 0 \\
1776— & 21,290 & 7 & 6 \\
1777— & 17,592 & 2 & 6 \\
1778— & 16,316 & 2 & 6 \\
1779— & 15,287 & 0 & 0 \\
1780— & 13,445 & 12 & 6 \\
1781— & 9,674 & 15 & 0 \\
\end{array}
$$

Total £155,939 16 10

The Third Report, 113, reproduces Smith's account of the herring bounty with a few minor variations, and excludes the number of empty barrels carried out and the bounty paid, the latter having, of course, been given earlier. The information on the bounties paid is stated in the Third Report (p. 58) to have been taken at Customs House, Edinburgh, 13 December 1784 and is signed by Cathcart Boyd, Examiner of Salt and Fishery Accounts. It is a reasonable assumption that Smith was supplied with similar information from the same source for the third edition of the WN. John Knox probably derived his information in the same way for *A View of the British Empire* (London, 1785), 233, which gives an account of the number of busses and barrels taken which is identical with those in the Third Report. Knox states that the information was 'extracted from the Customs House Books in Edinburgh, 1750–1783'.

Textual Schedules

SCHEDULE A. *Emendations of Accidental Readings*

THIS collation records all instances where the punctuation, spelling, or other formal characteristics of text *3* have been altered in the printer's copy for the present edition. The preferred reading now introduced appears first, without text reference if entered by the editors, with reference if transferred from some other text. After the rule the reading disallowed is then given, together with citation of *3* and any other editions where it occurs. In this second entry a tilde or curved dash (~) represents the same word as that first cited. In either entry a caret ($_\wedge$) denotes a punctuation mark there omitted but present in the other account.

Throughout in this and the following schedules the typography is so arranged to avoid line-end hyphenation of separable compounds, as the intrusion of hyphens not originally present would, in this circumstance, produce an ambiguous reading. Certain house-style and other features extraneous to the text are disregarded.[1]

10.4 always, 1|~$_\wedge$ 2–6. 14.20 taken 1–2, 4–6| tsken 3. 15.7 manufactories, 4–6| ~ $_\wedge$ 1–3. 15.35 man, 1–2|~ $_\wedge$ 3–6. 16.25 more, 1|~$_\wedge$ 2–6. 18.1 perform, 1–2|; 3–6. 20.24 valve, 1|~$_\wedge$ 2–6. 20.24 communication, 1|~$_\wedge$ 2–6. 21.8 is, 1|~$_\wedge$ 2–6. 21.12 a particular 1–2, 4–6| aparticular 3. 22.20 accommodation, 1|~$_\wedge$ 2–6. 48.14 purchasing; 3e, 4–6|~$_\wedge$ 2A–3. 55.18 conveniencies 1–2| conveniences 3–6. 149.19 scholars,' 6|~,$_\wedge$ 1–5. 149.19 'and 6| $_\wedge$~ 1–5. 149.22 wisdom,' 6|~,$_\wedge$ 1–5. 149.22 'ought 6| $_\wedge$~ 1–5. 155.26 obvious,' 5–6|~,$_\wedge$ 1–4. 155.27 'that 5–6| $_\wedge$~ 1–4. 193.12 *does,*|~ $_\wedge$ 1–6. 193.12 *not,*|~ $_\wedge$ 1–6. 234.30 *the real Price of*| om. 1–6. 240.1 cattle is 1–2, 4–6| cattleis 3. 242.26 butcher's-meat 4–6|~ $_\wedge$ ~ 1–3. 264.2 the 1–2, 4–6| the the 3. 310.33 premium. 2, 4–6|~ $_\wedge$ 3. 431.3 sovereign 1–2, 4–6| soreign 3. 435.15 never 1–2, 4–6| neevr 3. 556.4 *Motives* 4–6| *motives* 1–3. 564.29 *Prosperity* 5–6| *prosperity* 1–4. 586.27 place 1–2| places 3–6. 599.12–13 and sell 1–2, 4–6| andsell 3. 663.4 *Land,*|~ $_\wedge$ 1–6. 688.16 inconveniencies 6| inconveniences 1–5. 757.22–23 four trades 4–6| fourt rades 3. 764.36 Greek 1–2, 4–6| Greck 3. 797.34 allegiance to 1–2, 4–6|~ to to 3. 814.26 *Conclusion of the Chapter*| Conclusion 1–6. 828.4 *Rent*; 1, 5–6| *rent.* 2–4. 836.13 taille 1| tallie 2–6. 836.18 taille 1| tallie 2–6. 851.25 163, 166,|~. ~. 3–6. 858.15 *upon the Capital*| om. 1–6. 861.13 three-pence 1–2|~$_\wedge$~ 3–6. 862.25 ground-rents 1–2, 4–6|~$_\wedge$~ 3. 864.34 one-tenth 1–2, 4–6|~$_\wedge$~ 3. 877.37 conveniencies 1,6| conveniences 2–5. 890.20 3083*l*.6*s*.8*d*. 4–6|~*l*.~s.~d. 1–3. 892.19 twenty-five, 1–2, 4–6|~~~ 3. 904.29 vingtiemes 1–2, 4–6| vingtiems 3. 906.26 conveniencies 1–2, 4–6| conveniences 3. 921.27–923.22 [*l.s.d.* entries in italic type] 4–6| [entries in roman] 1–3. 922.17 72, 289, 673*l*. 1–2, 4–6|~, ~, ~ $_\wedge$.

---

[1] The collation excludes successive modifications of the titles in *1–6* and of Smith's own Table of Contents, but does represent the editors' necessary revision of chapter and section headings within text to bring these into conformity with the Contents as finally arranged for *3*. Also excluded are the volume caption headings for the three volumes of *3* (here beginning on pages 1, 330, 663) and all references originally appearing on or below the direction lines. Shoulder-notes have been transferred, in summary form, to the running-title line, abbreviated headings extended but terminal periods removed, paragraph numbers supplied in left margins, small capitals at the beginning of each paragraph reduced to lower case, reiterated quotation marks deleted, and long 's', digraphs and ligatures generally converted to modern style.

3. 924.2 fund 1–2, 4–6| und 3. 933.9 land-tax 1–2|~ ∧ ~ 3–6. 934.20 land-tax 1–2, 4–6|~ ∧ ~ 3. 941.34 History 1| Hist. 2–6. 942.12 Pennsylvania, 1–2, 5–6|~. 3–4. 949.18 wit ∧ 4–6|~, 3.

SCHEDULE B. *Excluded Variants*

THIS collation lists variant substantives adjudged to be misprints and accidentals of any kind as represented in some edition other than *3*, all of which are now excluded from the present text. Where the variation consists only of a point the text word is cited, the different punctuation then given, or a caret again used when punctuation now is lacking.

10.11 dexterity ∧ 1. 10.25 that ∧ 5–6. 10.25 or ∧ 6. 10.26 least ∧ 6. 11.6 supply, 1. 11.36 endeavoured ∧ 6. 11.39 In 1. 11.40 funds ∧ 1. 11.42 four 1. 12.1 book 4–6. 13.2 Productive 6. 13.8 Labour 1–2. 14.2 understood ∧ 6. 15.7 which ∧ 1–2. 15.27 though ∧ 6. 15.36 several, 1–2. 16.1 manufacturer ∧ 1. 17.12 becase 5. 17.14 hardware 1–2. 17.18 houshold 2. 17.20 which ∧ 1. 20.4 object ∧ 1. 20.11 work ∧ 1. 20.17 shown 1. 20.18 workmen ∧ 1. 22.2 dexterity ∧ 1–2. 22.7 occasions ∧ 1–2. 22.7 well ∧ governed 1–2. 22.8 society ∧ 1–2. 23.14 smelting ∧ house 1–2. 23.18 houshold 2. 23.21 kitchen ∧ grate 1–2. 23.36 to ∧ 1. 23.37 imagine ∧ 1. 24.2 true ∧ 1–2. 24.2 perhaps ∧ 1–2. 25.2 *Occasion* 1–2. 25.6 gradual, 5–6. 25.14 greyhounds ∧ 1–2. 26.17 animals, 6. 26.21 prevail, 1–2. 26.24 this: 5–6. 27.3 ourselves ∧ 1. 27.5 fellow ∧ citizens 1. 27.7 well ∧ disposed 1. 28.5 brazier; 5–6. 28.9 mens 1. 29.4 playfellows 5–6. 29.5 age ∧ 1–2. 30.5 tho' 1–2. 30.6 not ∧ 5–6. 30.6 least ∧ 5–6. 30.9 barter ∧ 2. 31.10 mens 1. 31.16 desart 1–2. 31.17 highlands 1. 32.6 cabinet ∧ maker 5–6. 32.6 wheel ∧ wright 5–6. 32.9–10 highlands 1. 32.16 sea ∧ coast 1, 6. 32.17 itself; 1. 32.20 men ∧ 1–2. 33.5 Edinburgh ∧ 1–2. 33.12 Whereas ∧ 1–2. 33.14 burthen 5–6. 33.15 risk ∧ 1. 33.8 other ∧ 1–2. 34.3 and, 1. 34.5 water ∧ carriage 1. 34.12 sea ∧ coast 1. 34.16 sea ∧ coast 1. 34.24 extreamly 1. 34.28 streights 1. 35.2 no where 1–2. 35.4–5 water ∧ carriage 1. 35.6 farm ∧ houses 1–2. 35.16 eastern 1–2. 35.17 too ∧ 1. 36.1 ancient 1. 36.8 inlets ∧ 1. 36.10 Bengal ∧ 1. 36.22 sea ∧ 1. 38.11 Diomed, 1–2. 39.8 sheep, 5–6. 39.21 bars ∧ 1–2. 39.24 copper, 5–6. 40.5 troublesome ∧ 1–2. 40.10 extreamly 1. 40.14 receive, 1–2. 40.22 public 4–6. 41.1 public 4–6. 41.3 public 4–6. 41.16–17 conqueror 5. 42.5 pondo 1. 42.5 podo 2. 42.8 sterling ∧ 5–6. 42.9 Edward I. ∧ 1–2. 42.17 first 1–2. 42.19 French ∧ 1–2. 42.21 two-hundred ∧ and ∧ fortieth 1–2. 43.4 forty, 1. 43.8 conqueror 1. 43.13 metal ∧ 1. 43.15 Republic 5–6. 43.15 twenty ∧ fourth 1. 44.11 public 5–6. 44.22 called, 1–2. 44.24 and ∧ 5–6. 46.10 price ∧ 2, 4–6. 47.10 it ∧ 1–2. 47.20 labour, 5–6. 48.2–3 purchase ∧ money 1. 48.5 it, 5–6. 48.11 both; 2A. 48.12 does necessarily 2A. 48.15 labour ∧ 2A. 48.26 exercised ∧ 1. 48.27 work, 6. 48.28 hour's 6. 48.29 industry, 6. 49.8 natural ∧ 5–6. 49.18 beer; 1–2, 4–6. 49.25 them, 2. 49.28 pass ∧ 1–2. 50.11 skill, 2. 51.1 alone ∧ 1–2. 51.13 Labour 1. 52.3 believe, 1–2. 52.8 though ∧ 4–6. 52.9 apprehend ∧ 4–6. 52.13 denomination, 1–2. 52.14 example ∧ 1–2. 52.21 public 4–6. 52.25 antient 1–2. 52.29 pence, 1. 53.4 ancient 4–6. 53.16 opulence, 4–6. 53.16 still, 4–6. 54.3 same ∧ 1–2. 54.4 same ∧ 1–2. 54.10 corn, 1–2. 54.26 century ∧ 2. 55.28 conveniences 5–6. 55.30 these, 5–6. 56.12 copper ∧ 1–2. 56.23 republic 4–6. 56.24 computed, 5–6. 57.4 kept ∧ 1–2. 57.8 believe ∧ 6. 57.9 metal ∧ 1. 57.10 England ∧ 1–2. 57.13 publick 1–2. 57.22 has, 1–2. 57.22 countries ∧ 1. 57.24 publick 1–2. 57.25 one ∧ and ∧ twenty 1–2. 57.29 standard, 4–6. 58.1 two ∧ and ∧ twenty 1–2. 58.12 difference ∧ 1–2. 58.12 however ∧ 1–2. 58.13 accounts ∧ 1. 58.15 five ∧ and ∧ twenty 1–2. 58.16 five ∧ and ∧ twenty 1–2. 58.22

keepieg 6. 58.30 seven-pence 5–6. 58.36 one∧and∧twenty 1–2. 59.3 publick 1–2. 59.4 so, 5–6. 59.6 one∧and∧twenty 1–2. 59.12 which∧ 1–2. 59.12 one∧and∧twenty 1–2. 59.14 10½*d*. 4–5. 59.14 10½*d* 6. 59.16 weight, 1–2. 59.24 sum∧ 1. 59.28 coin∧ 1. 59.29 reformation∧ 1. 60.7 fourpence 6. 60.8 sixpence 1,6. 60.11 market-price 6. 61.3 bullion∧ 1–2. 61.24 ten pence 1–2. 62.19 publick 1–2. 63.2 importation∧ 1–2. 63.13 price: 5–6. 63.35 experience, 1. 63.36 coin, 1–2, 5–6. 63.39 experience∧ 5–6. 63.41 money∧price 1. 64.1 Edward I.∧ 1–2. 64.1 money∧price 1. 64.2 contained∧ 1–2. 64.3 judge∧ 1–2. 65.10 labour∧ 1. 66.22 cent, 2. 68.11 part∧ 1. 68.22 meal∧ 6. 68.39 besides∧ 2. 69.3 number, 4–6. 69.11 sea∧shore 1. 69.16 other∧ 1–2. 69.21 other, 5–6. 70.36 materials∧ 1–2. 71.15–16 encrease 4–6. 72.2 *market* 1–2. 73.7 subsistence, 1. 73.27 said, 1–2. 73.27 sense, 1–2. 74.2 competitors∧ 2. 74.11 wages, 6. 75.37 deal, 4–5. 76.3 above, 5–6. 76.5 same, 4–6. 76.12 varies∧ 5–6. 76.23 produce; 5–6. 76.31 public 4–6. 76.32 occasions)∧ 1–2. 77.4 overstocked 1–2. 77.15 way∧ 1. 78.19 well∧cultivated 1. 78.26 forever 1. 78.35 occasion∧ 5–6. 79.9 together, 4–6. 79.16 well∧cultivated 1. 78.26 forever 1. 78.35 occasion∧ 5–6. 79.9 together, 4–6. 79.16 below, 5–6. 79.31 above, 5–6. 80.5 another, 4–6. 80.32 dependant 1–2. 81.1 place∧ 6. 81.3 place∧ 1–2. 83.17 completed 5–6. 83.20 independant 1–2. 83.22 completed 5–6. 83.28 independant 1–2. 83.32 labour, 4–6. 89.15–16 uniform, 5–6. 84.29 sometimes, 1–2. 84.31 defensive∧ 1–2. 85.14 rate, 5–6. 86.1 proportion∧ 6. 86.1–2 above∧mentioned 1–2, 4–6. 86.12 another∧ 1–2. 86.17 kinds: 5–6. 86.26 independant 1–2. 86.26 shoe∧maker 6. 87.7 thriving∧ 1. 87.15 bricklayers∧ 6. 87.17 ten-pence 1. 88.1 Britain∧ 1–2. 88.2 countries∧ 1–2. 88.4 five∧and∧twenty 1–2. 88.9 rewarded, 5–6. 88.10 burthen, 1–2, 4–6. 89.4 extent; 4–6. 89.14 labourer∧ 1–2. 89.18 industrious∧ 1–2. 89.20 industry∧ 1–2. 89.20–21 populousness∧ 1. 89.22 perhaps∧ 1–2. 89.22 time∧ 1–2. 90.6 street∧ 1–2. 90.10 nowhere 1. 90.11 cultivated, 5–6. 90.11 nowhere 1–2. 90.11 same, 5–6. 90.12 same, 5–6. 91.5 mortality, 5–6. 91.30 nowhere 1–2. 92.7 everywhere 1–2. 92.16 labour, 5–6. 92.20 same, 5–6. 92.20 same, 5–6. 92.26 five∧and∧twenty 1–2. 92.27 cent∧ 1–2. 92.29 ten-pence 1–2. 93.17 Scotch∧ 1. 93.18 reality∧ 1. 94.1 public 4–6. 94.12 six-pence 6. 94.14 western 1. 94.25 though∧ 1. 94.28 eight-pence 6. 95.7 arithmetic 4–6. 95.13 twenty-pence 1–2. 95.27 public 4–6. 95.29 anywhere 1. 95.29 things, 5–6. 96.9 household 1. 96.10 liquors∧ 5–6. 96.12 these∧ 1. 96.12 however∧ 1. 96.13 small∧ 1–2. 96.28–29 recompence∧ 1–2. 96.32 half∧starved 1–2. 97.3 weaken∧ 1–2. 97.3 altogether∧ 1–2. 97.4 extreamly 1–2. 97.7 soil, 5–6. 97.10 me∧ 1. 97.13 any where 5–6. 97.22 charities∧ 1. 98.14 understocked 1–2. 98.15 overstocked 1–2. 99.7 it, 5–6. 99.8 public 4–6. 99.15 cheerful 5–6. 99.17 declining∧ 5–6.

100.17 overwork 6. 100.35 subsistence∧ 5–6. 101.18 independant 1–2. 101.26 dependant 1–2. 101.33 independant 1–2. 101.36 separate, 1. 101.36 independant 1–2. 101.38 independant 1–2. 102.1 independant 1–2. 102.10 public 2, 4–6. 103.10 public 4–6. 103.10 men-servants 1–2. 103.11 independant 1–2. 103.13 independant 1–2. 103.14 public 4–6. 103.16 public 4–6. 103.16 registers, 6. 104.1 workmen∧ 1. 104.7 another∧ 1–2. 104.17 counter-balance 1–2. 104.17 every∧where 1–2. 105.13 labour, 6. 105.28 determine∧ 5. 105.30 ancient 4–6. 106.3 VIII, 1–2. 106.5 VI, 1–2. 106.8 VIII∧ 1–2. 106.8 Elizabeth∧ 1–2. 106.8 8, 1–2. 106.9 cent∧ 5. 106. 12 statutary 1–2. 106.20 VIII, 1–2. 107.5 another, 6. 107.31 public 1–2, 4–6. 108.10 country, 5–6. 108.11 ill-founded 5–6. 108.12 now, 4–6. 108.16 cent.∧ 1–2, 6. 108.18 England; 1. 108.28 latter; 1. 108.28 latter, 2. 108.29 exaggeration), 1. 109.13 stock∧ 1. 109.15 understocked 1–2. 109.16 under peopled 1–2. 109.38 nations, 6. 111.6 that∧ 1. 111.13 republic 4–6. 111.15 eight∧and∧forty 2. 111.18 climate∧ 1–2. 111.19 countries, 1–2. 111.29 every∧where 2. 111.29 every-where 5–6. 112.27 ancient 4–6. 113.27 awkward 4–6. 113.34 any∧where 1–2. 114.1 company 6. 114.8

cent.∧ 1–2,6. 114.9 interest∧ 1–2. 114.11 may∧ 1–2. 114.12 he 2. 114.25 people, 4–6. 114.26 day; 4–6. 114.35 stage 2. 114.36 would, 6. 114.36 flax, 6. 115.4 commodities, 6. 116.6 equal, 6. 116.15 advantageous∧ 1–2. 116.16 every∧where 1–2. 116.17 extreamly 1–2. 116.17 different, 6. 116.21–22 nowhere 1–2. 117.1 and∧ 5–6. 117.9 hours, 6. 117.14 shew 6. 117.16 al 6. 117.17 is, 1–2, 4–6. 118.34 every∧where 1–2. 118.16 The wages 1–2, 4–6. 118.16 cheapness∧ 1–2. 118.19 it, 1–2. 118.21 employments, 6. 119.5 mechanics 4–6. 119.25 mechanics 4–6. 119.40 liberal, 1–2. 120.5 domestic 4–6. 120.24 ten, 5–6. 121.1 accordingly∧ 1–2. 121.1 a∧day 5–6. 121.1 eighteen∧pence 4–6. 121.7 disagreeableness, 5–6. 121.16 coal∧ships 1–2. 121.22 a-day 1–2. 122.10 every∧where 1–2. 122.22 probity∧ 2. 122.26 The wages 1–2, 4–6. 122.30 mechanic 4–6. 122.32 but 6. 123.8 place∧ 6. 123.17 honouable 2. 123.18 under-recompensed 6. 123.27 public 4–6. 123.31 physic 4–6. 123.31 greater, 6. 123.31 perhaps, 6. 124.1 talents, 6. 124.4 public 4–6. 124.6 labour∧ 2. 124.13 public 4–6. 124.22 ancient 4–6. 125.20 mathematicks∧ 1–2. 125.20 mathematics 4–6. 125.23 tickets, 6. 125.27 sea∧risk 1–2. 125.35 alone∧ 1–2. 125.35 enough∧ 1–2. 125.36 this∧ 1–2. 125.40 rather, 5–6. 125.40 perhaps, 5–6. 126.3 seasons∧ 1–2. 126.4 sometimes, 1–2. 126.4 perhaps, 1–2. 126.16 soldiers∧ 1–2. 126.22 themselves∧ 1. 126.22 fancies∧ 1. 126.24 romantic 4–6. 126.31 Nobody 1–2. 126.32 public 4–6. 126.33 general; 6. 127.10 seamen's 4–6. 127.14 is, 6. 127.20 seven∧and∧twenty 1–2. 127.22 five∧and∧forty 1–2. 128.5 completely 5–6. 128.12 completely 5–6. 128.28 difference, 1–2. 128.30 greater∧ 5–6. 128.30 that∧ 5–6. 129.40 butcher's-meat 1–2. 130.6 butcher's∧meat 5–6. 130.7 therefore∧ 4–6. 130.8 butcher's-meat 1–2. 130.15 butcher's∧meat 5–6. 130.31 well∧known 1–2. 130.35 well∧known 1–2. 130.37 trade, 6. 131.17 quality 6. 131.29 fabric 4–6. 131.30 labour∧ 4. 132.6 This 4–6. 132.9 labour∧ 5–6. 132.17 seven∧and∧twenty 1–2. 132.37 public 4–6. 133.3 extreamly 1. 133.20 pot∧herbs 5–6. 133.23 sixteen∧pence 4–6. 133.29 ancient 4–6. 134.1 ancient 4–6. 134.5 any∧where 1–2. 134.9 five∧pence 4–6. 134.9 seven∧pence 4–6. 134.10 ten∧pence 4–6. 134.15 servants, 4. 134.18 twenty∧pence 4–6. 134.30 London, 1. 135.23 employment, 6. 136.10 any∧where 1–2. 136.13 public 4–6. 136.16 law∧ 1–2. 136.19 anciently 4–6. 139.21 anciently 4–6. 136.24 ancient 4–6. 136.29 ancient 4–6. 136.30 necessary∧ 1–2. 136.31 entitle 5–6. 136.31 master∧ 1–2. 137.1 anciently 4–6. 137.6 mistery 1. 137.9 public 1, 4–6. 137.12 market-towns 1. 137.16 set 4–6. 137.23–24 coach-wheels; 5–6. 138.14 butchers-meat 1. 138.15 apprenticeship∧ 1–2. 138.16 trades, 1–2. 138.29 law-giver, 6. 138.32 public 4–6. 139.15 public 4–6. 139.17 ancients 4–6. 140.4 completest 5–6. 140.7 mechanic 4–6. 140.13 aukwardness 1. 140.19 complete 5–6. 140.22 public 1–2, 4–6. 140.28 ancient 4–6. 141.13 over∧stocked 1–2. 141.15 reality, 1. 142.12 setts 1. 142.21 every∧where 1–2. 142.41 prohibit, 5–6. 143.2 wool-combers∧ 1. 143.2 perhaps∧ 1. 143.3 apprentices, 6. 143.20 mechanic 4–6. 143.21 completely 5–6. 143.27 judgement 1. 143.28 same, 6. 143.30 labour, 5–6. 143.31 mechanic 4–6. 143.33 temper, 4–6. 143.38 judgement 1. 144.1 judgement 1. 144.2 mechanic 4–6. 144.13 every-where 5–6. 144.15 every-where 5–6. 144.23 every-where 4–6. 144.38 ancient 4–6. 145.7–8 every-where 4–6. 145.10 shew 6. 145.17 inquiry 5–6. 145.19 public 4–6. 145.26 public 4–6. 146.6 sett 1. 146.7 account, 5–6. 146.10 workmen, 5–6. 146.24 public 4–6. 146.29 tedious, 5–6. 147.3 four∧pence 4–6. 147.5 three∧pence 4–6. 147.5 nine∧pence 4–6. 147.7 hve 4. 147.9 one∧third 4–6. 147.28 curates, 4–6. 148.5 Catholic 4–6. 148.7 Protestant 6. 148.8 us, 5–6. 148.10 decent∧ 1. 148.12 physic 4–6. 148.13 public 4–6. 148.17 public 4–6. 148.20 physic 4–6. 148.27 every∧where 1–2. 148.31 public 4–6. 148.32 and this 6. 148.36 knowledge∧ 1. 149.2 physic 4–6. 149.4 people, 1. 149.5 public 4–6. 149.6 public 4–6. 149.11 synonymous 1, 4–6. 149.14 ancient 4–6. 149.20 service, 6. 149.26

eight-pence 6. 150.7 rhetoric 4–6. 150.8 3∧333 1–2. 150.10 Didactron∧ 1–2.
150.17 Alexander, 4–6. 150.26 academic 4–6. 150.26 stoic 4–6. 150.28 public 4–6.
150.30 public 4–6. 151.2 public 4–6. 151.3 public 4–6. 151.4 public 4–6. 151.19
the other 6. 151.29 insignificant∧ 1–2. 152.17 another, 6. 152.17 every∧where 1–2.
152.33 2, 1–2. 153.2 raise, 5–6. 153.3–4 indispensibly 1. 153.7 enacted∧ 1–2 153.10
church-wardens 1–2. 153.30 III, 1–2. 153.31 church∧ 1–2. 153.36 them∧ 5–6.
154.10 office, 4–5. 154.14 public 4–6. 154.15 new∧comer 1–2. 154.19 married, 1–2.
154.27 because, 4–6. 155.35 None 1–2. 156.8 Author∧ 1–2. 156.8 Author, 5–6.
156.8 poor 1. 157.12 public 4–6. 157.17 opprest 1. 157.17 ill∧contrived 1. 157.19
anciently 1–2, 4–6. 157.22 intirely 1. 157.23 years,∧ 1–2. 157.23 ∧it 1–2. 157.30
prohibits, 6. 157.30 penalties, 6. 158.13 impartially∧ 1. 158.18 ancient 4–6. 158.29
one∧ 5–6. 159.4 public 4–6. 160.8 cattle, 6. 160.20 less, 5–6. 160.23 lett 1–2.
160.28 land∧ 2. 161.16 sea∧fish 1–2. 161.23 broguht 2. 162.11 profit∧ 6. 162.22
another, 1–2. 162.29 something∧ 1–2, 5–6. 162.18 town∧ 5–6. 164.3 ago, 4–6.
164.4 London∧ 4–6. 164.8 rents∧ 1–2. 164.15 butcher's∧meat 1–2, 6. 164.16–17
every∧where 1–2. 164.20 bread, ·5–6. 164.21 butcher's∧meat 6. 164.24
butcher's∧meat 6. 164.26–27 one∧and∧twenty 1–2. 164.31 no∧where 1–2. 164.36
butcher's∧meat 6. 164.37 butcher's∧meat 2, 6. 165.12 butcher's∧meat 2, 6. 165.13
oat-meal 4–5. 165.18 butcher's∧meat 6. 166.11 ancient 4–6. 166.11 Italy∧ 1, 4–6.
166.14 estate: 6. 166.16 ancient 4–6. 166.22 republic 4–6. 166.24 ancient 4–6.
166.26–27 well∧enclosed 1. 166.26–27 well-inclosed 4. 167.5 completely 5–6.
167.5 enclosed 1–2, 5–6. 167.22 butcher's∧meat 1–2. 167.22 bread, 4–6. 167.24 life
6. 167.25 butcher's∧meat 1–2. 167.27 shillings∧ 1–2. 167.29 November∧ 4–6.
167.31 March∧ 4–6. 167.31 inquiry 5–6. 168.3 March∧ 4–6. 168.5 year∧ 1–2.
168.6 1764∧ 4–6. 168.14 inquiry 5–6. 168.17 halfpenny 6. 168.18 March, 4.
168.20 suppose, 1. 168.29 butchers∧meat 1. 168.29 butcher's∧meat 2. 168.29
dearer, 4–6. 169.4 profit, 6. 169.23 ancient 4–6. 169.24 well∧watered 1–2. 169.27
ancients 4–6. 170.2 ancient 4–6. 170.8 enclosure 1–2, 5–6. 170.14 inclosure 1.
170.17 ancient 4–6. 170.19 ancient 4–6. 171.7 council∧ 1–2. 171.9 ones∧ 1–2. 171.9
years, 5–6. 172.7 wages, 1. 172.11 cultivation, 6. 172.18 any-where 5–6. 172.18
any where∧ 1–2. 172.23–24 fruit-tree 6. 172.30 profit, 1. 172.35 less∧ 1–2. 173.9
profit, 1. 173.12 piastres 1, 5–6. 173.13 by∧ 5–6. 173.13 Poivre*, 5–6. 173.29 said∧
1–2. 174.10 America, 5–6. 174.31 completely 1–2, 4–6. 174.32 and 6. 174.33 wages,
1. 175.5 Douglas*, 4–6. 175.5 informed)∧ 4–6. 175.14 and 6. 176.23 and 6. 176.37
follow∧ 1–2. 177.12 Lancashire, 6. 177.17 strong∧ 1, 5–6. 177.18 well∧ 1. 177.26
be∧ 4. 177.31 them∧ 1, 4–6. 178.12 materials, 1. 178.14 frequently∧ 1. 178.15
account∧ 1. 178.26 man∧ 1. 178.33 barbarons 4. 179.22 it∧ 4–6. 180.2 Baltic 4–6.
180.10 animals∧ 4. 180.12 nations∧ 6. 180.22 household 1–2. 181.2 lodging, 5–6.
181.2 household 1–2. 181.4 conveniences 4–5. 181.5 household 1. 181.20
ornamentally∧ 1–2. 182.1 household 1, 6. 182.2 earth, 5–6. 182.9 countries∧ 6.
182.20 coal-mines, 6. 182.30 no body 1–2. 182.31 no body 1–2. 182.32 country, 6.
182.33 mineral, 6. 182.35 but 6. 183.5 beginnings, 1. 183.26 no where 1–2. 183.29
well∧improved 1–2. 184.7 every∧where 1–2. 184.22 is∧ 1–2. 185.7 metallic 4–6.
185.11 sea-carriage 1. 185.20 metallic 4–6. 185.29 reduced, 6. 185.31 lodging, 1, 6.
185.33 ancient 4–6. 186.5 Cornwal 1. 186.6 Rev. 5–6. 186.11 acknowledgement 1.
187.2 tax, 1, 5–6. 187.5 Cornwal 1. 187.6 one∧twentieth 1. 187.7 proportion∧ 1.
187.8 one∧sixth 1. 187.9 Cornwal 1. 187.17 Cornwal 1. 187.21 proprietor∧ 1–2.
187.21 coarse∧ 1. 187.25 us∧ 1. 187.28 lottery∧ 1–2. 188.8 Cornwal 1. 188.9
ancient 4–6. 188.16 public 4–6. 188.20 silver, 1. 189.23 cloaths, 1, 4–5. 189.23
lodging, 1–2. 190.11 complete 4–6. 191.4 every-where 4–6. 191.5 independant 1.
191.19 up∧ 1. 192.3 public 4–6. 192.14 lodging∧ 1. 192.14 cloath∧ 1. 192.30

household 6. 193.2 any-where 5–6. 193.16–17 improvement 6. 194.9 if 1–2.
194.10 improvement, 1–2, 4–6. 194.26 accident, 6. 195.8 silver 1. 195.14 III. 6.
195.15 Statute of Labourers 6. 195.21 livery-wheat 6. 195.21 no-where 4–6.
195.24 had, 4–6. 195.24 III. 6. 195.29 III. 6. 195.30 silver 1. 195.36 years, 1–2.
196.2 judgement 1. 196.7 St. Augustine's 1. 196.8 installation day 1–2. 196.10
Fifty-three 5–6. 196.11–12 one and twenty 1–2. 196.12 sixpence 6. 196.12 money;
5–6. 196.20 accidentally, 6. 196.23 III. 6. 196.25 progenitors, 6. 196.27 Conquest
1. 197.5 silver 1. 197.7 must 1. 197.7 supposition 1. 197.13 silver 1. 197.17
silver 1–2. 197.23 silver 1–2. 197.25 Earl 1. 197.27 quarter; 1–2. 197.29 silver,
4–6. 198.11 and 6. 198.18 money, 1–2. 198.18 one-third 1–2. 198.19 III 5.
198.19 III.) 6. 198.36 preceeding 1. 199.4 silver, 6. 199.11 or 6. 199.27 ancient
4–6. 199.28 Caesar, 5–6.

200.8 ancient 4–6. 200.21 public 4–6. 200.22 judgement 1. 200.24 accoording 6.
201.1 ancient 4–6. 201.3 acknowledges 1. 201.3 occasion 1. 201.5
acknowledgement 1–2. 201.12 ancient 4–6. 201.13 sometimes, 6. 201.13 perhaps, 6.
201.14 ancient 4–6. 201.17 be 1. 202.3 sufficient 6. 202.7 III, 4–6. 202.11
preceeding 1. 202.24 statute: 6. 202.24 Et 6. 202.30 ancient 4–6. 203.1 Rudiman
1–2. 203.9 written, 1–2. 203.12 ancient 4–6. 203.15 ancient 4–6. 204.4 Society 6.
204.14 public 4–6. 204.23 College 5–6. 204.24 see, 4–6. 204.25 thirteenth 1–2.
204.36 corn, 6. 205.2 ancient 4–6. 205.7 ancient 4–6. 205.11 commodities, 1. 205.21
One and twenty 1–2. 206.5 set 4–6. 206.18 improvement 1. 206.20 or, 6.
206.22 counterbalanced 4–6. 206.23 continual 6. 206.30 set 4–6. 206.33 set 4–6.
207.1 every-where 4–6. 207.5 subsistence; 4–6. 208.3 commodities: 5–6. 208.8
encrease 1. 208.21 siver 4. 208.33 anywhere 4–6. 208.34 money price 1–2, 6.
209.9 England, 3. 209.38 same; 1. 210.2 necessaries, 6. 211.10 appears, 1–2.
211.11–212.17 [*l.s.d.* entries in Roman type] 1–2. 211.15 wheat, 1. 211.21 2*l*.10s
1–2. 211.21 which, 6. 211.29 completed 5–6. 212.17 which, 6. 212.22 corn 1–2.
212.25 home-market 1–2. 213.10 was 1. 213.11 five and twenty 1–2. 213.12
market price 1–2. 214.2 five and twenty 1–2. 214.3 is 1–2. 214.6 public 1–2,
4–6. 214.7 tillage 1–2. 214.8 bounty 5–6. 214.11 yet, 1–2. 214.11 as 1–2. 214.11
century 1–2. 214.18 century, 6. 214.20–215.3 [*l.s.d.* entries in Roman type] 1–2.
214.21 five and twenty 1–2. 214.23 sixpence 5–6. 215.3 eight and twenty 1–2.
215.9 eight and twenty 1–2. 215.20 is, 6. 215.23 eight and forty 1–2. 215.21 king
1. 216.14 If 1. 216.28 suppose 1–2. 216.32 proper 1–2. 216.32 perhaps
1–2. 216.36 silver 1–2. 216.37 When 1–2. 217.17 which 1. 217.17 years 1.
217.27–218.5 [*l.s.d.* entries in Roman type] 1–2. 218.1 preceeding 1. 218.5
6d*. 2. 218.10 preceeding 1. 218.11 tho' 1–2. 218.14 preceeding 1–2. 219.32 Peru,
5–6. 219.33 remains, 5–6. 219.39 one and forty 1–2. 220.26 preceeded 1. 220.33
well known 1. 220.33 V, 1. 221.5 which 5–6. 221.15 ancient 4–6. 221.17
agriculture 1. 221.24 cloathes 1. 221.31 every-where 4–6. 221.34 well cultivated
1–2. 221.37 improvement, 1, 6. 222.15 East-Indies 1–2. 222.19 East-Indies 1–2.
222.23 East-Indies 1–2. 222.26 century, 6. 222.27 East-India 1–2. 223.4 East-India
1–2. 223.7 East-India 1–2. 223.10 East-India 1–2. 223.10 Europe, 6. 223.10
great 1–2. 223.13 East-India 1–2. 223.17 too 1–2. 223.17–18 East-India 1–2.
223.22 East-India 1–2. 223.22 trade 1–2. 223.23 East-India 1–2. 223.25
East-Indies 2. 224.5–6 Indianmarket 2. 224.8 metals 1. 224.9 therefore 1.
224.24 tho' 1–2. 224.27 any where 1–2. 224.30 complete 4–6. 225.3 twelve 6.
225.5 silver, 6. 226.19–21 [*l.s.* entries in Roman type] 1–2. 226.24 which 2.
226.29 and 1. 226.29 sometimes 1. 226.29 well informed 1–2. 226.29 author 1–2.
226.30 philosophical 1. 226.30 political 1. 226.30 history 1. 226.30 Establishment

1–2. 226.35 which∧ 1–2. 226.35 4s.6d. 1–2. 226.36–227.12 [*l.* entries in Roman type] 1–2. 226.39 Postscript 6. 226.39 it 6. 227.14 tho' 2. 227.15 agree∧ 1. 227.29–30 hundred∧and∧twentieth 1–2. 227.31 silver∧ 1–2. 227.31 therefore∧ 1–2. 228.10 metals∧ 1–2. 228.11 and∧ 1–2. 228.13 wasted∧ 1. 228.32 metallic 4–6. 228.33 corn fields 1–2. 229.15 mint, 6. 229.15 perhaps, 6. 229.17 Japan∧ 1–2. 229.32 3s.6d. 1–2. 230.9 commonly, 1. 230.16 value, 4–6. 230.27 watch∧cases 1–2. 231.4 yet, 6. 231.7 and smallness 6. 231.15 king 1, 6. 231.29 king 6. 231.30 king 6. 232.3 tax∧ 5–6. 232.13 water, 6. 232.16 silver, 1. 232.18 it), 6. 232.29 retard∧ 2. 233.12 alledged 2. 233.16 that, 1. 233.18 place, 1. 233.29 manner, 2A, 4–6. 234.1 *value* 2. 235.21 wealth, 1–2. 235.36 republic 1–2, 4–6. 235.38 republic 1–2, 4–6. 236.3 sterling, 4–5. 236.5 one∧and∧twenty 1–2. 236.6 Eight∧and∧twenty 1–2. 236.9 ancient 4–6. 236.10 inversely; 4–6. 236.18 money, 1–2. 236.21 one∧third 6. 236.23 subsistence∧ 4–6. 236.24–26 [*l.s.d* entries in Roman type] 1–2. 236.26 9d.‡ 4–6. 237.27 butcher's-meat 1–2, 4–6. 237.28 high∧ 1–2. 238.6 to it *om.*6 239.6 grain; 1. 239.14 Under 2. 239.21 owing∧ 1–2. 239.26 completely 1–2, 4–6. 239.32 no-where 4–6. 239.39 completely 1–2, 4–6. 240.12 colonies∧ 1–2. 241.2 half∧starved 1–2. 241.10 milk∧ 4–6. 241.32 ancient 4–6. 241.32 us, 6. 241.33 ortolans 4–6. 242.22 butchers-meat 1. 242.26 butcher's-meat 4–6. 242.32 buck∧wheat 1–2. 243.28 forerunner 5–6. 244.6 height of 6. 245.2 any-where 4–6. 245.29 completely 2,4–6. 245.22 complete 2, 4–6. 245.24 corn∧land 1–2. 245.25 and∧ 5–6. 245.34 complete 2, 4–6. 245.35 public 4–6. 245.37 public 4–6. 245.37 fore-runner 1–2. 245.38 public 4–6. 245.39 money∧price 1–2. 246.20 improvement∧ 1. 246.22 which∧ 1. 246.28 extreamly 1. 246.29 every∧where 1–2. 246.37 little; 1–2. 247.14 improvement∧ 1. 247.29 same, 5–6. 247.30 should∧ 1. 247.30 however∧ 1. 248.2 butcher's∧meat 4. 248.6 authentic 4–6. 248.12–13 one∧and∧twenty 1–2. 248.17 ancient 1, 4–6. 248.18–19 one∧and∧twenty 1–2. 248.20 ancient 1–2, 4–6. 248.21 ancient 1, 4–6. 248.25 wool∧ 1. 248.28 England: 6. 248.29 free: 6. 249.10 authentic 4–6. 249.11 ancient 1, 4–6. 249.16 occasion: 1–2. 249.17–18 three-pence 1–2, 6. 249.20 four∧and∧twenty 1–2. 249.22 4s. 1–2. 249.26 51s.4d. 1–2. 250.2 ancient 1, 4–6. 250.5 pounds of 6. 250.6 ancient 1–2, 4–6. 250.8 February∧ 4–6. 250.10 ancient 1–2, 4–6. 250.26 ancient 1–2, 4–6. 250.35 ancient 1–2, 4–6. 250.37 clothiers∧ 1–2. 250.37 nation∧ 1–2. 251.4 only)∧ 1–2. 251.8 no-where 5–6. 251.10 hitherto∧ 1–2. 252.4 wool∧ 1–2. 252.4 falsely∧ 6. 252.15 country. 6. 252.25 domestic 2, 4–6. 252.32 lakes, 6. 253.11 tun 1. 253.14 extensive 5–6. 254.7 purchasing)∧ 1–2. 254.19 barrenness, 5–6. 255.15 ancient 4–6. 255.21 scarcity, 5–6. 256.2 the other 6. 256.4 industry∧ 4–6. 256.23 Europe; those 6. 256.28 general∧ 1. 257.13 money∧price 1–2, 5–6. 257.14 infer, 4–6. 257.39 public 4–6. 257.41 Messance∧ 1. 258.1 Duprè 1, 5–6. 258.1 complete 4–6. 258.19 account, 1. 258.21 public 2, 4–6. 258.30 fertility, 1. 258.30 or∧ 2. 258.31 cultivation∧ 2. 258.32 corn, 1. 258.36 publick 1. 258.36 Public 2, 4–5. 258.36 public 6. 258.39 publick 1. 258.39 Public 2, 4–5. 258.39 public 6. 259.13 corn∧land 1–2, 5–6. 259.14 because∧ 1–2. 259.19 perhaps∧ 1. 259.19 itself∧ 1. 259.21 food∧ 1. 259.22 kitchen∧garden 1–2. 259.28 butcher's∧meat 1. 259.28 height, 1–2. 259.29 except∧ 1. 259.29 perhaps∧ 1. 259.30 England∧ 6. 259.30 ago)∧ 1–2. 260.1 beer∧ 1–2. 260.7 diminishes∧ 1. 260.7 perhaps∧ 1. 260.11 though∧ 1–2. 260.27 preceeding 1. 260.35 watch∧work 1–2. 261.5 five∧and∧twenty 1–2. 261.13 now, 1–2. 261.20 imperfect, 4–6. 261.21 VIIth, 1–2. 261.21 VII∧ 4. 261.25 four∧and∧twenty 1–2. 262.1–2 eight∧and∧twenty 1–2. 269.9 IVth, 1–2. 262.11 clothing 4–6. 262.12 the IVth, 1. 262.12 the IVth∧ 2. 262.17 clothing 4–6. 262.18 ancient 4–6. 262.19 Ten∧pence 5. 262.27 clothing 4–6. 262.31 eight∧and∧twenty 1. 262.33 which∧ 1. 262.38 IVth, 1–2. 263.2 ancient 4–6. 263.5 are: 4–6. 263.6 spinning∧wheel 1–2. 263.12 extreamly 1. 263.13 the employment 6. 263.13 fulling-mill 1. 263.20 ancient 4–6. 263.24 ancient 4–6. 263.26 houshold 1, 5–6. 263.38 ancient 4–6. 263.39 tunnage 1. 264.7 may, 1–2. 267.7 perhaps, 1. 267.7 porhaps 5. 267.8 ancient 4–6. 265.23 great ᴧ 1. 265.28 public 2, 4–6. 265.36 indolence ᴧ 1. 265.39 public 2, 4–6. 266.13 connexion 5–6. 266.16 public 2, 4–6. 266.26 declension, 5–6. 266.29 connexion 5–6. 266.33 public 2, 4–6. 266.38 judgement 1. 266.38 candour, 1. 266.39 occasion), 1, 5–6. 267.1 public 2, 4–6. 267.5 public 2, 4–6. 267.6 public 2, 4–6. 267.8 to ᴧ 1. 267.8 public 2, 4–6. 267.11 public 2, 4–6. 267.14 fellow citizens 1. 267.20 public, 2, 4–6. 267.21 public 2, 4–6. 268.1 Average 5. 268.1 price 2. 270.2 XI 4. 272.2 *Lady-day* 1–2. 272.3 *Medium* 4–6. 272.4 *two* 6. 272.4 *days* 4. 272.4 *Market-days* 5–6. 273.1 Quarter 6. 273.1 Quarter 6. 274.1 Quarter 6. 274.1 Quarter 6. 275.1 Quarter 6. 275.1 Quarter 6. 276.8 beforehand, 5–6. 276.11 hunt: 1–2. 276.11 clothes 4–6. 276.12 kills; 6. 276.17 men's 6. 276.20 completed 2, 4–6. 276.27 work, 5–6. 277.4 completed 2, 4–6. 277.18 before-hand 6. 279.15 revenue ᴧ 1–2. 279.19 clothes 4–6. 279.21 houshold 1. 279.29 possession ᴧ 1. 279.33 circulation ᴧ 1. 279.33 exchanges ᴧ 1. 279.38 matters ᴧ 1. 280.5 shop ᴧ 1, 6. 280.5 warehouse ᴧ 1, 6. 280.12 circulated ᴧ 1–2. 280.16 slit-mill 6. 280.18 coal-works, 5–6. 280.22 fixed, 6. 280.26 their 6. 280.33 labour ᴧ 1. 280.36 come 2. 281.2 Tho' 1–2. 281.8 first 6. 281.9 characteristic 4–6. 281.10 clothes 4–6. 281.10 houshold 1. 281.12 dwelling ᴧ houses 1. 281.14 dwelling ᴧ house 1. 281.16 dwelling ᴧ house 1. 281.18 clothes 4–6. 281.18 houshold 1. 281.20 let 4–6. 281.24 public 4–6. 281.26 Clothes 4–6. 281.26 houshold 1. 281.29 lett 1–2. 281.30 let 4–6. 281.31 let 4–6. 281.32 let 4–6. 281.37 clothes 4–6. 282.1 clothes 4–6. 282.2 houshold 1. 282.3 second 6. 282.4 characteristic 4–6. 282.10 lets 4–6. 282.12–13 buildings, 1. 282.14–15 dwelling-houses 6. 282.17 on tin 2. 282.34 Third 1–2. 282.36 characteristic 4–6. 283.5 clothes 4–6. 283.7 mercers, 5–6. 283.9 completed 4–6. 283.12 ready ᴧ made 1. 283.14 consists, 1. 283.17 use ᴧ 1, 6. 283.18 parts, 6. 283.20 capital, 6. 283.36 clothes 4–6. 284.2 it ᴧ 1. 284.3 society, 1. 284.25 other ᴧ 6. 284.28 clothes 4–6. 284.31 part ᴧ 1–2, 4–6. 284.37 equal, 6. 285.1 command, 5–6. 285.8 own, 6. 285.13 safety ᴧ 1. 285.15 Turky 1–2. 286.5 book 1. 286.10 stock; 6. 286.13 one ᴧ 1. 286.13 other ᴧ 1. 286.24 country, 1–2. 286.25 inhabitants; 5–6. 286.35 labour; 4–6. 287.1 conveniencies ᴧ 1. 287.9 may, 1–2. 287.9 indeed, 1–2. 287.21 hands ᴧ 1. 287.29 cloathinᵱ, 1–2. 287.29 clothing ᴧ 4–5. 287.29 clothing, 6. 287.33 mechanics 4–6. 287.34 wo k ᴧ 5–6. 288.28 individual, 1–2. 288.33 who ᴧ 1. 288.34 him ᴧ 1. 288.35 their's 1. 288.36 society ᴧ 1. 288.43 expence ᴧ 1. 288.43 them ᴧ and 1. 289.33 computed ᴧ 1. 289.34 say, 6. 290.7 money's-worth 1. 290.14 former; 6. 290.14 guinea's-worth 1. 290.25 weekly ᴧ 5–6. 292.26 promissary 1. 292.30 promissary 1. 293.1 frequently, 1–2, 5–6. 293.6 promissary 1. 293.10 kind, 1–2. 293.18 promissary 1. 293.22 or, 1. 294.9 pounds, 6. 294.16 country ᴧ 1. 294.21 domestic 4–6. 295.2 consume, 1. 295.12 seems, 1. 295.12 probable, 1. 295.13–14 considerably, 6. 296.12 mechanics 4–6. 296.13 machinery, 1, 4–6. 297.4 five ᴧ and ᴧ twenty 1–2. 297.10 appears, 1–2. 297.18 public 4–6. 297.19 1695, 1. 298.2 Union 5–6. 298.2 which ᴧ 1. 298.2 it ᴧ 1. 298.3 411,117l.10s.9d. 1–2. 298.4 ancient 4–6. 298.8 Scotland; 1. 298.10 Union 5–6. 298.20 of of 6. 298.26 due. 5. 298.30 Rudiman's 1. 299.1 amount ᴧ 5–6. 299.1 finds, 6. 299.8 promissary 1. 299.9 called ᴧ 6. 299.9 is, 1,6. 299.10 sum, 1–2. 299.10 pounds, 6. 299.10 example,) 2. 299.17 repayment 6. 299.31 promissary 1. 299.39 Hence ᴧ 4–6.

300.30 thought, 6. 300.42 silver ᴧ 4–6. 301.11 shewed 5–6. 301.19 interest; and 6. 301.22 company ᴧ 1–2. 301.38 is ᴧ 6. 301.38 therefore, 1,6. 302.5 proportion, 5. 302.19 silver, 1–2. 302.29 or, 6. 302.31 age, 1–2. 302.34 3l.17s.10d.½ 1–2. 303.11 interest, 1. 303.14 set 4–6. 303.16 journies: 5–6. 303.16 debtor ᴧ 5–6. 303.19

extream 1. 303.31 but 6. 303.33 found, 6. 304.2 coin, 6. 304.2 therefore, 6. 304.10 over‿trading 1. 304.14 not‿ 5–6. 304.15 only. 5. 304.25 unemployed‿ 4–6. 305.6 unemployed, 4–6. 306.6 re-payments 1. 306.10 observed‿ 1. 306.11 re-payments 1. 306.16 that‿ 1. 306.16 consequently, 2, 4–6. 306.16 money‿ 1. 306.17 means‿ 1. 306.19 regularity, 6. 306.19–20 repayments 1. 306.22 him‿ 1, 4–6. 306.22 unemployed, 1. 306.28–29 re-payments 1. 306.37 country, 6. 307.3 them, 4–6. 307.4 money‿ 4–6. 307.17 dwelling‿houses 1. 307.36 judgement 1. 307.32 extreamly 1. 307.40 capiral 6. 308.5 five‿and‿twenty 1–2. 308.7 equal‿ 1. 308.21 trade, 1–2. 308.31 re-drawing 1, 4–5. 308.31 re‿drawing 6. 309.2 people, 1. 309.7 which, 6. 309.7 centuries, 6. 309.11 If‿ 1–2. 309.15 If‿ 1–2. 309.18 who‿ 4–6. 309.21 and‿ 1. 309.22 pay‿ 1. 309.33–34 Edinburgh‿ 4–6. 310.13 cent.; 4–5. 310.13 cent.‿ 6. 310.46 cent, this 5. 310.49 London, 4–6. 311.5 bills‿ 1–2. 311.10 because‿ 1–2. 311.15 which‿ 1–2. 311.23 money, 1. 311.27 and‿ 4–6. 311.34 people; 5. 312.10 that‿ 1–2. 312.13 situation‿ 6. 312.24 banks‿ 4–6. 312.31 those‿ 1. 312.34 public 2, 4–6. 313.13 public 4–6. 313.15 bank‿notes 4–6. 313.15 bank‿notes 4–6. 313.19 well‿filled 1–2, 4–6. 313.22 installments 1. 313.23 installment 1. 313.27 installments 1. 314.11 bank‿notes 4–6. 314.19 bank‿notes 4–6. 314.23 cent.‿ 1–2. 315.8 long‿run 6. 316.2 yet‿ 1–2. 316.38 complete 1–2, 4–6. 316.39 completed 2, 4–6. 317.7 encreasing 1. 317.13 which, 1. 317.13 imagined‿ 4–6. 318.7 pounds: 5–6. 318.7–320.18 [*l.s.d* entries in Roman type] 1–2. 318.8 4,000*l.* 1–2. 318.9–10 revolution 1–2. 318.12 1697, 6. 318.12–13 ingraftment 5–6. 318.13 1,001, 171*l.*10s. 1–2. 318.15 public 4–6. 318.15 1696‿ 1–2. 318.16 per cent.*. 1–2. 318.16 per cent.* 4–6. 318.23 Public 4–6. 319.16 George I.c.xxi. 1–2. 319.20 public 4–6. 319.22 public 4–6. 319.27 1746‿ 1–2. 319.27 public 4–6. 319.31 charter, 1–2. 319.36 public 4–6. 320.5 public 4–6. 320.10 public 4–6. 320.13 public 4–6. 320.29 banking, 1–2. 320.33 which‿ 4–6. 321.12 corn-fields 4–5. 321.12 cornfields 6. 322.5 other; 5–6. 322.16 Shilling 1–2. 322.29 goods; 5–6. 322.33–34 parliament‿ 6. 322.35 circulation, 1–2. 323.8 calamity 5–6. 324.1 yet‿ 1–2. 324.89 promissary 1. 324.12 them. 4. 325.3 discourses 1–2. 325.7–8 promissary 1. 325.26 promissary 1. 326.1 abuse, 1–2. 326.19 promissary 1. 326.36 money‿ 1. 327.29 sterling; 1. 328.9 less‿ 6. 328.27 alledge 1. 329.11 public 4–6. 329.14 public 4–6. 329.23 public 4–6. 329.26 public 4–6. 330.5 there 4–6. 330.7 adds‿ 1. 330.8 generally‿ 1. 330.16 he 4–6. 330.35 shew 6. 331.2 public 4–6. 331.8 defence‿ 4–6. 332.23 part‿ 2. 333.24–25 every-where 4–5. 334.9 independant 1. 334.10 anciently 4–6. 334.18 paltry 6. 334.30 ancient 4–6. 334.36 ancient 1–2, 4–6. 334.39 no-where 4–5. 335.2 no-where 4–6. 335.9 ground‿ 1–2. 335.32 Compeigne 6. 335.34 France, 6. 335.34 people‿ 1. 335.36 justice‿ 2. 336.13 industrious: 5–6. 336.30 Union 5–6. 337.1–2 every-where 4–6. 337.3 Wherever 1–2. 337.18 Parsimony‿ 1. 337.18 industry‿ 1. 338.2 sett 1–2. 338.7 sett 1–2. 338.10 clothing 4–6. 338.11 sett 1–2. 338.14 clothing 4–6. 338.19 public 4–6. 339.3 prophane 6. 339.15 home-made‿ 1–2. 339.18 clothing 4–6. 339.26 clothing 4–6. 339.27 re-produced 5–6. 339.32 money‿ 1. 339.32 besides‿ 1. 339.32–33 country‿ 4–6. 340.1 country, 4–6. 340.8 domestic 4–6. 340.8 circulation, 4–6. 340.19 even‿ 1–2. 340.28 public 4–6. 340.29 everywhere 4–5. 340.29 clothing 4–6. 340.39 public 4–6. 340.40 public 4–6. 341.10 some, 4–5. 341.12 principle‿ 4–6. 341.19 compleatly 1–2. 342.10 every-where 4–6. 349.19 public 4–6. 349.20 public 4–6. 343.2 public 4–6. 343.4 public 4–6. 343.22 only, 4–6. 343.34 public 4–6. 343.38 judgement 1. 344.6 ago‿ 6. 344.7 Though, 4–6. 344.10 public 4–6. 344.14 falsehood 4–6. 344.22 dissentions 4. 344.28 was‿ 1,6. 344.29 public 4–6. 345.3 forty‿five 1. 346.4 expence, 4–6. 346.10 public 4–6. 346.11 those‿ 4–6. 346.14 public 4–5. 346.19 alleviate, 1. 346.28 clothes 1, 4–6. 347.1 day: That 1–2. 347.7 compleatly 1–2. 347.11 clothing 4–6. 347.20

marriage∧bed 1. 347.20 the Ist 1–2. 348.1 public 4–6. 348.4–5 acknowledgement 1, 4–6. 348.20 work∧ 4–6. 348.20 mechanics 4–6. 349.19 public 4–6. 349.20–21 public 4–6. 350.16 interest, 1. 351.5 readily 6. 351.5 is∧ 4–6. 351.18 produce, 6. 352.2 coin, 1–2. 352.6 Y. 6. 352.12 as∧ 6. 352.12 time∧ 6. 352.14 or∧ 4–6. 352.21 it, 5–6. 352.32 or∧ 1–2. 353.13 diminished∧ 1. 353.13 were∧ 1. 353.14 is∧ 1. 353.16 Montesquiou 1. 354.18 cent.∧ 1–2. 354.20 any-where 4–6. 354.24 interest, 5. 355.9 cent.∧ 1–2. 356.26 every-where 4–6. 356.27 every-where 4–6. 357.7 four∧ 1–2. 357.7 half; 1–2. 357.8 cent.∧ 1–2. 357.8 is∧ 4–5. 357.12 cent.∧ 1–2. 357.24 sett 1–2. 357.24 people∧ 1. 358.3 cent.∧ 1–2. 358.4 cent.; 1–2. 358.5–6 every-where 4–6. 358.10 every-where 4–6. 359.2 cent.∧ 1–2. 359.4 cent.∧ 1–2. 360.5 extreamly 1. 361.5 transporting∧ 1. 361.5 rude, 2. 361.5 produce∧ 1. 361.19 month's 6. 361.20 capital, 1–2. 361.25 to hour, 4–6. 361.27 profit∧ 1. 361.28 way∧ 1. 361.31 necessary∧ 1. 361.31 them∧ 1. 361.32 public 4–6. 361.39 only: 6. 362.9 public 4–6. 362.22 capitals∧ 1. 362.29 profits∧ 6. 363.24 too, 4–6. 363.27 intended∧ 6. 364.7 or, 1, 6. 364.28 any-where 1–2, 4–6. 364.31 be, 1. 364.32 compleat 1–2. 364.36 clothed 4–6. 365.25 Baltick 1–2. 366.18 prematurely, 4–6. 366.34 household 6. 367.19 ancient 4–6. 367.19 ancient 4–6. 367.23 ancient 4–6. 368.14 country, 6. 368.21 domestic 4–6. 368.29 domestic 4–6. 368.30 capitals: 6. 368.31 domestic 4–6. 368.36 one∧ half 6. 369.7 domestic 4–6. 369.9 domestic 4–6. 369.10 for, 4–6. 369.14 round∧about 1. 369.21 repurchasing 5–6. 369.31 round∧about 1. 370.2 round∧about 1. 370.17 round∧about 1. 370.20 round∧about 1. 370.26 domestic 4–6. 370.29 compleatly 1–2. 371.10 motion∧ 1–2. 371.26 shipping∧ 6. 372.2 and, 1. 372.5–6 increase 6. 372.13 things∧ 1. 372.14 violence∧ 1. 372.25 sea–coast 1–2. 372.30 domestic 4–6. 373.9–10 round∧about 1. 373.18 wealth; 4–6. 373.27 round∧about 1. 374.26 publick 1–2. 374.36 cultivated, 4–6. 374.37 every-where 4–6. 377.30 particulrr 6. 377.32 no∧where 1–2. 377.35 completely 1–2, 4–6. 377.39 accidents, 4–6. 378.34 are, 4–6. 378.35 mutally, 4–6. 378.36 resort∧ 1, 4–6. 379.31 domestic 4–6. 379.33 completest 4–6. 379.37 ancient 1, 4–6. 380.15 has∧ 6. 380.16 intirely 1. 381.2 *ancient* 4–6. 381.7 ancient 4–6. 383.22–23 every∧where 1–2. 384.14 substitutions, 6. 384.16 ancient 4, 6. 384.22 compleatly 1–2. 385.3 fellow∧citizens 1. 385.13 forever 1. 385.31 household 5–6. 386.16 ancient 4–6. 386.17 af 5. 386.18 ancient 4–6. 388.1 ancient 4–6. 388.4 ancient 4–6. 388.5 republic 1–2, 4–6. 388.14 slave∧cultivation 5–6. 388.17 quakers 1–2. 388.17–18 Pensylvania 1–2, 6. 388.18 negroe 1. 389.7 slave∧cultivation 5–6. 389.10 ancient 4–6. 389.12 Latin∧ 1. 389.18 quitted∧ 1. 389.27 possible, 1. 390.14 out∧ 1–2. 390.19 one∧half 4–6. 390.21 proprietor: 1–2. 391.4 master's 6. 391.8 ancient 4–6. 391.8 chief 1. 392.4 extreamly 1. 392.8 extreamly 1. 392.25 no-where 4–5. 392.25 no∧where 6. 392.26 England, 4–6. 393.14 twenty∧seven 1. 393.16 anciently 4–6. 393.22 long∧run 1. 393.24 anciently 4–6. 393.27 want 6. 393.32 publick 1–2. 393.34 every-where 4–6. 394.1 houshold 1. 394.7 public 4–6. 394.8 ancient 4–6. 394.8 extreamly 1. 394.13 ancient 4–6. 394.22 gentleman∧ 1. 394.22 stock∧ 1. 394.25 ancient 4–6. 395.17 Europe, 6. 395.19 mechanics 4–6. 395.21 superior∧ 1. 396.1 ancient 4–6. 396.6–7 regraters 5. 396.11 ancient 4–6. 397.7 ancient 4–6. 397.7 republics 4–6. 397.8 public 4–6. 397.14–15 mechanics 4–6. 397.16 ancient 4–6. 397.18 show 1. 397.19 privilege∧ 6. 397.25 set 4–6. 398.14 made∧ 4–6. 398.16 protection, 1. 399.5 let 4–6. 399.10 let 4–6.

400.1 let 4–6. 400.7 let 4–6. 400.10 forever 1. 400.12 return, 5–6. 400.16 Free∧burgh 4–6. 400.17 Free∧burghers 5–6. 400.25 been∧ 6. 400.30 commonalty 4–6. 401.1 town∧council 1. 401.1 bye∧laws 1. 401.4 ward, 1–2. 401.4 anciently 4–6. 401.19 improved, 1. 401.21 republics 4–6. 401.23 this∧ 1. 401.24 Europe∧ 5–6. 401.26

themselves; 4–6. 401.33 Frederic 4–6. 401.34 Swabia 2. 402.29 first 1. 403.3 father 1. 403.23 republics 4–6. 403.26 republic 4–6. 404.2–3 republics 4–6. 404.7 considerable, 4–6. 403.8 farm ˄ rent 1. 405.2 cities, 4–6. 405.19 therefore. 6. 405.24 industry, 4–6. 406.2–3 subsistence, 6. 406.11 centre 5–6. 406.12 crusades 4–6. 406.12 though, 4–6. 406.14 extreamly 1. 406.16 holy land 1. 406.21 republics 1–2, 4–6. 407.3 times, 5–6. 407.16 Empire 6. 406.21 clothing 4–6. 406.25 cloths 4–6. 407.34 ancient 4–6. 408.3 anciently 4–6. 408.8 established, 4–6. 408.9 ancient 4–6. 408.11 silk. 4–6. 408.11 worms ˄ 2. 408.23 judgement 1. 408.23 judgment, 6. 409.9 produce ˄ 1–2. 409.10 side ˄ 1. 409.21 manufacture ˄ 1–2. 409.27 corn ˄ 1–2. 411.25 The 1–2. 411.25 other ˄ 1. 412.1 oeconomy, 6. 413.3 rustic 4–6. 413.13–14 Westminster ˄ hall 1. 413.14 dining ˄ room 1–2. 413.18 cloths 4. 413.18 clothes 5–6. 414.15 dependant 1–2. 414.18 dependant 1–2. 415.6 ancient 4–6. 415.11 ancient 4–6. 415.12 whom ˄ 1–2. 416.8 allodially ˄ 1. 417.4 public 4–6. 417.5 caaried 2. 419.6 ancient 4–6. 420.3 ancient 4–6. 420.12 thousandth ˄ 1. 420.14 independant 1. 420.20 rustic 4–6. 420.26 dependant 1–2. 420.32 it ˄ 1. 421.23 baubles ˄ 1–2. 421.23 children, 1–2. 421.32 Wales, 6. 422.1 Khan ˄ 1–2. 422.3 ancient 4–6. 422.13 law: 5–6. 422.16 public 4–6. 422.18 public 1–2, 4–6. 422.24 other ˄ 1–2. 423.1–2 Agriculture 2. 423.4 five ˄ and ˄ twenty 1–2. 423.15 purchase ˄ money 1–2. 423.16 every-where 4–6. 423.26 forever 1. 424.10 purchase ˄ money 1–2. 424.13 sea ˄ coast 1. 424.21 is ˄ 1–2. 424.21 whole ˄ 1–2. 424.29 part ˄ 1. 425.3 land-produce 1–2. 425.3 butcher's-meat 2. 425.3 butchers' 6. 425.9 primogenitute 6. 428.5 objects: 4–6. 428.8 public 2,4–6. 429.15 are ˄ 1. 429.16 language ˄ 1. 429.22 neighbourhood. 1–2. 429.26 says, 6. 429.26 him ˄ 1–2. 429.27 France. 1–2. 430.14 yet, 1. 431.16 anciently 4–6. 431.20 anciently 4–6. 431.22 extreamely 1. 431.24 wanted ˄ 1. 431.30 because ˄ 1. 431.32 and, 4–6. 431.34 seed ˄ time 1. 431.36 seed ˄ time 1. 432.14 only ˄ 5–6. 433.12 that 4–6. 433.16 Holland, 4–6. 433.22 too, 4–6. 434.8 nobles, 4–6. 434.16 The 6. 435.3 revenue ˄ 1. 435.23 commodities ˄ 1. 435.23 eommodities 2. 435.27 labour, 1. 435.30 because, 4–6. 435.35 gold, 1,2,4–6. 436.19 customs, 1. 436.20 Gottenburgh, 1. 437.5 understocked 1–2. 437.9 foundation ˄ 1. 437.10 constantly ˄ 1. 437.10 gradually ˄ 1. 437.16 If ˄ 1. 437.24 paper-money 4–6. 438.5 everywhere 1. 438.5 every-where 4–6. 438.10 over-trading 4–6. 438.12 credit, 6. 439.30 hard-ware 4–6. 439.31 hard-ware 4–6. 440.26 cloaths ˄ 1. 440.26 clothes 4–5. 440.30 managed ˄ 1. 441.1 domestic 1–2,4–6. 441.2 labour ˄ 1. 441.6 or ˄ 4–6. 441.39 expensive, 6. 441.39 perhaps, 6. 442.10 re-coinage 6. 442.26 cccasions 1. 442.26 over-trading 4–6. 442.28 over-trading 4–6. 443.28 republic 4–6. 441.30 republic 4–6. 443.34 republic 4–6. 444.1 republic 4–6. 444.18 republic 4–6. 445.13 it ˄ 1–2. 445.18 antient 1–2. 445.30 proportion, 1–2. 445.37 Independant 1–2. 446.6 Cossacs 4–6. 445.12 preceeding 1–2. 447.28 purchasers, 406. 447.28 no more 6. 447.29 no more 6. 447.31 present, 1. 448.11 ancient 2,4–6. 448.17 set 4–6. 448.34 ancient 2, 4–6. 449.1 monopolised 1–2. 449.29 public 4–6. 449.35 every-where 4–6. 450.14 home ˄ consumption 5–6. 450.15 domestic 4–6. 450.19 restraints 1. 450.19–20 home ˄ consumption 5–6. 450.22 restraints 1. 450.33 imported, 1. 451.7 above ˄ mentioned 1–2. 452.3 restraining ˄ 1. 452.3 prohibitions ˄ 1. 452.6 domestic 4–6. 452.9 butcher's-meat 4–5. 452.9 butchers'-meat 6. 453.13 society ˄ 1–2. 454.7 domestic 4–6. 454.11 Thus, 4–6. 455.3 emporium ˄ 1. 455.4 market ˄ 1. 455.12 when ˄ 1. 455.19 domestick 1. 452.26 domestic 2, 4–6. 452.29 domestic 2, 4–6. 456.3 domestic 4–6. 456.6 public 4–6. 456.7 domestic 2, 4–6. 456.8 industry, 4–6. 456.15 public 4–6. 456.18 domestic 4–6. 456.25 no where 1. 456.25 no-where 4–6. 456.28 domestic 4–6. 456.32 domestic 4–6. 457.1 clothes 4–6. 457.25 capital ˄ 4–6. 457.27 more ˄ 6. 458.4 country, 5. 458.6 total ˄ 6. 458.6 industry ˄ 1. 458.7 revenue ˄ 1. 458.11 revenue ˄ 4–6. 458.25 them, 1. 459.2

trade, 1. 459.6 home-market 4–6. 459.15 home-market 6. 459.29 too, 4–6. 460.6
which⋏ 1. 460.23 Wales⋏ 5–6. 461.1 butchers'-meat 6. 461.5 butchers'-meat 6.
461.6 butchers'-meat 6. 461.9 imported⋏ 5–6. 461.11 twenty-three-thousand 4.
461.18 tillage⋏ 4–6. 461.20 that⋏ 1. 461.22 corn⋏ 4–6. 461.31 Abbeville⋏ 4–6.
461.31 stipulated, 4–6. 462.17 home⋏market 1. 462.18 those, 1–2. 462.18 found⋏
1–2. 462.22 butchers'-meat 6. 463.6 domestic 4–6. 463.7 is, 4–6. 463.14 act: 1–2.
463.22 mariners⋏ 1. 463.36 oil⋏ 1. 464.8 parliament⋏ 1. 464.10 the IId. 1–2.
464.12 animosity, 6. 464.28 ancient 4–6. 465.4 domestic 4–6. 465.8 domestic 4–6.
465.12 domestic 4–6. 465.14 domestic 4–6. 465.26 domestic 4–6. 465.29 domestic
4–6. 465.33 domestic 4–6. 466.15 commodity⋏ 4–6. 466.18 foreign⋏ 1. 466.29
home, 1. 466.30 cafes, 1. 467.7 domestic 4–6. 467.10 far⋏ 1. 467.10 manner, 4–5.
467.19 Nations⋏ 5–6. 467.19 accordingly, 1–2. 467.28 minister⋏ 1. 468.22
ourselves⋏ 1. 468.28 home market 1. 468.28 home-market 2. 468.30 they, 1. 468.35
deliberation⋏ 1. 468.35 far⋏ 1. 469.1 manner, 4–6. 469.23 could⋏ 1. 469.23 things⋏
1. 469.26 hard-ware 5–6. 469.35 war, 4–6. 470.12 merchants service 1. 470.8
any-where 4–6. 470.10 merchant service 1. 470.28 kings 1. 470.31 please, 4–6.
470.33 public 4–6. 471.1 Onr 5. 471.6 Utopea 1. 470.7 public 4–6. 470.8 individuals⋏
1. 470.11 market, 1. 470.12 soldiers⋏ 1. 470.13 workmen⋏ 1. 470.14 regulation,
1. 471.26 public 4–6. 471.30 manufacture, 5–6. 471.34 legislature⋏ 1. 472.3 account⋏
1. 473.12 Britain, 2A, 4–6. 473.13 cambrics 4–6. 474.1 complete 2A, 4–6. 474.12
examining, 1–2. 474.13 monopoly: 1–2. 475.14 profit⋏ 2. 475.33 judgement 1.
477.13 way, 4–6. 477.13 besides, 4–6. 477.19 latter, 5–6. 477.30 first, 4–6. 477.34
proportion, 1–2. 478.21 government, 1–2. 478.30 workmanship, 4–6. 478.33 Sum
1. 478.34 commodities, 4–6. 480.13 when, 2. 480.26 cent, 1. 480.27 state⋏ 1.
480.29 coin⋏ 6. 480.29 with the 6. 480.38 inconveniences 6. 481.3 remained⋏ 1.
481.8 negotiated 4–5. 481.8 gilders 1. 482.8 re⋏transferring 5. 482.8 transferring 6.
482.11 one⋏half 2. 482.32 dollars), 4–6. 482.32 gilders, 1. 482.33 gilders; 1. 482.34
gilders 1. 482.34 gilders 1. 482.35 Proportions 1. 483.1 arenearly 1. 483.1 thesame
1. 483.4 happens⋏ 2. 483.9 gold⋏ 1–2. 483.21 credits⋏ 1–2. 483.21 receipts⋏ 1–2.
483.23 re⋏assigning 2. 484.12 gilders 1. 484.13 gilders 1. 484.17 gilders 1. 484.18
gilders 1. 483.18 decatoons 1. 483.13 ducatoons⋏ 1–2. 484.25 or, 5–6. 484.29 cent⋏
6. 484.31 as⋏ 6. 485.3 recipe 4. 485.10 receipt⋏ 1–2. 485.13 in titles 1. 485.15
public 1–2, 4–6. 485.15 invasion⋏ 6. 485.23 up, 4–6. 485.30 receipts⋏ 4–6. 485.31
books: 6. 485.42 granted, 5. 486.1 stock⋏jobbing 1–2. 486.8 intrinsic 1–2, 4–6.
486.13 gilder 1. 486.14 gilder 1. 486.23 gilder 1. 486.23 gilder 1. 486.27 set 4–6.
486.29 set 4–6. 487.3 bank⋏ 1–2. 487.8 accounts, 1. 487.9 allowance)⋏ 1. 487.11
gilders 1–2. 487.11 gilders 1–2. 487.12 circulation, 1–2. 487.15 above-mentioned
1–2. 487.12 gilders 1–2. 487.12 gilders 1–2. 487.14 gilders 1–2. 487.21 gilders 1–2.
488.2 gilders 1–2. 489.22 each⋏ 1–2. 489.22 therefore⋏ 1–2. 489.32 revenue⋏ 4–6.
489.32 case⋏ 5–6. 490.39 to, 4–6. 491.11 wine⋏ 1–2. 491.25–26 hard-ware 4–6.
491.29 consumption⋏ 1–2. 491.31 mines, 4–6. 492.4 for⋏ 1–2. 492.6 it⋏ 1–2.
492.6 little, 4–6. 492.10 workmen⋏ 1–2. 492.17 too, 4–6. 492.24 which⋏ 1. 492.27
tropicks 1. 493.3 Britain⋏ 1–2. 493.10 our's 1. 493.11 empire; 5–6. 493.22 preceeding
1. 493.23 Europe⋏ 1–2. 493.25 afraid⋏ 1. 493.27 be, 4–6. 494.2 question⋏ 1–2.
494.3 manufacturers, 6. 494.9 Britain⋏ 1–2. 494.9 countries⋏ 1–2. 494.18 politics
4–6. 494.31 capital, 4–6. 494.32 that⋏ 1–2. 494.32 circulates⋏ 1–2. 494.40 judgement
1. 495.2 trade, 4–6. 495.7 ancient 1–2, 4–6. 495.8 ancient 1–2, 4–6. 495.19 France,
4. 496.4 France⋏ 4–6. 496.4 therefore⋏ 4–6. 496.30 anxiety⋏ 1. 496.30 however⋏ 1.
497.3 nations, 4–6. 497.10 balance⋏ 1. 497.11 which⋏ 2. 497.24 and⋏ 1–2. 498.2
deals⋏ 1. 498.3 labour⋏ 1. 499.6 obliged⋏ 1. 499.7 therefore⋏ 1. 499.12 domestic
4–6. 499.20 destroy⋏ 1. 499.23 drawacks 1–2.

500.17 nearly∧ 6. 500.18 islands 5–6. 500.33 cambrics 4–5. 501.1 cent.∧ 5–6.
502.2 cent.∧ 6. 502.7 back; 2A. 502.31 war∧ 5–6. 503.1 mother-country 2A,
4–6. 503.3 12.)∧ 6. 503.23 perhaps, 1, 5–6. 503.39 domestic 4–6. 504.19
mother-country 4–6. 504.20 fellow∧subjects 1–2, 6. 504.22 Drawbacks∧ 1.
504.24–25 reimported 1–2. 505.4 domestic 4–6. 505.6 cheap∧ 1–2, 5–6. 506.8
well∧informed 1–2. 506.8–9 corn-trade 5–6. 506.17 public 4–6. 506.20 it, 4–6.
506.25 bounty∧ 1. 507.9 shew 6. 507.25 people, 1–2. 507.28 of, 2A. 507.28 and, 2A.
508.2 it∧ 1–2. 508.3 tillage, 2. 508.13 home∧market 4–6. 508.16 tax∧ 4–6. 508.19
home-market∧ 4–6. 508.25 well-informed 4. 508.26 corn∧trade 2A. 509.5
home∧market 4–6. 509.8 money-price 2A. 509.12 farmer∧ 1–2. 509.13 it∧ 1–2.
509.29 stationary, 1, 6. 510.4 complete 2,4–6. 510.11 yet, 1–2. 510.11 if∧ 1–2.
510.20 part∧ 2A, 4–6. 510.38 Portugal, 1. 512.18 or, 1. 513.15 labour∧ 1–2.
514.10 Mathew 1. 514.20 manufactures∧ 1–2. 514.35 both, 1–2. 514.35 scarcity∧
1. 515.2 sett 1. 515.8 home∧market 1–2, 4–6, 515.15 When, 4–6. 515.20 increase,
1. 515.20 increase 6. 515.26 money∧price 1. 516.1 market∧ 1–2. 516.8 determined;
corn 4–6. 516.27 complete 4–6. 517.1 public 2, 4–6. 517.3 not∧ 1–2. 517.3
commodity, 1–2. 517.4 silver∧ 1–2. 517.5 discouraged∧ 1–2. 517.5 degree∧ 1–2.
517.5 and∧ 1–2. 517.9 operation∧ 1–2. 517.14 least∧ 5–6. 517.17 believe∧ 1–2.
517.33 well∧ 1–2. 518.11 thought∧ 5–6. 518.14 bounties, 1–2. 518.15 expence∧
1–2. 519.16 cured∧ 6. 519.30 salt∧ 5–6. 520.3 together, 5–6. 520.3 find∧ 5–6. 520.4
salt, 2A. 520.5 11¼d.; 5–6. 520.6 3¾d.: 5–6. 520.7 5¾d.; 5–6. 520.9 twenty-
shillings 6. 520.16 seasteeks 2A, 4. 520.17 seasteeks 2A, 4. 520.26 Hebrides,
6. 520.21 burden 2A. 520.29 sea, 4–5. 521.2 resort∧ 5–6. 521.3 assured∧ 6.
521.5 Scotland: 5–6. 521.7 encouragement∧ 5–6. 521.10 boat∧fishery 4–6.
521.26 two-thirds 2A. 521.37 shillings∧ 4–6. 522.11 business∧ 5–6. 522.13 act∧
5–6. 522.15 fishery∧ 2A, 4–6. 522.15 24.), 2A, 4–6. 522.23 half-yearly 2A, 4–6.
522.25 fishing-chambers∧ 4–6. 522.39 otherwise 4–6. 523.2 British∧made 6.
523.7 public 4–6. 523.9 public 4–6. 523.15 exported∧ 1–2. 523.25 public 4–6.
523.25 excell 1. 523.33 complete 4–6. 523.35 public 4–6. 523.35 year∧ 5–6. 524.7
corn∧ 2. 525.14 inconsiderable, 4–6. 525.19–20 inconsiderable, 4–6. 525.32
Moluccas 4–6. 525.36 monopolised 1–2. 525.39 but∧ 5–6. 526.11 scarcity, 1, 6.
526.30 judgement 1–2. 526.24 preceeding 1. 526.27 sometimes∧ 1. 526.39 But∧ 6.
527.8 universal, 5–6. 527.17 famine, 1. 527.21 preventiv? 6. 527.36–37
eight∧and∧twenty∧shillings 1–2. 527.36–37 eight-and-twenty∧shillings 6. 528.6
sett 1–2. 528.7 mealmen∧ 1. 528.11 public 4–6. 529.1 ancient 4–6. 530.34 impolitic
4–6. 531.6 obstructed∧ 4–6. 531.23 farmer, 4–6. 532.15 VI.∧ 1–2. 532.17 trade∧
1–2. 532.18 inconveniences 2. 532.19 preventive 6. 533.1 antient 1. 533.4 authorizes
1. 533.10 people; 1–2. 534.4 can; 1–2. 534.8 home∧market 1, 4–6. 534.25 evet 2.
534.35 one∧and∧thirtieth 1–2. 535.1 arithmetic 4–6. 535.3 shew 6. 535.5–6
preceeding 1. 535.7 II.∧ 1–2. 535.8 five∧and∧twenty 1–2. 535.28 country∧ 1–2.
535.28 place∧ 1–2. 537.9 public 2, 4–6. 537.9 intire 1. 537.18 But∧ 5–6. 537.30
prince∧ 1–2. 537.35 four∧pence 4–6. 537.35 sixpence 1–2. 537.35 six∧pence 4–6.
538.3 was∧ 1. 539.8 dearth∧ 1. 539.23 public 1–2, 4–6. 539.32 public 1–2, 4–6.
539.35 corn, 1. 540.6 Britain∧ 1. 540.23–24 principle∧ 1–2. 541.29 quarter, 1.
541.31 sixpence 1. 542.4 six-pence 4–6. 542.7 six-pence 4–6. 542.10 cease∧ 1.
542.12 permits∧ 1. 542.12 prices∧ 1. 542.13 corn∧ 1. 542.13 free; 1. 542.13–14
meantime 1. 542.15 liberty∧ 1. 542.15 indeed∧ 1. 542.17 not∧ 1. 542.17 perhaps∧
1. 542.19 ancient 4–6. 542.31 bounty∧ 1. 543.1 ancient 2,4–6. 545.2 *treaties* 1.
545.2 *commerce* 1. 545.18 for∧ 1–2. 546.2 1703, 4–6. 546.6 admit∧ 2. 546.12 obliged∧
1–2. 546.15 Britain: 5–6. 546.27 treaty, 1. 546.28 months, 1–2. 546.30 prohibition;
4–6. 547.2 Holland∧ 4–6. 547.10 domestic 4–6. 547.13 abroad∧ 1–2. 547.18

packet-boat 1, 4–5. 547.29 imagined, 6. 548.3 which∧ 1–2. 548.10 England∧ 1–2. 548.17 markets∧ 1–2. 548.30 and, 1. 548.36 public 4–6. 549.6 more∧ 5–6. 549.31 turn 6. 549.33 forwards 1–2. 550.3 and, 1. 550.12 together∧ 1. 550.31–551.5 [*l.s.d.* entries in Roman type] 1–2. 551.30 mony 4. 551.34 January∧ 4–6. 551.34 1726,* 1–2. 552.1 livres, 1–2. 552.4 three∧fourths 2. 552.7 Louis∧d'ors 1. 552.10 deniers∧ 1–2. 552.11 livres, 1–2. 552.31 II∧ 1. 553.7 recoinage 5–6. 553.41 merchant, 1–2. 554.18 incurrs 1. 554.20 public 1–2, 4–6. 554.34 entirely∧ 1–2. 554.34 entirely∧ 1–2. 554.40 immediatly 2. 554.40 preceeding 1. 555.8 twenty∧one 1. 556.4 *colonies* 1. 556.7 antient 1. 556.9 antient 1. 556.15 which, 4–6. 556.16 preceeding 1. 556.18 minor 1. 556.19 sea 1. 556.23 child∧ 1–2. 556.26 independant 1–2. 556.26 state∧ 1–2. 556.30 antient 1. 556.30 republics 4–6. 556.31 public 4–6. 557.2 families, 1, 6. 557.8 citizens, 2. 557.10 independancy 1. 557.14 antient 1. 557.19 authority∧ 1. 557.19 protection, 1. 557.24 ancient 4–6. 557.26 republic 4–6. 557.34 public 4–6. 558.2 kind∧ 6. 558.9 latin 1. 558.10)∧ 1–2. 558.14 irresistable 1. 558.17 necessity; 1. 558.21 it; 5–6. 558.31–32 Portugueze 1. 558.38 traffic 1, 4–6. 559.2 and∧ 6. 559.3 completed 2, 4–6. 559.7 Protugueze 1. 559.9 west 1–2. 559.12 great∧ 1–2. 559.24 discovered∧ 6. 559.26 cultivation∧ 6. 559.32 him∧ 6. 559.38 discovered∧ 1–2. 560.6 and∧ 5–6. 560.11 West∧ 1. 561.1 production, 5–6. 561.14 account, 1. 561.15)∧ 1. 561.24 preceeded 1. 561.30 christianity 1. 561.41 completely 2, 4–6. 562.6 tenth, 1–2. 562.12 enterprises 5–6. 562.20 country, 1. 563.1 judgement 1. 563.2 extreamly 1. 563.17 us∧1. 563.19 jesuit 1. 563.29 enflame 1. 564.4)∧ 1–2. 564.16 Brazils∧ 6. 564.17 Dutch∧ 1. 564.21 there, 1. 564.26 north∧west 1–2, 4. 564.29 *colonies* 1. 564.31 country∧ 6. 565.18 him, 4–6. 565.21 children∧ 1. 565.21 infancy∧ 1. 565.27 countries∧ 6. 565.31 lands∧ 5–6. 566.13 ancient 4–6. 566.15 rivalled∧ 1–2. 566.16 surpassed, 6. 566.16 Aggrigentum 1–2. 566.17 lesser 1. 566.18 been, 1. 566.18 least, 1. 566.18 ancient 4–6. 566.20 eloquence∧ 2. 567.1 ancient 4–6. 567.2 Asiatic 4–6. 567.9 them∧ 1. 567.18 West-Indies 1. 567.18 surpass∧ 1–2. 567.18 ancient 2, 4–6. 567.20 antient 1–2. 567.24 overlooked 4–6. 567.30 population∧ 1. 568.17 York∧ 1. 568.19 draught∧ 4–6. 568.36 before, 1. 569.1 ancient 4–6. 569.21 connivance∧ 1. 569.22 Dutch∧ 6. 569.31 ocean: 4–6. 569.40 called∧ 1. 570.2 Danes∧ 1. 570.9 again∧ 1. 570.18 merchants∧ 1, 5–6. 570.37 less∧ 1–2. 270.37 smuggling∧ 1–2. 571.15 Mississipi 1–2. 571.25 encreased 1. 571.26 company∧ 1. 572.16 Pennsylvania 4–6. 572.25 land, 5–6. 572.28 Mayorazzo 1. 573.6 land, 1. 573.12 produce∧ 1–2. 573.28 public 2, 4–6. 573.29 Massachusets 1. 573.30–574.5 [*l.* entries in Roman type] 1–2. 573.33 Pensilvania 1. 573.33 Pennsylvania 4–6. 574.1 public 2, 4–6. 574.5–6 ever-memorable 5–6. 574.29 too, 4–6. 574.36 this∧ 1–2. 575.1 market∧ 1–2. 575.20 company∧ 1–2. 575.26 Fernumbuco 1–2. 576.11 six-pence 4–6. 576.16 ancient 2, 4–6. 576.19 subjects, 5–6. 576.31 Mississippi 1–2. 576.31 trade∧ 1–2. 576.31 therefore∧ 1–2. 577.4 too∧ 1–2. 577.7 Act 1–2. 577.10 ships∧ 1–2. 577.25 meer 1. 577.27 half∧peopled 1–2. 577.27 half∧cultivated 1–2. 577.33 market∧ 2. 578.3 New-England 1–2. 578.9 New-England 2. 578.11 Portugal∧ 1–2. 578.14 sugar∧planters 1. 578.17 colonies∧ 5–6. 578.19 fast, 5–6. 578.19 Jamaica, 5–6. 578.20 ceded islands 1. 578.26 provisions, 5–6. 578.32 provisions∧ 1. 579.12 produced∧ 1–2. 579.12 are∧ 1–2. 579.13 cocao-nuts 6. 579.14 fustic 4–6. 579.24 plantations 1. 579.25 plantations 1. 579.32 because∧ 1. 580.25 and, 1. 580.25 thereby, 1. 581.10–11 [*l.s.d.* entries in roman type] 1–2. 581.21 sugar∧ 1. 581.21 claying, 1. 582.12 horse-back 1. 582.16 houshold 1. 582.25 country∧ 6. 583.6 home∧market 1, 6. 583.7 tobacco∧ 1. 583.7 second, 1. 583.8 naval-stores 5–6. 583.8 stores∧ 2. 583.9 building∧timber 1. 583.28 goods∧ 6. 583.32 George IIId, 1. 583.32 George III. 2. 584.5 if∧ 1. 584.16 possible, 1–2. 584.17 and∧ 5–6.

584.38 compleat 1. 585.1 fellow‿citizens 1. 585.1 home. 2. 585.6 resentment‿ 1.
585.7 governor‿ 1. 585.15 house of lords 5–6. 585.20 descendent 4. 585.25 island
1. 586.17–18 Portugueze 1–2. 586.20 which, 5–6. 586.32 sugar‿cane 1–2. 586.34
Europe, 6. 586.36 sugar‿cane 1–2. 587.34 pieces, 6. 587.35 fish-pond 5–6. 587.37
republic 4–6. 589.7 catholics 4–6. 590.27 enterprising 4–6. 591.16 and‿ 5. 592.5
Poland, 1. 592.35 countries‿ 1. 594.16 England‿ 5–6. 594.19 commodities‿ 2.
594.20 theirs‿ 1. 595.21 would‿ 6. 596.11 trade, 1. 596.34 withholding 5–6. 597.30
desart 1. 597.32 Pennsylvania 6. 597.35 time, 4–6. 598.1 America, 4–6.
598.8)‿ 1. 599.11 country, 1. 599.14 less‿ 1–2. 599.14 disadvantage‿ 1–2.
599.31 more‿ 1.

600.29 maintain‿ 1. 600.33 employment‿ 1. 600.34 belongs‿ 1. 600.36 year‿ 1.
600.39 neighbouring‿ 1. 600.39 is‿ 1. 600.39 account‿ 1. 601.6 neighbouring‿
1. 601.10 neighbouring‿ 1. 602.38 Baltic 4–6. 603.14 domestic 4–6. 603.34 and‿
5–6. 603.35 probably‿ 5–6. 603.35 part, 6. 604.7 countries, 6. 604.20 supporting‿
1. 604.32 politic 4–6. 604.32 healthful‿ 1–2. 604.37 blood‿vessel 1–2. 605.2 politic
4–6. 605.4 armada‿ 1–2. 605.10 workmen‿ 1–2, 6. 605.14 blood‿ 6. 605.19 which,
1. 605.19 bounties‿ 4–6. 606.14 healthful‿ 1. 606.23 politic 1, 4–6. 606.24
occasioning‿ 1–2, 6. 606.24 time, 1–2. 606.34 December‿ 6. 606.36 colonies‿
1–2. 606.37 compleatly 1. 607.5 which‿ 6. 607.29 only‿ 1. 608.1 beneficial, 6.
608.6 Europe‿ 1–2. 608.7 state‿ 1. 608.19 employment‿ 1–2. 608.33 country‿ 1.
608.41–609.1 counter-balance 1. 609.2 altogether 5–6. 609.11 present, 4–6. 609.18
agriculture, 1. 609.25 Europe‿ 1. 609.26 employment‿ 1–2. 609.27 markets, 1.
609.27 markets: 6. 609.27 butcher's-meat 1, 4–5. 609.27 butchers'-meat 6. 609.28
Europe, 1,6. 609.35 world‿ 1–2. 610.8 re-payment 1–2. 610.12 restraints‿ 1.
610.14 domestic 4–6. 610.15 country, 1. 610.18 public 4–6. 611.1 diminishing‿ 1.
611.17 produces‿ 1. 611.28 too, 4–6. 611.32 monopoly‿ 1. 611.32 therefore‿ 1.
611.36 monopoly, 1, 5–6. 612.12 general‿ 1–2. 613.8 Portuguese 4–6. 613.13
London‿ 1. 613.13 indeed‿ 1. 613.24 men, 4–6. 613.34 clothes 4–6. 614.3 clothes
4–6. 614.5 price‿ 1. 614.5 indeed‿ 1. 614.8 reconnoitered 1–2, 6. 614.16
purchase‿money 1–2. 615.20 preceeded 1. 616.5 encrease 1. 616.10 which‿ 5–6.
616.19 adopted‿ 6. 617.3 and, 6. 617.5 whowould 6. 617.27 public 4–6. 618.5
public 4–6. 618.13 public 4–6. 618.19 order‿ 1. 618.21 impolitic 4–6. 618.22 show
1. 619.1 assemblies‿ 1. 619.4 public 4–6. 619.4 sufficient‿ 1. 619.23 home, 4–6.
619.30 seem 1. 619.34 intrusted 1. 619.42 super-intendancy 1. 620.3 super-intends
1. 620.9 super-intends 1. 620.21 fellow‿subjects 1. 620.23 tax; 1–2. 620.41 public
4–6. 621.4 colonies‿ 6. 621.5 France, 1–2. 621.8), 5–6. 621.11 raised‿ 1–2. 621.17
good‿humour 1–2, 4–6. 621.23 Great|Britain, 1. 621.23 empire‿ 1. 621.35 effec-
tual‿ 1. 621.41 it‿ 1. 622.2 public 1–2, 4–6. 622.8 domestic 1, 4–6. 622.10 imagine
1. 622.16 high‿spirited 1–2. 622.18 republic 1, 4–6. 622.19 born 1–2. 622.28 public
1–2, 4–6. 622.30 fellow‿subjects 1. 623.5 politics 1–2, 4–6. 623.10 is‿ 1–2. 623.11
fellow‿citizens 1–2. 623.20 become‿ 1. 623.25 America‿ 1. 623.25 present, 1–2, 6.
623.30 Henaut, 4–6. 624.2 times‿ 5–6. 623.10 antient 1. 623.14 ancient 1. 624.19
republic 1, 4–6. 624.23 republic 1, 4–6. 624.31 compleated 1. 625.1 principal, 1.
625.1 perhaps, 1. 625.1 arise‿ 6. 625.5 over-turn 1. 625.10 managing‿ 6. 625.20
parliament‿ 1–2. 625.21 it‿ 1–2. 625.22 good-will 5–6. 625.22 complaining‿
1–2. 625.28 population, 6. 626.3 America‿ 6. 626.10 events, 4–6. 626.12 encrease
5. 626.20 Europeans‿ 6. 627.6 splendour 5–6. 627.12 world, 1–2. 627.14 Baltic
4–6. 627.22 splendour 5–6. 628.35 itself, 1. 628.36 politics 4–6. 628.37 splendour
5–6. 629.6 risk‿ 1. 629.14 endeavour‿ 1–2. 629.30 that, 5. 630.10 public 4–6.
630.12 public 4–6. 630.15 public 4–6. 630.20 Bu 1. 630.27 system‿ 6. 631.11

dearer∧ 1. 631.20 thereby, 1. 631.38 kind∧ 1, 4–6. 631.39 established∧ 1. 632.22 public 1–2, 4–6. 632.24 round∧about 1. 632.27 tollerable 1. 633.1 If∧ 1–2. 633.4 if∧ 1–2. 633.10 circumstances∧ 1–2. 633.22 Portuguese 2. 633.34 sufficient∧ 1, 6. 633.34 on∧ 1. 634.8 belong, 5–6. 634.14 that∧ 1. 634.21 situation∧ 1. 635.4 Portuguese 2. 635.9 Portuguese 2. 635.16 half way-house 1. 635.28 Indians, 1. 635.29 Japan; 1. 635.29 Cochin-China∧ 1. 635.29 ar 2. 636.7 completely 1–2, 4–6. 636.18 Portuguese 2. 636.28 up∧ 1–2. 637.2 completely 1–2, 4–6. 637.31 sovereign, 6. 637.34 India∧ 1–2. 638.8 company∧ 5–6. 638.14 merchants, 5–6. 638.35 consequently 2. 638.38 completely 1–2, 4–6. 639.1–2 forever 1. 639.2 fortune∧ 1–2. 639.12 public 4–6. 639.15 this∧ 1–2. 639.15 perhaps∧ 1–2. 639.21 which∧ 1. 639.22 concealed∧ 1–2. 639.22 publicly 4–6. 639.24 public 4–6. 639.25 public 4–6. 639.30 which∧ 1. 639.30 trade∧ 1. 640.8 prejudice∧ 1. 641.7 would∧ 1–2. 641.7 probably∧ 1–2. 641.8 Madrass 1–2. 641.11 republic 4–6. 641.12 politics 4–6. 641.18 them; 1–2. 642.4 importation, 2A. 642.5 yet, 2A. 642.6 exportation, 2A. 643.4 importation, 4–6. 643.11 public 4–6. 643.27 employed, 2A, 4–6. 644.7–8 complete 2A, 4–6. 644.9 complete 2A, 4–6. 644.10 cheap, 2A. 644.10–11 legislature, 2A. 644.18 spinners; 2A. 644.20 complete 4–6. 644.23 Poor 6. 644.37 masting-timber 2A, 4–6. 645.2 continued, 2A. 645.9 pitch∧ 5–6. 645.24 March∧ 2A, 5–6. 646.1 Scotland, 2A, 5–6. 646.2 quantities, 2A. 646.7 kind∧ 2A. 646.12 timber, 2A, 6. 646.13 deals, 6. 646.17 kind, 5–6. 646.22 third, 2A, 6. 646.24 labour, 6. 646.27 kind∧ 2A. 646.34 seventh∧ 6. 646.34 kind∧ 2A. 647.6 another∧ 2A. 647.27 legislature, 2A. 647.35 which, 2A, 4–6. 648.18 may, 2A. 649.14 completely 2A, 4–6. 649.18 judgement 4. 649.18 years; 2A. 649.35 of∧ 4–6. 650.19 buy, 2A. 650.25 exchequer 6. 650.30 carrieth, 2A. 650.30 carried, 2A. 651.24 inquiries 2A. 652.23 that, 2A. 653.23 depends, 2A. 652.29 farmer, 6. 653.23 depends, 4–6. 653.33 do∧ 4–6. 653.34); 4–6. 654.27 perhaps∧ 2A. 655.2 statutes, 5–6. 655.5 two-thirds 4–6. 655.13 such∧ 4–6. 656.9 prohibition, 4–6. 656.11 III.∧ 4–6. 656.17 I.∧ 4–6. 656.18 Great-Britain 6. 656.21 wool, 6. 657.20 imported∧ 2A, 4–6. 657.21), 4–6. 657.36 six-pence 4–6. 658.7 exported∧ 2A. 658.8 Britan 5. 658.12 eight-pence 4–6. 658.12 a-piece 4–6. 658.14–15 sixteen-pence 4–6. 658.16 two-pence 4–6. 658.19 six-pence 4–6. 658.20 six-pence 4–6. 658.28 seven-pence 4–6. 658.29 eighteen-pence 4–6. 658.32 which, 2A. 658.33 four-pence 4–6. 658.33 five-pence 4–6. 659.10 manner, 2A. 659.22 parts, 4–6. 661.9 acknowledged, 4–6. 661.14 pay∧ 4–6. 661.16 home∧market 4–6. 661.33 trade, 4–6. 661.38 producers, 4–6. 662.3 consumers∧ 5–6. 663.3–4 Œconomy∧ 1–2. 663.10 country∧ 4–6. 663.17 XIVth, 1–2. 663.19 public 4–6. 663.21 public 4–6. 663.25 public 4–6. 664.3 public 4–6. 664.9 country 1–2. 6. 664.9 but∧ 1–2. 664.16 ancient 4–6. 664.22 inquiries 5–6. 665.36 completest 4–6. 665.40 completely 4–6. 666.9 completely 4–6. 666.15 well∧ordered 1–2. 666.16 completest 4–6. 667.3 completely 4–6. 668.1 extream 1. 668.7 complete 4–6. 668.18 completely 4–6. 668.33 artificers∧ 5–6. 668.38 circumstanced∧ 1. 668.29 kind∧ 1. 669.7 artificers, 1. 669.8 purchase, 2. 669.11 labour∧ 1. 669.11 employ∧ 1. 669.16 produce∧ 1. 669.19 artificers∧ 5–6. 669.30 supplied∧ 1. 669.30 goods, 1. 669.35 afterwards∧ 1. 669.37 surplus∧ 1. 670.1 artificers∧ 4–6. 670.3 maintained, 6. 670.6 artificers∧ 4–6. 670.4–6 which, 4–6. 670.31 merchants∧ 6. 670.39 home∧ 4–6. 670.41 the little 6. 670.42 great, 1, 4–6. 671.18 exporting∧ 1. 671.18 countries∧ 1. 671.19 country∧ 1. 671.36 fund, 4–6. 672.2 which∧ 1–2. 672.17 merchants, 1–2. 672.30 class∧ 5–6. 673.5 manner, 5–6. 673.9 which∧ 1. 673.13 less∧ 1. 673.13 another∧ 1. 673.20 system, 1, 4–6. 673.24 every∧ 1. 673.24 smallest∧ 1. 673.26 show, 4–6. 674.14 correcting∧ 1. 674.14 respects∧ 1. 674.15 oeconomy 1. 674.15 degree∧ 1, 6. 674.23 body∧ 1. 674.26 manufacturers, 2. 674.27 shew 6. 675.7 artificers, 2. 675.11 manufacturers, 2.

675.11 merchants∧ 6. 675.22 manufacturers, 2. 675.26 manufacturers, 2. 675.30 production; 5–6. 675.32 who, 4–6. 676.13 assert, 4–6. 676.14 manufacturers, 2. 676.17 asserted, 4–6. 676.19 reader∧ 1–2. 676.27 manufacturers, 2. 676.35 subdivided∧ 2. 676.36 operation∧ 1. 676.38 degree. *In 1–2. 677.4 revenue∧ 1. 678.3 imperfection, 5–6. 678.3 perhaps∧ 1–2. 678.20 republic 4–6. 678.24 public 4–6. 678.29 ancient 4–6. 678.33 works∧ 2. 679.10 ancient 4–6. 679.11 ∧There 1. 678.11 began,∧ 1. 679.12 ∧three 1. 679.14 first∧ 1–2. 679.16 transmitting∧ 1–2. 679.21 benefit.∧ 1. 679.29 artificer, 6. 680.6 on∧ 1. 680.6 themselves∧ 1–2. 680.7 bottoms∧ 1. 680.15 are∧ 1. 680.15 countries∧ 1. 680.16 countries∧ 1. 680.16 besides∧ 1. 680.19 flourish∧ 1. 680.21 difficult∧ 1. 681.6 is∧ 2. 681.7 perhaps∧ 1. 681.7 extent∧ 1. 681.19 too∧ 1. 681.20 Indostan∧ 1. 681.20 agricultrue 6. 681.35 ancient 4–6. 682.2 countries∧ 1–2. 682.4 extreamly 1. 682.4 yet∧ 1. 682.5 plenty∧ 1. 682.7 ancient 4–6. 682.29 or∧ 1. 682.29 most∧ 1. 682.33 ancient 4–6. 682.35 opened∧ 1. 682.35 manner∧ 1. 682.40 ancient 4–6. 683.2 Indostan∧ 1–2, 5–6. 683.5 Ancient 4–6. 683.9 ancient 1, 4–6. 683.12 land∧rent. 4. 683.14 kind∧ 1–2. 683.16 natural∧ 4–5. 683.21 ancient 4–6. 683.21 republics 4–6. 683.24 ancient 4–6. 684.4 were∧ 1. 684.4 Rome∧ 1. 684.6 power∧ 1. 684.7 work∧ 1. 684.10 work, 5–6. 684.17 work∧ 1. 685.6 linen∧ 1. 685.10 awkwardness 5–6. 685.14 pence, 1–2. 685.23 author† 2. 686.1 ancient 4–6. 686.2 ancient 4–6. 686.8 rich, 1. 686.31 markets, 1. 686.34 it∧ 1. 687.19 man∧ 1–2. 687.23 super-intending 1–2. 688.1 public 4–6. 688.1 public 4–6. 688.10 commonwealth 5–6. 690.4 labour∧ 1. 690.10 live∧ 1. 690.11 tents∧ 1. 690.19 children, 5–6. 691.4 children∧ 1–2. 691.10 javeling 1. 691.12 maintained∧ 1. 692.2 Thucidides 1. 692.6 havoc 4–6. 692.14 society, 1,4–6. 692.15 commerce, 4–6. 692.15 manufactures∧ 4–6. 692.16 household 2. 692.17 use, 1. 692.17 warrior∧ 1–2. 693.16 least∧ 1. 693.17 and∧ 1. 693.18 kind∧ 1. 693.21 seed∧time∧ 1–2. 693.27 ancient 4–6. 693.30 Thucidides 1. 693.30 summer∧ 1. 694.2 kings∧ 1. 694.2 republic 4–6. 694.2 republick∧ 1. 694.3 they∧ 1. 694.3 home∧ 1. 694.4 those, 2. 694.5 monarchies∧ 5. 694.7 lords∧ 1. 694.8 dependents∧ 1. 694.13 they∧ 1. 694.13 field∧ 1. 694.17 seed∧time 1. 695.5 public 4–6. 695.6 public 4–6. 695.9 public 4–6. 695.16 public 4–6. 695.17 public 4–6. 695.22 troops, 6. 695.22 consisting∧ 1. 695.22 indeed∧ 1. 695.24 Veii∧ 1–2. 695.30 civilized∧ 1. 695.34 maintaining∧ 1. 695.34 stations∧ 1. 695.36 Agrarian 1. 695.36 ancient 4–6. 696.10 republics 4–6. 696.10 ancient 4–6. 696.11 exercises∧ 1. 696.12 public 4–6. 696.13 public 4–6. 696.15 institution∧ 1. 696.16 at∧ 1. 696.16 ancient 4–6. 696.18 ancient 4–6. 696.19 public 4–6. 696.27 republics 4–6. 696.27 ancient 4–6. 696.29 separate∧ 1. 696.30 trade∧ 1. 697.3 himself∧ 1. 697.3 occasions∧ 1. 697.7 arts∧ 1. 697.12 this∧ 1. 697.18 peace∧ 1–2. 697.19 public 4–6. 697.25 such∧ 1. 698.1 account, 1. 698.3 public 4–6. 698.5 circumstances∧ 1. 698.5 methods∧ 1. 698.6 public 4–6. 698.24 artificer∧ 1. 698.32 republics 4–6. 698.33 ancient 2, 4–6. 698.33 Rome∧ 1–2. 699.11 only∧ 1. 699.13 school∧ 1. 699.18 awkward 1–2, 5–6. 699.24 battles∧ 1. 699.30 ancient 4–6. 699.38 ancient 4–6.

700.1 well-disciplined 4–6. 700.1–2 well-exercised 4–6. 700.3 week∧ 1. 700.5 day∧ 1–2. 700.6 ancient 4–6. 700.6 times; 1–2. 701.29 well∧regulated 1. 702.7 struggle∧ 1–2. 702.8 galant 1. 702.8 well-exercised 6. 702.8 republics 4–6. 702.8 ancient 4–6. 702.9–10 ill∧exercised 1–2. 702.10–11 republics 4–6. 702.13 mankind, 5–6. 702.16 republics 4–6. 702.21 son∧in∧law 1. 702.26 Romans∧ 1. 702.30 Thrasymenus∧ 5–6. 703.4 well-disciplined 6. 703.5 well-exercised 6. 703.15 well∧disciplined 1–2. 703.15 well∧exercised 1–2. 703.20 Annibal, 5. 703.21 republics 4–6. 703.23 republic 4–6. 703.25 grandeur∧ 1. 703.28 ancient 1–2, 4–6. 703.39 judged∧ 1. 703.40 while∧ 1,5–6. 703.41 ancient 4–6. 704.2 ancient 1–2,

4–6. 704.28 nations∧ 4–6. 704.30 ancient 4–6. 704.32 barbarous∧ 1. 704.33 shepherds∧ 1. 705.5 settlements∧ 1. 705.33 well∧regulated 1–2. 705.39 superiority∧ 1. 705.39 barbarous∧ 1. 705.40 well∧regulated 1–2. 706.6 well∧regulated 1–2. 706.7 defended, 1. 706.7 it∧ 1. 706.14 well∧regulated 1–2. 706.16 peace∧ 1. 706.19 so∧ 1. 706.21 Cesar 1. 706.22 republic 4–6. 706.22 Cromwel 4–6. 707.3 jealousy∧ 1. 707.4 republics 4–6. 707.4 republicks∧ 1. 707.12 well∧regulated 1–2. 707.17 well∧regulated 1–2,5. 707.17 only∧ 1. 707.18 public 4–6. 707.18 require∧ 1. 707.19 power∧ 1. 707.23 expensive∧ 1. 707.28–29 fire∧arms 1–2. 708.3 powder∧ 1,6. 708.3 review∧ 1. 708.5 ancient 2,4–6. 708.8 expence∧ 1. 708.9 artillery, 6. 708.9 too∧ 1. 708.10 ancients 4–6. 708.10 ancients∧ 1,4–6. 708.11 rown 1. 708.11 resist, 5–6. 708.12 weeks, 5–6. 708.14 improvement, 6. 708.19 consequently∧ 1. 708.19 civilized∧ 1. 708.20 ancient 4–6. 708.25 pernicious∧ 6. 709.1 justice∧ 4–5. 709.1 two very 6. 710.5 envy∧ 1. 711.5 man, 4–6. 711.6 who∧ 1,6. 711.6 body∧ 1,6. 711.10 precedency∧ 4–6. 711.21 whom∧ 1. 711.21 therefore∧ 1. 711.23 estate, 6. 712.6 produce, 5–6. 712.20 that∧ 1. 712.20 age∧ 1. 712.24 superiority∧ 1. 712.25 age∧ 1. 712.25 qualities∧ 1–2. 713.2 shepherds∧ 5. 713.9 ancient 4–6. 713.10 antient 1. 713.14 commonly, 2. 713.14 wealth∧ 1. 713.15 ancient 2,4–6. 713.16 ancient 4–6. 713.16 are∧ 1. 713.17 measure∧ 1. 713.22 submitted, 1. 713.30 fool, 5–6. 714.2 intirely 1. 715.10 things∧ 1. 716.5 revenue∧ 1. 716.13 instructions *1–2. 716.18 justice∧ 1. 716.23 person∧ 1. 716.24 hand∧ 1. 716.24 he∧ 1. 716.25 one∧ 1. 716.28 Tyrrel's 5–6. 717.3 ancient 4–6. 717.10 only∧ 1. 717.16 ancient 4–6. 717.30 is∧ 1. 717.30 manner∧ 1. 717.32 what∧ 1. 717.33 Europe∧ 1. 717.33 subjects∧ 1. 717.34 occasions∧ 1. 717.37 occasions∧ 1. 718.3 it∧ 1. 718.7 proposed, 4–6. 718.22 stipulated, 4–6. 718.26 judges, 1–2, 4–6. 718.28 ancient 4–6. 718.36 no-where 4–6. 719.15 public 1–2, 4–6. 719.37 Public 1–2, 4–6. 720.1 Epices 1. 720.8 Epices 1–2. 720.10 moderate∧ 1. 720.24 alledging 1–2. 720.30 originally, 6. 720.30 measure∧ 1. 720.31 emulation∧ 1. 720.31 anciently 2, 4–6. 720.34 specific 1–2, 4–6. 720.36 specific 1–2, 4–6. 721.17 court∧ 1. 722.3 forever 1–2. 722.9 power∧ 1. 722.12 state∧ 1. 722.17 office∧ 1. 722.17 ignoble, 2. 723.10 *public* 2, 4–6. 723.10 *public* 2, 4–6. 723.12 public 2, 4–6. 723.12 public 2, 4–6. 723.16 it∧ 1, 4–6. 723.16 therefore∧ 1, 4–6. 723.20 public 4–6. 723.20 public 4–6. 723.27 public 4–6. 724.2 *public* 4–6. 724.6 public 4–6. 724.10 public 4–6. 724.14 carriages∧ 1. 724.16 lighters∧ 1. 724.19 public 4–6. 724.20 public 4–6. 724.22 public 4–6. 724.23 managed∧ 1. 724.28 port∧duty 1–2. 724.32 post∧office 1–2. 724.37 public 4–6. 725.6 public 4–6. 725.10 gains, 1. 725.25 magnificence∧ 1. 725.33 happen∧ 1. 726.11 have∧ 1. 726.11 therefore∧ 1. 726.12 commissioners∧ 1. 726.27 completest 4–6. 726.34 controlling 5–6. 727.2 which∧ 1–2. 727.2 oeconomy∧ 1–2. 727.8 trustees∧ 1. 727.10 million∧ 1–2. 727.25 may∧ 1. 727.25 perhaps∧ 1. 727.26 doubtful∧ 1. 727.28 them∧ 1. 727.28 them; 6. 727.28 doubled, 1. 727.29 millions∧ 1. 727.33 encumbrance 1. 727.35 goods∧ 1. 728.1 consequently∧ 1. 728.1 narrowed, 1, 5–6. 728.3 domestic 1–2, 4–6. 728.20 difficult∧ 1. 728.20 present∧ 1. 728.23 purpose∧ 1. 728.28 France∧ 1. 728.30 consist∧ 1. 728.34 ancient 4–6. 729.8 post∧roads 1–2. 729.12 cross∧roads 1–2. 729.17 splendour 5–6. 729.18 highway, 4–6. 729.19 applauses∧ 4–6. 729.24 paltry 6. 729.31 judgement 1. 729.33 public 1–2, 4–6. 729.39 travellers, 1. 730.1 not∧ 1. 730.1 perhaps∧ 1. 730.3 travellers∧ 1. 730.4 too∧ 1. 730.4 perhaps∧ 1. 730.17 country, 1. 730.19 not∧ 1–2. 730.19 Europe∧ 1–2. 730.21 perhaps∧ 1. 730.21 perhaps∧ 1. 730.28 public 1–2, 4–6. 730.32 public 1–2, 4–6. 730.35 revenue∧ 1. 731.2 expence∧ 1. 731.10 trifling∧ 1. 731.21–22 communauté 1. 731.23 *Public* 4–6. 731.25 public 4–6. 732.10 public 4–6. 732.22 ancient 2A, 4–6. 732.23 fifteenth, 2A. 733.2 commonwealth; 2A. 733.12 persuade 4–6. 733.22 not, 2A. 733.27 not,

5–6. 734.1 manage∧ 4–6. 734.2 themselves∧ 5–6. 734.2 ancient 2A, 4–6. 734.4 intitled 2A. 734.15 Britain, 2A, 4–6. 734.15 ancient 2A, 4–6. 734.17 Turky 2A. 735.3 north∧side 5–6. 735.3 Baltic 4–6. 735.15 Turkey 4–6. 735.19 Turkey 4–6. 735.22 traders∧ 6. 735.22 Geo. 2A. 735.36 Turkey 4–6. 736.2 Turkey 4–6. 736.17 Committee 2A. 736.17 Council, 2A. 736.17 council, 4–6. 736.27 not, 2A, 5–6. 736.28 Turkey 4–6. 736.34 Turkey 4–6. 736.36 Turkey 4–6. 736.36 Company 5–6. 736.38 publick 2A. 737.2 public 4–6. 737.17 garrisons∧ 4–6. 737.29 public 4–6. 738.8 trade, 2A. 738.12 Bristol, 2A. 738.22 Bristol, 2A. 738.22 house-rent 5–6. 738.26 constitution∧ 2A. 738.32 following∧ 2A, 5–6. 738.32 Geo. 2A. 738.32 44.), 2A, 5–6. 738.33 coast∧ 4–6. 738.33 South 2A. 738.39 Geo. 2A. 739.3 nine∧ 5–6. 739.3 factors∧ 5–6. 739.4 settlements∧ 5–6. 739.27 public 4–6. 740.2 Turkey 4–6. 740.14 king 2A. 741.5 control 2A. 741.34 Royal 5–6. 743.20 charters, 4–6. 745.8 contract, 2A. 746.28 goods, 2A. 747.26 public 2A, 4–6. 748.20 public 4–6. 749.1 parliament, 2A, 4–6. 749.7 joint∧stock 5–6. 749.15 pounds∧ 4–6. 749.15 sustained, 2A. 749.28 war∧ 5–6. 750.15 period, 6. 750.16 cent.∧ 2A. 750.28 settlements. 6. 750.29 trade, 6. 751.3 them∧ 5–6. 751.15 India∧ 4–5. 752.6 enacted, 2A. 752.26 dividend, 2A. 752.36 regulations∧ 5–6. 753.4 exehequer 5. 753.5 public 4–6. 753.15 have, 2A. 753.16 embezzling, 2A. 753.17 cent.∧ 2A. 753.20 proprietors∧ 2A. 753.20 sometimes, 2A. 753.21–22 committed∧ 2A. 753.23 court∧ 2A. 753.24 consequence∧ 2A. 753.27 Notwithstanding, 2A. 753.28 had, 2A. 753.28 time, 2A. 753.29 sterling, 2A. 753.29–30 notwithstanding, 2A. 753.30 that, 2A. 753.31 depredations∧ 5–6. 754.3 garrisons∧ 4–6. 754.15 public 4–6. 755.40 companies, 6. 756.5 routine 5–6. 756.30 Companies 2A. 757.12 thriving, 6. 757.21 produce, 4–6. 757.23 above-mentioned 4. 757.23 above mentioned 2A, 5–6. 757.24 trade∧ 4–6. 757.25 Inquiry 2A. 757.26 public 4–6. 757.26 public 4–6. 758.1 utility, 6. 758.1 while, 2A. 758.1 time, 2A. 758.1 expence∧ 4–6. 758.3 above-mentioned 4. 758.17 public 4. 758.17 public-spirited 5–6. 758.31 may∧ 1. 758.31 manner∧ 1. 759.5 society∧ 1. 759.5 is∧ 1. 759.6 countries∧ 1. 759.7 Europe∧ 1–2. 759.7 accordingly∧ 1–2. 759.14 public 1–2, 4–6. 759.18 public 1–2, 4–6. 759.21 profession∧ 1. 759.21 it∧ 1–2. 760.7 profession? 5–6. 760.19 instructions, 1. 760.28 same∧ 1–2. 761.3 are∧ 1. 761.4 teachers, 1. 761.7 public 1–2, 4–6. 761.8 teaching, 1–2. 761.11 diocese, 1–2. 761.12 state, 1. 761.14 do∧ 1. 761.15 is∧ 4. 761.16 week, 6. 761.19 kind∧ 4. 761.22 judgement 1. 762.14 physic 1–2, 4–6. 762.17 universities∧ 1. 763.9 teacher∧ 1–2. 763.11 if∧ 1. 763.13 another∧ 1. 763.18 them∧ 1. 763.25 contempt∧ 1. 763.28 upon,∧ 4–6. 763.30 himself∧ 4–6. 763.36 this, 4–6. 763.37 of saying 6. 763.38 college∧ 1. 763.38 time∧ 1. 764.1 contrived∧ 1. 764.2 or, 6. 764.3 is∧ 1. 764.3 cases∧ 1,6. 764.11 where-ever 1–2. 764.12 may∧ 1. 764.12 doubt∧ 1. 764.13 children∧ 1. 764.13 boys∧ 1. 764.18 that∧ 6. 764.22 public 4–6. 764.24 public 4–6. 764.25 not∧ 1, 4–6. 764.25 indeed∧ 1, 4–6. 764.29 public 4–6. 764.31 public 4–6. 764.34 public 4–6. 764.36 Latin; 4–6. 764.39 sciences∧ 1. 765.1 public 4–6. 765.5 may∧ 1. 765.5 perhaps∧ 1. 765.7 public 1, 4–6. 765.17 was∧ 4–6. 765.19 latin 1–2. 765.21 Bible, 1. 765.22 latin 1–2. 765.22 Latin; 4–6. 765.24 latin 1–2. 765.28 latin 1–2. 765.32 ancient 4–6. 765.33 prophane 6. 765.35 latin 1–2. 766.1 made∧ 1. 766.1 beginning∧ 1. 766.3 Greek∧ 1. 766.4 latin 1–2. 766.12 New 6. 766.13 testament∧ 1. 766.13 Testament 6. 766.13 old∧ 1. 766.13 Old 6. 766.14 opinions, 4–6. 766.16 catholic 1, 4–6. 766.16 themselves∧ 1. 766.16 therefore∧ 1. 766.17 catholic 1, 4–6. 766.21 embraced∧ 1. 766.21 rejected∧ 1. 766.24 catholics 1, 4–6. 766.26 universities∧ 1. 766.26 therefore∧ 1. 766.28 latin 1–2. 766.39 ancient 4–6. 766.39 nto 4. 766.40 physics 1–2, 4–6. 766.40 ethics 1–2, 4–6. 766.40 logic 1–2, 4–6. 767.2 revolutions, 1. 767.3 meteors, 1. 767.4 animals, 1. 767.5 curiosity, 4–6. 766.6 curiosity, 4–6. 767.12 philosophers∧ 1. 768.1

accordingly $_\wedge$ 1. 768.5 life $_\wedge$ 6. 768.18 deducible $_\wedge$ 1. 769.1 ancient 4–6. 769.15 judgement 1. 770.5 Logic 1–2, 4–6. 770.7 origin, 4–6. 770.8 physics 1–2, 4–6. 770.8 ethics 1–2, 4–6. 770.9 ancient 4–6. 770.13 ancient 4–6. 770.13 was, 6. 770.15 ancient 4–6. 770.17 physics 1–2, 4–6. 770.19 could, 2. 770.20 conclude $_\wedge$ 1. 770.20 conjecture $_\wedge$ 1–2. 770.20 them $_\wedge$ 1. 770.31 Metaphysics 1–2, 4–6. 770.31 Pneumatics 1–2, 4–6. 771.1 Physics 1–2, 4–6. 771.13 Metaphysics 1–2, 4–6. 771.14 Pneumatics 1–2, 4–6. 771.15 Metaphysics 1–2, 4–6. 771.18 antient 1. 771.24 ancient 4–6. 771.30 generous. 6. 771.31 up $_\wedge$ 1. 771.31 cases $_\wedge$ 1. 772.2 Logic 1–2, 4–6. 772.5 Moral 1. 772.9 Physics 1–2, 4–5. 772.9 physics 6. 772.12 ancient 4–6. 772.13 ecclesiastics 1–2, 4–6. 772.23 universities $_\wedge$ 1. 772.29 improvements $_\wedge$ 1. 772.31 remain $_\wedge$ 1. 772.31 time $_\wedge$ 1. 773.3 public 2, 4–6. 773.7 profession; 6. 773.22 travels $_\wedge$ 1. 773.25 respects, 4–6. 773.28 time $_\wedge$ 1. 773.31 habit $_\wedge$ 1. 774.11 republics 1–2, 4–6. 774.11 ancient 4–6. 774.12 public 1–2, 4–6. 774.13 music 1–2, 4–6. 774.16 public 1–2, 4–6. 774.18 music 1–2, 4–6. 774.21 public 1–2, 4–6. 774.22 ancient 4–6. 774.23 ancient 4–6. 774.26–27 public 1–2, 4–6. 774.27 been $_\wedge$ 1. 774.27 but, 1, 4–6. 774.29 life $_\wedge$ 1. 775.1 Halicarnassus; 1–2. 775.3 public 1–2, 4–6. 775.5 public 1–2, 4–6. 775.9 republic 1–2, 4–6. 776.3 respect $_\wedge$ 1. 776.3 ancient 4–6. 776.4 ancestors $_\wedge$ 1. 776.5 ancient 4–6. 776.6 continued $_\wedge$ 1. 776.6 interruption $_\wedge$ 1. 776.6 societies $_\wedge$ 1. 776.8 Music 1–2, 4–6. 776.11 ancient 4–6. 776.12 ancient 4–6. 776.13 ancient 4–6. 776.14 republics 1–2, 4–6. 776.15 should $_\wedge$ 1. 776.15 time $_\wedge$ 1. 776.16 public 1–2, 4–6. 776.17 music 1–2, 4–6. 776.19 Rome, 1. 776.19 republic 1–2, 4–6. 777.1 purpose $_\wedge$ 1. 777.1 public 1–2, 4–6. 777.3 republics 1–2, 4–6. 777.5 account, 1. 777.5 arithmetic 1–2, 4–6. 777.6 home $_\wedge$ 1. 777.7 pedagogue, 1, 4–5. 777.7 generally $_\wedge$ 1. 777.7 slave $_\wedge$ 1. 777.8 citizens $_\wedge$ 1. 777.13 age, 4–6. 777.15 rhetoric 1–2, 4–6. 777.19 public 1–2, 4–6. 777.20 rhetoric 1–2, 4–6. 777.24 rhetoric 1–2, 4–6. 777.25 state $_\wedge$ 1. 777.26 however $_\wedge$ 1. 778.2 Citta, 4–6. 778.4 Antoninus $_\wedge$ 1. 778.5 public 1–2, 4–6. 778.15 authority $_\wedge$ 1. 778.16 people $_\wedge$ 1, 4–6. 778.20 people $_\wedge$ 1. 778.21 public 1–2, 4–6. 778.21 it $_\wedge$ 1. 778.24 were $_\wedge$ 1. 778.24 them $_\wedge$ 1. 778.25 ancient 4–6. 778.25 republics 1–2, 4–6. 778.26 republic 1–2, 4–6. 778.26 ancient 4–6. 778.28 republics 1–2, 4–6. 778.29 ancient 4–6. 778.30 numerous, 4–6. 778.30 and $_\wedge$ 1, 4–6. 778.30 therefore $_\wedge$ 1, 4–6. 778.30 disorderly, 4–6. 778.31 faction, 1. 779.2 people, 1. 779.2) $_\wedge$ 1. 779.5 public 1–2, 4–6. 779.8 example $_\wedge$ 1. 779.8 precedent $_\wedge$ 1. 779.9 them $_\wedge$ 1. 779.9 same $_\wedge$ 1. 779.10 attention $_\wedge$ 1, 4–6. 779.10 precedent $_\wedge$ 1. 779.20 well $_\wedge$ informed 1–2. 779.23 abilities $_\wedge$ 1. 779.23 military $_\wedge$ 1. 779.23 Romans $_\wedge$ 1. 779.24 been $_\wedge$ 1. 779.27 believe, 4–6. 780.8 ancient 4–6. 780.12 public 1–2, 4–6. 780.24 professions; 4–6. 780.26 public 1–2, 4–6. 780.29 sciences, 6. 780.33 have $_\wedge$ 1. 780.33 manner $_\wedge$ 1. 780.34 public 1–2, 4–6. 780.36 public 1–2, 4–6. 780.38 it $_\wedge$ 4–6. 780.39 fashionable, 4–6. 780.40 teaching $_\wedge$ 1,6. 781.2 pedantic 1–2, 4–6. 781.3 where $_\wedge$ 1. 781.6 public 1–2, 4–6. 781.7 through $_\wedge$ 1. 781.8 education $_\wedge$ 4–6. 781.12 public 1–2, 4–6. 781.18 oeconomy; 4–6. 781.22 man $_\wedge$ 1. 781.22 life $_\wedge$ 1. 781.25 public 1–2, 4–6. 782.10 judgement 1. 782.12 country $_\wedge$ 4–6. 782.18 strength, 2. 782.18 perseverance $_\wedge$ 1. 782.20 seems $_\wedge$ 1. 782.20 manner $_\wedge$ 1. 783.5 stupidity $_\wedge$ 1–2. 783.6 which $_\wedge$ 1. 783.6 society, 1. 783.9 judgement 1. 783.13 society, 6. 783.14 understanding $_\wedge$ 1. 783.18 does $_\wedge$ 1. 783.19 ingenuity $_\wedge$ 1. 783.25 few $_\wedge$ 1–2. 783.29 understandings $_\wedge$ 1. 783.30 degree $_\wedge$ 1. 784.1 be $_\wedge$ 1. 784.4 public 1–2, 4–6. 784.10 public 1–2, 4–6. 784.12 are $_\wedge$ 1. 784.13 cases $_\wedge$ 1. 784.18 is $_\wedge$ 1. 784.19 things $_\wedge$ 1. 784.20 lives $_\wedge$ 1. 785.2 understanding, 1. 785.2 while $_\wedge$ 1. 785.3 time $_\wedge$ 1. 785.6 cannot $_\wedge$ 1. 785.6 society $_\wedge$ 1. 785.11 public 1–2, 4–6. 785.15 public 1–2, 4–6. 785.18 public 1–2, 4–6. 785.18 because, 4–6. 785.24 books $_\wedge$ 1, 6. 785.26 are; 1–2, 5–6. 785.26 Latin, 1, 4–6. 785.28 them, 1. 785.28 them; 2, 4–6. 785.29 mechanics 1–2, 4–6. 786.2 mechanics 1–2, 4–6. 786.6 public 1–2, 4–6. 786.9 public

1–2, 4–6. 786.12 republics 1–2, 4–6. 786.23 public 1–2, 4–6. 786.25 republics 1–2, 4–6. 786.26 exercises∧ 1. 786.28 games∧ 5–6. 786.28 illustration∧ 1. 786.31 republic 1–2, 4–6. 786.32 exercises, 4. 787.4 well∧disciplined 1. 787.5 not∧ 1. 787.5 perhaps∧ 1. 787.7 spirit∧ 1. 787.7 besides∧ 1. 787.13 ancient 4–6. 787.14 effectual∧ 1. 787.15 people∧ 1. 787.18 maintain, 4–6. 787.19 execution, 4–6. 787.21 influence∧ 1. 787.22 besides∧ 1. 787.22 ancient 4–6. 787.23 completely 1–2, 4–6. 787.28 mind∧ 1, 5–6. 787.36 deformity, 4–6. 787.36 wretchedness∧ 1. 788.2 though∧ 1. 788.2 perhaps∧ 1. 788.3 public 1–2, 4–6. 788.4 public 1–2, 4–6. 788.7 man∧ 4–6. 788.17 besides, 4–6. 788.18 themselves∧ 1. 788.18 individually∧ 1. 788.25 judgement 1. 788.39 land-tax 1. 789.2 ancient 4–6. 789.7 well∧endowed 1–2. 789.15 full-fed 1, 4–6. 789.19 adversaries∧ 1. 789.21 land∧ 1. 789.30 culitivated 1. 789.33 trust-rights 1. 789.38 Rome∧ 1. 789.39 interest∧ 1. 790.6 armies, 1. 790.8 pupils; 4–6. 790.13 Dominic 4–6. 790.14 revived∧ 2. 790.15 catholic 1–2, 4–6. 790.16 catholic 1–2, 4–6. 790.22 says, 1–2. 790.27 artizans, 4–6. 791.1 public 2, 4–6. 791.7 ecclesiastics 1–2, 4–6. 791.13 people∧ 2. 791.18 because∧ 1–2. 792.1 occasions∧ 1–2, 792.1 for his 6. 792.2 interest∧ 1. 792.3 adpoting 5. 792.18 weary∧ 1–2. 792.18 besides∧ 1–2. 792.24 take∧ 1. 792.28 politics 1–2, 4–6. 792.39 necessity; 1–2. 792.41 is∧ 1. 793.5 public 4–6. 793.8 tenets, 5–6. 793.19 because∧ 1–2. 793.28 Pennsylvania 6. 793.29 quakers 1. 794.2 public 6. 794.2 tenets, 1–2. 794.13 the latter 4–6. 794.41 morality, 6. 796.8 sects∧ 1. 796.9 indeed∧ 1. 796.28 public 1–2, 4–6. 796.31 music 1–2, 4–6. 796.33 dissipate∧ 1. 796.33 them∧ 1. 796.35 Public 1–2, 4–6. 797.3 Dramatic 1–2, 4–6. 797.4 public 1, 4–6. 797.5 public 1–2, 4–6. 797.5 accounts∧ 1. 797.5–6 diversions∧ 1. 797.10 do∧ 1. 797.10 appointing∧ 1. 797.13 them∧ 1. 798.7–8 Constantinople∧ 1. 798.19 public 1–2, 4–6. 798.28 Christian 4–6. 798.36 violence, 4–6. 798.36–37 freeholds, 4–6. 799.1 them∧ 1. 799.3 them∧ 1. 799.3 soften∧ 1. 799.5 parliaments∧ 1. 799.5 justice∧ 1. 799.8 Steuart 1. 799.8 Stuart 6. 799.12 experiment, 4–6. 799.26 are∧ 1. 799.26 governments∧ 1. 799.32 public 1–2, 4–6. 799.35 ancient 4–6.

800.12 bishoprics 4–6. 800.19 quarters∧ 1. 800.27 dependant 1–2. 800.31 ancient 4–6. 800.34 estates∧ 1. 801.2 clergy, 1. 801.2 bailiffs∧ 1. 801.22 ancient 4–6. 802.12 dominions∧ 1. 802.16 ancient 4–6. 802.17), 4–6. 802.24 religion? 4–6. 802.31 twelfth∧ 1. 803.1 reason∧ 1. 803.7 superstition, 6. 803.10 well∧built 1–2. 803.11–12 over-turned 1. 803.14 perhaps∧ 1. 803.15 manufactures∧ 1. 803.18 manufactures∧ 1. 803.25 clergy∧ 1, 4–6. 804.24 ancient 4–6. 804.26 antient 1 804.26 pragmatic 1–2 804.26 Pragmatic 4–6. 804.33 him∧ 1. 805.5 catholic 1–2, 4–6. 805.11 Prince 1. 805.18 shaken∧ 1. 805.25 declension∧ 1. 805.26 reformation∧ 1. 805.30 party∧ 1. 806.6 passionate, 4–6. 806.7 rustic 1–2, 4–6. 806.7 rustic, 5–6. 806.12 enabled∧ 2. 806.13 over-turn 1–2. 806.13 which∧ 1. 806.24 Frederic 1–2, 5–6. 806.31 affairs∧ 1. 806.35 altogether∧ 1. 806.38 times∧ 1–2. 807.14 tribunal∧ 1–2. 807.30 bishoprics 4–6. 807.37 never∧ 1. 807.37 accordingly∧ 1. 808.29 clergy∧ 2. 808.31 become∧ 1–2. 808.38 republic 1–2, 4–6. 808.39 republic 1–2, 4–6. 809.1 republics 1–2, 4–6. 809.2 public 1–2, 4–6. 809.8 parish∧ 1. 809.8 purchase∧ 1. 809.8 price∧ 1. 809.11 Anne 4–6. 809.15 Anne 4–6. 809.32 difference∧ 1–2. 810.2 worst∧ 1. 810.2 perhaps∧ 1. 810.9 t may 2. 810.28 completely 1–2, 4–6. 811.42 it∧ 1. 811.1 Voltaire∧ 1–2. 811.2 republic 1–2, 4–6. 811.5 singular, 4–6. 810.6 Cassendi 6. 811.7 genius∧ 1. 811.8 him∧ 1. 811.12 catholic 1–2, 4–6. 811.14 physic 1–2, 4–6. 811.16 England, 1–2. 811.20 catholic 1–2, 4–6. 811.30 public 1–2, 4–6. 811.30 rhetoric 1–2, 4–6. 812.3 completely 1–2, 4–6. 812.13 letters∧ 6. 812.14 public 1–2, 4–6. 812.24 and∧ 5. 812.32 anciently 4–6. 812.33 catholic 1–2, 4–6. 812.34 sufficient∧ 1. 812.35 defray, 4–6. 813.2 public 1–2, 4–6. 813.3 public

1–2, 4–6. 813.9 dwelling∧houses 1. 813.15 a∧year 1–2. 813.20 completely 1–2, 4–6. 813.31 roman 1. 813.31 catholic 1–2, 4–6. 813.32 complete 1–2, 4–6. 813.32 tolerated, 1–2. 814.22 republic 1–2, 4–6. 814.22–23 fellow∧citizens 1–2. 814.24 king∧ 1–2. 814.33 too∧ 1–2. 815.3 those, 1–2. 815.6 justice, 2. 815.6 rights∧ 1. 815.8 one, 2. 815.8 other∧ 1. 815.9 persons∧ 1. 815.27 setts 1–2. 815.37 public 1–2, 4–6. 816.2 society∧ 1–2. 816.4 public 1–2, 4–6. 817.2 *public* 4–6. 817.14 consist∧ 1. 817.14 stock∧ 1. 817.16 case, 1–2. 817.16 profit; 1–2. 817.16 other, 1–2. 817.20 super-intends 1. 817.23 public 1–2, 4–6. 817.24 republics 1–2, 4–6. 817.25 republic 1–2, 4–6. 817.25 public 1–2, 4–6. 817.26 apothecaries 1. 818.2 public 1–2, 4–6. 818.19 which∧ 1. 818.19 peace∧ 1. 818.23 project, 4–6. 818.30 advanced, 2. 819.7 republic 1–2, 4–6. 819.17 only∧ 6. 819.24 in their 5–6. 819.26 public 1–2, 4–6. 819.31 states, 1–2. 819.31 public 1–2, 4–6. 820.8 public 1–2, 4–6. 820.12 four∧and∧sixpence 1–2. 820.12 33,750l 1–2. 820.13 Pensylvania∧ 2. 820.17–18 transferrable 5–6. 820.21 4500l 1–2. 820.25 money, 1. 820.26 stock∧ 1. 820.32 circulation∧ 1. 820.33 colonies; 1. 821.1 to∧ 1. 821.1 steady, 1. 821.4 public 1–2, 4–6. 821.7 public 1–2, 4–6. 821.7 public 1–2, 4–6. 821.9 public 1–2, 4–6. 821.9 antient 1–2. 821.10 republics 1–2, 4–6. 821.10 derived∧ 1. 821.10 time∧ 1. 821.13 antient 1–2. 821.14 War, 6. 821.16 antient 1–2. 821.16 republics 1–2, 4–6. 821.22 antient 1–2. 821.24 field∧ 1–2. 821.25 maintained∧ 1. 821.30 people∧ 1. 821.32 public 1–2, 4–6. 822.16 public 1–2, 4–6. 822.18 land∧tax 1, 5–6. 822.19 land∧tax 4–6. 822.22 public 1–2, 4–6. 822.25 land∧tax 6. 822.26–28 [*l.s.d.* entries in Roman type] 1–2. 822.28 land∧tax 5–6. 822.29 coporate 4–6. 822.30 altogether∧ 1. 822.30 houses∧ 1. 822.35 is∧ 1, 4–6. 822.35–36 public∧ 1. 822.35–36 public 2, 4–6. 823.12 rent∧ 1. 823.13 them∧ 1, 4–6. 823.14 probable∧ 1, 5–6. 823.22 people∧ 1. 823.24 anywhere 4–6. 823.38 public 1–2, 4–6. 824.8 public 1–2, 4–6. 824.23 revenue, 6. 824.29 public 1–2, 4–6. 824.31 public 1–2, 4–6. 824.34 public 1–2, 4–6. 824.40 public 1–2, 4–6. 824.40 common-wealth 1. 825.4 Inquiry 4–6. 825.5 one, 2. 825.15 fund∧ 1. 825.16 revenue∧ 1. 825.26 consists∧ 1. 825.28 above-mentioned 1. 825.28 above∧mentioned 5–6. 826.8 manner, 4–6. 826.16 too∧ 1. 826.16 buy∧ 1. 826.17 buy, 4–6. 826.21 public 1–2, 4–6. 826.23 public 1–2, 4–6. 826.30 destroy, 4–6. 826.30 funds∧ 4–6. 827.4 visits∧ 4–6. 827.13 judgement 1. 827.13 equal, 1. 827.15 and∧ in proportion 5–6. 828.1 show, 4–6. 828.4 *Rent* 1, 5–6, 828.4 *Rent* 1, 5–6. 828.10 land-tax 4–6. 828.13 time∧ 1. 828.16 Mary, 4–6. 829.35 coined∧ 1. 829.36 sevenpence 6. 829.37 fourpence 1. 829.37 four pence 2. 830.12 themselves, 1. 830.19 appear, 4–6. 830.24 public 1–2, 4–6. 830.26 estimation, 4–6. 830.29 land-tax 1–2, 4–6. 830.30 not∧ 1. 830.30 perhaps∧ 1. 830.34 would∧ 1. 830.34 measure∧ 1. 831.2 public 1–2, 4–6. 831.7 public 1–2, 4–6. 831.13 frequently∧ 1–2, 4–6. 831.18 down∧ 1. 831.18 been∧ 1. 831.21 discouraged∧ 1–2. 831.26 landlords 1. 831.28 knowledge, 1. 831.37)∧ 1. 831.28 rent, 6. 831.36 former∧ 1. 832.3 money-rents 1–2. 832.8 him∧ 1–2. 831.16 importance∧ 1. 832.18 should∧ 1. 832.18 them∧ 1. 832.19 country, 1. 832.20 tenants∧ 2. 832.23 cultivation∧ 1. 832.26 might∧ 1. 832.26 perhaps∧ 1. 832.27 occasion, 2. 832.27 oppression, 2. 832.29 land, 1–2. 832.29 policy∧ 1–2. 833.2 taxes∧ 1. 833.6 land∧ 1. 833.8 improve∧ 1. 833.12 lands∧ 1. 833.13 neighbourhood∧ 1. 833.19 landlord∧ 1. 833.23 encitement 1. 833.23 counter-balance 1. 833.33 judgement 1. 833.35 produce∧ 1. 834.13 call'd 1. 834.19 public 1–2, 4–6. 834.20 Doomsday∧book 1. 834.22 ancient 4–6. 834.22 Prussia∧ 1. 834.23 valuation∧ 1. 834.28 valuation, 4–6. 834.31 order∧ 1–2. 834.32 one-third 1–2, 4. 834.33 one-third 1–2, 4–6. 835.3 VI.∧ 1. 835.5 Piemont 1. 835.13 reasonable, 4–6. 835.19 Silesia∧ 1. 835.25 countries∧ 1. 835.27 real 4–6. 836.19 actual-state 1. 836.33 *Produce* 4–5. 837.6 church-tythe 1. 837.20 four∧tenths 2. 837.29 one-fifth part 1–2, 4–6. 837.30 whereas∧ 4–6. 838.11 Asia∧ 1. 838.16

land-rent 5–6. 838.18 company 1–2, 5–6. 838.19 ancient 4–6. 838.24 ancient 4–6. 839.8 fraud∧ 1, 4–6. 839.13 public 1–2, 4–6. 839.26 land∧ 5–6. 839.27 way, 6. 839.40 modus 5–6. 840.1 company 1–2, 5–6. 840.2 public 1–2, 4–6. 840.2 publie 6. 840.5 public 1–2, 4–6. 840.6 been∧ 1. 840.21 building, 1, 4–6. 840.26 cent.∧ 1. 840.26 cent, 2. 840.36 completely 1–2, 4–6. 841.2 ground-rent 6. 841.6 Ground-rents 6. 841.17 ground∧rent 1–2. 841.18 fall∧ 6. 841.18 house∧ 6. 842.12 ground∧rents 1–2. 824.14 houses, 6. 842.27 public 1–2, 4–6. 842.35 from, 1. 842.35 of, 1. 843.1 not, 1, 5–6. 843.7 it∧ 1. 844.6 inhabitant∧ 1. 844.18 are∧ 1. 844.33 funds∧ 1. 844.40 building-rent 5–6. 845.2 land∧tax 1–2. 845.8 land-tax 4–6. 845.14 rent, 4–6. 845.21 revenue, 5–6. 845.24 houses∧ 6. 845.27 improved∧ 5–6. 846.4–5 dwelling-house 6. 846.14 window∧tax 1–2. 846.15 window∧tax 1–2. 846.15 present, 1–2. 846.15)∧ 1–2. 846.18 which∧ 6. 846.18 England∧ 6. 846.36 Britain∧ 1. 847.38 land∧ 1. 847.39 completely 1–2, 4–6. 848.13 employed∧ 4–6. 848.35 removed, 5–6. 849.3 could∧ 1, 4–6. 849.4 business∧ 1. 849.8 revenue∧ 6. 849.14 and∧ 1. 849.14 therefore∧ 1. 849.22 one∧fifth 4. 850.3 Whatever, 6. 850.10 beeen 2. 850.13 is∧ 1. 850.14 perhaps∧ 1. 850.23 public 1–2, 4–6. 850.24 upon. 4. 850.27 republic 1–2, 4–6. 850.33 underwold 1. 850.37 orders∧ 1. 850.37 that∧ 1–2. 850.37 necessity∧ 1. 851.1 which, 5–6. 850.3 fellow∧citizens 1–2. 850.11 publicly 4–6. 852.5 per. 2. 852.5 cent.∧ 2. 852.10 public 1–2, 4–6. 852.10 capital∧ 1. 852.13 completely 1–2, 4–6. 852.14 taxupon 1. 852.14 tho' 1–2. 852.33 merchants, 4–6. 853.3)∧ 1–2, 5–6. 853.3 free, 1–2, 5–6. 853.4 profit, 1–2, 5–6. 853.6 over-charge 1–2. 853.7 kind, 1. 853.28 inquisition, 1–2. 854.9 land, 1. 854.9 Europe, 1. 854.9 were∧ 1. 854.9 them∧ 1. 854.13 ancient 4–6. 854.15 years, 4–6. 854.17 independency, 6. 854.36 present, 1–2. 854.36 1775,) 1–2. 855.4 circumstances∧ 1–2. 855.27 complain, 4–6. 856.34 cultivation, 6. 856.38 public 1–2, 4–6. 857.3 Inquiry 4–6. 857.6 negroe 5–6. 857.11 cultivation∧ 6. 857.11 anciently 4–6. 858.2 Vingtieme∧ 1–2. 858.2 twentieth-penny 1–2. 858.4 stock, 1–2. 858.9 rent, 1–2. 858.11 bnt 6. 858.12 vingtieme 1–2. 858.25 public 1–2, 4–6. 858.27 stock∧ 1–2. 858.28 property∧ 1–2. 858.32 parchment, 1–2. 858.34 public 1–2, 4–6. 858.37 transfering 6. 858.38 transfering 6. 859.2 ancient 4–6. 859.5 legacies∧ 1–2. 859.9 donations∧ 1–2. 859.26 might∧ 4–6. 859.29 living, 4. 859.30 ancient 4–6. 860.5 dowager, 1. 860.9 ancient 4–6. 850.9 splendour 5–6. 860.14 to he 5. 860.27 indirectly∧ 1. 860.31 transferred, 1. 861.4 proceedings; 1–2. 861.6 officers, 1–2. 861.11–12 stampt-paper 1–2. 861.11–12 stamped paper 4–6. 861.18 bonds∧ 1–2. 861.28 stamp∧duties 2. 861.37 another, 4–6. 862.17 new∧built 1. 862.36 labourers, 1. 862.37 people∧ 1. 863.15 farmers-general 5–6. 863.18 contrôle 1–2. 863.19 Uncertainty, 1–2, 5–6. 863.26 public 1–2, 4–6. 863.28 public 1–2, 4–6. 863.41 wine, 4–6. 863.42 intended∧ 1. 863.42 perhaps∧ 1. 864.1 callcd 2. 864.21 such∧ 1. 865.8 wages∧ 1. 865.11 who∧ 1. 865.12 before∧ 1. 865.14 or, 6. 865.19 cases∧ 1, 4–6. 865.20 long-run 4–6. 865.36 farmer's 4–6. 866.11 two-and-twenty 4–6. 866.12 9l. 7s. 6d. 1–2. 866.12 villages∧ 1. 866.26 perhaps∧ 1. 866.2 public 1–2, 4–6. 867.3 envy, 6. 867.6 *should*, 2. 867.21 proportioned, 1–2. 868.1 England, 1–2. 868.10 Sergeants 1. 868.13 tax, 1–2. 868.35 pay, 1. 868.41 before. 4–6. 869.4 assessment∧ 4–6. 869.6 perfectly-well 1. 869.6 well∧informed 1–2. 869.17 were 5. 869.19 public 1–2, 4–6. 869.26 tax∧ 1. 869.27 proportionably∧ 1. 870.1 indispensibly 1. 870.7 public 1–2, 4–6. 870.12 public 1–2, 4–6. 870.16 publicly 1–2, 4–6. 870.17 necessaries, 1, 6. 870.20 things∧ 4–6. 871.1 nowhere 5–6. 871.3 regulated∧ 1. 871.15 hand; 1. 872.5 eighteen∧pence 5. 872.26 public 1–2, 4–6. 873.4 declining, 1. 873.27 Mathew 1. 873.28 are∧ 1. 873.28 goods∧ 1. 873.35 candlemaker 2. 874.4 antient 1–2. 874.15 leather∧ 1–2. 874.15 cent; 1–2. 874.17 cent; 1–2, 6. 874.17 cent; 1–2. 875.4 where 5–6. 875.16 which∧ 1. 875.17 scarcity∧ 1. 875.21 public 1–2, 4–6. 875.30 guilders

4–6. 875.31 nine-pence 1–2, 6. 876.4 French∧ 1–2. 876.4 author† 1–2. 876.6 taxes∧ 1. 876.11 oil∧ 1. 876.24 the greater 5–6. 877.15 well∧known 1–2. 877.15 Mathew 1–2. 877.15 Decker∧ 1–2. 877.36 licenee 2. 878.31 above-mentioned 1–2. 878.31 above mentioned 5–6. 878.33 antient 1–2. 879.6 times∧ 1. 879.6 understood∧ 1. 879.8 overcharge 1. 879.16 distinction∧ 1, 6. 879.16 antient 1. 879.22 antient 1–2. 879.23 antient 1–2. 879.28 which, 4–6. 879.29 which∧ 4–6. 879.31 six-pence 1. 879.35 but, 1. 879.35 six-pence 1–2. 880.24 antient 1. 880.31 importation, 6. 881.3 These∧ 1. 881.7 flax∧ 6. 881.10 duties∧ 6. 881.18 Inquiry 4–6. 882.4 arithmetic 1–2, 4–6. 882.6 imposed∧ 1. 882.7 us∧ 1. 882.7 cases∧ 1. 882.12 public 1–2, 4–5. 882.12 pubic 6. 882.15 re-landed 1–2. 882.19–26 [*l* entries in Roman type] 1–2. 882.19 January, 1–2. 882.22 certificates∧ 1–2. 882.22 together∧ 1–2. 882.24 which∧ 1–2. 882.27 amounts, 1–2. 882.27 manner, 1. 883.12 4s. 9d. 1–2. 883.19 custom-house 1–2. 883.20 expence∧ 1–2. 883.21 precision∧ 1. 883.24 public 1–2, 4–6. 883.26 revenue∧ 1. 883.26 excise∧ 1. 883.27 contributors, 2. 883.30 people∧ 1–2. 883.31 public 1–2, 4–6. 883.33 articles∧ 1. 883.36 cacao-nuts 1–2. 883.37 piece∧goods 1–2. 883.38 afford∧ 1. 883.38 perhaps∧ 1. 883.38 present∧ 1–2. 884.5 taxes∧ 1. 884.6 public 1–2, 4–6. 884.34 public 1–2, 4–6. 884.40 public 1–2, 4–6. 885.5 excise∧duties 1–2. 885.8 always, 1–2. 885.11 public 1–2, 4–6. 885.15 smuggling∧ 1. 885.16 extent∧ 1. 885.16 duties, 1. 885.20 revenue∧ 1. 885.21 customs∧ 1. 885.24 certainty∧ 1. 885.25 loses∧ 1. 885.26 re-landed 1–2. 885.29 home-produce, 1. 885.32 might∧ 1. 885.32 kind∧ 1. 885.34 public 1–2, 4–6. 885.34 loss; 1–2. 885.41 home-market 1–2. 886.13 independant 1–2. 886.16 public 1–2, 4–6. 886.21 goods∧ 1. 886.24 consumption, 6. 886.31 Faction∧ 6. 887.12 people∧ 1. 887.20 Fourthly∧ 6. 887.27 remains∧ 1. 887.28 ranks∧ 1. 887.32 than∧ 1, 4–6. 888.1 July, 1–2. 888.2 [*l.s.d.* entries in Roman type] 2. 888.17 brewed∧ 1–2. 888.29–30 alehouse 4–6. 889.14 brewery, 1, 4–6. 889.14 beer, 1, 4–6. 889.30 [*l.s.d.* entries in Roman type] 1–2. 890.22 having, 4–6. 890.22 year, 4–6. 890.27 secondly∧ 2. 890.30 the produce 4–6. 890.32 tax, 1–2. 891.5 opportunity, 1. 891.17 reduce, 4–6. 891.17 respect, 4–6. 891.24 Doctor 1. 892.3 beer, 4–6. 892.9 dearer, 2. 892.9 taxes∧ 2. 892.31 system∧ 1. 893.5 wines, 1–2. 893.15 tax∧ 1. 893.17 show 1. 893.17–18 demonstrated∧ 1. 893.18 perhaps∧ 1. 893.22–23 well-cultivated 1–2, 4–6. 893.24 barley, 1–2. 893.28 or, 6. 893.32 exemption∧ 1. 893.33 enjoy∧ 1. 894.2 Peages 1–2. 894.2 duties 1–2. 894.4 tolls∧ 1. 894.4 rivers; 1–2. 894.9 eases 6. 894.18 expence, 6. 894.20 weight, 6. 894.31 another∧ 1. 895.2 humour∧ 1–2, 4–6. 895.6 contribute 4. 895.6 little∧ 1–2. 895.6 consumption∧ 1–2. 895.8 nothing∧ 1. 895.8 consumption∧ 1. 895.9 country∧ 1. 895.20 might∧ 1. 895.20 perhaps∧ 1. 896.13 public 1–2, 4–6. 896.18 custom-house 1–2. 896.22 July, 1–2. 896.24 [*l.s.d.* entries in Roman type] 2. 897.5–6. perquisites: 5–6. 897.6 revenue, 1–2. 897.8 authorised 5–6. 897.24 domestic 1–2, 4–6. 897.26 domestic 1–2, 4–6. 897.36 no increase 1. 898.10 public 1–2, 4–6. 898.12 smuggling∧ 1–2. 898.16 pedantic 1–2, 4–6. 898.20 public 1–2, 4–6. 898.25 becomes, 1. 898.33–34 tax∧gatherers 1–2. 898.34 doubt∧ 2. 899.2 customhouse 4–6. 899.25 cent.∧ 1–2. 899.25 cent.∧ 1–2. 899.25 cent, 4. 899.28 sold*. 6. 899.28 revenue-officers 4–6. 899.30 subjects∧ 1. 899.33 tax∧ gatherers 1–2.

900.16 visit∧ 1. 900.20 duty∧free 6. 900.29 revenue-officers 4–6. 901.20 farms, 1–2. 901.21 ancient 5–6. 901.23)∧ 1–2. 901.27 much∧ 1. 901.34 restraints∧ 1–2. 902.4 nothing∧ 1. 902.5 climate∧ 1, 6. 902.8 government, 1. 902.8 an are 2. 902.11 let 5–6. 902.22 inspection∧ 1. 902.23 profit∧ 1–2. 902.24 public 1–2, 4–6. 902.29 few∧ 1. 902.30 competitors∧ 1. 902.31 auction∧ 1. 902.33 public 1–2, 4–6. 902.34 public 1–2, 4–6. 903.1 public 1–2, 4–6. 903.9 public 1–2, 4–6. 903.12 public

1–2, 4–6. 903.28 because ₍ 1–2. 903.31 irresistable 1. 903.37 lett 1. 904.3 tobacco, 1. 904.12 that ₍ 1. 904.32 would, 5–6. 904.37 excises ₍ 1. 905.7 abbe 1. 905.7 Abbè 4–6. 905.9 probable ₍ 1–2. 905.11 great 1. 905.17 advantages, 5–6. 905.21 imperfect, 4–6. 905.32 ship ₍ building 1–2. 906.11 republic 1–2, 4–6. 906.21 influence, 5–6. 906.29 public 1–2, 4–6. 907.2 *public* 2, 4–6. 907.5 introduce ₍ 6. 907.7 inquiry 1–2. 907.7 Inquiry 4–6. 907.12 clothing 4–6. 907.13 commerce, 1. 907.16 clothe 4–6. 907.17 clothe 4–6. 907.20 show 1–2, 5–6. 907.21 not ₍ 1–2. 907.21 perhaps ₍ 1–2. 907.23 Bu 1. 907.28 family ₍ 1. 907.29 rustic 1–2, 4–6. 907.29) ₍ 1. 907.30 land-holders ₍ 1. 907.30 not ₍ 1. 907.31 times ₍ 1. 907.35 money ₍ 1. 907.35–36 perhaps ₍ 1. 907.36 luxury ₍ 1. 908.2 usury, 6. 908.5 home ₍ 1. 908.6 violence ₍ 1. 908.8 treasure ₍ trove 1. 908.26 ancient 5–6. 909.1 passions ₍ 1. 909.1 conduct ₍ 1. 909.13 Europe, 5–6. 909.16 monarchcial 2. 908.16 republics 1–2, 4–6. 908.18 republic 1–2, 4–6. 909.19 republics 1–2, 4–6. 909.21 public 2, 4–6. 909.22 republic ₍ 1. 909.22 republic 2, 4–6. 909.32 taxes ₍ 1. 909.33 drawn ₍ 1. 909.38–39 ammunition, 4–6. 910.7 hands, 1. 910.13 merchant ₍ 1. 910.30 government, 6. 911.10 individuals, 5–6. 911.14 no body 5. 911.15 willing ₍ 1–2. 911.20 ruin ₍ 1–2. 911.26 bears ₍ 1. 911.27 bear ₍ 1. 911.35 seamen's 4–6. 911.36 exchequer 1–2. 911.37 debts, 1. 911.38 exchequer 1–2. 911.40 value; 1–2. 912.4 état*) 4–6. 912.7 exchequer 1–2. 912.9 revolution 1–2. 912.13 public 1–2, 4–6. 912.15 year ₍ 1. 912.16 case, 5–6. 912.17 other, 5–6. 912.21 annuity ₍ 1–2. 912.23 funding, 5. 912.27 revolution 1–2. 912.31 public 1–2, 4–6. 912.37 king 1, 4–6. 912.37 queen 1–2, 4–6. 913.3 time, 1. 913.3) ₍ 1. 913.11 August ₍ 4. 913.14–914.4 [*l.s.d.* entries in Roman type] 1–2 913.16 1701, 5–6. 913.16 duties ₍ 1–2. 913.17 August, 1–2, 5–6. 913.21 August, 1, 5–6. 913.27 August, 1–2, 5–6. 913.31 August, 1–2, 5–6. 913.34 August, 1–2, 5–6. 914.1), 5–6. 914.1 others, 5–6. 914.3 Company 6. 914.9 Company 5–6. 914.11 land ₍ bank 4–6. 914.12–28 [*l.s.d.* entries in Roman type] 1. 914.15 cent. ₍ 1. 914.35 public 1, 4–6. 915.3 it ₍ 1. 915.10 public 1, 4–6. 915.17 public 1, 4–6. 915.25 public 4–6. 915.34 [*l.s.d.* entries in Roman type] 1–2. 915.35 public 1–2, 4–6. 916.15 cent. ₍ 1–2. 916.16–917.9 [*l.s.d.* entries in Roman type] 1–2. 916.16 year, 5–6. 916.24 cent. ₍ 1–2. 917.2 South ₍ Sea 4–6. 917.10 1739, 1–2. 917.13 should ₍ 1–2. 917.16 public 1–2, 4–6. 917.19 years ₍ 1–2. 917.19 intrinsic 1–2, 4–6. 917.25 same ₍ 1–2. 917.26 same, 1–2. 917.26 makes ₍ 1–2. 917.27 therefore ₍ 1–2. 917.28 annuities ₍ 1–2. 917.29 lives ₍ 1–2. 917.37 public 1–2, 4–6. 917.39 public 1–2, 4–6. 918.13 public 1–2, 4–6. 918.14 public 1–2, 4–6. 918.16 public 1–2, 4–6. 918.19 eighth ₍ part 5–6. 918.19 public 1–2, 4–6. 918.26 public 1–2, 4–6. 919.16–17 public 1–2, 4–6. 919.23 splendour 5–6. 919.29 than, 1–2. 919.33 comes, 4–6. 919.35 who ₍ 5–6. 920.5 them, 1–2. 4–6. 920.7 news-papers 1–2. 920.12 conquest, 1–2. 920.16 debt ₍ 1–2, 4–6. 921.9 public 1–2, 4–6. 921.12 public 1–2, 4–6. 921.21 public 1–2, 4–6. 921.26 December ₍ 4–6. 921.26 public 1–2, 4–6. 921.29 December ₍ 4–6. 921.31 public 1–2, 4–6. 921.32 public 1–2, 4–6. 921.36 public 1–2, 4–6. 921.37 December ₍ 4–6. 921.39 public 1–2, 4–6. 921.39 December ₍ 4–6. 922.2 December ₍ 4–6. 922.4 public 1–2, 4–6. 922.7 encrease 1. 922.8 December ₍ 4–6. 922.13 public 1–2, 4–6. 922.16 public 1–2, 4–6. 922.18 January ₍ 4–6. 922.21 though ₍ 1–2. 922.22 January ₍ 4–6. 922.26 debt, 1, 6. 922.27 public 1–2, 4–6. 922.32 public 1–2, 4–6. 923.4 Pelham ₍ 6. 923.7 January ₍ 4–6. 923.13–14 independant 1. 923.16 Company 4. 923.21 are, 1–2, 4–6. 923.22 Fench 5. 923.30 pound, 1–2. 924.4 cents. 1–2. 924.4 cents., 4–6. 924.5 million ₍ 1. 924.5 perhaps ₍ 1. 924.9 as. 6. 924.14 public 4–6. 924.17 public 1–2, 4–6. 924.19 super-added 1. 924.23 public 1–2, 4–6. 924.29 advanced, 6. 924.30 public 1–2, 4–6. 925.1 employed ₍ 5–6. 925.18 public 1–2, 4–6. 925.18 expence ₍ 1. 925.21 public 2, 4–6. 925.28 burthened 1. 925.32 public 1–2, 4–6. 926.15 Those,

1. 926.26 it as 5–6. 926.29 public 1–2, 4–6. 927.6 public 1–2, 4–6. 927.9 public 1–2, 4–6. 972.13 public 1–2, 4–6. 927.16 sets 4–6. 927.24 conveniences 4–5. 927.31 When 1–2. 927.31 conveniences 5. 927.34 conveniences 4–6. 927.35 other, 4–6. 927.37 manufacturers, 1–2, 4–6. 927.39 tax gatherers 1. 927.39 tax-gatherers, 4–6. 928.7 sett 1. 928.8 persons, 1. 928.8 public 1–2, 4–6. 928.9), 4–6. 928.11 public 1–2, 4–6. 928.17 public 1–2, 4–6. 928.20 public 1–2, 4–6. 928.24 republics 1–2, 4–6. 928.27 republics 1–2, 4–6. 928.33 republic 1–2, 4–6. 928.41 republic 1–2, 4–6. 929.3 public 2, 4–6. 929.4 irresistable 1. 929.32 completely 1–2, 4–6. 929.32 public 1–2, 4–6. 929.37 public 1–2, 4–6. 930.7 public 1–2, 4–6. 930.9 public 1–2, 4–6. 930.12 public 1–2, 4–6. 930.12 public 1–2, 4–6. 930.14 public 1–2, 4–6. 930.15 public 1–2, 4–6. 930.17 fellow citizens 1. 930.19 public 1–2, 4–6. 930.20 public 1. 930.20 public 2, 4–6. 930.24 capital, 1–2. 930.25 encrease 1. 930.30 when 6. 930.34 ancient 4–6. 930.36 punic 1. 930.38 ounces: 5–6. 930.40 republic 1–2, 4–6. 931.4 ancient 4–6. 931.5 republics 1–2, 4–6. 931.14 republic 1–2, 4–6. 931.26 that 1–2. 931.27 public 1–2, 4–6. 931.30 millions, 1. 931.30 thousand, 1. 930.31 pounds, 1. 931.32 punic 1. 931.37 millions, 1. 931.37 thousand, 1. 932.1 pounds, 1. 932.1–10 penny-weight 5–6. 932.32 coin, 1. 932.32 augmentation, 1. 932.42 du 1. 933.1 public 1–2, 4–6. 933.1 completely 1–2, 4–6. 933.7 public 1–2, 4–6. 933.8 public 1–2, 4–6. 933.16 hopes 1. 933.16 public 1–2, 4–6. 933.19 public 1–2, 4–6. 933.23 scarce 1. 933.23 perhaps 1. 933.25 states general 1. 933.25 empire 5–6. 934.13 land tax 5. 934.13 stamp-duties 4–6. 934.23 completely 4–6. 934.25 complete 1–2, 4–6. 934.26 Ireland, 1. 934.31 Indies 6. 934.36 manner 2. 935.5 customhouse 1. 935.12 cape 1. 936.1–2 necessary 6. 936.11 tax gatherers 1. 936.12 public 1–2, 4–6. 936.21 eight pence 5. 936.22 Carolina 1. 936.29 Mathew 1. 936.36 extreamly 1. 937.1 public 1–2, 4–6. 937.5 home consumption 1. 937.6 exporter; 1. 937.32 public 1–2, 4–6. 937.32 amounts 1. 937.33 March, 1–2. 938.4 Ireland 5–6. 938.8 public 1–2, 4–6. 938.15 completely 4–6. 938.16 meantime 1–2. 938.30 burdens 6. 938.38 England, 5–6. 938.41 excise 1. 939.11 themselves, 6. 939.17 duties 6. 939.28 smuggling 4. 939.33 and if 5–6. 940.1 province, 5–6. 940.3 said 5–6. 940.16 metals, 1–2. 940.18 domestic 1–2, 4–6. 940.20 domestic 1–2, 4–6. 940.21 Inquiry 4–6. 940.29 cloathing 1. 940.29 houshold 1–2. 940.29 iron work 5–6. 940.34 domestic 1–2, 4–6. 940.35 Pensylvania 1. 940.37 Massachuset's 1. 940.38 public 1–2, 4–6. 941.3 paid 5–6. 941.3 public 1–2, 4–6. 941.6 domestic 1–2, 4–6. 941.9 paper-money 4–6. 941.10 domestic 1–2, 4–6. 941.11–12 domestic 1–2, 4–6. 941.13 enterprising 1–2, 5–6. 941.15 paper-money 4–6. 942.2 sett 1. 942.8 domestic 1–2, 4–6. 942.11 rich, 4–6. 942.12 Pensylvania 1. 942.16 balance 5–6. 942.16 therefore 5–6. 942.22 grcat 2. 942.30 balance 4–5. 942.30 therefore 4–6. 943.7 uncertain, 4–6. 943.9 completely 1–2, 4–6. 943.15 occasions 2. 943.22 clothing 4–6. 943.22 household 4–6. 943.25 appears, 4–6. 943.28 enterprise 5–6. 943.40 enterprise 5–6. 944.7 public 1–2, 4–6. 944.9 revolution 1–2. 944.15 property, 1. 944.15 public 1–2, 4–6. 944.24 complete 1–2, 4–6. 944.26 Britain, 4–6. 944.27 complete 1–2, 4–6. 944.30 which 1. 944.31 other 1. 945.9 mother country 1. 945.14 provinces, 1–2. 945.14 center 1. 945.24 public 1–2, 4–6. 945.25 public 1–2, 4–6. 945.31 abundant 1. 945.31 perhaps 1. 945.33 and, 4–6. 945.33 extent 1. 945.35 necessary 1, 5–6. 945.37 might 1. 945.37 perhaps 1. 945.37 lighten 1. 946.1 aggravate 1. 946.5–6 above-mentioned 1–2. 946.7 collecting 1. 946.7–8 public 1–2, 4–6. 946.28 time 1. 946.28 completely 2, 4–6. 946.42 have 1. 947.1 past 1. 947.5 which 1. 947.6 cost, 4–6. 947.13 completed 2, 4–6. 948.2 accounts 6. 949.26 herrings 4, 6. 950.1 exported, 6. 950.5 *Duty* 4–6. 950.6 *Year* 4–6.

SCHEDULE C. *Line-End Hyphenation*

1. *Hyphens in basic texts.* The separable compounds recorded in this first list,[1] all hyphenated at the ends of lines in editions *1* or *3*, as indicated, are now cited in the form given in the present text. Ordinarily that form has been established, for *1* by the word as it appears within the line of *3*, for *3* by the corresponding entry in *1*, and for those words hyphenated in both *1* and *3*, by the form prevailing elsewhere in the text. Compounds with starred reference, identifying line-end words both in *3* and in the present edition, may be further represented in the second list under this schedule.

12.3 commonwealth 3. 14.12 workhouse 1. 22.11 workman 3. 22.24 wool-comber 3. 23.8 workmen 3. 23.15 bricklayer 3. 30.3 greyhound 3. 32.7 plough-wright 1. 33.8 land-carriage 3. 33.17 land-carriage 1. 33.24 land-carriage 1. 34.32 shipbuilders 3. 38.18–19 ale-house 3*. 42.21 two-hundred 3. 59.11 forty-four 1. 59.13 six-pence 3. 60.7 five-pence 3. 60.8 seven-pence 1. 61.34 ten-pence 3. 64.1 money-price 3. 68.29 flax-dresser 3. 70.19 landlord 1. 76.36 journeymen 1. 78.29 under-stocked 3. 82.20 tenfold 1. 83.15 workmen 3. 83.20 workman 1. 85.12 ringleaders 3. 85.31 able-bodied 3. 87.15 bricklayers 3. 89.29 work-houses 1. 90.23 workmen 3. 92.26 five-and-twenty 3. 94.16 eight-pence 3. 98.29 journeymen 1. 99.25 workmen 3. 102.1 workmen 3. 104.1 workmen 3. 111.29 everywhere 3. 112.24 over-run 1. 117.7 journeyman 3. 120.21 one-half 1. 120.28 bricklayers 3. 121.3 country-villages 3. 121.16 coalships 3. 125.4 over-valued 3. 125.25 under-valued 3. 127.15 workmen 3. 130.40–41 well-known 3*. 131.21 workmen 1. 133.18 out-servants 3. 134.25 house-rent 3. 134.38 dwelling-house 3. 135.4 ground-floor 1. 137.26 coach-maker 1. 138.12 reel-makers 3. 141.15 under-stocked 1. 146.5 workmen 1. 146.10 workmen 3. 146.28 churchmen 3. 150.1 thirty-three 3. 156.17 church-wardens 3. 157.32 seven-pence 3. 158.6 workmen 3. 158.16 workmen 3. 158.17 workmen 3. 160.25 landlord 1. 160.32 landlord 3. 168.3 twenty-five 3. 168.7 eight-pence 3. 169.10 landlord 3. 169.24 vineyard 3. 171.14–15 super-abundance 3*. 173.16 seventy-five 1. 177.16 oatmeal 3. 178.14 super-abundance 1,3. 179.11 super-abundant 3. 179.16 super-abundant 3. 179.21 well-cultivated 1. 180.15 ninety-nine 3. 181.5 houshold 1. 184.25 landlord 3. 186.11–12 undertaker 3*. 188.4 forty-six 3. 196.11 two-pence 1,3. 196.12 six-pence 1. 197.13 Tower-weight 3. 197.27 eight-pence 1, 3. 198.16 eight-pence 3. 198.17 four-pence 3. 202.27 six-pence 3. 211.17 one-third 3. 211.23 two-thirds 3*. 213.29 fifteen-pence 3. 214.17 sixty-four 1. 214.26 twenty-six 3. 215.9 eight-and-twenty 3. 219.39 one-and-forty 3. 222.27 East India 1. 223.7 East India 1. 223.37 super-abundance 3. 228.33 cornfields 3. 231.12 landlord 3. 232.8 one-fifth 3. 236.6 Eight-and-twenty 3. 242.22 butcher's-meat 3. 244.33 butcher's-meat 1. 247.3 butcher's-meat 3. 248.11 twenty-pence 3. 248.11 Tower-weight 3. 248.14 money-price 3. 248.18 twenty-eight 3. 249.20 four-and-twenty 3. 252.16 butcher's-meat 3. 257.35 sixty-four 1. 260.31 locksmiths 1. 262.30 fourteen-pence 1. 263.33 workman's 3. 265.15 landlord 3. 276.8 beforehand 3. 277.18 beforehand 3. 279.37 suchlike 3. 281.30–31 undertakers 3*. 282.12 workhouses 3. 282.31 workman 1. 283.7 timber-merchants 3. 283.8 brickmakers 3. 288.2 workmen 3. 292.4 undertaker 3. 293.33 overflow 3.

---

[1] Not cited in this or the subsequent list are the following words, all of which appear invariably, in the WN editions, as inseparable compounds: afterwards, apprenticeship, extraordinary, hardship, highland, however, likewise, mankind, mortgage, nevertheless, otherwise (occasionally spelled 'otherways'), sometime, somewhat, somewhere, therefore, troublesome, understand, understood, undertake, withdrawn, within, without.

295.5 workmen 3. 295.43 workmen 3. 307.17 workmen 3. 307.20 waggon-ways 1. 308.11–12 over-traded 3*. 313.15 bank-notes 3. 327.27 three-pence 1. 331.11 opera-singers 1. 332.20 landlord 3. 338.19 workhouse 3. 355.11 one-fourth 3. 362.14 ale-houses 3. 371.36 home-trade 3. 372.21 home-market 3. 378.15 wheel-wrights 1. 388.13 freemen 3. 392.24 landlords 3. 400.17 Free-traders 3. 408.2 workmen 3. 416.1 bye-laws 3. 420.1 footmen 3. 420.9 workmen 1. 437.36 Overtrading 1,3. 442.2 seventy-five 3. 452.10 butchers-meat 1. 457.1 shoemaker 3. 461.6 fourpence 1. 461.28 undertaker 3. 461.30 undertaker 3. 463.15 three-fourths 1. 468.28 home-market 3. 468.28 workmen 1. 469.26 hardware 1. 470.2 merchant-service 3. 470.10 merchant-service 3. 473.13–14 warehoused 3*. 482.16–17 warehouse 3*. 482.32 twenty-two 3. 484.16 one-fourth 3. 484.27 warehouse-rent 1, 3. 487.11 thirty-three 3. 487.23 over-drawn 1,3. 491.28 round-about 1. 491.37 workman 3. 494.29 under-selling 1. 502.17 non-enumerated 3. 504.7 drawbacks 3. 504.10 drawback 3. 508.26 corn-trade 3. 510.13 sixpence 1. 511.12 dam-head 3. 515.8 home-market 3. 515.9–10 over-stocked 3*. 515.15 home-market 3. 516.14 home-made 3. 517.30 undertakers 1. 519.29 eighty-four 3. 521.16 boat-fishery 3. 523.19 gunpowder 1. 523.21 drawbacks 3. 527.36–37 eight-and-twenty 3. 529.8 shop-keeper 1, 3. 529.25 workhouse 3. 530.22 shop-keeper 3. 532.23 twenty-four 1. 532.26 forty-eight 3. 534.10 forestalling 3. 537.22 understocked 1. 538.7 forty-eight 1. 541.28 forty-eight 3. 542.4 sixpence 3. 542.26 forty-four 3. 546.18 hogsheads 1. 546.19 third part 1. 549.28 round-about 1. 550.32 forty-eight 1. 557.20 freeman 1. 557.36 bye-laws 3. 565.23 over-pays 3. 572.26 quit-rent 3. 577.11 three-fourths 3. 578.5 whale-fishery 3. 582.1 customhouse 1,3. 583.30 drawbacks 3. 585.1 fellow-citizens 3. 588.14 overflowed 3. 601.7 round-about 1. 602.36 eighty-two 3. 603.17 outports 3. 606.20 hogsheads 3. 625.22 good-will 3. 629.32 understocked 3. 637.12 land-rent 3. 644.36 bowsprits 3. 651.6 outwards 3. 655.1 shoe-makers 3. 655.17 comb-maker 3. 666.6 landlord 1. 667.28 pennyworth 3. 676.33 workman 1. 678.29 twenty-seven 3. 683.12 land-tax 1. 683.12 land-rent 3. 693.10 commonwealth 3. 694.17 seed-time 3. 701.29 well-regulated 3. 703.15 well-exercised 3. 707.12 well-regulated 3. 719.29 law-suit 3. 720.37 non-payment 1. 723.7 good-will 1. 725.15 post-chaises 1. 727.6 turnpikes 3. 732. 34 freebooters 3. 733.18 long-run 3. 736.4 bye-laws 3. 747.7 forty-four 3. 755.31 fellow-subjects 3. 779.25 over-rate 3. 798.36–37 free-holds 3*. 801.28 lay-lords 3. 802.21 clergyman 1. 810.24 well-endowed 1. 815.25 turnpike 1. 820.8 pawn-shop 1. 824.35 commonwealth 1. 824.40 commonwealth 3. 828.16 land-tax 1. 829.10 landlords 1. 831.10–11 spendthrift 3*. 833.5 land-tax 3. 837.15–16 landlord 3*. 837.33 landlord 3. 838.19 land-tax 3. 839.17 tax-gatherers 3. 841.24 seventy-two 3. 842.12 ground-rents 3. 844.10 ground-rents 1. 846.18 two-pence 3. 851.3 fellow-citizens 3. 853.24 ale-houses 3. 857.9 landlords 1. 857.18 freemen 3. 858.6 land-tax 3. 861.13 three-pence 1. 861.14 twenty-seven 3. 862.25 ground-rents 1. 863.4 stamp-duties 3. 864.2 stamp-duties 3. 864.7 workmen 3. 870.6 day-labourer 3. 870.17 bare-footed 3. 871.22 landlord 3. 873.24 over-charge 1. 873.35 salt-maker 3. 878.5 workman 1. 878.6 halfpence 3. 878.8 piece-meal 3. 883.36 cocoa-nuts 3. 885.5 warehouses 3. 886.12 workmen 3. 886.19 home-consumption 3. 887.1 home-produce 3. 889.25 twenty-four 3. 890.29 eleven-pence 1, 3. 890.31 counterbalance 1. 891.3 two-thirds 3. 892.15 twenty-four 1. 892.33 twenty-five 3. 893.11 vineyard 3. 894.14 turnpike 3. 894.33 transit-duty 3. 899.1 warehouse 1. 899.33 tax-gatherers 3. 900.19 coast-cockets 1. 903.37 twenty-two 1. 907.30 land-holders 1. 912.33 spendthrift 3. 915.3 overload 3. 916.29 thirty-two 3. 916.30 ninety-eight 1. 918.17 twenty-four 1. 929.40 sixpences 3. 930.2–3 sixpences 3*. 930.4 twenty-eight 3. 931.29

twenty-eight 3. 931.31 eight-pence 3. 932.1 eight-pence 3. 934.20–21[2] land-tax
1. 934.34 rent-roll 1. 937.37 forty-one 1. 940.33 paper-money 1. 945.12 bloodshed
3.

2. *Hyphens in present text.* In quotations from this edition no line-end hyphens are
to be retained except those listed below. With few exceptions these hyphens are
previously represented within line of edition *3*, an issue carefully pointed by the
author. In the exceptional cases, here starred, where the line-end break occurs
both in the present edition and in *3*, the practice is determined ordinarily by the
form in *1*. In all instances, though the compound word extends to the subsequent
line, page-line citation here simply refers to the line on which the word begins.
22.7 well-governed. 22.17 day-labourer. 22.21 day-labourer. 26.14 co-operation.
27.5 fellow-citizens. 32.6 wheel-wright. 38.18 ale-house*. 48.2 purchase-money.
76.29 under-stocked. 76.34 under-stocked. 116.21 no-where. 118.3 every-where.
127.22 five-and-forty. 130.15 butcher's-meat. 130.40 well-known*. 137.22
coach-maker. 137.23 coach-wheels. 137.25 wheel-wright. 147.17 shoe-makers.
166.26 well-enclosed. 171.14 super-abundance*. 173.20 Cochin-china. 182.36
water-carriage. 183.29 well-improved. 185.4 coal-mine. 187.12 one-tenth. 196.11
one-and-twenty. 196.12 Fifty-eight. 197.17 Tower-weight. 211.23 two-thirds*.
227.29 hundred-and-twentieth. 247.4 two fifths. 262.1 eight-and-twenty. 299.22
piece-meal. 308.11 over-traded*. 348.17 one-half. 362.10 ale-houses. 373.9
round-about. 383.22 every-where. 398.13 Domesday-book. 404.13 counter-balance.
408.5 Spital-fields. 474.2 seventy-five. 478.24 sixty-two. 482.11 one-half. 504.24
re-imported. 509.23 home-made. 515.9 over-stocked*. 549.38 round-about.
550.25 forty-four. 571.20 free-booters. 586.8 over-awes. 603.4 round-about.
622.30 fellow-subjects. 650.10 sea-coast. 651.5 coast-ways. 654.38 boat-makers.
655.12 fellow-citizens. 702.9 ill-exercised. 707.28 fire-arms. 738.12 committee-man.
749.36 a-year. 750.2 twenty-eight. 750.3 ninety-two. 757.36 attorney-general.
798.36 Free-holds*. 814.22 fellow-citizens. 836.19 under-taxed. 840.34 ground-rent.
842.1 ground-rent. 842.15 house-rent. 844.9 ground-rent. 844.36 ground-rents.
845.2 land-tax. 846.11 tax-gatherer. 850.19 one-fourth. 852.30 ale-houses. 857.17
poll-tax. 860.27 stamp-duties. 863.38 news-papers. 873.35 candle-maker. 888.30
ale-house. 893.22 well-cultivated. 894.27 transit duties. 895.10 land-tax. 898.33
tax-gatherers. 927.22 land-taxes. 931.35 twenty-eight. 940.29 iron-work.

[2] Of the ninety-five edition *1* line-end compounds here recorded this is the only word
occurring also at the end of the line in the present edition.

Table of Corresponding Passages

THE first column gives part and paragraph numbers from the present edition. The second and third columns give the corresponding pages in the (5th) Cannan edition (Methuen, 1930) and in the Modern Library version (New York, 1937).

I.i	1930	1937
1	5	3
2	5–6	3–4
3	6–7	4–5
4	7–9	5–7
5	9	7
6	9–10	7–8
7	10	8–9
8	10–11	9–10
9	12	10
10	12–13	11
11	13–14	11–12

I.ii	1930	1937
1	15	13
2	15–16	13–14
3	17	15
4	17–18	15–16
5	18	16

I.iii	1930	1937
1	19	17
2	19–20	17–18
3	20–21	18–19
4	21	19
5	21–22	19–20
6	22	20
7	22	20
8	22–23	20–21

I.iv	1930	1937
1	24	22
2	24–25	22–23
3	25	23
4	25–26	23–24

I.iv	1930	1937
5	26	24
6	26	24
7	26–27	24–25
8	27–28	25–26
9	28	26
10	28–29	26–28
11	29–30	28
12	30	28
13	30	28
14	30	28
15	30	28
16	30	28
17	30	29
18	30–31	29

I.v	1930	1937
1	32	30
2	32–33	30–31
3	33	31
4	33	31
5	33–34	31–32
6	34	32
7	34–35	32–33
8	35	33
9	35	33
10	35–36	33–34
11	36	34
12	36	34
13	36–37	34–35
14	37	35
15	37–38	35–36
16	38	36
17	38–39	36–37
18	39	37
19	39	37

I.v	1930	1937
20	39–40	37–38
21	40	38
22	40	38
23	40–41	38–39
24	41	39
25	41	39
26	41	39–40
27	42	40
28	42–43	40–41
29	43	41
30	43	42
31	43–44	42
32	44	42
33	44	42–43
34	45	43
35	45	43–44
36	45–46	44
37	46	44
38	46	44–45
39	47	45
40	47–48	45–46
41	48	46
42	48	46

I.vi	1930	1937
1	49	47
2	49	47
3	49	47
4	49–50	47–48
5	50	48
6	50–51	48–49
7	51	49
8	51	49
9	52	50
10	52	50
11	52	50
12	53	51
13	53	51
14	53	51
15	53	51–52
16	54	52
17	54	52
18	54–55	52–53
19	55	53

I.vi	1930	1937
20	55	53
21	55	53
22	55	53
23	55	53–54
24	56	54

I.vii	1930	1937
1	57	55
2	57	55
3	57	55
4	57	55
5	57–58	55–56
6	58	56
7	58	56
8	58	56
9	58–59	56
10	59	57
11	59	57
12	59	57
13	59	57
14	60	57–58
15	60	58
16	60	58
17	60–61	58–59
18	61	59
19	61	59
20	62	59
21	62	60
22	62	60
23	62	60
24	62–63	60–61
25	63	61
26	63	61
27	63	61
28	63–64	61
29	64	62
30	64	62
31	64	62
32	64	62
33	65	62–63
34	65	63
35	65	63
36	65	63
37	65	63

I.viii	1930	1937
1	66	64
2	66	64
3	66	64
4	66–67	64–65
5	67	65
6	67	65
7	67	65
8	67	65
9	67–68	65–66
10	68	66
11	68	66
12	68	66
13	68–69	66–67
14	69	67
15	69–70	67–68
16	70	68
17	70	68
18	70–71	69
19	71	69
20	71	69
21	71	69
22	71–72	69–70
23	72–73	70–71
24	73–74	71–72
25	74	73
26	74–75	73
27	75	73–74
28	75	74
29	76	74
30	76	74
31	76–77	74–75
32	77	75
33	77–78	75–76
34	78–79	76–78
35	79–80	78
36	80	78–79
37	80–81	79
38	81	79
39	81	79
40	81–82	80
41	82–83	80–81
42	83	81
43	83	81
44	83–84	81–82

I.viii	1930	1937
45	84	82–83
46	85	83
47	85	83
48	85	83–84
49	86	84
50	86	84
51	86–87	84–85
52	87	85
53	87	85
54	87	85–86
55	87–88	86
56	88	86
57	88	86

I.ix	1930	1937
1	89	87
2	89	87
3	89	87
4	90	88
5	90–91	88–89
6	91	89
7	91	89–90
8	92	90
9	92–93	90–91
10	93–94	91–92
11	94–95	92–93
12	95	93–94
13	95–96	94
14	96	94–95
15	96–97	95
16	97	95–96
17	97	96
18	97–98	96
19	98	96
20	98	96–97
21	98	97
22	98–99	97
23	99	97
24	99–100	97–98

I.x.a (Of Wages and Profit in the different Employments of Labour and Stock)

	1930	1937
1	101	99

I.x.a	1930	1937
2	101	99
3	101	99

I.x.b (Inequalities arising from the Nature of the Employments themselves)

	1930	1937
1	102	100
2	102	100
3	102–03	100–01
4	103	101
5	103	101
6	103	101
7	103	101
8	103–04	101–02
9	104	102
10	104	103
11	105	103
12	105	103
13	105	103–04
14	105–06	104
15	106	104
16	106	105
17	107	105
18	107	105
19	107	105
20	107	105
21	107	106
22	107–08	106
23	108	106–07
24	108	107
25	108–09	107
26	109	107
27	109–10	108
28	110	108–09
29	110–11	109
30	111	109
31	111–12	109–10
32	112	110
33	112–13	110–11
34	113	111
35	113	112
36	114	112
37	114–15	112–13

I.x.b	1930	1937
38	115	113–14
39	116	114
40	116	114
41	116	114
42	116	114–15
43	116	115
44	117	115
45	117	115
46	117–18	115–16
47	118	116
48	118	116
49	118	116–17
50	119	117
51	119	117
52	119–20	117–18

I.x.c (Inequalities occasioned by the Policy of Europe)

	1930	1937
1	120	118
2	120	118
3	120	118–19
4	120	119
5	120–21	119
6	121	119
7	121–22	120
8	122	120
9	122–23	120–21
10	123	121
11	123	121
12	123	121–22
13	123–24	122
14	124	122
15	124	122–23
16	124–25	123
17	125–26	123–24
18	126	124
19	126–27	124–25
20	127	125
21	127	125–26
22	127–28	126
23	128	126–27
24	128–29	127
25	129	127–28
26	129–30	128

I.x.c	1930	1937
27	130	128
28	130	128–29
29	130	129
30	130–31	129
31	131	129
32	131	129
33	131	129
34	131–33	129–31
35	133	131
36	133	131
37	133	131–32
38	133–34	132
39	134–35	132–34
40	135–36	134
41	136	134
42	136	134
43	136–37	134–35
44	137	135
45	137	135
46	137	135–36
47	137–38	136
48	138	136
49	138	136–37
50	138	137
51	138–39	137
52	139	137
53	139	137–38
54	139–40	138
55	140	138–39
56	141	139–40
57	141	140
58	141–42	140
59	142	141
60	142–43	141
61	143–44	141–42
62	144	142–43
63	144	143

I.xi.a (Of the Rent of Land)	1930	1937
1	145	144
2	145–46	144–45
3	146	145
4	146	145
5	146	145

I.xi.a	1930	1937
6	146	145
7	146	145
8	147	145–46
9	147	146

I.xi.b (Part I)	1930	1937
1	147	146
2	147	146
3	147–48	146–47
4	148	147
5	148–49	147–48
6	149	148
7	149	148
8	149–50	148–49
9	150	149
10	150	149
11	150	149
12	150–51	149–50
13	151	150
14	151	150–51
15	152	151
16	152	151
17	152	151
18	152	151
19	152–53	151–52
20	153	152
21	153	152
22	153	152
23	153	152
24	153	152
25	153–54	152–53
26	154	153–54
27	155–56	154–55
28	156	155
29	156	155
30	156	155
31	156–57	155–56
32	157–58	156–57
33	158–59	157–58
34	159	159
35	159–60	159
36	160	159
37	160	159–60
38	160	160

I.xi.b	1930	1937
39	161	160
40	161	160
41	161–62	160–61
42	162	161

I.xi.c (Part II)		
1	162	161
2	162	161
3	162	161–62
4	163	162
5	163–64	162–63
6	164	163
7	164–65	163–64
8	165	164
9	165	164–65
10	165	165
11	165	165
12	166	165
13	166	165
14	166	165
15	166	165
16	166–67	165–66
17	167	166
18	167–68	166–67
19	168	167
20	168	167
21	168	167–68
22	168–69	168
23	169	168
24	169	168
25	169–70	168–69
26	170–71	169–70
27	171	170
28	171–72	170–71
29	172	171
30	172	171–72
31	172–73	172
32	173	172–73
33	173–74	173
34	174	173
35	174	173–74
36	174–75	174

I.xi.d (Part III)		
1	175–76	174–75

I.xi.d	1930	1937
2	176	175
3	176	175
4	176	176
5	176	176
6	177	176
7	177	176

I.xi.e (Digression on Silver. First Period)		
1	177	176
2	177–78	176–77
3	178	177–78
4	178–79	178
5	179	178
6	179	178–79
7	179	179
8	179	179
9	180	179
10	180	179
11	180	179–80
12	180–81	180
13	181	180
14	181–82	180–81
15	182	181
16	182	181
17	182–83	181–82
18	183	182
19	183	182–83
20	183	183
21	183–84	183
22	184	183–84
23	184–85	184–85
24	185–86	185
25	186–87	185–86
26	187	186
27	187	186
28	187	186–87
29	187–88	187
30	188	187–88
31	188	188
32	188	188
33	188–89	188
34	189	188–89
35	190	189–90
36	190	190

I.xi.e	1930	1937
37	190	190
38	190–91	190
39	191	190–91

I.xi.f (Second Period)		
1	191	191
2	191	191
3	191–92	191
4	192	191–92
5	192	192

I.xi.g (Third Period)		
1	192	192
2	192–93	192
3	193	192–93
4	193–94	193
5	194	194
6	194–96	194–96
7	196	196
8	196	196
9	196	196
10	196–97	196–97
11	197	197
12	197	197
13	197	197
14	197	197
15	197–98	197–98
16	198	198
17	198–99	198–99
18	199–200	199–200
19	200	200
20	200	200–01
21	201	201
22	201	201
23	201–02	202
24	202	202
25	202	202
26	202–04	202–04
27	204–05	204–05
28	205–07	205–07
29	207	207
30	207	207–08
31	207	208

I.xi.g	1930	1937
32	208	208
33	208–09	208–09
34	209	209
35	209	209–10
36	209–10	210
37	210	210

I.xi.h (Variation in . . . the respective values of Gold and Silver)		
1	210–11	211
2	211	211
3	211	211–12
4	211	212
5	211–12	212–13
6	212–13	213–14
7	213	214
8	214	214–15
9	214	215
10	214–15	215
11	215	215–16
12	215	216
13	215	216

I.xi.i (Grounds of the Suspicion that the Value of Silver still continues to decrease)		
1	216	216
2	216	216–17
3	216	217

I.xi.j (Different Effects of the Progress of Improvement upon . . . different Sorts of rude Produce)		
1	216–17	217

I.xi.k (First Sort)		
1	217–18	218–19

I.xi.l (Second Sort)		
1	219	219–20
2	219–20	220
3	220–22	220–22

I.xi.l	1930	1937
4	222–23	222–23
5	223	224
6	223	224
7	223	224
8	223–24	224–25
9	224–25	225–26
10	225	226
11	225–27	226–27
12	227	227–28
13	227	228

I.xi.m (Third Sort)

	1930	1937
1	228	228
2	228	228–29
3	228	229
4	228	229
5	228	229
6	228–29	229–30
7	229–30	230
8	230	230–31
9	230–31	231
10	231–32	231–32
11	232–33	232–33
12	233–34	233–34
13	234	234
14	234	234–35
15	234–35	235
16	235	235
17	235	235–36
18	235	236
19	235–36	236
20	236	236
21	236–37	236–37

I.xi.n (Conclusion of the Digression)

	1930	1937
1	237–38	237–39
2	238	239
3	238–39	239
4	239	239–40
5	239–40	240
6	240	240
7	240	240
8	240	240–41
9	240	241

I.xi.n	1930	1937
10	241	241–42
11	242	242

I.xi.o (Effects of the Progress of Improvement upon . . . manufactures)

	1930	1937
1	242	242–43
2	242	243
3	242	243
4	242–43	243
5	243	243–44
6	243	244
7	243–44	244
8	244	244
9	244	245
10	245	245
11	245	245
12	245–46	246
13	246	246
14	246	246–47
15	246	247

I.xi.p (Conclusion of the Chapter)

	1930	1937
1	247	247
2	247	247
3	247	247–48
4	247	248
5	247	248
6	248	248
7	248	248
8	248	248–49
9	248–49	249
10	249–50	249–50

II

	1930	1937
1	258	259
2	258–59	259
3	259	260
4	259	260
5	259	260
6	259–60	260–61

II.i	1930	1937
1	261	262
2	261	262
3	261	262
4	261–62	262–63
5	262	263
6	262	263
7	262	263
8	262	263
9	262	263
10	262–63	263–64
11	263	264
12	263–64	264–65
13	264	265
14	264	265
15	264	265
16	264	265
17	264–65	265–66
18	265	266
19	265	266
20	265	266
21	265	266
22	265	266
23	265	266
24	265–66	266–67
25	266	267
26	266	267
27	266	267
28	266–67	267–68
29	267	268
30	267	268
31	267–68	268–69

II.ii	1930	1937
1	269	270
2	269	270
3	269	270
4	269–70	270–71
5	270	271
6	270	271
7	270–71	271–72
8	271	272
9	271	272
10	272	273
11	272	273

II.ii	1930	1937
12	272	273
13	272	273
14	272–73	273–74
15	273	274
16	273	274
17	273	274
18	273–74	274–75
19	274	275
20	274	275
21	274	275
22	274–75	275–76
23	275	276
24	275	276
25	275	276
26	275	276
27	276	277
28	276	277
29	276	277
30	276–77	277–78
31	277	278
32	277	278
33	277–78	278–79
34	278	279
35	278	279
36	278	279
37	278–79	279–80
38	279	280
39	279	280
40	279–80	280–81
41	280	281
42	280–81	281–82
43	281	282
44	281–82	282–83
45	282	283
46	282–83	283–84
47	283	284
48	283–84	284–85
49	284	285
50	284	285
51	284–85	285
52	285	285–86
53	285	286
54	285	286
55	286	286–87

II.ii	1930	1937
56	286–87	287–88
57	287	288
58	287	288
59	287	288
60	288	288–89
61	288	289
62	288–89	289–90
63	289–90	290–91
64	290–91	291–92
65	291–92	292–93
66	292	293
67	292–93	293–94
68	293	294
69	293–94	294–95
70	294–95	295–96
71	295	296
72	295–96	296–97
73	296–98	297–99
74	298–99	299–300
75	299	300
76	299	300
77	299–300	300–01
78	300–01	301–02
79	301	302
80	301	302–03
81	302	303
82	302	303
83	302	303–04
84	303	304
85	303	304
86	303–04	304–05
87	304	305–06
88	305	306
89	305–06	306–07
90	306	307
91	306	307
92	306	307
93	306–07	307–08
94	307	308
95	307	308
96	307–08	308–09
97	308	309
98	308–09	309–10
99	309	310
100	309–10	310–11

II.ii	1930	1937
101	310	311
102	310	311–12
103	310–11	312
104	311	312
105	311–12	312–13
106	312	313

II.iii	1930	1937
1	313–14	314–15
2	314	315
3	314	315
4	315	315–16
5	315	316
6	315	316
7	315–16	316–17
8	316	317
9	316–17	317–18
10	317	318
11	317–18	318–19
12	318–19	319–20
13	319–20	320–21
14	320	321
15	320	321
16	320	321
17	320	321
18	320–21	321–22
19	321	322
20	321	322
21	321	322–23
22	322	323
23	322	323
24	322–23	323–24
25	323	324
26	323	324
27	323	324
28	323–24	324–25
29	324	325
30	324–25	325–26
31	325	326
32	325–26	326–27
33	326	327
34	326	327
35	326–27	327–28
36	327–28	328–29

II.iii	1930	1937
37	328	329
38	328–29	329–30
39	329–30	330–31
40	330	331
41	330	331–32
42	331	332

II.iv	1930	1937
1	332	333
2	332–33	333
3	333	334
4	333	334
5	333–34	334–35
6	334	335
7	334–35	335–36
8	335	336
9	335–36	336–37
10	336	337
11	336–37	337–38
12	337–38	338–39
13	338	339
14	338	339
15	338–39	339–40
16	339	340
17	339	340

II.v	1930	1937
1	340	341
2	340	341
3	340	341
4	340	341
5	340–41	341
6	341	342
7	341–42	342–43
8	342	343
9	342	343
10	342–43	343–44
11	343	344
12	343–44	344–45
13	344	345
14	344	345
15	344	345
16	344–45	345–46

II.v	1930	1937
17	345	346
18	345	346
19	346	346–47
20	346	347
21	346–47	347–48
22	347	348
23	347	348
24	347–48	348–49
25	348	349
26	348	349
27	348	349
28	349	350
29	349–50	350–51
30	350–51	351–52
31	351–52	352–53
32	352	353
33	352	353
34	352–53	353–54
35	353	354
36	353	354
37	354	355

III.i	1930	1937
1	355–56	356–57
2	356	357
3	356–57	357–58
4	357–58	358–59
5	358	359
6	358	359
7	358–59	359–60
8	359	360
9	359	360

III.ii	1930	1937
1	360	361
2	360	361
3	360–61	361–62
4	361	362
5	361–62	362–63
6	362	363
7	362–63	363–64
8	363–64	364–65
9	364	365
10	364–65	365–66

III.ii	1930	1937
11	365	366
12	365–66	366–67
13	366–67	367–68
14	367–68	368–69
15	368	369
16	368	369
17	368	369–70
18	368–69	370
19	369	370
20	369–70	370–71
21	370	371–72

III.iii	1930	1937
1	371	373
2	371–72	373–74
3	372–73	374–75
4	373	375
5	373	375
6	373–74	375–76
7	374	376
8	374–75	376–77
9	375–76	377–78
10	376	378
11	376	378–79
12	376–77	379
13	377–78	379–80
14	378	380
15	378	380
16	378	380–81
17	378–79	381
18	379	381
19	379–80	381–82
20	380–81	382–83

III.iv	1930	1937
1	382	384
2	382	384
3	382–83	384–85
4	383	385
5	383–84	385–86
6	384	386
7	384–85	386–87
8	385–86	387–88

III.iv	1930	1937
9	386	388
10	386–87	388–89
11	387	389
12	387–88	389–90
13	388	390
14	388	390
15	389	390–91
16	389	391
17	389–90	391–92
18	390	392
19	390–91	392–93
20	391–92	393–94
21	392–93	394–95
22	393	395
23	393	395
24	393–94	395–96

IV	1930	1937
1	395	397
2	395	397

IV.i	1930	1937
1	396	398
2	396–97	398–99
3	397	399
4	397	399
5	398	400
6	398	400
7	398	400
8	398–99	400–02
9	400	402
10	400–01	402–03
11	401–02	403–04
12	402	404
13	402–03	404–05
14	403	405
15	403	405–06
16	404	406
17	404	406
18	404–05	406–07
19	405–07	407–09
20	407	409
21	407	409

IV.i	1930	1937
22	407	409
23	407–08	409–10
24	408	410
25	408	410
26	408–09	410–11
27	409	411
28	409–10	411–12
29	410–11	412–13
30	411–12	413–15
31	413	415
32	413–14	415–16
33	414–15	416–17
34	415–16	417–18
35	416	418
36	416	418
37	416	418
38	416	418
39	416	418
40	416	418–19
41	417	419
42	417	419
43	417	419
44	417	419

IV.ii		
1	418	420
2	418–19	420–21
3	419	421
4	419	421
5	419	421
6	419–20	421–22
7	420	422–23
8	421	423
9	421	423
10	421	423
11	421–22	423–24
12	422	424
13	422–23	425
14	423	425
15	423–24	425–26
16	424	426
17	424–25	426–27
18	425	427
19	425	427–28

IV.ii	1930	1937
20	425–26	428
21	426–27	428–29
22	427	429
23	427	429
24	427	429–30
25	427	430
26	428	430
27	428	430
28	428	430
29	428–29	430–31
30	429	431
31	429–30	431–32
32	430	432
33	430	432–33
34	430	433
35	431	433
36	431	433
37	431	433–34
38	431–32	434
39	432–33	435
40	433	435–36
41	433–34	436
42	434–35	436–37
43	435–36	437–38
44	436	438–39
45	436	439

IV.iii.a (Part I)		
1	437–38	440–41
2	438–39	441–42
3	439	442
4	439	442
5	439–40	442–43
6	440	443
7	440–41	443–44
8	441	444
9	441–42	444
10	442	445
11	442–43	445–46

IV.iii.b	(Digression	concerning
	Banks of Deposit)	
1	443	446
2	443–44	446–47

IV.iii.b	1930	1937
3	444	447
4	444–45	447
5	445	447–48
6	445–46	448–49
7	446–47	449–50
8	447	450
9	447–48	450
10	448	451
11	448–49	451
12	449	451–52
13	449	452
14	449–50	452–53
15	450–51	453–54
16	451	454
17	451–52	454–55

IV.iii.c (Part II)	1930	1937
1	452–53	455
2	453	456
3	453	456
4	453	456
5	454	456–57
6	454	457
7	454–56	457–59
8	456–57	459–60
9	457–58	460
10	458	461
11	458–59	461–62
12	459–60	462–63
13	460	463
14	461	463–64
15	461	464
16	461	464
17	461–62	464–65

IV.iv	1930	1937
1	1	466
2	1–2	466
3	2	466–67
4	2	467
5	2	467
6	2–3	467
7	3	467–68

IV.iv	1930	1937
8	3	468
9	3–4	468–69
10	4–5	469–70
11	5	470
12	5	470
13	6	470–71
14	6	471
15	6	471
16	6	471

IV.v.a (Of Bounties)	1930	1937
1	7	472
2	7–8	472
3	8	473
4	8	473
5	8–9	473–74
6	9	474
7	9	474
8	10–11	475–76
9	11	476
10	11	476
11	11	476
12	11	476–77
13	11–12	477
14	12	477
15	12	477
16	12	477–78
17	12–13	478
18	13	478
19	13–15	478–80
20	15	480–81
21	15–16	481
22	16	481
23	16–17	481–82
24	17–18	482–83
25	18–19	483–84
26	19	484
27	19	484
28	20	485
29	20	485
30	20	485
31	20–21	485–86
32	21	486
33	21–22	486–87

IV.v.a	1930	1937
34	22	487–88
35	22–23	488
36	23	488–89
37	24	489
38	24	489
39	24	489–90
40	24	490

IV.v.b (Digression concerning the Corn Trade)

	1930	1937
1	25	490
2	25	490
3	25–26	490–91
4	26–27	491–92
5	27	492–93
6	27–28	493
7	28	493
8	28–29	493–94
9	29	494
10	29	494
11	29–30	494–95
12	30	495
13	30–31	495–96
14	31	496
15	31–32	496–97
16	32	497
17	32–33	497–98
18	33	498
19	33	498
20	33	498–99
21	33–34	499
22	34	499
23	34	499
24	34	499–500
25	34–35	500
26	35	500–01
27	36	501
28	36	501
29	36	501
30	36	501
31	36	501
32	36–37	501–02
33	37–38	502–03
34	39	504

IV.v.b	1930	1937
35	39	504
36	39	504–05
37	40	505
38	40–41	505–06
39	41–42	506–07
40	42	507
41	42	507
42	42	507–08
43	42–43	508
44	43	508
45	43	508–09
46	44	509
47	44	509
48	44	509–10
49	44–45	510
50	45	510
51	45	510
52	45	510
53	45	510

IV.vi	1930	1937
1	46	511
2	46–47	511–12
3	47	512
4	47	512
5	47–48	512–13
6	48	513
7	48	513
8	48	513–14
9	49	514
10	49	514
11	49	514
12	50	515
13	50	515
14	50–51	515–16
15	51	516
16	51	516
17	51	516
18	51–52	516–17
19	52–53	517–18
20	53	518
21	53–54	518–19
22	54	519
23	54–55	519–20

IV.vi	1930	1937
24	55	520
25	55	520
26	55	520
27	55	520
28	55–56	520–21
29	56	521
30	56–57	521
31	57	521–22
32	57	522

IV.vii.a (Part I)

	1930	1937
1	58	523
2	58	523
3	59–60	523–25
4	60	525
5	60	525
6	60–61	525–26
7	61	526
8	61–62	526–27
9	62	527
10	62	527
11	62	527
12	62	527
13	62–63	527–28
14	63	528
15	63	528
16	63–64	528–29
17	64	529
18	64–65	529–30
19	65	530
20	65–66	530–31
21	66	531
22	66	531

IV.vii.b (Part II)

	1930	1937
1	66	531–32
2	67	532
3	67–68	532–33
4	68	533
5	68	533–34
6	68–69	534
7	69–70	534–35
8	70–71	535–36

IV.vii.b (Part II)	1930	1937
9	71	536
10	71	536–37
11	71–72	537
12	72	537–38
13	72–73	538
14	73	538
15	73	538
16	73	538
17	73	538–39
18	73–74	539
19	74–75	539–40
20	75–76	540–41
21	76	541–42
22	76–77	542
23	77–78	542–43
24	78	543
25	78	543–44
26	78	544
27	79	544
28	79	544
29	79	544
30	79	544–45
31	79–80	545
32	80	545
33	80	545
34	80	545–46
35	80–81	546
36	81–82	546–47
37	82	547
38	82	547
39	82	547
40	82	547–48
41	82–83	548
42	83	548
43	83	548–49
44	83–84	549
45	84	549
46	84	549
47	84	549–50
48	84–85	550
49	85–86	550–51
50	86	551
51	86–87	551–52
52	87	552–53
53	87–88	553

IV.vii.b	1930	1937
54	88	553–54
55	89	554
56	89	554–55
57	89	555
58	89	555
59	90	555
60	90	555
61	90	555
62	90	555–56
63	91	556
64	91	556

IV.vii.c (Part III)	1930	1937
1	91	557
2	91	557
3	91–92	557
4	92	557
5	92	557
6	92	557
7	92–93	557–58
8	93	558
9	93–94	558–59
10	94	559
11	94	559
12	94	559–60
13	94	560
14	95	560
15	95	560–61
16	95	561
17	95–96	561
18	96	561–62
19	96–97	562
20	97	562
21	97	562
22	97–98	562–63
23	98–99	563–64
24	99	564
25	99	564–65
26	100	565
27	100	565
28	100	565
29	100	565–66
30	100	566
31	100	566

IV.vii.c	1930	1937
32	100–01	566
33	101	566
34	101	566
35	101	566–67
36	102	567
37	102	567
38	102–03	567–68
39	103	568
40	103–04	568–70
41	105	570
42	105	570
43	105–06	570–71
44	106–07	571–72
45	107–08	572–73
46	108	573
47	108	573
48	108–09	574
49	109	574
50	109	574–75
51	109–10	575
52	110	575
53	110	575–76
54	110–11	576
55	111	576
56	111	576–77
57	111	577
58	112	577
59	112	577–78
60	112	578
61	112–14	578–79
62	114	579
63	114–15	579–80
64	115–16	580–81
65	116	581
66	116–17	581–82
67	117–18	582–83
68	118	583
69	118	583–84
70	118–19	584
71	119	584–85
72	119–20	585
73	120–21	585–86
74	121	586–87
75	121–22	587–88
76	122–23	588

IV.vii.c	1930	1937	IV.viii	1930	1937
77	123–24	588–89	11	145	611
78	124	589	12	145	611
79	124	589–90	13	145	611
80	125	590–91	14	145–46	611–12
81	125–26	591	15	146	612
82	126	591–92	16	146	612
83	126–27	592	17	146	612
84	127	592	18	146–47	612–13
85	127	592–93	19	147	613
86	127–28	593	20	147–48	613–14
87	128–29	593–94	21	148	614
88	129	594–95	22	148–49	614–15
89	129	595	23	149	615
90	129–30	595	24	149–50	615–16
91	130	595–96	25	150	616
92	130	596	26	150–51	616–17
93	130	596	27	151–52	617–18
94	130–31	596	28	152	618
95	131	596	29	152	618
96	131	596–97	30	152	618
97	131–32	597	31	152	618–19
98	132	597–98	32	153	619
99	132–33	598–99	33	153	619
100	133–34	599–600	34	153–54	619–20
101	134–36	600–01	35	154	620
102	136	601–02	36	154	620–21
103	136–37	602–03	37	155	621
104	137	603	38	155	621
105	138–39	603–04	39	155	621
106	139–40	604–05	40	155–56	622
107	140	605–06	41	156–57	622–23
108	140	606	42	157	623
			43	157–58	623–24
IV.viii			44	158	624
			45	158	624
1	141	607	46	158	624
2	142	607–08	47	158	625
3	142	608	48	159	625
4	142–43	608–09	49	159	625
5	143	609	50	159	625
6	143	609	51	159	625
7	143–44	609–10	52	159–60	625–26
8	144	610	53	160	626
9	144	610	54	160	626
10	144	610			

IV.ix	1930	1937
1	161	627
2	161	627
3	161–62	627–28
4	162	628
5	162–63	628
6	163	629
7	163–64	629–30
8	164	630
9	164	630
10	164–65	630–31
11	165	631
12	165–66	631–32
13	166–67	632–33
14	167	633
15	167–68	633–34
16	168	634
17	168	634
18	168	634
19	168	634
20	168–69	634–35
21	169	635
22	169	635
23	169–70	635–36
24	170	636
25	170	636–37
26	171	637
27	171–72	637–38
28	172	638
29	172	638–39
30	172–73	639
31	173	639
32	173–74	639–40
33	174	640
34	174	640–41
35	174–75	641
36	175	641
37	175–76	641 42
38	176–77	642–43
39	177	644
40	177–78	644
41	178–79	644–45
42	179	645
43	179	645–46
44	179	646

IV.ix	1930	1937
45	180–81	646–47
46	181	647
47	181–83	647–49
48	183–84	649–50
49	184	650
50	184	650–51
51	184–85	651
52	185	651–52

V.i.a (Part I)

	1930	1937
1	186	653
2	186	653
3	186–87	653–54
4	187	654
5	187–88	654–55
6	188	655
7	188–89	655–56
8	189	656
9	189–90	656–57
10	190	657
11	190–91	657–58
12	191	658
13	191	658
14	191–92	658–59
15	192	659
16	192	659
17	192–93	659–60
18	193	660
19	193	660
20	193	660
21	193–94	660–61
22	194	661
23	194	661
24	194–95	661–62
25	195	662
26	195	662
27	195–96	662–63
28	196	663
29	196	663
30	196	663
31	196–97	663–64
32	197	664
33	197	664
34	197	664

V.i.a	1930	1937
35	197–98	664–65
36	198–99	665–66
37	199	666
38	199–200	666–67
39	200	667
40	200	667
41	200–01	667–68
42	201	668
43	201–02	668–69
44	202	669

V.i.b (Part II)

	1930	1937
1	202	669
2	202–03	669–70
3	203	670
4	203	670
5	204	671
6	204	671
7	204–05	671–72
8	205	672–73
9	206	673
10	206	673
11	206	673–74
12	207	674
13	207–08	674–75
14	208	675
15	208–09	675–76
16	209–10	676–77
17	210	677
18	210	677
19	210	677
20	210–11	677–78
21	212	679
22	212–13	679–80
23	213	680
24	213–14	680–81
25	214	681

V.i.c (Part III)

	1930	1937
1	214	681
2	214–15	681–82

V.i.d (Article 1st)	1930	1937
1	215	682
2	215	682
3	215	682
4	216	683
5	216	683
6	216	683
7	216–17	683–84
8	217	684
9	217–18	684–85
10	218	685
11	218	685
12	218–19	685–86
13	219	686
14	219	686
15	219	686–87
16	220	687
17	220–22	687–89
18	222	689
19	222	689

V.i.e

	1930	1937
1	223	690
2	223	690–91
3	224	691
4	224	691
5	224	691
6	224–25	691–92
7	225	692
8	225	692
9	225–26	692–93
10	226–28	693–95
11	228–29	695–96
12	229	696
13	229–30	696–97
14	230–32	697–99
15	232	699
16	232	699
17	232	699
18	232–33	699–700
19	233	700
20	233–34	700–01
21	234–35	701–02
22	235–36	703
23	236	703

V.i.e	1930	1937
24	236–37	704
25	237	704–05
26	237–44	705–11
27	244	711
28	244	711–12
29	244–45	712
30	245–46	712–13
31	246	713
32	246	713
33	246	713–14
34	247	714
35	247	714
36	247	714–15
37	247	715
38	248	715
39	248	715
40	248	715–16

V.i.f (Article 2d)

	1930	1937
1	249	716
2	249	716
3	249	716
4	249–50	717
5	250	717
6	250	717
7	250	717–18
8	250–51	718
9	251	718–19
10	251	719
11	252	719
12	252	719
13	252	719–20
14	252–53	720
15	253	720–21
16	253–54	721
17	254	721
18	254	721
19	254	722
20	254–55	722
21	255–56	722–23
22	256	723
23	256	723
24	256	723–24
25	256–57	724

V.i.f	1930	1937
26	257	724–25
27	258	725
28	258	725–26
29	258	726
30	259	726
31	259	726–27
32	259	727
33	259–60	727
34	260	727
35	260	727–28
36	260–61	728
37	261	728
38	261	728
39	261	728–29
40	261–62	729–30
41	262–63	730
42	263	730
43	263–64	730–31
44	264–65	731–32
45	265–66	732–33
46	266	733
47	266–67	734
48	267	734
49	267	734
50	267–68	734–35
51	268–69	735–36
52	269	736–37
53	269	737
54	270	737
55	270	737–38
56	270	738
57	270	738
58	271	738
59	271	738–39
60	271–72	739
61	272–73	739–40

V.i.g (Article 3d)

	1930	1937
1	273–74	740–41
2	274–75	741–42
3	275	742
4	275	742–43
5	275–76	743
6	276	743

V.i.g	1930	1937
7	276–77	743–44
8	277–78	744–45
9	278–79	746
10	279	746–47
11	279–80	747
12	280	747–48
13	280	748
14	281	748
15	281	748
16	281–82	748–49
17	282–83	749–50
18	283	750
19	283–84	750–51
20	284–85	751–52
21	285	752
22	285–87	752–54
23	287	754
24	287–88	754–55
25	288	755–56
26	289	756
27	289–90	756–57
28	290	757
29	290	757
30	290–91	757–58
31	291	758
32	291	758–59
33	291–92	759
34	292–93	759–60
35	293	760
36	293–94	760–61
37	294–95	761–62
38	295	762
39	295–96	762–64
40	296–97	764
41	297–98	764–66
42	299	766

V.i.h (Part IV)	1930	1937
1	299	766
2	299	766
3	299	766–67

V.i.i (Conclusion)	1930	1937
1	300	767

V.i.i	1930	1937
2	300	767
3	300	767
4	300	767–68
5	300–01	768
6	301	768

V.ii	1930	1937
1	302	769

V.ii.a (Part I)	1930	1937
1	302	769
2	302	769
3	302	769
4	302–03	769–70
5	303	770–71
6	304	771
7	304	771
8	304	771
9	304–05	772
10	305	772
11	305	772–73
12	306	773
13	306	773
14	306	773
15	306–07	773–74
16	307–08	774–75
17	308	775
18	308–09	775–76
19	309	776
20	309	776
21	309	776–77

V.ii.b (Part II)	1930	1937
1	310	777
2	310	777
3	310	777
4	310–11	778
5	311	778
6	311–12	778–79
7	312	779

V.ii.c (Article 1st)	1930	1937
1	312	779–80
2	313	780
3	313	780–81
4	313–14	781
5	314	781
6	314	781–82
7	314–15	782
8	315	782
9	315	782
10	315	782
11	315	782–83
12	315–16	783
13	316	783
14	316	783
15	316–17	783–84
16	317	784
17	317	784
18	317–18	784–85
19	318	785
20	318	785–86
21	318–19	786
22	319	786
23	319	786
24	319	786–87
25	320	787
26	320	787
27	320–21	787–88

V.ii.d (Taxes which are proportioned ... to the Produce of Land)		
1	321	788
2	321	788–89
3	322	789
4	322	789
5	322–23	789–90
6	323	790
7	323	790
8	323–24	790–91
9	324	791

V.ii.e (Taxes upon the Rent of Houses)		
1	324	791

V.ii.e	1930	1937
2	324–25	791–92
3	325	792
4	325	792
5	325–26	792–93
6	326–27	793–94
7	327	794
8	327–28	794–95
9	328	795
10	328	795–96
11	329	796
12	329	796
13	329	796–97
14	330	797
15	330	797
16	330	797
17	330	797
18	330–31	797–98
19	331	798
20	331	798

V.ii.f (Article 2d)		
1	331	798
2	331–32	798–99
3	332–33	799–800
4	333	800
5	333	800
6	333	800
7	333–34	800–01
8	334	801
9	334	801
10	334–35	801–02
11	335	802
12	335–36	802–03
13	336	803
14	336	803

V.ii.g (Taxes upon the Profit of particular Employments)		
1	336	803–04
2	336–37	804
3	337	804
4	337–38	804–05
5	338	805

V.ii.g	1930	1937
6	338–39	805–06
7	339–40	806–07
8	340	807
9	340–41	807–08
10	341	808
11	341	808
12	341–42	809
13	342	809

V.ii.h (Appendix to Articles 1st & 2d)

	1930	1937
1	342	809
2	343	810
3	343	810
4	343–44	810–11
5	344	811
6	344	811
7	344–45	811–12
8	345	812
9	345	812
10	345	812–13
11	345–46	813
12	346	813
13	346–47	813–14
14	347	814
15	347	814
16	347	814
17	348	815

V.ii.i (Article 3d)

	1930	1937
1	348–49	815–16
2	349	816–17
3	350	817
4	350	817
5	350	817
6	350	817–18
7	351	818

V.ii.j (Article 4th)

	1930	1937
1	351	818–19
2	351–52	819
3	352	819
4	352	819

V.ii.j	1930	1937
5	352	819–20
6	352–53	820
7	353	820–21
8	353	821
9	354	821

V.ii.k (Taxes upon Consumable Commodities)

	1930	1937
1	354	821
2	354	821
3	354–55	821–22
4	355	822
5	355	822–23
6	355–56	823
7	356	823–24
8	356–57	824
9	357	824–25
10	357	825
11	358	825
12	358	825–26
13	359	826
14	359–60	826–27
15	360	827
16	360	827
17	360	827–28
18	360–62	828–29
19	362	829
20	362	829–30
21	362	830
22	363	830
23	363–64	830–31
24	364–65	831–32
25	365	832
26	365	832
27	365	832–33
28	365–66	833
29	366	833
30	366–67	833–34
31	367	834
32	367	834
33	367	835
34	367	835
35	367–68	835
36	368	835

V.ii.k	1930	1937	V.iii	1930	1937
37	368	835–36	1	392–93	859–60
38	368–69	836	2	393–94	860
39	369–70	836–37	3	394	861
40	370	837	4	394–95	861–62
41	370	837	5	395	862
42	370	837–38	6	395	862
43	370–71	838	7	395–96	862–63
44	371–72	839	8	396	863
45	372	839–40	9	396	863
46	372	840	10	396–97	863
47	372–73	840	11	397	863–64
48	374	840–41	12	397–98	864–65
49	374	841–42	13	398	865
50	374–75	842	14	398	865
51	375	842	15	398	865
52	375	843	16	398–99	865
53	376	843	17	399	865–66
54	376–77	843–44	18	399	866
55	377	844–45	19	399	866
56	377–78	845	20	399	866
57	378	845–46	21	399	866
58	378–79	846–47	22	399	866
59	379	847	23	400	866–67
60	379–80	847	24	400	867
61	380	847	25	400	867
62	380–81	847–48	26	400–01	867–68
63	381	848–49	27	401	868
64	381–82	849	28	401	868
65	382–83	849–50	29	401	868
66	383	850	30	402	868–69
67	383–84	850–51	31	402–03	869–70
68	384	851	32	403	870
69	384	851–52	33	403	870
70	384–85	852	34	403–04	870–71
71	385	853	35	404	871
72	385–86	853	36	404–05	871–72
73	386	853–54	37	405	872
74	387	854	38	405–06	872–73
75	387–88	854–55	39	406	873
76	388	855	40	406	873
77	388–89	855–56	41	407	873–74
78	389–90	856–57	42	407	874
79	390	857	43	407	874
80	390–91	857–58	44	407	874

V.iii	1930	1937	V.iii	1930	1937
45	407–08	874–75	69	419	887
46	408–09	875–76	70	420	887
47	409–10	877	71	420	887
48	410–11	877–78	72	420–21	887–88
49	411	878	73	421	888
50	411	878–79	74	421–22	888–89
51	412	879	75	422	889
52	412	879	76	422–24	889–91
53	412	879	77	424–25	891–92
54	412–13	879–80	78	425	892
55	413	880	79	425	892–93
56	413	880–81	80	426	893
57	414	881	81	426	893–94
58	414–15	881–82	82	427	894
59	415	882	83	427	894
60	415–16	882–83	84	427	894–95
61	416–17	883–84	85	427–28	895
62	417	884	86	428	895
63	417–18	884–85	87	428–29	896
64	418	885	88	429–30	896–97
65	418	885	89	430	897
66	418–19	885–86	90	430–31	897–98
67	419	886	91	431	898
68	419	886–87	92	431–33	898–900

Index of Statutes

and of

THE ACTS OF THE PARLIAMENTS OF SCOTLAND

INDEX OF THE ACTS OF THE PARLIAMENTS OF SCOTLAND

Index of Authorities[1]

(cited in text and notes)

ADAM, C. E. (ed.). *View of the Political State of Scotland in 1788* (Edinburgh, 1887) 393

ADAMS, J. *A Voyage to South America* (London, 1807). See under G. Juan and A. de Ulloa

ADDISON, W. I. *The Snell Exhibitions* (Glasgow, 1901) 148

ANDERSON, A. *Historical and Chronological Deduction of the Origin of Commerce* (London, 1764) 322, 444, 475, 487, 580, 585, 651, 732, 734, 740, 741, 742, 743, 744, 745, 746, 747, 749, 758, 915, 917, 920 [ASL]
   Historical and Chronological Deduction etc (London, 1789) 753

ANDERSON, JAMES. *Observations on the Means of Exciting a Spirit of National Industry* (Edinburgh, 1777) 515–6

ANDERSON, JAMES. *Selectus diplomatum et numismatum Scotiae thesaurus*, ed. T. Ruddiman (Edinburgh, 1739) 203, 230, 298 [ASL]

ANDERSON, JOHN. *Commonplace Book* 90, 97, 121, 689, 711, 722

ANON. *A Letter from a Gentleman in Edinburgh to his Grace the Duke of Buccleugh on National Defence, with Some Remarks on Dr. Smith's Chapter on that Subject in his Book, entitled 'An Inquiry into the Nature and Causes of the Wealth of Nations'* (London, 1778) 700

ANTOINE, M. *Le Conseil du Roi sous le règne de Louis XV* (Geneva, 1970) 171

ARBUTHNOT, C. *Table of Ancient Coins, Weights and Measures* (London, 1727) 149, 150, 685 [ASL]

ARISTOTLE. *Politics.* 40, 388, 775 [ASL]

ASHTON, T. S. *An Economic History of England: the Eighteenth Century* (London, 1955) 167

BALL, V. *Travels in India* (London, 1889). See under J. B. Tavernier

BARETTI, J. *Journey from London to Genoa through England, Portugal, Spain, and France* (London, 1770) 547

BARKER, T. C., McKENZIE, J. C., and YUDKIN, J. *Our Changing Fare* (London, 1966) 93

BAZINGHEN, M. Abot de. *Traité des Monnoies et de la jurisdiction de la Cour des Monnoies en forme de dictionnaire* (Paris, 1764) 551 [ASL]

BELL, J. *Travels from St. Petersburg in Russia to diverse parts of Asia* (Glasgow, 1763) 680 [ASL]

BENTHAM, J. *Defence of Usury* (London, 1787) 351, 357, 358 [ASL]

BERESFORD, M. W. *The New Towns of the Middle Ages: Town Plantations in England, Wales and Gascony* (London, 1967) 402

BERGERON, N. *Voyages faits principalement en Asie dans les xii, xiii, xiv, et xv siècles* (La Haye, 1735) 429 [Q]

BERNIER, F. *Voyages* (1710), translated by I. Brock as *Travels in the Mogul Empire by F. Bernier* (London, 1826) 730 [ASL]

BIBLE 41, 838 [ASL]

BINDON, D. *A Political Essay upon Commerce* (Dublin, 1738). See under J. F. Melon

BIRCH, T. *The Life of Henry Prince of Wales* (London, 1760) 167 [ASL]

---

[1] Where Smith owned *an* edition of a book (or the collected works of some author) cited in this index, it is marked 'ASL' to signify that it was in his library—as reported by either James Bonar or H. Mizuta in their respective catalogues. Where Smith purchased a book for Glasgow University Library during his period as Quaestor, it is marked 'Q'. Smith's accounts as Quaestor are reprinted in W. R. Scott's *Adam Smith as Student and Professor* at pp. 179–84.

BLACKSTONE, W. *Commentaries on the Laws of England* (Oxford, 1765–69) 52, 391 [ASL]
BOLTS, W. *Considerations on India Affairs, particularly respecting the Present State of Bengal and its Dependencies* (London, 1772) 637, 639–40 [ASL]
BONAR, J. *A Catalogue of the Library of Adam Smith* (London, second ed., 1932) 170
BORLASE, W. *The Natural History of Cornwall* (Oxford, 1758) 186, 188
BOSWELL, J. *London Journal, 1762–3,* ed. F. A. Pottle and C. Marley (London 1950 and 1966) 134
BOUCHAUD, M. A. *De l'impôt du Vingtième sur les successions et de l'impôt sur les merchandises chez les Romains* (Paris, 1766) 859 [ASL]
BRADY, R. *An Historical Treatise of Cities and Burghs or Boroughs* (London, 1711) 394, 398, 400, 403 [ASL]
BRITISH PARLIAMENTARY PAPERS, 1868–69 (366) XXV. *Public Income and Expenditure* 822, 878
BROCK, I. *Travels in the Mogul Empire by F. Bernier* (London, 1826). See under F. Bernier
BUFFON, *Histoire Naturelle,* translated as *Barr's Buffon's Natural History* (London, 1797) 243, 560 [ASL]
BURMAN (BURMANNUS), P. *De vectigalibus populi Romani dissertio* (1714) 859 [ASL]
BURN, R. *Ecclesiastical Law* (London, 1763) 147 [ASL]
—— *Justice of the Peace* (London, eds. of 1764 and 1776) 154, 156 [ASL]
—— *History of the Poor Laws* (London, 1764) 95, 156, 157 [ASL]
BYRON, J. *Narrative of the Hon. John Byron, containing an account of the Great Distresses suffered by himself and his companions on the Coast of Patagonia from the Year 1740 until their Arrival in England 1746* (London, 1780) 205

Caldwell Papers (Maitland Club, 1854). See under W. Mure.
CAMPBELL, R. H. *Carron Company* (Edinburgh, 1961) 313
—— 'The Law and the Joint-Stock Company' in P. L. Payne (ed.) *Studies in Scottish Business History* (London, 1967) 741
—— *States of the Annual Progress of the Linen Manufacture, 1727–1754* (Edinburgh, 1964) 102
—— 'Diet in Scotland: An Example of Regional Variation' in T. C. Barker, J. C. McKenzie and J. Yudkin, *Our Changing Fare* (London, 1966) 93
CANTILLON, R. *Essai sur la Nature du Commerce* (1755) 32, 38, 39, 40, 45, 47, 50, 51, 66, 75, 85, 86, 90, 97, 106, 112, 117, 119, 139, 160, 180, 184, 189, 210, 225, 229, 291, 320, 331, 354, 358, 405, 425, 432, 436, 442, 505, 512, 535, 581, 691 [ASL]
CARRERI, J. F. G. *A Voyage round the World.* See under A. and J. Churchill, *A Collection of Voyages and Travels.*
CARR, C. T. *Select Charters of Trading Companies, 1530–1707* Selden Society, xxviii (London, 1913) 742
CATO, *De re rustica* 462 [ASL]
CHALMERS, G. *Comparative Strength of Great Britain to 1803* (London, 1804) 88, 95, 215, 296 [ASL]
CHAMBERS, E. *Cyclopaedia* (fourth ed. 1741) 15 [ASL]
CHARLEVOIX, F. X. de. *Histoire de l'isle espagnole ou de S. Domingue* (Paris, 1730) 559, 560
—— *Histoire et description générale de la nouvelle France* (Paris, 1744) 571 [ASL]
CHILD, J. *New Discourse of Trade* (London, 1694) 432, 735, 737 [ASL]
CHURCHILL, A. and J. *A Collection of Voyages and Travels* (London, 1704) 568 [ASL]
CICERO. *Ad Atticum* 111 [ASL]
—— *De Divinatione* 876 [ASL]
—— *De Officiis* 166, 683–4 [ASL]
—— *In Verrem* 236 [ASL]
CLAPHAM, J. H. *The Bank of England* (Cambridge, 1944) 318, 319, 320, 322, 915–16
—— *A Concise Economic History of Britain* (Cambridge, 1949) 137, 151
COBBETT, W. *Parliamentary History,* xiv (1747–53) 218
COLUMELLA. *De re rustica* 169, 170, 241, 388 [ASL]
CONRAD, A. H. and MEYER, J. R. *Studies in Econometric History* (London, 1965) 387

FIRTH, C. H. and RAIT, R. S. (eds.) *Acts and Ordinances of the Interregnum 1642–1660* (London, 1911) 464

FLEETWOOD, W. *Chronicon Preciosum* (London, 1707) 43, 51, 196, 199, 201, 203, 204–5, 249, 267, 268, 269, 270, 271 [ASL]

FOLKES, M. *A Table of English Silver Coins* (London, 1745) 42, 195–6

FORSTER, J. R. *Travels into North America* (Warrington, 1770) [ASL] See under P. Kalm

FRÉZIER, A. F. *A Voyage to the South Sea and along the Coasts of Chili and Peru in the years 1712, 1713 and 1714* (London, 1717) 186, 222

GEE, J. *The Trade and Navigation of Great Britain Considered* (Glasgow, 1760) 476 [ASL]

GESNERUS, (GESNER) J. M. *Scriptores rei rusticae* (1735) 170 [ASL]

GILBERT, G. *A Treatise of Tenures* (London, 1757) 391 [Q]

GILBOY, E. W. 'The Cost of Living and Real Wages in Eighteenth Century England', *Review of Economic Statistics*, xviii, 218

GRANT, I. F. *Social and Economic Development of Scotland before 1603* (Edinburgh 1930) 138

GRAS, N. S. B. *The Evolution of the English Corn Market from the Twelfth to the Eighteenth Century* (London, 1915) 204

GRAY, M. *The Highland Economy* (Edinburgh, 1957) 133

GREEN, T. H. and GROSE, T. H. (eds.) D. Hume, *Essays Moral, Political, and Literary* (London, 1882) See under D. Hume

GREIG, J. Y. T. *The Letters of David Hume* (Oxford, 1932) 425

GRENVILLE, G. See under T. Whateley

GROTIUS. *De Jure Belli ac Pacis* 40, 45 [ASL]

GUICCIARDINI, F. *Della Istoria d'Italia* (Venice, 1738) 426 [ASL]

GULVIN, C. 'The Union and the Scottish Woollen Industry, 1707–1760', *Scottish Historical Review*, l. 252

GUMILLA, J. *Histoire naturelle, civile et géographique de l'Orenoque* (Avignon, 1758) 563

GUTTRIDGE, G. H. 'Smith's Thoughts on the State of the Contest with America', *American Historical Review*, xxxviii. 605, 615, 616, 617, 622, 623, 625, 707

HABAKKUK, H. J. *American and British Technology in the Nineteenth Century* (Cambridge, 1962) 87

HAILES, LORD (DAVID DALRYMPLE) *An Examination of Some of the Arguments for the High Antiquity of Regiam Majestatem* (Edinburgh, 1769) 203 [ASL]

HALE, M. *Discourse touching Provision for the Poor* (London, 1683) 95

HAMILTON, H. 'The Failure of the Ayr Bank, 1772', *Economic History Review* (second series) viii. 313

—— 'Scotland's Balance of Payments Problem in 1762', *Economic History Review* (second series), v. 304

HAMILTON, SIR W. (ed.) D. Stewart, *Works* (Edinburgh, 1856) See under D. Stewart

HANWAY, J. *An Historical Account of the British Trade over the Caspian Sea* (London, 1753) 346 [ASL]

HARRIS, J. *An Essay upon Money and Coins* (London, 1757) 13–14, 28, 38, 40, 42, 43, 44, 45, 47, 54, 57, 58, 86, 117, 207, 233–4, 430, 476, 477, 480, 512, 581 [ASL]

HARTE, W. *Essays on Husbandry* (London, 1764) 395–6 [ASL]

HALKETT, S. and LAING, J. *Dictionary of Anonymous and Pseudonymous Literature of Great Britain* (Edinburgh, 1882–88) 700

HAWKINS, W. *A Treatise of the Pleas of the Crown* (London, third ed., 1739) 648 [ASL]

HEATON, H. *The Yorkshire Woollen and Worsted Industries* (Oxford, 1920) 102

HÉNAULT, C. J. F. *Nouvel Abrégé chronologique de l'histoire de France* (Paris, 1768) 624

HERBERT, C. J. *Essai sur la police générale des grains, sur leur prix et sur les effets de l'agriculture* (Berlin, 1755) 199, 216 [ASL]

HIGGS, H. (ed.) R. Cantillon, *Essai sur la Nature du Commerce* (London, 1931) See under R. Cantillon

HOBBES, T. *Leviathan* (1651) 48 [ASL]

KING, G. *Natural and Political Observations and Conclusions upon the State and Condition of England*, (1688) 88, 95, 215, 296
KIPPAX, J. *The Theory and Practice of Commerce* (London, 1751) See under G. de Uztariz [ASL, Q]
KITCHEN, A. H. and PASSMORE, R. *The Scotsman's Food* (Edinburgh, 1949) 93
KNOX, J. *A View of the British Empire* (London, 1785) 950
KNOX, W. (attributed to). *The Present State of the Nation* (1768) 108, 442, 443 [ASL]
KOEBNER, R. *Empire* (Cambridge, 1961) 625
KUCZYNSKI, M. and MEEK, R. L. (eds.). *Quesnay's Tableau Economique* (London, 1972) 672
KYD, J. G. *Scottish Population Statistics* (Edinburgh, 1952) See under A. Webster

LAW, J. *Money and Trade Considered* (Edinburgh, 1705) 39, 45, 194, 317, 353 [ASL]
LEHMANN, W. C. *John Millar of Glasgow* (Cambridge, 1960) 710, and see under J. Millar
LESTER, R. A. 'Currency Issues to overcome Depressions in Pennsylvania, 1723 and 1729' *Journal of Political Economy*, xlvi. 326
LINDSAY, J. E. (ed.). *New Cambridge Modern History*, vii. (Cambridge, 1957) 745
LIVY. *History* 694 [ASL]
LOCKE, J. *Essay on Civil Government* (1690) 24, 430 [ASL]
—— *Some Considerations of the Consequences of the lowering of Interest and raising the Value of Money* (1691) 54, 353, 357, 358, 430
—— *Further Considerations concerning raising the Value of Money* (1695) 60
LOWENTHAL, D. (ed.). Montesquieu, *Considerations on the Causes of the Greatness of the Romans and their Decline* (London, 1965) See under Montesquieu
LOWNDES, W. *Report containing an Essay for the Amendment of the Silver Coins* (London, 1695) 41, 213 [ASL]
LOYN, H. R. *Anglo-Saxon England and the Norman Conquest* (London, 1962) 41
LUCIAN. *Eunuchus* 778 [ASL]

MACHIAVELLI, N. *History of Florence* (translated London, 1851) 819 [ASL]
—— *Discourses on the First Decade of Titus Livius*, translated by N. H. Thomson (London, 1883) 790 [ASL]
MACKAY, D. *The Honourable Company* (Toronto, 1938) 743, 744
MACKENZIE, W. M. *The Scottish Burghs* (Edinburgh, 1949) 140
MADOX, T. *Firma Burgi* (London, 1726) 136, 141, 399, 401, 402 [ASL]
—— *History and Antiquities of the Exchequer of the Kings of England. From the Norman Conquest to Edward II* (London, 1711) 199, 399 [ASL]
MAGENS, N. (ed. Horsley). *The Universal Merchant* (London, 1753) 60, 108, 226, 229, 320, 444, 487 [ASL]
MANDEVILLE, B. *The Fable of the Bees* (1723) 13, 20, 21, 22, 24, 26, 27–8, 38, 45, 48, 73, 99, 118, 124, 126, 256, 337, 338, 339, 341, 342, 388, 432, 454, 464–5, 512, 759, 760, 777, 870, 906
MARION, M. *Dictionnaire des Institutions de la France aux XVII et XVIII Siècles* (Paris, 1923) 358, 496
MARSHALL, D. 'The Old Poor Law, 1662–1795', *Economic History Review*, viii. 152
MEEK, R. L. *The Economics of Physiocracy* (London, 1962) 663, 673, 679, 689
—— *Turgot on Progress, Sociology and Economics* (Cambridge, 1973) 14, 689, and see also under Turgot
MELON, J. F. *Essai Politique sur le Commerce* (Paris, 1734) translated by D. Bindon, *A Political Essay upon Commerce* (Dublin, 1738) 924, 926, 932 [ASL]
MERCIER DE LA RIVIERE. *L'ordre naturel et essentiel des sociétés politiques* (1767) 679 [ASL]
MESSANCE. *Recherches sur la population des généralities d'Auvergne, de Lyon, de Rouen et de quelques provinces et villes du royaume, avec des reflexions sur la valeur du bled tant en France qu'en Angleterre, depuis 1674 jusqu'en 1764* (Paris, 1766) 102, 199, 216, 257 [ASL]
MILLAR, J. *Origin of the Distinction of Ranks* (1771) 388–9, 412, 689, 710 [ASL]
MINGAY, G. E. *English Landed Society in the Eighteenth Century* (London, 1963) 392

POSTLETHWAYT, J. *History of the Public Revenue from 1688 to 1753, with an Appendix to 1758* (London, 1759) 318, 912, 913, 921, 922 [ASL, Q]

POSTLETHWAYT, M. *Dictionary of Commerce* (London, 1774) 108 [ASL]

POWNALL, THOMAS *Letter to Adam Smith, being an Examination of Several Points of Doctrine laid down in his Inquiry, into the Nature and Causes of the Wealth of Nations* (London, 1776) 25, 47, 48, 50, 72, 87, 293, 294, 321, 327, 362, 370, 452, 457, 461, 507, 594, 599, 601, 602, 605, 613, 614-5, 616, 768-9

—— *Administration of the Colonies* (1764) 613 [ASL]

The Precipitation and Fall of Messers Douglas, Heron and Company, late Bankers in Air, with the Causes of their Distress and Ruin, investigated and considered by a Committee of Inquiry appointed by the Proprietors (Edinburgh, 1778) 313 [ASL]

The Present State of the Nation (1768) [ASL] See under W. Knox

PRICE, R. *Observations on Reversionary Payments* (London, 1772) 88 [ASL]

PUFENDORF *De Officio Hominis et Civis Juxta Legem Naturalem* 40, 45 [ASL]

—— *De Jure Naturae et Gentium* 40, 45, 54, 175, 180, 754 [ASL]

QUESNAY, F. *Analyse* (1766) 673 See under Dupont

—— *Probleme Economique* (1766) 673

—— *Tableau Economique* (1757-8) 673

—— (ed. A. Oncken). *Oeuvres Economiques et Philosophiques* (Paris, 1888) 89, 391, 681

RAE, J. *Life of Adam Smith* (London, 1895) 171, 357-8, 663, 811

RALEIGH, W. *The Discovere of the large and bewtiful Empire of Guina* (1596) 563

RAMAZZINI, B. *De morbis artificum diatriba*, translated by R. James, *A Treatise of the Diseases of Tradesmen* (London, 1705) 100

RAYNAL, G. T. F. *Histoire philosophique et politique des établissemens et du commerce des Européens dans les deux Indes* (Amsterdam, 1775) translated by J. Justamond, *A Philosophical and Political History of the Settlements and Trade of the Europeans in the East and West Indies* (Edinburgh, 1777) 225, 227, 444, 511, 575, 589, 626 [ASL]

LE REFORMATEUR (1756) 876

Regiam Majestatem. See under Lord Cooper, and Sir J. Skene

The Regulations and Establishment of the Household of Henry Algernon Percy, the Fifth Earl of Northumberland, at his castles of Wresill and Lekinfield in Yorkshire, begun A. D. MDXII (London, 1827) 197

Report from the Committee . . . appointed to inquire into the Causes of the High Price of Provisions, 1764, 168

ROBERTSON, W. *History of Charles V* (1769) 412 [ASL]

ROUSSEAU, J. J. *Origin of Inequality* (1755) 689 [ASL]

RUDDIMAN, T. *An Introduction to Mr. James Anderson's Diplomata Scotiae* (Edinburgh, 1782) 203, 230, 298 [ASL]

RUFFHEAD, O. *Statutes at Large from Magna Charta to the Twentieth Year of the Reign of King George III*, 13v. (London, 1769-80) 42-3, 202

SANDI, V. *Principj di Storia Civile della Republica de Venezia* (Venice, 1755) 407 [ASL]

SAXBY, H. *The British Customs* (1757) 248, 501, 536, 642, 643, 874, 875, 881, 883 [ASL]

SCHUMPETER, E. B. *English Overseas Trade Statistics, 1697-1808* (Oxford, 1960) 372-3

SCOTT, SIR W. *Thoughts on the Proposed Change of Currency . . . First Letter of Malachi Malagrowther* (1826) 315

SCOTT, W. R. *Adam Smith as Student and Professor* (Glasgow, 1937) 412

—— *Constitution and Finance of English, Scottish and Irish Joint Stock Companies to 1720* (Cambridge, 1912) 298, 318, 742, 744, 747, 748, 756

—— (ed.). *Minute Book of the Managers of the New Mills Cloth Manufactory 1681-1690*, Scottish History Society (first series), xlvi (Edinburgh, 1905) 252

SEN, S. R. *The Economics of Sir James Steuart* (London, 1957) 751

SENECA. *De ira* 588 [ASL]

SHANNON, H. A. 'The Coming of General Limited Liability', *Economic History*, ii. 741

SINCLAIR, SIR J. *The History of the Public Revenue of the British Empire* (London, 1803) 442 See under Correspondence of the Rt. Hon. Sir John Sinclair.

SKENE, SIR J. *Regiam Majestatem. The Auld Laws and Con-stitutions of Scotland. Faithfullie collected furth of the Register, and other auld authentick Bukes, from the Dayes of King Malcome the Second untill the Time of King James the First* (Edinburgh, 1609) 203 [ASL]

SKINNER, A. S. (ed.). Sir James Steuart, *Principles of Political Oeconomy* (Edinburgh, 1966). See under Sir James Steuart

SMITH, A. *Thoughts on America*. See under G. H. Guttridge.

SMITH, C. *Three Tracts on the Corn Trade and Corn Laws* (second ed., London, 1766) 199, 211, 217, 218, 272, 461, 506, 508, 534, 536, 538 [ASL]

SMITH, J. *Chronicon Rusticum Commerciale; or Memoirs of Wool, etc.* (London, 1747) 248, 252, 652 [ASL]

SMOUT, T. C. 'Lead-Mining in Scotland, 1650–1850' in P. L. Payne (ed.) *Studies in Scottish Business History* (London, 1967) 186

—— 'Scottish Landowners and Economic Growth, 1650–1850', *Scottish Journal of Political Economy*, xi. 182

SOLORZANO-PEREIRA *De Indiarum Jure* (Madrid, 1777) 219

STAIR, LORD (JAMES DALRYMPLE) *Institutions of the Law of Scotland*, (1681) 383 [ASL, Q]

STARK, W. *Jeremy Bentham's Economic Writings* (London, 1952) See under J. Bentham

STEPHENS, W. WALKER *Life and Writings of Turgot* (London, 1895) 689 and see under Turgot

STEUART, SIR JAMES *Principles of Money Applied to the State of the Coin in Bengal* (London, 1772) 751

—— *Considerations on the Interest of the County of Lanark in Scotland* (Glasgow, 1769) 870

—— *Principles of Political Œconomy* (London, 1767). 9, 19, 44, 46, 62, 73, 74, 94, 97, 133, 139, 181, 317, 325, 331–2, 357, 409, 412, 414, 425, 436, 456, 479, 581, 612, 689, 691, 733, 751, 795, 827, 870, 876 [ASL]

STEWART, D. *Works* (Edinburgh, 1856) 67

SUTHERLAND, L. S. *The East India Company in Eighteenth Century Politics* (Oxford, 1952) 751

SWIFT, J. *An Answer to a Paper called a Memorial of the Poor Inhabitants and Labourers of the Kingdom of Ireland* (Dublin, 1728) 882 [ASL]

TAVERNIER, J. B. *Travels in India*, translated by V. Ball (London, 1889) 191 [ASL]

THEOCRITUS. *Idylls* 118 [ASL]

THOM, W. *Defects of an University Education, and its Unsuitableness to a Commercial People* (Glasgow, 1762) 761

THUCYDIDES. *History of the Peloponnesian War* 692, 693–4 [ASL]

TURGOT, A. J.[2] *Reflections on the Formation and Distribution of Riches* (1766) 14, 73, 276, 337, 338, 358, 360, 391, 672–3, 689 [ASL]

TYRRELL, J. *General History of England both Ecclesiastical and Civil* (London, 1700) 716 [ASL]

DE UZTARIZ, G. *The Theory and Practice of Commerce*, translated by John Kippax (London, 1751) 222, 511, 899–900 [ASL]

ULLOA. See under Juan G. and De Ulloa

---

[2] It is reported by H. Mizuta that Adam Smith owned numbers of the *Ephémérides du citoyen ou bibliothéque raisonée des sciences morales et politiques* for the years 1766–69. He thus owned the first two (out of three) parts of Turgot's *Reflections*. See above, p. *23* and P. D. Groenewegen, 'Turgot and Adam Smith', *Scottish Journal of Political Economy*, xvi. (1969), 275.

Professor Mizuta has reported that a separate copy of the *Reflections* was in Smith's library and bound with *New and old principles of trade compared* (London, 1788). This edition of the *Reflections* is dated London, 1793. *Adam Smith's Library*, p. 59.

Index of Subjects*

This index is the original index, which appeared first in edition 3, with (in square brackets) additions by Edwin Cannan. It covers only the text and the author's notes.

A

[Abassides, opulence of Saracen empire under, 406]

[Abbeville, woollen monopoly, 461–2]

[Abraham, weighed shekels, 41]

Absentee tax, the propriety of, considered, with reference to Ireland, 895.

[Abyssinia, salt money, 38]

[Academy, the, assigned to Plato, 778]

[Academy of Sciences, *Description des Arts et Métiers faites ou approuvées par Messieurs de l'académie royale des sciences*, 1761, 143]

[Acapulco ships, sailing between America and East Indies, 222, 225, 227]

Accounts of money, in modern Europe, all kept, and the value of goods computed, in silver, 57.

[Accumulation, early state preceding, 65, 82; title of Bk. ii., 276; previous and necessary to division of labour, 277]

[Achilles, Agamemnon's offer to, 717–8]

Actors, public, paid for the contempt attending their profession, 124

[Adriatic, favourable to commerce, 36]

[Adulteration of coin, worse than augmentation 932]

[Adulterine guilds, 141]

[Ægean sea, islands of, 556]

[Æolian colonies, 556]

[Æsop's Fables, apologues, 768]

Africa, [powerful king much worse off than European peasant, 24,] cause assigned for the barbarous state of the interior parts of that continent, 35–6. [Trade to America consists of slave trade, 571; receives rum in exchange for slaves, 578; manufactures from European towns, 627; no thriving colonies, 634; natives being shepherds could not be displaced, ib.; gum senega export, 657; necessity of forts for commerce, 731; music and dancing, 776.]

African company, [one of five regulated companies, 734;] establishment and constitution of, 737[–40]. Receive an annual allowance from parliament for forts and garrisons, 739. The company not under sufficient controul, ib. History of the Royal African company, 741–3. Decline of, ib. Rise of the present company, 743.

[Agamemnon's recommendation of his cities, 717–18]

Age, the foundation of rank and precedency in rude as well as civilized societies, 711

[Agen, land tax in, 854]

Aggregate fund, in the British finances, explained, 914

Agio of the bank of Amsterdam [how accounted for by some people, 328;] explained, 479. Of the bank of Hamburgh, 480. The agio at Amsterdam, how kept at a medium rate, 486.

* We are grateful to Methuen and Co., for permission to reproduce Cannan's entries to this index. The original index is based on the text of edition 3, whose italic, spelling, punctuation (and where possible paragraphing) have been retained. There were no substantive changes in the index as between editions 3–5. Such changes in spelling as were effected have been recorded in the notes.

ᵃ⁻ᵃ completely 5

ᵇ⁻ᵇ land 5

Amsterdam, [209, 454, 479, 613, 652, 818] agio of the bank of, [how accounted for by some people, 328;] explained, 479. Occasion of its establishment, 480. Advantages attending payments there, 481. Rate demanded for keeping money there, 482. Prices at which bullion and coin are received, 482–3, *Note*. This bank, the great warehouse of Europe for bullion, 484. Demands upon, how made and answered, 485. The agio of, how kept at a medium rate, 486. The treasure of, whether all preserved in its repositories, ib. The amount of its treasure only to be conjectured, 487. Fees paid to the bank for transacting business, ib.

[Anderson, Adam, quoted 744]

[Anderson, James, quoted, 203, 230, 298]

[Angola, 558, 635]

Annuities for terms of years, and for lives, in the British finances, historical account of, 915–17.

[Antigua, 597, 943]

[Antoninus, Marcus, 778]

[Antwerp, 427, 479]

[Aperea of Brazil, 560]

[Ἀποικία, 558]

Apothecaries, the profit on their drugs unjustly stigmatized as exorbitant, 28–9.

[Apothecary's shop a source of profit to Hamburg, 817]

[Apples imported from Flanders in seventeenth century, 96]

[Apprenticeship statutes raise wages more permanently than they lower them, 79]

Apprenticeship, the nature and intention of this bond servitude explained, 119. The limitations imposed on various trades, as to the number of apprentices, 135–6. The statute of apprenticeship in England, 137. Apprenticeships in France and Scotland, 137–8. General remarks on the tendency and operation of long apprenticeships, 138–40 [obstructs free circulation of labour from one employment to another, 151; means of gaining a settlement, 154].

The statute of, ought to be repealed, 470 [Relation to privileges of graduates, 762].

[Arabia, hospitality of chiefs, 414; histories full of genealogies, 421; riches long in the same family, 422]

[Victorious when united, 692; militia, 700; despotic authority of scherifs, 713; revenue of chiefs consists of profit, 817]

[Arabia, Gulf of, favourable to commerce, 36]

Arabs, their manner of supporting war, 690–1

[Aragon, 561]

[Arbuthnot, Dr. John, quoted, 685]

[Archipelago, 607]

[Argyle, the Duke of, 416]

[Aristotle, munificently rewarded by Philip and Alexander, 150; Lyceum assigned to, 778; a teacher, 811; quoted, 388, 775]

[Arithmetic, political, untrustworthy, 535; of the customs, two and two make one, 882]

[Armada, the defeat of, stopped Spanish obstruction of colonisation, 569–70; less alarming than the rupture with the colonies, 605]

Army, [a disadvantageous lottery, 126;] three different ways by which a nation may maintain one in a distant country, 441.

Standing, distinction between and a militia, 698. Historical review of, 701. The Macedonian army, 702. Carthaginian army, 702–3. Roman army, 703–4 [courageous without active service, 705]. Is alone able to perpetuate the civilization of a country, 705–6. Is the speediest engine for civilizing a barbarous country, 706. Under what circumstances dangerous to, and under what, favourable to liberty, 706–7 [small, would be sufficient if martial spirit prevailed, 787; no security to the sovereign against a disaffected clergy, 798].

Artificers, prohibited by law from going to foreign countries, 659. Residing abroad, and not returning on notice, exposed to outlawry, 660 [serving in an army must be maintained by the public, 695]. See *Manufactures*.

---

[1] This entry appears before 'Bounties' in the original index.

ᶜ⁻ᶜ completed *4–5*   ᵈ⁻ᵈ public *4–5*

dustry and idleness, 337. How it is increased or diminished, ib. National evidences of the increase of, 343. In what instances private expences contribute to enlarge the national capital, 346–7. The increase of, reduces profits by competition, 352. The different ways of employing a capital, 360. How replaced to the different classes of traders, 362. That employed in agriculture puts into motion a greater quantity of productive labour, than any equal capital employed in manufactures, 364. That of a manufacturer should reside within the country, ib. The operation of capitals employed in agriculture, manufactures, and foreign trade, compared, 365–6. The prosperity of a country depends on the due proportion of its capital applied to these three grand objects, 367–8. Different returns of capitals employed in foreign trade, 369. Is rather employed on agriculture than in trade and manufactures, on equal terms, 377. Is rather employed in manufactures than in foreign trade, 379. The natural progress of the employment of, 380. Acquired by trade, is very precarious until realized by the cultivation and improvement of land, 426. The employment of, in the different species of trade, how determined, 453–4 [industry proportioned to, 457]. [Distributed among inferior ranks annually, 887; and land, the two original sources of revenue, 927]

[Capital values, taxes on, 858]

Capitation taxes, the nature of, considered, 867. In England, 868. In France, 868–9 [and see Poll taxes].

[Carlisle, exchange between London and, 326]

[Carnatic, 749]

[Carneades, 150]

[Carolina, planters both farmers and landlords, 176; plantation of, 597]

[Carreri, Gemelli, see under Gemelli]

Carriage, land and water, compared, 32–3. Water carriage contributes to improve arts and industry, in all countries where it can be used, 34, 163, 224 [absence of cheap, causes settlement of finer manufactures, 408–9].

    Land, how facilitated and reduced in price, by public works, 724–5.

[Carriage tax, 728]

[Carron, 94]

[Carrots reduced in price, 95–6]

Carrying trade, [defined, 294;] the nature and operation of, examined, 370–1. Is the symptom, but not the cause, of national wealth, and hence points out the two richest countries in Europe, 373. Trades may appear to be carrying trades, which are not so, ib. The disadvantages of, to individuals, 454. The Dutch, how excluded from being the carriers to Great Britain, 463. Drawbacks of duties originally granted for the encouragement of, 503.

[Carthage, mariners sailed beyond Gibraltar, 34; the fate of, great historical revolution, 702]

[Carthagena, 705, 746]

Carthaginian army, its superiority over the Roman army, accounted for, 702.

[Cash account at Scotch banks explained, 299]

[Castile, 561]

[Castracani, Castruccio, drove out manufactures from Lucca, 407]

[Casuistry taught as moral philosophy, 771]

[Catholics established Maryland, 589]

[Cato, advised good feeding of cattle, 166; on communication of agricultural knowledge, 462]

Cattle, [at one time used as money, 38] and corn, their value compared, in the different stages of agriculture, 164. The price of, reduced by artificial grasses, 167. To what height the price of cattle may rise in an improving country, 237. The raising a stock of, necessary for the supply of manure to farms, 238. Cattle must bear a good price to be well fed, ib. The price of, rises in Scotland in consequence of the union with England, 239–40. Great multiplication of European cattle in America, 240. Are killed in some countries, merely for the sake of the hides and tallow, 247. The market for these articles more extensive than for the carcase, ib. This market sometimes brought nearer home by the establishment of manufactures, ib. How the extension of cultivation raises the price of animal food, 259 [labouring, are a fixed capital, 280; importation prohibited, 424].

Is perhaps the only commodity more expensive to transport by sea than by land, 459. Great Britain never likely to be much affected by the free importation of Irish cattle, ib.

[Ceded Islands, 578, 923, 943]

[Celebes, 635]

[Celtes cultivated music and dancing, 776]

Certificates, parish, the laws relating to, with observations on them, 155.

[Chance of gain overvalued, 125]

[Charles V., remark on the abundance of France and poverty of Spain, 220; befriended the Pope, 806]

[Charles VI. surveyed Milan, 835]

[Charles VIII., expedition to Naples, 425, 426]

[Charles XII. of Sweden 446]

[Charlevoix, Francois, quoted, 571]

[Chastity, in the liberal morality, 794]

[Chatham, Lord, his account, 923]

Child, Sir Josiah, [quoted, 735] his observation on trading companies, 737.

Children [value of, in North America, 88, 565] riches unfavourable to the production, and extreme poverty to the raising, of them, 96–7. The mortality still greater among those maintained by charity, 97.

[Chili, takes Spanish iron, 185; rent of gold mines, 188; price of horses in, 205; growth of towns of, 222; cattle killed for sake of hide and tallow, 247; conquest of, 562, 589–90]

China, to what the early improvement in arts and industry there was owing, 35. Concurrent testimonies of the misery of the lower ranks of the Chinese, 89–90 [one of the richest countries in the world, 89]. Is not however a declining country, 90 [stationary population, 98; long stationary and as rich as possible, 111]. High rate of interest of money there, 112 [country labourers higher paid than artificers, etc., 144; price of silver affected by price in Peru, 185; richer than any part of Europe, 208, 255]. The price of labour there, lower than in the greater part of Europe, [209] 224 [trade with, 223]. Great state assumed by the grandees, 223 [not much inferior to Europe in manufacturing, 224]. Silver the most profitable article to send thither, 224–5. The proportional value of gold to silver, how rated there, 229 [quantity of precious metals affected by the abundance of American mines, 254]. The value of gold and silver much higher there than in any part of Europe, 255 [wonderful accounts of wealth and cultivation, 367; never excelled in foreign commerce, ib; wealthy without carrying on its own foreign trade, 379–80; without mines richer and better off than Mexico or Peru, 448; replacement of capital employed, 490; acquired wealth by agriculture and interior commerce, 495].

[Importance of the Cape and Batavia to the trade with Europe, 635] Agriculture favoured there, beyond manufactures, 679. Foreign trade not favoured there, 680. Extension of the home-market, 681. Great attention paid to the roads there, 729 [land tax the principal source of revenue, 730]. In what the principal revenue of the sovereign consists, 838 [consequent goodness of roads and canals, ib.]. The revenue of, partly raised in kind, 839 [silk, 886].

[Chocolate, a luxury of the poorest Spaniards, 871; duty on, 886]

[Choiseul, Duke of, managed the parliament of Paris, 799]

[Christianity established by law, 765]

[Christiern II., Reformation in Sweden assisted by his tyranny, 806]

Church, [of England not successful in resisting enthusiasts, 789; loyal, 807; drains the universities, 811] the richer the church, the poorer the state, 812. Amount of the revenue of the church of Scotland, 813. The revenue of the church heavier taxed in Prussia, than lay proprietors, 835. The nature and effect of tythes considered, 837.

[Cibao, 559]

[Cicero, quoted, 111, 166, 876]

[Cipango, 559]

Circulation, the dangerous practice of raising money by, explained, 309–10. In ᵉtraffickᵉ the two different branches of, considered, 322.

ᵉ⁻ᵉ traffic 5

ᶠ⁻ᶠ Ancient 4-5   ᵍ⁻ᵍ Ancient 4-5   ʰ⁻ʰ enterprises 5   ⁱ⁻ⁱ ancient 4-5

627. Review of the plan by which it proposes to enrich a country, 642[–62]. The interest of the consumer constantly sacrificed to that of the producer, 660. See *Agriculture, Banks, Capital, Manufactures, Merchant, Money, Stock, Trade,* &c.

Commodities, the barter of, insufficient for the mutual supply of the wants of mankind, 37. Metals found to be the best medium to facilitate the exchange of, 38. Labour an invariable standard for the value of, 50. Real and nominal prices of, 51. The component parts of the prices of, explained and illustrated, 67. The natural and market prices of, distinguished, and how regulated, 72. The ordinary proportion between the value of any two commodities, not necessarily the same as between the quantities of them commonly in the market, 229. The price of rude produce, how affected by the advance of wealth and improvement, 235.

Foreign, are primarily purchased with the produce of domestic industry, 368. When advantageously exported in a rude state, even by a foreign capital, 379. The quantity of, in every country, naturally regulated by the demand, 435. Wealth in goods, and in money, compared, 438. Exportation of, to a proper market, always attended with more profit, than that of gold and silver, ib. The natural advantages of countries in particular productions, sometimes not possible to struggle against, 458.

[Commons, the House of, not a very equal representation of the people, 585; untrustworthy reports of debates in, 738–9]

Company, [government of an exclusive, the worst of all governments, 570; most effectual expedient for stopping growth of a colony, 575] mercantile, incapable of consulting their true interests when they become sovereigns, 637. An exclusive company, a public nuisance, 641.

Trading, how first formed, 733. Regulated, and joint stock companies, distinguished, ib. Regulated companies in Great Britain, specified, 734. Are useless, 735. The constant view of such companies, 736. Forts and garrisons, why never maintained by regulated companies, 737. The nature of joint stock companies explained, 740, 755 [seldom successful without an exclusive privilege, 741; account of several companies, 741–53]. A monopoly necessary to enable a joint stock company to carry on a foreign trade, 754 [Morellet's list of fifty-five failures, 755]. What kind of joint stock companies need no exclusive privileges, 756. Joint stock companies, why well adapted to the trade of banking, ib. The trade of insurance may be carried on successfully by a [joint] stock company, ib. Also inland navigations, and the supply of water to a great city, 756–7. Ill success of joint stock companies in other undertakings, 758.

Competition, the effect of, in the purchase of commodities, 73–4. Among the venders 74, 105 [restraint of, causes inequalities of wages and profits, 135, 146; the only cause of good management, 163–4; of shopkeepers, cannot hurt the producer or the consumer, 362].

[Compiègne, 335]

[Conceit, men's overweening, often noticed, 124]

Concordat, in France, its object, 804–5.

[Condom, 854]

[Congo, 558, 635]

Congress, American, its strength owing to the important characters it confers on the members of it, 623.

[Connecticut, expense of, 573; governor elected by the assembly, 585]

[*Considerations on the Trade and Finances of Great Britain,* quoted, 922]

[Constantine, 704]

[Constantinople, 798]

[Consumable goods, taxes on, finally paid by the consumer at convenient time, 826; paid indifferently from the three kinds of revenue, 867; incidence of, &c., 869–906]

[Consumption the sole end of production, 660]

[Contrôle, the French stamp duties on registration, 863]

Conversion price, in the payment of rents in Scotland, explained, 200–1.

[Copartnery, difference between it and a joint-stock company, 740–1]

[Copenhagen, 336]

Copper, [Romans used unstamped bars of, as money, 39] the standard measure of value among the ′antient′ Romans, 56. Is no legal tender in England, 57 [rated above its value in the English coinage, 60; not legal tender for more than a shilling, 61].

[Copyholders, 854]

[Copyright, a monopoly granted to an author, 754]

Cori, the largest quadruped on the island of St. Domingo, described, 560.

Corn, the raising of, in different countries, not subject to the same degree of rivalship as manufactures, 16–17. Is the best standard for reserved rents, 52. The price of, how regulated [varies more from year to year than silver, 53]. The price of, the best standard for comparing the different values of particular commodities at different times and places, 55–6. The three component parts in the price of, 68. Is dearer in Scotland than in England, 93 [corn-field produces more food than pasture of equal extent, 164]. Its value compared with that of butchers meat, in the different periods of agriculture 164, 168. Compared with silver, 195. Circumstances in a historical view of the prices of corn, that have misled writers in treating of the value of silver at different periods, 200 [at all stages of improvement costs the price of nearly equal quantities of labour, 206]. Is always a more accurate measure of value, than any other commodity, ib. Why dearer in great towns than in the country, 209. Why ᵏdearᵏ in some rich commercial countries, as Holland and Genoa, ib. Rose in its nominal price on the discovery of the American mines, 210. And in consequence of the civil war under king Charles I., 212. And in consequence of the bounty on the exportation of, ib. Tendency of the bounty examined, 215–16 [recent high price due to bad seasons, 217]. Chronological table of the prices of, 267.

The least profitable article of growth in the British West Indian colonies, 389. The restraints formerly laid upon the trade of, unfavourable to the cultivation of land, 396 [bounty on exportation and duties on importation, 424]. The free importation of, could little affect the farmers of Great Britain, 459. The policy of the bounty on the exportation of, examined, 506. The reduction in the price of corn, not produced by the bounty, 507. Tillage not encouraged by the bounty, 507–9. The money price of, regulates that of all other home-made commodities, 509. Illustration, 511. Ill effects of the bounty, 513–4. Motives of the country gentlemen in granting the bounty, 515. The natural value of corn not to be altered by altering the money price, ib. The four several branches of the corn trade specified, 524. The inland dealer, for his own interest will not raise the price of corn higher than the scarcity of the season requires, ib. Corn a commodity the least liable to be monopolized, 525. The inland dealers in corn too numerous and dispersed to form a general combination, 526. Dearths never artificial, but when government interferes improperly to prevent them, ib. The freedom of the corn trade, the best security against a famine, 527. Old English statute to prohibit the corn trade, 528. Consequences of farmers being forced to become corn dealers, 529. The use of corn dealers to the farmers, 531. The prohibitory statute against the corn trade softened, 532. But still under the influence of popular prejudices, 533. The average quantity of corn imported and exported, compared with the consumption and annual produce, 534. Tendency of a free importation of corn, 535. The home market the most important one for corn, 536. Duties payable on the importation of grain, before 13 Geo. III., ib., *note*. The impropriety of the statute 22 Car. II. for regulating the importation of wheat, confessed by the suspension of its execution, by temporary statutes, 536. The home-market indirectly supplied by the exportation of corn, 537. How a liberal system of free exportation and importation, among all nations, would operate, 538. The laws concerning corn, similar to those relating to religion, 539. The home-market supplied by the carrying trade, ib. The system of laws connected with the establishment of the bounty, undeserving of praise, 540. Remarks on the statute 13 Geo. III., 541 [restrictions on French corn trade removed, 678; bounty on corn worse than a tax on necessaries, 875.].

[*Corn, Essay on the Legislation and Commerce of*, quoted, 905]

[Cornwall, 186–8]

Corporations, tendency of the exclusive privileges of, on trade, 79, 135. By what authority erected, 140. The advantages corporations derive from the surrounding country, 141. Check the operations of competition, 144. Their internal regulations, combinations

---

ʲ⁻ʲ ancient *4–5*   ᵏ⁻ᵏ dearer *5*

against the public, 145. Are injurious, even to the members of them, 146. The laws of, obstruct the free circulation of labour, from one employment to another, 152.

The origin of, 400. Are exempted by their privileges from the power of the feudal barons, 401. The European East India Companies disadvantageous to the eastern commerce, 449. The exclusive privileges of corporations ought to be destroyed, 470.

[Cortez, 562]

[Corvée, a principal instrument of tyranny, 731]

[Cossacks, treasures of their chief, 446]

[Cost, real, defined, 72]

Cottagers, in Scotland, their situation described, 133. Are cheap manufacturers of stockings, 134. The diminution of, in England, considered, 243.

[Cotton, most valuable vegetable production of the West Indies, 560; bales of, exhibited by Columbus, 561]

[Cotton manufacture not practised in Europe in 1492, 560-1]

[Country, the charms of, attract capital, 378]

[Country gentlemen, imposed on by the arguments of merchants, 434; imitated manufacturers, 462]

[Courts, see Justice]

Coward, character of, 788.

Credit. [of a person does not depend on his trade, 122; might supply the place of money, 437] See *Paper-money*.

[Creoles, 569]

[Cromwell, 597, 706]

[Crown lands should be sold, 824]

Cruzades to the Holy Land, favourable to the revival of commerce, 406.

[Cruttenden East Indiaman, 750]

[Cuba, 185, 589]

[Curaçoa, 571]

[Curate, 146]

Currency of states, remarks on, 479.

[Custom-house books untrustworthy, 475-6]

Customs, the motives and tendency of drawbacks from the duties of, 499. The revenue of the customs increased, by drawbacks, 503.

Occasion of first imposing the duties of, 732. Origin of those duties, 878. Three ancient branches of, 879. Drawbacks of, 880. Are regulated according to the mercantile system, 881. Frauds practised to obtain drawbacks and bounties, 882. The duties of, in many instances uncertain, 883. Improvement of, suggested, ib. Computation of the expence of collecting them, 896.

[Cyder, tax on, 890]

[Cyprus, 111]

D

[Daedalian wings of paper money, 321]

Dairy, the business of, generally carried on as a save-all, 244. Circumstances which impede or promote the attention to it, ib. English and Scotch dairies, 244-5.

[Daniel, Gabriel, quoted, 403]

[Dantzig, 209, 477]

Danube, the navigation of that river why of little use to the interior parts of the country from whence it flows, 36.

[Darien, 560]

[Dauphiné, 854]

Davenant, Dr. [quoted, 95] his objections to the transferring the duties on beer to the malt, considered, 891.

[Dear years enable masters to make better bargains with servants, 101]

Dearths, never caused by combinations among the dealers in corn, but by some general calamity, 526. The free exercise of the corn trade the best palliative against the incon-

¹⁻¹ public *4–5*

E

ᵐ⁻ᵐ ancient 4–5

$^{n-n}$ Public *4–5* $^{o-o}$ public *4–5*

ᵖ⁻ᵖ public 5

a regular administration of justice to cause manufactures and commerce to flourish, 910. Origin of a national debt, 910-11. Progression of public debts, 911. War, why generally agreeable to the people, 920.

Governors, political, the greatest spendthrifts in society, 346.

[Gracchi, 775]

[Grapes might be grown in Scotland at sufficient expense, 458]

Grasses, artificial, tend to reduce the price of butcher's meat, 167.

Graziers, subject to monopolies obtained by manufacturers to their prejudice, 655.

Greece, [ancient, had no work for apprentice, 139; slavery harsher than in the middle ages, 386; cultivation of corn degenerated, 388; citizens consisted of landed proprietors, 397; opulent and industrious, 406] foreign trade promoted [prohibited] in several of the ʳantientʳ states of, 683 [trade and manufactures carried on by slaves, 683-4; citizens long served in war without pay, 693]. Military exercises, a part of general education, 696. Soldiers not a distinct profession, in, ib; [individual military exercises, 698; militias defeated by Macedonian and Roman standing armies, 702-3; but had defeated Persian militia, 704-5; just beyond the shepherd stage at the Trojan war, 717]. Course of education in the republics of, 774. The morals of the Greeks inferior to those of the Romans, ib. [779; sanguinary factions, 775; exercises and elementary education, 776-7]. Schools of the philosophers and rhetoricians, 777. Law no science among the Greeks, 778. Courts of justice, ib. [abilities of people equal to those of modern nations, 779]. The martial spirit of the people, how supported, 787 [great men of letters were teachers, 811; public revenue largely obtained from state lands, 821].

[Greek clergy, turbulent, 798]

Greek colonies, [reasons for sending them out, 556] how distinguished from Roman colonies, 558. Rapid progress of these colonies, 566 [plenty of good land, 567; sometimes contributed military force but seldom revenue, 593; England and America might imitate the tie between mother country and colony, 593-4].

Greek language, how introduced as part of university education, 766. Philosophy, the three great branches of, ib.

[Green glass, tax on, 878]

[Greenland seal fishery, 643; South Sea Company's whale fishery, 745]

[Grenada sugar refinery, 581; new field for speculation, 943]

[Grocer, high profits of, explained, 129]

Ground rents, great variations of, according to situation, 840-1. Are a more proper subject of taxation than houses, 843 [tax on the sale of, 862].

[Guastalla, 876]

[Guernsey, 620]

[Guicciardini, quoted, 426]

[Guienne, 171]

[Guilds, adulterine, 141]

[Guinea coast, 492, 558, 739]

[Guineas not used in computation, 57; Drummond's notes for, 58]

Gum senega, review of the regulations imposed on the trade for, 657-8, [881].

[Gumilla, 563]

Gunpowder, great revolution effected in the art of war by the invention of, 699, 707-8. This invention favourable to the extension of civilization, 708.

Gustavus, Vasa, how enabled to establish the reformation in Sweden, 806.

[Gymnazium, 696, 774, 786]

H

[Hackney coaches and chairs, taxes on, 852-3]

[Hale, Lord Chief Justice, quoted, 95]

[Halifax, 409]

Hamburgh, [houses of, supported by Bank of England, 320; goods imported from, paid

ʳ⁻ʳ ancient *4-5*

for by bills on Holland, 477; exchange with, formerly unfavourable, 479; a small state which must use foreign coin, 480] agio of the bank of, explained, ib.

[British colonial monopoly hampers the merchants, 628; type of mercantile state, 668]. Sources of the revenue of that city, 817–18, 820. The inhabitants of, how taxed to the state, 850.

[Hamburgh Company, some account of, 734]

[Hamilcar, 702]

[Hannibal, 702–3]

Hanseatic league,² causes that rendered it formidable, 403. Why no vestige remains of the wealth of the Hans towns, 426.

[Harbours, cost of, should be defrayed by a port duty on tonnage of ships, 724]

[Hardware, 439–40, 491; Birmingham manufacturers buy wine with, 897]

[Hasdrubal, see Asdrubal]

[Hawkers, tax on, 852]

[Hawkins, Serjeant, quoted, 648]

[Hazard, capitalist paid for incurring, 66]

Hearth money, why abolished in England, 845–6.

[Hebrew language not a part of common university education, 766]

[Hebrides, wages in, 94; herring fishery, 520]

[Hénault, President, quoted, 623–4]

Henry VIII. of England, prepares the way for the reformation by shutting out the authority of the Pope, 806–7 [adulterated the coin, 932].

[Henry IV. of France, siege of Paris, 624; had a treasure, 909]

[Henry, Prince, 167]

[Heptarchy, 344]

[Herbert, quoted, 199, 216]

Herring buss bounty, remarks on, 519. Fraudulent claims of the bounty, 520. The boat fishery the most natural and profitable, 521. Account of the British white-herring fishery 522. Account of the busses fitted out in Scotland, the amount of their cargoes, and the bounties on them, 948[–50].

[Hesiod, quoted, 768]

Hides, the produce of rude countries, commonly carried to a distant market, 246. Price of, in England three centuries ago, 249. Salted hides inferior to fresh ones, 250. The price of, how affected by circumstances, in cultivated and in uncultivated countries, 251.

[Higgling of the market, 49]

Highlands of Scotland, [could not support a nailer, 32; wages in, 94] interesting remarks on the population of, 97 [high mortality of children, ib.; cattle of, admitted to England by the Union, 165, 237–40; old families common in, 421]. Military character of the Highlanders, 701.

[Highways originally maintained by six days' labour, 821]

[Hippias, lived in splendour, 150; peripatetic, 777]

[Hispaniola, 247]

Hobbes, Mr. remarks on his definition of wealth, 48.

Hogs, circumstances which render their flesh cheap or dear, 243.

Holland, [water carriage afforded by the Maese, 35; ratio of silver to gold, 14 to 1, 60] observations on the riches and trade of the republic of, 108 [richer than England, wages high, profits low, gained carrying trade of France, holds large amount in French and English funds, not decaying, 108–9]. Not to follow some business, unfashionable there, 113 [corn chiefly imported, 166; spices burnt to keep up the price, 175, 525, 636]. Cause of the dearness of corn there, 209 [improved since the discovery of America, 220; expelled the Portuguese from India, 222, 449; tea smuggled from, 223; houses supported by Bank of England, 320; operation of carrying trade, 370–1].

enjoys the greatest share in the carrying trade of Europe, 373 [farmers not inferior to those of England, 395; legislature attentive to commerce and manufactures, 424; exchange with, 433; East India Company's tea smuggled into England, 436; imports

² This entry appears before 'Hamburgh' in the original index.

lean cattle, 460; Dutch undertaker of woollen manufactures at Abbeville, 461]. How the Dutch were excluded from being the carriers to Great Britain, 463 [supplied other nations with fish, 464; bad terms with England, ib.]. Is a country that prospers under the heaviest taxation, 467 [French wine smuggled, 475; computation of state of credit and debit, 477–8]. Account of the Bank of Amsterdam, 480 [market price of bullion above the mint price, 482]. This republic derives even its subsistence from foreign trade, 497.

[Buys English corn cheaper and can sell manufactures cheaper in consequence of the British corn bounty, 514; must carry on herring fishery in decked vessels, 520; position in regard to the Methuen treaty, 547; no gold, silver or diamonds in the American colonies, 564; attack on Brazil, 569; settlements in 17th century, 570; Curaçoa and Eustatia free ports, 571; exclusive company for colonial commerce, 575; naval power in 1660, 597; possessed New York and New Jersey, ib.; tobacco imports, 602; linen exported to America, 604, 627; maintains monopoly of trade to the spice islands, 631; would send more ships to the East Indies if the trade were free, 632; settlements at the Cape and Batavia the most considerable in Africa and the East Indies, 635; destructive policy in East Indies, 637, 638; English duty on yarn, 643; gum senega clandestinely exported from England, 658; type of mercantile state, 668; subsistence drawn from other countries, 677; great cities the capitals of little republics, 808; respectable clergy, 810; eminent men of letters often professors, 811; monopoly of madder owing to existence of tithe elsewhere, 838].

tax paid on houses there, 845 [rate of interest, ib.; 2 per cent. tax on capital paid voluntarily, 851–2; a tax intended to fall on capital, 852; servants' tax, 857]. Account of the tax upon successions, 859. Stamp duties, 861 [tea and sugar luxuries of the poorest, 871; taxes on bread and necessaries ruined manufactures, 875–6]. High amount of taxes in, 875, 905–6 [tea taxed by licence to drink, 878; expense of preserving from the sea, 906]. Its prosperity depends on the republican form of government, ib.

[Holstein, cattle of, exported to Holland, 677]

[Holy Land, 406]

[Homer, quoted, 38, 718]

Honoraries from pupils to teachers in colleges, tendency of, to quicken their diligence, 760.

[Hop-garden, high profit of, 169]

Hose, in the time of Edward IV. how made, 262.

Hospitality, ᵃantientᵃ, the cause and effect of, 412–13, 907.

[Hottentots, 634]

House, different acceptations of the term in England, and some other countries, 134–5, [180]. Houses considered as part of the national stock, 281. Houses produce no revenue, 281, 282.

the rent of distinguished into two parts, 840. Operation of a tax upon house rent, payable by the tenant, 841. House rent the best test of the tenant's circumstances, 843. Proper regulation of a tax on, ib. How taxed in Holland, 845. Hearth money, 845–6. Window tax, 846 [tax on sale of, 862].

Hudson's bay company, the nature of their establishments and trade, 743. Their profits not so high as has been reported, 744.

[Hume, quoted, 247, 325, 354, 412, 445, 790–1]

[Hungary, Danube little use to, 36; serfs still exist in, 387; industry encouraged by colonisation of America, 591–2; mines worked by free men, 684]

Hunters, war how supported by a nation of, 690. Cannot be very numerous, 691. No established administration of justice, needful among them, 709. Age the sole foundation of rank and precedency among, 711. No considerable inequality of fortune, or subordination to be found among them, 712. No hereditary honours in such a society, 713 [minds kept alive by absence of division of labour, 782–3].

Husbandmen, war how supported by a nation of, 692–3.

Husbandry. See *Agriculture.*

[Hutchinson, quoted, 941]

[Hyder Ali, 753]

ᵃ⁻ᵃ ancient 4–5

---

³ In the original index, entries in this and the following section are listed under 'J'.

J

K

L

---

4 In the original index, this entry appears after the two which follow.

in England, 87. Is cheap in countries that are stationary, 89. The demand for, would continually decrease in a declining country, 90. The province of Bengal cited as an instance, 91. Is not badly paid for in Great Britain, ib. An increasing demand for, favourable to population, 98. That of freemen cheaper to the employers than that of slaves, ib. The money price of, how regulated, 103. Is liberally rewarded in new colonies, 109. Common labour and skilful labour distinguished, 118–19. The free circulation of, from one employment to another, obstructed by corporation laws, 152. The unequal prices of, in different places, probably owing to the law of settlements, 156. Can always procure subsistence on the spot where it is purchased, 162. The money price of, in different countries, how governed, 209. Is set into motion by stock employed for profit, 266. The division of, depends on the accumulation of stock, 276. Machines to facilitate labour, advantageous to society, 287.

productive and unproductive, distinguished, 330. Various orders of men specified, whose labour is unproductive, 330–1. Unproductive labourers all maintained by revenue, 333. The price of, how raised by the increase of the national capital, 353. Its price, though nominally raised, may continue the same, 355. Is liberally rewarded in new colonies, 565. Of artificers and manufacturers, never adds any value to the whole amount of the rude produce of the land, according to the French agricultural system of political œconomy, 667. This doctrine shewn to be erroneous, 675–6. The productive powers of labour, how to be improved, 676 [forced, 731, 821; division of, see Division of labour].

Labourers, useful and productive, every where proportioned to the capital stock on which they are employed, 11. Share the produce of their labour, in most cases, with the owners of the stock on which they are employed, 67. Their wages a continued subject of contest between them and their masters, 83–4. Are seldom successful in their outrageous combinations, 85. The sufficiency of their earnings, a point not easily determined, ib. Their wages sometimes raised by increase of work, 86. Their demands limited by the funds destined for payment, ib. Are continually wanted in North America, 88. Miserable condition of those in China, 89–90. Are not ill paid in Great Britain, 91. If able to maintain their families in dear years, they must be at their ease in plentiful seasons, 92. A proof furnished in the complaints of their luxury, 96. Why worse paid then artificers, 119. Their interests strictly connected with the interests of the society, 266. Labour the only source of their revenue, 279. Effects of a life of labour on the understandings of the poor, 781–2.

[Labourers, statute of, 195]

[Lace, £30 worth made of a penny-worth of flax, 667]

[Lacedæmon, 436]

[Lancashire, oatmeal diet, 177]

Land, [appropriated, 65] the demand of rent for, how founded, 67. The rent paid, enters into the price of the greater part of all commodities, ib. Generally produces more food than will maintain the labour necessary to bring it to market, 162–3. Good roads, and navigable canals, equalize difference of situation, 163. That employed in raising food for men or cattle, regulates the rent of all other cultivated land, 168, 175. Can clothe and lodge more than it can feed, while uncultivated, and the contrary when improved, 178. The culture of land producing food, creates a demand for the produce of other lands, 192. Produces by agriculture a much greater quantity of vegetable, than of animal food, 206–7. The full improvement of, requires a stock of cattle to supply manure, 238. Cause and effect of the diminution of cottagers, 243. Signs of the land being 'compleatly' improved, 245. The whole annual produce, or the price of it, naturally divides itself into rent, wages, and profits of stock, 265.

the usual price of, depends on the common rate of interest for money, 358. The profits of cultivation exaggerated by projectors, 374. The cultivation of, naturally preferred to trade and manufactures, on equal terms, 377. Artificers necessary to the cultivation of 378. Was all appropriated, though not cultivated, by the northern destroyers of the Roman empire, 382. Origin of the law of primogeniture under the feudal government, ib. Entails, 384. Obstacles to the improvement of land under feudal proprietors, 385–6.

ᵗ⁻ᵗ completely, 4–5

ᵘ⁻ᵘ ancient *4–5*

⁵ In the original index the order of the next two entries is reversed.

Levity, the vices of, ruinous to the common people, and therefore severely censured by them, 794.

[Lewis the Fat, 403]

Liberty, [perfect, necessary for correspondence of market and natural price, 73, 79; and for equality of advantages of different employments, 116, 135; flagrantly violated by the laws of settlement, 157] three duties only necessary for a sovereign to attend to, for supporting a system of, 687-8.

[Licences to consume, Decker's plan of taxation by, 877-8]

['Light come light go,' applicable to high profits, 613]

[Ligue, 623]

Lima, computed number of inhabitants in that city, [222] 568.

Linen manufacture, [open to everybody, 152] narrow policy of the master manufacturers in, 643-4 [high price in ancient Rome, 685; use of, makes soap necessary, 874; duty on Scotch, 913].

[Lionnois, 185]

[Liquors dearer owing to taxes, 96; brewed and distilled for private use, 888]

[Lisbon, gold and silver imported to, 226; both residence of a court and a trading city, 336; gold could easily be brought from, 435; carrying trade example, 454; bills paid in common currency, 479]

    [Weekly amount of gold brought from, to London, 547; Vasco de Gama sailed from, 559; exorbitant profits, at, 612; merchants magnificent lords, 613]

Literature, the rewards of, reduced by competition, 148. Was more profitable in ancient Greece, 149-50. The cheapness of literary education an advantage to the public, 151.

[Liverpool represented on the African Company's committee, 738]

[Loango, 558]

Loans of money, the nature of, analysed, 350-1. The extensive operation of, 351-2.

[Local revenue, the proper source of maintenance for public works and services, 730, 815; sometimes maintains schools and colleges, 759; péages and duties of passage formed part of, 894]

[Lochaber, 416]

[Lochiel, Cameron of, 416]

Locke, Mr. remarks on his opinion of the difference between the market and mint prices of silver bullion, 60. His account of the cause of lowering the rates of interest for money, examined, 353. His distinction between money and moveable goods, 430.

[Locri, 566]

Lodgings, cheaper in London, than in any other capital city in Europe, 134.

Logic, the origin and employment of, 769-70.

[Lombardy, 426]

[London, road and sea traffic to Edinburgh and Calcutta, 32-3; price of silver, 55; wages lower than in New York, 87; wages, 92; early decay of carpenters, 100; bankers pay no interest, 107; great companies borrowed at 5 per cent. after the late war, 110; wages of labourers and bricklayers and masons, 120; chairmen employed as bricklayers, ib.; employment from day to day, ib.; tailors often out of employment, 121; coalheavers, ib.; wages of common labour, ib; wages of seamen and other labourers compared with those paid at Edinburgh, 127; lodging cheap, 134; silkweavers' byelaw, 136; counties near, petitioned against turnpikes, 164; meat fallen in price compared with bread, 167; societies of merchants buy land in sugar colonies, 174; chairmen, porters, coalheavers and prostitutes, Irish, 177; stone quarry near, affords considerable rent, 179; paving stones from Scotland, ib.; civil war raised the price of corn, 212; price of meat, 238, 243; merchants have not the advantage of Scotch cash accounts, 300; transactions of Scotch banks, 303; drawing and redrawing, 309; no bank notes under £10, 322, 323; exchange with Carlisle and Dumfries, 326; residence of a court, but a trading city, 336; fire and plague, 344; trade with Scotland, 368; coal trade with Newcastle, 371; French cambrics may be imported, 473; exchange with Paris, 476; and other foreign towns, 479]

    [Herring fishery company, 522; fifth of gold and silver found in colonies reserved to the king in the patent of the London Company, 564; merchants not so magnificent as those of Cadiz and Lisbon, nor so parsimonious as those of Amsterdam, 613; entrepôt

79. The deductions made from labour employed on manufactures, 83. Inquiry how far they are affected by seasons of plenty and scarcity, 101. Are not so materially affected by circumstances in the country where they are carried on, as in the places where they are consumed, 103 [price of, more raised by high profits than by high wages,] 114. New manufactures generally give higher wages than old ones, 131. Are more profitably carried on in towns than in the open country, 142. By what means the prices of, are reduced, while the society continues improving, 260. Instances in hard ware, ib. Instances in the woollen manufacture, 261. What fixed capitals are required to carry on particular manufactures, 280.

for distant sale, why not established in North America, 378–9. Why manufactures are preferred to foreign trade, for the employment of a capital, 379. Motives to the establishment of manufactures for distant sale, 407–8. How shifted from one country to another, ib. Natural circumstances which contribute to the establishment of them, 408–9. Their effect on the government and manners of a country, 412. The independence of artisans explained, 420 [best commodities wherewith to pay armies in foreign parts, 444]. May flourish amidst the ruin of a country, and begin to decay on the return of its prosperity, 445 [particular, may be acquired earlier by means of regulations, 458]. Inquiry how far manufacturers might be affected by a freedom of trade, 469. Those thrown out of one business can transfer their industry to collateral employments, 470. A spirit of combination among them to support monopolies, 471. Manufacturers prohibited by old statutes from keeping a shop, or selling their own goods by retail, 529. The use of wholesale dealers to manufacturers, 531. British restraints on manufactures in North America, 580–2. The exportation of instruments in, prohibited, 659.

Manufacturers, an unproductive class of the people, according to the French agricultural system of political œconomy, 666. The error of this doctrine shewn, 674. How manufacturers augment the revenue of a country, 677. Why, the principal support of foreign trade, 680. Require a more extensive market than rude produce of the land, 682. Were exercised by slaves in ancient Greece, 683. High prices of, in Greece and at Rome, 684–5. False policy to check manufactures in order to promote agriculture, 686. In Great Britain why principally fixed in the coal countries, 874 [can lend money to governments, 910].

Manure, the supply of, in most places depends on the stock of cattle raised, 238.

[Marannon, 575, 576]

[Marco Polo, quoted, 559, 560]

[Maria Theresa, 835]

Maritime countries, why the first that are civilized and improved, 34.

[Marriage, discouraged but not always prevented by poverty, 96; encouraged by high wages, 565]

[Marseilles treated as foreign by France, 901]

Martial spirit, how supported in the ᵛantientᵛ republics of Greece and Rome, 786. The want of it now supplied by standing armies, 787. The establishment of a militia little able to support it, ib.

[Maryland, retail stores often belong to residents in England, 367; tobacco exports, 500, 595, 602; expense of civil establishments, 574; established by Catholics, 589; revenue, 937]

[Massachusetts, expense of civil establishment, 573; tax on importation of molasses, 936; paper money, 940]

[Mazeppa, 446]

[Meat, see Butchers' meat]

[Mechanics should be taught in the parish schools, 785]

[Medici, Lorenzo de', 819]

Mediterranean sea, peculiarly favourable for the first attempts in navigation, 34 [carries commerce of Europe and Asia, 36; British carrying trade between ports of, 373; expense of last war partly laid out in, 442]

[Venetian fleets scarcely went beyond, 569; American fish sent to, 578; British trade

ᵛ⁻ᵛ ancient 4–5

$^{w-w}$ tallie 3–5 $^{x-x}$ ancient 4–5

O

ʸ⁻ʸ ancient 4–5

Plate [sterling mark on, gives greater security than apprenticeship, 139; annual consumption of, 225] of private families, the melting it down to supply state exigencies, an insignificant resource, 441 [profusion of, in Spanish and Portuguese houses, 512]. New plate is chiefly made from old, 550 [tax on, most conveniently paid as an annuity 876].

[Plato, quoted, 150, 388, 775; the Academy assigned, to, 778; a teacher, 811]

[Play for nothing, better than to work for nothing, 335]

[Pliny, quoted, 39, 56, 236, 388, 685]

Ploughmen, their knowledge more extensive than the generality of mechanics, 143–4.

[Plutarch, quoted, 150; a teacher, 811]

[Plymouth Company, 564, 576]

Pneumatics, the science of, explained, 770–1.

[Pneumatology, 772]

[Po River, transit duties, 894]

[Poacher everywhere in Great Britain a very poor man, 118]

[Pocock, Dr., quoted, 413]

Poivre, M., his account of the agriculture of Cochin China, 173.

Poland, [corn as cheap as that of France, 16; disorders have raised the price of corn, 217] a country still kept in poverty by the feudal system of its government, 256 [annual produce declining, 258; trade, 371; serfs still exist in, 387; corn exchanged for wines and brandies of France, 407].

[Industry encouraged by colonisation of America, 591; partition and pacification of, 607; Russian invasion, 705].

[Police, regulations of keep market price above natural, 77, 79; violent, of Indostan and ancient Egypt, 80; rules of, consequent on statute of apprenticeship, 137; laws of settlement the greatest disorder of, in England, 152; wrong regulation of, not likely to be advised by landlords, 265]

[Vigilant and severe, will not retain gold and silver in Spain and Portugal, 512; of Spain and Portugal lowers value of precious metals there, 541; maintenance of roads and canals a branch of, 730; particular town or district should pay for its own, 815]

[Police of grain, quoted, 199, 216, see Herbert]

[Policy of Europe, favourable to the industry of towns, 11, 679; nowhere leaves things at perfect liberty, 116, 135; considers country labour as common labour, 119]

[Political arithmetic, Gregory King's skill in, 95; author has no great faith in, 535]

Political œconomy, [private interests and prejudices of particular orders of men have given occasion to different theories of, 11; system of, which represents national wealth as consisting in abundance of gold and silver, 255, 429–30; the great object of, is to increase the riches and power of the country, 372] the two distinct objects, and two different systems of, 428 [Mun's title a maxim in the, of England and other countries, 434; under the mercantile system, object of, to diminish imports and increase exports, 450]

the present agricultural system of, adopted by French philosophers, described, 663. Classes of the people who contribute to the annual produce of the land, 664. How proprietors contribute, 665. How cultivators contribute, ib. Artificers and manufacturers, unproductive, 666. The unproductive classes maintained by the others, 668. Bad tendency of restrictions and prohibitions in trade, 671–2. How this system is delineated by M. Quesnai, 672–3. The bad effects of an injudicious political œconomy, how corrected, 674. The capital error in this system pointed out, ib. [this system the best yet published on the subject of, 678; very important science, ib.; deals with the nature and causes of the wealth of nations, 678–9; of Europe favours manufactures and foreign trade, 679; to promote cheapness and encourage production, the great business of, 748; Morellet's great knowledge of, 755].

[Politician, insidious and crafty animal, 468]

Poll taxes, origin of, under the feudal government, 398 [on negro slaves, a tax on particular profits, 857].

why esteemed badges of slavery, ib. The nature of, considered, 867 [French, 904].

[Polybius, quoted, 774, 775, 779]

[Pondicherry, 749]

[Pondo, 42]

[Pontage, 398]

Poor, history of the laws made for the provision of, in England, 152–3 [see Settlement].

Pope of Rome, the great power formerly assumed by, 800. His power how reduced, 803–4. Rapid progress of the reformation, 805.

Population, riches and extreme poverty, equally unfavourable to, 96–7. Is limited by the means of subsistence, 97, 180 [encouraged by high wages in colonies, 566; taxation of luxuries of the poor, no discouragement to the increase of useful, 872].

[Porrée, Father, 811]

Porter, [tax on, has not raised wages, 872; price of a pot of, 878] the proportion of malt used in the brewing of, 889.

[Porters, compared with philosophers, 28–9; can only find employment in a town, 31; Irish, in London, 177]

[Portico assigned to Zeno, 778]

[Porto Bello, 746]

Portugal, [small part of Europe, 220; in 16th century the only nation regularly trading with East Indies, 222; lost that trade to the Dutch, ib., 449; annual produce of land and labour declining, 258; trade with Britain, 368; and with Poland, 371] the cultivation of the country not advanced by its commerce, 426 [expense of last war laid out in, 442; British duties on wines, 473, 493; foreign trade, 475]. The value of gold and silver there, depreciated by prohibiting their exportation, 511–12. Translation of the commercial treaty concluded in 1703 with England, 546. A large share of the Portugal gold sent annually to England, 547. [examination of the advantages of the trade with, to Great Britain, 547–9]. Motives that led to the discovery of a passage to the East round the Cape of Good Hope, 558 [settlement of Brazil, 569; exclusive companies recently established for Fernambuco and Marannon, 575; prohibition of import of tobacco except from the colonies, 583; banished Jews to Brazil, 589]. Lost its manufactures by acquiring rich and fertile colonies, 609 [trade with East Indies open, 631; and none the less prosperous, 633, 635; African colonies resemble the American, though there is no exclusive company, 634–5; summary of effect of Methuen treaty, 661; slave trade unprofitable, 745; see Spain and Portugal].

[Postlethwayt, quoted, 318, *note*; 922]

Post-office, [affords a revenue to the state, 724] a mercantile project well calculated for being managed by a government, 818.

Potatoes, remarks on, as an article of food, 176–7. Culture, and great produce of, ib. The difficulty of preserving them, the great obstacle to cultivating them for general diet, 177.

[Potosi, mines of, 164, 211, 220]

[Pots and pans, 439–40]

Poultry, the cause of their cheapness, 242. Is a more important article of rural œconomy in France than in England, ib.

[Pounds, various, 42–3; accounts kept in, 57]

Poverty[6] sometimes urges nations to inhuman customs, 10. Is no check to the production of children, 96. But very unfavourable to raising them, 97.

Pragmatic sanction in France, the object of, 804. Is followed by the concordat, ib.

Preferments, ecclesiastical, the means by which a national clergy ought to be managed by the civil magistrate, 798. Alterations in the mode of electing to them, 799–800, 804.

Presbyterian church government, the nature of, described, 809. Character of the clergy of, 810, 813 [countries exempt from tithe, 838].

[*Present State of the Nation*, quoted, 443]

[Press-gang, 132]

Prices, [natural, real, market, and nominal, 46, 47–64, 72–81] real and nominal, of commodities distinguished, 51 [of labour, 53, 162, 218]. Money price of goods explained, 63 [component parts of, 65–71]. Rent for land enters into the price of the greater part of all commodities, 67. The component parts of the prices of goods explained, 67. Natural and market prices distinguished, and how governed, 72–4, [79] 104. Though raised at

---

[6] In the original index, this entry appears before 'Poultry'.

²⁻² ancient 4–5

ᵇ⁻ᵇ completed *4–5*

219. The value of silver kept up by an extension of the market, 220. Is the most profitable commodity that can be sent to China, 224–5. The value of, how proportioned to that of gold, before and after the discovery of the American mines, 228–9. The quantity commonly in the market in proportion to that of gold, probably greater than their relative values indicate, 230 [a proper subject of taxation, 232]. The value of, probably rising, and why, 232. The opinion of a depreciation of its value, not well founded, 258.

the real value of, degraded by the bounty on the exportation of corn, 509 [tax on, in America, 562; has not varied since the imposition of the English land-tax, 829; not necessary to the Americans, 940; see Gold and Silver].

Sinking fund in the British finances, explained, 915. Is inadequate to the discharge of former debts, and almost wholly applied to other purposes, 920. Motives to the misapplication of it, 920.

Slaves, the labour of, dearer to the masters than that of free men, 98.

under feudal lords, circumstances of their situation, 386–7. Countries where this order of men still remains, 387. Why the service of slaves is preferred to that of free men, 388. Their labour why unprofitable, 389. Causes of the abolishing of slavery throughout the greater part of Europe, 389–90. [Cultivation under the Romans by, 557]. Receive more protection from the magistrate in an arbitrary government, than in one that is free, 587.

why employed in manufactures by the ᶜantientᶜ Grecians, 683–4. Why no improvements are to be expected from them, 684 [domestic pedagogues usually slaves in Greece and Rome, 777].

[Smith, Charles, *Tracts on the Corn Trade*, quoted, 218, 461, 506, 508]

[Smith, John, *Memoirs of Wool*, quoted, 248, 652]

Smuggling, a tempting, but generally a ruinous employment, 128 [of tea, 223; moderate tax does not encourage, 553]. Encouraged by high duties, [826] 881–2. Remedies against, 884 [excise laws obstruct more than those of the customs, 886]. The crime of, morally considered, 898 [more opportunities for, in thinly peopled countries, 939].

[Soap, dearer in consequence of taxes, 96; rendered necessary by the use of linen, 874]

[Society, human, the first principles of, 26–7]

Soldiers, remarks on their motives for engaging in the military line, 126. Comparison between the land and sea service, ib.

why no sensible inconvenience felt by the disbanding of great numbers after a war is over, 469–70.

reason of their first serving for pay, 694–5 [possible proportion of, in civilised society, 695–6]. How they became a distinct class of the people, 698. How distinguished from the militia, ib. Alteration in their exercise produced by the invention of fire-arms, 699.

[Solomon, Proverbs of, 768]

[Solon, laws of, 543, 777]

[Solorzano, quoted, 219]

[Sou, 43]

[Sound, the transit duty, 894]

[South Carolina, expense of civil establishment, 573; duty on molasses, 936]

South Sea company, amazing capital once enjoyed by, 741 [744]. Mercantile and stock-jobbing projects of, 745. Assiento contract, ib. Whale fishery, ib. The capital of, turned into annuity stock, 746, 914, [915].

Sovereign and trader, inconsistent characters, 819.

Sovereign, three duties only, necessary for him to attend to, for supporting a system of natural liberty, 687. How he is to protect the society from external violence, 689, 707. And the members of it, from the injustice and oppression of each other, 708–9. And to maintain public works and institutions, 723.

Spain [mark on ingots of gold, 41; tax of one fifth on Peruvian mines, 186–7, 219; avidity for gold in St. Domingo, 192–3; declension not so great as is commonly imagined, 220; saying of Charles V. that everything was wanting, ib.; colonies, 221; sheep killed for fleece and tallow, 247] one of the poorest countries in Europe, notwithstanding its rich

ᶜ⁻ᶜ ancient 4–5

mines, 256 [wool, 261, 365, 408, 410, 651; ambassador gave Queen Elizabeth stockings, 262].

its commerce has produced no considerable manufactures for distant sale, and the greater part of the country remains uncultivated, 425–6. Spanish mode of estimating their American discoveries, 429 [wealth according to the Spaniards consisted in gold and silver, 430; prohibition of English woollens in Flanders, 468; sober, though wine is cheap, 492]. The value of gold and silver there, depreciated by laying a tax on the exportation of them, 511. Agriculture and manufactures there, discouraged by the redundancy of gold and silver, 512. Natural consequences that would result from taking away this tax, 513 [attempt to deprive Britain of Portugal trade, 549; representations of Columbus to the court, 560]. The real and pretended motives of the court of Castile for taking possession of the countries discovered by Columbus, 561. The tax on gold and silver, how reduced, 562. Gold, the object of all the ᵈenterprizesᵈ to the new world, 562[–4. Crown derived some revenue from colonies, 567]. The colonies of, less populous than those of any other European nation, 568. Asserted an exclusive claim to all America, until the miscarriage of their invincible armada, 569. Policy of the trade with the colonies, 576. The American establishment of, effected by private adventurers, who received little beyond permission from the government, 589–90 [Flota drained Germany of many commodities, 607]. Lost its manufactures by acquiring rich and fertile colonies, 609 [veterans equalled by the American militia, 701; united with France by the British acquisition of Gibraltar and Minorca, 740; transaction with South Sea Company, 745; Greek not taught in universities, 766. The alcavala tax there explained, 899. The ruin of the Spanish manufactures attributed to it, ib. [large national debt, 928; see Spain and Portugal].

[Spain and Portugal, supposed to have gone backwards, 220; beggarly and misgoverned countries though the value of gold and silver is low, 256; ineffectual attempts to restrict exportation of gold and silver, 431, 436, 541; quantity of gold and silver annually imported, 444]

[Gold and silver naturally a little cheaper there than elsewhere, 510–11; exports of gold and silver nearly equal to the imports thereof, 512; agriculture discouraged by the cheapness of gold and silver, ib.; would gain by abandoning the restrictions, 513; history of the American colonies, 567–9; colonies have more good land than the British, 572; right of majorazzo in the colonies hinders improvement, ib.; some revenue drawn from the colonies, 574, 593; colonial commerce confined to one port and to licensed ships, 575–6; American fish trade, 578; absolute government in colonies, 586; benefited by colonisation of America, 591; colonial monopoly has not maintained manufactures, 609; and its bad effects have nearly overbalanced the good effects of the trade, ib.; capital not augmented by the exorbitant profits of Cadiz and Lisbon, 612–13; the colonies give greater encouragement to the industry of other countries, 627; only the profits of the linen trade with America spent in, ib.]

[Sparta, iron money at, 39]

Speculation, a distinct employment in improved society, 21. Speculative merchants described, 130.

[Spices, Dutch are said to burn, in plentiful years, 175, 525, 636; imported into Great Britain, 883]

[Spirits, licence to retail, 852; wages not affected by taxes on, 872; taxes on, paid by consumers, 877; policy of Great Britain to discourage consumption of, 891]

[Spitalfields, silk manufacture, 408]

Stage, public performers on, paid for the contempt attending their profession, 124; the political use of dramatic representations, 796.

[Stallage, 398]

[Stamp Act, the American, 102, 605]

Stamp duties [on proceedings in law courts might maintain the judges, 721; loans taxed by, 858] in England and Holland, remarks on, 860–1 [on wills in Holland, 861; in France, ib., 863; have become almost universal in Europe in the course of a century,

ᵈ⁻ᵈ enterprises 5.

ᵉ⁻ᵉ ancient 4–5

f–f ancient *4–5*

[7] In the original index entries in this and the following section appear under 'V'.

V

W

⁹⁻⁹ ancient 4–5   ʰ⁻ʰ ancients 4–5